Second Edition

Two Nations, Many Cultures

Ethnic Groups in Canada

Second Edition

Two Nations, Many Cultures

Ethnic Groups in Canada

EDITED BY

Jean Leonard Elliott
Department of Sociology and Anthropology
Dalhousie University

Prentice-Hall Canada Inc., Scarborough, Ontario

Canadian Cataloguing in Publication Data

Two nations, many cultures

Bibliography: p.

ISBN 0-13-935205-8

1. Canada – Population – Ethnic groups – Addresses,
essays, lectures.* 2. Canada – Foreign population –
Addresses, essays, lectures. I. Elliott, Jean
Leonard, 1941-

FC104.T86   301.45'1'0971   C78-001486-3
F1035.A1T86

Prentice-Hall, Inc., Englewood Cliffs, New Jersey
Prentice-Hall International, Inc., London
Prentice-Hall of Australia, Pty., Ltd., Sydney
Prentice-Hall of India, Pvt., Ltd., New Delhi
Prentice-Hall of Japan, Inc., Tokyo
Prentice-Hall of Southeast Asia (PTE.) Ltd., Singapore
Editora Prentice-Hall do Brasil Ltda., Rio de Janeiro

Design by John Zehethofer

Printed and bound in Canada by Webcom Limited

ISBN 0-13-935205-8

1 2 3 4 5 W 86 85 84 83

Contents

Acknowledgements

I am indebted to Marta Tomins and Linda Findlay of Prentice-Hall and Ernest Hillen for their interest in my project, their editorial assistance, and expedition of the book's publication.

Preface

The debate on ethnicity in Canada has become intwined with the concept of *nation*. The term *nation* is being used quite ambiguously by Canadians; to a large extent this lack of clarity can be traced to the two standard dictionary definitions of the word. On the one hand, a nation is defined as an aggregate of persons of the same ethnic family, speaking the same language or cognate languages; on the other hand, a nation is defined as a body of people in a particular territory who are sufficiently conscious of their unity to seek or to possess a government peculiarly their own.

Given the lack of uniformity in the everyday usage of a key concept like nation, there is little wonder that there is disagreement concerning the existence and status of nations within Canada. This book of readings on Canadian ethnic groups focuses on the theme of "the nations within." Attempting to come to grips with the reality of the nations within, it is hoped, is not in the nature of a sterile, academic exercise. The recognition of the existence of nations within Canada and a resolution of their status are matters of great urgency and moral concern.

A consideration of the ethnic group *qua* nation is not encapsulated by Canada's historic French/English dualism. In fact, both the French and English spheres of Canadian life are undergoing redefinition to the point that to speak of French Canada or English Canada today does not indicate a precise referent. Both entities – French Canada and English Canada – have assumed mythical proportions in Canadian life. In reality, francophones and anglophones in Canada are split by regional factionalisms and a heterogeneous ethnicity. A francophone from Manitoba may have little in common with a francophone from Quebec City, Toronto, or Moncton; the case of an anglophone from these regions may be similar. Regions in Canada are *real* factors contributing to the identity of people. When region and ethnicity combine, as is the case with the Scots in Nova Scotia or the French in Quebec, we have perhaps a more dramatic effect on the level of an individual's ethnic identity than is found when an ethnic group is spread thinly across regions or when a single region contains a potpourri of ethnic groups.

In addition to the traditional French/English cleavage in Canada and the matter of regional loyalties, there is a third division within Canadian society that pits Native Peoples against non-Natives. In both a moral and a legal sense, the Native Peoples have strong arguments supporting their struggle for the recognition of their nations in the Northwest Territories and elsewhere. Although the Native Peoples may be relatively few and fragmented by language, culture, and region, they are attempting to unite in their struggles to decolonize their lands.

The organization of this book reflects the three basic divisions within Canada that may serve as catalysts for change – Native Peoples, French Canada, and the non-British segment of English-speaking Canada. In their own way, each is seeking self-definition and an ultimate accommodation to the federal system – even if this means an attempt at "opting out." For this reason, the mainstream of Canadian society, the dominant British charter group, has not been included in this collection. While the British charter group at some time may have to react to the forces of change put into motion by the non-British segments of the Canadian population, the former's role may tend to be one of reaction rather than action.

Within each division, articles were selected to illustrate the range of strategies ethnic groups use in the process of working out their identities and accommodations to the larger society. Some of the newer Third World groups, or "visible minorities," such as the Haitians and some Asian groups, are included. Unfortunately, it was not possible to include all established groups or groups of recent origin; sampling within region and within Canada's ethnic mosaic was necessary. Given the enormous diversity of cultures within Canada, it is hoped that some representativeness was achieved. Groups such as the Icelanders who have been somewhat neglected to date with respect to their inclusion in ethnic collections were sought, while larger groups such as the Dutch or the German were omitted as they have appeared more frequently in readily available, published material. Similarly, ethno-religious minorities such as the Amish and Hutterites were omitted. The voluntary segregation of the communal sects has effectively removed them from the general arena of debate concerning the status of ethnic groups in Canada.

As much as possible, an attempt was made to have the people who belong to an ethnic group or nation speak for themselves. Thus there are, for example, Native People articulating the identity and aboriginal rights issues of concern to Native People; a Polish Canadian examining multiculturalism among Poles; a Franco-Ontarian writing on the subject of ethnic boundaries among *Ontarois*; and a member of the Montreal Greek community sharing her perceptions on life and social organization among Greek Canadians. Also in keeping with the attempt to have authors addressing topics internal to groups they have empathy with, female contributors have interpreted the experiences of (1) Native women with the discriminatory Indian Act and (2) Acadian women face to face with disruptive social change in the Maritimes.

In these studies of ethnic groups various theoretical perspectives have been employed to reflect the choice of the contributor as well as the particular problem or issue under focus. The Procrustean bed of forcing all data to a single perspective has been avoided. There has been minimal reliance on a single imported or professional perspective. The intent was to deal with the Canadian reality rather than to apply a pre-existing theory to Canadian society or test particular versions of standard ethnic behavior models. Ethnic groups have different histories in Canada. Consequently, with respect to some of the more recent and smaller ethnic groups like the Indochinese and the Arabs, our analyses are at the simple level of description. With other ethnic groups more numerous and longstanding, such as the Jews and the Ukrainians, our analyses are more complex and our theories more broadly based and logically compelling. Through this variety of perspectives it is hoped that a better understanding of the aspirations of Canadians as well as a range of potential options concerning ethnicity and nationhood will emerge.

Since the first edition of *Two Nations, Many Cultures* was published, Canada has concluded the historic era in which the British North America Act functioned as a constitution. In 1981, a new, made-in-Canada constitution was authored, and in the following year, Great Britain agreed to its patriation – notwithstanding the objections of the government of Quebec and some Native groups. What will be the impact of this new constitution on the quality and diversity of ethnic life in Canada? Many of the ultimate consequences must await the Supreme Court of Canada's interpretation of various sections of the Charter of Rights and Freedoms. Generous interpretations by the Court will advance multiculturalism in Canada.

Although the concept of an ethnic group *qua* nation may be a stumbling block for some, the intensity or political forcefulness of an ethnic group's aspirations does not necessarily diminish to conform to the wishes of "outsiders." For Canadians who wish to view Canada as a *modern* society, ethnic group membership may seem passé or antithetical to what it means to be modern in the sociological sense. In a modern society, one's membership in the larger society is based on citizenship – equally extended to all, rather than upon such ascribed characteristics as age, sex, race, or ethnic group membership. These latter characteristics are thought to describe the social organization of traditional or primitive societies. Inasmuch as people will act in terms of the labels or categories that are meaningful to them, the study of ethnic groups in Canada is fundamentally relevant to Canada's future – regardless of one's particular view of the importance of the "ethnic factor" in the life of modern societies. Ethnicity seems to persist in modern societies long after sociologists have heralded its demise.

J.L. ELLIOTT

Introduction
Canada: Two Nations, Many Cultures?

This collection of readings was compiled in the immediate wake of the patriation of the Constitution – the Canada Act – from Great Britain. The process of patriating the Constitution from Great Britain involved years of rancorous debate between the provinces and the Federal government culminating in the government of Quebec's refusal to endorse the agreement and the people of Quebec being divided on the issue. Did the patriation of the Constitution ring the death knell for any viability that the *deux nations* concept, the supposed backbone of the Canadian Confederation, might have had? In what sense may we speak meaningfully of "two nations" in post-patriation Canada?

Although Canadians would agree that the *concept* of "two nations" refers to the two founding peoples or charter groups (the French and the English), consensus ends there. Interpretations differ concerning the implications of the historic French/English dualism for present-day Canada. If we turn to the Constitution for clarification, we see that while the position of the official minority, the French, has been strengthened across Canada in such vital areas as educational guarantees, the Province of Quebec not only has lost ground with respect to internal powers such as the control over the language of education, but also, and perhaps more importantly, it no longer enjoys the traditional veto it has held concerning amendments to the federal Constitution. On balance, one could argue either way with respect to whether Canadian dualism is healthier today than it was previously when we were governed under the distant authority of the British North America Act.

The fact that some Canadians might argue that Canada has been strengthened by patriation and some might argue the reverse is indicative of the divergent views and expectations we have concerning Canada. Perhaps the fundamental question that persists is: Are there two nations in Canada? Our response to this question – aside from depending on one's definition of nation – reflects our knowledge of Canadian history as well as our thoughts on self-determination and perhaps our own ethnic background as well. Essentially there are three positions voiced:

(1) Canada is one nation in the sense of being a nation-state, a political unit, that has representation in such international bodies as the United Na-

1

tions. Although attitudes toward institutional bilingualism may vary, it is acknowledged that Canada is officially bilingual on the federal level. The Official Languages Act received the support of all major parties as did the new Constitution. Within this view of Canada, Quebec is a province like all others.

(2) The federalist view, as articulated by such spokesmen as Prime Minister P.E. Trudeau, is compatible to some extent with the above view, but it acknowledges the two-nation principle. It considers the French nation as not coterminous with Quebec but extending throughout Canada wherever communities of French-Canadians are found. This view of Canada as two nations stresses the partnership element in the confederation of French and English that rests on mutual cooperation for the good of the whole. Institutional bilingualism is fully supported inasmuch as it guarantees that Canadians can receive certain federal services in the language in which they are taxed as they travel and live throughout Canada. The Charter of Rights and Freedoms in the Canadian Constitution buttresses this view.

(3) A third position, which has become identified with such groups as the Parti Québécois, considers Quebec as the French nation in Canada. Within this view, a nation is defined as a territory inhabited by those of the same ancestral or ethnic background who share a common language and culture and regard themselves as a people. Quebec is not a province like the others; it is the homeland of the French-Canadians, a distinct nation within Canada. The new Constitution is not congruent with this position.

Quebec

From the perspective of the Parti Québécois, the Canadian Confederation is a failed partnership. Quebec occupies the status of a colony within Canada. Such Quebec nationalists would be inclined to entitle this volume: *Canada and her Internal Colony or English Canada and the French Colony within*. The model of Quebec as a colony refers to the perceptions that Québécois are controlled unduly by Ottawa; that they are not "masters in their own house"; that they lack autonomy in cultural and economic affairs, and, as importantly, that the Province of Quebec has been bled systematically by anglophone economic elites. The Constitution only exacerbates this condition.

The Parti Québécois government of René Lévesque was voted in to office in 1976 on a "good government" platform with the matter of independence (sovereignty association) to be decided at a later date by referendum. Just as the writing of the Constitution was an exercise in self-definition for Canadians, so also the 1980 referendum on sovereignty association in Quebec served a similar function. While it was generally agreed that Quebec deserved a more advantageous political arrangement vis-à-vis Canada, voters were asked to decide whether the road to take was sovereignty association or federal renewal through constitutional reforms. The electorate chose the latter in a 60/40 split. It is dubious to what extent those voting against the referendum and for renewal would be satisfied with the current constitutional arrangement which has left the government of Quebec feeling "outraged" and "betrayed." Ironically, rather than federal renewal as called for by the referendum, the constitutional events of 1982 may give new impetus to the Parti Québécois or other nationalistic social movements. Indeed, Quebec Liberal Party leader, Claude Ryan has argued this eventuality.

Over the years English Canada has not been oblivious to the dissatisfaction in Quebec and elsewhere in French Canada which has developed steadily since the signing of the original partnership in Charlottetown in 1867. The commitment of English Canada to this partnership and its desire to strengthen the two-nation foundation sparked such ameliorative measures as The Task Force on National Unity (the Robarts/Pepin Commission) which sprung into being on the heels of the first Parti Québécois electoral success and the earlier Royal Commission on Bilingualism and Biculturalism formed during the government of Lester Pearson. The cry for the Royal Commission was heard as a result of the changes wrought by the Quiet Revolution in Quebec. Following a recommendation from the Commission, the federal Official Languages Act was proclaimed. Subsequent legislation in the 1970s was directed at instituting bilingualism in the federal civil service. By 1978, bilingualism priorities were shifting to the "youth option" whereby it was thought that more school children in Canada should have the opportunity to learn two official languages. In the era following the Quebec referendum, ameliorative measures aimed at righting the unequal balance between French and English Canada tended to be discussed within the framework of entrenching the rights of the official minority within the Charter of Rights and Freedoms of the new Constitution. Now that such rights have been entrenched, time will tell to what extent, if any, the Charter will be able to restore even a semblance of a balance between the two nations. The role of the Supreme Court of Canada in this matter looms large.

English Canada

So far I have addressed the problem of circumscribing the French nation in Canada in a way agreeable to all Canadians. To delimit the parameters of the English Canadian nation also is not without its share of problems. In 1838, when Lord Durham surveyed the dissension between the French and the English in the Canadas, he summed up what he saw in Lower Canada as "two nations warring in the bosom of a single state." As a solution he recommended the assimilation of the French by the English. However, the

Confederation that followed some 30 years later was *not* a strategy on the part of the English to assimilate the French. Leaders like Cartier from Lower Canada were principal participants in the forging of the Confederation agreement. In fact, Lower Canada was in many respects more convinced concerning the benefits to be accrued from Confederation than was Nova Scotia which feared domination from Upper Canada. English Canada at the time of Confederation was rife with many of the same regional disparities that plague it today. It would be grossly inaccurate to assume that English Canada spoke with a strong, single voice and foisted Confederation upon a weaker Lower Canada (Quebec).

To the regional differences in English Canada that existed at the time of Confederation are added the regional differences that stem from the populating of the West with immigrants who were largely non-British and non-French. European immigration canceled the Anglo-French alliance in the West that was hoped for by Lower Canada. With the settlement of the West, Canada went from an essentially bicultural land to one that was decidedly multicultural. So-called English Canadians today are more accurately referred to as "anglophones" as their language may be the most prominent cultural characteristic shared.

The problem of correct terminology for the Canadian people was noted by Hugh MacLennan in the course of his writing *Two Solitudes*. "No single word exists, within Canada itself, to designate with satisfaction . . . a native of the country. When those of the French language use the word *Canadien*, they nearly always refer to themselves. They know their English-speaking compatriots as *Les Anglais*. English-speaking citizens act on the same principle. They call themselves Canadians; those of the French language French-Canadians." Since the writing of this novel set during World War I, the terminology dilemma has intensified. Our solitudes, reinforced by regional differences and history, have multiplied.

The lack of communication between regions is sometimes discussed in the context of the elusive Canadian identity. Anglophones are missing a core identity that unites them and sets them apart from the British and the Americans. Just as Quebec has been subjected to the status of a colony vis-à-vis the anglophone economic community, so also has English Canada experienced the economic and cultural dependency characteristic of a colony in many of its relations with the mother country and with the powerful neighbor to the south.

In addition to the question of identity and the facts concerning cultural and economic dependency, the realities of regional economic disparaties are responsible for rifts within English Canada. The phenomenon of Western alienation is well known. So intense is this alienation from Ottawa on such matters as the control and ownership of provincial resources that two political parties – the Western Canada Concept and the West Feds – have come into being by squarely proposing "separation" as an end to the alienation. While it is the case that separatist parties in the West are not widely supported, their very existence indicates that something is awry. Alienation of the West from the Liberal government in Ottawa is further evidenced by the fact that in 1982, there are no federal Liberal Members of Parliament west of Winnipeg. The Liberal party is currently moribund in the West.

In Eastern Canada, Newfoundland has a similar axe to grind as the Western provinces on the matter of resource ownership and control. Central Canada is often the culprit responsible for Newfoundland's woes. While no separatist party *per se* has been formed in Newfoundland, the sentiment does not go unvoiced from time to time, even if only in a nostalgic way given the fact that Newfoundland was independent from Canada until the late 1940s.

Suffice it to say, it would be meaningless to think of English Canada as a monolithic entity. The provinces in English Canada also have responded in different ways to the presence of the official minority residing within their borders. New Brunswick, in large measure owing to the Acadian population resident there, has a relatively sterling record inasmuch as New Brunswick is the only province in English Canada to recognize both French and English as official languages on the provincial level. The Charter of Rights and Freedoms in the Constitution does *not* require the expansion of French as an official language on the provincial level. Clearly, so-called English Canada is in reality composed of a myriad of ethnic groups, regions, and interest groups all contributing to the Canadian whole and all vying for a fair share of the proverbial pie.

Native Peoples

It has been convenient for Canadians to overlook the fact that their country was built on land on which the Native People hold prior claim. Although Europeans have used the words "Indian" and "Eskimo" to refer to the original occupants of North America, the original people call themselves, for example, Inuit, Dene, Micmac, Malecite, Montagnais, Algonquin, Mohawk, Ojibway, Cree, Sioux, Chipeway, Huron, Tlingit, Salish, Haida, Nishga, and Kwakiutl. Given their long tenure in North America, it is understandable that Native People resent the "founding peoples" mythology which pervades the development of the Canadian nation-state inasmuch as the "founding peoples" refers to the French and English – never acknowledging the presence or contribution the Natives have made in North America.

There has been a gradual evolution of consciousness and political organization on the part of Canadian Native Peoples. The National Indian Brotherhood, which represents more than 300 000 status and treaty Indians in Canada, changed its name in 1982 to the Assembly of First Nations. The "first nation" imagery signifies both their struggle for self-determination and their awareness of their aboriginal rights. Just as the writing of the Constitution was an exercise in self-definition for the larger Canadian society so also did the Native People benefit from their efforts to get their aboriginal and treaty rights entrenched in the Constitution. This uphill struggle had the effect of "radicalizing" many moderate Natives and functioned to weld together native groups across the country in their pursuit of a common objective.

While the new Constitution affirms existing aboriginal and treaty rights, the Native Peoples have a long way to go in their establishment of a just and lasting peace with the larger Canadian society. Aboriginal rights must be "identified and defined." Native leaders are adamant in their insistence that this dialogue take place between Natives and the federal government to the exclusion of the provincial governments. The provincial governments, however, are reluctant to accept any decisions that the federal government and the Natives might reach if the provinces have had no representation at or input into the discussions. Attending a federal-provincial conference (in May, 1982) on Indian rights preliminary to the constitutional conference on Indian affairs guaranteed under Canada's new Constitution to take place within the year, the elected National Chief of the Assembly of First Nations, David Ahenakew declared:

> By virtue of the trust relationship between Indians and the federal government arising out of the Royal Proclamation, the federal government of Canada is responsible for providing and protecting the resources that will enable Indian governments to maintain and enhance Indian cultural, economic and political self-determination. This is confirmed in the treaties and in the Constitution Act. By section 91, sub-section (24) of that act, the federal government has the exclusive 'legislative' authority for Indians and Indian lands. There is therefore no legal basis for the involvement of any provincial government in our affairs. Yet today, some of us are being asked to sit down to observe provincial governments discussing our affairs, our rights with the federal government. This is absurd and totally repugnant to us.
>
> (*Indian News* Vol. 23, No. 3, p. 3, June 1982)

Thus future discussions will have to iron out what role, if any, provincial governments are to play in the identification and definition of those existing aboriginal rights entrenched in the Constitution.

While it is the case that Native Peoples insist upon their recognition as "first nations" and reject "founding peoples" ideology as it pertains to the French and English, this is not to say that some Natives may not be sympathetic to the self-determining process of the Québécois. At the time of the national unity debate prior to the referendum in Quebec on the matter of a mandate to negotiate sovereignty association, John Amagoalik, director of

Inuit land claims in the Northwest Territories, drew strength from this Quebec parallel:

> When the Prime Minister says to the Québécois that it is possible for them to be self-determining within Confederation; when he gives them assurances of the survival of their language and culture; when he promises a new Canadian federalism, we take him at his word. We, too, believe these things are possible, and we will stand as testimony to this truth as we move toward the conclusion of our negotiations.

(*Globe and Mail*, January 28, 1978)

In the interim, the issue has not been resolved. The hope that John Amagoalik expressed remains in the hearts of many. Canada as a nation-state contains within its borders the aspirations of many "nations." Canada, an experiment in the confederation of nations, will continue to evolve until the matter of nationhood for its many peoples is resolved.

PART ONE
Native Peoples

Introduction

The Native Peoples in Canada today are attempting to redirect, if not reverse, the historical process that has left them, in effect, colonies of the larger society. Through decolonization, Native People hope to regain control over their own lives, institutions, and the development of their own land, and to resolve such basic questions as who is a member of their community or nation. The legal leverage the Native People hope to employ in their struggle toward decolonization and the reclamation of their cultural heritage rests upon the definition of their aboriginal rights and title to land that has been occupied since prehistoric times. If the Native People are able to achieve a successful outcome in their negotiations with Ottawa and the provinces, they will stand to reclaim not only their land, but their pride and sense of self as well. Thus the intent of this section is to describe: (1) the goals of the decolonization process from the point of view of the Native Peoples; (2) some achievements in the establishment of aboriginal rights and land claims; and (3) the discriminatory aspects of the Indian Act that erode native culture.

George Manuel and Michael Posluns use the term Fourth World to describe as a collective entity indigenous people in various countries who have experienced European intrusion. The Native Peoples in Canada are uniting with other Fourth World members in a common struggle. In fact, a World Assembly of First nations attended by Native Peoples from 24 countries was held in Regina in 1982.[1] In line with the Assembly's theme of self-determination for Native Peoples, Manuel and Posluns previously have argued the necessity of defining aboriginal rights within the Canadian context.

Thomas R. Berger reviews the path followed toward the establishment of aboriginal rights in Canada by recounting the legal action taken by the Nishgas in British Columbia. The fact that (the as yet undefined although acknowledged to be *existing*) aboriginal rights have been entrenched in our new Constitution, the Canada Act,[2] owes much to the ground-breaking decision of the Supreme Court of Canada giving partial support to the Nishgas' land claims. While the role the Nishgas have played in this process deserves to be highlighted, one should not overlook the continuing and substantial contributions made over the years by the grass-roots provincial, national, and territorial native organizations.

One such grass-roots organization is the Dene Nation. The Dene first called attention to their Fourth World status in their Statement of Rights issued at Fort Simpson in the Northwest Territories in 1975. The Dene are the approximately 11 000 people of native ancestry who live in the Mackenzie District, including the Dogribs, Loucheux, Slaveys, and Chipewyans who speak the Athapascan or Dene dialects. The word *Dene*, which is common to all the languages of the Mackenzie, means "all the people." *Denendeh* refers to the territory of the Dene. While the Dene Declaration has not been recognized formally by the larger society, it has served to unite Native Peoples, and thus, has signaled the start of the long, slow process of decolonization.

The Eastern Arctic Inuit refer to their land as *Nunavut*. Their position on aboriginal rights and the principle of political sovereignty is put forth by the Inuit Tapirisat of Canada, the organization which represents about 17 500 Inuit in the NWT. Unlike the treaty Indians, the Eastern Arctic Inuit have never signed a treaty with the federal government. Inuit in the Western Arctic, however, numbering about 2 500, and negotiating under the banner of the Committee of Original People's Entitlement (COPE), signed an agreement in principle in 1978. This agreement which has not been implemented to date calls for the Inuit to give up all claims to aboriginal rights in exchange for money, legal title over a limited amount of land, and a limited form of municipal government.

Since the Eastern Arctic Inuit have never signed an agreement with the federal government, they are negotiating from a position of relative strength. Their unity of purpose was witnessed in the April, 1982, plebiscite held in the Northwest Territories. At issue was the future of the Territories as a political unit. Although the vote was not binding on the federal government, a slight majority of 56 percent of the Northerners voted "yes" in favor of splitting the Territories into two jurisdictions – Nunavut and Denendeh. In the Eastern Arctic, however, the vote was overwhelmingly in favor of division. The Inuit number about 16 000 in the Eastern Arctic as opposed to about 6 000 non-Inuit. In the Western Arctic, the native and non-native population are more evenly balanced with the non-native population likely to expand as a result of natural resource development in the area. The non-native majority in Yellowknife, Inuvik and Hay River voted "no" by a wide margin. The Dene were urged by their leaders to vote "yes," but the turnout was low in Dene communities. Nevertheless, the Inuit are encouraged by the results. The president of the Inuit Tapirisat, John Amagoalik, stated, "The people in the east are more determined than ever to see the creation of Nunavut."[3] If Nunavut were eventually to become a province with Frobisher Bay as its capital, it would be the only province in which Native People would be in a majority.

The Inuit's political steps toward the creation of Nunavut are contrasted and compared with the political strategies of other aboriginal peoples in circumpolar countries by Peter Jull. First, the Inuit are placed within the context of a larger "native movement." Secondly, Jull examines the situation within Canada. The Quebec Inuit, for example, are a "minority within a minority." Their mother tongue is Inuktitut, and English, not French, tends to be their second language. The future of the Quebec Inuit is dependent upon their negotiations in Ottawa as well as in Quebec City. Their situation is further complicated by the fact that Quebec is not a signatory to the Canada Act or the Charter of Rights which guarantees the protection of "existing aboriginal and treaty rights."

Until the aboriginal rights that "exist" are defined and agreed to by all parties concerned – the Native Peoples, the federal government and the provinces – the Indian Act will continue to serve as the closest formal arrangement Native Peoples have with the federal government.[4] While the Indian Act is far from satisfactory from the native point of view, it remains and functions as a constitutional document. Native Peoples, as a matter of principle, are opposed to any changes in the Indian Act which are not made through native initiative or consultation.

One problem with the Indian Act, however, is that the Act confers unequal status on native men and women in certain instances. For example, native women who marry non-natives lose their status under the Act and no longer qualify for such privileges as reserve housing; on the other hand, native men who marry non-Natives do not forfeit their band membership and all the rights and privileges it entails; furthermore many of these rights like housing are extended to the non-native spouse.

The sexism inherent in the Indian Act, it should be remembered, is not an attribute of native culture, in general, but of the Canadian society that authored it. Given the constraints of the Indian Act, Sally Weaver addresses issues relevant to the status of native women. The Equality Rights Section in the Canadian Charter of Rights and Freedoms in the Constitution of Canada, unfortunately, does not apply to native women who fall under the jurisdiction of the Indian Act; regarding those matters in which the Indian Act is in conflict with the Charter of Rights and Freedoms, the Act has precedence over the Charter. Although Ottawa is committed to amending the discriminatory clauses in the Indian Act, it is not clear how or when native consent will be obtained. As a compromise, Ottawa has, since July, 1981, been granting exemptions to the discriminatory marriage clause (Section 12-1b of the Indian Act) at the request of Indian bands. In the months immediately following the announcement of the exemption, only 18 of Canada's 575 bands took advantage of it. Furthermore the request has to originate from the band rather than from the individual women involved, and such requests are not retroactive. It is estimated that 15 000 women and their 45 000 children have had their status taken away as a result of Section 12-1b since 1920. The United Nations Human Rights Committee ruled in July, 1981, that Canada is violating international law in denying native women their full cultural rights.[5]

END NOTES

1. George Manuel was the founder and first President of the World Council of Indigenous People. He also has been President of the Union of British Columbia Chiefs and the National Indian Brotherhood. The First World Conference of Indigenous Peoples in Canada was held in Port Alberni, British Columbia in 1975. For more information, see *WAFN '82: An Introduction to the World Assembly of First Nations*, (Regina, Saskatchewan: W.A. Print Works Ltd., 1982).
2. Constitution of Canada, Part II, "Rights of the Aboriginal Peoples": 35 (1) The existing aboriginal and treaty rights of the aboriginal peoples of Canada are hereby recognized and affirmed. (2) In the act, "aboriginal peoples of Canada" includes the Indian, Inuit and Metis.
3. Jeff Sallot, "NWT division backed; vote shows racial split," *Globe and Mail* (Toronto), April 16, 1982.
4. Part IV of the Constitution of Canada is entitled, "Constitutional Conference." In section 37 (2) it is stated that a conference "shall have included in its agenda an item respecting constitutional matters that directly affect the aboriginal peoples of Canada, including the *identification and definition* [emphasis added] of the rights of those peoples to be included in the Constitution of Canada, and the Prime Minister of Canada shall invite representatives of those peoples to participate in the discussions on that item."
5. David Folster, "An ancient injustice revisited," *Maclean's* (Toronto), Sept. 28, 1981, p. 13.

SELECTED REFERENCES

Berger, Thomas R. *Northern Frontier, Northern Homeland: The Report of the Mackenzie Valley Pipeline Inquiry.* Ottawa, 1977.

Bertelsen, Judy S., ed., *Nonstate Nations in International Politics.* New York: Praeger, 1977.

Brand, Johanna. *The Life and Death of Anna Mae Aquash.* Toronto: James Lorimer, 1978.

Brody, Hugh. *The People's Land: Eskimos and Whites in the Eastern Arctic.* Markham, Ont.: Penguin Books, 1975.

Campbell, Maria. *Halfbreed.* Toronto: McClelland and Stewart, 1973.

Cumming, Peter A. and Neil H. Mickenberg. *Native Rights in Canada*, Second Edition. Toronto: General Publishing, 1972.

Cowan, Susan, ed., *We Don't Live in Snow Houses Now: Reflections* from Arctic Bay. Ottawa: Canadian Arctic Producers, 1976.

Dosman, Edgar J. *Indians: The Urban Dilemma.* Toronto: McClelland and Stewart, 1972.

Frideres, J.S. *Canada's Indians: Contemporary Conflicts.* Scarborough, Ont.: Prentice-Hall of Canada, 1974.

Graburn, Nelson. *Eskimos without Igloos.* Boston: Little, Brown, 1969.

Hutchison, George and D. Wallace. *Grassy Narrows.* Toronto: Van Nostrand, 1977.

Ponting, J. Rick and Roger Gibbins. *Out of Irrelevance: A Sociopolitical Introduction to Indian Affairs in Canada.* Toronto: Butterworths, 1980.

Ryan, Joan. *Wall of Words: The Betrayal of the Urban Indian.* Toronto: Peter Martin, 1978.

Sawchuk, Joe. *The Métis of Manitoba: Reformulation of an Ethnic Identity.* Toronto: Peter Martin, 1978.

Smith, Derek G. *Canadian Indians and the Law: Selected Documents, 1663-1972.* Toronto: McClelland and Stewart, 1975.

Watkins, Mel, ed., *Dene Nation: The Colony Within.* Toronto: University of Toronto, 1977.

Weaver, Sally M. *Making Canadian Indian Policy: The Hidden Agenda, 1968-1970.* Toronto: University of Toronto Press, 1981.

GEORGE MANUEL
MICHAEL POSLUNS

The Fourth World in Canada*

The Fourth World has always been here in North America. Since the beginning of European domination its branches, one by one, have been denied the light of day. Its fruit has been withered and stunted. Yet the tree has not died. Our victory begins with the knowledge that we have survived.

The celebration of the Fourth World, its real test of strength, and its capacity to endure, lies more with our grandchildren than with our ancestors. It is they who must cultivate the tree as a whole and honor the unique qualities of each root and branch.

Our grandfathers faced and endured the physical violence of wars, famine, and disease. They survived. We endured the social violence of legal disabilities and administrative oppression. We survived. Now there is the possibility that our grandchildren may yet face the danger of material success. They shall survive. Our history and our faith in the future are united. We are neither the beginning nor the end.

Constitutions are a collection of customs and practices that are recorded in whatever way seems suitable at the time that the practice was found good to the people who lived under it. Yet, however loosely recorded, however many sources must be consulted to put together all the pieces, that constitution does stand as a valid symbol of the hopes and aspirations, customs and beliefs, traditions and taboos of the people who live under it at the present moment. It is more than a symbol; it is the very substance of the nation and its culture.

Why then should it be so hard to understand the root and branch of the Indian nations? Our claim to a special place in the past and future history of North America? Our belief that if the Canadian mosaic arises sensibly out of the history and culture of Canada, the case for Indian nationhood arises at least as clearly out of the history and culture that the Indian nations of North America have shared?

The way to end the custodian-child relationship for Indian people is not to abolish our status as Indians, but to allow us to take our place at the table with all the rest of the adults. Indian status has too often been described as

* Reprinted from George Manuel and Michael Posluns, *The Fourth World: An Indian Reality,* Don Mills, Ontario: Collier-Macmillan Canada, 1974, by permission of authors and publisher.

"special" by those who want to create an argument to get rid of it. Indian status is neither more nor less special than those special provisions that have been made for different provinces, at Confederation and since, in order to make it possible for them to work within the partnership of Canada. These provisions recognized the unique needs of different peoples and groups and have been preserved because the differences have been found real. Yet everyone insists that they do not confer special status because they only create conditions for the different groups to become equal partners.

Why should there be a different kind of equality for us as Indian people than for the other groups of Canadians who share both a common history and a common territory that distinguish them from other Canadians? It is true that not all Indian people share a common territory in the way that a province occupies a single territory. Yet we can only imagine that our relationship with this land and with one another is far deeper and more complex than the relationship between the people of any province and their land, their institutions, or one another.

The Indian peoples cannot be brushed off with the multicultural broom to join the diverse ethnic groups that compose the Third Element of Canada, that is, those who are neither French nor English. When the Englishman speaks of "the Mother Country," the French-Canadian can still reply "Maîtres Chez Nous"; the Jew can build his freedom in North America with the faith that if it fails there is yet another Promised Land; and the Eastern European who becomes an ardent Canadian nationalist still believes himself to be in exile from his native land. It seems as if every element in the Canadian mosaic is carved from a split personality. This itself is enough to distinguish the Indian peoples from the multicultural society.

When we say, "The Earth is Our Mother," we are saying that Canada is our Promised Land. Where other people look "homeward" for the medicines to heal themselves, this is our home. If the exiled condition in which Eastern Europeans believe themselves can only be ended with a change in the relationship between their Mother Country and the neighboring Great Powers, our exile can be ended only with a change in our relationship with Canada. We know that many of those people who have come to our shores to find freedom will not go home when their country is liberated. On that day their freedom will be the freedom to choose. This is the freedom of the Fourth World. We ask no more for ourselves than the many immigrant groups ask for themselves. We do expect the same freedom and autonomy in our Mother Country as they demand in theirs, and ours. This is equality.

We are neither an ethnic group nor a province of Canada. Although there are elements in both models that are useful, neither one will really work very well for us. The imposition of models on those who did not have a hand in the design has been the problem throughout our history. Clearly, the right to design our own model is the first step toward the Fourth World.

Home rule begins with the opportunity to build that model with all the ingredients that the tides of history have washed up on our shores.

What is useful in the provincial model is that it teaches us that constitutional provisions and agreements have commonly been used to guarantee local autonomy and preserve the customs, traditions, and values of those people who have been able to make their political presence felt. The basic concept of making special provisions for special needs, far from being a strange anomaly as some contemporary political leaders have led us to believe, has been an accepted way of making room at the table for those whom the present partners were prepared to welcome.

The ethnic model teaches us that a Confederation founded on the belief in "two founding groups" can broaden its perspective when it appears to be politically expedient to do so. That is a source of enormous hope and confidence. If Confederation can endure past the racial myths that were the midwives at its birth, there can be no finer proof that institutions survive through the will of men as much as through their purely economic virtues.

If there is no single model on which to build either a route or a vehicle into the Fourth World there is both a common philosophy and a common fuel. The philosophy has been born from the desire to resolve two dilemmas that have been imposed through the conditions of unilateral dependence. We know that no Canadian government will ever deal fairly with the Indian peoples until we can negotiate from a position of strength. We also know that the kind of integration based on mutual respect and acceptance of each other's values as valid for the other will never happen until Indian people achieve the same standard of living as that enjoyed by city-dwelling, middle-class, White Canadians. The political and social dilemmas meet every time the Canadian taxpayers are told of the vast sums spent by their Department of Indian Affairs. Led to believe that this money is somehow directed for our benefit, the taxpayer resents the expenditure and wonders how people can be so foolish that they fail to benefit when millions of dollars are spent on their behalf.

The energy to move away from this situation comes from the realization that the way to remain Indian is to dispel the myths that have given rise to these false dilemmas in the first place. Most Indian people not only want to remain Indian but do not believe that there is any conflict between wanting to live decently and even comfortably, and wanting to maintain and develop our own way of life as Indian people. Remaining Indian does not mean wearing a breech-cloth or a buckskin jacket, any more than remaining English means wearing pantaloons, a sword, and a funny hat. Yet on ceremonial occasions all people dress in the manner of their forefathers to remind themselves where they came from and who they are.

Remaining Indian means that Indian people gain control of the economic and social development of our own communities, within a framework of legal and constitutional guarantees for our land and our institutions.

Without those guarantees, our people and our institutions remain in a defensive position, and our only weapon is passive resistance. With the constitutional and material support to carry on that development, there would be no dilemma. The racial myths that were created to justify the seizure of our land base will only be fully dispelled when we have received the legal recognition of our effective title to the lands that remain to us, and sufficient grants to compensate for what is lost that we can afford to develop what does remain. Only then will we be able to demonstrate that there is no conflict between wanting to live comfortably and wanting to develop within our own traditional framework.

The desire for legal recognition of our aboriginal and treaty rights has taken on a religious perspective. But, as in most natural or traditional religions, the spiritual has not been separated from the material world. Recognition of our aboriginal rights can, and must be, the mainspring of our future economic and social independence. It is as much in the long-term interest of the non-Indian peoples of North America as in our own interest that we be allowed our birthright, rather than that governments and churches perpetuate the Christian conspiracy that renders us the objects of charity while others enjoy the wealth of our land.

Immigrants to North America have long been considered on the basis of their skills and their usefulness to the economic development of the country. Unfortunately for the Gross National Product, we did not apply at the Immigration Office. The skills that those immigrants brought with them were at least the portable portion of their birthright. We, the first people of the land, must recover our birthright so that we can choose whether to become a part of the North American economy or to develop within our own value system.

THOMAS R. BERGER

The Establishment of Aboriginal Rights:
The Case of the Nishgas in British Columbia*

1. Introduction

The issue of aboriginal rights is the oldest question of human rights in Canada. At the same time it is also the most recent, for it is only in the last decade that it has entered our consciousness and our political bloodstream. It began with the White occupation of a continent already inhabited by another race, a race with its own cultures, its own languages, its own institutions, and its own way of life. Today the members of that race are advancing claims to the lands they once occupied and calling for self-determination and self-government. These claims give rise to fundamental issues, and we have come to understand that these issues are somehow bound up with what happened long ago. And they are: for the claims of the present day are founded on aboriginal rights.

Aboriginal rights are simply the rights to which Native Peoples are entitled because they are the original peoples of Canada. Until recently, the idea of aboriginal rights seemed irrelevant to Canadian concerns. But during the 1970s we began to realize that aboriginal rights are the axis upon which our relations with the Native Peoples revolve. To recognize aboriginal rights is to understand the truth of our own history, while, for the Native Peoples, such recognition is the means by which they may achieve a distinct and contemporary place in Canadian life.

The emergence of Native Peoples as a political force in the 1970s occurred because of initiatives that Indians, Inuit, and Metis all over Canada have taken themselves. One thing is common to all of these initiatives: the idea of aboriginal rights. The Native Peoples own idea of themselves has acquired a sharper focus. At the same time, our own ideas about Native Peoples are undergoing a great change: once thought to be peoples on the margins of our history and irrelevant to present-day concerns, they are now seen by a growing number of Canadians as having a moral, indeed, a constitutional right to fashion a future of their own.

* From *Fragile Freedoms* by Thomas R. Berger © 1981 by Clarke, Irwin & Company Limited. Used by Permission.

2. The Struggle of the Nishgas

The history of White-Native relations in Canada may be epitomized in the history of relations between the Whites and the Indians of British Columbia. There the Native protest over the loss of their lands has been more audible than elsewhere, and the Indian land question has agitated the province for more than a century. One tribe, the Nishgas, has been in the forefront of this controversy. The story of the Nishga Indians illustrates the quest of all Canadian Indians for legal recognition of their aboriginal rights. Their story takes us back to the beginnings of European colonization of North America, and it brings us forward to the very center of the present conflict over land claims, Indian self-determination, and the concept of Indian government.

The Nishgas are one of the tribes of the northwest coast. Here the sea and the forest have always offered a good life and, before the Whites arrived, the Indian population along the northwest coast was one of the densest in North America. Here the Nishgas had their settlements, fishing places and hunting grounds. They regarded the Nass River valley as their own. They defended it before the White man came, and they have defended it since. Today they have four villages in the Nass valley: Kincolith, Greenville, Canyon City and New Aiyansh. They say that they, as the people who have occupied this valley since time immemorial, are entitled to claim it as their own today. There was never any question in the minds of the Europeans that the Indians might retain sovereignty over the lands that had been theirs. The Europeans based their assumption of power over the Indians on the supposed moral superiority of European culture and religion over those of the Indians and on the undoubted superiority of European arms. Nevertheless, the European powers did acknowledge that the Indians retained an interest – a legal interest – in their lands because they had been the original occupants. This legal interest came to be known as aboriginal title, or Indian title.

Having acknowledged that the Indians had a legal interest in their lands, the Europeans had to consider how the Indians could be persuaded to give it up. So treaties were made with the Indians providing for the surrender of their title. In the United States, when the government could not acquire land by negotiation, it acquired it by war. Yet each time the United States government subjugated an Indian tribe, it made a treaty to obtain the surrender of Indian title. In Canada, although few treaties were made in the Atlantic provinces and in Quebec, the British, by the mid-18th century, had established a policy of treating with the Indians for their land. This policy was enshrined in the Royal Proclamation of 1763. Thus, by 1850, treaties had been made with the Indians for the surrender of virtually the whole of southern Ontario; as settlement proceeded westward across the Prairies, treaties were made (beginning in the 1870s) with the Indians there to enable the construction of the Canadian Pacific Railway to proceed, opening the country to agriculture. Treaties were also made to open up natural resources on the frontier. The prospect of extracting oil from the Athabaska tar sands, first mooted in the 1880s, led to a treaty with the Stonies in 1899, and in 1921 treaties were made with some of the northern tribes as a consequence of the discovery of oil at Fort Norman in the Northwest Territories. In 1974, the Cree and Naskapi Indians and the Inuit of northern Quebec signed the James Bay Agreement, whereby they surrendered aboriginal title to their lands, so that the James Bay Project, a vast hydroelectrical development, could proceed. All of these treaties were intended to achieve one main purpose: to extinguish the aboriginal title of the Native Peoples so that agricultural or industrial development could go ahead.

When the White fur traders arrived, the Indians of the northwest coast already had a sophisticated culture, a culture that was at first enriched and refined by contact with the Whites. Chisels and axes, for instance, made possible great advances in the carving of totem poles. Claude Lévi-Strauss, the great French anthropologist, has described the Indian culture of the northwest coast as one of the great efflorescences of mankind, and the Indians themselves as fit to be compared with the ancient Greeks and Romans. The collapse of that culture is seen by many as one of the great tragedies of modern times. How did it happen?

The Indians were indispensable partners in the fur trade. They collected the furs and brought them to the forts. All that changed with the abandonment of the fur trade and the advance of settlement. Under the new dispensation Indian labor was not needed. What was wanted was Indian land. As White settlement encroached on Indian land, Indian society and the Indian economy were transformed. Hunting and fishing continued to be the base of the Indian economy, but the Indians were prepared to enter other occupations. Some became farm laborers. Others were seasonally employed in logging camps and sawmills, in road and railway construction, and on fishing boats and in fish canneries. But the extent to which Indians could adapt to the new circumstances was limited: when they left their reserves, they encountered many forms of prejudice, barriers that made it difficult for them to adapt, and impossible to adapt completely.

Indian society was unstable for other reasons, too. The Indians were defenseless against the diseases brought by the Europeans. Smallpox and tuberculosis took an enormous toll of lives. Alcohol became a manifestation of and contributed to disintegration and decay. By 1900, the Indian population of the northwest coast, which at mid-century had stood at about 50 000, was reduced to 10 000, many of whom were enfeebled by disease. The appalling decline in the Indian population led to the conclusion, widely held among Whites, that the Indians were a people condemned by history, who would soon become extinct. Any sense of urgency about coming to grips with the question of aboriginal title diminished year by year.

The Indians were not completely excluded from various forms of wage labor, and their hunting and fishing activities were not totally prohibited or curtailed, but Indian unemployment and underemployment, their dependence on reserves, and their economic deprivation stem from this period. Perhaps even more damaging to the Indians than these losses was the denigration of their way of life that was implicit in every relation they had with White society, from the abolition of the potlatch to the refusal to allow them to vote. (The Indians, along with the Chinese and the Japanese, were denied the right to vote in British Columbia in 1895. They did not get it back until 1949. It is astonishing to think that Indians in Canada did not receive the right to vote in federal elections until 1960, when John Diefenbaker was prime minister.) The White presence, from the fur trade and the missions, to the advent of agriculture and industrial development, to the proliferation of government institutions, has dominated and it continues to dominate Indian society. There is an intrinsic relationship between this domination and the cluster of social pathologies and economic difficulties that afflict Indian communities today.

White attitudes common in British Columbia a century ago persist even today. The policies we pursued in the past were designed to suppress Indian languages, Indian culture, and the Indian economy. During the 19th century, we believed – and many persons still believe – that the Indian economy and, indeed, Indian society, was moribund, that Indian culture was at best a colorful reminder of the past and that what we see of it today is only a pathetic remnant of an age now gone.

Nevertheless, in the midst of these hammer blows, the Indians of the northwest coast continued to cling to their beliefs and to their own idea of themselves. And they remained determined to insist upon their aboriginal rights. In 1887, the provincial government appointed a royal commission "To Enquire into the Conditions of the Indians of the Northwest Coast." When the commission visited the Nass valley, the Nishga chiefs raised the question of aboriginal rights. David Mackay, one of the chiefs, summed up the Nishga point of view:

> What we don't like about the Government is their saying this: "We will give you this much land." How can they give it when it is our own? We cannot understand it. They have never bought it from us or our forefathers. They have never fought and conquered our people and taken the land in that way, and yet they say now that they will give us so much land – our own land. These chiefs do not talk foolishly, they know the land is their own; our forefathers for generations and generations past had their land here all around us; chiefs have had their own hunting grounds, their salmon streams, and places where they got their berries; it has always been so. It is not only during the last four or five years that we have seen the land; we have always seen and owned it; it is no new thing, it has been ours for generations. If we had only seen it for twenty years and claimed it as our own, it would have been foolish, but it has been ours for thousands of years.

Nevertheless, White encroachment on Indian lands continued. In 1885 the completion of the Canadian Pacific Railway had brought a rush of new immigrants. British Columbia, formerly easily accessible only by sea, could now be reached by rail from the east. By the turn of the century, the province's White population had greatly increased, and the resource industries and the road and rail networks had been greatly extended. These developments further limited the territory on which the Indians could hunt and fish. As early as 1895, the federal department of fisheries began to restrict the Indian food fishery, that is, the right of Indians to fish for food for themselves and their families, and by 1915 Indian hunting and trapping was brought under provincial regulation.

The Indians still had their reserves, of course. But these, too, came under attack after the turn of the century. Since 1874, the federal and provincial authorities had jointly laid out new Indian reserves, but in 1908 the province refused to lay out any more. The province insisted, instead, that the existing reserves must be reduced in size and that lands already held by the Indians must be made available for agricultural and commercial uses.

All this time, the Indians continued to press for recognition of their aboriginal title. In 1906 and again in 1909, delegations of Indian chiefs from British Columbia went to London to present their demands to the King himself. But the Imperial government was powerless to intervene, even if it were disposed to do so. In any event, the province would not change its position. In 1909, the premier, Richard McBride, said, "Of course it would be madness to think of conceding to the Indians' demands. It is too late to discuss the equity of dispossessing the Red man in America." McBride believed that the question of aboriginal title would never have been raised were it not for the "pernicious advice of some unscrupulous whites." This theme recurs again and again in our dealings with the Native Peoples. Many Canadians have found it convenient to believe that Native Peoples would not have thought of asserting their claims to the land, if it were not for the influence of subversive Whites. Thus historians have argued that the Métis would not have advanced a claim to aboriginal title in 1816, if they had not been put up to it by the Nor'Westers; while in the 1970s White radicals were supposed to have persuaded the Dene who, it was said, would not themselves have advanced such a position, to insist upon a settlement of their land claims before a pipeline could be built along the Mackenzie Valley.

In 1910, Prime Minister Wilfrid Laurier met representatives of the Indians at Prince Rupert. "The only way," he told them, "to settle this question that you have agitated for years is by a decision [of the Privy Council], and I will take steps to help you." The federal government then prepared a list of questions, to which the Indians agreed, to be submitted to the Privy Council. But Premier McBride rejected the whole idea. He would never agree, he asserted, to any adjudication of the question of aboriginal title.

On April 26, 1911, a deputation of the Indian chiefs of the northwest coast again met with Laurier at Prince Rupert. Laurier told them,

> The matter for us to immediately consider is whether we can bring the Government of British Columbia into Court with us. We think it is our duty to have the matter inquired into. The Government of British Columbia may be right or wrong in their assertion that the Indians have no claim whatever. Courts of law are just for that purpose – where a man asserts a claim and it is denied by another. But we do not know if we can force a government into court. If we can find a way, I may say we shall surely do so. . . . The Indians will continue to believe they have a grievance until it has been settled by the court that they have a claim, or that they have no claim.

But in the autumn of 1911, Laurier's government was defeated. His successors, Conservative and Liberal, refused for the next 50 years to consider the question of aboriginal claims in British Columbia and refused to intercede on the Indians' behalf with the province's intransigent politicians. Only in 1969 were the Indians finally able to force the government of British Columbia into court to have the question of aboriginal title adjudicated.

The case for the province rested on a series of ordinances passed during the pre-Confederation era by the Crown colony of Vancouver Island and the colony of British Columbia, which provided for the Crown grants and other forms of tenure. The contention of the province was that this exercise of legislative power had operated to extinguish whatever interest the Indians may have had in the lands comprising the province, albeit without compensation. After all, how could it be said that Indian title still subsisted, when the pre-Confederation governments had assumed the power to dispose of the very lands the Indians claimed.

The trial judge, Mr. Justice Gould, accepted this argument and dismissed the Nishga Indians' claim. He held that, if aboriginal title had existed, it had been extinguished by the ordinances passed by the old colonial governments of Vancouver Island and British Columbia.

The Nishgas carried their case to the British Columbia Court of Appeal. There they suffered another setback. Mr. Justice Gould had not determined whether or not there is such a thing as aboriginal title. He had simply held that, if there were such a title, it had been extinguished before the colony had entered Confederation. He left to the higher courts the determination of whether or not aboriginal title is a concept recognized by Canadian law. The British Columbia Court of Appeal was ready to address the question. The judges of that court held that the law had never acknowledged any such concept as aboriginal title, that while governments might choose as a matter of policy to deal with Indians as if they did have a legal interest in land, there was, in reality, no such legal interest – no Indian title – and there never had been. Thus the Nishga Indians had never had aboriginal title. They went on to say that, if they had had such a title, it had been extinguished during the pre-Confederation era (as Mr. Justice Gould had held). Chief Justice H. W. Davey demonstrated the attitude of the court. Observing the Nishgas across an ethnographic gulf, he declined to believe that the Nishgas had their own ideas of land ownership, saying, "They were undoubtedly at the time of settlement a very primitive people with few of the institutions of civilized society, and none at all of our notions of private property."

It has been difficult to convince lawyers and judges that the Native Peoples of Canada have certain rights based on the indisputable fact that they occupied vast areas if not the whole of this continent before the Europeans discovered, then colonized it. They had their own cultures, their own social institutions, their own laws. But of this lawyers and judges remained unaware. Chief Justice Davey was one of British Columbia's finest judges: he was patient, scholarly, and upright. Yet he could not understand that Native Peoples had sophisticated concepts of legal relations and legal rights. He could not accept that people without a written language can, nevertheless, have an elaborate legal system of their own. And, as for their aboriginal title, how could the court acknowledge it? It was ill defined, it was not recorded in a system of title deeds, and it was not a form of private property but property held communally by the tribe.

Chief Justice Davey's inability to comprehend the true nature of native culture and native claims is widely shared. It results in an attitude toward Native People that infuriates them. This attitude is sometimes manifested in an attempt to preserve native culture and sometimes in an attempt to eradicate it, but it is always manifested in a patronizing way. It assumes that native culture cannot be viable in a contemporary context, that it cannot have a place in an urban, industrial society. This is the crux of the matter. Native Peoples insist that their culture is still a vital force in their own lives, that it informs their own view of themselves, of the world about them, and of the dominant White society. We too easily assume that native culture is static and unchanging. We see the Native Peoples as locked into their past. Such an assumption may become self-fulfilling: by refusing to give Native People the means to deal with present problems in their own terms, their culture may, in fact, become static. But they are not locked into the past: we are excluding them from the present.

The culture of Native Peoples amounts to more than crafts and carvings, dancing and drinking. Their tradition of decision-making by consensus, their respect for the wisdom of their elders, their concept of the extended family, their belief in a special relationship with the land, their respect for the environment, their willingness to share – all of these values persist in one way or another among them today, despite unremitting pressure to abandon them.

Thus Indian culture is not moribund. Indian ideas about their relationship with the land are the foundation of aboriginal title. But the Nishgas could not persuade the British Columbia Court of Appeal that they had ever in their long past had title to the Nass valley, or that they could assert any title in the present. Neither could the Nishgas nor any other of the Native

Peoples of Canada persuade the federal government to recognize aboriginal title. *The Statement of the Government of Canada on Indian Policy*, 1969, declared:

> Aboriginal claims to land . . . are so general and undefined that it is not realistic to think of them as specific claims capable of remedy except through a policy and programme that will end injustice to Indians as members of the Canadian community.

Prime Minister Trudeau, speaking on this subject in Vancouver on August 8, 1969, said, "Our answer is no. We can't recognize aboriginal rights because no society can be built on historical 'might have beens'." So there was no relief to be had in the courts, and no acknowledgment of their claims by the federal government.

But the Native Peoples' conviction that their future must lie in the assertion of their common identity and in the defense of their common interests has proved stronger than anyone could have anticipated. Government policy was overthrown by the determination of the Native Peoples to reject it. And the Nishga Indians' appeal to the Supreme Court of Canada was one of the principal instruments of that overthrow.

But wasn't Trudeau right? Shouldn't Native Peoples be treated as any other minority? Why should there be a special place for them in Canadian life? The reason is simple. To refuse to acknowledge a special status for the Natives is to repudiate Canada's constitutional history. In the British North America Act, the Fathers of Confederation provided that Parliament should have exclusive legislative jurisdiction over the Native Peoples of Canada. Why should the Native Peoples be given special consideration? No such provision was made for the Ukrainians, the Swedes, the Italians, or for any other ethnic group or nationality. The Indians, the Inuit and the Métis did not immigrate to Canada as individuals or families who expected to be assimilated. Immigrants chose to come here and to submit to Canadian laws and institutions; their choices were individual choices. The Indians, the Inuit, and the Métis were already here: they have been forced to submit to the laws and institutions, be they anglophone or francophone, of the dominant White society. And they have never relinquished their claim to be treated as distinct peoples in our midst.

To affirm the simple reality of this ancient truth – that the Native Peoples are the aboriginal peoples of Canada and therefore have aboriginal rights – the Nishgas appealed to the Supreme Court of Canada. They urged the federal government to intervene on their behalf in the proceedings in the Supreme Court. Here at last was the opportunity, sought since Laurier's day, to bring the province of British Columbia before the Supreme Court of Canada and to resolve the question of Indian title in British Columbia. Jean Chrétien, then Minister of Indian Affairs and Northern Development, although personally sympathetic to the Nishgas' cause, declined to intervene, because he felt constrained by the federal policy enunciated in 1969 to refuse recognition of aboriginal rights.

The chiefs of the four villages in the Nass valley, together with village elders wearing their traditional sashes, travelled to Ottawa for the hearing in November, 1971. Seven judges of the Supreme Court of Canada sat on the case. The argument of the appeal took five days. The judges of the Supreme Court reserved their decision for 14 months. When finally the court handed down its judgment in February, 1973, the Nishgas appeared to have lost, four to three. At last they had reached the end of the road. But careful study of the reasoning of the seven judges who heard the case soon made clear that, although technically the Nishgas had lost their case, they had in fact won a moral victory. Moral victories are not usually of any tangible value, but this victory had a great deal to do with bringing about a fundamental change in federal government policy.

Mr. Justice Wilfred Judson, speaking for three judges, found that the Nishgas, before the coming of the White man, had aboriginal title, a title recognized under English law. But, he went on to say, this title had been extinguished by pre-Confederation enactments of the old colony of British Columbia. Mr. Justice Emmett Hall, speaking for three judges, found that the Nishgas, before the coming of the White man, had aboriginal title, that it had never been lawfully extinguished, and that this title could be asserted even today. On this reckoning, the court was tied.

Mr. Justice Louis-Philippe Pigeon, the seventh judge, expressed no opinion on the main issue. He held against the Nishgas on the ground that they had proceeded by issuing a writ against the Province of British Columbia. They should, he said, have proceeded by way of a petition of right, a procedure which was unavailable to them since it was necessary to have the consent of the province to issue a petition of right against the province. Mr. Justice Pigeon's vote meant that the Nishgas had lost, four to three.

Here is the crucial point. All of the six judges who had addressed the main question supported the view that English law in force in British Columbia when colonization began had recognized Indian title to the land. Here, for the first time, Canada's highest court had unequivocally affirmed the concept of aboriginal title. Mr. Justice Judson, in describing the nature of Indian title, relied on the passages from Professor Duff's *The Indian History of British Columbia* that were quoted above. He concluded,

> The fact is that when the settlers came the Indians were there, organized in societies and occupying the land as their forefathers had done for centuries. This is what Indian title means. . . . What they are asserting in this action is that they had a right to continue to live on their lands as their forefathers had lived and that this right has never been lawfully extinguished.

Mr. Justice Judson went on to hold that the old colony of British Columbia had effectively extinguished the aboriginal title of the Nishga Indians. But he had no doubt that there is such a thing as aboriginal title.

Mr. Justice Hall, speaking for the three judges who were prepared to uphold the Nishgas' claim, urged that the court should adopt a contemporary view and not be bound by past and mistaken notions about Indians and Indian culture. In the judgment of Mr. Justice Hall you will find that sense of humanity – that stretch of the mind and heart – that enabled him to look at the idea of aboriginal rights and to see it as the Indian people see it. This required some idea of the place of Indian history in our own history. He suggested that Chief Justice Davey, in asserting that the Nishgas were at the time of settlement "a very primitive people with few of the institutions of civilized society, and none at all of our notions of private property," had assessed the Indian culture of 1858 by the same standards that the Europeans applied to the Indians of North America two or more centuries before. Mr. Justice Hall rejected this approach:

> The assessment and interpretation of the historical documents and enactments tendered in evidence must be approached in the light of present-day research and knowledge disregarding ancient concepts formulated when understanding of the customs and culture of our original people was rudimentary and incomplete and when they were thought to be wholly without cohesion, laws or culture, in effect a subhuman species. This concept of the original inhabitants of America led Chief Justice Marshall in his otherwise enlightened judgement in *Johnson vs. McIntosh* (1823) 8 Wheaton 543, which is the outstanding judicial pronouncement on the subject of Indian rights, to say: "But the tribes of Indians inhabiting this country were fierce savages whose occupation was war. . . ." We now know that that assessment was ill-founded. The Indians did in fact at times engage in some tribal wars but war was not their vocation and it can be said that their pre-occupation with war pales into insignificance when compared to the religious and dynastic wars of "civilized" Europe of the 16th and 17th centuries.

Mr. Justice Hall concluded that the Nishgas had their own concept of aboriginal title before the coming of the White man and were still entitled to assert it today. He said:

> What emerges from the . . . evidence is that the Nishgas in fact are and were from time immemorial a distinctive cultural entity with concepts of ownership indigenous to their culture and capable of articulation under the common law, having "developed their cultures to higher peaks in many respects than in any other part of the continent north of Mexico."

Emmett Hall's contributions to Canadian life are numerous. But none is more important than his strong and stirring judgment in the Nishgas' case. For he held that the Nishgas' title could be asserted today. No matter that the province would be faced with innumerable legal tangles. What was right was right.

The Supreme Court's judgment, although it was not handed down until 14 months after the hearing in the case, came at a propitious moment. The election of 1972 had returned the Liberals to power, but as a minority government. To remain in office, the Liberals depended on the good will of the opposition parties. The Nishga decision now catapulted the question of aboriginal title into the political arena. In Parliament, both the Conservatives and the New Democrats insisted that the federal government must recognize its obligation to settle native claims. The all-party Standing Committee on Indian and Northern Affairs passed a motion that approved the principle that a settlement of native claims should be made in regions where treaties had not already extinguished aboriginal title. On August 8, 1973, Jean Chrétien announced that the federal government intended to settle native land claims in all parts of Canada where no treaties had yet been made. Mr. Justice Hall's judgment can now be seen to be the basis for the assertion today of native land claims throughout Canada.

3. A Look to the Future

Of course the Nishgas were not alone in effecting this fundamental change in federal government policy. The National Indian Brotherhood and many provincial and territorial native organizations had worked steadily toward the same end – but the Nishga case was a crucial development in the long process.

The land claims movement has given rise to a call among the Native People for self-determination. After years of poor achievement in our schools, after years of living on the fringes of an economy that too often has no place for them as workers and no need of them as consumers, and without the political power to change these things, the Native Peoples have decided that they want to substitute self-determination for enforced dependency.

The Nishga Indians, like the rest of Canada's Native Peoples, are re-entering Canadian history. They are not some ghostly rabble whose former presence had left too faint a mark to catch the attention of our political leaders today. For more than two centuries, the history of Canada was the history of an encounter between the French and the Native Peoples, then of an encounter between the English and the Native Peoples. Only during the last century and a half have the Native Peoples been relegated to a place off center stage. Now they are returning from the wings to demand a speaking part again.

But what about the provinces? The federal government has agreed to settle aboriginal claims. But, unless the provinces are obligated by the Constitution to negotiate a settlement of native claims, their governments will no doubt continue to deny, as they have in the past, the existence of aboriginal rights or of any obligation to negotiate a settlement of aboriginal claims.

Settlement of their claims ought to offer the Native Peoples a whole range of opportunities. In some cases priority should be given to local renewable resource activities – not because such activities are universally desirable, but because they are on a scale appropriate to many native communities.

These are activities that local people can undertake, that are amenable to local management and control, and that are related to traditional values. Development need not be defined exclusively in terms of large-scale, capital-intensive technology. But there is no reason why native peoples should not have access as well to the economy of the dominant society where large-scale technology pre-dominates. The settlement of native claims ought to provide the means to enable Native Peoples to thrive, and native cultures to develop, in ways denied them in the past. They can become hunters, trappers, fishermen, lawyers, loggers, doctors, nurses, teachers, workers in the oil and gas fields, or in the sawmills and the stores. But most important of all, the collective fabric of native life will be affirmed and strengthened. The sense of identity of individual Native People – their very well-being – depends upon it.

The Native Peoples do not want to recreate a world that has vanished. They do, however, want to find a place in the world that we have forced upon them. Indian treaties, Indian reserves, the Indian Act – these are all institutions that we have devised to manage the Native Peoples primarily for our own convenience. Now they want to develop institutions of their own fashioning; they are eager to see their cultures grow and change in directions they have chosen for themselves. They do not wish to be objects of sentimentality. They do not want native culture, native communities, and the native economy to be preserved in amber for the amusement and edification of others. They do not want to return to live in tents and igloos. Like us, they are residents of the 20th century. They, too, live in a world in which progress has an industrial and technological definition. However, because the Native Peoples use the technology of the dominant society, that fact does not mean that they should study only English or French in school, that they should learn no history except ours, or that they should be governed by our institutions alone.

It will take time for the Native Peoples to limn their claims, for their claims are not limited to land and resources. They wish to achieve a measure of self-determination and self-government, and they see their claims as the means by which these things will be achieved. They are already undertaking to define their claims in the fields of education, health, and social services – claims as significant to the urban Native as the rural Native. For instance, Native People complain that in school their children are told about the kings and queens of England and about the brave band of settlers who established the colony of New France on the shores of the St. Lawrence River. All that, they say, is your history. What about our history? They want schools in which their children can study native history, native languages, native lore, and native rights. Of course they also want their children to speak English or French, as the case may be, to understand the history of our European antecedents and their expansion into the New World, and to study mathematics, natural sciences, and everything else a person needs to know to function in the dominant society. But they must have schools in which they can learn about who they are as well as who we are. The Nishga Indians now have their own school district; it is one of the first in Canada to embrace a predominantly native population. In June, 1979, 10 years after the trial of their land claim before the Supreme Court of British Columbia, the first class graduated from the Nishga Secondary School.

If, in working out settlements of native claims, we try to force native development into moulds that we have cast, the whole process will end in failure. No tidy, bureaucratic chart will be of any use; and no governmental policy or program can succeed unless it takes into account the Native Peoples' determination to remain themselves – Indian, Inuit, or Métis. For this reason, the Native Peoples must have distinct social, economic, and political institutions. At the same time, they must have access to the social, economic and political institutions of the dominant society. When we are devising such arrangements, it is important to understand precisely what we are talking about. We are not talking about apartheid. In South Africa, the Blacks have been confined to *bantustans;* they have no right to live, to vote, or to work in South Africa except on sufferance. What Native Peoples in Canada are asking for is the right to their own institutions, to the extent that they require them to preserve their culture and their sense of collective identity, and access to the institutions of the dominant society. Only if we were to deny them such access could our policy be said to be one of apartheid.

Canada is committed to a fair settlement of native claims. This has come about because our institutions have offered the means for redress, and our tradition of tolerance has demanded that redress be made. Of course, this is only a beginning. But it offers to Canada an opportunity to make a contribution to human rights for indigenous peoples everywhere. Pierre Trudeau has suggested that,

> Canada could become the envied seat of a form of federalism that belongs to tomorrow's world. . . . Canada could offer an example to all those new Asian and African states who must discover how to govern their polyethnic populations with proper regard for justice and liberty. . . . Canadian federalism is an experiment of major proportions; it could become a brilliant prototype for the moulding of tomorrow's civilization.

It is all very well to say that Canadian institutional arrangements may speak to the emerging nations of Asia and Africa. But why not to our own hemisphere? There are 50 million Native People in North and South America, almost everywhere dispossessed, everywhere poor, everywhere powerless. In the past they refused to die; today they will not be assimilated. They insist that we must address the issues that have pursued us for almost 500 years, since Columbus set foot in the New World. How can we work out a just relationship between the dominant societies established by the White Europeans and the indigenous peoples of North and South America? In Canada this can be achieved through a fair settlement of native claims. The settlement of these claims may, therefore, be important to men and women in many countries, truly a "prototype for tomorrow's civilization."

The Dene Declaration*

We the Dene of the N.W.T. insist on the right to be regarded by ourselves and the world as a nation.

Our struggle is for the recognition of the Dene Nation by the Government and people of Canada and the peoples and governments of the world.

As once Europe was the exclusive homeland of the European peoples, Africa the exclusive homeland of the African peoples, the New World, North and South America, was the exclusive homeland of the Aboriginal peoples of the New World, the Amerindian and the Inuit.

The New World, like other parts of the world, has suffered the experience of colonialism and imperialism. Other peoples have occupied the land – often with force – and foreign governments have imposed themselves on our people. Ancient civilizations and ways of life have been destroyed.

Colonialism and imperialism is now dead or dying. Recent years have witnessed the birth of new nations or rebirth of old nations out of the ashes of colonialism.

As Europe is the place where you will find European countries with European governments for European peoples, now also you will find in Africa and Asia the existence of African and Asian countries with African and Asian governments for the African and Asian peoples.

The African and Asian peoples – the peoples of the Third World – have fought for and won the right to self-determination, the right to the recognition as distinct peoples and the recognition of themselves as nations.

But in the New World the Native Peoples have not fared so well. Even in countries in South America where the Native Peoples are the vast majority of the population there is not one country which has an Amerindian government for the Amerindian peoples.

Nowhere in the New World have the Native Peoples won the right to self-determination and the right to recognition by the world as a distinct people and as Nations.

While the Native People of Canada are a minority in their homeland, the Native People of the N.W.T., the Dene and the Inuit, are a majority of the population of the N.W.T.

---

* Reprinted by permission of the Indian Brotherhood of the Northwest Territories.

The Dene find themselves as part of a country. That country is Canada. But the Government of Canada is not the government of the Dene. These governments were not the choice of the Dene, they were imposed upon the Dene.

What we the Dene are struggling for is the recognition of the Dene Nation by the governments and peoples of the world.

And while there are realities we are forced to submit to, such as the existence of a country called Canada, we insist on the right to self-determination as a distinct people and the recognition of the Dene Nation.

We the Dene are part of the Fourth World. And as the peoples and nations of the world have come to recognize the existence and rights of those peoples who make up the Third World the day must come and will come when the nations of the Fourth World will come to be recognized and respected. The challenge to the Dene and the world is to find the way for the recognition of the Dene Nation.

Our plea to the world is to help us in our struggle to find a place in the world community where we can exercise our right to self-determination as a distinct people and as a nation.

What we seek then is independence and self-determination within the country of Canada. That is what we mean when we call for a just land settlement for the Dene Nation.

PETER JULL

Aboriginal Peoples and Political Change in the North Atlantic Area*

Introduction

The plight of aboriginal or Native Peoples is of increasing interest to the world community, even if not yet the subject of enlightened action in many countries. The misfortunes of Latin American Indians in the face of ruthless industrialization and large-scale farming have, with the help of modern communications media, shocked the European peoples on both sides of the Atlantic. However, when strong clear voices in our own time and our own country tell us we are "racist" or that our present actions are as brutal as those of the past, we are apt to shake our heads at such "radicalism."

If we cannot accept the accusations of a Harry Daniels, President of Canada's national organization representing the Métis and non-status Indians, and hence the largest body of Canadian Native People,[1] or the analysis of northern development policies quietly put forward by a George Erasmus, President of the Dene Nation,[2] the Indian and Métis organization in the Mackenzie Valley which has been the leading edge of the aboriginal fight against insensitive development interest, where do we turn? It may be useful to compare our experience with that of other countries faced with similar questions and to attempt to identify common difficulties. In this process, I believe, we will discover that far from being a local aberration or an adventure of restless youth, the voices we hear are authentic expressions of universal problems and ones, therefore, which may require different solutions than may be dictated by current political fashion or by our cultural prejudices.

The three countries to be discussed are Canada, Danish Greenland and Norway. These three circumpolar countries not only include a wide variety of experience, but immediately concern international relations experts studying the North Atlantic area. Indeed, it is the very fact that "the native movement" has begun to impinge on the considerations of strategic studies that makes serious discussion of the questions addressed here so important.[3] But these three national situations are only part of the whole circumpolar experience; examples from northern Finland or Iceland, Shetland or Alaska would equally serve the purposes of the discussion.

* Reprinted from *Journal of Canadian Studies* Vol. 16, No. 2 (Summer, 1981).

Before examining the specific cases, it may be useful to describe a few of the most general characteristics of the political culture of the region under consideration. Three uniquely Canadian situations – northern Quebec, Nunavut and the national constitutional review process involving Native People – will then be analysed. A tentative conclusion will follow an exploration of Greenland's home rule and Norway's rapidly evolving native rights movement.

General Characteristics

All of the areas under discussion are "northern." Just how difficult it is to define what that means in practical terms is suggested in Louis-Edmond Hamelin's *Nordicité Canadienne*[4] by his complex mixture of physical and cultural indices which determine degrees of "northernness" or "nordicity." At its simplest, we generally understand a northern community to include a small population, living in a harsh climate and inadequately linked to the societies, services and infrastructure of the state which exercises political control over it.

A second feature of our areas is that they all lie within Western liberal democracies. This has considerable significance, as the Canadian Inuit were quick to notice when defining the goals and format of the international organization (Inuit Circumpolar Conference) which they have jointly created with Alaska and Greenland Inuit.[5] The possibilities for overt political expression and action are there, as presumably are opportunities for non-violent change. For this reason official appeals to "higher causes" (such as military security, territorial integrity, or the energy needs of the whole state) are inherently problematic and destabilizing insofar as they change the rules of the game and impose limitations prematurely on political processes in areas where – our third point – political processes are underdeveloped and seeking expression.

The third point is the heart of our story, but it need not be discussed at length here. It is sufficient to point out that because of small populations, remote locations vis-à-vis national decision centers and, indirectly, unsettled land and resources regimes, these areas do not dispose of the full rights of political citizenship enjoyed by other inhabitants of the state. The reasons given are generally of two types: that small numbers and other administrative inconveniences do not warrant or permit the highest levels of political participation until some future time established perhaps by some future review; or, that the great wealth potential to be found in the regions where so few people live could not responsibly be shared or controlled by so few. This double bind is particularly familiar to the people of northern Canada.

Linked to the preceding is the obvious importance of land and resources, including marine and seabed resources. The two main features of this problem are jurisdictional and proprietary rights and conflicting resource uses.

In the first case, there may be limited ownership of land, as in Finnmark county of northern Norway or in Greenland, and hence limited control by the people of the region. Or there may be a fundamental dispute, again as in Greenland, but also in all other aboriginal areas, as to who should hold the powers over lands and resources and on what terms. Resource use conflicts often occur between resident communities dependent economically, and for social and cultural continuity, upon renewable resource activities (fishing or reindeer herding, sea mammal or land hunting), and interests which would, or could, damage this renewable resource base. Far from there being anything sentimental about these environmental battles, they are basic to economic and social self-interest. The impact of big money and inflation, influxes of outside transient workers and pollution all threaten the stability of the community, and for communities which have survived many hundreds or even thousands of years, the trade-offs for a 10-year mining project may be unexciting.

Finally and perhaps obviously, these northern regions contain culturally and linguistically separate communities whose distinctiveness becomes both a rallying point and a cause of political development. This very distinctiveness becomes a major datum with its own set of demands. When all the factors mentioned are found in conjunction, as they are not only in the aboriginal areas under specific discussion here, but in all the other small societies of the circumpolar world, including the European peoples of the North Atlantic area, one might expect that special political circumstances would obtain.

Northern Quebec[6]

In northern Quebec 15 Inuit villages account for a rapidly expanding population of 5 200. The families from these villages have used and occupied about one third of Quebec since ancient times, and their ancestors much of the north shore of the St. Lawrence in early historic times. It is estimated that about 80 percent of the food needs of these people still derive from traditional sources, and indeed traditional hunting and fishing activities are the main occupations of the people. Quebec Inuit are a minority within a minority; not only an aboriginal minority within a predominantly European Society, they also, by historical accident, speak English as a second language after their native Inuktitut and are hence classed as part of the Anglophone minority – with all its political signification – by the Quebec Francophone majority. Nevertheless, in their villages and in their overall territory, the Inuit constitute the overwhelming majority of the population. The "two solitudes" of Inuit and Francophone Quebec could not be more clear, separated as they are by many hundreds of miles of boreal forest and tundra.

The relations between Quebec Inuit and Francophone Quebecers are a worthy subject for study. The history of suspicion and tension is more complex, although not more unpleasant, than the usual run of dismal Native-

White relations in Canada. In the 1930s, when the Quebec government of the day rejected bills for payment of Inuit famine relief and took the case to the Supreme Court of Canada, the resulting decision (the so-called Eskimo Reference of 1939) specified that Inuit were Indians within the constitutional meaning and hence a special responsibility of the federal government. It is this very particular status, shared by other Native Peoples in Canada, that has offended Quebec nationalist sentiment in recent years. Unique perhaps among its constitutional positions, Quebec spokesmen argue that legalisms like the James Bay and Northern Quebec Agreement and related legislation should not be taken literally but as tokens of a new era of trust between Native Peoples and the provincial government.[7] Quebec officials, meanwhile, find themselves continually faced with Anglophone advisers to the Inuit, often former federal officials, and are suspicious of their presumed federalist sympathies. In short, the nationalism of a Francophone Quebec vis-à-vis a predominantly Anglophone Canada is the special context which complicates the situation of Quebec Inuit and must be understood. But the other features are more universal.

When the Bourassa government was elected in 1970 it linked the province's destiny to the vast hydro-electric potential lying in the many wild rivers which fell off all sides of the great Quebec peninsula. In a chronically difficult economic and employment situation, the vision of new wealth and an engine for Quebec economic growth beckoned. Plans to begin development in the James Bay region were pushed ahead for the largest-ever hydro-electric project in the world. The views of Native People and the impact of these plans on their lives were little known and not thought important. But a successful court injunction won by the Inuit and the Cree temporarily stopped the project. As a result, Quebec was prepared to negotiate a comprehensive agreement to free not only the areas around the project from further legal action but to establish clearly the title of Quebec to the whole of its territory (other than Labrador, still disputed by Quebec). The result in 1975 was the James Bay and Northern Quebec Agreement.

Although the Agreement was widely criticized by other native groups across Canada, and especially by those who hoped to negotiate their own agreements with government later, the Inuit and the Cree obtained under its terms cash compensation, elective regional government and school board structures, lands reserved under various regimes, development agencies, as well as continuing opportunities to participate in environmental decisions relating to the hydro-electric or other developments in the region. These arrangements are, in all cases, utterly separate, Cree from Inuit, although the Inuit often speak of their regional government structures as being "non-ethnic."

The Agreement spawned two primary agencies – the Kativik Regional Government and the Makivik Corporation. The latter is an economic development corporation and trustee of the cash compensation owed to all the Inuit of Northern Quebec. It is also the central political and social representative body for the Inuit. (The Makivik principals were the members of the Northern Quebec Inuit Association who had negotiated the Agreement.) Since the signing of the Agreement, much of the activity in northern Quebec has been initiated by the financially independent Makivik Corporation whose elected leaders have become the dominant Inuit politicians in northern Quebec. These dynamic leaders have emphasized economic development over ideology with the result that the political climate of the region is characterized by strong personalities working for practical community interests.

Meanwhile, the Kativik Regional Government, with few funds and denied the powers or resources for which the Inuit had traded away aboriginal rights, is the vehicle which is supposed to deliver most of the housing, water, sewage and health services. Since early 1980 an argument, which shows no signs of resolution, has divided the Inuit, Quebec and federal governments over the question of actual levels of service. In March 1981, a House of Commons standing committee reviewing Inuit and Cree grievances in this area took extraordinary all-party action to obtain direct federal assistance for the Inuit and to bring greater pressure to bear on Quebec.[8] For its part, Quebec argues that most of the issues of concern are strictly internal matters. Because this federal-provincial stalemate has persisted in one form or another since 1963, Inuit community services are often alarmingly poor and certainly far below the standards established in the Northwest Territories.

The Inuit failed to obtain rights to resource taxation or any formula financing which might assist their revenue picture through development in the region. With only business licenses and other such inauspicious possibilities for revenue, the Inuit fear that they may have a difficult financial future. To date they have been unable to generate serious talks with Quebec about revenue sharing. The cash compensation, which gives an illusion of wealth, cannot be used for capital requirements. The interest from the compensation fund provides the operating budget for Makivik and its subsidiary companies which, in turn, are intended to create jobs, training and more wealth in the Inuit north. These many difficulties have maintained a small but persistent dissident movement centered in two communities and in the association of Cooperatives. The dissidents seek to delay any agreements with governments and look to a day when their children can bargain more effectively, an approach dismissed by Makivik partisans as unrealistic.

Two points are worth emphasizing in conclusion. During the testimony of March 26, 1981, before the House standing committee in Ottawa, both Inuit and Cree leaders continued to stress that they regarded the Agreement itself as sound; they did not, however, believe that it was being implemented in good faith. Whereas they had clearly understood that normal government programs would be available as before – a view supported by the Hon. Warren Allmand, the man who, as Minister of Indian and Northern Affairs at the time, had piloted the Agreement legislation through Parliament – their experience indicated that they were often left on their own with only their compensation funds. To quote Makivik vice-president Mark R. Gordon, one of the negotiators of the Agreement,

> . . . in the negotiation of the James Bay Agreement we had to negotiate for many of the programs and normal services that are available to other Canadians under the normal laws of application. We were supposed to get those programs in the first place, but we had to negotiate for those essential services. We had to trade them off for aboriginal rights. Sure, we could have got a hell of a lot more in land but we had to fight to be able to get basic municipal services. Even those have not been implemented today.[9]

Nunavut[10]

If the James Bay and Northern Quebec Agreement bears a strong resemblance to the Alaska land claims settlement, Nunavut is strictly a made-in-Canada model. In fact, the scrupulous adherence to Canadian political norms was a conscious attempt by Inuit leaders to ensure greater credibility for their political aspirations than had been allowed those of other native groups meeting public hostility or incomprehension with their talk of nationhood, sovereignty and self-determination.

Nunavut, meaning, "our land" in Inuktitut and therefore a most potent concept for the Inuit, would divide the Northwest Territories along the tree-line (which also separates the Indians [Dene] from the Inuit). The principal official opposition to the idea seems to be based on the belief that drawing such a boundary line would create an "ethnic jurisdiction," something said to be repugnant to Canadian norms – although of course the southern provinces are no more monoethnic with large Anglo-Celtic or French-descended majorities than would be Nunavut with its non-Inuit minority (whose rights would be guaranteed under the Inuit proposal). The other argument, that a divided NWT would not be administratively practical or economical, loses force when it is recalled that both the Conservative and Liberal governments of the early 1960s had proposed precisely this division on the grounds of such efficiency. Nevertheless, nobody in the Inuit movement believes that the realization of Nunavut will be easy.

The first and perhaps most important step in the creation of Nunavut would be the division of the NWT. Inuit politicians are working vigorously to that end and have the sympathetic report of an NWT Legislative Assembly committee set up to study the matter last year,[11] plus a unanimous Assembly vote favoring a referendum on the concept to support them. The federal Cabinet has given no positive indications on the question.

Although Nunavut has been proposed by the Inuit since 1974, the present detailed proposal was approved by the Annual General Meeting of the Inuit Tapirisat at Igloolik, NWT, in September 1979. As with the James Bay Agreement and Indian treaties of the past, it was resource development which mobilized the Inuit to start organizing their political concerns around the concept of Nunavut. Beginning in the Mackenzie Delta region, the search for oil, gas, uranium and other minerals, the damage done by exploration crews to ecologically sensitive landscapes, and the threats to the marine life on which most Inuit rely for their food and livelihood, could not be ignored. When appeals directed through the normal channels of government bureaucracy failed to yield an adequate response to their concerns, the Inuit began to develop a sophisticated political platform.

The Nunavut proposal integrates the settlement of Inuit land claims with political structures. Rather than divide the northern lands into different categories of ownership and administration, the Inuit would turn to the kind of multiple-use planning favored by modern environmentalists and encouraged by the Inuit values of collective ownership and sharing. Despite similar land use management schemes in provinces like British Columbia, Inuit spokesmen are finding that they must explain their proposal in considerable detail.

The proposal for a self-governing Nunavut territory along lines previously advocated by federal government northern affairs officials would seem unexceptional. However, the misunderstanding which has surrounded the proposal to date has led many observers in Canadian native groups to see its fate as a test of Canadian sincerity in the amelioration of the conditions of aboriginal peoples.

The Canadian Constitution [12]

Constitutional reform has exercised Canadian governments for many years. But when the present phase opened in June 1978, with the publication of Prime Minister Trudeau's white paper, *A Time for Action*, and Bill C-60, the federal government repaired some of the damage done by its earlier, offensive proclamations about "two founding peoples," a notion which had incensed Native Canadians for years. Now Ottawa stated as one of its cardinal principles that:

> The renewal of the Federation must fully respect the legitimate rights of the native peoples, recognize their rightful place in the Canadian mosaic as the first inhabitants of the country, and give them the means of enjoying full equality of opportunity. [13]

More important, however, was a sentence which appeared in the Explanatory Document, a small booklet accompanying Bill C-60:

> An elaboration of rights particular to the native peoples could, of course, be added to the Charter [of Rights] if at the close of ongoing discussions between governments and the native peoples, agreement is reached that this should be done.

These words went largely unnoticed, and indeed the daily press and broadcast media virtually ignored the native consitutional dimension until Indian chiefs visited London a year later in the hope of presenting their constitutional views to the Queen. Nevertheless, native newspapers and radio programs across the country actively stimulated discussion and debate on the question.

Native leaders had long been aware that many of the problems they were trying to negotiate with governments were tied to constitutional problems. The first Inuit Circumpolar Conference in June 1977 passed a resolution supporting Canadian Inuit involvement in any process of constitutional reform. The Indian leadership learned from lengthy discussions of a new India Act that a more fundamental recognition of their status was needed if their cultural and other objectives were to be met. The Métis and non-status Indians suffered the worst privations of any group precisely because of the federal discretion which refused to acknowledge them as Indians within the constitutional meaning of that term, even if many tens of thousands of them lived every day of their lives with the culture and burdens of Canadian aboriginal peoples.

Following the June 1978 opening of constitutional talks, the national native leaders began to press for direct meetings with government leaders. In autumn 1978, the federal government failed to win provincial support for a hearing of native presentations at the First Ministers' Conference of October 30 – November 1, but native observers were allowed to circulate position papers. At that meeting more than half the heads of government noted the presence of the native leaders, and one, Premier William Davis of Ontario, said they should be involved in constitutional revision. After a winter of lobbying by the native groups and an increased federal political awareness of native views, resulting from a recruitment drive by the Liberals to attract native candidates for the impending general election, Prime Minister Trudeau pushed for the inclusion of native issues on the constitutional working agenda when the First Ministers reconvened in February 1979. Along with Premier Davis, the Prime Minister urged his colleagues to meet directly with native leaders for a thorough discussion of native constitutional concerns. When the final session of the conference was televised, Premier Davis brought this agreement from the closed session to light and there the native constitutional hopes rested for some time.

Following a general election which saw the defeat of the Trudeau government and the reaffirmation of the February agreement by the Clark government on June 29, 1979,[14] native leaders sought to clarify the extent of their involvement in constitutional work. They feared that although they would be allowed to discuss some topics deemed suitable by government officials, they would lose by default on their major concerns because of ongoing federal initiatives in areas where conflicts of concern to natives had not yet been resolved. For example, despite the failure to settle native political rights, Ottawa was continuing discussions about the extension of new institutional arrangements to the Yukon government. Ottawa was also exploring with certain provinces a possible redefinition of jurisdiction over offshore resources, even while these were subject to native claims accepted for negotiation by the federal government. That Native People had a legitimate cause for concern was amply demonstrated by federal abandonment of the painfully negotiated Inuit land claims agreement-in-principle in the Mackenzie River Delta area. The federal compromise, which was sustained when the Trudeau Liberals returned to power in February 1980, stated that Native People would be able to discuss constitutional matters with "direct legal impact" on them through a special agenda item, "Canada's Native Peoples and the Constitution." Unlike other agenda items, this would be a forum rather than a subject heading.

The prospects were challenging. Constitutional conferences were notoriously unproductive despite intensive preparation and the continuity of the federal-provincial "club." What would happen with new and inexperienced actors, entirely new subject matter like aboriginal rights, for which no definitions existed, and with no agreed vocabulary or even shared legal concepts between native and government sides? At the first meeting of federal and provincial ministers and the national native leaders, Conservative constitutional minister, the Hon. Bill Jarvis, clearly delineated the problem and gave some advice:

> I have no doubt that many of the achievements from this process will be in the form of intangible benefits or "spinoffs". As much as we may eventually want to find new words for the Constitution, we are here as well to take account of the broad relationship of governments and native peoples and seek to improve it. . . . Work has to be done together. Everyone knows that we are not dealing with subjects where someone can walk into a room and deliver a position and expect people to agree and go home. *All* of us, and I stress the word *all*, are going to need to explore each other's concerns and vocabularies. One of the reasons we will need to do this is because there exists no generally accepted language or experience for some of the work we must undertake. Such a process requires a commitment to meetings, however informal, to discussions, and to patience. . . . The challenge for all of us is that here we may have to come to terms with perceptions of history, society, even law, which are new to many of us. It is clear that our past practices have not adequately permitted this, and I need hardly refer to some depressing social statistics to illustrate this point. . . . Canadians are coming to realize that the problems of alienation are not simple but often rooted in long periods of unresolved grievances and thwarted aspirations. All governments have experienced the costs of failing to solve these difficulties; what we must do now is show that our Canadian federalism provides opportunity for all peoples to fulfill themselves. Our legal and political systems have always been flexible enough to accommodate such diversity. Our only guarantees of success, however, are open minds, understanding and goodwill.[15]

Following the Trudeau government's return to power, new priorities emerged. In the winter election campaign and in preparation for the Quebec referendum in May, Trudeau avoided the constitutional issue. But when Parliament opened in mid-April he returned to it with vigor. On April 29, 1980, he asked for the help of national native leaders to defeat the Parti

Québécois option and suggested that the native constitutional talks open with such subjects as aboriginal rights, treaty rights, native self-government within Canada, native political representation (e.g. in Parliament) and federal and provincial responsibilities in providing services to Native Peoples.[16] The importance of this suggestion lay not only in the substance of the items, but in the fact that a native agenda which cut across the usual categories familiar to participants in constitutional talks had apparently been accepted.

However, after the federalist victory in the Quebec referendum, the Prime Minister moved quickly with his own plans. An intensive summer of constitutional work was scheduled, to be capped with a First Ministers' Conference in September to discuss a package of items on which Ottawa believed there to be a reasonable hope of achieving federal-provincial consensus. In this high-speed move to demonstrate Canadian responsiveness to demands for constitutional change, there was no room for the Native People and their difficult questions. In August the Native People did have a half-day hearing with the constitutional ministers to discuss the summer agenda items, but little was achieved except the reminder that Native People had a wide range of constitutional interests.

On October 2, 1980, after the collapse of the September First Ministers' Conference, Prime Minister Trudeau proceeded with his unilateral federal constitutional "patriation package." Native groups, alarmed once again at being left out of a process in which they had been promised a part, became especially worried by the proposal of new constitutional amending procedures which could make provincial opposition to native hopes a sure obstacle to constitutionally entrenched rights. One of the axioms of Indian and Inuit political opinion in Canada is a fear of the provinces, as explained by the Inuit in a paid advertisement which appeared in the London *Times* during the constitutional lobbying:

> The British Government placed administrative and jurisdictional responsibility for native concerns with the Federal Government, rather than the Provincial Governments, when our constitution was written in 1867. Provinces in Canada have power over lands, resources and local matters. While the Federal Government certainly does not have an activist record in employing its powers on behalf of native peoples, the Federal responsibility has been the closest thing native Canadians have had to any guarantee of rights.[17]

After an intensive lobbying effort in which the federal government slowly gave way before the demands of various minority, civil rights and other interest groups through the winter of 1980-81, the Trudeau government, joined by both federal Opposition parties, supported critical amendments to the partriation scheme. Most dramatic was the simple clause: "The aboriginal and treaty rights of the aboriginal peoples of Canada are hereby recognised and affirmed."[18] In addition, other provisions effectively "constitutionalized" the Royal Proclamation of 1763, which Native People often call their "Magna Carta," guaranteed protection from the non-discrimination provisions of the charter of rights and also the political commitment to include an item on the agenda for discussion with native leaders at First Ministers' conferences in the next two years.

Despite the dramatic changes won by Indians and Inuit, and indeed by other Canadians who for the first time had been able to participate significantly in a constitutional process, the native intervention was only a prelude to the promised direct negotiations on matters such as those listed by the Prime Minister on April 29. Clearly a most important political precedent had been established. The quality of the Native interest is a fundamental one, and was described by the Inuit in the following terms for members of the parliamentary constitutional committee:

> There is nothing so fundamental to a people or a state as the Constitution which determines the nature of political and social relationships by which those peoples choose to live with each other. At the same time, a Constitution is a basic statement of the values and traditions of the peoples within a state.
>
> The present Canadian Constitution has often been criticised for being more of an "administrative" document than a clear statement of national will. Inuit believe, as do other native groups, that as native people we can make special contributions to this fundamental statement of Canadianness. We think that this is the spirit with which governments have tried to approach the essential redefinitions in the Constitution over recent years. In this light it would be a severe mistake to leave out of consideration the first peoples of the lands now making up the Canadian state and to ignore the importance of clarifying their historical, legal and cultural place as aboriginal peoples. The past failure to set these matters clearly in the constitutional framework has resulted in the unsatisfactory social conditions and political and economic opportunities which are acknowledged by all parties in Parliament.[19]

Greenland[20]

The question of home rule in Greenland is particularly worthy of Canadian interest because it involves a Canadian population, the Inuit, and because it has occurred in a state politically similar to Canada. The northern territories constitute one third of all Canada, a country rich in resources. But Greenland is many times larger than European Denmark and contains almost all the non-renewable resources that the state can claim. The amicable nature of the Danish-Greenlandic relationship is also impressive.

With the German occupation of Denmark during World War II, the consequent detachment of Greenland from the norms of colonial government, plus the breaking of Denmark's quarantine policy by the American occupation of Greenland, the colony began to press for greater local autonomy and improved material conditions. In the post-war era the Danes were almost over-enthusiastic in their efforts to respond to the latter, in the process causing a cultural and political shock which is still evident. They failed to understand the plea for greater autonomy at first; indeed, the very shape and size of the the vast Inuit island seemed to demand a highly centralized, European direction if all the needs of a modernized infrastructure and its attendant services were to be met. The population of small coastal settlements was relocated to large, alienating "growth centers" where life revolved around a sophisticated fishing industry. The well-paid Danish work force which was reshaping the world around them was so oblivious to Greenlandic preferences that Danish-Greenlandic relations became severely strained.

After 1970 a younger generation of nationalist, well-educated Greenlanders began to demand serious political changes. Their efforts led to the creation of a study committee of Greenland politicians who, in turn, recommended the creation of a home rule commission to be composed of an equal number of elected indigenous leaders and Danish Members of Parliament. This commission went on to produce a study, draft legislation and detailed administrative proposals. A referendum held in January 1979 endorsed the home rule plan which was put into effect in May of the same year.

The Greenlanders, a largely mixed-blood Inuit people who speak an Inuktitut dialect easily understood by many Canadian Inuit, number about 40 000 people, with another 10 000 Europeans in their midst. In an area so geographically distinct and so far removed from Denmark, Danes have harbored few illusions about "melting pot" politics, showing little reluctance to recognize the Greenlanders as unique. The Faroe Islands of the North Atlantic, settled originally by Vikings, had already obtained home rule from Denmark and so constituted a precedent. Denmark reserved some powers – defense, currency, foreign policy – and, through the home rule commission, negotiated a phased transfer of others, including the financing of their administration. Most economic, social, cultural and environmental matters are coming under Greenlandic control subject to general conditions similar to the universality and portability clauses written into Canada's federal-provincial shared-cost programs. Greenlandic Inuktitut is the main language but public officials must also be able to work in Danish; both languages are taught in the schools.

Denied aboriginal title or other ownership, but acknowledged to "have certain fundamental rights," the Greenlanders share a double veto on policy and projects with Denmark. A joint Danish-Greenlandic committee, working with the resources administration, is designed to achieve compromises which will avoid exercise of the veto.

Home rule is not constitutionally entrenched, although it is well understood by Danish convention that having been achieved by negotiation, any amendments would also require negotiation. And even before home rule, Danish bills and regulations affecting Greenland were submitted to the elected Greenland assembly for advice. Greenland Premier Jonathan Motzfeldt reports that the opposition to and even fear of home rule among some Greenlanders has now evaporated in a mood of optimism and dynamism.[21] His government's priorities, apart from completing the complex administrative transfers, including the takeover of a large state-owned commercial and transportation complex, the Royal Greenland Trade Department, are economic development and diversification, coupled with strict protection of the Arctic environment.

Some Canadian academics and advisers in native groups have greeted Greenland home rule with scepticism and view it as "indirect rule," but their qualms are not shared by even the most radical Greenland leaders who had earlier opposed its establishment on similar grounds. Greenlanders prefer the reality of self-government and national development to the delays of abstract political speculation. As leading Greenland minister and a chief architect of home rule, Lars-Emile Johansen, acknowledges:

> The independent, Greenlandic society does not simply spring into existence from one day to the next and it cannot be introduced merely by memoranda in a commission. The only way in which it can exist is through a development of the people, and Home Rule is a step in this direction, a possibility for further growth.[22]

Norway[23]

In Norway the types of situations discussed above seem to have been telescoped in time. Moreover, the emergent native rights situation has sparked fundamental controversy perhaps greater than has yet occurred in Canada or in Denmark. A European population long used to taking for granted northern territory has suddenly found itself challenged and its political and constitutional norms questioned. The Norwegian public has not responded to this unfamiliar situation with any more understanding than one would expect of other majorities.

Of the estimated 50 000 Sami (Lapps) living in northern Norway, Sweden, Finland and the USSR, half are found in Norway. This population, not physically distinct from other Scandinavians, is best known for its reindeer herding economy, an activity which involves only about 10 percent of Sami families today. However, the reindeer herders have played a vital role in promoting cultural continuity and providing leadership in recent times. The progam of the main Sami political groups includes familiar themes such as respect for aboriginal land and resource rights, protection of language and culture and collective political identity. But as the most prominent Sami reindeer association leader, Ole Henrik Magga, stated recently, the Sami are not questioning Norway's territorial integrity or national unity.

Controversy over construction of a hydro-electric dam on the Alta River, one of the last great Norwegian salmon rivers cutting through unspoiled areas of the Sami reindeer heartland, has solidified the native rights movement. Joining a large environmentalist outcry against a project relatively insignificant in terms of meeting energy needs, the Sami have taken their struggle into the south where police action against their peaceful protest in the parliamentary park in Oslo two years ago shocked the Norwegian public and temporarily delayed action on the dam project. Civil disobedience and mass arrests in 1981 focussed the conflict. Government leaders and others, meanwhile, have insisted on the formal propriety of the official decisions taken, in spite of embarrassing court findings about the poor or distorted information employed to justify them. In practice, the government has used various postponements and "further studies" to defuse tension while continuing to deny the existence of a native rights issue in the Alta case.

In the autumn of 1980, the Norwegian government established a committee to study Sami cultural and educational needs. At the same time another committee with wide representation was created to look at land and water rights, possible Sami political structures and constitutional questions. Norwegian anthropologist Helge Kleivan has said that until Norway accepts the fact of two peoples living together within the Norwegian state there can be no real resolution of outstanding problems. Meanwhile, many Norwegians continue to deny that the Sami are an aboriginal people or that past Norwegian support for aboriginal rights in United Nations forums is relevant to their own situation.

Conclusions

It would be irresponsible to draw too many conclusions on the basis of the limited study which has been given circumpolar political development to date. Meanwhile, northern peoples are rushing ahead with their own programs for change, experimenting, discussing and trying to resolve problems which, as has been suggested, may be visited upon them by the source, shape and size of external pressure for resource development.

At the very least, one may suggest that the relationship between land and resource rights (or lack of them) and outside proposals for development in northern societies, aboriginal or European, is such that government ministers and their advisers should think carefully before announcing that regional interests affected by them will not be considered in the context of political development. Northern societies with their strong sense of territoriality and cultural continuity may not be amenable to the general political assurances which are the norm in the more southerly, populous and powerful portions of circumpolar states.

Premier Jonathan Motzfeldt of Greenland recently said that Inuit of whatever country must regard themselves as the "soldiers and police" of the Arctic environment if the peoples of the northern parts of the world are to survive.[24] While not opposing development *per* se, he saw the question as one of the *type* of development. If developers and southern governments would understand the origins and legitimacy of such northern views, much of the political ferment in the circumpolar world could be more positively directed at solutions to the many interrelated problems in the area.

END NOTES

1. "Native group reviewing BNA stand," Toronto *Globe and Mail,* April 21, 1981.
2. On April 30, 1980, at the First Nations Constitutional Conference in Ottawa, George Erasmus delivered a talk on northern development at a panel chaired by the Hon. Marc Lalonde. This was taped by CBC Northern Service and is perhaps the classic exposition of northern development problems in Canada.
3. E.g., the terms of reference of the University of Calgary's new northern studies program marrying strategic studies with northern and native political studies.
4. Translated as *Canadian Nordicity* by William Barr, (Montreal: Harvest House, 1978).
5. P. Jull, "Diplomats of a New North" in *Policy Options,* Vol. 2, No. 2 (May-June 1981), p. 24.
6. The author has inevitably drawn on his experience as an employee of Makivik Corporation. All the material presented is found in the various briefs submitted by Makivik (and available on request) to Quebec and federal governments, the most recent and therefore up-to-date being the comprehensive "Brief to the Standing Committee on Indian Affairs and Northern Development, House of Commons: Position of the Inuit of Quebec with respect to the Implementation of the James Bay and Northern Quebec Agreement, March 20, 1981." The proceedings of that Committee for March 26, 1981 also contain much useful material. The James Bay and Northern Quebec Agreement is published in French and in English by the Editeur Officiel du Québec.
7. A view put forward regularly by Quebec government officials in meetings with Makivik, especially by the head of SAGMAI, the Quebec government secretariat in the Executive Council office responsible for native affairs.
8. "Statement from the House of Commons Standing Committee on Indian Affairs and Northern Development to the Ministers of Indian Affairs and National Health and Welfare on the Government's Failure to Implement Major Provisions in the James Bay and Northern Quebec Agreement of 11 November 1975," March 31, 1981. See also "MPs planning new drive for native rights," Montreal *Gazette*, March 27, 1981, and "Ottawa may act to end James Bay wrangling," Montreal *Gazette*, April 1, 1981.
9. *Minutes of Proceedings and Evidence of the Standing Committee on Indian Affairs and Northern Development, March 26, 1981,* p. 17.
10. The two best and most complete sources are the detailed Nunavut proposal itself, *Political Development in Nunavut* (Ottawa: Information Services, Inuit Tapirisat of Canada, 1979), and an interview with the chief Nunavut negotiator, Thomas Suluk, in an unattributed article, "The Nunavut Concept" in *Arjungangimmat*, Winter 1981 (Inuit Cultural Institute, Eskimo Point, NWT).
11. Report of the Unity Committee of the NWT Legislative Assembly, tabled and debated in November 1980 at Frobisher Bay.
12. The most complete documentary summary of the native/constitutional work is an unpublished paper by the author, widely circulated among native groups and Canadian governments, "Canada's Native Peoples and the Constitutional Reform Process: a brief background paper," July 18, 1980. Published articles which summarize events are the author's "Canada's Native Peoples and the Constitution" in *IWGIA Newsletter*, No. 24, April 1980 (published in Copenhagen), and Simon McInnes, "Inuit win historic recognition of aboriginal rights" in *Inuit Today*, Vol. 9, April 1981.

13. *A Time for Action,* Government of Canada, June 1978.
14. Letter from the Hon. William Jarvis to Noel Starblanket, President of the National Indian Brotherhood, copied to other native leaders and published as a press release on July 30, 1979.
15. Opening Remarks by the Hon. William Jarvis, December 3, 1979, at the CCMC Sub-committee meeting with national native presidents, published as a press release by the Federal-Provincial Relations Office, Ottawa.
16. In the two succeeding days, the Hon. Marc Lalonde and the Hon. John Munro elaborated on this statement in the name of the Prime Minister during sessions of the First Nations Constitutional Conference in Ottawa to ensure that the commitment did not go unnoticed.
17. Advertisement in *The Times*, London, December 3, 1979, placed by the Inuit Committee on National Issues, signed by Charlie Watt and Eric Tagoona, Co-Chairmen.
18. Adopted unanimously by the Joint Parliamentary Committee on the Constitution, January 30, 1981.
19. Contained in a letter from the Inuit Committee on National Issues to all Senators and MPs on the Joint Parliamentary Committee on the Constitution, dated January 15, 1981.
20. A thorough study of the home rule provisions by a most knowledgeable source, the Secretary to the Home Rule Commission, Ole Olesen, is *Home Rule for Greenland* (Ottawa: Department of Indian and Northern Affairs, 1979). A good short article is Hans Christian Gullov's "Home Rule in Greenland" in *Inuit Studies,* Vol. 3, No. 1 (Laval, 1979). An excellent discussion is Helge Kleivan's "Greenland from Colony to Home Rule" in *IWGIA Newsletter*, No. 22, June 1979. A Canadian observation is the author's "Greenland: Lessons of self-government and development," *Northern Perspectives*, Vol. VII, No. 8 (1979). The best background available on Greenland in English is Hubert Schuurman's *Greenland: Canada's Eastern Neighbour* (Ottawa: Department of Indian Affairs and Northern Development, 1976). Much of the author's information derives from talks with Danish and Greenlandic officials, politicians, academics and observers, from the autumn of 1977 when I began to follow home rule.
21. Private interview with Premier Motzfeldt, March 1981.
22. Cited in Gullov, "Home Rule."
23. The best background book is Harald Eidheim's *Aspects of the Lappish Minority Situation* (Oslo: Universitetsforlaget, 1971). For my material I owe everything to Helge Kleivan and Eva Solem of the International Working Group on Indigenous Affairs (IWGIA) in Copenhagen and Oslo who set up my visit to Norway in April 1981, and who put me in touch with persons and resource materials. Especially I wish to thank Rune Stormo of the Oslo Samiid Saer'vi; Professor Carsten Smith who heads the government-appointed native rights study committee and other legal experts to whom he introduced me in Oslo; Arne G. Arnesen, lawyer for the Nordic Sami Institute; and for the general situating of the questions which occurred to me, Norwegian anthropologists Helge Kleivan of the University of Copenhagen, Georg Henriksen of the University of Bergen, and Harald Eidheim and Eva Solem of the University of Oslo. The *IWGIA Newsletter* is the best English-language source for information on the rapidly evolving Norwegian Sami rights and Alta River situations.
24. Personal interview with Premier Motzfeldt, March 1981.

Nunavut — "Our Land"*

Introduction

Inuit Tapirisat of Canada, or Eskimo Brotherhood, was founded in 1971 when an organizing committee of Inuit decided it was time for the Native People of the Arctic to speak with a united voice on a host of issues concerning development of the North, education of their children, and preservation of their culture.

Initially, headquarters were established in Edmonton, but in 1972 the offices were moved to Ottawa when it became obvious the ITC needed better access to the federal government and closer communication with government officials.

A lot has happened since then. The Committee for Original People's Entitlement (COPE) representing the Inuit of the Western Arctic, became an affiliate of ITC. Other affiliated organizations are the Northern Quebec Inuit Association, the Labrador Inuit Association, the Baffin Region Inuit Association, Kitikmeot Inuit Association (representing the Central Arctic from offices in Cambridge Bay), and the Keewatin Inuit Association with headquarters in Rankin inlet.

The affiliated organizations look after day-to-day problems and concerns in their communities and regions, but their presidents also sit as members of the ITC board of directors. The national organization concentrates on national issues but helps out with community or regional problems when requested to do so. For example, ITC head office frequently goes to bat for Arctic communities when the government is asked to restrict development or exploration work in areas where local residents believe the environment and wildlife are threatened.

In short, Inuit Tapirisat is dedicated to preserving the culture, identity, and way of life of the Inuit and to helping them find their role in a changing society. To that end, an Inuit Cultural Institute has been established at Eskimo Point, and a language commission is exploring the possibility of adopting a standard system of writing in the Inuktitut language. A legal aid office has been opened at Frobisher Bay. A major communications research project is under way.

---

* Reprinted with permission from the *Inuit Tapirisat of Canada.*

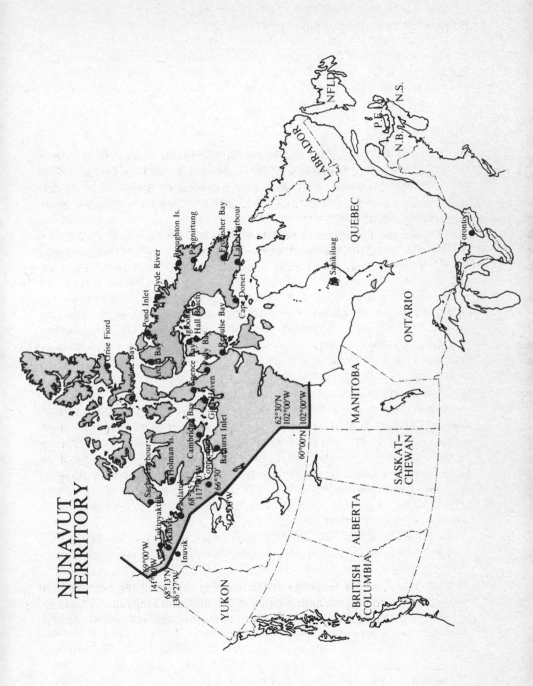

NUNAVUT
TERRITORY

A non-profit housing corporation has been established, and a $48 000 contract has been signed with Frontier College of Toronto to draw up a management training program designed to fit the special needs of Inuit. An Inuit Development Corporation is being established as the business arm of ITC to enable the people of the Arctic to administer the resources and assets which will come under their control when a land claims agreement is reached with the government of Canada.

Land Claims

In the short history of Inuit Tapirisat, by far its most significant project is the Inuit land claims proposal for the Northwest Territories. It is probably the most comprehensive proposal of its kind ever presented in North America, the product of three years of intensive research and field work covering the legal aspects, renewable and non-renewable resources, and the documentation of actual land use and occupancy over the centuries.

The land use and occupancy study, directed by Dr. Milton Freeman of McMaster University, shows that from prehistoric times the Inuit have used and occupied virtually all of the 750 000 square miles of land generally north of the treeline, and an estimated 800 000 square miles of northern ocean. This research, along with an exhaustive study of renewable resources directed by Dr. Gordon Nelson of the University of Waterloo, and a survey of non-renewable resources by geological consultant Pedro Van Meurs of Ottawa, went into the preparation of a proposed agreement in principle drawn up by ITC's legal consultant, Prof. Peter Cumming of York University.

But lest there be any misunderstanding, ITC's land claims proposal is not another example of White man in the South deciding what is best for Inuit in the North. At successive annual meetings of Inuit Tapirisat, delegates from all regions of the Arctic gave their organization's board of directors a strong mandate to proceed with the land claims project. And while the consultants were preparing their studies, ITC field workers were actively seeking the views of the people in the communities, talking to them about the issues and collecting their suggestions.

All of this hard work and effort culminated in a historic meeting of Inuit held at Pond Inlet, Northwest Territories, from October 28 to November 2, 1975. More than 100 voting delegates from 32 Arctic communities attended. Resolutions passed by their community councils empowered them to vote on behalf of their people. For six days and some long nights, the delegates plodded through the lengthy land claims document clause by clause, questioning some of the points, voting to make amendments to some of the important sections, and finally passing a resolution authorizing ITC to begin negotiations with the federal government. What the delegates did, in effect, was declare that the Inuit are willing to share the land which they have never surrendered by treaty or otherwise.

Because the Inuit are neither greedy nor unreasonable, they are not asking for outright ownership of their entire 750 000 square miles of traditional lands; in fact, ownership of land as southern Canadians understand it is a concept that had always been foreign to the Inuit. The land had always been there for the people to use and occupy. However, the people realize now that if their native environment is to be preserved for future generations, they must have a piece of paper establishing ownership under Canadian law of enough land to ensure their survival. So they are asking for ownership of 250 000 square miles of land, which will be selected in such a way that each Arctic community has at least 2 500 square miles. The remaining 500 000 square miles north of the treeline would be surrendered, but with certain conditions attached. Among those conditions, the Inuit would retain exclusive hunting, fishing and trapping rights. And the Inuit want a share of the revenue from development of natural resources. A royalty of 3 percent has been suggested.

The Inuit want to be self-sufficient. One really unique feature of their land settlement proposal is that it will not cost the taxpayers of Canada anything. They are not asking for a cash settlement, because the Inuit land is not for sale. In fact, they are offering to pay back, with interest, the money provided by the federal government (more than $2 million) to finance their land settlement research.

The revenue from resources would go toward financing a comprehensive social and economic development program, and operations of the new Inuit Development Corporation. The whole philosophy behind ITC's proposal is to permit the Inuit to gain some control of their social, cultural and economic destiny. To that end, they are also suggesting a first step toward self-government by the creation of a new territory to be known as Nunavut, which means "Our Land." Nunavut would comprise all 750 000 square miles of the traditional Inuit lands, and its system of government would be similar to that of the existing Northwest Territories, with an appointed commissioner and an elected council. Since the majority of electors would be Inuit, Native People would assume a degree of control over industrial development and such things as environmental protection and wildlife conservation.

And then eventually, perhaps there will be a Province of Nunavut. The Inuit are not separatists. They are Canadians. But they don't want to be colonial subjects. They want to be partners in Confederation. When one considers the unbelievably barren nature of the Arctic terrain and the effects of a climate that is harsh and cruel by southern standards, 250 000 square miles is really not very much.

Look at it this way. In the fertile agricultural areas of Ontario, according to Statistics Canada, the average farm earning 51 percent or more of its revenue from livestock covers an area of 209.1 acres. In Alberta, where the grazing land is not quite as lush and the climate somewhat more severe, the average livestock operation requires 1 025.5 acres. In the Arctic, it takes up to tens of square miles of land to support one caribou. That is why it is so unreasonable to think in terms of five square miles per family, as has been suggested for native land settlements in other parts of the North.

In an exhaustive study of Arctic renewable resources carried out for Inuit Tapirisat, Dr. Gordon Nelson of the University of Waterloo says that "Inuit hunters range over hundreds of thousands of square miles, so land settlement must be thought of on an entirely different scale than elsewhere in Canada."

There are lessons to be learned from history when it comes to negotiating a land agreement with the Inuit. In the 19th century, when the arid plains of western Canada were being settled, homesteaders were allowed 160 to 320 acres for farming. This size was based on the experience of raising crops on the moist lands of eastern Canada, but was totally unrealistic for the dry land of the west. It took decades of trial and error, countless farm failures and untold human misery before farms of 1 000 acres or more – large enough to support a family – could be established by those lucky enough to emerge as winners in the long struggle against other settlers and the environment.

Dr. Nelson conludes in his report that the same principle applies in the Far North. "Much land must be placed in control of the Inuit and conservation agencies of government if wildlife and environment are to be protected and traditional hunting and fishing as well as modern commercial renewable resource-based enterprises are to have a second opportunity to grow in the Arctic."

Why an Inuit Land Settlement?

There are good, solid reasons why the people of Canada through their elected government should reach a land sharing agreement with the Inuit of the Northwest Territories. Old-fashioned fair play is one of them. It can be argued that Canada owes a large debt to the Inuit, after so many years of intruding into their land, uninvited, imposing changes in their way of life, exploiting the natural resources of the Arctic without consulting the original inhabitants.

The government of Canada has adopted an enlightened and generous policy of assistance and support for the emerging countries of the Third World. In fairness, can Canadians be any less generous with the first citizens of their own country? But if apathy and indifference should rule out fairness as an argument, how about enlightened self-interest?

The politicians churn out hundreds of thousands of inspired words about maintaining sovereignty over that vast and magnificent land that stretches north beyond the treeline, through the Arctic Islands, almost to the North Pole. But to have sovereignty, one must have occupancy. The Inuit are the occupants. They are the only occupants who want to, or indeed are able to live in the extreme environment of Canada north of the treeline. They are happy to live there, and struggling desperately to preserve what is left of their unique way of life. In fact, until the White man came and imported the southern comforts of home, the Inuit were the only ones who knew how to survive in the North.

Recently, southern Canada has been showing a great interest in the Arctic. But this has not been reflected in any eagerness among large numbers of southern Canadians to actually live in the Arctic. They are interested in the North for what they can take out of it.

Canadians are on the threshold of one of the most significant decisions since Confederation. They can help the Inuit achieve self-sufficiency – socially, culturally, and economically. The alternative is continued colonial rule at ever-increasing cost to the Canadian taxpayer, coupled with destruction of the Inuit culture and the consignment of a proud and independent people to a marginal existence on poor wages and government handouts. For the Inuit, it is still not too late to avoid the mistakes which have blighted the history of White society's relationships with Native People.

SALLY M. WEAVER   University of Waterloo

The Status of Indian Women

Introduction

In recent years some Indian women in Canada have become increasingly dissatisfied with the membership section of the Indian Act which they believe discriminates against them and not against Indian men. The membership section of the Act not only affects the status of Indian women, but it also affects the families of the Indian women who marry non-Indians and the community as a whole. The intent of this article is to examine the nature of the linkage between marriage and legal Indian status as it relates primarily to Indian women.[1] The historical reasoning behind the contentious membership provisions in the Indian Act will be explained and the current dissatisfaction with the legislation described, focusing upon why efforts at reform have failed to date.

Traditionally Canadian Indians reckoned membership in their tribes by a variety of principles of descent, marriage, residence, and adoption, and among some bands the process of determining membership was a very fluid one due to the practice of intermarriage. Generally speaking, the predominant principle of descent was bilateral and the most common form of marriage was monogamy. Post-marital residence patterns covered a variety of forms including neolocal, patrilocal, and matrilocal.[2] With the coming of the Europeans, however, kinship patterns began to change and band membership took on new meaning. As reserves were set aside specifically for Indians, attempts were made to keep these lands protected from unscrupulous White settlers who disregarded the laws. Over time it became necessary to define more precisely who was an Indian and who, therefore, had the right to occupy the reserve lands that had been assigned to each band. Beginning in the mid-19th century, the Canadian government developed policies and legislation to cope with the problem of defining Indian status. Family relationships always provided the basis from which legal status as a band member derived and under the century-old Indian Act this right has been defined patrilineally, through the male line. As a result of this law, Indian women who "married-out," that is, who married non-Indians, lost their right to band membership and therefore their legal status. In the language of the Indian Act they became "enfranchised."[3] In addition, their children were also denied the right to legal status. Thus the Indian woman and her children assumed the non-Indian status of the husband, giving each member of the nuclear family the same legal status. However, the consequence of marrying-out for Indian men was not the same. Instead of losing their legal status they retained it and their White wives became legally Indian under the Indian Act. Unlike the United States, where the criteria for band membership is largely the responsibility of the tribe and where the percentage of Indian blood is often the basic criterion, Canada has always coped with the membership question under a single piece of federal legislation (the Indian Act) that applied a nationally uniform system of criteria to all bands. Bands did not have the choice of retaining their traditional pattern of membership.

In the early 1970s, under the encouragement of the women's liberation movement, some enfranchised Indian women became increasingly dissatisfied with the feature of the Indian Act that removed their Indian status upon marriage to non-Indians. They felt the consequences of marrying-out were more harsh and unreasonable for them than for the Indian male and they argued that the provision in the Indian Act maintaining this inequity (Section 12 (1) (b)) was a clear-cut case of sexist discrimination. They sought the help of the courts to reinstate them on the band lists but, although they raised public consciousness about the problems they faced, they did not succeed in getting the support of Indian provincial and national organizations for status Indians.

The Evolution of Legal Status

With the coming of Europeans to the continent, native Indian populations faced many disruptions in their way of life. One of the most serious was the loss of their lands to White settlers. In an effort to halt unscrupulous land dealings, the colonial powers developed a policy of setting aside specific parcels of land (reserves) for the sole use and occupancy of Native People. It was believed that the reserve system (today totalling over 2 240 reserves) would guarantee enough land for the continuation of subsistence activities and protect the Indian people from the disadvantages of "civilization" until they could successfully adopt the farming economy and other features of Euro-Canadian society. Even when the reserves were set aside, however, unethical land dealings continued. White squatters sometimes established a foothold on reserves and it was both difficult and costly to remove them even when they were willing to relocate. Furthermore, Indian lands were sometimes illegally sold or rented to Whites and the absence of a system for recording individual Indian land holdings on reserves made it difficult to determine the nature and extent of these land dealings. Consequently, a system of legislation gradually developed by which the federal government could more accurately define who had the right to occupy Indian lands and more effectively exclude non-Indians from gaining access to these lands. As a result, the definition of legal status for Indians emerged in the mid-19th century. At the outset the definition of membership in a band was reasonably broad, but as pressures on Indian lands and resources persisted, it became necessary to sharpen the criteria and draw a firm line for inclusion and exclusion.

In the earliest legislation the definition of band membership was treated in a simple and almost self-evident fashion. Thus in the 1850 and 1857 legislation of Upper Canada, those who had the right to occupy reserve lands were "Indians" of that particular band and "those inter-married with Indians."[4] But greater precision was necessary as White settlement, particularly in Ontario and Quebec, began to press in on Indian lands. Consequently, in 1868 the criteria for band membership were refined and three conditions for status as a band member were spelled out.[5] A person was considered a member of a band under the Indian Act if (1) he or she was of "Indian blood" and locally acknowledged to be a member of the band, or (2) if he or she was the descendent "on either side from Indians" of that band, or (3) if in the case of a non-Indian woman she were legally married to a member of that band. The children of all three classes mentioned above were also legally deemed to be band members under the Act. Under this legislation a White man married to an Indian woman was not considered a band member but he did have the right to reside on the reserve with his Indian wife and his children who did have legal status.[6] In practice, however, the exclusion of the White husband from band membership was not always firm and on some reserves, such as the large Six Nations Iroquois Reserve in southern Ontario, these men were sometimes "added to" the band list by the band council with the subsequent approval of the Department of Indian Affairs.[7] Thus the 1868 legislation did not involuntarily enfranchise Indian women for marrying-out, nor did it deny their children legal status.

Within a year, however, the legislation was changed specifically to deny Indian women their legal status if they married non-Indians, and to remove the right to transfer legal status to their children. The broader principle of bilateral affiliation was replaced by the more restrictive one of patrilineal affiliation for the children, and the married-out woman assumed the same status (non-Indian) as her husband.[8] This also applied in the case of an Indian woman marrying a member of another tribe and in this instance her name was simply transferred to her husband's band list.

The immediate question that arises is why was the exclusion of married-out women adopted in 1869? The answer is evident in the archival records and it reveals the government's basic fear that intermarriage with White men and the related right of residence traditionally granted them, would lead to White male dominance of Indian land.[9] This dominance could occur in either its use or its ownership indirectly through their Indian wives. Indian policy at that time was explicitly geared to encourage the Indian male to adopt the farming practices of the period, and to protect Indian lands so these practices would produce economically viable Indian families and communities. It was feared that enterprising and aggressive White men might buy up much of the reserve lands through their wives and diminish the opportunity for Indian men to practice agriculture, or equally disturbing, that Indians would rent out much of their land to Whites and thereby not farm it themselves. The intent of the legislation was clear and in the words of the Superintendent General of Indian Affairs responsible for the 1869 amendments it was seen as "preventing men not of Indian Blood having by marrying Indian women either through their Wives or Children any pretext for Settling on Indian lands."[10] It is evident from the correspondence of the day that White men married to Indian women were regarded as a basic threat to the band's resources while the White wife was not seen to pose similar problems.

Since 1869 the Indian Act regulations have retained the provision of excluding married-out Indian women. But the exclusion in itself posed some threat to the corporate resources of the band. A band is essentially an administrative unit under the Indian Act to which certain lands have been assigned. When traditional Indian territory was surrendered to the Crown in return for the reserves, whether it be by treaty or more simple land surrenders, the monies from the sale of these lands were deposited in a capital fund for that particular band and these monies accrued interest for the band. Such was also done when portions of the reserved lands were themselves sold by the Crown. When an Indian woman married-out, she was given her per capita share of the capital funds and the revenues, and if she were a member of a band that had signed a treaty (about half of the legal status Indians in Canada are treaty Indians), she was also entitled to receive a sum of money equal to a 20-year payment of the annuities from that treaty,[11] and her per capita share of any capital payments under the treaty. Thus upon marriage to a non-Indian, she relinquished all her rights as a legal status Indian under the Indian Act, but she received her portion of the capital and annuity assets.

Although, as Sanders has carefully noted, it is not always clear what legal status under the Indian Act entails for the individual, there are some features which generally have universal acceptance.[12] These are: (1) the right to reside on the reserve that is assigned to the individual's band, (2) freedom from estate taxes, (3) freedom from land taxes on reserve lands, (4) freedom from income taxes on income earned on a reserve, and (5) the right to vote in band council elections. There are also other important consequences of legal status and these pertain to eligibility for certain social programs that the federal government has established from time to time for status Indians in the fields of education, health care, and housing. The financial benefits in each of these cases can be, and have been, very substantial. Lower interest rates on mortgages can amount to considerable savings. By the government's covering a good portion of the cost of tuition, books, clothing, and boarding for eligible secondary and post-secondary students, financial pressures in the household can be lessened. In the past the cost of hospital and doctor care was in practice covered by the Department of Indian Affairs as well, but this has changed and today only indigent Indians are eligible for these benefits. All these rights and benefits are denied Indian women who marry non-Indians, and their children. But more significant for some women is the loss of their right to reside in the community among kinsmen and friends that they have been raised with. In this sense "home" is denied them although temporary visits are not and in some communities by practice the permanent residence of a non-status woman and her children will be overlooked by the authorities. Indeed, some critics argue that the exclusion of married-out women is a factor in discouraging legal marital unions and fostering common law unions. The extent to which this is accurate is an unexplored feature of the legislation.

While these and other effects of the Indian Act on the family deserve close examination in any attempt to alter the laws, there are also certain long-standing assumptions in the legislation that merit critical reappraisal. A few of these can be briefly mentioned.

The 1869 legislation was based on the belief that the White husband was of far greater threat to the reserve's resources and community life than the White wife. In the days of a farming economy it was possible to argue that an aggressive White man could occupy and monopolize disproportionate amounts of reserve lands. But even then White wives could be, and on many reserves in Ontario definitely were, powerful forces behind their Indian husbands' farming activities. With the changing economy, White married-in women on many reserves today play strong roles as assertive and enterprising entrepreneurs, craft specialists, teachers, and nurses. Historically, some of these White wives have played dominant roles in voluntary associations in the communities and their influence has been felt far beyond their immediate family. Their participation, moreover, has often been the subject of considerable hostility and resentment. Having gained legal status through marriage they can purchase and develop Indian lands and operate family enterprises. They are also eligible for a variety of federal grants for economic development. Given the social changes in the role of women, the likelihood of these activities increasing in the future can not be avoided. The assumption that the White wife of an Indian man poses a limited threat to the band's resources is no longer tenable, if it ever was. The case for her exclusion from legal status merits as much careful consideration as the case for the exclusion of the White husband, if an equitable evaluation of the membership criteria is to be achieved.

The historic assumption of the "less threatening White wife" and the "more threatening White husband" must also be questioned in a different circumstance. It is interesting to note that historically the role of the Indian woman as socializing agent and mother has never been a consideration in the arguments surrounding the question of band membership and legal status. Although the current Indian movement focuses much of its attention on retaining and enhancing Indian cultural patterns, irrespective of how traditional or modified these patterns are, this basic priority has not been related by Indian spokesmen to the role of mother. Despite the variety of kinship patterns among Indian people, including those modified by acculturation, the salient function of the mother in teaching the children the community's cultural patterns has been consistently overlooked. Although it is not impossible for a married-out Indian woman to transfer these beliefs and customs to her children, she does not have the option of doing so within the supportive community environment where reinforcing sanctions exist. In the case of the White wife who gains legal status, she is usually not familiar with local tribal customs and therefore can not be a link in the process of cultural continuity. While the patrilineal kinsmen of the children can certainly influence the children's socialization process, this contact is rarely as close and intimate as that with the mother. This is also the case when the question of language transference to the new generation is considered. The White wife cannot provide this linguistic link, nor can she converse with the husband, thereby providing a spoken language milieu for the child. While she can certainly learn to speak the local language there is no evidence that this in fact occurs except in rare cases. The high value generally placed on retaining Indian languages as a medium of cultural expression – as living languages – by Indian people consequently becomes more difficult to realize in the face of already strong pressures from the mass media and from the educational system where English or French is the operative language. In general, and not excluding valuable contributions by other kinsmen, the fundamental role of the Indian mother as a basic link in cultural and linguistic continuity cannot be easily dismissed if the retention of the Indian way of life is indeed a priority to the Indian people.

Historically, the rather curious absence of this concern reflects the basic approach taken to membership since the mid-19th century. Membership has been viewed by the government primarily in terms of access to the reserve's physical resources, not in terms of cultural resources and their continuity within the community.

The long-standing preoccupation by both the government and Indians with securing the reserve lands and other resources from alienation is understandable given the steady attrition of these assets in the past. In addition, the band's resources are usually finite. Unlike non-Indian communities, reserves do not annex new land and expand their land base, and unless oil, gas, or other resources are found, or reserve lands are sold, the capital assets of the band remain finite, increased only by the interest that accumulates on these funds annually. However, even if the land base were extended, the process of defining who has the right to occupy and use it could not be avoided. The need to develop criteria, however, does not bring with it the need to discriminate against Indian women. Nor does it necessarily bring with it the need to deplete the corporate resources when a member leaves the band whether voluntarily or involuntarily. Like the legal arrangements made by Hutterites in western Canada, corporate resources can be secured for the community against the efforts of individuals to claim a share of the assets. With the corporate resources made secure in this or some similar fashion, the criteria for membership could be equalized by a series of different procedures.

The concern that the Indian population increase, over time, will outstrip the reserve lands has in itself yet to be fully demonstrated. Much reserve land is neither farmed nor developed and it remains unclear in what respects the land has been or is inadequate for the communities' needs. While this aspect of the problem deserves serious attention, taking into consideration the increasing urban residence of Indian people and the use of reserves at the time of retirement, the finite land base for reserves cannot be dismissed as a minor concern of Indians.

During the century following Confederation there was no pressure from either the Indians or the federal government to change the regulations that related to the status of Indian women. The native population became increasingly dependent upon the patronage and protection of the expanding federal Indian bureaucracy and the Indian Act. Despite the ambivalent attitude of dependency and resentment held by Indians toward the Act, parts of it became internalized in the communities. The boundary-maintaining mechanisms of the Act were to become custom law in many bands and were seen as the major protective devices for their resources which were dwindling despite official legal safeguards. The anxiety over preserving these resources (land, band funds, timber, etc.) increased the utility of excluding White men from the reserves and giving them no claim to the corporate property. Over the years, hostility to any enfranchisement became strong because the corporate whole could suffer the loss of either land (according to early statutes) or funds when a member relinquished legal status whether it was voluntary or involuntary. In the face of continued acculturation, land became an emotionally charged symbol of Indian rights. Security of the land was used as an index of society's respect for the agreements that had been made with Indians, and denial of these agreements (whether by treaty or regular land surrender) was viewed as symbolic disregard for the welfare and rights of Indian people. Furthermore, land was a finite resource. Rarely has the land base of reserves been increased despite the rapid population growth in the mid-20th century. These sentiments toward land and rights were tenacious and deep-rooted and gained full expression in the 1960s as the Indian rights movement emerged.

The Collision of Two Social Movements

The 1960s was a time of social ferment and among the social movements that emerged to capture public attention were the Indian rights movement and the women's rights movement. These soon clashed over the status of Indian women, and in particular, over that section of the Indian Act that excluded Indian women from legal status upon marriage to a non-Indian.

The Indian movement was given impetus in 1967 when the federal government decided to revise the Indian Act (1951). Greater flexibility was sought in the provisions of the Act so it could more readily accommodate the varied needs of Canada's then 230 000 status Indians.[13] Consultation meetings were held with Indians across the country in 1968 and early 1969 to obtain their opinions on possible amendments, but the membership sections of the Act, and particularly those involving the status of Indian women, attracted little attention from Indian delegates. Some band spokesmen felt that an Indian woman should continue to lose her status if she married-out, others felt she should retain it, while still others thought a waiting period of possibly five years should be instituted to insure that the marriage was stable before she relinquished her status.[14] In addition, some felt that the band itself should play a more significant role in determining issues of band membership, but proposals in this regard were not specific. To the extent that the status of Indians was treated at the consultation meetings (or at all during the 1960s[15]), the approach was at best segmental. The complex relationship between legal status, family, residence, rights, and corporate property was not dealt with in any coherent fashion by either the government or Indian groups. Indian concern, to the extent it formed a consistent pattern at the consultation meetings, focused on band membership in general, the consequences of relinquishing membership on corporate property of the band, illegitimacy, and adoption. Discussions on the subject produced mixed opinions and dangling recommendations. For example, the recommendation that Indian women should retain status upon marrying-out did not question the consequences of this on the status of the children, the residence of the children, the residence of the husband on Indian land, or his participation in Indian community life. When the consultation meetings ended in the spring of 1969 no Indian consensus had emerged on the matter.

In June of 1969 the federal government's response to the consultation meetings was to come forward, not with a revised Indian Act as Indians had been led to expect, but with a policy that proposed terminating all special rights for Indians.[16] The Indian Act was to be repealed and legal status for Indians was to become a thing of the past. The policy had a traumatic effect on Indian people who highly prized their special rights and it acted to catalyse the Indian movement as no event in the recent past had done. Indians revitalized their provincial and national organizations in an effort to prevent the implementation of the policy and the Indian movement became sharply focused on retrenching their special rights.[17] Indian spokesmen had been highly critical of the Indian Act, but they had sought its retention in modified form. More especially they had demanded that their special rights be more firmly retrenched in law and that they be given the opportunity to participate in decisions that affected their future. They asked that no action be taken by the government to change the Act until their historic rights could be researched by themselves and their own case presented to the government. Both the Prime Minister and the Minister of Indian Affairs publicly stated that the termination policy would not be forced on them,[18] but Indians remained skeptical. From their experience the Indian Act consultation process had been deceptive and they feared that termination policy remained as a hidden agenda within government. As a consequence, Indians became preoccupied with examining their historic rights and defending the Indian Act which contained some of these rights. The priorities of the status Indian organizations, moreover, did not include the subject of the status of Indian women.

While the Indian movement was focusing on special rights, the women's liberation movement had taken hold primarily among urban professional women. Unlike the Indian movement, it demanded radical changes in the status quo and basic social reforms in the social order that would bring equality to men and women. In 1967, the federal government had appointed a Royal Commission to assess the status of women within the federal domain and its 1970 Report took note of the circumstances of enfranchising Indian women who married non-Indians. It observed the disproportionate number of involuntary enfranchisements due to marriage compared to the voluntary enfranchisements, noting that between 1958 and 1968, 4 605 women automatically became enfranchised through intermarriage in contrast to only 891 adult Indians of both sexes who chose to relinquish Indian status.[19] The Report of the Royal Commission recommended an equalizing arrangement by suggesting that the "Indian Act be amended to allow an Indian woman upon marriage to a non-Indian to (a) retain her Indian status and (b) transmit her Indian status to her children."[20] This was essentially the condition that had prevailed in the 1868 legislation, but the recommendation was as incomplete in its comprehension of the social and legal dimensions of the problem as were earlier recommendations by Indian spokesmen at the consultation meetings. In the end the recommendation was not implemented. The failure of the government to take action disappointed some enfranchised Indian women and they proceeded to take their cases to the courts for redress, but not before a potentially significant challenge had already been made to the validity of the entire Indian Act.

While Indian leaders were trying to defend the Indian Act and to prevent the termination policy from being implemented in late 1969, a case came before the Supreme Court of Canada which resulted in the liquor sections of the Indian Act being declared inoperative.[21] The case had been argued under the Bill of Rights and its success opened up the question that if one section of the Act could be removed because it was discriminatory on the basis of race (and contrary to the Bill of Rights), was the entire Act not vulnerable to further challenge under the Bill? In 1971 this question was answered.

Impatient with certain provisions in the Indian Act and motivated by certain local-level factors, two Indian women who had been enfranchised because of marriage to non-Indians proceeded independently to take their claims of sexist discrimination against the Indian Act to the courts. They did so as individuals, without the support of regional Indian associations and against the wishes of their own band councils and bands.

The Case of Jeannette Lavell

The first to begin proceedings before the courts was Jeannette Corbiere Lavell, an Ojibwa woman from Manitoulin Island in southern Ontario. Lavell, then living in Toronto where women's rights groups were active, had lost her Indian status in 1970 at the time of her marriage to a non-Indian. According to the procedures in the Indian Act, the Registrar in the Department of Indian Affairs and Northern Development removed her name from the band list. She appealed the ruling to the Department asking that her name be reinstated on the band list, and after failing to win the appeal she took her case to the Ontario courts. Beginning in the lower court, her lawyer argued that her loss of Indian status was an instance of sexist discrimination in the Indian Act (Section 12 (1) (b)), pointing out that Indian men marrying-out did not suffer enfranchisement under the same circumstances. The court was not sympathetic to the argument and, indeed, it was evident that the judge felt the question was properly a parliamentary matter, not one that was rightly the domain of the judiciary. The judge argued that "If Section 12 (1) (b) is distasteful or undesirable to Indians, they themselves can arouse public conscience and thereby stimulate parliament by legislative amendment to correct any unfairness or injustice."[22] This belief was equally shared by many status Indians and their organizations. Following the Indians' rejection of the termination policy, the government had publicly agreed to leave the Indian Act unrevised until native organizations concluded their research on treaty and historical rights. This research was still going on when Jeannette Lavell brought her case forward. Because the political arena was effectively closed on the matter of revising the Act this left the courts as the only realistic avenue through which changes in the legal status of Indian women might be effected.

Although Lavell lost her first court case, she appealed the decision with success.[23] The judge ruled that the membership section that caused Lavell to lose her Indian status was discriminatory on the basis of sex and contrary to the Bill of Rights. The judgment called for that section of the Act to be made inoperative and that Lavell's name be reinstated on the band list. Lavell's case had been built entirely around her own status and it had not included any demands for her young son or her non-Indian husband. Nor did the judgment refer to the consequences of the ruling for the son or the husband.

The Case of Yvonne Bedard

While Jeannette Lavell was proceeding with her appeal, a second Indian woman began legal action. Yvonne Bedard had been born on the Six Nations Reserve (Iroquois) in southern Ontario and in 1964 had married a non-Indian and moved to the city where she remained until 1970 when she separated from her husband.[24] At that point she returned to the reserve with her two children to live in the house that had been willed to her by her mother. She sought and was granted permission from the band council to reside on the reserve for a period of six months during which time, according to the Indian Act provisions, she was to dispose of her property which as a non-band member she had no right to retain. At the end of the six months she was granted a further six-month extension. After that the band council was firm in its determination that she vacate the reserve. Fearing formal eviction by the band council, Bedard took her case to the courts asking for a temporary injunction to prevent the band council from forcing her off the reserve. Unlike Jeannette Lavell, Yvonne Bedard was seeking legal right to reside on the reserve with her children, and her lawyer was arguing a broader case against the Indian Act. He claimed that the entire Act was discriminatory on the basis of race and that with few exceptions it should be entirely repealed. If he were to succeed in his argument, legal status would no longer exist as an issue and Bedard would have the right to residence in the community.

Yvonne Bedard did not receive public support for her case from her reserve or from the Indian association to which her band council belonged, despite the interesting fact that the Iroquois were traditionally a matrilineal and matrilocal society. The prevailing local attitude toward such women who returned home was one of limited sympathy, especially if they needed social welfare assistance from the band council as Bedard had temporarily required. The band council's position was accurately reflected in a position paper presented to the Minister of Indian Affairs in 1971:[25]

> The latest Court decision, (Lavell's successful appeal) that an Indian woman, by marrying a non-member of the Band, does not lose her Indian status, poses more problems for her children than it solves. It is the legal and moral duty of the husband to support his wife. Consequently by the Indian Act, the Indian woman lost her Indian status and took the status of the husband. This section in the Indian Act was merely a legislative embodiment of what had become Indian custom.

The Bedard case was heard shortly after Lavell had succeeded in getting her name reinstated on the band list and Yvonne Bedard was successful on the basis of the Lavell judgment. But the judge avoided the larger question of whether the entire Indian Act should be declared inoperative on the basis of racial discrimination.

A Period of Indecision

With the two judgments in favor of the Indian women, public attention was more clearly focused on the matter, but the social consequences of these decisions to the family, its individual members and the band did not receive critical attention from either the public or the courts. Indeed it was not clear if the judgment would be retroactive, and if so, it was uncertain where the break-off point would come, if at all. To reinstate all Indian women who had lost status upon marrying-out would be a complex task and it would still leave open the question of the implications of this for the children and husbands.[26] Action was taken, however, by the Department of Indian Affairs following the judgment and the removal of Indian women from the band lists upon marriage to a non-Indian was suspended.

Politically, the two judgments raised deep concern among the provincial Indian associations and their federated national body, the National Indian Brotherhood. Leaders from these associations feared that the Indian Act was now even more vulnerable to abrogation than it had been in the past, and that their efforts to secure the Act in the face of the termination policy might be nullified by further judicial rulings that the Act was racially discriminatory and contrary to the Bill of Rights. Their hard-won battle to save the Indian Act and the special rights it supplied might fall before the courts.

A short time after the two judgments in favor of the Indian women were made, the Minister of Justice announced that he would appeal the decision to the Supreme Court of Canada.[27] He stated that the consequences of the rulings on both the rights of Indians and of women were so far-reaching that further clarification from the courts was necessary. The Lavell and Bedard cases were heard jointly before the Supreme Court in January of 1973 but unlike the earlier cases the court was packed to overflowing with supporters for both women's rights and Indian rights. In political terms, the case was seen as women's rights versus Indians' rights, but the public sentiment and support for the former was not as strong or as well organized.

Defense of the Indian Act

Intervening on behalf of Jeannette Lavell and Yvonne Bedard, were private individuals and the Native Council of Canada, the national organization for Métis and Non-Status Indians. The group known as Indian Rights for Indian Women, initially formed by non-status Indian women in 1972, was not yet legally incorporated and as Sanders has noted, it was unable to intervene in the case in a collective capacity.[28] More forceful intervention against Lavell and Bedard was made by the National Indian Brotherhood, the national organization for status Indians. While acknowledging that the membership sections of the Indian Act needed revision, the National Indian

Brotherhood argued that the proper route for such reform was legislative, not judicial.[29] Behind this argument, however, lay a more powerful historical fact. Status Indians have not supported efforts by non-status and Métis groups to gain equivalent status or rights from the federal government, fearing that their own position and limited resources might be endangered in the process. The strains between status and non-status Indian groups has a long tradition. The Indian Rights for Indian Women group also suffered from the same problems, primarily because the government required, as a condition of funding, that both status and non-status women be represented.[30] Status Indian women have not supported the efforts of enfranchised Indian women to regain their legal status and in general Indian people, during the last century, have come to accept the legal definition of Indian. The exclusion of married-out Indian women is often seen as a voluntary act for which the consequences are known and must be accepted. As one status Indian woman said of Yvonne Bedard, "You have made your bed – now lie in it."[31]

The results of the government's appeal of the Lavell and Bedard cases proved to be a major disappointment for the two women and the women's rights movement in general. In a decision that is now regarded as "virtually unintelligible" by lawyers and legal academics,[32] the Supreme Court of Canada ruled that the Indian Act was not discriminatory against Indian women who married non-Indians.[33] The judgment, brought down in August of 1973, was seen as a major defeat for women's equality under the Bill of Rights, but for Indians it was a victory in defending the Act against the Bill. The contentious section on membership in the Act remained in force and the Department of Indian Affairs resumed its procedure of enfranchising Indian women who marry non-Indians. Thus the judicial forum, initially sympathetic to the Indian women's cases, had proved, in the end, to be an unproductive arena in which to secure legal changes in the Indian Act.[34]

Broader Implications of the Law

Because the *legal status* of Indian women became the focus of public concern, the more general ways in which the Indian Act affected Indian women and their families did not receive attention. The setting up of reserves had provided for unique community enclaves in which Indian families could socialize their children in the cultural traditions of the tribes without the overwhelming presence of non-Indians in their communities. In this sense the Act provided some protection for the continuation of their cultures although the acculturative forces were nevertheless strong. In the case of the Indian women who married-out, however, this cultural milieu was denied them and their children. By marrying-out, the Indian woman and her family were severed from her kinsmen, friends and community. The prohibition against residence in the community meant that the woman herself could no longer participate in the cultural traditions in any sustained, day-to-day fashion. Her role in community life in religious and political affairs was effectively terminated. Nor could she systematically provide this cultural milieu as a socialization experience for her children. The effect of the Indian Act in her case was to truncate the extended family and cut her off from daily contact with her kinsmen. As she raised her children, she did not have the option of easy and informal exchange and guidance from her mother or sisters to assist her in her new role as mother. Nor did she have the economic support often provided a new couple by the parents in sharing residences or assisting in the securing of land for establishing a new household. In general the significant emotional support of the parental family was denied her at the time she became a wife and more importantly as she became a mother. If her marriage broke down, she had no right to return to her parents' household for help in a time of crisis and readjustment. In a reciprocal fashion, if her parents were elderly and in need of assistance she was in no position to offer them accommodation and daily support within the confines of their own community. If she were willed property in land or buildings on the reserve, she was forced to sell these within a short period of time, risking the chance of a low market value. In general, although the warm and nurturing sentiments in the family relationships may well be retained, the daily acting out of these in a mutually supportive fashion is no longer possible. The grandparent-grandchild relationship is likewise weakened and this entails a further cost, for the grandparents are likely to be more knowledgeable about the cultural traditions of the community than the parents.

These and other implications of the legislation were largely unresearched by the government or academics, the notable exception being Sanders' thorough analyses of the legal cases.[35] Harold Cardinal's discussion of the matter in *The Rebirth of Canada's Indians* in 1977,[36] and Jamieson's book *Indian Women and the Law in Canada: Citizens Minus* in 1978, sponsored by the Advisory Council on the Status of Women and Indian Rights for Indian Women,[37] provided the public with a better understanding of the issue, but by that time the matter had moved from the judicial to the political forum where it was already encountering difficulties.

The Political Forum

Following the defeat of Indian women in the Supreme Court case in 1973, it became evident that any subsequent attempts to alter the contentious provision in the Indian Act would have to be made through political channels. But in the three years following the judgment, neither the federal government nor the National Indian Brotherhood (NIB) gave the matter serious attenton. The NIB, after the 1969 White Paper, had concentrated its resources on questions of treaty and aboriginal rights, education, and other matters. Even though its president, Noel Starblanket, endorsed the government's decision to fund the IRIW research program in 1977 and publicly expressed his personal opinion that section 12 (1) (b) was discriminatory, the NIB has not officially supported the efforts of non-status Indian women for reform.[38] The government, moreover, took the position in these years that it could not alter the membership section in the Act until the entire Act was revised. Consequently, neither the government nor the NIB were receptive to the plight of non-status Indian women. During these years, however, public pressure from women's groups, both native and non-native, continued to mount, being directed at the government which was publicly committed to equal rights for women in its own policies. As a result, the issue of the status of Indian women surfaced prominently again in 1977 in three contexts.

(a) Indian Rights for Indian Women

The first context, in the fall of 1977, was a meeting between IRIW and the government at which the IRIW put forward a series of brief recommendations. The major ones were:[39]

1. That all Indian women should keep their Indian status and that no Indian woman should be evicted from a reserve until the Indian Act is amended.
2. That Indian women who have lost their status because of marriage should have their Indian rights restored to them under the revised Indian Act.
3. That the non-Indian spouse of any Indian should be allowed to live on the reserve and that all children of a mixed marriage should be granted Indian status.
4. That Indians with one-quarter native ancestry should qualify for Indian status.

Although the IRIW received no commitment from the government on its proposals, their meeting affirmed their determination to continue pressuring the government until the Act was amended. The Cabinet, however, was already committed to discussions with the NIB on revising the Indian Act in the Joint Cabinet/National Indian Brotherhood Committee, the second context in which the issue arose.

(b) National Indian Brotherhood

In 1974, the federal government and the NIB had embarked on an unprecedented policy advising experiment in what was called the Joint Cabinet/NIB Committee.[40] Composed of the governing council of the NIB and several Cabinet ministers, the Joint Committee was created to develop mutually acceptable policies for Indians. In 1975 it had begun exploring possible amendments to the Act but special representation by IRIW in the Joint Committee had been denied by the NIB, a position which led to criticism of the NIB as "unrepresentative" of Indian women by certain members of Parliament and the Human Rights Commissioner, Gordon Fairweather.[41] By 1977, however, relations in general between the NIB and the government were becoming strained over many issues, and within the Joint Committee they were reaching a breaking point because the government had evaded discussion of Indian rights issues, the central purpose for which the NIB had entered the Joint Committee experiment initially. A confrontation was inevitable in the Joint Committee and it occurred in the final December 1977 meeting over the matter of Indian educational rights. The ministers expressed the view that they were unconvinced that Indians had the rights to education that the NIB had claimed, and when the next agenda item, the status of Indian women, came forward, the NIB refused to discuss it, arguing that if Indian rights in general were uncertain, the rights of Indian women were even more tenuous.[42] When the Joint Committee experiment collapsed in April 1978, with the NIB withdrawal, the issue of the status of Indian women remained unresolved. Indeed no mutual policy agreements had emerged during the Joint Committee's three-and-a-half year history.

(c) Human Rights Act

The third context in which the issue of the status of Indian women arose was the passage of the federal Human Rights Act legislation in 1977. Justice Minister Ron Basford had been under increasing public pressure to amend the contentious section of the Indian Act on women, but in 1977 the Cabinet was still committed to the Joint Committee forum for discussing changes in the Act. The government's resolution of this dilemma, although a temporary one until the Act could be amended, was to exempt the Indian Act from the application of the Human Rights Act which came into force in 1978. This led to further criticism from members of the House of Commons Standing Committee on Justice and Legal Affairs in reviewing the Human Rights Bill,[43] but it also pre-empted the possibility of Indian women using the new Human Rights Commission as a vehicle for redress and reform.

Consequently, by early 1978, there had been no substantive gain in changing the legislation affecting Indian women. Political channels for seeking reform had been exhausted and the government together with the NIB had not advanced the issue. There was no clear movement even within government for amending the Indian Act other than the dissemination to the public of various "Discussion Papers" whose status was uncertain.[44]

The International Forum

Perhaps inevitably, the issue of the status of Indian women moved into yet another arena in 1978, that of the United Nations, in the form of the Sandra Lovelace "case." An Indian woman from the Tobique reserve in New Brunswick, Sandra Lovelace had married-out in 1970, later separating from her non-Indian husband and returning to live on the reserve with her children. In mid-1978, she took her case to the United Nations Human Rights Committee, arguing that Canada was in violation of the International

Covenant on Political and Civil Rights on the grounds of sexual discrimination, section 12 (1) (b) of the Indian Act. In 1981, the Human Rights Committee ruled, under article 27 of the covenant, that Canada was contravening this international treaty because Lovelace was denied the right to live in her "ethnic community."[45] This ruling, however, was not made under articles of the covenant dealing with sexual inequality because of a technicality, namely, that Sandra Lovelace had married *before* 1976 when Canada signed the convention. This raised the question of the retroactivity (prior to 1976) of the denial of rights under the covenant, even though it was recognized that a case could be made for the continuing denial (post-1976) of her rights. Since then, several additional cases have been filed before the same United Nations committee by Indian women who married non-Indians after 1976, and the decision of the committee is still pending at the time of writing.

The Lovelace case functioned to embarrass the Canadian government, a discomfort government members may well have welcomed given their desire to remove the discriminatory sections of the Indian Act. The government's determination in this regard was most recently affirmed in December 1981 when it ratified the United Nations Convention on the Elimination of All Forms of Discrimination against Women.[46] In announcing this ratification, the government confirmed its intention to amend the discriminatory section of the Indian Act after consultation with Indians "within the context of the Charter of Rights and Freedoms."[47] In the meantime, as an interim measure, the government had announced a new policy in July 1980 of suspending the application of section 12 (1) (b) to Indian women if it receives a formal request to do so from individual Indian band councils.[48] In these instances, Indian women who marry non-Indians retain their legal status and their children also have legal status. Predictably, this measure has not proven popular with bands, and to date only 46 of the 573 band councils (8 percent) have chosen this option.[49] The band response reflects the lower status accorded Indian women at the reserve level, as well as the absence of general support for married-out Indian women in the status Indian community at large. And it contrasts dramatically with the behavior of band councils to the option of suspending the "double mother" provisions in the Indian Act.

The "double mother" provision, section 12 (1) (b) (iv) of the Indian Act, automatically enfranchises all children at 21 years of age, whose parents married after September 1951 and who have a non-Indian mother and grandmother (father's mother). Suspending this provision was also an interim measure, and it was precipitated by bands in Quebec where sons of influential band members or chiefs were affected by the section. Concerted pressure was put on the federal government by these bands to change this provision, but unlike the issue of the status of Indian women, the matter attracted little public attention. Since 1980, 260 of the 573 bans (45 percent) have requested the suspension of the "double mother" section, and officials estimate that an additional 70 bands are likely to follow suit, their members, being affected by this section through more extensive intermarriage with non-Indians.[50] The Indian preference for patrilineal descent (although not universal) and for the rights of band membership for males is clear in this behavior at the band level, behavior which the NIB represents politically at the national level in its resistance to Indian women's rights.

Finally, in turning to the most recent developments on the status of Indian women it becomes evident that the matter is being perceived by Indian women and the government more in terms of its broader implications than it has been in the past. Internal organizational problems, including those of accounting for government funding,[51] led to the collapse of the IRIW organization in the fall of 1981. The IRIW has been succeeded by the National Native Women's Association of Canada as spokesman for native women. This organization continues to advocate for amendments to the Indian Act; it has become increasingly vocal in its demands for improved socio-economic conditions for native families and communities. This broader based advocacy was best illustrated in the native women's march from Oka, Quebec, to Ottawa in July 1979, protesting inadequate housing as well as discrimination in the Indian Act.[52] These demands have continued to emanate from NNWA's active regional associations, including the new one formed in British Columbia following the Indian women's occupation of DIAND's Regional Offices.[53]

Within government, the issue of Indian women has finally become subject to more detailed policy research which has revealed the complexity of the problem as options for amending the membership provisions of the Indian Act are considered by various departments.[54] More significantly, in terms of legislative changes to section 12 (1) (b), the issue has become enmeshed in the uncertain implications of the new constitution's Charter of Rights and Freedoms, and in the more pragmatic aspects of fiscal restraint in government. In short, the issue of Indian women now engages the attention of several departments and it is being examined in two contexts: the human rights field of the constitution and the United Nations, and the practical field of financial costs which the government is likely to incur with various amending options. The option of reinstating married-out Indian women has received considerable attention, and the government is currently attempting to determine how many of the Indian women who were deprived of their status through marriage would likely return to live on reserves, and what costs this renewed residence would generate for the government in terms of housing, welfare, health and educational programs.[55] Such predictions are precarious because, among other reasons, Indian women may return to their reserves in times of economic hardship, unemployment, and high inflation, but retain their current residency in a more favorable economic climate, and because there is no history of similar behavior patterns on which to formulate such projections. Nor is there any reason to assume that legislative changes, when they occur, will be retroactive.

Although the climate of fiscal restraint has not completely destroyed the issue of Indian women as a matter of principle, it has made the issue increasingly one of practical costs and policy forecasting. This development has forced into the open the longstanding NIB concern that if Indian women were reinstated without government provisions beyond those currently provided to communities, the quality of services on reserves, which is already problematic, would decline even more. Although the concern of status Indians with finite resources, whether they be corporate reserve lands, oil and gas revenues, or government program monies, has rarely been articulated with any clarity, there is some evidence that this may be changing. The current president of the NIB, Del Riley, for example, recently predicted that any government effort to reinstate married-out Indian women and their children would meet with firm opposition from bands across the country which were already experiencing severe cut-backs in government programs.[56] This concern is supported by the more generally disturbing fact that in the past 10 years the federal government's per capita spending on Indians has fallen drastically below its expenditures on a per capita basis in other federal social programs; in real terms, federal government expenditures for Indians increased only 14 percent per capita between 1970/71 and 1978/79 in contrast to a 128 percent per capita increase in the federal government's other social programs.[57] Any future policy to reinstate Indian women, or to have them retain legal status despite marriage, will require large government program expenditures if both the Indian women and the reserve communities are not to be handicapped in their quality of life.

Still unresolved is the matter of revising the Indian Act. Although ministers of Indian Affairs have, since 1978, indicated their desire to amend the Act, the 1951 Act remains in force. Consideration has been given, for example, to amending only the membership sections of the Act while passing an entirely new piece of legislation into which individual bands could opt to enhance their local governing powers. However, at the time of writing (February 1982), Cabinet has yet to approve a timetable and an amending process for the Act or any new legislation. Since 1978, the patriation of the constitution has taken priority over amendments to the Indian Act in the field of Indian policy, as it has within the NIB.[58] Because the Indian Act is largely an administrative vehicle which does not embody Indian aboriginal and treaty rights, Indian associations have not supported the attempts of ministers of Indian Affairs to amend the Act. In contrast, Indian women, who continue to marry-out at a reasonably even rate (see Table 1), have placed first priority on the Indian Act amendments. Under the new constitution, the government will have three years in which to correct discriminatory legislation, and this deadline may well become the effective pressure which will finally lead to the reform that enfranchised Indian women have sought for over a decade.

TABLE 1 *Number of Indian marriages*

	Indian women to Indian men[1]		Non-Indian women to Indian men		Indian women to Non-Indian men		Total
	No.	%	No.	%	No.	%	
1972	971	52.4	442	23.9	440	23.8	1853
1973	1026	48.2	564	26.5	538	25.3	2128
1974	886	44.0	544	27.0	582	28.9	2012
1975	836	47.8	500	28.6	410	23.5	1746
1976	1082	50.5	611	28.5	451	21.0	2144
1977	1035	50.0	561	27.1	474	22.9	2070
1978	948	48.5	566	29.0	439	22.5	1953
1979	1089	54.2	494	24.6	428	21.3	2011

Source: Indian and Northern Affairs, Ottawa.
1. Includes marriages between Indian women and Indian men of the same band and of different bands.

Conclusion

The issue of the status of Indian women has maintained political momentum, without resolution, for over a decade, shifting from the judicial to the political arena within Canada, and finally to the international forum of the United Nations. The issue was spearheaded by individual Indian women who, because of intermarriage with non-Indians, lost their legal status and sought reinstatement. These women experienced the fate of double jeopardy because they suffered not only the loss of Indian status and the special rights it provided, but they also suffered the general disprivileges of women in society. Politically, these enfranchised Indian women were trapped in the middle of two clashing social movements. The urban-based middle class women's rights movement singled out their discrimination and supported their efforts to reform the legislation. The rural-based nationalistic Indian rights movement gave priority to Indian determination of their unique ethnicity as aboriginal peoples; a determination which included the right to define their membership, whether it be by endorsing the century-old provisions in the Indian Act or by decisions of the band councils in some future form of Indian government. The view of many Whites that status Indian organizations are opposing the cause of married-out Indian women because they are male dominated is simplistic. This view not only ignores the reserve-based preference for patrilineal membership, it also disregards the understandable concern among status Indians for their finite resources (e.g. land, oil and gas revenues, and government program monies). Furthermore, the complexity of the issue of enfranchised Indian women was initially ignored by advocates and critics alike, and when the govenment began to examine seriously the options for changing the legislation, the overriding fiscal policies in Ottawa were recasting the issue from one of principle to one of pragmatic financing, and the matter of the new constitution was overshadowing any immediate action to amend the Indian Act. Hence, although the government's policy is to eliminate the discrimination in the Indian Act, implementing interim measures until this can be achieved, the Act itself invokes larger problems of its own. Among these problems are those of whether the Indian Act can ever become "living" legislation which is regularly amended in response to Indian needs and, secondly, whether the Act, as it now exists, can endure an uncertain future in the context of the new Charter of Rights and Freedoms. Those who advocate women's rights are often the same persons who label the entire Indian Act as discriminatory legislation.[59] While this need not be the case under the new Charter, the Charter will undoubtedly call for some more extensive interpretation of the Act not only in its sexually discriminatory aspects, but in its overall formulation.

END NOTES

1. I wish to thank Tom S. Abler, J. William Hill, and Douglas Sanders for their very helpful comments on this work.
2. Harold E. Driver, *Indians of North America*, Chicago: University of Chicago Press, 1961, Chs. 15 and 16, and Maps 31 and 32.
3. The term "enfranchised" is a confusing one unless it is understood that historically, with minor exceptions, Indians did not have the franchise if they held legal status. Only by relinquishing their legal status could they become "enfranchised," thereby gaining the right to vote in federal and provincial elections. In 1960 this situation changed when the federal government amended its election laws and since then Indians have had the federal franchise without having to relinquish their legal status. In the same decade most of the provinces followed suit. The term "enfranchisement", however, is still retained in the Indian Act to describe the process of giving up one's legal Indian status (Revised Statutes of Canada, 1970, Chs. 1-6, Sections 109-113).
4. Statutes of Upper Canada, 1850, Ch. 74, Section 10; and Statutes of Upper Canada, 1857, Chapter 26, Section 1.
5. Statutes of Canada, 1868, Chapter 42, Section 15.
6. *Ibid.*, Section 17.
7. Sally M. Weaver, research notes from the Six Nations Band Council Minutes, 1847-1890. Six Nations Indian Agency Archives, District Office, Department of Indian and Northern Affairs, Brantford, Ontario.
8. Revised Statutes of Canada, 1869, Ch. 6, Section 6.
9. Sally M. Weaver, "Report on Archival Research Regarding Indian Women's Status, 1868-1869", Prepared for B. Kellock, legal counsel to the Six Nations Band Council, Nov. 9, 1971.
10. Letter, Hector Langevin, Superintendent General of Indian Affairs, to Sawatis Anionkiu, Peter Karenho and Other Iroquois Indians; Caughnawaga, P.Q., Aug. 20, 1869. Public Archives of Canada, Record Group 10, Volume 528.
11. Revised Statutes of Canada, 1970, Chs. 1-6, Section 15, sub-section 1.

12. Douglas E. Sanders, "The Bill of Rights and Indian Status", *UBC Law Review*, Vol. 7, No. 1, (1972), pp. 89-90.

13. Department of Indian Affairs and Northern Development, *Choosing a Path*, Ottawa: DIAND, 1968.

14. Department of Indian Affairs and Northern Development, *Résumé of the Reports of the Indian Act Consultation Meetings*, Ottawa: DIAND, March 1969, pp. 1-2.

15. Minutes of the Second and Third Meetings of the National Indian Advisory Board, Ottawa: DIAND, 1966; and Sally M. Weaver, "Proposed Changes in the Legal Status of Canadian Indian Women: The Collision of Two Social Movements," Paper presented at the 1973 Annual Meeting of the American Anthropological Association, New Orleans.

16. *Statement of the Government of Canada on Indian Policy 1969*, Ottawa: Queen's Printer, 1969; and Sally M. Weaver, *Canadian Indian Termination: A Case Study in Policy-Making*, 1977, unpublished manuscript.

17. *Citizens Plus* (The Red Paper) printed by the Indian Chiefs of Alberta, Edmonton, 1979; *Wahbung: Our Tomorrows*, printed by the Manitoba Indian Brotherhood, Winnipeg, 1971; and *Position Paper*, printed by the Association of Iroquois and Allied Indians, Brantford, Ontario, 1971.

18. Pierre E. Trudeau, "Statement by the Prime Minister at a Meeting with the Indian Association of Alberta and the National Indian Brotherhood, Ottawa, June 4, 1970". Toronto: Indian-Eskimo Association; and Jean Chrétien, "The Unfinished Tapestry – Indian Policy in Canada", Speech given at Queen's University, Kingston, Ontario, March 17, 1971. Ottawa: DIAND Press Release.

19. *Report of the Royal Commission on the Status of Women*, Ottawa Queen's Printer, 1970, p. 238.

20. *Ibid.*

21. Douglas E. Sanders, "The Indian Act and the Bill of Rights," *Ottawa Law Review*, Vol. 6, (1974), pp. 400-403, and Douglas E. Sanders, "Indian Act – Status of Indian Woman on Marriage to Person Without Indian Status", *Saskatchewan Law Review*, Vol. 38 (1974), p. 243.

22. *Lavell v. Attorney General of Canada*, Ontario County Court, (Grossberg, J), 22 Dominion Law Record, (3rd), 1971, pp. 182-186.

23. *Lavell v. Attorney General of Canada*, Federal Court of Appeal, judgment dated Oct. 8, 1971.

24. Sally M. Weaver, "Judicial Preservation of Ethnic Group Boundaries: The Iroquois Case," In *Proceedings of the First Congress of the Canadian Ethnology Society*, Ottawa: National Museum of Man, Mercury Series, 1974. Paper No. 17, pp. 48-66.

25. Association of Iroquois and Allied Indians, *Position Paper*, Brantford, Ontario, 1971, pp. 63-64.

26. Letter, Jean Chrétien to John Turner, October 26, 1971, in DIAND records division, Ottawa, file no 1/18-26, Vol. 3.

27. Statements in the House of Commons by John Turner, Minister of Justice, Debates of the House of Commons, Dec. 1, 1971, p. 10045.

28. Douglas E. Sanders, "Indian Women: A Brief History of Their Roles and Rights," *McGill Law Journal*, Vol. 21, No. 4, (1975), p. 667.

29. National Indian Brotherhood, Press Release, "Resolution on the Lavell Case, Indian Status and the Indian Act", September 27, 1973, Ottawa.

30. *Ibid.*, footnote 28, p. 666.
31. Letter to the Editor from "Forbidden Voice," *Brantford Expositor*, Sept. 14, 1971.
32. Personal communication, Douglas Sanders, Jan. 29, 1978.
33. *Attorney General of Canada v. Lavell* and *Isaac v. Bedard*, judgement of Aug. 27, 1973 reported in the *Dominion Law Report* 38 (3d), 1973.
34. At a later date yet another case was brought to the courts but it did not have the political consequences of Lavell and Bedard. Mrs. Canard, an Indian woman in Manitoba, charged that the denial of her right to act as executor of her husband's estate constituted sexist discrimination in the Indian Act. Her case failed before the Supreme Court of Canada in 1975. See David W. Elliott, "Canard: A Triad Returns," *University of Toronto Law Journal*, Vol. 25 (1975), pp. 317-332.
35. Doulgas E. Sanders, *Family Law and Native People*, unpublished Report of the Law Reform Commission of Canada, Ottawa, 1975.
36. Harold Cardinal, *The Rebirth of Canada's Indians*, (Edmonton: Hurtig, 1977), p. 101.
37. Kathleen Jamieson, *Indian Women and the Law in Canada: Citizens Minus*, Ottawa, Minister of Supply and Services, Canada, 1978).
38. "Non-Status Native Women Promised Aid in Rights Fight," *Ottawa Citizen*, October 24, 1977; and "Starblanket Wins Election," *Indian News* (DIAND) 1978, 19(6):2, and "NIB: No Equality for Women Just Yet," *Indian News* 1980, 20(9):7.
39. "Indian Rights for Indian Women Resolutions," *Indian News*, 1978, 19(3):7. "The Federal Cabinet and the National Indian Brotherhood: A Unique Experiment in Pressure Group Relations."
40. Sally M. Weaver, "Pressure Group Relations between the Federal Government and the National Indian Brotherhood," paper presented at the Seminar on 'Governing Under Pressure,' Sponsored by the Institute of Public Administration of Canada, Chateau Montebello, Oct. 5-7, 1981.
41. House of Commons Standing Committee on Justice and Legal Affairs, Minutes of Proceedings and Evidence, May 25, 1977, No. 15, p. 44; "Interview with Gordon Fairweather," *Indian News*, 1978, 19(1):1,3; "Indian Brotherhood Attacked Over Rights," *Ottawa Citizen*, October 10, 1978.
42. Minutes of the Joint Cabinet/National Indian Brotherhood Meeting, Canadian Indian Rights Commission, Dec. 12, 1977, p. 12-13.
43. House of Commons Standing Committee on Justice and Legal Affairs, Minutes of Proceedings and Evidence, May 25, 1977, No. 15, pp. 42-47.
44. "Revision Process Planned," *Indian News*, 1978, (Summer edition, no volume or number cited), p. 1-2; "Special Edition: Discussion Paper for Indian Act Revision," *Indian News,* Nov. 1978.
45. United Nations Committee on Human Rights, 1981, xxxx.
46. "Text of Joint Communique of Federal and Provincial Ministers Responsible for Human Rights concerning Ratification of the Convention on the Elimination of All Forms of Discrimination Against Women," Secretary of State, Ottawa, Dec. 10, 1981.
47. "Canada Ratifies Pact to Counter Discrimination Against Women," News Release, Secretary of State, Ottawa, Dec. 10, 1981, p. 2.

48. Announcement of the Minister of Indian Affairs, John Munro, July 24, 1980, DIAND News Release; "Gov't Ready to Lift Controversial Clause: Section 12(1)(b)," *Indian News*, 1980, 21(4):1,6.

49. I am grateful to Jim Allen of the Membership Division of DIAND for these figures.

50. *Ibid.*

51. "Bickering Will End," *Indian News*, 1981, 22(5):8: "Sec. of State Checking IRIW," *Native People*, 1981, 14(41):1-2.

52. "Women and Children Walk for Change," *Indian News*, 1979, 20(5):1,7.

53. "B.C. Chief Speaks Out for Indian Women's Rights," *Indian News*, 1980, 21(2):5; "Women's Plight Ignored," *Indian News*, 1981, 22(4):5: "Indian Women Won't Sit Back," *Indian News*, 1981, 22(6):3,5.

54. In October 1981 a 'leaked' document, titled "The Legislation Proposals," provided some indication of possible options government was considering in eliminating the discriminatory provisions on Indian women. Various cost estimates were made for the reinstatement option, and the heaviest demands on government programs were seen to fall on DIAND and the Department of Health and Welfare. See also, "Changes Would be Expensive," *Indian News*, 1981, 22(7):1,4.

55. "Gov't Fence Sitting on Indian Act Changes," *Native People*, 1981, 14(49):1-2.

56. "Stiff Resistance to Government Plans," *Indian News*, 1981, 22(8):9,10.

57. Department of Indian and Northern Affairs, *Indian Conditions: A Survey*, 1980, Ottawa, p. 5.

58. *Resolutions* of the National Indian Brotherhood's Assembly of First Nations Constitutional Conference: Constitutional Strategies for Entrenchment of Treaty and Aboriginal Rights, Nov. 30 to Dec. 2, 1980, Ottawa.

59. See, for example, comments made in the House of Commons Standing Committee on Justice and Legal Affairs, Minutes of Proceedings and Evidence, May 25, 1977, No. 15, p. 42.

PART TWO

The Second Nation:
The French in Canada

Introduction

When Prime Minister Trudeau addressed the U.S. Congress in 1977, he observed, "The success of our efforts in the first century following Confederation was promising but by no means complete. . . . We have not . . . created the conditions in which French-speaking Canadians have felt fully equal or could fully develop the richness of the culture they had inherited. And therein is the source of our *central problem today* [emphasis added]." This section examines the "central problem" from a regional and historical perspective.

Quebec Society

The historical background to the so-called central problem as it concerns Quebec is presented through the eyes of a Quebecer, Marcel Rioux. Quebec is the homeland of about 80 percent of the francophones in Canada. Rioux's article highlights the rise of the Quebec State (as opposed to the French Canadian nation), the objectives of the Royal Commisson on Bilingualism and Biculturalism, the federalist's definition and response to the Quebec question, and the alternative offered by Quebec.

In order to secure the boundaries of the Quebec State or Nation, another Quebecer, Pierre Laporte, details Quebec's recent efforts in the area of language planning. Language legislation is a deliberate attempt on the part of Quebec to instigate social change, particularly in the institutions of work and education. By raising the status of French in Quebec life, both the status of francophones and Quebec society have, in turn, improved. Laporte presents some empirical data pertaining primarily to the language of work.

The language of instruction vis-à-vis the relative statuses of anglophones and francophones is explored by Ann Denis. Language planning has had an impact both on education in Quebec and ethnic relations within Quebec society. It is too soon to say – since Quebec was not a signatory to the November 5, 1981, constitutional accord with Ottawa – what effect, if any, the new Constitution will have on Quebec's continuing ability to fortify itself through the vehicle of language planning.

Ethnic Minorities in Quebec

Recent expressions of nationalism in Quebec – of which language planning is a concrete example – coupled with immigration have led to questions being raised by the anglophone community concerning its status in the Quebec of the future. Newspapers are rife with such sensational headlines as "Ryan to fleeing English: 'Don't' ".[1] In fact, the reality behind the headlines is that in Quebec, the number of people claiming English as a mother tongue dropped by about 12 percent in 1981 in comparison with its 1976 standing according to Statistics Canada.[2] The anglophone communities that remain are attempting to organize in their defense and rally around such movements as Alliance Quebec. Such rear guard action on the part of the "charter group" in Quebec indicates that *les anglais* are rapidly developing a besieged minority group mentality.

However, recent immigrant groups – the so-called ethnic minorities – are coping with the political climate in Quebec in various ways. The party currently in power, le Parti Québécois, is trying to face any fears of intolerance that may exist and put them to rest. In a 1982 internal party referendum, le Parti Québécois membership voted overwhelmingly (95 percent) to endorse the continuing leadership of its head, René Lévesque, and such party principles as, "an open attitude toward Quebec's cultural and ethnic minorities."[3] The necessity of making such public pronouncements would seem to indicate that uncertainty and tension characterize the relationship between the current provincial government in Quebec and the non-francophone Québécois origin communities.

The four ethnic minorities chosen for attention in this section are the Greeks, the West Indians, and the Haitians in Montreal and the Portuguese within the province as a whole. Efie Gavaki, a sociologist who is an immigrant from Greece, describes her community. We see that it is institutionally complete and politically active, electing one of its members to the Quebec National Assembly in 1981. A somewhat different set of political strategies are employed, according to J. Antonio Alpalhao and M.P. DaRosa, within the Portuguese communities. Given the political events in Portugal at the time of heavy emigration to Canada, the Portuguese lacked experience with democratic institutions. Rather than being politically active in Quebec to the extent that the Greek community reportedly is, Alpalhao and DaRosa suggest that the Portuguese have tended to adopt a stance of studied neutrality. No doubt as the ethnic community matures within Quebec society, Portuguese political opinion will become more vocal and find expression within Quebec's political parties.

Various Black ethnic groups in Montreal are in a state of flux. West Indians, for example, have traditionally been English speakers, sending their children to English schools. The Haitians, on the other hand, have been tracked typically to the French schools even though they are Creole-speaking people. With The Charter of the French Language in Quebec, Bill 101, West Indians no longer have the option of English schools with some noted exceptions. The question becomes the following: Will the West Indians and the Haitians over time within a francophone milieu come to share a common identity as "Black" or will they retain their primary identities as

West Indians and Haitians? If the former, how will this Black identity be formed? These are some of the questions underlying the research conducted by Michel Laferrière in the Montreal school systems.

Francophones Outside Quebec: The Official Minority

Francophones outside Quebec participate in a broad range of social and political contexts. Even within the same province, they may have in common only their language and the reality of a larger society that may be alternatively supportive, disinterested, or, perhaps, aggressively hostile. Such variations in the social milieu, coupled with ethnic differences among francophones, make francophone organizational efforts somewhat problematic. Taking the case of francophones in Ontario, Danielle Juteau Lee and Jean Lapointe discuss the presence of a francophone identify in some areas and absence in others, and the societal factors that tend to explain this. Lee and Lapointe analyze the structural changes that have taken place in the ethnic boundaries of the Franco-Ontarians. For the most part, the latter trace their ancestry to the founding French settlers in Canada. Many Franco-Ontarians are related to the Québécois as both groups are descended from very old French-Canadian families. Because of the divergent histories of Quebec and Ontario, unique ethnic identities are emerging in each province. Lee and Lapointe relate the changes in ethnic boundaries to the new modes of Franco-Ontarian ethnicity they encompass.

In the West, French ethnicity was weakened by an influx of Central European immigrants. Cornelius Jaenen offers a historical account of the cultural battle for survival that francophones have waged in the West on behalf of the "two nation" concept of Confederation. French Canada's survival in the West – if only in a token way – has been achieved seemingly against all odds. French was only briefly recognized as an official language on the provincial level in Manitoba, and throughout the West. French language instruction in the schools assumed the status of a foreign language. The linguistic factor was cross-cut by religious sentiments. While English Protestants tended to oppose French Catholics, non-French speaking Catholics tended to support the French Catholics on some political issues on the assumption that Catholics of all languages should band together. The net effect of this support may have been a weakening of the francophone position. Nevertheless the remnants of French ethnicity persist in the West in such communities as St. Boniface Manitoba.[4]

Even in a province like New Brunswick with its official policy of bilingualism, the future of the Acadian culture is in doubt. The Acadians, descendants of the early 17th-century French settlers who were expelled in the mid-18th century by the British, and who subsequently returned after the Peace of Paris, are struggling to keep their culture intact. Recent attempts at modernizing fish-processing have had an impact on the Acadian life style. Nanciellen Davis investigated the effects of modernization on the traditional status of men and women in a small New Brunswick community. It was assumed that ethnicity mediates the modernization process. Acadian culture and traditional sex roles stand to be eroded by economic development with women perhaps benefiting less than men.

The picture of French ethnicity in the Atlantic provinces is yet again different. Eric Waddell and Claire Doran recount the situation in Newfoundland where French-speaking indigenous communities were virtually extinct until recent attempts were made from both within and outside the province to revive them. What is the future of the francophone in Newfoundland in light of the complete absence of institutional community supports and an indifferent provincial government? Is the Charter of Rights in the Constitution with its guarantees to the official minority a classic example of "too little, too late?"

END NOTES

1. Victor Malarek, "Poll foresees new exodus. Ryan to fleeing English: 'Don't.' " *Globe and Mail* (Toronto), January 20, 1982.
2. "Anglophones leaving Quebec," *Globe and Mail* (Toronto), July 7, 1982.
3. *Globe and Mail* (Toronto), February 10, 1982.
4. For an excellent analysis, see Leo Driedger, "The Maintenance of Urban Ethnic Boundaries: the French in St. Boniface," *The Sociological Quarterly* 20 (Winter, 1979): 89-108.

SELECTED REFERENCES

Beattie, Christopher. *Minority Men in a Majority Setting: Middle-Level Francophones in the Canadian Public Service.* Toronto: McClelland and Stewart, 1975.

Breton, Raymond, Jeffrey G. Reitz and Victor Valentine. *Cultural Boundaries and the Cohesion of Canada.* Montreal: Institute for Research on Public Policy, 1980.

Cartwright, Donald G. *Official Language Populations in Canada.* Montreal: Institute for Research on Public Policy, 1980.

Clark, Andrew Hill. *Acadia.* Madison: University of Wisconsin Press, 1968.

Clement, Wallace. *The Canadian Corporate Elite: An Analysis of Economic Power.* Toronto: McClelland and Stewart, 1975.

Clift, Dominique and Sheila McLeod Arnopoulos. *Le Fait Anglais au Quebéc.* Montreal: Libre Expression, 1979.

Cook, Ramsay. *French-Canadian Nationalism.* Toronto: Macmillan, 1969.

Dejean, Paul. *Les Haïtiens au Québec.* Montreal: Les Presses de l'Université du Québec, 1978.

Dion, Léon. *Nationalismes et politique au Québec.* Montreal: Hurtubise H.M.H., 1975.

Dorge, Lionel. *Introduction à l'étude des Franco-Manitobains.* Saint Boniface: La Societé Historique de Saint Boniface, 1973.

Henripin, Jacques. *Immigration and Language Imbalance.* Ottawa: Information Canada, 1974.

Henripin, Jacques and E. Lapierre-Adamyck. *La fin de la revanche des berceaux.* Montréal: Presses de l'Université de Montréal, 1974.

Jackson, John D. *Community and Conflict: A Study of French-English Relations in Ontario.* Toronto: Holt, Rinehart and Winston, 1975.

Joy, Richard. *Languages in Conflict.* Toronto: McClelland and Stewart, 1972.

Milner, Henry. *Politics in the New Quebec.* Toronto: McClelland and Stewart, 1978.

Morris, Raymond N. and C. Michael Lanphier. *Three Scales of Inequality: Perspectives on French-English Relations.* Don Mills, Ont.: Longman, 1977.

Pepin, Jean-Luc and John P. Robarts, *The Task Force on Canadian Unity: A Future Together,* Ottawa, 1979.

Piotte, J.M. (ed.), *Québec occupé.* Montreal: Editions Parti-Pris, 1971.

Trudeau, Pierre E. *Federalism and the French Canadians.* Toronto: Macmillan, 1968.

Wade, Mason. *The French Canadians* Vol. 1 1760-1911; Vol. 2 1911-1967. Toronto: Macmillan, 1968.

Quebec Society

MARCEL RIOUX   University of Montreal

Quebec in Question*

In his year-end speech in 1968, General de Gaulle expressed the hope that the French people of Canada would obtain a free hand in the management of their national life. The journalists at once remarked that the General had been more insistent on this point than the previous year. When asked to comment on this statement, Prime Minister Trudeau was said to have agreed with the General. How was this posssible? "The General was speaking of French Canada," Trudeau is said to have replied, "not of Quebec." The essence of the Quebec problem lies, in fact, in this distinction.

To speak of French Canada (or of the French people of Canada) is to speak of Canadians who speak French and who live in all parts of Canada. The problem is therefore one of bilingualism or, at the most, of biculturalism, and the solution is to be reached through the agency of the central government, the Canadian State. Federalists are happy to grant the name "French Canada" to the totality of French-speaking people scattered throughout the Canadian territory. Ottawa could, at the outside, even tolerate that this population be called the French-Canadian nation, because so defined, the word "nation" refers only to characteristics of language and culture; moreover, Ottawa remains the government of these two "nations" because the population referred to is distributed over the entire territory of Canada. The French-speaking people thus remain the traditional minority of about 28 percent defending their minority rights while experiencing a progressive anglicization. All is safe and sound. No attack has been made on the political and economic power structure, nor on the important sectors of government and administration which continue to be controlled by the central government in Ottawa, the capital of the two "nations." Here is the most perfect status quo, the very thesis of Trudeau. For the federalists, Quebec is one province out of 10; it can make no claims to represent the French-Canadian nation because there are still French-speaking people living in the other nine provinces.

---

* Reprinted from Marcel Rioux, *Quebec in Question*, Toronto: James Lewis and Samuel, 1971, with permission of author and publisher.

In the 1960s a great change occurred, revolutionizing the situation. Quebecers began to make a distinction between Quebec and French Canada. On the one hand, there is a population of French-speaking people distributed throughout Canada. This population has, in varying degrees, a common heritage of language, religion, tradition, and custom. This cultural element represents about 28 percent of Canada's total population. Federal government statistics show that outside of Quebec this population is becoming anglicized at various rates of speed; in British Columbia 60 percent of this group have been assimilated. For Canada as a whole, it will be a lost cause sooner or later; the steamroller of English-speaking North American culture will soon leave nothing but a few remnants of this language and culture.

On the other hand, there is a vast land three times larger than France where the French-speaking people are a great majority, namely Quebec. Since 1867, this territory has had a government and an administration with limited constitutional powers, but still perhaps capable of exercising enough leverage to safeguard most of what we call French-Canadian culture. On the evidence, to do this requires a reevaluation of the Quebec State, the only collective instrument that the French-Canadians possess. In Quebec the French-speaking people own only a small share of the economy, the industry, and commerce. All they have is a mini-state, a territory, a culture, and the desire to live together and to develop themselves. Under the pressure of public opinion, Quebec provincial governments have timidly endeavored, since 1960, to affirm the existence of the Quebec State and to control, as far as possible, those economic and political decisions which affect the life of their people. They have adopted measures to strengthen the role of the State in economic life. They soon realized, however, that the most important powers required by a modern industrial state were held by the national government of the other nine provinces, in all of which the English-speaking people were in the majority. Quebec public opinion showed a surprising degree of unanimity that favored more power for the Quebec State, and a significant part of the population now demanded full political powers. It is here that the Quebec question arises. We are no longer dealing with French Canada, with bilingualism and biculturalism, but with the powers of the State of Quebec and with the collective life of the people of Quebec. The issue is not merely that of nationalism, racism, or prejudice towards anyone; it is also a question of life or death for a nation of six million people. The fate of Canada's French-speaking people will be decided in Quebec itself. French Canada's culture is finished – in Newfoundland, in British Columbia, and even in Ottawa. A century of Confederation has proved that.

Trudeau's rise to power in Ottawa was the federalists' most spectacular reply to the separatists, but the central government had been actively working against separatism many years before the appearance of Trudeau. In July 1963, well aware of the seething discontent in Quebec, the Canadian government, in the best British tradition, appointed a Royal Commission "to enquire into and report on the present state of bilingualism and biculturalism in Canada and to recommend measures that would be taken to ensure the development of Confederation according to the principle of equality between the two founding nations, taking into account the contribution of other ethnic groups to the cultural enrichment of Canada, as well as measures to be taken to safeguard this contribution."

In 1965, in their first public document, the commissioners opined that "Canada, without being fully conscious of the fact, is passing through the greatest crisis in its history." Curiously enough, Quebec is no exception to the rule; as in every colonial situation, the dominant power is always behind the times, and unaware of how conscious its subjects are of the society that is made for them. For a century, French-speaking people have fought for an acceptance of bilingualism by the federal government. If Ottawa had been aware of this problem before, events might have taken a different course. The federal government was prepared to accept bilingualism only at a time when Quebecers, declaring themselves a majority in their own country, were taking on attitudes and political stances which went far beyond bilingualism. As in every other colony, it's a case of too little or too late. The problem that interests Quebecers at the moment is the question of monolingualism in Quebec; the bilingualism that Quebecers had frequently demanded for Canada as a whole no longer seems a worthwhile goal to many French-Canadians.

Let us recognize clearly, here in Quebec, that when the members of any group – nation or class – are subjugated to another group and see that they are considerably weaker than their masters, they ask only for equality. When the dominated group becomes more and more aware of its strength and the balance of power seems to shift in its favor, it demands all the power and all the culture for itself. This is plainly what is happening in Quebec today.

Almost everyone who lives here agrees that there are serious problems in Quebec, but there are many conflicting explanations for this state of affairs and many proposals to remedy it. The supporters of the status quo, i.e., the Canadian Confederation, say that Quebec has not quite caught up with the rest of Canada, that the problem of Quebec is a problem in regional economic disparity, more or less the normal situation in any federated system, as certain regions develop more rapidly than others. The remedy is equally simple: apply the appropriate economic policies to correct this state of affairs. Most federalists see Quebecers as the authors of their own misfortune: if instead of electing so many reactionary governments and investing so much energy in defense of their collective rights, each one of them had striven to succeed in his particular field, Quebecers would be in much better economic shape today. If instead of holding fast to outmoded practices and obsolete values they took an active part in the modern life of North America, they would not have to complain about being oppressed.

This view implies the thesis (openly stated, moreover) that Canada is one people, one nation, one State composed of several ethnic strains – the English- and French-speaking being the two principal ones – and that the government will take all necessary measures to ensure the continued existence of one nation. This is one of the chief replies made to the Quebec question.

The other reply – given by the great majority of Quebecers – is that a French-speaking nation exists in Quebec and that it has the right to a great measure of political autonomy; for many Quebecers, this nation has been dominated continually since 1760. Today, in spite of occasional fits of frustration and impatience, it has become aware of this state of domination and is struggling for political independence. This is the reply which explains why there should be a Quebec question.

PIERRE-E. LAPORTE

Language Planning and the Status of French in Quebec*

I. The Goals of Language Planning

1. Introduction

Prior to the early 1960s, state intervention in language problems in Quebec had been limited in scope and sporadic in occurrence. The responsibility for language problems of promotion and purification was left to various patriotic and religious organizations rather than with the State. State intervention proper coincides with what has become known as the Quiet Revolution and the politicization of language programs parallels that of many other spheres of social and economic activities.

Three major pieces of language legislation have seen the light of day since 1969; the number of public and private organizations concerning themselves with language planning has multiplied fivefold, in the past 15 years – as have their personnel and budget. The reasons behind this growth are, moreover, very similar to those which have given rise to the expansion of language planning elsewhere in the world where it has been studied: the rise of nationalism, which some have linked to the phenomenon of decolonization, and the defense of native tongues from the widespread domination of English.

The objective of this paper is the analysis of language planning in Quebec in relation to the status of French in Quebec society. In this essay, "language planning" refers to decision-making in the area of language problems – problems related either to the social position of language in society or to the internal structure of languages as such. Thus I recognize the distinction made by Kloss (Fishman, 1974) between status planning and corpus planning. I also believe it is useful to keep in mind the suggestion made by Das Gupta (Fishman, 1974) that language planning means decision-making in conformity with State policy. Although the State is not the only actor, it is nonetheless the central figure from whom the initiative tends to come in most cases of language planning. Finally, I intend to limit

---

* This paper is a revised version of "Language Planning In Quebec: An Evaluation," presented to the 76th Annual Meeting of the American Sociological Association, Toronto, 1981.

my remarks to "status planning"; the question of "corpus planning" (or issues of linguistic purity) would require an entirely different discussion which is beyond the scope of this essay.

2. The History of Language Planning

The Lavergne Law of 1910 was aimed at requiring public utility companies to place the French version alongside the English one in printed matter sent to their customers; previously the script appeared in English only. The Duplessis Law of 1937 granted priority to the French text in the interpretation of certain laws. It caused such an outcry among anglophones that it was rescinded a year after its passage (Bouthillier, 1978). Indeed, it was only with the creation of the Office of the French Language in 1961, that State intervention on matters of language began its fuller institutionalizaton. The initial mandate of the Office, however, was almost exclusively centered on corpus planning – namely, the issue of purification.

Preoccupations with questions of status, especially legal and economic, had yet to arise, but they were soon to appear when, in 1965, the Government tabled a white paper that proposed the first Quebec policy on language. In this white paper there emerged, for the first time, some of the key ideas which have inspired language planning to this day. The subsequent development, especially after 1970, proceeded at a rapid pace; after the Commission of Inquiry on the situation of French and Linguistic Rights tabled its report at the end of 1972, the sphere of State action in language matters greatly expanded: the Official Language Law in 1974, the White Paper on Language policy in 1977, and finally the Charter of the French Language that same year, were the major actions in that expansion. Thus, a veritable system of language planning has arisen in Quebec in 20-odd years, and especially within the last 10 years, a system in which the State plays a central but not exclusive role. The system has in fact a pluralistic character: it allows for intervention by private and semi-private organizations as well as by the State which continues to play a major role in the initiation and the monitoring of change.

3. Areas of Concern

The aims of language planning are comprehensive. They touch not only the legal status of French as Quebec's official language but all major domains of public life, including politics and governmental administration, the working world, the public media – advertising and labelling – and education. In all these domains, the goal is to make French a language of universal use consistent with the concept of Quebec as an "essentially francophone society" (Laurin, 1977). The Quebec language policy, then, is one of resolute "francization" with broad implications for the linguistic organization of institutional life, especially economic life, for the demography of languages and, more generally, the linguistic identity of Quebec in Canada and in North America.

(a) Demographic. In order to understand the reasons for the developments which have occurred during the past 20 years, one must be familiar with the language situation in Canada and in Quebec. The late '50s and early '60s were a time of fundamental change in Canadian linguistic demography. It is in fact during this period that the proportion of francophones among the Canadian population was to decrease for the first time since the mid-19th century. While the proportion of francophones in Canada had hovered around 30 percent since 1871, the date of the first Canadian census, it declined to 28 percent during the 1951-56 period, down to 25.9 percent in 1971 and to 25.6 percent in 1976 (Henripin, 1977). These changes, which have been recently described as "a rupture of the demographic equilibrium," are attributed to the drastic decline in francophone fertility since World War II. Added to this first major transformation of Canadian language demography was the observation of the rapid linguistic assimilation of French Canadians everywhere in Canada except for Quebec, the Acadian part of New Brunswick and the sections of Ontario adjacent to Quebec (Joy, 1972, Castonguay and Marion, 1974).

The impact of these changes on the collective consciousness of francophones cannot be neglected. Historically, their sense of strength as a national minority rested upon their hopes for a stable and even growing demographic position as a language group (Siegfried, 1907) and signs of decline of this demographic position were to exacerbate the francophone sense of vulnerability. Among francophone Quebecers this dynamic factor was certainly a crucial element in the movement which in the late '60s gave birth to state intervention on the status of the French language. Made more vulnerable than ever in Canada, French Quebecers opted for maximum linguistic protection in Quebec where they could expect to remain the majority. Language planning was the response to this felt need for protection.

(b) Social status and economic power. Other dynamic factors have to do with the Quebec language situation itself. This situation was characterized by the fact that English was the dominant language while French was spoken by the vast majority of the population. Ferguson has argued that language situations where dominance is not based on demographic supremacy tend to produce social tensions (Ferguson, 1971). This has certainly been the case in Quebec. The dominance of English in Quebec was partly demographic since its status as a majority language in Canada and North America gave to English locally, and to the local anglophone community, a weight and, psychologically, a sense of strength which they would not have had otherwise. But, much more important, given that Quebec is 80 percent French, is the economic basis of language dominance. It is simply a fact that for most of Quebec's history, and still today, English has been the language of the economically powerful. Alexis de Tocqueville was quick to perceive that reality when he wrote in 1831 that "the worst unhappiness for a people was to be conquered" (Bouthillier and Meynaud, 1972). Similar observations were made by E.C. Hughes in the '30s. In his minute description of labor conditions in Cantonville, Hughes showed that for all practical purposes the use of French as a language of administrative and technical communication in anglophone-controlled industrial firms stopped just below the foreman level (E.C. Hughes, 1943). The situation has certainly changed over the last 50 years or so but only in the sense that the domains and functions of English dominance have been reduced in span and strategic significance, not that they have disappeared altogether. The great centers of commercial, financial, industrial, and technological power in Quebec function in English even today (Sauve, 1977, Inagaki, 1980, Jannard, 1981). The concrete manifestations of English dominance are numerous, and I will limit myself only to those that have had a dynamic effect on the development of language planning activities over the last 15 years or so.

First, there are manifestations having to do with the status of English and French as languages of communication in the public domain: advertising, labelling of products, official names of corporations and, generally speaking, what in Quebec is known as "visage linguistique," linguistic ambiance. The dominance of English here has always been masked by the practice of institutional bilingualism which has contributed to raise the status of French over the years. However, Montreal has remained for many years a metropolis whose linguistic ambiance was heavily English and it is only recently that things have begun to change. An indication of the dominance of English as a public language, especially in Montreal, is the fact that it was only around 1978 that large Quebec-based commercial firms began to spend more on translations from French to English than from English to French in their commercial advertising (Taneau, 1980). One should add that complaints about the English ambiance of Montreal have been a constant feature of the Quebec language situation over many years. These complaints by numerous categories of "défenseurs de la langue" amply testify to, if not always the strength of English as a public language in Quebec, at least the dissatisfactions with the status of French. This was an important element of the movement leading to State intervention.

Second, *and much more important*, is the status of English and French in economic life. Here again, English clearly dominated, and we will look at a few indicators of the usage level and the social role of the two languages.

In Quebec's economic life, English tended to dominate both as a language of communication and of economic advancement.[1] This was notably so despite the fact that French was, for instance, widely used as a language of work. However, the economic activities that are most highly valued socially, tended to be conducted in English rather than French. Table 1 is an illustration of this phenomenon of language dominance. It shows that the use of English by francophones increases, the higher they are up the ladder in the working world. As for the use of French by anglo-

TABLE 1 *Language use at work by anglophones and francophones —*
Quebec, 1971

	Anglophones using French	Francophones using English
	%	%
Administrators	28	45
Office Staff	28	48
Salespeople	31	37
Workers in secondary industry	39	25
Workers in primary industry	31	5

Source: Laporte (1974, p. 12).
Note: We have used only the occupational categories that refer to the corporate world where
language groups are most likely to meet and the pressures for bilingualism likely to be felt.
(Further details concerning this research may be obtained by contacting the author.)

phones, the table shows it increases but in the opposite direction – the lower
they are in the job hierarchy, the more anglophones make use of French.
Thus the social structure of bilingualism in Quebec was a quite different
reality for anglophones and francophones. The social pressures for using
French as a language of communication at work are more strongly felt by
lower status anglophones, while the higher status francophones experienced
more strongly the pressure to work in English.

As mentioned earlier, the economic dominance of English in Quebec was
more than a matter of the social stratification of languages as a means of
communication. The social evaluation of languages as resources for
economic advancement was also involved. This, by the way, is to be
expected in a society where one language dominates another since, as
Bourdieu would put it, one kind of cultural capital – in this case particular
linguistic knowledge – will be of greater strategic value (Bourdieu, 1980). I
think that convincing proof of the superior position of English as a
language of economic advancement in Quebec in the early '70s is provided
by the answer of salaried professionals to this question: "In the business
where you work, is knowledge of English more essential for advancement
than knowledge of French?" Table 2 shows the results.

(c) Immigrant choice. Finally there is the status of English and French as
languages of adoption by non-English and non-French language groups. As
a language of adoption by these groups, English was much stronger than
French. This was so in Montreal where most of the English population is
located as well as outside Montreal where the linguistic environment is overwhelmingly French. Table 3 shows there were clearly great pressures to
choose English as a language of adoption on the part of the non-English
and non-French language groups.

Although English won out over French in 1971 as the language of adoption by Quebecers of other tongues, such was not always the case. There
was a time when the opposite was taking place, and it is only towards the
end of the 1951-61 period that the turnaround occurred. In 1931, 52 percent

TABLE 2 *The Social evaluation of English*

Type of work milieu	Percent seeing English as more essential than French
	%
Control of the business	
Quebec Francophone	13
Quebec Anglophone	46
Canadians	80
Americans	82
Where they do business	
Quebec	12
Canada	65
Canada/U.S.	68
International	59
Kind of business	
Government	22
Professional	30
Commercial	45
Industrial	71
Number of employees	
1-49	43
50-1449	46
1500 and over	60

Source: Laporte (1974, p. 58).

of Quebecers whose origin was other than British or French had adopted French as mother tongue: by 1961, their number had fallen to 29 percent (Charbonneau and Maheu, 1974). Two language minorities, the Italian and the Portuguese, had until about the end of the '50s a stronger tendency to adopt French than English. This tendency became less marked over the years until by 1971 the speakers of these two minor tongues adopted English as the language of everyday use almost as often as French. Thus, over a 25-year period, the adoption of French by these two communities had almost been supplanted by English (Kralt, 1976).

A corollary to this movement of anglicization of language minorities deserves mention. Added to the preference of parents for the use of English in everyday life, was the growing anglicization of minority language children through English schooling. By the early '70s, about one quarter of the student population of anglophone schools was made up of pupils whose mother tongue was other than English. These included a small percentage of francophone pupils and a much greater proportion of students from language minorities. For the year 1970-71, 8.3 percent of the student population of Montreal English schools was of French mother tongue while 22.5 percent was from various language minorities. In 1972-73, the percentages were respectively 8.7 percent and 23.4 percent. The comparison with French schools is revealing: in 1971-72, 1.9 percent of students in these

TABLE 3 *Adoption of English and French by speakers of other mother tongues, 1971*

| | Language of adoption | |
	English	French
	%*	%
Quebec as a whole	22.7	9.3
Montreal	23.1	8.2
Quebec excluding Montreal	19.2	17.8

Source: Kralt (1976, p. 37).
*Percentage distribution; each cell in the table is a fraction of 100%.

schools were English mother tongue and 0.9 percent came from language minorities. One year later, the percentages were 1.2 percent and 0.9 percent. This is a very convincing indicator of language dominance since the attraction of the English schools upon non-English mother tongue children was much greater than that of the French schools on non-French mother tongue children (Vanasse, 1981).

4. Objectives and Implementation

The language situation just described caused State intervention in Quebec. Language planning in Quebec can be seen as a response to dissatisfactions expressed with the language situation by the French. As noted, these dissatisfactions were many, as were their social consequences. First, there was a socioeconomic question. One can well imagine that a situation where the dominant language is not that of the majority poses a real problem of social equality: anglophones and francophones cannot have the same chances of social success in Quebec as long as English remains the main language of communication and the essential means of access even to lower and middle levels of the economic hierarchy. Many studies have revealed the economic inequalities between Quebec anglophones and francophones with like education and job experience. These inequalities were germane to the phenomenon of language domination and, indeed, were seen by the francophone majority as resulting from it. One of the objectives of linguistic planning in Quebec is the elimination of this inequality and its effects by making French the language generally used in economic life, especially within the large corporations where English dominates. The priority set by the State on the use of French in the workplace is undoubtedly aimed at the resolution of that social problem.

Second, it has been noted that it is numbers that determine the strength of French in Quebec. It is political strength, because in a democracy a community's size is related to its political influence, but also a sociolinguistic strength because the preservation of a language and its influence undoubtedly requires an adequate demographic base. The demographic base of French remains solid in Quebec, though we have seen it gradually eroding elsewhere in Canada. By the mid-'60s, the signs could be observed of the beginning of its slow decline in greater Montreal where the linguistic currents described above were strongest. So action was initiated. During the past 10 years that action has consisted above all of legislative interventions limiting access to English schools to anglophone children only.

Third, there is a sociolinguistic problem involved in making French a language of widespread use in every sphere of social activity in Quebec. There is, for example, the problem of giving a French look to Quebec's linguistic face: billboards, labelling, firm names, place names and other eye-catching elements which enable a community to clearly reflect its linguistic composition. There is also the problem of promulgating French administrative, scientific, and technical terms; the terminology in use has been and still is highly anglicized. Here we are touching on the great challenge to corpus planning. Quebec's interventions in this area are highly ambitious, both from the point of view of the goal of generalized French use and the means set out to accomplish it.

State intervention has been the main means of achieving the goals of language planning. The State first intervened in 1974 with Bill 22, then in 1977 with Bill 101 which changed the legal status of English and French. With Bill 101, The Charter of the French Language, French became *the* official language of Quebec. This was highly symbolic for it granted French a prestige it formerly did not have. And, as importantly, Quebec became committed to the promotion of the use of French in its day-to-day legal and administrative practices throughout society. The Charter intended to affect the status of English as a language in the Courts and Legislature; that is, French was to become the only language in these two domains. However, these dispositions of the Charter were declared unconstitutional by the Supreme Court of Canada in December 1979 and have not been enforced since. Consequently, both English and French remain as official languages in the Courts and Legislature of Quebec.

Having described the language situation and the broad goals of language planning in Quebec, I will now consider the impact of language planning on the areas of concern already identified – demographic patterns, social status and economic power, and immigrant adoption patterns. I will consider such indices of impact as mass perceptions and patterns of language use.

II. The Tentative Impact of Language Planning on the Status of French in Quebec

1. Introduction

What has been the impact of Quebec's policy of francization as it has been gradually adopted over the last 15 years? To what extent has the language situation developed in the direction of the broad goals set by the State?

These questions are difficult to answer for at least two reasons. First, there is the lack of data permitting a comparison over time of the language situation. However, some data exist which indicate that the situation has changed and these data will be examined with their limitations in mind. Second, there is the problem of "effect lag" which complicates all attempts at evaluating change. Experience shows that the effects of any institutional intervention are felt only after a certain lapse of time. In the case of language planning in Quebec, the lag is due in part to the fact that in spite of sustained efforts made over a 15-year period, the great interventionist push has really only come about in the last few years. Thus the principal language law which is the Charter of the French Language has only been implemented since 1977 and we must assume that its results will become more evident in the future.

2. Mass Perceptions

Indicators of change in the status of French are provided by mass perceptions of the language situation. A first set of indicators concerns the status of French as a public language; that is, a language used in commercial transactions with strangers, to obtain public services of all kinds, and printed on commercial posters and public signs generally. What is at stake here are linguistic opportunities, but not less relevant is what I have called "ambiance." The data seem to show that French is making gains in this area.

A survey conducted in 1979 of language use for commercial and public services shows that 71.2 percent of Quebecers perceived that French is more widely used than it was five years ago. The same survey reports on what are recognized to be opportunities to obtain services in one's own language in 1979 compared to 1971. The results are revealing: among francophones the percentage of respondents reporting that they experienced difficulties obtaining services in French went from 13 percent in 1971 to 8.8 percent in 1979. Among anglophones, however, the percentage was higher in 1979 than in 1971, that is 34 percent compared to 26.0 percent. This is perhaps as good an indicator as any that francization is gaining ground (Bouchard and Beauchamp – Achim, 1980, p. 79-80).

Conceivably even more convincing are the results of a survey conducted in 1980 among tourists in Quebec. First, 51.2 percent of respondents were of the opinion that commercial posters were now more frequently in French than they were the last time they came to Quebec. Second, among tourists who had visited Quebec in 1979, 40 percent reported a wider use of French while the percentages were 66 percent, 90 percent and 62 percent among tourists whose last visit dated three, four, or six and more years back. The case of Montreal seems to confirm this change in linguistic ambiance. When tourists were asked if, judging by the use of languages in commercial posters and public signs generally, Montreal looked more like a French than

TABLE 4 *Mass perceptions of change in the use of French by francophone and non-francophone Quebecers*

1. Would you say that the use of French, as a language of work, is more prevalent, less prevalent or equally prevalent today than it was two years ago?

	Francophones (453)	Non-francophones (108)
More prevalent	66 %	75 %
Less prevalent	2	2
Equally prevalent	30	22
Don't know	1	1

2. During the last two years, would you say that you used more French in your work?

	Francophones (287)	Non-francophones (69)
More French	34 %	33 %
Less French	3	4
As much	62	61
Don't know	1	1

Source: Centre de recherche sur l'opinion publique (CROP), 1980.

a bilingual or English city, 59.3 percent answered a French city, 39.0 percent a bilingual and 1.7 percent an English city (Bourgeois and Girard, 1981).

Other indicators concern mass perceptions about the changing status of French as a language of work. Breton and Grant (1981) have summarized the results of surveys conducted during the '70s saying that "a solid majority of francophones and anglophones perceive that French is making gains, whether as a language of employment, as a language of communication with the employers or as the administative and business language of firms." This observation is confirmed by recent surveys of mass perceptions and by studies of the changing roles of languages on the labor market.

A recent survey of a general sample of the Quebec population reports not only that people perceive that French is more used as a language of work today in Quebec than it was two years ago, but that they also say that they use it more in their own work. This is shown in Table 4 wherein a cross-section of work milieus is represented.

The same survey, however, warrants a note of caution. While mass perceptions indicate an improvement in the status of French as a *language of communication*, they do not seem to allow the same conclusion about its status as a *language of advancement*. This is at least what is suggested by mass perceptions concerning the role of English on the labor market. These perceptions indicate that "knowing English" has remained a strategic resource and, perhaps, that the role of French compared to English in this respect has not changed as significantly as might have been expected. Here one recalls that Breton and Grant (1980) have argued that change in the

TABLE 5 *Mass perceptions of the utility of knowing English to make a living and getting promoted by francophone and non-francophone Quebecers*

1. Compared to two years ago, would you say that knowing English is more useful, less useful or equally useful to making a living in Quebec?

	Francophones (453)	Non-francophones (108)
More useful	19 %	13 %
Less useful	18	39
Equally useful	60	48
Depends	2	—
Don't know	1	1

2. Compared to two years ago, would you say that it is more useful, less useful or equally useful to have a good knowledge of English to get a promotion at work?

	Francophones (453)	Non-francophones (108)
More useful	35 %	22 %
Less useful	16	37
Equally useful	46	38
Depends	3	2
Don't know	1	1

Source: CROP 1980.

status of French as a language of communication may be distinct from change in its status as a language of advancement. I think that Table 5 suggests that the two do not necessarily go together and that the gains in the social mobility function of French are perhaps not as significant – and certainly not as socially visible – as the gains in its function as a means of social communication.

3. Patterns of Representation and Language Use

One piece of evidence concerning the changing status of French as a language of work comes from a study of 10 large business firms where the representation of language groups at the managerial level, language knowledge, and language requirements had been measured first in 1964, and again in 1979. We thus have an extraordinary basis for comparison of language conditions studied at a 15-year interval. It should be noted that the use of French here is measured indirectly. The study's authors presumed that if the presence of francophones at the executive and managerial levels and the French language requirements at these levels had increased during the past 15 years, then the use of French throughout the business world would have increased in comparable proportions. This seems a valid and even ingenious assumption, considering the difficulty of directly measuring the use of language over a period of time. Thus we will keep in mind the in-

TABLE 6 *Change in the presence of francophones among managerial staff, 1964-1979*

| | Percentage | |
	1964	1979
	%	%
All corporations	50	63
Head offices	32	40
Local branches	69	75

Source: Société d'études en Changement Organisationnel (SECOR), 1980.

dictors that the study gives us on the change in the percentage of francophones and the language requirements at those levels; we will use those indicators to measure the advancement in the status of French use in business during the last 15 years.

The study first notes that the presence of francophones among supervisory staff in Quebec's large corporations has increased. This growth has been in the order of 1 percent per year over the past 15 years. The results appear in Table 6. Note that the changes undergone remain below the ideal of having francophones represented in the business hierarchy in proportion to their demographic presence in Quebec. It is nonetheless true that among managers of local branches, a 75 percent representation has already been achieved.

Table 7 deals with an important aspect of francophone presence in Quebec businesses of anglophone origin: francophones are better represented among lower-level management than among management as a whole, including higher-level executives. Moreover, it's on the lower level that progress is most rapid. Finally, need it be emphasized that in the head offices, where the strategic decisions are made, francophones remain all but invisible? In local branches the presence of francophones is really very high.

Table 8 brings closer the phenomenon of French use in large Quebec corporations. It deals with language requirements in the exercise of a function and with language competence. There are three facts to be noted. First, there is an obvious increase in the French language requirements for anglophones. Second, bilingualism is less often required of francophones at the local level in 1979 than it was in 1964, which allows us to suppose that one of the results of state intervention was the elimination of the bilingual requirement often artificially imposed on francophones by English-speaking employers. Third, knowledge of French among managerial anglophone personnel has increased between 1964 and 1979, which permits us to assume that many anglophone employees have become bilingual over the last 15 years. This is specially noteworthy in head offices where knowledge of French on the part of anglophones in 1964 was very low.

TABLE 7 *Francophone presence among managerial staff according to hier-archical level, 1964-1979*

	Percentage	
	1964	*1979*
	%	%
Head offices		
All executive and managerial staff	18	30
Lower-level management	22	45
Branch Offices		
All management staff	71	78
Lower-level management	73	84

Source: Société d'Études et de Changement Organisationnel (SECOR), 1980.

I must emphasize once again that the data just discussed do not bear directly on the use of French as such, but on corporate requirements and job performance. The results are consistent, however, with those of other studies concerning the same subject. There seems to be no question, for instance, that knowing French is becoming more and more a condition of employment for anglophones in a great many business firms operating in Quebec (Bourbonnais, 1979; Mc Kinnon and Miller, 1981; Vaillancourt and Daneau, 1980).

One last piece of evidence of the changing status of French at work concerns the language use pattern itself. In two labor market surveys, one in 1970 and the other in 1979, people were asked the percentage of time they use French at work. Table 9 reports the findings for several occupational categories. It shows that from 1973 to 1979, for both men and women of all occupational categories, the percentage of time at work when French is used has increased.

It appears that the status of French as a language of work has improved over the last decade. Not only is this systematically shown by mass perceptions but the change is equally indicated by data on corporate linguistic representation, corporate language practices, and the language use pattern.

4. Immigrant Adoption

The gains made by English as a language of adoption by immigrants coming to Quebec during the late '50s and early '60s was, as mentioned already, a dynamic factor in the emergence of State intervention of the language situation. It was anticipated at the time that such gains could result in a slow but steady erosion of the demographic dominance of the French language in Quebec, especially in the Montreal area where most non-francophone Quebecers were concentrated (Henripin and Charbonneau, 1971). Thus

TABLE 8 *Language requirements and knowledge, 1964-1979*

	Percentage	
	1964	*1979*
	%	%
Second language requirement		
Head offices		
Anglophones	10	39
Francophones	72	71
Local branches		
Anglophones	46	63
Francophones	91	23
Language Familiarity		
of French by anglophones		
Head offices	36	62
Local branches	73	92
of English by francophones		
Head offices	82	88
Local branches	91	53

Sources: Société d'Études et de Changement Organisationnel (SECOR), 1980.

there was the fear that francophones would lose control over the only territory where they were and could ever expect to be the majority.

The main issue here was the choice by an increasing number of immigrants (of non-French and non-English mother tongue) of English as the language of schooling for their children. This choice, which was seen as the source of anglicization of a growing sector of the Quebec population, became the target of language policies. Crucial aspects of state intervention on the language situation over the last 15 years, therefore, have been various attempts to limit access to English language instruction. The last such attempt is contained in the French Language Charter of 1977 which restricts English language instruction at the primary and secondary levels to many fewer categories of Quebecers than used to be the case.[2]

Studies of the evaluation of school attendance by language groups over the last 10 years or so tend to show that as a consequence of state intervention, French is making gains as a language of instruction. However, these gains still look small even if their cumulative effects could be substantial in the long run.

Most impressive perhaps is the growing number of non-francophone children attending francophone schools. At the nursery school level, the change has been rapid, moving from 17 percent of such children in French nurseries in 1977-78, to 30 percent a year later. The change is even more visible if only children of non-French and non-English mother tongues are taken into account. In 1971-72, 23.9 percent of these children were attend-

TABLE 9 *Percentage of time at work where French is used, 1970 and 1979 for five occupations*

	Managers	Teachers, Health workers	Office workers	Sales people	Production workers
	%	%	%	%	%
1970					
Men	63	75	70	72	83
Women	68	82	63	82	85
1979					
Men	75	89	81	83	90
Women	80	88	82	86	92

Source: Vaillancourt (1981, p. 16).

ing French nursery schools, while in 1978-79 the attendance was up at 57.9 percent. This is, it should be emphasized, change taking place among the youngest school children since for higher school levels, English instruction remains predominant for children whose mother tongue is neither English nor French: in 1978-79, 72.8 percent of these were in English school, a drop of 1.2 percent over the preceeding year.

Perhaps, it is worth mentioning that changes that can now be seen in the status of French as a language of instruction are not entirely the result of coercion. A convincing sign of this is the increase since 1977 of the number of children eligible for English school instruction who are attending francophone schools – from 3 690 in 1977 to 7 956 in 1979. This is probably as good an indicator as any that the status of French is changing in Quebec and that people are perceiving the benefits of adjusting to that change (St-Germain, 1980; Vanasse, 1981).

Conclusion

Our purpose was to analyse the emergence and the impact of language planning in Quebec over the last 15 years. We have shown that the status of French relative to that of English has improved: French is more extensively used in several domains of social life and its place in society has been strengthened. All the indicators – mass perceptions, use patterns, and measures of the advance of French as a language of adoption – support that generalization. However, it is much more difficult to evaluate the significance of the change: mass perceptions would seem to indicate that it has been substantial, while the evaluation of the use patterns seems to indicate that change has been slow even if self-sustained.

One finding that is troubling concerns the status of English as a language of economic advancement in Quebec: mass perceptions suggest not only that it has not changed but also that English has become an even more important language of advancement over the last few years. This finding is unexpected given the many recent studies which have shown that the socioeconomic status of francophones has improved over the last 10 years (Bernard, 1979; Boulet, 1981; Vaillancourt, 1979). Moreover these studies indicate that the share of managerial jobs held by francophones is increasing (Vaillancourt, 1981); one had expected that the salience of English as a language of advancement should have declined. However, mass perceptions suggest the opposite. Maybe this is another case of the well-known phenomenon of relative deprivation: as the socioeconomic status of francophones improves, social expectations rise, and what aspects of the dominance of English remain, become even more socially visible than before.

We have assumed throughout this paper that change in the status of French is the consequence of language planning. However, how do we know that this is so? In a logical sense, can we establish the linkage between the growth over the years of language planning activities and the improvement of the status of French?

Indeed, it could be argued that such linkage does not exist in a casual sense, and that the changing status of French is the product of much more basic social trends over a longer period than the one we have envisaged. Laponce has argued, for instance, that language groups have a natural tendency for concentration. In the case of Quebec, such concentration, which was supported by industrialization and urbanization, has created forceful social demands for the use of French in an increasing number of social domains with the resulting change in the status of French and francophones occurring quite independently of conscious interventions by the State (Laponce, 1980). Another argument simply could be that the changing status of French has resulted from the improved educational level of francophones over the last 20 years, and what is seen are the many adjustments to such changes, especially on the part of business firms. In this case, the supply of qualified francophones and the anticipatory adjustments of business firms would have been more important than language planning per se (Vaillancourt, 1981). One can mention, finally, the growing francophone market as a powerful source of social pressures for "francization."

A conclusion that a rise in the status of French is primarily the result of language planning obviously would be hard to support. However, here again, mass perceptions leave no doubt that some sort of relationship exists. When people are asked what accounts for the changing status of the French language, State intervention is spontaneously and systematically seen as an important factor. This is especially so for mass opinion surveys conducted since the last language legislation – the Charter of the French language – was adopted (Multi-Reso, 1978; CROP, 1979; CROP 1980).

Another aspect of the linkage between language planning and the changing language situation is the institutionalization of language planning itself.

As this approach to planned change becomes more and more important in terms of budgets and staff, and as language planning is "professionalized" in Quebec, it becomes more difficult to discard its influence (Breton and Grant, 1981). Finally, it would seem that successive language legislations, by increasing the cost of moving to Quebec on the part of non-francophones and the cost of remaining in Quebec for unilingual anglophones, have had an effect on the status of French especially as a language of communication. At best, however, these are rough ways of measuring the linkage which we have assumed exists between language planning and the changing status of French in Quebec. Until more research is done, our evaluation of the impact of language planning must remain as an approximation.

END NOTES

1. This useful analytical distinction was first made by Breton and Grant in their recent book on the language of work in Quebec (Breton and Grant, 1980). The distinction points to two functions of language in work organizations: as instruments for transmitting information, and as skills that one is expected to possess to be eligible for advancement and promotion in work organizations. Breton and Grant argue that the two functions need not be strongly correlated. For instance, French can become generalized as a language of communication while English remains essential as a language of advancement.

2. With few exceptions having to do with temporary resident status, the Charter of the French Language (Bill 101) grants access to schools where English is the language of instruction to the following categories of children:

   a) Children whose fathers or mothers have completed their primary school education in English in Quebec;

   b) Children whose fathers or mothers have had a primary school education in English outside of Quebec but who were residents of Quebec the day the law was passed;

   c) Children who are already in kindergarten and primary English schools in Quebec and their younger brothers and sisters.

   One must add, however, that college and university level access is not affected by the Charter.

SELECTED REFERENCES

Bouchard, Pierre, Sylvie Beauchamp-Achim, *Le français, langue des commerces et des services publics:* Dossier du Conseil de la langue française, Etudes et recherches, No. 5, Gouvernement du Québec, Editeur officiel du Québec, 1980.

Bourbonnais, Jean-Pierre, *L'Evolution de la demande de cadres bilingues dans l'entreprise privée anglophone, au Québec, de 1974 à 1978:* Gestion, Vol. 4, No. 1, février 1979, pp. 60-67.

Bourdieu, Pierre, *Les trois états du capital culturel,* Actes de la recherche en sciences sociales, Vol. 30, Juin 1979, Paris.

Bourgeois, Manon, Benoit Girard, *Réactions des touristes à la francisation de l'affichage et de la publicité commerciale au Québec,* STUDAX, Inc., Octobre 1980.

Bouthillier, Guy, *Aux origines de la planification linguistique québécoise,* Unpublished paper 1979.

Bouthillier, Guy et Jean Meynaud, *Le choc des langues au Québec 1760-1980,* Presses de l'Université du Québec, 1972.

Breton, Raymond and Gail Grant, *La langue de travail au Québec, Synthèse de la recherche sur la rencontre de deux langues:* Institut de recherches politiques, 1981.

Castonguay, Charles et Jacques Marion, *L'anglicisation du Canada,* Bulletin de l'Association des démographes du Québec – 3 (1): 19 à 40, 1974.

Charbonneau, Hubert et Robert Maheu, *Les aspects démographiques de la question linguistique,* Décembre 1973, Editeur officiel du Québec.

Centre de recherche sur l'opinion publique. Les bulletins Crop, novembre 1979 et 1980.

Ferguson, Charles A., "The Language Factor in National Development," in F.A. Rici, ed. *Study of the Role of Second Languages*, Center for Applied Linguistics, Washington, D.C., 1962, pp. 8-14.

Fishman, Joshua, A., *"Language Planning and Language Planning Research: The State of the Art." Advances in Language Planning,* ed. Joshua A. Fishman, Mouton, 1974, pp. 15-27.

Henripin, Jacques, "Quebec and the Demographic Dilemma of French Canadian Society," in J.R. Mallea Ed. *Quebec's Language Policies Background and Response*, Presses de l'Université Laval, Quebec, pp. 41-54.

Hughes, E.C., *French Canada in Transition*, Chicago: University of Chicago Press, 1939.

Inagaki, Morido, *La situation linguistique dans les CRDI au Québec*, Vol. 2, Simulex Inc., Montréal, Avril 1980.

Jannard, Maurice. *Les cadres supérieurs francophones: Très lente percée dans les grandes entreprises.* La Presse, Montréal, Samedi, 20 juin 1981.

Joy, Richard J., *Languages in conflict*, Toronto: McClelland and Stewart, 1972.

Kralt, John, "Profile Studies," *Languages in Canada* Vol. 5, Part 1, (Bulletin 5. 1-7) Ottawa: Statistics Canada, August, 1976.

Laponce, Jean, *"Le comportement spacial des groupes linguistiques: solutions personnelles et territoriales aux problèmes de minorités"* International Political Sciences Revue, Vol. 1, No. 3, 1980 pp. 478-495.

Laporte, Pierre-Etienne, *L'usage des langues dans la vie économique au Québec: Situation actuelle et possibilités de changement.* Synthèse 7, Commission d'enquête sur la situation de la langue française et sur les droits linguistiques au Québec. L'Editeur officiel du Québec, 1974.

Laurin, Camille, *La politique québécoise de la langue française*: Gouvernement du Québec, mars 1977.

McKinnon and Roger Miller, *Some Aspects of Recruitment Policies and Practices of French in Quebec* – SECOR Inc., June 1981.

Multi-Réso, Survey of Opinions on the French Language Charter, Office de la langue francaise, Gouvernement du Quebec, Montreal, 1978.

Sauvé, Maurice, *Les Canadiens français et la direction des entreprises au Québec*. Unpublished Paper. Mai 1976.

Sigfried, André, *The Race Question in Canada*, London, Eveleigh Nash, 1907.

Société D'études et de Changement Organisationnel (SECOR), *Le processus de francisation dans 10 grandes entreprises établies au Québec*, Montréal, 1980, Mimeograph.

Taneau, Vonick, *French is Money*, Opération Solidarité Économique, août 1980, p. 13-19.

Vaillancourt, François, *Les cadres québécois et la présence des francophones*: *L'évolution récente et la situation en 1971*, Montréal: SECOR Inc., 1979.

Vaillancourt, François, "*The Economies of Language Planning: An Application to the Case of Quebec (1960-1980)*," Paper read at the Sixth International Congress of Applied Linguistics, Lund, Sweden, July 1981.

Vaillancourt, François ct Alain Daneau, *L'évolution des exigences linguistiques pour les postes de cadres et d'ingénieurs au Québec – 1970 à 1979*. Cahier 8035, Département des sciences économiques, Université de Montréal, 1980.

ANN B. DENIS   University of Ottawa

Education and Ethnic Relations*

Introduction

Since the 1960's successive provincial governments in Quebec have attempted through legislation to alter the ethnic stratification of the province that placed the French in a subordinate economic position to the English. Schools and the work place have been major targets and consequently centers of ethnic conflict. Bills passed by both Liberal and Parti Quebecois governments during the 1970s showed that a French hegemony over the language of work and education had become a crucial strategy. In 1977, the Charter of the French Language, Bill 101, made French the only official language of Quebec. Only through such language policies, it was thought, could French Quebecers become "masters in their own house."

Since education falls under provincial jurisdiction, Quebec has been able to make significant strides with respect to institutionalising the French language as the language of instruction for almost everyone in the province. While opposition on the part of anglophones and other ethnic minorities greeted the government every step of the way, accommodation was being worked out and the fundamental right of Quebec to pass legislation affecting educational structures was not in question until the patriation of the Canadian Constitution in 1982. Since then the constitutionality of the Charter of the French Language, as it affects education, has been challenged in the courts, and is still (November 1982) under consideration.

With the ethnic conflict and accommodation in the past two decades in the areas of work and schooling as background, we can appreciate Quebec's refusal to join the other provinces in entrenching the official minority language rights of school children in the November 5, 1981 Constitutional accord. For Quebec, the adoption of the new minority language guarantee, if not a step backward, would mean that the province was no longer absolute in its power to determine the nature of its educational policies. Progress made in recent years would be subject to erosion.

In this paper it will be argued that the controversies swirling around education in Quebec can best be understood in the context of the broader societal changes that have occurred in ethnic relations in Quebec since the

---

* Written expressly for *Two Nations, Many Cultures: Ethnic Groups in Canada*, second edition. This article extends an analysis which was initially developed in "Nationalism and Multiculturalism in Quebec," *Canadian and International Education*, 6:1 (1977), pp. 1-13.

advent of the Quiet Revolution in the early 1960s. R.A. Schermerhorn's perspective[1] will serve as a framework for the analysis. I will first summarize Schermerhorn's theory of ethnic relations and then attempt to apply it to the empirical reality of education in Quebec.

The Schermerhorn Model

Schermerhorn's model of ethnic relations applies to societies in which there is a dominant ethnic group and one or more subordinate groups. The former is the "collectivity within a society which has preeminent authority both as guardians and sustainers of the controlling value system, and as prime allocators of rewards in the society . . . [When] . . . units or elements of society are brought into an active and coordinated compliance with the ongoing activities and objectives of its dominant group"[2], the society is characterised by integration; otherwise there is conflict. In explaining the conditions that encourage or prevent integration between ethnic groups in a society, Schermerhorn posits that three independent and three intervening or contextual variables should be considered.[3] The independent variables are: (1) the type of sequence of interaction between ethnic groups (migration, annexation, colonisation); (2) the degree of structural pluralism – that is, the degree of enclosure of subordinate group(s) from the society-wide network of institutions and associations; and (3) the power differential between groups, specifically the degree of control exercised by the dominant group over access to resources by the subordinate group. The two intervening variables which will be considered are: (1) whether the political or the economic institutions in the society are predominant; and (2) whether or not the dominant and subordinate groups agree on the collective goals for the latter. These goals can entail assimilation, with all adopting the dominant culture and participating in a single set of institutions, or pluralism, where distinctive cultures and/or parallel non-complementary sets of institutions coexist.

Without developing a series of closely interwoven general hypotheses, Schermerhorn endeavors to highlight the complex interrelations among these variables, interrelations which should be considered, he argues, in attempting to specify sets of relationships more systematically. He suggests, for example, that pluralism is a more likely form of ethnic relations when annexation or colonisation has occurred than when there has been voluntary immigration. In the former cases, minorities may, as charter members of the society, legitimate certain rights in terms of their historical residence in the region.[4] On the other hand, in voluntarily seeking admission to the host society, a subordinate group has no basis for legitimizing a greater degree of pluralism than the host society has agreed to accord to *any* newcomers. Thus one would predict assimilation would be a more likely result in the case of voluntary migrants than in the case of a charter group, and that where pluralism occurred as a long-term form of interaction, its legitimation would be wholly in terms of collective societal goals, whereas in the case of the charter groups, reference might also be made to historical rights.

Schermerhorn suggests that the greater the degree of enclosure of subordinate groups, the greater the likelihood that societal integration will be on a coercive rather than a consensual basis, unless there is little power differential between the groups.[5] He also argues that structural enclosure is more likely to be extensive in an agricultural than in an industrial economy, regardless of the level of cultural enclosure. Indicators of structural pluralism or enclosure include "endogamy, ecological concentration, institutional duplication, associational clustering, the rigidity and clarity of group definitions."[6]

Where there is small power differential between ethnic groups, Schermerhorn argues that there will be endemic, periodic conflict, regardless of the cultural congruency between the groups. The subordinate group shifts back and forth between an acknowledgement of the partial legitimacy of the dominant group's exercise of power and a total denial of its legitimacy, while the dominant group affirms its own legitimacy throughout. Where there is a large power differential (as in the case of voluntary migrants) and cultural congruity, Schermerhorn argues, one typically notes a shift from the dominant group fully acknowledging its own legitimacy with the subordinate group partially acknowledging this, to a situation where both perceive it as only partially legitimate.[7]

Finally, turning to the contextual variable of agreement about collective goals, Schermerhorn hypothesises that the more the dominant and subordinate groups agree on the collective goals for the subordinate group, the more integration will characterise the intergroup relations, and the less they agree, the more conflict will characterise the relations. The collective goals may be either assimiliation or autonomy and pluralism. In the case of disagreement, enforced assimilation or enforced segregation results.[8]

An ethnic group is a status group sharing a real or putative common ancestry and history, a cultural focus on one or more symbolic elements defined as the epitome of its peoplehood, and a feeling of consciousness of kind.[9] The crucial symbolic elements, though relatively stable, may change over time. In the case of the French in Quebec, such a change, reflected in changes in the "goals" for self and for other ethnic groups, resulted in changes in the educational and work structures, and in the degree of conflict between ethnic groups.

Identification of the dominant ethnic groups presents some problems in the case of Quebec. Schermerhorn argues that power is more salient than size for dominance. Within Quebec, those of French origin are dominant in the sphere of provincial power,[10] but not with regard to the economy, where those of British origin (both in Quebec and elsewhere in Canada) continue to be dominant,[11] together with the multinational corporations.[12] Some provincial legislation, including the nationalisation of the hydro-electric system, the groundwork for nationalisation of asbestos mining, and the specification of the language of work suggest that, although the political system is strongly influenced by the economic, the former is, in the last analysis, more powerful and is being used increasingly as a means of influencing the overall social structure, notably the economy. Consequently the French are treated here as the dominant group, although their dominance has not always been accepted as wholly legitimate by other ethnic groups in Quebec, who consider Canada as a whole, with its British economic and political dominance, as the salient unit of reference.

The relationship of the aboriginals to the French is one of colonisation, as is that of the French to the British in one sense (although one might also make a case for the latter as annexation of the North American territory of one coloniser by another). The other ethnic groups have arrived as voluntary migrants.

Social Structure and Ideology in Traditional Quebec and the Resulting Educational Structure

Three major periods are distinguished with regard to dominant definitions of nationalism[13]: traditional Quebec, the Quiet Revolution, and autonomy. The first extends into the 1950s, when about 14 percent of the population was of British origin and about 6 percent of non-charter origins. The ideal of the dominant French ethnic group was to maintain a Roman Catholic, French, agricultural society, that had minimal contact with the continently dominant, largely non-Catholic, English-speaking, more industrialised society. There was a high degree of enclosure of the subordinate group[14] from Quebec society-wide institutions and associations. Furthermore, the dominant group exercised relatively little control over access to scarce resources by subordinates. In general, the power differential between the two groups was small. Overall, however, the two ethnic groups agreed that the collective goals of the society should be pluralist and the economy was characterised by ethnic stratification as well as structural pluralism.[15]

In education this structural pluralism – analagous, parallel, non-complementary but distinguishable sets of institutions[16] – was particularly evident. Although there was nominally a coordinating council at the top of the educational structure, it did not meet between 1908 and 1960.[17]

The effective decision-making bodies were the Protestant and Catholic subcommittees, the latter with somewhat autonomous English and French branches. As a result, there were three parallel, distinguishable educational systems – Protestant, English Catholic, and French Catholic – with separate (Protestant and Catholic) tax bases, feeding into structurally distinguishable English and French university systems. The parallel educational structures permitted the English minority to provide itself with an education that facilitated participation in the non-manual sector of an industrial economy as well as interprovincial mobility, either during or after studies. No doubt in large part because of the socioeconomic composition of Protestant Quebecers, this group had a higher proportion of their young people in school than in any other province. The French Catholic system included a quality education for the elite and limited mass education. The latter was an outcome both of the nationalist ideology's emphasis on agricultural endeavor and, probably, the socioeconomic composition of the dominant group. Religious isolation was also reinforced, since easy movement from Quebec's French Catholic system was only possible to parochial educational systems in other provinces.

Changes of the Quiet Revolution

By the late 1940s changes were beginning to occur in the content of French Canadian nationalism, although these only became widespread during the Quiet Revolution that followed the death of Premier Maurice Duplessis in 1959. During the decade that this nationalism was important, there were crucial changes both in the overall educational structures and in the degree of ethnic autonomy in education.

In the ideology of this period the traditional isolationist, agrarian perspective based on the goal of cultural survival was rejected. Instead a partnership within Canada of the two "founding" (English and French) groups was advocated, and more equal division of control over resources in order that both might flourish within an industrial, secular society.[18] Thus in a rapidly industrialising Quebec there was an initiative on the part of the dominant group to lessen the degree of enclosure and to exert greater control over and to equalise the access to resources of all in the society. Although there continued to be plural structures, the division of resources among them was to be based on more universalistic criteria than in the past.

In education, for instance, the Royal Commission on Education (Parent Commission) was established in 1961. The resulting legislation, passed in 1964,[19] aimed at establishing a structure that would extend access to education, and equalise the costs for and choices in education regardless of one's ethnic or religious background, sex, socioeconomic background, or region of residence. It was opposed by both francophones and anglophones. The francophones, typically upholders of the traditional nationalism, were concerned that religious enclosure and autonomy in education were being threatened, while the anglophone opposition feared that the legislation would threaten their ability to maintain religious and fiscal autonomy to the detriment of their minority education.[20] Thus enclosure was perceived as a protection for traditional values and for minority privileges respectively.

By the late 1960s, the percentage of immigrants in Quebec had increased, so that about 2.5 percent of the population was of Italian origin and a further 7.5 percent of other non-charter group origins. On the whole, these groups were selecting English as their language of communication and attending Catholic schools. This resulted in increasing demands on the English Catholic school system, at a time when there were competing demands to improve the quality of French Catholic education. That the Catholic School Commission decided to restrict English facilities and expand French ones in a section of Montreal with a heavy concentration of Italians suggests that these new users of the English system – non-British immigrants – were defined by the dominant group as qualitatively different from (and inferior to) the British minority.

As a result of the ensuing crisis, in which the British supported the Italians against the French, Bill 63 was passed. It institutionalised the right of parents to choose English or French as the language of instruction for their children, a right that had not previously existed, since only minority religious rights in education had been dealt with in the B.N.A. Act. Thus, linguistic pluralism was institutionalised and with it, for immigrant groups, the choice of assimilation linguistically to either of the charter groups. Distribution of education resources (based on enrolment) was determined by the choices of *individuals* (the parents) rather than those of the dominant group acting as a collectivity. French had precedence to the extent that the default choice (where no choice had been formally stated) was for French. The English perceived this as an erosion of their traditional rights, since it had not been necessary previously to state one's choice independently of the action of enrolling one's child. Had Bill 62 also been passed, there would have been more basis for this perception. Bill 62 proposed a reorganisation of the Montreal school boards which, by eliminating the enclosure of religious and linguistic groups, would have severely restricting the ability of the English to influence decisions in education. Although the Liberal government introduced it at the same time as Bill 63, they withdrew it in the ensuing controversy, and never reintroduced it. In the opinion of French critics, this was a drastic error in legislative strategy, since, by itself, Bill 63 meant that the will of the politically subordinate (i.e. the ethnically heterogeneous non-French) group had prevailed to a considerable extent. The French opposition to Bill 63 demonstrated its awareness of this, focussing as it did on the legitimation of English as a language of instruction and on the according to it of a formal legitimacy it had never previously enjoyed.

Autonomy . . . or separation

By the late 1960s a new ideology of nationalism, stressing the autonomy of a linguistic group (the French) within the territory of Quebec, became widespread. Drastic reductions in the French Quebec birthrate during the Quiet Revolution, coupled with expansion of the non-charter group immigrant population resulted in concern that the numerical (and hence political) predominance of the French and use of the French language within Quebec was being threatened.[21] Whereas elsewhere in Canada immigrants in fact had little choice in their language of work and the language of education of their children, in Quebec the choice between English and French existed, and, for education, had even been institutionalised in Bill 63. Since most immigrants selected English,[22] the francophone population was not enjoying the same expansion through incorporation of immigrants and their children as the anglophone population did. In order to counter these trends, the separate-but-equal ideology was replaced by one based on language as the salient criterion for ethnic identity with a culturally and economically autonomous territorial unit, Quebec. There are separatist (full political independence) and federalist (greater political and fiscal autonomy within Confederation) versions of this ideology, but general agreement exists on the preponderance of political over economic and other structures, and on the necessity of institutionalising the promotion of the French language.

Bill 23, passed in 1974 by the Liberal government, was a federalist attempt to legitimize (and impose) a new set of norms minimizing the amount of enclosure permitted in the economy for all non-francophones and in education for those who were not aboriginals or members of the (linguistically defined) English charter group. The French language was accorded precedence in public spheres, such as work, and also became the language of instruction for all except aboriginals of northern Quebec and anglophones. Those with mother tongues other than English who wished to attend English school had to pass an English language test. Provision of instruction in English was permissive, not obligatory for the school boards, and all in English schools also had to master French adequately. The Bill aroused opposition from both francophones who thought it was too permissive and from ethnic minorities who rejected the legimacy of the dominant group's action, arguing that since Quebec was part of Canada, all its residents had a right to education in English, one of the country's official languages.

Considered analytically, this Bill resulted in a number of changes in ethnic relations within Quebec. The dominant group began restricting structural pluralism and exerting much greater control over access to resources by subordinate groups. For the first time it differentiated among them. Continued linguistic rights in education for the English and aboriginals seemed to derive from their charter group status and, in the case of the English, probably from their economic power as well. At the same time legislating French as the language of work was a policy aimed at reversing the power differential between the French and the British in the economic sphere, and increasing it, so it approached that between the French and non-charter immigrant groups. The collective goal for the minorities became a large measure of assimilation. In the face of minority opposition, this goal could best be characterized as forced assimilation, a situation tending towards conflict in Schermerhorn's view. Part of the minority groups' opposition stemmed from their contention that Canada, with its two official languages, was the relevant territorial unit. The Bilingualism and Biculturalism Commission's[24] rejection of territoriality as the sole basis for linguistic rights made the Quebec language legislation seem all the more illegitimate. Differentiation between English-speaking and other groups was also rejected on the basis that it implied unequal choice of resources. It also, of course, threatened to divide the subordinate group.

The Parti Québécois, elected to power in 1976, did not feel that Bill 22 was proving an effective vehicle for change.[25] The French language charter, Bill 101, was consequently passed the following year. Through its various provisions Bill 101 has reinforced and sharpened the changes already begun under Bill 22 regarding the significance of language, Quebec as a territorial unit, economic autonomy, *cultural* pluralism being the only legitimate form of pluralism and increasing power differentials between dominants and subordinates. For education this has been accomplished by redefining in a more restrictive manner the population eligible for instruction in English. This has been done in such a way that the English language and British origin populations have been subdivided. Now at least one parent must have attended English language primary school in Quebec, an easier criterion to apply than the language tests were, and one which clearly emphasizes entrenched rights *within Quebec* as the basis for the exception. Since the Quebec-educated English population is an aging one, one can anticipate reductions in the number of children eligible for English schools. Children of those who are temporarily in Quebec may attend English school for up to two years, an indication of the continued economic power of English language capital in Quebec. The right to English education could be extended to those coming from provinces which accord a reciprocal right to French education to former Quebecers, but so far no such agreements have been made. These new regulations eliminate the possibility of francophones opting for school in English.

In addition to differentiating within the subordinate group of "non-French" in terms of their access to English language education, various other measures indicate a change in both ideology and practice: now the assimilation of non-francophones into the dominant group is actively encouraged, in contrast with the encouraging (in the traditional period) or permitting (during the Quiet Revolution) of structural pluralism. Thus immigrants and their adaptation have become a subject of academic analysis[26] and policy concern.[27] Cultural pluralism (to enrich Quebec society) is officially encouraged,[28] and a ministry concerned with cultural minorities has been established.

There have been interesting contrasts in the minority responses to the bill. Both Protestant and English Catholic school boards initially enrolled "illegal" students, who were now ineligible for instruction in English. Not only did the government refuse to give per capita grants for these students, it also stated that they would not be able to get certification of their studies. At the same time other provisions of Bill 101 specified more stringently the implementation of French as the language of work. For anyone planning to work in Quebec over the long term, it is clear that being able to work in French is now an economic necessity, as it is an economic necessity to be able to work in English in most other parts of Canada. The erstwhile economically dominant English group, after vociferous protests and the "rebellion" of enrolling students illegally, has within its Protestant sector greatly expanded the French language program offered, a recognition of the inevitability, if not the legitimacy, of the dominant group's policy. Thus they can tap the clientele that must be taught in French, and at the same time ensure that other anglophones who intend to remain in Quebec can have good quality French and English instruction. Their graduates may have a linguistic advantage in the job market in which case the insistence on French usage by non-francophones may serve to reduce the power differential again between the dominant and at least some of the subordinate ethnic communities in Quebec. The English Catholic schools seem to have adapted in this way to a lesser extent, perhaps because language is the crucial ethnic boundary in their case, as against the English Protestants, where it is combined with religion. Also a larger proportion of their clientele is already studying in a second language in which they want to become sufficiently competent to be geographically mobile within Canada.

Comparatively, one could argue that there has been a certain symmetry between the status quo elsewhere in Canada and the direction of change in Quebec. The eventual linguistic assimilation of non-charter groups to the dominant charter group of the region has been an overall goal. Where instruction of (and occasionally in) non-charter group languages has been tolerated, this has been either as a means of facilitating integration into the dominant school system of those of other mother tongues,[29] as an optional subject, or, very recently, as one language in optional bilingual programs. Effectively, in no other province have as extensive educational possibilities been available in the minority official language as in Quebec. This remains the case even since Bills 22 and 101, although the latter's long-term consequences may alter this, as may the guarantees of education in either official language (where numbers warrant) in the patriated Canadian Constitution. At the same time there is a significant difference in the status of majority language between Quebec and the rest of Canada. Both the Royal Commission on Bilingualism and Biculturalism[30] and the Gendron Commission[31] have highlighted the extent to which within Quebec francophones, but not anglophones, have been obliged to work in their second language. In fact, prior to Bills 22 and 101 neither inside nor outside Quebec have there been great economic incentives to the learning of French, with the bilingualism program of the federal civil service representing a minor exception,[32] as may the guarantees of education in either official language in the patriated

Canadian Constitution. If autonomy for the French as a linguistic group within an industrialized society is to be realized, measures to increase the value of French as the language of communication are probably necessary. Given the high degree of interdependence which characterizes industrialized societies, decreases in the degree of structural pluralism are no doubt inevitable. Equally, though, this reduced enclosure represents a change in the collective aims for the minority ethnic groups, a change which restricts their choices and generally increases the power differential between them and the dominant group.

We can also see during this last period changes in the perceived legitimacy of the dominant group's goals for the minorities regarding educational policy, changes which generally support Schermerhorn's hypotheses. When the power differential was small, the dominant groups voiced no doubts about the legitimacy of its policy. The subordinate groups, acting as a single entity, shifted (as control over them increased) from defining the policies as partially legitimate (even if unpopular) to illegitimate (to be challenged in the courts and to be disobeyed). As the power differential has increased with the overall application of Bill 101, both groups, particularly the subordinate, seem to be treating the policies as partially legitimate. Greater acceptance of Quebec territorial boundaries as salient, reduction or elimination of programs for "illegal" students, and establishment of French Protestant schools are examples of the subordinate group's increasing acceptance of the partial legitimacy of the dominant group's policies, while the establishment of the ministry for cultural communities and of non-charter language studies in schools[33] could indicate the same for the dominant group.

Two factors may, however, produce a resurgence of opposition and of claims that the dominant group's policies are illegitimate. The first is the institutionalisation of minority education rights in the Charter of Rights of the Canadian Constitution, which became law in 1982. Henceforth, where numbers warrant, any Canadian citizen who has received primary school instruction in Canada in the minority language of his or her current province or residence may have his or her children educated in that language. Similarly, if any children in the family have been educated in the minority language, all brothers and sisters have the right to be educated in that language. There is an interesting similarity between this law and Bill 101, in that both make parental education in the minority official language a basis for claiming the right of having children educated in that language. The Constitution is more restrictive than Bill 101 in that the right applies to Canadian citizens only, but more open in that the geographical unit of reference is Canada (not Quebec), and, in addition to parental primary education, parental secondary schooling, siblings' schooling, or (except in Quebec) parental mother tongue give the right to minority language education. The provisions in Quebec's Bill 101 restricting access to education in

English have been appealed on the basis of the Charter of Rights. The court's ruling in favor of wider access to education in English has been appealed by the Quebec government, which also denied the affected children access to minority schools until a final ruling has been handed down. In the meantime school boards will not receive their per capita grant for any such children. The Quebec government's actions on this matter have been strongly denounced as illegitimate by the English minority.

The second factor which is eliciting opposition from a wide cross section of Quebecers is the Quebec government's white paper on education, issued in June 1982.[34] It proposes a restructuring of schools and school boards aimed at increasing the autonomy of individual schools and creating non-confessional school boards unifying both official linguistic groups. The latter idea has been proposed sporadically since the Parent Report and to date had been effectively opposed. The current White Paper proposes that schools be governed by school councils, including representatives of parents, staff, the community and, in secondary schools, students.

Each School Council would decide how to offer its services, necessarily in conformity with Ministry of Education guidelines and, ideally, at the same time, reflecting the needs and preoccupations of its community base. School boards, which would deal with staff employment, would include representatives of the schools within their jurisdiction and of the affected municipal councils. In conformity with Bill 101, a number of English schools would be established, and in conformity with the B.N.A. Act, there would be Protestant and Catholic School Boards in Montreal and Quebec, and the possibility of "dissident" (i.e. minority religious) boards elsewhere. However Minister Laurin explicitly hopes that, with greater school autonomy, the religious groups will agree to common (non-confessional) school boards, combined with the possibility of appropriate religious instruction in all schools. The White Paper is currently under discussion. Not surprisingly there is some opposition from religious and minority language groups because of the reduced enclosure such reform would entail. There is also a more widespread opposition based on fears that the proposed structures would unduly increase central Ministry of Education control over all schools. Should this legislation be passed, minority residential concentration would seem indicated as the most effective way of ensuring that the "cultural democracy" of the schools represent minority as well as majority interests. Even so, minority autonomy could be reduced, without impinging on the minority rights which are assured by law.

Either of these factors could produce a resurgence of ethnic conflict in educational matters.

END NOTES

1. R.A. Schermerhorn, *Comparative Ethnic Relations* (New York: Random House, 1970).
2. *Ibid.*, pp. 12-13; p. 66.
3. *Ibid.*, pp. 14-16.
4. *Ibid.*, p. 157.
5. *Ibid.*, pp. 125-7.
6. P. van den Berghe, *South Africa, A Study in Conflict* (Middletown, Conn.: Wesleyan University Press, 1965), pp. 78-9.
7. Schermerhorn, *Comparative Ethnic Relations*, pp. 72-6.
8. *Ibid.*, pp. 77-85.
9. *Ibid.*, p. 12.
10. D. Juteau Lee, *The Impact of Modernisation and Environmental Impingements upon Nationalism and Separatism: The Quebec Case* (Toronto: unpublished Ph.D. dissertation, University of Toronto, Department of Sociology, 1974).
11. J. Porter, *The Vertical Mosaic* (Toronto: University of Toronto Press, 1965).
12. W. Clement, *The Canadian Corporate Elite* (Toronto: McClelland and Stewart, 1975). Niosi discusses the advent of a francophone bourgeoisie in Quebec. J. Niosi, "La nouvelle bourgeoisie canadienne-française," *Les Cahiers du Socialisme*, 1 (1978) pp. 5-50. Although important in some sectors of the economy, this bourgeoisie is not predominant according to K. McRoberts and D. Posgate, *Quebec: Social Change and Political Crisis.* rev. ed. (Toronto: Mc-Clelland and Stewart, 1980).
13. Lee, *The Impact of Modernisation and Environmental Impingements upon Nationalism and Separatism*, M. Rioux, *La Question du Québec* (Paris: Editions Seghers, 1969, and McRoberts & Posgate, *Quebec*.
14. which, from the dominant group's perspective, was generally socially undifferentiated into its ethnic components.
15. Porter, *Vertical Mosaic*.
16. P. Van den Berghe, *Race and Racism* (New York: John Wiley, 1967).
17. Royal Commission of Inquiry of Education in the Province of Quebec (Parent Commission), *Report* (Quebec: Editeur Officiel, 1963).
18. H. Guindon, "Social Unrest, Social Class and Québec's Bureaucratic Revolution," *Queen's Quarterly*, LXXI (1964) pp. 150-62.
19. Bill 60, originally introduced in 1963, elicited extreme opposition. It was reintroduced in amended form in 1964 and passed.
20. L. Dion, *Le Bill 60 et le Public* (Montréal: l'Institut Canadien d'Education des Adultes, 1966), Les Cahiers de l'I.C.E.A. No. 1.
21. J. Henripin, *Immigration and Language Imbalance*, Canadian Immigration and Population Study (Ottawa: Manpower and Immigration, 1974), R. Maheu, *Les Francophones au Canada, 1941-1991* (Montréal: Parti Pris, 1970).
22. P. Bernard, A. Demers, D. Grenier, J. Renaud, *L'évolution de la situation socioéconomique des francophones et des non-francophones au Québec, 1971-1979.* (Québec: Gouv. du Québec, Office de la langue française, 1979), R. Didier, *Le Processus des choix linguistiques des immigrants au Québec.* Etude E6. (Québec: Editeur Officiel, 1973).
23. McRoberts & Posgate, *Québec*, L. Delorme, *Bill 22: Le Waterloo du Bou Bou* (Laval: Editions du Duvernay, 1974).

24. Royal Commission on Bilingualism and Biculturalism, *Report* (Ottawa; Queen's Printer, 1967-70).
25. McRoberts & Posgate, *Québec*, D. Clift and S. Arnopoulos, *Le Fait anglais au Québec* (Montréal: Libre Expression, 1979), C. Laurin, "Le sort des minorités dans un Québec indépendant", in D. Juteau Lee, ed, *Emerging Ethnic Boundaries* (Ottawa: University of Ottawa Press, 1979), pp. 175-84.
26. Association Canadienne des Sociologues et Anthropologues de Langue Française, *La Transformation du Pouvoir au Québec* (Montréal: Editions coopératives Albert Saint-Martin, 1980.)
27. For example, establishment of special language classes for non-French speaking students, as well as language and general orientation programs for adults.
28. Laurin, "Le sort des minorités." *Ibid.*
29. A Wolfgang, ed., *Education of Immigrant Children* (Toronto: O.I.S.E., 1975).
30. Royal Commission on Bilingualism and Biculturalism, *Report*, volume 3, (Ottawa: Queen's Printer, 1969).
31. Commission d'enquête sur la situation de la langue française et sur les droits linguistiques au Québec (Commission Gendron), *Rapport*, Livre 1. (Québec: Editeur officiel, 1972).
32. P. Lamy, "The Management of Ethnic Diversity: Canada's Multiculturalism Within a Bilingual Framework" (Ottawa: University of Ottawa, 1976), mimeo.
33. Clift & Arnopoulos, *Le fait anglais*, McRoberts & Posgate, *Québec*.
34. Ministry of Education, *The Québec School: A Responsible Force in the Community* (Québec, 1982).

Ethnic Minorities in Quebec

EFIE GAVAKI' Concordia University

Urban Villagers: The Greek Community in Montreal*

I. Introduction

The purpose of this paper is to provide a brief description and analysis of the institutional development of the Greek community in Montreal.[2] It will seek out the sociohistorical factors and processes that have made this ethnic community not only "institutionally complete," but also an important sociological entity within the Quebec and Canadian societies. The data has been secured from available records and interviews with leaders and members of the Greek community in Montreal during 1980 and 1981 (Appendix A).

In the now classic article on interpersonal relations of immigrants, Breton (1964) looked at the ethnic communities' institutions and their functions with respect to the personal and cultural integration of immigrants within their communities. "Institutional completeness would be at its extreme whenever the ethnic community could perform all the services required by its members (p. 194)." The concept of institutional completeness includes such organizations as religious, educational, political, recreational, national, professional, welfare and mutual aid societies, mass media, and financial institutions. Such organizations help integrate the individuals into their ethnic communities and mediate between the individuals and the larger society.

The Greek ethnic group in Montreal today is an "institutionally complete" group, although one may debate on its institutional effectiveness and maturity. It has more than 60 organizations with a variety of support mechanisms, all claiming to serve the social, cultural, religious, educational, economic and linguistic needs of the members of the ethnic group. In

---

* This article is a revised version of a paper, "Urban Villagers: Institutional Development and Ethnic Identity among Greeks in Montreal," presented to the Annual Conference of the Canadian Sociology and Anthropology Association, Halifax, N.S., May-June, 1981.

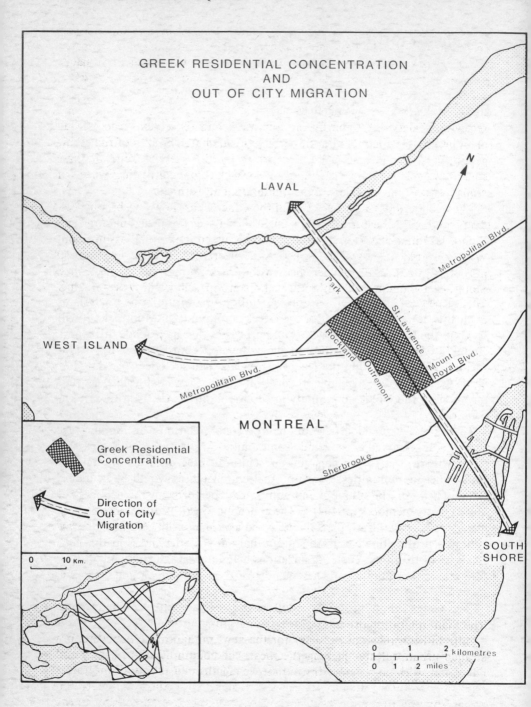

GREEK RESIDENTIAL CONCENTRATION
AND
OUT OF CITY MIGRATION

LAVAL

WEST ISLAND

MONTREAL

SOUTH
SHORE

Metropolitan Blvd.

Park

St. Lawrence

Rockland

Outremont

Mount
Royal Blvd.

Metropolitain Blvd.

Sherbrooke

Greek Residential
Concentration

Direction of
Out of City
Migration

0   10 Km.

0   1   2 kilometres
0   1   2 miles

addition, some of them serve as entry points for formal and informal interaction with the Quebec and Canadian societies. Currently, this organizational process is at a dynamic, developmental stage as it struggles to mature in terms of functions and, particularly, in terms of effectiveness. Many factors have contributed to this development. Some have been generated: a) by the uniqueness of the sociocultural environment and structure of the receiving society; b) some by the migration and settlement process; and c) others by the social, cultural, and historical characteristics of the ethnic group. It is the interaction and interplay of the factors from all these sources together that may explain the existence, degree, and effectiveness of ethnic institutions, in the process of immigrant adjustment.

We will attempt to discuss some of these factors as they have become evident from our research of Greek institutional development in Montreal. Figure 1 summarizes those factors to be discussed making no assumption, of course, that they exhaust the list. And, whereas the Greeks in Montreal may share some similar experiences with Greek immigrants in the United States, and Canada, and with other ethnic groups, they still have a distinct institutional development (as with the church) that makes them unique not only in North America, but in the entire recent history of Greek immigrant community development. On the other hand, Montreal itself may share similar sociocultural elements with North American cities; still, it stands unique in its dominant cultural structures and ethnic relations ideologies.

II. Socio-Historical Background

1. Immigration

Greek immigration to Canada began late in the 19th century as an offshoot of the larger migration to the United States. By 1895, a small number of Greeks had settled in Montreal. Between 1895 and 1900 that number rose to 300. By 1906 it is reported that there were 1 000 Greeks in Montreal whereas Toronto numbered around 200 (Nagata, 1970: 48). The newly-arrived immigrants were primarily coming from Laconia, Arcadia, and Macedonia, the mainland regions of Greece that even today provide Canada with the bulk of Greek immigrants. They could be found working in factories, the fur trade, small stores, small businesses, restaurants, and as taxi drivers. The chain migration process was then soon to start.

Life in Montreal was not easy for the new immigrants. They were in a strange urban culture, lacking the means of communication, skills, and education, with no religious institutions to perform basic rites of marriage, baptism, and burial. In addition, they were faced with a hostile climate and social isolation that made both social and psychological adjustment to the new land extremely painful. It was basically for the fulfillment of those

FIGURE 1 *Preliminary list of factors contributing to Greek ethnic institutional development in Montreal*

A. Factors generated by the receiving society
  1. Sociocultural dominance and power struggle of charter groups
  2. Ethnic relations ideologies of charter groups
  3. Existence of other distinct ethnic groups
  4. Prejudice and discrimination
  5. Federal-Provincial governments
  6. Language legislation
  7. Others

B. Factors generated by the migration and settlement process
  1. Size
  2. Residential concentration
  3. Recency of immigration — old immigrants vs. new immigrants
  4. Immigrant characteristics
  5. Others

C. Factors generated by the Greek ethnic group
  1. *Uniting factors*
     a. Hellenism
     b. Language
     c. Religion
     d. Family and social interaction needs
     e. Church
     f. Traditions of Greeks in Diaspora (examples of)
     g. Greek issues
     h. Others
  2. *Dividing factors*
     a. The "Greek personality"
     b. Regionalism
     c. Greek politics, Federal-Provincial politics
     d. Church
     e. Power struggle-special interests
     f. Others

Note: Factors are assumed distinct for presentation purposes only.

needs that the first informal efforts at organization were made early in the 1900s. Petritis (1972:10) reports that the first informal associations formed were *Patris* (Fatherland), *Anagenisis* (Resurrection), and *Panhellinios Enosis* (Panhellenic Union). Membership was open to all Greeks with the primary objectives of providing cultural, social, and economic support. These associations, however, were short-lived.

After the devastation of Greece by World War II and the Civil War (1950), large waves of immigrants arrived. The Greek immigrants, although mainly rural in origin, tended to settle in urban areas, with Montreal and Toronto receiving the bulk of them. Table 1 shows the distribution of Greek

TABLE 1 *Immigrants to Canada, Ontario and Quebec and having Greece as the country of last permanent residence, 1971-1979*

		Ontario		Quebec	
Year	Canada	Number	Per Cent of total	Number	Per Cent of total
	#	#	%	#	%
1971	4 769	2 565	54	1 685	35
1972	6 297	2 494	40	516	8
1974	5 632	2 984	53	—	—
1975	4 062	2 312	57	1 142	28
1976	2 487	1 350	54	846	34
1977	1 960	1 016	52	559	29
1978	1 474	768	52	435	30
1979	1 247	606	49	407	33

Source: Statistics Canada, *Immigration 1963-1979*.

immigration in Ontario and Quebec since 1971.

In 1976, Statistics Canada reported that of the 91 530 Greeks in Canada (counted by mother tongue), 90 440 (or 98.8 percent) lived in urban areas. Of the 34 655 residing in Quebec, 98.2 percent lived in Montreal. Today, estimates of the number of Greeks in Montreal vary from 60 000 to 80 000.

2. Socioeconomic Characteristics

The most recent data on socioeconomic variables are provided by the 1971 Census. Tables 2, 3, and 4 present a comparative picture of education, income, and occupation among Greeks in Quebec, Ontario, and Canada.

It is recognized that such data may not accurately represent the relative distribution of the Greeks on the social ladder today. Many factors may have contributed to some changes in the ethnic group during the 1970s. For example, immigrants arriving during the 1970s were slightly different from those of the previous years. They were the ones who had worked in the industrial cities of Europe during the late '60s and early '70s. They had acquired some skills, and organizational abilities, and had been exposed to urban living. In addition, since 1976, Greek immigration has been significantly reduced, (see Table 1), with an 1980 estimate of approximately 500 Greeks arriving in Canada. Furthermore, the 1976 elections in Quebec and the language policy of the Parti Québécois may have precipitated some internal movement of mobile Greeks from Montreal to Toronto. What is evident, however, from Greek statistics, is that return migration to Greece from overseas (which includes Canada) is on the rise. In 1975, 2 719 Greeks returned from overseas and that number increased to 3 425 in 1976 and is still rising.

Finally, in the 10 years since 1971, a socioeconomic growth has occurred that may have slightly changed the picture of the group. However, it is believed that any changes in the 1970s will reflect quantitative rather than significant qualitative differences in the ethnic group.

The overall picture of Greeks living in Montreal is that of urban villagers,[3] with no or few skills, low education and income, struggling for both physical and cultural survival.

Of the 26 955 Greeks in Montreal of 15 years and over, 43 percent of the males and 58 percent of the females had only elementary education or no schooling at all; 45 percent of the males and 36 percent of the females had completed high school; and only 4 percent of the males and 1 percent of the females had university degrees. Compared to other ethnic groups in Montreal, according to Table 2, Greeks have the third lowest educational level after the Portuguese and the Italians, whereas Japanese have the highest followed by the Blacks, Dutch, and Jews.

Of the 19 700 Greeks in the 1971 labor force only 4 percent hold professional and business occupations in Montreal. These are usually fluent in two or all three languages (Greek, French, English) and occupy middle positions in both Greek and Canadian institutions. A number of Greeks are small business owners, mainly restaurants, groceries, and small corner stores, the latter two serving mostly Greek clientele and located in areas densely populated by Greeks. However, the majority, approximately 60 percent, work as factory workers, restaurant help, hospital service personnel, cleaners, and janitors. Compared to other ethnic groups in Montreal, we can see from Table 3, Greeks, along with the Portuguese and Italians occupy the lower levels of the occupations ladder, while the Jews, Dutch, and British concentrate at the higher levels. Unemployment runs high with estimates ranging from 20 percent to 30 percent of the labor force.

In Montreal in 1971, 20 005 Greeks, 15 years and over, were earning some income. Of those, 71 percent were reporting earnings of less than $10 000 whereas only 2 percent reported earnings of $15 000 and over. The average income for the group was $3 291 with the Chinese and Portuguese also earning below both provincial and national averages as shown in Table 4.

III. Institutional Development

The primary needs for establishing ethnic organizations by Greeks mainly stem from the age-old desire of Greeks in the Diaspora to maintain their "Hellenism," historical links and traditions, cultural customs, language, and religion. Culture and religion are intertwined in Hellenism; and being Greek means being Greek Orthodox Christian. Preserving Greekness, then, means preserving the Greek Orthodox faith, and the reverse is also true.

TABLE 2 *Educational distribution of selected ethnic groups in Montreal, 1971 (Percent of total)*

Education (15 yrs. & over excluding those attending full-time)	Greeks	Italians	Jews	Dutch	Portuguese	Negro West Indians	Japanese	Chinese	American	British	French
Total	26 955	99 925	77 545	5 570	8 690	6 065	1 075	6 110	565	290 000	1 113 680
	%	%	%	%	%	%	%	%	%	%	%
1. With degree	3	2	12	13	1	13	21.9	11	6	9	4
2. 1 or more year university	5	3	13	13	3	14	16	8	9	10	5
3 Grades 7-13	36	41	64	69	44	67	54	49	66	72	70
4. Grades 1-6	46	49	8	4	44	5	7	21	20	8	20
5. No schooling	4	5	3	—	9	—	1	11	1	—	1

Source: Statistics Canada, Special Report No. 6001-00175AC-2B 1971

TABLE 3 *Occupational distribution in major categories of selected ethnic groups in Montreal, 1971 (Percent of total)*

	Greeks	Italians	Jews	Dutch	Portuguese	Negro West Indians	Japanese	Chinese	American	British	French
Labor force	19 700	66 505	52 130	4 035	6 050	4 840	780	4 280	380	184 255	654 465
Managers/ Administration	1	2	12	11	1	3	6	3	5	10	5
Other Professional	5	5	15	22	4	28	24	17	12	17	13
Clerical	6	11	20	19	6	20	17	14	26	27	19
Sales	12	7	22	11	4	3	10	5	12	10	10
Service	29	11	4	8	24	15	9	30	8	7	10
Farms	—	2	—	1	1	—	—	—	1	—	1
Processors/ Machinery	7	10	2	5	10	3	4	2	5	4	6
Production/ Fabrication	24	23	8	6	23	9	14	10	12	6	9
Construction/ Transportation	6	14	4	7	9	5	6	3	11	9	14
Other and not stated	10	15	13	10	18	14	20	16	8	10	13

Source: Statistics Canada, Special Report No. 6001-00175AC-2B-1971.

TABLE 4 *Income distribution of selected ethnic groups in Montreal, 1971 (Age 15 and over)*

Ethnic group (in rank order)	Total number	Average income	Earning $0.0 - 9 999	Earning $10 000 - 14 999	Earning $15 000 and over
		$	%	%	%
Jews	91 065	5 733	62	8	9
Dutch	6 345	5 581	58	12	7
Japanese	1 210	5 322	61	9	7
British	329 260	4 950	64	9	6
American	615	4 092	72	7	2
Negro/West Indians	6 975	3 787	70	5	2
French	1 262 750	3 770	66	5	2
Italians	110 460	3 638	71	4	1
Greeks	29 005	3 291	71	3	2
Chinese	7 375	3 258	67	3	2
Portuguese	9 470	3 182	71	3	1

Quebec average income: $4 969
Canada average income: $5 043
Source: Statistics Canada, *Special Report No. 6001-00175AC-2B-1971.*

As the yearbook of one of the community associations puts it: "There are many among us (the Greeks) that worry about the very essence of "Hellenism" in our area, about the maintenance and transmission of our morals and customs (which protect our youth from foreign influence), and finally, about the absence of a church", (Communauté Greque de la Region Sud-Ouest de Montréal, Yearbook, 1981). Of the estimated 20 million Greeks, only nine million live in Greece proper. The others are scattered around the world, and have been ever since antiquity, one of the *least assimilated* groups by host cultures. The Greeks of Montreal are no different in this respect. Early life in Canada was, and still is, hard for many immigrants. Although they left poverty behind them, they also left their social, cultural, and social-psychological support systems that were the buffers in time of adversity, need, and social control.

The first formal organizations to be formed were centered around the church. As the size of the group grew, so did the number of ethnic organizations. Individual and sub-groups felt that their needs were not met by the existing organizations and the church, and thus formed new ones. Regionalism, special interests, and, above all, political differences generated conflict and split up groups who formed their own organizations. As a Montreal *Gazette* reporter so aptly put it, "The Greek Canadians are originally the most political and most socially conscious of Montreal's ethnic groups." He went on to add, ". . . Canadian affairs get the occasional mention . . . but the deepest concerns for many are in their homeland and in their community." (*Gazette*, October 15, 1980:5).

Finally, when one community leader was asked to single out the most important factor that divides Greeks in Montreal today, he promptly answered: "The Greek character," pointing out the cultural inability of Greeks for team work, their preference for confrontation rather than cooperation, and their strong sense of individualism and dogmatism for dealing with personalities rather than issues. Thus the combination of the Greeks' preoccupation with homeland, communal and provincial politics, and the "Greek character" have brought about disunity and conflict.

Conflict, on the one hand, when managed, contributes to the institutional growth of the group. On the other hand, such conflict has at times threatened the very existence of the community's basic institutions, weakened the community's bargaining power with other groups and government institutions, and kept the young, more educated and skilled Greeks from joining and participating in such organizations.

Immigration experience in Canada, while similar in many ways to that of the United States, differs in some significant aspects. Greek immigration to Canada reached large numbers when entrance to the U.S. was limited. It is mainly a post-World War II population with the majority still being Greek-born. In the U.S., the large waves of Greek immigrants arrived before and shortly after World War I (Vlachos, 1975:7). From the beginning, Greeks in the U.S. found themselves in the massive Americanization process of the 1920s and 1930s where they had to suppress typically ethnic behavior and avoid identifying themselves as Greek if they were to be accepted and progress. The only organizational effort not disapproved of was the establishment of the Greek Orthodox Church, on a parish basis, and dominated by the clergy. This organizational tradition still dominates in the U.S.

In Montréal, however, the post-World War II immigrants had also gone through the experience of the Civil War, with a radical leftist and trade union movement orientation. Recent immigrants, as stated earlier, have arrived from urban centers in Greece and elsewhere in Europe, and are more skilled and educated than the early immigrants. They have found themselves in a society adhering to a pluralistic ideology, and two dominant – and in their cultural and social institutions distinct – governments and charter groups locked in a continuous power struggle. The legal, cultural, and social climate was favorable to any ethnic organizational development, as long as it did not violate the laws of the land. In addition, the numerous other ethnic groups already in existence, some of them with strong and effective ethnic organizations (i.e. Jewish), provided an example for imitation and competition for scarce resources (such as government funds). Finally, prejudice and discrimination by the receiving society will dictate a state of closed or open institutional membership and growth or absence of ethnic organizations. French Québécois institutions and culture were not open to the newly-arrived immigrants and English institutions accepted them only in the labor market. Thus it was against the threat of cultural extinction that ethnic groups in Montreal organized themselves.

New waves of immigrants have constantly rejuvenated the "Greekness" of the group. They tend to concentrate in heavily populated areas, thus reinforcing each other's cultural identity, values, customs, and traditions. The St. Lawrence Boulevard (the divider of the French-English Solitudes) became the launching area of Greek immigrant settlement, extending eastwards to Park Avenue and northwards to Park Extension. Families, friends, and relatives from the old village tend to live in the same neighborhoods and when one moves out, the rest tend to follow as economic means allow. Such residential concentration tends to make contact and mobilization of the ethnic members much easier.

As important as the receiving environment and the immigration process are, however, it is the needs and the strength of the desire to alleviate those needs that will motivate a collectivity to organize itself into a community. Such needs may unite the ethnic members into forming "universal" organizations (for all of the ethnic members), or divide them into sub-groupings (for the needs of or according to the definition and/or the priority of needs of certain sub-groupings). A multiplicity of ethnic organizations results, sometimes cooperating among themselves and sometimes competing for membership, resources, or status. Both such cohesive and divisive factors have led to the organizational development of the Greeks in Montreal. In the next section of this paper, the specific concerns and needs of Montreal's Greeks, the establishment of organizations to satisfy them, and the role that conflict and cooperation have played, will be more explicitly discussed.

Ethnic structures are necessary, but not always sufficient for an ethnic group to maintain and transmit ethnic identity and ethnic culture. Forces, processes, and structures of the receiving society must also be taken into consideration for any meaningful sociological analysis of ethnic relations. The Montreal society, with its unique social and cultural structure in North America, must always be taken into consideration in a discussion of ethnic institutional development in Montreal.

IV. Selected Greek Institutions in Montreal

1. The Hellenic Community of Montreal

The Hellenic Community of Montreal today constitutes one of the major institutions of the ethnic group, although many may like to dispute its importance. Its strength comes in part from its universality of membership (any Greek Orthodox, of 18 years and over), but mainly from its association with and ownership of the four churches on the Island of Montreal, and from being the single Greek institution most used by the federal and provincial governments as a communication link and entry point into the community or for the dissemination of funds. The legitimacy of this function has generated conflict at times.

In 1906, in order to preserve Hellenism, the Greek Orthodox religion, and the Greek language, 1 000 Greeks (Montreal's entire Greek population) constituted themselves into the Greek Orthodox Community of Montreal. They received a Charter from Quebec City and bought property at 735 St. Lawrence Boulevard to erect a church. The money was raised through donations and bond issues (which were never redeemed). They applied for a priest to the Patriarch of Constantinople, who in turn directed them to apply to the Holy Synod of Greece, and on October 25, 1906, Father Agathodoros Papageorgopoulos arrived to become the first priest of the newly-established community. The cornerstone for the first Greek Orthodox Church to be built in Canada was laid on May 5, 1910, at the St. Lawrence property where Greeks, after work, began carrying stones, mixing cement, laying bricks, or doing odd chores for their first church. Seven months later they celebrated the Divine Liturgy at the church named Evangelismos (Annunciation).

Shortly after, the first Greek parochial school was established at the church with some 35 students. A year later, in 1911, a house at the back of the church was bought and converted into a school. It was named Plato and was fully supported and sponsored by the church. The school followed the curriculum of the Montreal public schools and taught Greek, English, and French. In its early life, the community was dominated by the church in the decision-making process, selection of programs, administration, and the Greek curriculum.

However, the politics of the homeland were soon to reach the community and threaten its very existence. By 1925, the community was split by the same political partisanship that divided Greece. After the destruction of the Greek army by the Turks in Asia Minor right after World War I, Greece was split into two camps, pledging each other's destruction. The Royalists, under King Constantine in Athens, and the Venizelists, under Venizelos in Salonica, brought the land to the brink of disaster. The event was echoed in Montreal. The Royalists and Venizelists split the community and the result was the establishment of a second Greek Orthodox Community in Montreal. The second community (Venizelists) purchased and chartered the Holy Trinity Greek Orthodox Church at 8 Sherbrooke Street West, and chartered the Socrates Anglo-Greek School Inc. in the building next door. This school followed the curriculum of the Protestant School Board of Greater Montreal and taught Greek, English, and French. Several months later, the newly-organized church and school were amalgamated by an act of legislature of the Province of Quebec into the Holy Trinity Greek Orthodox Congregation of Montreal (18th Biennial Ecclesiastical Congress: 1966: 31).

From accounts of interviewees who experienced the split, we learn that the conflict, accentuated by the financial crisis which resulted from the 1920 "Crash," almost disintegrated the communities. Businesses went bankrupt; fighting erupted, leading to court trials; members of opposing factions would not talk to each other; and churches would refuse to perform "mixed" marriages (Royalists and Venizelists). The divided ethnic group, faced with the additional effects of the Great Depression, was torn by conflict and incapable of supporting two organizations, two churches, and two schools. As one priest put it, ". . . so many people lost their business during the fights and the split. It was bad not only from a religious point of view, but also from a financial, social, business, health, or family point of view. I know, because I used to be a bookkeeper, and I know how business went down and this was the only cause."

It was through the efforts of the Archdiocese and specifically of the Archbishop of North America, Athenagoras, that on December 3, 1931, the two communities reached an agreement of unification. A new committee was formed, half from the one church and half from the other. They sold the Evangelismos church, and only the Holy Trinity Church and the Socrates school were retained.

With the influx of new immigrants after World War II and the Civil War, the needs of the population grew and so did its organizational structures.

In 1956, the Holy Trinity Greek Orthodox Congregation of Montreal petitioned Quebec and assumed the name of the Hellenic-Canadian Community of the Island of Montreal. In October of the same year the Community purchased property for the purpose of erecting a new church, a school, and a community center that would fill the needs of the growing Greek Community. By 1961, St. George's Cathedral had been built on that land, and in 1962 St. George's School was established as a branch of the Socrates school. A community center is now under construction.

It was in the late '60s and early '70s that the Hellenic Community experienced functional growth. Ironically, it was during these same years that the organization experienced a period of low membership and once again came into dangerous conflict with many other community organizations and ethnic members. The 1967 military coup in Greece created a political turmoil, and again Greek was turned against Greek. The clergy and many of the Hellenic Community leaders and members sided with the Junta in opposition to the majority of the immigrants who were against it. New associations were formed in Montreal like Makrygiannis with the prime objective to oppose the Junta, to actively influence the members of the group, and force the Canadian media and governments to censor or take punitive measures against the military government. This conflict again caused financial hardships and fights in the community. Church services were disrupted, and angry feelings ran high between opposing factions. In 1974 the Turkish invasion and occupation of Cyprus helped bring down the military government in Greece. The Cyprus problem has always united Greeks everywhere.

It is significant to note that this period was one of growth for the Hellenic community. The immigrants had given signs that increased domination by the clergy, specifically in political and non-church issues, would be constant points for confrontation and conflict. The lay members increased their power so that, in 1980, the organization's name was changed to simply Hellenic Community of Montreal, it was *restructured and took over the ownership and administration of its four churches.* The power of the clergy became restricted to matters of religion only, with a consultative function on other issues. It is this move that made the structure and administration of the church in Montreal unique. Everywhere else, in Canada and outside Greece, churches are owned by parishes, membership to churches is by parishes and the clergy has dominance on decisions and administration of church and parish issues. The parishes are usually small in number, thus clergy control is easier. In Montreal, however, the Hellenic Community owns its churches, membership is to the community, not to any given church – community members can marry, be baptized, and receive services in any of the four churches, and the non-religious affairs are decided by laity. Although the clergy is still consulted on non-religious matters (i.e. education), it has no vote on such issues.

During the same period, that is the '70s, the Hellenic Community, having reorganized itself internally, brought in outside funds for the first time (federal and provincial funds) and made serious attempts to cooperate and unify policy and decisions on similar functions and activities with the other community organizations. Such effects have helped the Greek community to present a united front to outsiders, thus increasing its bargaining power.

Today the Hellenic Community of Montreal owns four churches and operates the Socrates Elementary School, the Aristotle High School, 26 afternoon schools, a day care center, a school of Home Economics, social services, a senior citizens' club and a ladies' charity association.

As impressive as the list of its organizations is however, the Hellenic Community has not succeeded in involving and reaching a significant membership. It receives its power from its association with the church – churches overflow with worshippers on Sundays and holidays – and at the same time, it becomes a target of attack because of the interference of the clergy with non-religious matters. It is the institution that receives most government funds (80 percent of the day school budget is financed by the provincial government, 100 percent of the non-Greek programs), and is one of the main institutions through which the government gains indirect entry into the ethnic community. Finally, it is mostly associated with the "Greek immigrant establishment," an impression that has caused class conflict with those organizations that claim to represent the masses of Greek immigrant workers.

The Hellenic Community of Montreal has gone through the processes of cooperation and conflict and has experienced, along with the immigrant group, the pains of institutional growth. It is central to the life of the ethnic community and its institutional importance is not disputed. However, as the number of Greek immigrants grew, so did the complexity of their needs and the inability of one organization to fulfill them. As the immigrants moved outside the City of Montreal, they formed their own communities and parishes. Presently, there are the Greek Orthodox Communities of Laval, South Shore, Montreal North, South West and West Island. The church is at the heart of each community.

Greeks and Hellenism in Diaspora have survived for centuries. And the Greeks of Montreal have established more organizations to help them in this effort of survival.

2. The Hellenic Federation of Parents and Guardians of Greater Montreal

Even the most optimistic estimates show that the Hellenic Community's educational facilities reached less than 10 percent in 1970, and reach less than 15 percent of the ethnic group's school-age children today (800 in the day schools and approximately 1 800 in the afternoon schools). The need to educate the young in the Greek language, religion, and traditions was not really fulfilled until the establishment of the federation in 1969, with its principal stated goal: ". . . to unite all parents of Hellenic origin and guardians of Greek children in a common effort for the better education of their children and better understanding and adaptation to the Canadian Society and way of life, and generally their social development. Furthermore, to support and promote among its members the love, study and development of the Hellenic culture of the Greek language in particular."

The federation operates Greek afternoon classes, after regular school, in the Protestant schools of Greater Montreal. It claims to be the largest Greek institution in Montreal, reporting a membership of 2 500 families, and 3 500 students. Its curriculum includes instruction in the Greek language, Greek geography, Greek history, and Greek Orthodox religion. In addition, for those children who are interested, it offers a program of Greek folk dances and songs.

Student enrollment has constantly increased since the schools started operating in 1970. So has the number of schools and teachers which, by 1980, had reached 38 and 74 respectively. Financially, the organization mainly supports itself, and it is only since the late 1970's that some funds have been secured from the federal and provincial governments.

The federation, in addition to the formal class instruction of language, religion, and culture, has systematically promoted and transmitted "Hellenism" and has attempted a smooth entrance of the children into the larger Montreal society. It organizes celebrations on Greek holidays by presenting theatrical and dance performances, its annual gymnastics display, and its "Mini-Olympics."

The federation has also organized what it calls an "Exchange of Culture" (F. Katma, 1980:9) with French Canadians at Place des Jardins where children's school activities, such as painting, artcraft, and poetry are demonstrated. During July and August, tours of summer camps are organized.

The federation commands the respect and social recognition of the ethnic community because of its functions. However, it solidified that respect and approval by showing opposition to the Greek military Junta and by refusing to accept any favors or interacting in any cooperative way with the Junta or its embassy and consulate. It was this anti-Junta stand that brought the federation in open friction with the Hellenic Community which supported the Junta and followed its educational dictates.

There have been many attempts at reconciliation and cooperation, at least regarding schools and education, between these two organizations. The community's recognition of the Junta and the clergy's participation and dominance on educational matters, however, prevented success. The fall of the Junta, the cooperation of the organizations over the Cyprus issue – which brought them together and at least opened the channels of communication – and, most importantly, the clergy's gradual removal from overt power in educational matters have brought the two organizations into a closer cooperative status. Realizing that outside organizations, especially governments, were playing them against each other for funds – with the result that neither of the organizations were to receive much – the two decided to cooperate internally on policy issues and present a united front to outside agencies. Thus, now, only one organization at a time seeks out governmental funds for afternoon schools.

However, even with the tremendous work of these two organizations, there were still Greeks in the community who felt that their special needs were not satisfied. As stated earlier, the majority of the Greeks have low education, are mostly factory and service workers, and there is over 25 percent unemployment. To meet their needs a labor organization was established in Montreal.

3. The Hellenic-Canadian Labour Association of Metropolitan Montreal

The Labour Association was constituted formally in March, 1971. As stated in its charter, the necessity for such an association stemmed from the needs of "securing the protection and expansion of the rights and interests" of its members. The charter also states that this need was generated from the ". . . lack of linguistic skills, knowledge of the social and labour legislature, the low quality and the nature of occupations that mainly absorb the newly-arrived immigrants in addition to the other social and personal problems of adaptation. It does not constitute a union, but an advisory organization that urges its members to unionize and assists them with job-related and adaptation problems" (the Greek-Canadian Labour Association of Montreal, Charter 1978).

Among its goals, the association also aims at cultivating and perpetuating the "cultural and intellectual interests" of its members. Membership is open to all laborers and clerks of Greek origin 16 years and over. It is organized and administered by an administrative council and seven committees responsible for public relations, media, finance, syndicalism, programs, women's issues, and the association's center. Its strength is derived not only from its own membership, but also from the overlapping membership of the federation and the other regional associations.

The Labour Association has an expressed political ideology – Marxist – and is known as the most "militant" association of the ethnic community. It commands acceptance by the ethnic community, not only by offering assistance to the Greek immigrant worker, but also because of its early stand against the Greek Junta. It has its own monthly newspaper which is distributed to all members by mail and deals mostly with association issues and achievements. In addition, it sponsors a one-hour radio program (Centre Ville) once a week, informing listeners of its latest news.

The association maintains a purely ethnic character. It offers its members a placc to socialize and communicate. Discussions focus upon political ideologies, Greek politics, and immigrant interests and problems. It is, of course, this preoccupation with political ideology and politics that sets the association against other organizations in the community which dispute the legitimacy of its cultural contribution to the group. However, this association has mobilized large participation in ethnic events and celebrations, Greek issues of unity, such as the Cyprus issue, and has supported the education of youth through their federation membership. They also have their own theatrical chorus and folk dance groups.

4. The Cretans' Association of Montreal

After politics, the second major factor that divides the Greeks but does not necessarily produce conflict, is regional in origin. Residential neighborhoods are "ethnic villages" with family and compatriots living in proximity. It has been a long established pattern of the Greek migration process, both internal and external to Greece, that when a "sufficient" number from the same geographic region of origin moves to a new place, it tends to form an association. Greeks in Montreal have also followed this pattern.

There are approximately 50 chartered organizations in the Greater Montreal area with the basic objective of bringing "compatriots" together, mainly for social interaction and social support, celebration of regional holidays, the maintenance of a link with the "home region," and for the occasional financial assistance to the village. They send money for schools, churches, roads, water works, health programs, and for any emergency. The main social event of such association is their annual gathering, where they dance to Greek and regional music, interact, and hope that their children will make friends and marry within the group. The most important organizations, from the point of view of the community's institutional development and because of its size and functions, is the Cretans' Association of Montreal.

This is the oldest and largest of the Greek Brotherhood Associations in Montreal. It was established on January 12, 1912, the night after the death of a Cretan's wife. The event brought Cretans together in soul-searching and in assessing their lives and future in a foreign land. It was to support each other socially and financially, that they decided to form the Cretans Brotherhood Association, "O Minos".

Within a short time, the association claimed a membership of 35, all the immigrants in Montreal from the island of Crete. Today, the brotherhood reports a membership of 1 500 to 2 000 from among the 5 000 Cretans in Montreal.

The stated objectives of this organization as published in their Yearbook (1972-1973:3) are ". . . the maintenance of the Greek identity in general, and the Cretans' identity in particular, among its members. It aims at cultivating the spirit of brotherhood, the perpetuation of the Greek language, and the morals and customs and traditions of the motherland, Crete – and most particularly, the transmission of these, along with the island's history and tradition, to their youth.''

They have bought their own "Cretans' Shelter," a building on Park Avenue which is daily crowded with Cretans and friends conversing on politics – of course – or on news from Crete and Greece, the economy, and so on. It is the only brotherhood association that has established its own Greek school where children of Cretan origin are exposed to the Greek language, history, and tradition. In addition, since the early 1970s, and with the assistance of the Canadian Government, it operates daily schools for free French and English lessons to its members. It offers instruction in Cretan folk dances and music, and has its own dance groups and bands that often perform for Greek and Canadian audiences – on stage and on television. Finally, it publishes an annual yearbook that deals with literature, art, and the cultural pursuits of the Island of Crete.

The brotherhood has always provided assistance to the island of Crete. In 1948 it offered all its financial resources to parents who lost their children in World War II and bought clothes for children devastated by the war (F. Katma, 1980:5). For members, it has provided social and financial support whenever needed, particularly to newcomers. As Katma reports, the association has lately made available to its members many types of insurance, such as life, home, and car. It has also made donations to hospitals and to the sick, both in Montreal and Crete. It has occasionally paid air fares to Greece for some families who could not afford the trip.

Being a Cretan comes first in the affairs of the association. When in 1970 it was proposed to open its school to all Greek children, the motion was defeated. And it was out of this dispute that the Hellenic Community and the Federation of Parents established the afternoon schools. However, the brotherhood has been generous in cooperating with the community's other Greek institutions.

5. Travel agencies

An institution that has played an important role in the ethnic community in Montreal, but isn't talked about much, is the travel agency. Travel agencies were very useful during the peak of the Greek immigration to Montreal, from 1950 to 1960 as, mediators between sponsors in Montreal and immigration authorities and transportation companies. They helped the sponsors every step of the way, at a price, of course, filling in applications, visiting immigration offices with them, translating and guaranteeing loans for the immigrants' fares. Their head offices in Greece assisted candidates through the screening process, passport acquisition, and embarkation. The agencies were the only ones who could help the immigrants make sense of their new world, translate papers, provide advice in general, and help many find jobs. The agencies, in effect, became immigration brokers.

TABLE 5 *Emigrant remittances in the Greek balance of payments (US $ millions)*

Year	Total goods and services	From emigrant remittances	Remittances as per cent to total G. & S.
	$	$	%
1967	890.4	232.1	26.1
1968	954.6	239.4	25.1
1969	1 048.3	277.0	26.0
1970	1 218.0	344.7	28.3
1971	1 455.1	469.6	32.3
1972	1 870.0	571.4	30.1
1975	3 885.1	733.6	18.9
1976	4 454.1	803.2	18.0
1977	5 102.0	924.8	18.1
1978	6 147.9	984.4	16.0

Source: *Statistical Yearbook of Greece*, 1971, 1973 and 1979; Tables XXIV, XXIII, and XXIII, respectively.

There are about 22 Greek travel agencies in greater Montreal today. Some have been operating for as long as 30 years. They were first established in Greece and then set up branch offices in Montreal. Besides encouraging and facilitating travel to Greece, which keeps the immigrants in constant touch with the homeland and helps them re-establish ties and reaffirm their identity, the travel agencies mediate in the issuance of visas, passports, travel, and citizenship documents; they translate government documents, provide immigrants with all sorts of information, and prepare their income tax reports. The agencies, through necessity and practice, have become the unofficial mediators between the immigrant and his new society.

The rest of this section will deal with a Greek financial unstitution – the Hellenic Canadian Trust – and the mass media. The research on these institutions is not yet complete and the discussion will be sketchy at best.

6. The Financial Institution

One of the most significant sources of the Greek National Product comes from remittances of the Greeks in Diaspora. History supports the statement that, wherever Greeks settle, through hard work and ingenuity, they tend to progress, save, and never forget those whom they left behind. Immigrant remittances have always been a significant component to the Greek balance of payment. Table 5 gives a summary picture of Greek immigrant remittances relative to the total amount from current transactions of goods and services in the balance of payments.

Of the remittances, $18.7 million U.S. came from Canada in 1970, whereas in 1972, it had reached $32.5 million with nearly double that amount, $61.0 coming in 1978. These amounts are a significant indication of the links, not only emotional but also structural, between Greeks in Canada and in Greece. In addition, it has always been the dream of the Greek in Diaspora to "make it big," and then return to the homeland's sunny skies and blue sea to retire.

The reward for handling the finances of the Greeks in Montreal and encouraging them to invest their savings in Greece has prompted the Greek Government to establish in April, 1972 the Hellenic Canadian Trust, a subsidiary of the National Bank of Greece. It provides mainly savings and investment services.

Greeks basically tend to distrust financial institutions. They would prefer to hold on to their money themselves, and the use of cheques is looked upon with suspicion. Greeks are leery of foreign financial institutions most of all. The Hellenic Trust, therefore, provides a compromise of mistrust and necessity. A mainly Greek staff offers its services in Greek, and the managers take a personal approach to their customers' affairs. In an industrialized-urban environment, where savings and investment constitute a business "must," it is easier to deal with one of your own kind. Thus the institution not only provides the formal services of a trust organization, but also helps to socialize the thrifty immigrant and the successful small businessman into the world of financial dealings of both Canadian and Greek societies.

7. The Mass Media

The community is currently served by two weekly newspapers, the *Hellenic Postman* (since 1958) and the *Hellenic Canadian Tribune* (since 1964), a monthly, *Drasis* (since 1971) and the short-lived *The Greek News*, a bi-weekly paper started in April, 1981 and now defunct. The community also published for a brief period in 1981 a joint New York-Montreal issue of *Proini*, a publication that aimed at filling in the journalistic gaps of the existing publications. Finally, there is *O Metoikos, Le Meteque*[4] (since 1980), a monthly political review sympathetic to the Parti Québécois.

The community is also served by CHCR (since 1965), the only Greek station, and by radio programs provided by the multi-ethnic stations CFMB (since 1962) and Centre Ville (since 1968). The programs broadcast Greek music exclusively and inform the listeners of news and events. Finally, one can watch a half hour on Sunday televison on CFCF, which presents summaries of Greek news, documentaries on Greece, and Greek music. The emphasis is mostly on Greek news, with community and Canadian news given secondary exposure.

No other institution in the community has collectively experienced more ups and downs than the Greek mass media in Montreal. Lack of capital investment, poor journalism, community politics, and personal involvements have seen many newspapers close down. At times, some of them become instruments of attack and "character assassination" in the settlement of personal and political scores. Also, since direct Montreal-Athens flights, Montreal has been flooded with Athens' newspapers and magazines that reach readers with fresh and better quality news presentations on the day of publication.

As a whole, then, the community abounds in ethnic print and Greek language media. It is a common sight to see Greeks in their cafés or association halls, drinking Greek coffee, listening to Greek music on the radio, and reading Greek newspapers. The latter provide close contact with the events in Greece and food for Greece's national pastime – "discussing politics."

IV. The Future

This paper has attempted to describe the Greek community in Montreal and delineate the sociological forces and factors that enter the institutional development process of the ethnic group. Cooperation and conflict seem to be the most dominant of such forces. In tracing the establishment and development of the group's most important institutions, these forces were seen to constantly interplay and account for the major oscillations in the community structures. Factors significant to the structural development of the group seems to originate from the sociocultural environment of the Montreal society and its ethnic relations ideology, the dynamics of the immigration process, and the needs and characteristics of the ethnic group.

It is through these institutions that individuals and family maintain and transmit cultural symbols, traditions, values and customs, the language, and religion as well as provide social support to alleviate cultural and social needs. It is through these institutions that the sense of "peoplehood," the "consciousness of kind," and the "we" feelings are reinforced which dictate culturally appropriate behavior and preserve Greek identity.

However, this question remains: Will the Greek ethnic group mature in its organizational structure and effectiveness and succeed in passing it, along with the ethnic culture and identity, to the younger generations, or, as the inevitable acculturation occurs, will the younger generations opt for membership into the larger society? On the one hand, the answer will depend on the changes in the receiving societies such as in the ethnic relations ideologies and policies, the constitutional structure of Quebec and Canada, and the decline of English power and institutions. On the other hand, changes in the immigration process and context, such as the interruption of inflow of new immigrants, the outflow of returning immigrants, residential dispersion, and changes in the presence and structures of other ethnic groups will also affect the Greek community. Finally, changes in the Greek group, such as linguistic decline, church language policies, links with Greece, upward mobility, perception of prejudice and discrimination, the

FIGURE 2 *Tentative list of processes and factors that may affect the future of Greek institutions and ethnicity among Greeks in Montreal*

A. Processes
 1. Conflict
 2. Cooperation
 3. The process of immigrant adjustment (acculturation, integration, assimilation)
 4. Others

B. Factors
 1. *Generated by the receiving society*
    a. Changes in Quebec ethnic relations ideologies and policies
    b. Constitutional structure of Quebec (federalism or separation)
    c. Decline or extinction of English power and of vital English institutions
    d. Language legislation
    e. French maturity in its own dominant position
    f. Urbanization-urbanism (effects of on family and kinship structure — emphasis on pecuniary and achievement values)
    g. Others
 2. *Generated by the immigration process*
    a. Interruption of immigrant in-flow
    b. Outflow of immigrants (to Canada or returning to Greece)
    c. Residential dispersion
    d. Changes in the presence and structures of other ethnic groups
    e. Others
 3. *Generated by the ethnic group*
    a. Socioeconomic mobility
    b. Decline of linguistic ability (ethnic language)
    c. Changes in church language
    d. Links with Greece and other Greek communities
    e. Absence of desirable Greek models for the socialization of youth
    f. Class characteristics confused as cultural characteristics by the youth and rejected
    g. Ability to manage political and institutional conflict
    h. Relative deprivation
    i. Perception of prejudice and discrimination
    j. Others

Note: Processes and factors are assumed distinct for analytical purposes only.

absence of desirable Greek role models and relative deprivation, all these will affect the ability of the group to maintain its growth and the effectiveness of its institutional development. Figure 2 summarizes the forces and factors that will have a continuing impact on Montreal's Greek community.

Traditionally, the majority of immigrants have become acculturated by the English rather than the French community in Montreal. However, as a result of Bill 101, the Charter of the French Language, immigrant youth are being directed towards French educational institutions. For the most part, both the Greek leadership and clergy in Montreal tend to dismiss the linguistic issue. The lay leaders see the usefulness and the necessity of the French language. In 1971, the Hellenic community was the first to change its school curriculum by making French the primary educational concern in terms of instruction against the outcry of some members of the community that accused them of "selling our children to the French." However, the bishop and the majority of the clergy hold that the Greek language, as one of them put it, "will always be the language of the church, thus we need not worry about English and French." Montreal may possibly end up with three factions: Greeks, Franco-Greeks, and Anglo-Greeks. And once the factors leading to possible division increase, so could the conflict and fragmentation in the Greek community.

Overall, the Greeks in Montreal seem to be organizationally dynamic, cohesive, and institutionally complete. Organizations interact and interlock in terms of membership and functions. They are becoming more politically oriented and they have challenged the establishment and the church effectively. With the coming to power of the Parti Québécois, these organizations also have entered into provincial and federal politics. Current, provincial politics are significantly gaining participants. And as the ethnic minorities have become political assets to provincial and federal policy makers, the Greek organizations have seen an influx of politicians and power brokers promising the preservation of the Greek culture, the dissemination of funds and grants, and political power in return for votes and acceptance of programs and policies. It is because of these reasons that the Greek group saw its first member to the National Assembly elected during the 1981 Quebec elections.[5]

Finally, if the current trend of almost negligible Greek immigration to Canada continues and Greece experiences some political stability, provincial and local community politics will continue to grow as significant factors in the community, especially when competition for funds may be associated with community status, functions, and programs.

Appendix A

The Research Method

The information in this paper has been secured from available records and extensive, in-depth interviews by the author and her research assistant with knowledgeable leaders and members of the Greek community in Montreal during 1980 and 1981.

At the beginning, a list of knowledgeable people was drawn from public information on current leadership of the major Greek organizations. Then we were referred to individuals in past and current key positions in the affairs and politics of the community. All of those contacted eventually agreed to talk with us, indicating interest and care for our efforts.

Whenever resistance was encountered, other leaders, personal friends and family mediated on our behalf. Thus we interviewed most of the current and some past leaders of the major organizations.

The interviews were held in community centers and other public places. A list of general, open-ended questions was used to allow the informants to elaborate on their own while giving us a focus for the interviews. Such questions generally aimed at the historical development of the community structures, the needs and forces of their development, functions and accomplishments, membership and finances, politics and relations with other organizations, the church, the community at large, Greece, other ethnic communities, Quebec, and Canada. All interviews were taped.

END NOTES

1. The author wishes to express her gratitude to the Quebec Ministry of Education, Professors F. Bird, A. Synnott, M. Downing and M. Rosenberg. Special thanks to D. Manolakos, A. Maris, Bishop Sotirios, Father Salamis, Father Chalkias, Father Saitanis, L. Bombas, D. Dimakopoulos, F. Komborozos, G. Papadakis, P. Ferentinos, K. Georgoulis, M. Manoukian, N. Georgiadis, J. Chilakos, Ch. Kolyvas, S. Giousmas, K. Spiliadis, I. Daperis, the Women's Committee of the Greek Labour Association, and finally my research assistant Fotini Katma, for her professionalism and diligence in securing most of the interviews.

2. This constitutes part of a larger study carried out by the Ethnic Groups Research Project of Concordia University. The objectives of this project were to determine the institutional development of seven ethnic groups in Montreal (Greeks, Dutch, Jews, Italians, Portuguese, Haitians, Moslems); their functions; their contributions to the maintenance and transmission of ethnic identity; and finally, the factors behind such development. During the preliminary analysis of basically qualitative data which were secured through interviews with community leaders and knowledgeable persons in the ethnic communities, the Greeks were found to be on a relatively high level of institutional development (along with the Jews and Italians), assessed by the number of types of institutions, their functions, ethnic participation and community linkages. The Dutch, on the other hand, were found at the lowest levels of such institutional development.

3. The term "urban villagers" was first used by H.J. Gans *Urban Villagers* (London: Free Press, 1962) to refer to individuals living in urban slums, usually "European immigrants – (who) try to adapt their non-urban institutions and cultures to the urban milieu" (p. 4). In my usage, the term slightly differs in the sense that I place emphasis on the rural, socioeconomic and cultural characteristics of the Greek immigrants, who, however, attempt to live in an urban city, and establish national and urban institutions to maintain an ethnic culture with rural values and attitudes.

4. Franco-Greek media are more visible since the election of Le Parti Québécois.

5. Chris Sirros is the first member of the Greek community to serve in the Quebec National Assembly.

SELECTED REFERENCES

Breton, R. "Institutional Completeness of Ethnic Communities and the Personal Relations of Immigrants," *American Journal of Sociology,* Volume 70, pp. 193-205, 1964.

Chimbos, P. *The Canadian Odyssey: The Greek Experience in Canada.* Toronto: McClelland & Stewart, 1980.

Chimbos, P., "The Greek Canadian Family: Tradition and Change," in K. Ishwaran, *Canadian Families: Ethnic Variations,* Toronto: McGraw-Hill, 1980.

Cretans' Association of Montreal, *Yearbook*, 1972-73.

Eighteenth Bicentennial Ecclesiastical Clergy-Laity Congress and Philoptohos Conference of the Greek Archdiocese of North and South America. Montreal, June 25-July 2, 1966.

Gans, H.J. *The Urban Villagers* London: Free Press, 1962.

Gavaki, E., "The Greek Family in Canada: Continuity and Change and the Process of Adjustment," *International Journal of Sociology of the Family,* Vol. 9, No. 1, Jan.-June, 1979.

Gavaki, E., *The Integration of Greeks in Canada*, San Francisco, R. & E. Research Associates, 1977.

Montreal *Gazette*, October 15, p. 5, 1980.

The Greek-Canadian Labour Association of Montreal, *Charter*, 1978.

Katma, F. "The Hellenic Community: An Institutional Analysis," Paper submitted to the Ethnic Studies Research Project, Concordia University, 1980.

Lieberson, S. *Language and Ethnic Relations in Canada* Toronto: John Wiley & Sons, Inc., 1970.

Nagata, J.A. "Adaptation and integration of Greek Working class immigrants in the city of Toronto, Canada: a situational approach," *International Migration Review,* 1970.

Ontario Ministry of Culture and Recreation, *Ontario Ethnocultural Profiles: Greeks,* ISBN O-7743-3925X, 1979.

Petritis, J., "The Greek Immigrants in Canada," in Cretans' Association of Montreal, *Yearbook*, pp. 5-11, 1972-73.

Reitz, J.G., *The Survivial of Ethnic Groups.* Toronto: McGraw-Hill, 1980.

Saloutos, Theodoros, "The Greek Orthodox Church in the United States and Assimilation," *International Migration Review*, No. 7 Winter, 1973.

Statistics Canada, *Special Reports*, Nos. 6001-2B-1971; 8917-13549A-2B-1971, 1971. *Immigration Statistics*, 1963-1979.

Statistical Service of Greece, *Statistical Yearbook of Greece*, Athens, Greece, 1971, 1973, 1979.

Vlachos, E. "Greek American Perspective: Social, Psychological and Historical." Paper presented to the Greek-American Bilingual-Bicultural Education Conference, New York, April 25, 1975.

Vlassis, G. *The Greeks in Canada.* Ottawa, 1953.

J. ANTÓNIO ALPALHÃO
VICTOR M.P. DA ROSA

The Portuguese in a Changing Society*

Portuguese Emigration

From the 17th century onwards, it was Brazil that attracted the Portuguese. In the last quarter of the 19th century, Africa offered them a new horizon. In the 20th century, South America, North America, and even Europe became the lands of hope for Portuguese emigrants. During the last 100 years, almost three million Portuguese have emigrated. This exodus has now been stepped up. In the last 20 years two million individuals have left Portugal, a million of them in the last decade.[1] This means that close to one-quarter of all Portuguese live in foreign countries, a phenomenon without precedent in the history of Portugal.

Under all regimes, past and present, Portuguese emigration policy has been very ambiguous. Generally speaking, emigration is a personal or collective solution, adopted in a situation of extreme emergency. At the individual level, the decision to emigrate appears logical because it means choosing a lesser evil. However, at the collective level, the attitude of governments is paradoxical insofar as they bemoan the exodus of workers without doing anything to put an end to the situation.

Emigration is today more than ever linked to the labor market and dependent on this market at the international level. "Emigration, though it has multiple characteristics, is today one of the facets of the international division of labor, and is imposed by the dominant social organizations and by the most industrialized economies, that is to say, by imperialist capital and its production logic.[2] We can thus understand why the countries supplying manpower are countries whose economy is somewhat backward and whose political regimes are frequently totalitarian.

To attribute Portuguese emigration solely to internal causes would be to consider only one part of the problem. The "push-pull" theory also applies to the Portuguese case. Foreign countries' utilization of Portuguese manpower obeys economic and political criteria which are linked to their interests. The aim of those countries which import manpower is to increase their production potential by using a labor force which can be requested at their own convenience.

---

* Adapted from *A Minority in a Changing Society: The Portuguese Communities of Quebec*, J. António Alpalhão and Victor M.P. Da Rosa (Ottawa: University of Ottawa Press, 1980.)

In the specific case of Quebec, we would list as the main elements of the "pull" factor a high economic level, high wages, the advantages of social security, better prospects for education and, in general, greater potential for children's development. The choice of Quebec may be attributed also to the testimony of immigrants already established there, to its politico-social image, and to advertising abroad.

Some tens of thousands of Portuguese live in Quebec today. Their destiny is bound to two continents, two peoples, and several governments. It is clear that the governments of Canada and Quebec have serious obligations to those whom they called upon when they experienced a shortage of manpower.

Places of Settlement

1. Montreal

The metropolitan region of Montreal is the main pole of attraction for immigrants settling in Quebec. Large numbers of Portuguese in metropolitan Montreal have been evident since the beginning of 1950s and are presently estimated at 40 000.[3] Almost 60 percent of them come from the Azores.[4]

Even though there are Portuguese in all the districts of greater Montreal, they are particularly numerous in the area bounded by Sherbrooke Street to the South, St. Joseph to the North, St. Denis to the East and Park Avenue to the West. In the heart of this area is the St. Louis district where almost 12 000 Portuguese live.[5] This district has for a long time been the gateway for successive waves of immigrants from several countries.[6]

The different parts of the city in which Portuguese immigrants choose to settle may serve as a test of the socioeconomic status achieved. We find that the most evolved strata tend to settle in the suburbs. This leaves room for the new arrivals, who are more deprived, to use the old St. Louis district as their "gateway." Among the new settlements with a high density of Portuguese residents is Longueil, where there are about 500 at present.[7]

2. Hull

The second largest Portuguese settlement in Quebec is situated in Hull, the twin city of Ottawa, a privileged location which is particularly important within the context of Quebec and of Canada in general. For the purposes of this study, when we speak of Hull, we include the entire surrounding area situated on Quebec territory, and more specifically, Wrightville, Mont-Bleu, Gatineau, Touraine, and Aylmer. Some of the first Portuguese to settle in Hull did so at the beginning of the 1950s, following their departure from the La Tuque region where they had worked in the lumber industry. Today, the Portuguese population of the Hull region is estimated at close to

3 000, 70 percent of whom live in the center of the city in what is called the Island of Hull, 25 percent in Wrightville, and the rest in the suburban areas mentioned above. Displacement towards these areas usually implies a rise on the socioeconomic ladder.

We should emphasize the homogeneity of the Portuguese of Hull, in that 95 percent to 98 percent of them are natives of the Azores and more specifically come from the Parish of Maia on Sao Miguel Island.

3. Laval

Under the name Laval, we include all the territory of Île Jésus. The Portuguese community scattered throughout this island is concentrated mainly in the area of Chomedey. Other Portuguese groups of lesser importance live in the vicinity of Laval, in particular in Fabreville, Vimont, and Laval-des-Rapides.

The Portuguese began settling in Laval around 1953 and presently total 2 000. The vast majority of them are from the Azores. It should be pointed out that a certain number of families had emigrated to Brazil before coming to settle in Laval.

4. Quebec City

There were Portuguese in Quebec City from the beginning of colonization. However, it was only in the 1950s that their presence began to make itself felt. The Portuguese population of Quebec City and the surrounding area, which includes Beauport, Cap-Rouge, Charlesbourg, Giffard, and Lévis, is estimated at about 750. They are mainly Azoreans who emigrated to Canada after the eruption of the Capelinhos volcano (Faial Island).

5. Ste. Thérèse

The settlement of the first Portuguese immigrants in the Ste. Thérèse region dates back to the beginning of the 1950s. Initially destined for farm work in the outlying areas, they gradually moved to the urban centers where large industries are located. Today, it is in the urban region that almost all the area's Portuguese are to be found. According to the leaders of the Ste. Thérèse community, the first and second generation Portuguese population totals 2 500 persons. The centers with the highest concentration of Portuguese are Ste. Thérèse, Blainville, and Boisbriand. The vast majority (90 percent) of these immigrants come from the Azores.

In spite of regional differences, Portuguese from the islands and from the continent consider themselves members of the same group. However, the number of people from a given region is one of the factors which must be taken into account in assessing the degree of social participation or the rate of integration and acculturation. In areas with a high concentration of

Portuguese immigrants, there is a tendency to create an imaginary, bygone Portugal. Where numbers are small, isolation limits the possibilities of sharing and transmitting culture and easily leads to anomie, above all in the case of more deprived immigrants.

Adaptation to Quebec

1. Political Factors

The present political situation in Quebec means constant pressure on ethnic groups to support one or the other of the dominant groups. Although the attitude of most Portuguese seems to be one of non-alignment, we must nevertheless conclude that these pressures do affect them. As Claude Ryan suggested:

> When the immigrants feel that we accept them for what they are, that we love them as they are, they will feel more drawn to us. So long as we give them the impression that we want to use them as hostages of sorts in conflicts for which there is not even agreement among ourselves we shall drive them psychologically further away from the Francophone community instead of bringing them closer.[8]

In the battle of the dominant cultures, it becomes well-nigh impossible to resist the temptation of enlisting minorities. It is clear that any form of conflict requiring a taking of sides creates distasteful situations, and it is understandable that ethnic minorities should feel uncomfortable when it comes to stating their convictions or when they must suffer the unpleasant effect of "non-alignment."

The attention shown by the different parties to immigrant minorities at election time in an effort to win their votes is well known.[9] The Portuguese ethnic group, though aware that it is not well represented on the Quebec political scene, seems attentive to the main political forces at work, while remaining sensitive to all the manipulations that would use it as a pawn on the political chess board.

Considering the large number of Portuguese immigrants, many of whom are naturalized Canadians, we could expect a certain political representation at the administrative level, but this is not the case.[10] Many factors can explain this absence. On the one hand, the Portuguese ethnic group is still first generation and thus is a population still in the process of adapting. On the other hand, the majority of Portuguese immigrants now living in Quebec have suffered in their country of origin from the effects of certain political taboos existing under the dictatorship which lasted from 1926 to 1974. They have been victims of the obscurantism of a dictatorial political regime which never encouraged them to participate in the social and political life of the community. We can thus better understand why there is not yet a single Portuguese deputy in Quebec or a single political leader issuing from the Portuguese community.

2. Economic Factors

Either because they lack special skills, or because they have not mastered the language, Portuguese immigrants almost always find themselves on the lowest rungs of the occupational ladder.

On arrival, the immigrant easily falls victim to certain kinds of exploitation.[11] Women working in clothing manufacturing are particularly vulnerable. Employers often limit salaries to the minimum permitted by law and almost always organize production so as to pay workers by the piece, which is deleterious to both the dignity and health of the workers.[12] To say that immigrants accept these working conditions (long hours, piece work, unhealthy surroundings, low wages, etc.) out of a spirit of cupidity is both unjust and illogical. More to the point is the fact that immigrants cannot defend themselves because of their ignorance of labor laws and workers' rights or because of the lack of sufficiently strong representation in union organizations.

Once settled in the new milieu, they view their economic level in comparative terms. An economic improvement over the country of origin may not be an improvement in the context of Quebec society. In general, however, we do find a rise in living standards within the Portuguese ethnic group at the level of the individual or the family.

The financial status of the immigrant rises not only in comparison with the wages paid in the country of origin, but also in terms of the buying power achieved in the new country. We find that the purchasing power of the Portuguese immigrants in Quebec is by far superior to that of their compatriots in Portugal. However, it would be ridiculous to say that the Portuguese community is rich. Thanks to their hard work and their thriftiness, the Portuguese generally achieve a satisfactory standard of living, which is almost always proportional to the length of time in the province and also depends on the type of activity in which they are engaged.

The economic factor acts as a double-edged sword in both the public and the private sectors. Neoclassical economists consider migratory movements as occurring in answer to the law of supply and demand, which, on the international migration market, threatens to make commercial objects of human beings. The procedures and official decisions of the countries which export or which import manpower risk turning immigrants into simple production machines designed to promote the economy of these manpower importing countries. Seen in this optic, even the attention given to immigrants is perhaps motivated more by the desire to have them produce than by any altruistic concern. When this is the case both in the country of origin and in the receiving country, the immigrant becomes an object of capitalist manipulation, which threatens his identity and his sociocultural integration.

The Portuguese immigrant is, by nature, attached to his country of origin and tries to invest his savings there. For more than a century, money sent home by emigrants has meant a substantial contribution to the Portuguese balance of payments. These remittances have been estimated "by Herculano (1873) at close to three million escudos per year [. . .]; at the time of Oliveira Martins (1891) at more than twelve million escudos; and during this century by Bento Carqueja at twelve million escudos and by Fernando Emidio da Silva (1917) at a sum ranging from twenty to twenty-four million escudos."[13] In the course of recent years, the following figures were recorded:

TABLE 1 *Money sent by Portuguese emigrants, 1968-1979*

Year	Amount in escudos	Year	Amount in escudos
1968	7 902 000 000	1974	22 913 000 000
1969	11 812 000 000	1975	20 975 000 000
1970	14 343 000 000	1976	26 566 000 000
1971	18 848 000 000	1977	43 232 000 000
1972	22 188 000 000	1978	74 226 000 000
1973	26 452 000 000	1979	119 758 000 000

Sources: *Estatisticas Financeiras*, Instituto Nacional de Estatistica (Lisbon) and *Relatorios*, Banco de Portugal (Lisbon).

These remittances, which are destined essentially to aid family members, represent considerable revenue for the Portuguese economy. The presence of Portuguese banks in the Portuguese communities abroad only confirms Portuguese government policy, which is to profit from the money sent home by emigrants.

This raises a question: What basic reasons lead a country to open or to close its door to immigration? It would be naive to think that these decisions are made chiefly for altruistic reasons. In principle, the country of immigration has the means of production but lacks cheap manpower. Its products are more competitive because they are cheaper to manufacture and are more numerous, which permits it to increase its margin of profit and its export capacity. We are thus forced to conclude that one can doubly exploit the country of origin of the immigrants by importing its cheap manpower on the one hand and exporting high-priced manufactured goods to it on the other.

We might also ask, just how high are the economic profits realised by the province of Quebec through the presence of Portuguese immigrants? Though we know of no other studies which could clarify this, suffice it to say that, between 1951 and 1974, "the national revenue of Quebec would have dropped by 11 percent without international immigration."[14] For reference purposes, we might also cite the VIth French Plan according to which: "France realises net profits of five billion francs per group of one hundred thousand immigrant workers."[15]

A policy which aimed at manipulating the labor force based on purely economic interests would be as reprehensible as the attitudes of those who, like the wolf in the fable of the wolf and the lamb, blame the immigrant for things which could not possibly be his fault. The goal of improving one's financial status, which the Portuguese immigrant considers essential, has nothing in common with the Machiavellian manipulations of the world capitalist system of which he is a victim. For him, earning his daily bread honestly is a sacred principle. "Making good" is both a goal and a stimulus which brings him to put forward an extra effort and which often translates into numerous hours of work carried out in a spirit of true abnegation.

There is nothing more humiliating for the immigrant worker than to see himself viewed positively or negatively according to his profitability for the exploiting organisation. "We import immigrants to offset our deficiencies, and, when an economic crisis comes, we accuse them of being their cause."[16]

The cultural differences between the majority and minority groups are sometimes exaggerated in times of conflict between these two groups, when in reality, economic factors are at the source of these antagonisms. In effect, the capitalist system fosters divisions within the working class by its recourse to immigration. This recourse guarantees the availability of cheap labor and also makes it possible to meet the demands of the elite of the organised working class.[17] Since the majority of immigrants are in the cheap labor category, certain conflicts which seem to have an ethnic character are in fact basically class conflicts.

One of the essential factors in immigrant sociocultural integration is financial security, both collective and individual. We can recognise the importance of the economic factor without considering it to the exclusion of all others or accepting its arbitrary aspects. Economic development must be subjected to a political code regulating the process of migrations and their short- or long-term evolution. The Parliamentary Committee on Immigration Policy points out the danger of linking immigration to economic development on the short term: "immigration is a long term investment in human resources."[18]

Human Resources

Quebec's economic situation is directly dependent on the presence of the ethnic groups which determine it. "For Quebec, immigration may represent a contribution in terms of men, manpower, and know-how, and may possibly be a source of economically profitable investments."[19]

The ethnic groups of Quebec, for their part, are at the mercy of government, which must be able to make optimum use of the human resources it imports. "Quebec's difficulties will increase in the coming years because of its inability to industrialise effectively. In order for a country to become industrialised, it must be able to readily find the human resources needed by modern business, and to use them rationally and effectively."[20]

Immigrant workers, acting both as producers and as consumers, benefit the receiving country. As producers, they contribute to the development of natural resources by increasing production potential. On the other hand, they may improve the local economy by introducing new production methods. According to the Minister of Manpower and Immigration: "immigrants are a source of wealth insofar as they contribute their talents and their education and become consumers of Canadian products. Their impact on the economy has been considerable. Among the principal economic advantages of immigration, we should mention: growth of the domestic market, contribution to Canadian industrial expansion, enrichment of the country by new know-how and new art forms."[21]

The greatest wealth of a people is its human capital. For this reason, it would seem that manpower-importing countries are poor compared to manpower-exporting countries. Unfortunately, economic potential is becoming more and more the mark of distinction between rich and poor nations, thus creating an inhumane order in the scale of values. On this scale, man takes second place to the goods which he processes. In fact, the rich countries' potential in natural wealth has been realised because the recourse to imported human labor has made possible the transformation of this wealth.

We must conclude that the Quebec economy is strongly dependent on immigrant labor. We must not forget that human capital is the primary resource in a nation's economy. However, in immigration policy, whatever the interests of the parties concerned, it is essential that immigrants be regarded first and foremost as human beings and not as simple machines in the service of economic interests.

END NOTES

1. Cf. Eduardo Sousa Ferreira, *Origens e formas da emigraçao* (Lisboa: Iniciativas Editoriais, 1976) p. 78. Also Joaquim A. Pires de Lima, *A emigraçao portuguesa em França.* (Lisboa: Editorial Estamps, 1974) p. 29.
2. Carlos Almeida and António Barreto, *Capitalismo e emigraçao em Portugal,* 2nd ed. (Lisboa: Prelo, 1974) p. 241.
3. In 1971 official Canadian statistics showed that there were 14 500 Portuguese immigrants in Montreal. However, according to the Consulate General of Portugal, the number of Portuguese established in this region in fact totalled 40 000 persons. However it must be emphasized that official statistics do not include children born in Canada, who obviously must be considered Portuguese in the case of the first generation.
4. The percentage of natives of the Azores is lower in Montreal than anywhere else in Quebec.
5. *Le groupe portugais à Montréal: la situation sociologique, la problématique et les lignes d'intervéntion,* (Montreal: Centre Portugais de Référence et de Promotion Sociale, 1976) p. 10.

6. Although it is located in the center of Montreal, the St. Louis district is one of the poorest areas of the city, with a lack of green space and old and run down buildings. The monotonous brick has been painted in bright colors by the Portuguese, giving the district a more cheerful look. Cf. Pierre Beaupré, "Rénovations des Portugais au quartier Saint Louis," *Décormag*, March, 1976, Vol. 4, No. 7 p. 10.

7. Estimate provided by the Municipality of Longueuil in 1978.

8. Anselme Mvilongo *et. al. Les Minorities ethniques à Montreal* (Montreal: Bureau de la Consultation Jeunesse, Inc., 1972) p. 16.

9. See especially Paul Cappon, *Conflict entre les Neo-Canadiens et les francophones de Montreal* (Quebec City: Les Presses de l'Universite Laval, 1974) p. 75 where he states: "Immigrants' neutrality often goes to the extreme of refusing to express an opinion on intercommunity relations in Montreal, because they fear the consequences of aligning themselves on one or the other side".

10. We estimate the percentage of Portuguese in Quebec who have taken out Canadian citizenship at 25 percent.

11. In Romao's sample of Portuguese living in Montreal, two-thirds of immigrant workers stated that at some time or other during their stay in Montreal, they had been victims of exploitation. See Isabel Romao, "Le processus de migration, la mobilite professionnelle, la mobilité sociale et l'acculturation chez les ressortissants d'origne Portugaise à Montreal" (M.A. thesis in Sociology, University of Montreal, 1972) p. 119.

12. According to the data of the Employment and Immigration Commission, immigrant women make up approximately half of the workers in the textile sector and almost all of the workers in the clothing sector, of which the most important centers are in Montreal, Toronto and Winnipeg. There are approximately 200 000 workers in these sectors throughout the country. More than any other group of workers in Canada, immigrant women hold jobs in the sectors paying the lowest wages: maid, chambermaid, cleaning woman, dishwasher, waitress, sewing machine operator, plastics manufacturing worker. See Françoise Côte in *Le Devoir*, Dec. 8, 1978 p. 2. Also Sheila McLeod Arnopoulos, *Problems des femmes immigrants sur le marché du travail Canadien* (Ottawa: Conseil consultatif Canadien de la situation de la femme, 1979) p. 5 and Bernard Bernier, "Main-d'oeuvre féminine et ethnicité dans trois usines de vêtement de Montreal," Anthropologie et Societés, Vol. 3, No. 2, 1979.

13. Joel Serrao, *A emigvaçao portuguesa,* 2nd ed. (Lisboa: Livros Horizonte, 1974) p. 175.

14. Côté, *Le Devoir,* p. 2.

15. Máximo Loizu, *Capitalisino europeo y emigracion* (Barcelona: Avance, 1975) p. 50.

16. Kévork Baghdjian, "Pourquoi voudrait-on que les immigrants soient à jamais 'les autres' parmi nous?" *Le Devoir*, June 8, 1976 p. 5.

17. Cf. Edna Bonacich, "A Theory of Ethnic Antagonism: The Split Labour Market," *American Sociological Review*, Vol. 37, 1972 p. 547-559.

18. Cf. Special Joint Committee of the Senate and the House of Commons on Immigration, *Report to Parliament* (Ottawa: 1975) p. 6.

19. *Une problématique des Ressources humaines au Québec* (Montreal: Ministère de Immigration, 1974) p. 168.
20. Jean-Claude Lenormand, *Québec Immigration: Zéro* (Montreal: Les Editions Parti Pris, 1971) p. 16.
21. *Fiche d'information de l'immigration Canadienne* (Ottawa: Ministère de la Main-d'Oeuvre et de l'Immigration, 1974) p. 1-2.

SELECTED REFERENCES

Almeida, Carlos and Barreto, António. *Capitalismo e emigraçao em Portugal.* 2nd ed. Lisboa: Prelo, 1974.

Arnopoulos, Sheila McLeod. *Problèmes des femmes immigrantes sur le marché du travail canadien.* Ottawa: Conseil consultatif canadien de la situation de la femme, 1979.

Baghdjian, Kévork. "Pourquoi voudrait-on que les immigrants soient à jamais 'les autres' parmi nous?" *Le Devoir*, Montreal, 8 juin 1976, p. 5.

Beaupré, Pierre. "Rénovations des Portugals au quartier Saint Louis," *Décormag,* March 1976, Vol. 4, No. 7, pp. 16-20.

Bernier, Bernard. "Main-d'oeuvre féminine et ethnicité dans trois usines de vêtement de Montréal," *Anthropologie et Sociétés,* Vol. 3, No. 2, 1979, pp. 117-139.

Bonacich, Edna. "A Theory of Ethnic Antagonism: The Split Labour Market," *American Sociological Review*, Vol. 37, 1972, pp. 547-559.

Cappon, Paul. *Conflit entre les Néo-Canadiens et les francophones de Montréal.* Québec: Les Presses de l'Université Laval, 1974.

Centre Portugais de Référence et de Promotion Sociale. *Le groupe portugais à Montréal: la situation sociologique, la problématique et les lignes d'intervention.* Montréal, 1976.

Ferreira, Eduardo Sousa. *Origens e formas da emigraçao.* Lisboa: Iniciativas Editoriais, 1976.

Lenormand, Jean-Claude. *Québec-Immigration: Zéro.* Montréal: Les Editions Parti Pris, 1971.

Lima, Joaquim A. Pires de. *A emigraçao portuguesa em França.* Lisboa: Editorial Estampa, 1974.

Loizu, Máximo. *Capitalismo europeo y emigración.* Barcelona: Avance, 1975.

Mvilongo, Anselme *et al. Les Minorités ethniques à Montréal.* Montréal: Bureau de la Consultation Jeunesse, Inc., 1972.

Romao, Isabel. "Le processus de migration, la mobilité professionnelle, la mobilité sociale et l'acculturation chez les ressortissants d'origine portugaise à Montréal." M.A. thesis in Sociology, University of Montreal, 1972.

Serrao, Joel. *A emigraçao portuguesa.* 2nd ed. Lisboa: Livros Horizonte, 1974.

MICHEL LAFERRIÈRE   McGill University

The Education of West Indian and Haitian Students in the Schools of Montreal: Issues and Prospects*

Introduction

Haitians and anglophone West Indians'[1] come from the same geographical area and share several historical and social experiences: their countries were colonies of European powers where a plantation system based on slavery was the dominant mode of production; now independent, these countries retain commercial and/or cultural ties with the *ex-metropole*. Haitians and West Indians are non-White, although their backgrounds vary, and both groups have been migrating to Canada in the last two decades, mostly for economic reasons.

These similarities, however, are offset by differences: Haiti was colonized by France, but has been politically independent since 1804 while the anglophone West Indies were colonized by Britain and, most of them gained their independence recently through a peaceful process. One major difference between the two groups is the dominant language: while all Haitians speak Creole, French is the prestige language of the small dominant group; in the anglophone West Indies, most people speak a "patois"[2] and in a few cases, such as Domenica, a Creole quite close to Haitian Creole, but the dominant language is English.[3]

As immigrants to Quebec, both groups have tended to reproduce the province's linguistic division by sending their children to different schools and by interacting, in most aspects of social life, with the linguistic group which spoke the dominant language of their home country, i.e. French for the Haitians, and English for the West Indians. In education, West Indians have traditionally preferred English public schools, usually Protestant, and sometimes Catholic, while Haitians send their children to the French Catholic public schools.[4]

Recent political and social events in Quebec have led to legislation restricting access to English primary and secondary education and pro-

* Written expressly for *Two Nations, Many Cultures, Ethnic Groups in Canada,* second edition. Data presented in this paper were gathered as part as the Minority Education Research Project, Faculty of Education, McGill University. It is funded by the Direction générale de l'enseignement supérieur, Ministère de l'éducation du Québec, the Fonds F.C.A.C. The views presented here are not necessarily shared by other project members, McGill University, or the Ministère de l'éducation du Québec.

moting French in all areas of social life, including education. In 1974, Bill 22, passed by the predominantly Liberal National Assembly, made French the official language of the province; required that a French text accompany any English public notice; and subjected immigrant children who wanted to enter English schools to a linguistic test, to prove they were really English-speaking. In 1977, Bill 101, passed by an Assembly led by the Parti Québécois, went still further than Bill 22 by making only a French text official in a public notice; preventing linguistic discrimination against francophones in the workplace; requesting that French be the only language used in public signs (except when a specific linguistic group was the target of the sign, in which case French and another language could be used); and sending all children to French schools, except if one of their parents had received his or her primary education in English in Quebec, or if the child was attending an English school or had a sibling in such a school at the time of the passing of the law, or if his or her family were temporarily, i.e. for three years or less, in Quebec (Assemblée Nationale du Québec, 1977). This law, aimed at protecting the French language, attempted to prevent immigrant parents from sending their children to English schools, the schools of the dominant minority group, and it attempted to integrate immigrants into the French system. One could wonder about the present or future impact of language legislation on the Black immigrant groups in the province, particularly in Montreal, where nearly all of them live. Over time, will this legislation tend to solidify them as a community sharing the same racial status and able to communicate in the same language, or will historical, cultural, and class differences be more important? Before speculating on the possible future of Black education in Quebec, this paper will examine the divergent experiences of West Indians and Haitians in the different parts of the Montreal school system.

The History of Black Education

The education of Blacks in Quebec has been defined as a "problem" since the late 1960s (Laferrière, 1976). Until then, most of the Quebec's few Blacks were of Canadian, American, or, more rarely, West Indian backgrounds. Nearly all of them were English-speaking, and most were Protestant. They did not, therefore, create the institutional problems that the children of other immigrant groups, especially the Jews (Kage, 1975), presented in public schools legally based on religious confessionality and *de facto* divided along linguistic lines. The system discriminated against those who were neither Catholic nor Protestant, or who did not speak English or French. Blacks, however, fitted into those categories. As for issues of school achievement and equality of educational opportunities, these issues concern mainly the huge French lower-class population and have only been seriously considered for the last two decades.

In 1975, Black pupils in the Protestant School Board of Greater Montreal (PSBGM) numbered about 4 000 among more than 50 000 anglophones. There were also Black students in the English sectors of several Catholic school commissions, particularly in the Commission des Ecoles Catholiques de Montréal-Montreal Catholic School Commission (CECM-MCSC), but, although exact figures aren't available as no census was ever taken in the Catholic English schools, there could not have been more than a few hundred at most. The Black pupils have been given special attention because of the problems perceived by teachers, and especially by certain groups in the anglophone Black community such as the Quebec Board of Black Educators, the Negro Community Center, or the Black Studies Center. The position of Black Liaison Officer was created in 1969 (along with that of Greek Liaison Officer, for the approximately 6 000 children of Greek origin in the Board). The Liaison Officer serves as a link between the community and the schools, and works with teachers, administrators, social services agencies, and community groups. In 1974, the PSBGM instituted a special committee, the Ad Hoc Committee on Personnel Practices as They Relate to Racial and Minority Peoples' Issues. This committee submitted a report in 1975 recommending that Greek and Black teachers be hired and that ethnic studies be taught. In 1976, the PSBGM created welcoming classes for anglophone immigrants aimed at easing the adaptation of immigrant West Indian children by teaching them standard Canadian English and introducing them to the Canadian school culture. These classes can now only exist in the French sector of the PSBGM as Bill 101 forces immigrant children to attend French schools.[5] Black students who need help, however, may receive assistance under programs for the "disadvantaged" established for schools in the "grey zones" (i.e. poverty areas). They also receive help from programs established by the Black community, such as the Da Costa Hall program.[6]

As far as the francophone school system is concerned, the CECM only acknowledged the presence of francophone Blacks, primarily from Haiti, when it took a census of students and teachers of Haitian origins in its schools in the mid-1970s. Such a census is difficult to establish: while many lower and lower-middle class anglophone Blacks are found in certain districts (for example, the old Saint Antoine "Black neighborhood," which had always been predominantly White in fact, Notre-Dame de Grâce-Walkley, Côte des Neiges-Barclay, and some areas of Ville LaSalle), the Haitians are lost among the francophones of French-Canadian origin. Déjean (1978: 68) estimated that, at the beginning of 1977, there were at least 22 500 Haitians in Quebec, and Pierre-Jacques (1981: 74) guesses that presently there are at least 4 000 Haitian children in Quebec schools. Legal immigration has been sharply reduced, but it is likely that illegal immigration has continued; moreover, families have been reunited and Quebec's Haitian population seems to have a higher birthrate than many other ethnic groups. Some community leaders estimate that there are at least 30 000 Haitians in Quebec, including 6 000 school-age children. Haitian children, however, are lost among the numerous White French children, close to 140 000, that the major French school board, the CECM, serves. A number of Haitian students are also found in the Jerôme Le Royer School Commission, which serves Montréal's north end.

The CECM has only recently begun paying attention to its Haitian students. In 1977, a report (the Ravary Report) noted that among the 1 800 Haitian students the various school administrations reported on, 56 percent were one year late in their studies and 27 percent more than one year late; i.e. 83 percent were not at the normal school-age for their grade. It is likely that this report under-represented the total Haitian school population, since the isolated or "no-problem" children were often left out, as were the children in other school commissions or in private schools. Since 1977, Haitian students have been an object of concern principally for Haitian community organizations. Two main organizations, the Bureau de la Communauté Chrétienne des Haitiens de Montréal (BCCHM) and the Maison d'Haiti, provide various social services for the community and represent its interests. In education, they have created compensatory programs, and programs on Haiti and in Creole to teach children about their cultural heritage. The BCCHM also created the Centre haitien d'information et d'orientation scolaire (CHOIS) to test, place, and counsel Haitian students. These bodies serve as links with the school commissions. Social services agencies, have begun to offer the services of a few Haitian social workers. Research on Haitian immigrants is underway, particularly at the Centre de Recherches Caribes of the Université de Montréal and at the McGill Minority Education Research Project.

One should stress, however, that in the French school commissions, teachers have not been trained to deal with racial and cultural diversity since, until the last few years, the schools' population was culturally homogenous. Even teachers in the "class d'accueil," the "welcoming classes," have been trained in second-language teaching, but have little, if any, knowledge of the social and cultural characteristics of students with immigrant backgrounds. In fact, up until the last few years, Haitian students were classified as francophones and could not be admitted to the welcoming classes; they can, now, but do present specific problems to be examined below because of some similarities between French and their mother tongue, Creole, and because of the dominant social status of French. It seems that the *classe d'accueil* teachers, their administrators, or the professors preparing them[7] have little notion of the overall situation.

Haitian children also may benefit from the compensatory education program "Operation Renouveau," launched by the CECM in 1970, and by other types of inner-city intervention programs subsidized since 1975 by the newly-created School Council of the Island of Montreal.[8] One should emphasize, however, that "inner-city" and "disadvantaged" are not, in Montreal, euphemisms for Blacks, as they are in many school systems in the

Northeastern United States. For the CECM, nearly all of the "disadvantaged" are poor French-Canadians, and for the PSBGM, they are usually children of immigrant origins in schools where Blacks very rarely constitute more than 50 percent of the student body. Consequently, these programs are not adapted to some of the specific characteristics of the Haitians or the West Indians.

Why was there no educational problem for Blacks in Quebec schools up until recent years? One reason may have been that teachers and school administrators were insensitive to students' needs and, because of racist feelings, did not feel they could succeed. In interviews conducted with Blacks who received part or all of their education in Quebec before the 1960s, most stressed that teachers and students were rarely racist, that the major problems encountered were outside the school – discrimination in the workplace was common, for example. In contrast, adolescents interviewed in 1978 reported racism and discrimination in their school experience more often. Educational problems of Blacks in Quebec also have been defined first in the anglophone Black community because that group not only was much more numerous than the Haitian community, and still is, numbering nearly 80 000 people, although their exact number is not known (Winks, 1971: 484-496)[9], but also because that group had long-established, active community organizations and groups and individuals who acted as "social problem definers," to adopt one of the paradigms of the sociology of social problems (Spector and Kitsuse, 1977). Research on Black education in English, coming from the U.S., Britain, and, in Canada, Ontario and Nova Scotia, was also available. In contrast, Haitian immigration to Quebec is more recent and has undergone drastic changes: while in 1968, 71 percent of Haitian immigrants were independent immigrants, in 1976 this group represented less than 25 percent, the others being nominated or sponsored immigrants; while in the early 1970s immigrants were equally divided between while-collar and blue-collar workers, as of 1974 blue-collars outnumbered white-collars 2 to 1; and while in 1976, 82 percent of the Haitians had less than 13 years of education, 10 years before, most had had professional training (Déjean, 1978). Thus Haitian immigration changed from one of educated, professional, and semi-professional people, often escaping their country for political reasons, to an immigration of much less educated working-class people, fleeing mostly for economic reasons.[10] Haitian professionals offered their children educational advantages, such as an intellectual environment, educational help, and the opportunity to attend excellent French private schools; because of family and class background, these students as a group had no educational problems. Newly arrived lower-class Haitians, on the other hand, encountered problems due to their race, social class, and immigrant status, which were compounded by the fact that they could only attend lower-class public schools in depressed areas.

I shall now examine some of the specific problems Haitian students encounter, and compare them with the situation of anglophone West Indian children.

Educational Problems of Black Students

Different sources of data can be tapped to present the educational problems of Black students in Quebec: we interviewed teachers, administrators, students themselves, and community leaders and activists. More recently, publications have also dealt with that issue (Déjean, 1978; Pierre-Jacques, 1981 and Pierre-Jacques, ed., 1982; Dehoux-Tardieu, 1979; Hayes, 1979, for instance), as have some community briefs (Groupe de Travail sur l'Education de la Communauté Noire, 1978). These problems may be grouped under three general headings: linguistic problems, social and cultural problems, and racial issues.

1. Linguistic problems

Practically all Haitian-born students raised in Haiti, and nearly all of those born outside, speak and understand Creole. It is difficult to define Creole in general, but it can be considered as a language comprising elements of the European lexicon in a syntaxical pattern of African origin. Creole is often denigrated as if it were a European language poorly spoken. This commonly held view has been criticized by linguists, who have shown that Creole is a language with its own lexicon and syntax. It is not scientifically accepted that a whole cultural group uses, as a means of socialization and communication, a "poor" language. Thorough research on Creole, such as Hymes' (1971) or, specifically, Pompilus' (1973), Valdman's (1970), or Déjean's (1980) for Haitian Creole, coupled with actions by Haitian intellectuals and, recently, by the Haitian government, have enchanced its status: thus, for instance, Creole is becoming the language of instruction for the early grades of public education in Haiti (République d'Haiti, Département de l'éducation nationale, 1982). Anglophone West Indians also often speak a patois, which is in fact a language but is not in the process of gaining recognition as Haitian Creole is. The anglophone West Indies have been independent for only a short time; their educational system is patterned on Britain's, and the colonizer's language is still very dominant. Moreover, anglophone West Indians usually understand, and very often speak, a form of standard West Indian English which differs from international or British English much less than Creole does from French. Education is also much more prevalent in the formerly British West Indies than it is in Haiti, and the school served as a way of denigrating, and sometimes eliminating, the local patois in the West Indies as in many other societies.

Without denigrating Creole, one should note that creolophones encounter specific educational problems in Canadian schools (Domingue et Laferrière, 1978; Alleyne, 1976). Craig (1971) has distinguished four categories of creolophone comprehension with reference to the colonial or dominant European language:

(a) The creolophones are able to understand and utilize the dominant language.

(b) The creolophones are able to understand the dominant language but will only use it when forced. They have learned the language through contact with the mass media and through contact with those who speak the dominant language but they do not customarily speak it.

(c) The creolophones have a passive knowledge of the dominant language. They are able to understand it in a general sense, but are unable to express themselves.

(d) The creolophones have no knowledge of the dominant language.

In Haiti, most of the peasants would fall in category (d); the masses of Port au Prince, the capital city, in (c). The middle class mostly in (b); and the intellectual middle class and the upper class would fall in category (a), i.e., complete fluency in both languages. While a knowledge of French usually indicates upper class membership, the upper class also knows Creole (Valdman, 1968).

What are the consequences of the above for the Haitians in Montreal? First, Haitian pupils were, until recently, considered to be francophones, while in fact, the only true francophones in category (a) comprise a very small fraction of the total Haitian population (less than 5 percent). Because of the changes in immigration patterns, most Haitians in Montreal now fall into categories (b), (c), and (d). In the last few years, some school systems have been testing the Haitian students' abilities in French and have put those who needed it in "classes d'accueil" to teach them French. This has met with opposition from some administrators, because of the costs involved, and also from some Haitian students who would not admit that they do not speak French fluently, since it would mean admitting lowly social standing in a society which is very class- and color-conscious. The classes d'accueil are also geared towards the teaching of French as a second language, and not as a second dialect, and specific methods and contents should be devised for creolophones, since their lexicon has much in common with French.

When young Haitians go to a Quebec school, regardless of how well they speak French, they see Creole, i.e., their mother tongue in most cases, disparaged. One student told me, for instance, that he was forbidden to "speak Black" by one of his Québécois teachers. Young Haitians frequently take refuge among their fellow Haitians and speak Creole. This behavior is often viewed as defiance by teachers and administrators, and the Haitian students are suspected of making fun of their teachers and Québécois friends. It seems that many Québécois of different ethnic backgrounds should be taught languages other than their own, be they one of the two official languages or one of the unofficial languages. Languages have their own value and should be considered as a source of enrichment. Moreover, the often denigrated Creole has become, for many Haitian nationalists, the essence of Haitian culture and a mother tongue to be proud of (Mathelier, 1976), especially while encountering the hardships of migration.

Finally, some young Haitians consider the French spoken by the Québécois difficult for them to understand because of the accent, vocabulary, and syntax. Some Québécois speak a French which has evolved since the British conquest, and some Montrealers speak a French which is influenced by English. (See, for instance, Corbeil and Guilbert, eds, 1976; *Cahier de linguistique* No 6, 1976). Some (Wittman, 1974) have debated whether "joual," the lower-class dialect of French spoken in Eastern Montreal, could be considered a Creole born from the contact between a dominated French dialect and a dominant English language. These difficulties in mutual comprehension often may be real, and they also provide young Haitians with an opportunity to criticize the dominant White group they are in contact with, and to show that the Québécois, too, do not speak the prestigious "standard" French.

It would seem that an educational effort could be undertaken to show students in both the minority and the majority groups that Creole, just as the French spoken in different parts of Quebec, is a language of integrity. There is a Haitian literature in French as well as in Creole. Similarly, while some Quebec French writers use standard international French, most use a language closely resembling that labeled standard Québécois French, but only a minority attempts to transcribe the popular language, joual. It is interesting to note that, particularly in the last 20 years, group pride for both Haitians and French Québécois has relied on a rehabilitation of their real mother tongue. It seems that this commonality, the reappropriation of a beleaguered mother tongue, as well as contributions from literature, linguistics, and socio-linguistics could play a modest but effective role in furthering transcultural understanding.

Anglophone West Indians have suffered from similar difficulties: children often are said to speak a poor, ungrammatical English, and are frequently classified as linguistically, socially, and culturally deprived. It seems that the patois they speak is closer to standard Canadian English and the problems they face may be less acute. Some individual teachers, however, have been trying approaches dealing with bi-dialectalism which have been used in the U.S. for Black English or in Britain for West Indian children. Black community organizations have also stressed the Black and West Indian heritage to their youth[11]; some schools and some groups have introduced courses on West Indian and/or Black literature, but always in standard English. Perhaps because of the domination of British education in the West Indies and, until recently, in Canada, it seems that the patois is seen more as a hinderance to educational success than as a valuable means of communication and symbol of group identity.

2. Social and Cultural Problems

Young immigrant Haitians and West Indians encounter a school system in Quebec which is very different from the one they may have experienced in their home country. The Haitian case is perhaps the more striking. In Haiti, education is a privilege. As recently as 1950, over 90 percent of the population was illiterate (Moore, 1972). Only the good private schools for the wealthy provide a quality education. Thus, many students who emigrate to Quebec have incomplete schooling; indeed, many adolescents are unable to read and write at all when they arrive, and it is impossible to place them in classes that would correspond with their age. Their parents, often barely literate themselves, cannot help them either (Pierre-Jacques, ed., 1982). While poor anglophone West Indians usually have a better educational level than poor Haitians, they are still not able to provide their children with much continuous intellectual support. For this last group, parental concerns can also have detrimental effects. For example, parents often leave their children behind in the West Indies so that they can be better cared for when small, and only have them come to Canada to start high school as Canadian secondary public schools are free and better than many West Indian schools. Unfortunately, this total uprooting compounds the inevitable difficulties of puberty for the youngsters having to make the difficult adjustment to a strange, cold, White society.

Even when they are not scholastically behind their age peers, Haitians and West Indians find themselves in schools vastly different from their native milieu. In both Haiti and the West Indies, teachers have total authority: they dictate the courses to be studied, are to be addressed only after they authorize the student to do so, and may use physical punishment. In contrast, Quebec schools must seem like anarchy. Following the Parent report, the structures and cultures of education in Quebec were greatly changed, a modified version of the philosophical outlook of progressive education was adopted, and schools now favor student participation and individual autonomy.

The curriculum and teaching methods in Quebec are also very different from Haiti or the West Indies. In the islands, a good student obeys and learns the lessons by heart; examinations are designed to show how well students have memorized their lessons. For the Québécois teacher, anglophone or francophone, this is not a creative approach to learning.

Course content differs as well. Technical and vocational education is rarely offered and education serves the function of status maintenance for the elite and social mobility for a select few from the middle class. Professional studies, particularly in law and medicine, are favored. Students wishing to undertake courses in other fields must usually leave their home countries to obtain them. All in all, education in the West Indies consolidates the position of dominant families and does little to contribute to the country's economic development (Chancy, 1972, for Haiti). This is in sharp contrast with Quebec, where education is seen as preparing students for the world of work and where the ideology of equal opportunity and education for all prevails.

Young Haitians or West Indians are often unable to participate in school because they do not understand well what is being said, or what the rules of the educational game are. Therefore, they appear dull and lacking in intelligence and motivation to their Québécois teachers. To the students, the teachers appear undignified and not very respectable. As for the parents, they are often seen by teachers and administrators as not interested in participating in the life of the school. There are several reasons for the absence of parental participation. First, parents are not required to participate in the life of the school in their countries of origin; on the contrary, the teacher has the authority. Second, some parents do not wish to be noticed: they may be illegal immigrants or, and this applies to particularly Haitians, they have suffered for expressing their ideas under an authoritarian and repressive regime. Third, some West Indian and Haitian adults have accepted and internalized an educational system in which those in positions of authority have complete control; they have blind confidence in the teacher and would consider it rude to question his or her educational competence. Finally, some parents may feel intimidated by a middle-class teacher, when they themselves are uneducated, speak poor French, or a different dialect of English.

A last point, the children can identify with little in their textbooks. Some anglophone teachers have been trying to introduce West Indian material or Black studies courses, but very few French teachers have done so. The introduction of such material is not easy, since it should be non-stereotypical, and give an accurate, diversified, and non-"folkloric" view of the group (Laferrière, 1982, for instance). One could mention here the attempts made by the New York City and New York State Boards of Education to use elements of the Haitian culture in schools with a bilingual Creole-English or French-English program, attended by a significant number of Haitian students. For example, *vévés* (traditional figures drawn during Voodoo ceremonies, usually familiar to the students) were used to teach geometry (because of their symmetry), art, and religion.

3. Racial Issues

Black students in Montreal schools often encounter covert, and sometimes overt, racism, although this has been denied. (Quebec is contrasted with the U.S. or Ontario as having few racial problems.) Examples of discrimination in the past (Winks, 1971, for instance) and more recent incidents, such as racial tensions in the taxi business in 1982 and the beating of Haitian youths by the Montreal police in 1979, are evidence to the contrary. In the early 1970s, racial fights in some anglophone lower-class schools were reported but these seem to have ceased. In French Catholic schools, "foreigners" and "immigrants" had been traditionally absent and the schools had been homogenous – obviously, new Haitian students are then particularly noticeable. They are the only Black students in the system and the few Black teachers often do not teach them.

Several actors in the system are not prepared to properly help and educate the Black students. First, the school frequently reflects some of the attitudes of the larger society. There exist anti-immigrant feelings among French Québécois, since immigrants are seen as *voleux de jobs* (job snatchers) and English upper-management very often used anglicized people of immigrant backgrounds as middle-level managers of French-Canadian workers. This view of immigrants as allies of the English reinforced feelings against them. This only partly applies to Haitians, as they are often perceived as French-speaking and live in French neighborhoods, but it does apply in the larger society to West Indians who are seen as anglophones. Haitians, however, may have a very ambivalent attitude toward White society. On the one hand, they know they are in a foreign country and may be fearful of racism; on the other hand, the foreign element in Haiti was White, and skin color has always been important in the social stratification system in Haiti, in addition to social class of origin and education. Perhaps more than in the anglophone West Indies, light skin is favored over dark in Haiti, and offers an avenue for prestige and mobility (Labelle, 1978), although this may be changing today. These feelings of ambivalence will no doubt be modified by the length of time the Haitians live in Quebec. It should be stressed that my research revealed that Haitian and West Indian students rarely express anti-White attitudes associated with the more militant American Blacks, although Black American culture is rapidly penetrating the lives of Haitian migrants through the Quebec media, U.S. influence in Haiti itself, and more frequent contact with Haitians in the U.S., the principal country of immigration. In the late '60s, the most militant among West Indians adopted a Black Power ideology, and also answered racism through mass protest, as the occupation of Sir George Williams University in 1969 illustrates (Tunteng, 1973; Forsythe, ed., 1971). However, it seems that in the last decade the community tackled issues of racism in a more indirect way or used the Quebec Human Rights Commission.

It should be noted that little is known about the real state of race relations in Quebec schools. While racism is often denied, one cannot help noticing that Haitian or West Indian students often congregate and that few spontaneous groupings are integrated racially. It is also interesting to note that little, if any, research is being done on the subject, most likely because it could be seen as socially explosive, and that few programs are instituted in the schools or in faculties of education to attempt to alleviate eventual problems, although some government agencies provide guidelines (Gouvernement du Québec, 1978).

Racism in the schools may not be an intentional effort by individuals or groups, but may be linked to the organization and the practices of the institution itself. For instance, testing, especially IQ testing, often discriminates against poor or culturally different children. Haitians and West Indians frequently fall in these two categories and may be given tests which do not correspond to their previous educational and social experiences. When these evaluation procedures are followed, students are often placed in sections and classes which do not correspond to their actual potential. No studies comparable to Samuda's (1975) for the U.S. and Samuda and Crawford's (1980) for Ontario are found in Quebec. It should be noted, however, that teachers and administrators often refuse to use testing, particularly in the French sector among politically and socially conscious professionals.

Finally, some practices are seen as racist although they may not be so intentionally. Haitian students who arrive in Quebec with a poor educational attainment level often have high educational aspirations. Because of their age and their poor previous education, they cannot be placed in the grade where they should be, and are placed in "easy" programs, such as short vocational ones. These programs do not give access to higher education, and the placement is then seen by parents and students as discrimination. Parents sometimes do not even realize their children have been placed in such programs, since these are labelled in French "professionnel court," which the parents associate with "professionnel", i.e., professional. These discrepancies between parents' and students' aspirations and between the opportunities offered by the educational system often accentuate the maladjustment of the students and their families. The educational system could provide special programs aimed at illiterate young adults and special continuing education programs, but these are virtually non-existent.

Conclusion

Haitian and anglophone West Indians experience similar problems due to their race, dialect, and immigrant status. Since the passing of Bill 101, anglophone West Indians also have to send their children to French schools; this measure often has been perceived by immigrant parents as discriminatory, and West Indians are no exception, although many do now accept that French will be more and more necessary to reside, and especially to work, in Quebec. One wonders if the future commonality in language, with both groups speaking French, will increase communication between the two communities. While contact may be increased, the relationship to the French language will probably be quite different. For West Indians, as for other anglophones, the French language will be seen as merely instrumental; their affective and cultural ties will be with the English group and with their own group. The relationship of Haitians to the French language, however, is much more complicated, and is often a love-hate affair. French is the dominant language in Haiti, socially and culturally. A part of the intellectual elite wants to rehabilitate Creole, but at the same time speaks French fluently and has been educated in the francophone tradition. Most of Haitian literature is still written in French, and works from the *francophonie*, especially from France, the French Antilles and francophone West Africa, are particularly appreciated by Haitian intellectuals. Whether one looks at the writing of Roumain, Senghor, or Fanon, one finds closer ties to French Marxist, existentialist, or phenomenological thought than to Carmichael's and Hamilton's views of Black Power.

Even if anglophone Blacks come to speak French in school and at work, it is likely that their social and intellectual life will continue in English, as they usually live in English areas, read the English press and tune in to the other English media. They now rarely come into contact with francophones, Black or White; by the same token, Haitians also rarely come into contact with anglophones. I suspect the situation will remain as it is at present, unless racial relations in Montreal take a dramatic turn and Blacks have to unite to fight discrimination, putting aside linguistic and cultural differences.

END NOTES

1. For the sake of brevity, I shall label anglophone West Indians as "West Indians," although Haitians also come from the same geographical and cultural area, the Caribbean or West Indies.
2. The term "patois" is used in the English West Indies. In French, the term has a pejorative connotation and describes local dialects of French, usually spoken by peasants. Because of a return to local and regional cultures, patois are now often being rehabilitated.
3. This information was provided by Dr. Dorothy Wills, a prominent figure in the Montreal anglophone Black community. Dr. Wills, whose mother tongue is Dominican Creole, told me that she could perfectly understand speeches in Haitian Creole, but not all speeches in French.
4. For historical reasons, public education in Quebec has a confessional basis: most public schools are either Catholic or Protestant, following Article 93 of the British North America Act. These schools are also divided along linguistic lines.
5. The French sector of the PSBGM has recently expanded. Protestant schools have grouped children from several religious faiths for several decades.
6. Da Costa is said to have been the first Black to arrive in Canada. He was Samuel de Champlain's interpreter and spoke several Indian languages.
7. In the last two years, the School Council of the Island of Montreal has prepared small booklets describing different immigrant groups one of which includes a description of the characteristics and problems of Haitian students. The *classe d'accueil* teachers are trained at the Université du Québec à Montréal where there are very few foreign students or students from ethnic minority groups.
8. This body was created in 1975 as a "super" school commission. It groups the several school boards found on the Island of Montreal. Its mandate is to prepare

a restructuring of education on the island, and to prepare budgets and distribute money for special compensatory education programs in poor areas.

9. Winks has an interesting appendix on the problem of counting Blacks in Canada. The category "Negro-Nègre" did not always appear in the census, and Blacks could be found in diverse categories such as "Canadian," "American," "West Indian," "British," etc., according to their birth places. Winks' comments are still valid, but one should also add that some immigrants are in Canada illegally and attempt to avoid census takers.

10. Of course, the distinction between political and economic reasons is partly fallacious, since the dismal economic state of Haitian society is partly due to its social and political regime.

11. For instance, the Negro Community Center since the 1920s and especially the Black Studies Center since the late 1960s have had programs of that kind.

SELECTED REFERENCES

Alleyne, Mervin C. "Dimensions and Varieties of West Indian English and the Implications for Teaching," *T.E.S.L. Talk*, Special Issue on Black Students in Urban Canada: 35-62, 1976.

Assemblée Nationale du Québec. Trente et unième législature, deuxième session. *Projet de loi no 101. Charte de la langue française*. Québec: Editeur officiel du Québec, 1977.

Craig, Dennis. "Education and Creole English in the West Indies: Some Sociolinguistic Factors," in Dell Hymes, ed., *Pidginization and Creolization of Languages*. New York: Cambridge University Press: 371-392, 1971.

Cahier de Linguistique. *La sociolinguistique au Québec*. Cahier No 6. Montréal: Les Presses de l'Université du Québec, 1976.

Corbeil, Jean-Claude et Louis Guilbert. "Le français au Québec." *Langue française*, volume 31, septembre, 1976.

Dehoux-Tardieu, Charles. "L'évaluation et l'orientation des étudiants immigrants haitiens à Montréal," Montréal: Thesis in the Department of Education, Educational Technology, Concordia University, 1979.

Déjean, Paul. *Les Haitiens au Québec*. Montréal: les presses de l'Université du Québec, 1978.

Déjean, Yves. *Comment écrire le créole d'Haiti*. Outremont: Collectif Paroles, 1980.

Domingue, Nicole et Michel Laferrière. "Créole Speakers and Education," *McGill Journal of Education*, XIII, 2: 166-174, 1978.

Forsythe, Dennis, ed. *Let the Niggers Burn. The Sir George Williams University Affair and Its Caribbean Aftermath*. Montreal: Black Rose Books, 1971.

Groupe de Travail sur l'Education de la Communauté Noire. "Rapport final des aspirations et attentes de la communauté noire du Québec par rapport à l'éducation," soumis au Comité d'étude sur les Affaires Interconfessionnelles et Interculturelles du Conseil supérieur de l'éducation, 1978.

Gouvernement du Québec. Conseil supérieur de l'éducation. Comité catholique. *Dans ce pays*. A l'école catholique l'accueil des enfants de traditions religieuses et culturelles diverses. Québec: Ministère de l'éducation, 1978.

Hayes, Victor A. "Social and Educational Adjustment of West Indian Students in a Montreal High School," M.A. thesis, Social Foundations of Education, McGill University, 1979.

Hymes, Dell, ed. *Pidginization and Creolization of Languages.* Cambridge: Cambridge University Press, 1971.

Labelle, Micheline. *Idéologie de couleur et classes sociales en Haiti.* Montréal: les Presses de l'Université de Montréal, 1978.

Laferrière, Michel. "Lecture et situation minoritaire," *Lecture Jeunesse* (Paris), janvier, 21: 2-9, 1982.

Mathelier, Georges. *Pédagogie et Bilinguisme en Haiti.* Thése de Doctorat, Faculté des Lettres, Université de Fribourg (Switzerland), 1976.

Moore, Ernest O. *Haiti: Its Stagnant Society and Shackled Economy.* Jericho, N.Y.: Exposition Press, 1972.

Pierre-Jacques, Charles. *Le jeune haitien et l'école québécoise.* Montréal: Centre de Recherches Caraibes, Université de Montréal, 1981.

Pierre-Jacques, Charles, sous la direction de *Enfant de migrants haitiens en Amérique du Nord.* Montréal: Centre de Recherches Caraibes, Université de Montréal, 1982.

Pompilus, Pradel. *Contribution à l'étude comparée du créole et du français à partir du créole haitien. Phonologie et lexicologie.* Port au Prince: Editions Caraibes, 1973.

République d'Haiti. Départment de l'éducation nationale. *La réforme éducative. Elements d'Information.* Port au Prince: Comité de curriculum, Institut Pédagogique National, Direction de la Planification, 1982.

Samuda, Ronald J. *Psychological Testing of American Minorities: Issues and Consequences.* New York: Dodd, Mead and Company, 1975.

Samuda, Ronald J. and Douglas H. Crawford. *Testing, Assessment, Counselling and Placement of Ethnic Minority Students. Current Methods in Ontario.* Toronto: Ministry of Education, 1980.

Spector, Malcolm and Kitsuse, John. *Constructing Social Problems.* Menlo Park, Calif.: Benjamin-Cummins, 1977.

Tunteng, P. Kiven. "Racism and the Montréal Computer Incident," *Race*, XIV, 3: 229-240, 1973.

Valdman, Albert. "The Language Situation in Haiti," in Schaedel, R., ed., *Research Resources in Haiti.* New York: Institute for Modern Man: L55-203, 1968.

Valdman, Albert. *Basic Course in Haitian Creole.* Bloomington, Indiana: Indiana University Publications, Language Science Monographs, 1970.

Winks, Robin W. *The Blacks in Canada.* Montreal: McGill-Queen's University Press and New Haven, Conn.: Yale University Press, 1971.

Wittman, Henri. "Le joual, c'est-tu un créole?" *La linguistique*, 9,2: 83-93, 1974.

Francophones Outside Quebec: The Official Minority

DANIELLE JUTEAU-LEE University of Montreal
JEAN LAPOINTE University of Ottawa

From French Canadians to Franco-Ontarians and Ontarois: New Boundaries, New Identities*

In recent years, both insiders and outsiders have increasingly used the term "Franco-Ontarian" rather than "French Canadian" in referring to the French community living in Ontario. Since 1980, yet a newer term has emerged as members of the community began to call themselves *"Ontarois."* These new appellations reflect the changes presently affecting the collective identity of the community. In exploring this new identity phenomenon, a case will be made that the identity of an ethnic community is conditioned by its boundaries and that fluctuations in the boundaries of such a community bring about changes in its collective identity.

This analysis, which focuses on the French community in Ontario, will examine the criteria that define the boundaries of an ethnic group, identify the factors responsible for their fluctuation and determine the impact of such fluctuations on changes in collective identity. Some attention will be given to the type of people most susceptible to acquiring this new identity.

Ethnic Boundaries

Existing definitions of the concept "ethnic group" are numerous, contradictory, and often confusing. In discussing this problem, Vallee (1975: 162-202) has suggested an approach that will be retained in this analysis. The distinction he makes between ethnicity and ethnic group is crucial:

> . . . ethnicity refers to descent from ancestors who shared a common culture or subculture manifested in distinctive ways of speaking and/or acting. This common culture may have been carried by many different kinds of grouping, such as

---

* Revised version (by Danielle Juteau-Lee) of "The Emergence of Franco-Ontarians: New Identity, New Boundaries," in *Two Nations, Many Cultures: Ethnic Groups in Canada,* first edition.

religious, political, geographical, but in all cases the kinship networks are crucial bearers of the culture (Vallee, 1975: 165-166).

Thus we say that an ethnic group is made up of people who share ethnicity (as previously defined), who share some sense of peoplehood or consciousness of kind, who interact with one another in meaningful ways beyond the elementary family, and who are regarded by others as being in the one ethnic category (Vallee, 1975: 167).

Ethnicity thus constitutes the main factor of inclusion/exclusion. When it leads to the emergence of an ethnic group, this group can be examined in terms of its existing system of interaction. A distinct system of interaction implies the presence of cultural and structural factors which define boundaries sharply enough to differentiate the group from surrounding collectivities.

Cultural factors are the cognitive, expressive, and evaluative dimensions of ethnicity and include, among others, religion, language, and lifestyle. They refer mainly to the content of the system. Structural factors pertain to those institutions which embody culture.

Ethnic communities with parallel and compartmentalized sets of institutions are characterized by structural pluralism (van den Berghe, 1967: 34). In other words, the level of structural pluralism can be determined from the number and type of parallel institutions – educational, religious, economic, and political. By examining the institutional completeness and the organizational capacity of an ethnic community (Breton, 1964: 1974), it is possible to determine its level of enclosure. The meaningful interaction referred to by Vallee can be studied in terms of the structural criteria outlined here.

Communities based on ethnicity, therefore, can be classified on a continuum ranging from ethnic groups that possess a few voluntary associations to nation-states where there is a complete congruence between cultural and structural factors. Although these factors are empirically interwoven, they are analytically distinguishable and mutually irreducible. It follows that the goal of survival, which can be defined as the maintenance of distinct boundaries (Juteau-Lee, 1974), can be understood in terms of the maintenance of cultural and/or of structural boundaries. Finally, an ethnic group has a subjective dimension which consists of a common identity, a feeling of solidarity, loyalty, belongingness, and "we-ness." Because this collective identity is conditioned by the boundaries of the system, there exists an identity which is predominantly cultural and an identity which is predominantly structural.

The transition from a French-Canadian to a Franco-Ontarian identity must be examined in terms of changes in group boundaries that fluctuate over time (Barth, 1969) and in many ways. Horowitz differentiates between the processes of ethnic fusion (where boundaries between one group and another are erased) and ethnic fission (where boundaries are narrowed by the creation of additional groups). In the first case, which is a process of assimilation, fusion may take the form of amalgamation, where "two or more groups may unite to form a new group, larger and different from any of the component parts" (Horowitz, 1975: 115); or it may take the form of incorporation, where "one group may lose its identity by merging into another group which retains its identity" (Horowitz, 1975: 115). In the second case, which is a process of differentiation, fission may take the form of proliferation, where "a new group comes into existence without its 'parent group' losing its identity" (Horowitz, 1975: 115); or that of division, when a group separates into its component parts. The process examined here corresponds to differentiation-division. The French-Canadian nation is separating into component parts, namely Québécois, Franco-Ontarians, Franco-Manitobans, Acadians, and so on. When one talks of French-Canadians, the criteria emphasized are *cultural*, such as language, religion, and life style, and they separate the French from the English. When one talks about the Québécois, Franco-Ontarians, Franco-Manitobans, it is the *structural* criteria underlying group boundaries which are emphasized. They outline different institutional spheres and refer to different territories and states.

The identity of an ethnic community is inseparable from its boundaries, and changes in this identity can only be understood in terms of changes in its boundaries. Two main sets of factors are responsible for the fluctuations in the boundaries of the French-Canadian collectivity in Ontario: (1) the emergence of a Québécois nation-community (the external factor) that has modified the relations between the French of both provinces; and (2) the industrialization and urbanization of the French collectivity in Ontario (the internal factors) that have modified its former means of maintaining boundaries. Because Franco-Ontarians pursue the goal of boundary-maintenance, they will tend to choose means better suited to achieve this goal and will emphasize mainly the criteria which delineate the sharpest boundaries.

Changing Boundaries of the Collectivity

The Collectivity

By 1971, the population of French origin (ethnicity) in Ontario had reached 737 360 (Census of Canada, 1971, Bulletin 1 3-2), and constituted 9.6 percent of the total population in that province. It is unevenly distributed within the province; the most important cluster can be found in the Ottawa-Carleton area where there are 117 465 people of French origin (Census of Canada, 1971, Bulletin 1. 3-2, Table 4). There are also many smaller centers in the North and in the East which are predominantly French. The lowest concentrations of French are found in the South; in spite of their relatively

TABLE 1   *Distribution of those of French mother tongue, by selected regions in Ontario, 1976*

Region	Total population	French mother tongue	
		Number	%
North East	583 725	157 780	33.3
North West	233 390	9 150	2.0
East	1 149 265	175 330	37.9
Center	5 050 830	87 245	18.9
South West	1 247 140	36 685	7.9
Ontario	8 264 350	462 190	100

Source: "Les Franco-Ontariens," Conseil des Affaires franco-ontariennes, p. 1.

large numbers, the proportion of French is lower since they are scattered in heavily populated areas. This pattern has previously been described by Joy (1972) who referred to it as the bilingual belt.

Although certain settlements were established at the beginning of the 18th century in Essex County, most communities were set up during the last century by immigrants from Quebec. Because of population pressures on the land, many Québécois settled in Ontario, along the railroad tracks that were being built, in pulp and paper areas such as Hawkesbury and Sturgeon Falls, and eventually in mine towns such as Timmins. By 1971, 22.3 percent of the population of French mother tongue residing in Ontario was born in Quebec (FFHQ, 1977: 30).

The goal of survival (boundary-maintenance) was also a predominant one for the French in Ontario. The emphasis was on maintaining linguistic and cultural patterns, and the church played a major role in attaining this goal. The school system was also crucial to the survival of the collectivity, and most of the battles fought by the French community centered around the establishment of French instruction in the province. Regulation 17 in 1912 barred the francophones from receiving a primary education in their own language. Although this regulation was modified in 1927, it was not until 1968 (Jackson, 1975: 31) that the Ontario Legislature officially recognized the existing primary schools and allowed for the establishment of French Language Secondary Schools. Language represents one of the major criterion delineating boundaries, and the capacity of the group to resist linguistic assimilation indicates its vitality. This capacity, as indicated in Table 1, varies in different areas. Obviously, both the absolute and relative numbers of francophones influence the collectivity's capacity to establish the structural basis (meaningful interactions which extend beyond the elementary family) which is essential for boundary-maintenance. Of course, the capacity of a group to maintain boundaries is also determined by the overall political, legal, and constitutional framework within which it operates.

Boundary Changes

A transformation in the group boundary criteria has brought about a fluctuation in group boundaries and a change of emphasis from cultural to structural factors. The emergence of a Québécois collectivity and the changes in the social organization of the French collectivity in Ontario constitute the two main factors responsible for this transformation. This boundary change process has been reinforced by the dynamic relationship between the French and English in Canada.

Industrialization, urbanization, and political modernization are mainly responsible for the emergence of a Québécois collectivity (Juteau-Lee, 1974; 1978: 10). French Canadians were French in ancestry, spoke French, adhered to Catholicism and lived mostly on farms. Cultural factors were emphasized in the definition of group boundaries and were the main basis of identification until the advent of industrialization. Industrialization diminished the importance of religion (decrease in religious practice and in the size of the clergy, secularization of norms and values), accelerated urbanization, and modified the occupational structure. These trends led to the erosion of the main components of the French-Canadian social structure as well as of the former basis of "we-feeling", group-sentiment, and belongingness (Juteau-Lee, 1974: 170-74). The gradual disappearance of the boundaries underlying identification is responsible for the collective identity crisis examined by many authors (Bellah, 1970; Eisenstadt, 1966; Rioux, 1969; Smelser, 1968), Although ethnicity remains, the criteria which serve as the basis of this community weaken and are replaced by new ones.

Political modernization is a criterion which will serve as a new basis for defining group boundaries and solidarity. This process corresponds to the growing scope and intensification of the power of the central, legal, and administrative agencies of the society (Eisenstadt, 1966: 4). First, the more active role of the state in provincial matters increases the importance of territoriality, since by definition, a state has jurisdiction over certain boundaries. Since political modernization also involves the penetration of the provincial level of government into local and regional sectors, it modifies institutional boundaries and sensitizes the overall population to such changes. Second, political modernization increases the emphasis on self-steering because it brings about the institutionalization of change. As a result, survival (i.e., boundary-maintenance) is no longer defined in terms of maintaining existing patterns, as the emphasis shifts to the capacity of controlling internal functioning in terms of existing goals and resources (Juteau-Lee, 1974: 130). As industrialization and urbanization eroded the criteria underlying group boundaries, political modernizaton supplied new ones by increasing the salience of the territorial basis of *l'Etat du Québec* and of the collectivity it governed. Consequently, the basis and boundaries of the collectivity were transformed.

TABLE 2 *Distribution of rural-urban population, for French mother tongue and Ontario as a whole, 1971*

Ontario	% Urban	% Rural		Total
		Non-farm	Farm	
French mother tongue	76.6%	18.9%	4.5%	100
Total population	82.4%	12.9%	4.7%	100

Source: Adapted from FFHQ, 1977: 28.

The emergence of the Québécois nation-community constitutes the external factor responsible for the changes in the boundaries of the French-Canadian nation. Previously, all the French in Canada belonged to the French-Canadian nation. The changing of the francophone collectivity in Quebec meant that the Québécois excluded from their "we" the francophones in other parts of Canada. This process of differentiation-division, which is painful both for the excluded groups and those who remain, was formally recognized at the 1969 meetings of "les Etats généraux du Canada français." In his analysis, Arès (1969; 100) identified the strong conflicts between the francophones of Quebec and those of the other provinces. The initial tension subsided only when the existence of two parallel collectivities and systems of solidarity was accepted.

Nevertheless, the French in Ontario could have kept their French-Canadian identity. To account for the emergence of a new identity, one must examine internal factors such as industrialization and urbanization. The percentage of people with a French mother tongue who live in an urban area as compared with the population as a whole is presented in Table 2. As a result of the rural-to-urban transition, the occupational structure has been modified; francophones are now represented at all occupational levels.

The resulting breakdown of isolation as a mechanism for maintaining relative closure and group boundaries has required that strong action be taken to develop greater autonomy in education, health services, and the courts. To achieve a certain level of structural pluralism, the French in Ontario had to exert pressures at the level of *their* provincial government; this course of action has strengthened *their* territorial basis of identification. Thus, the means employed for boundary-maintenance shifted from the defense of traditional patterns to the development of structural pluralism. Consequently, the territorial criterion has been emphasized and has become operative in the definition of group boundaries.

Finally, the ensuing reinforcement of this transition must also be examined in terms of the overall political-legal framework within which French-English relations have evolved in Canada. Although the birth of the Canadian federation can only be understood with reference to the economic context at that time (Naylor, 1972; Clement, 1975), the type of federal system which emerged was adopted in order to solve the political stalemate between

TABLE 3 *Percentage of labor force (15 years and over) in occupational categories, French mother tongue and Ontario as a whole, 1971*

Occupations	French mother tongue Ontarians	Total Ontario
Managerial, administrative and related occupations	3.2	4.7
Professional and semi-professional	7.4	9.0
Religion	0.3	0.2
Medicine and Health	2.6	3.7
Clerical and related occupations	14.7	17.6
Sales and Services	19.5	20.2
Primary sector	7.4	5.2
Processing occupations	32.9	29.5
Not elsewhere classified	2.2	2.3
Not stated	9.9	7.7
All occupations	199 385	3 354 360

Source: FFHQ, 1977: 41.

Canada East and Canada West in the mid-19th century. The division of the country into provinces each with its own government implied that the British North American Act did not recognize politically the existence of two nations. The areas of jurisdiction were distributed between the federal and provincial levels of government, with the latter controlling mainly the cultural sphere. Since more French Canadians resided in Quebec, the granting of autonomy on a territorial basis constituted a solution at the time; French Canadians in Quebec were relatively safe, since their provincial government had some control over cultural matters and could defend their rights against federal and anglophone encroachments. But historical developments modified the basis of this agreement. Many French Canadians moved to other provinces only to face the abolition of existing privileges. The expansion of provincial jurisdiction into areas such as education, health, and welfare led to increased conflicts between federal and provincial governments. The growing scope of provincial government jurisdiction also heightened the provincial basis of identification.

The Franco-Ontarian Identity

The modification of the criteria defining group boundaries has led to a process of differentiation-division and to the emergence of the Franco-Ontarian identity which can be gauged by a variety of indicators. Spokespersons of the collectivity often make statements which explicitly define or implicitly reflect the collective identity of their community; the various expressions of these people, be they leaders of organizations or poets, constitute useful indicators.

Associations and Organizations

The name chosen by an association or its statement of goals usually reflects the collectivity's definition of itself. At the beginning of this century, the collective identity was definitely French-Canadian. The most important association, founded in 1910, was called *L'Association canadienne-française d'éducation en Ontario* (ACFEO); this name reflects the identity of its founders. In 1914, the *Fédération des femmes canadiennes-françaises* adopted a similar name. Between 1910 and 1960 many associations sprang up throughout the province with regional and local representatives in almost every French-speaking area. These associations operate under the patronage of the ACFEO to which they are affiliated and share its definition of a French-Canadian collectivity. In 1960, there were nine such associations in Ontario (ACFEO, 1960: 169-70).

Many associations adopted the terms "French" and "Catholic" in their names. The term "French-Canadian" was also used by groups like the *Association des hommes d'affaires canadiens-français de Welland*, founded in 1955 (ACFO, 1976: 199). During that period, only the *Union des cultivateurs franco-ontariens* (1929) and *l'Association de la jeunesse franco-ontarienne* (1949) used the term "Franco-Ontarian."

At the beginning of the 1960s, the designation "Franco-Ontarian" was used by new associations or old ones involved in a name change. The *Fédération des clubs sociaux franco-ontariens* was founded in 1959. The *Association de l'enseignement français de l'Ontario* (1939) became, in 1963, *l'Association des enseignants franco-ontariens*. In 1969, the *Union catholique des fermières* (1937) changed its name to the *Union culturelle des franco-ontariennes*. The *Association des surintendants franco-ontariens* (school boards) was founded in 1968. Other local organizations also adopted the term "Franco-Ontarian" to identify themselves; for example, the *Club franco-ontarien de l'unviversité d'Ottawa,* founded in 1975, the *Centre franco-ontarien de folklore* of the University of Sudbury, established in 1964 and *Les Campeurs franco-ontariens* of Hamilton, founded in 1967 (ACFO, 1976: 6-50, 279, 473, 267). The term "Franco-Ontarian" also found greater use at the governmental level to designate official organizations. The Ontario Art Council opened a Franco-Ontarian section in 1970. In 1975, the Ministry of Culture and Recreation, in conjunction with the Ministry of Colleges and Universities, created an *Advisory Council for Franco-Ontarian Affairs*. Other recent organizations, such as the *Mouvement c'est l'temps* (1975), *Théâtre-Action* (1971), the *Editions Prise de Parole* (1973) among others, adopt this new collective identity explicitly in their statement of objectives (ACFO, 1976: 156, 372; Cano: 1973).

All these examples, drawn at the level of the organizations and associations of the collectivity, reflect the change that has occurred at the identity level. Of course, the French-Canadian identity has not disappeared.

L'ACFE0, now *l'Association canadienne-française de l'Ontario* (ACFO), did not change the term of reference in its name; and as late as 1975, a new organization created in Welland was called *Le Club canadien-français de Welland* (ACFO, 1976: 201).

Analysis of Speeches

An examination of the speeches and writings of the leaders of the community also shows that the term "French Canadian" was replaced by the term "Franco-Ontarian" at the beginning of the 1960s. This tendency is confirmed in a study done by R.G. Guindon (1971). His content analysis of communications presented at the founding meeting (1910) of the ACFEO and at its 50th anniversary meeting (1960) supports our view (Guidon, 1971: 38, 64). If we analyse the four-page circular distributed to thousands of people living in French parishes during the organization of the 1910 meetings, we see that there were two references to "Franco-Americans" (who have already set up an association) but no reference to "Franco-Ontarians." The emphasis lies on the terms French Canadian or French Canadian of Ontario which were repeated six times and which were associated with expressions such as "notre gloire nationale" ("our national glory"), "nos intérêts nationaux" ("our national interests"), "L'avenir de notre nationalité" ("the future of our nationality"), "si nous voulons être un peuple" ("if we want to be a nation") (ACFEO, 1960: 86-90). On the other hand, the subtitle of the report of the celebration of the 50th anniversary of the ACFEO read: "Cinquante années de vie franco-ontarienne" (ACFEO, 1960). In the foreword, the author referred both to "Franco-Ontarians" and "French Canadians". In a one-page speech, one honorary president mentioned the term "Franco-Ontarian" four times and did not refer once to "French Canadians" (ACFEO, 1960): 164-65. Appendix B, which summarized the accomplishments of the association, referred in less than two pages to "Franco-Ontarians" seven times and only once to French Canadians (ACFEO: 168-70).

Artistic Expression

This dimension is important as we believe that artists express the soul and life of a collectivity. In recent years, the Franco-Ontarian collectivity has produced its own poets and musicians who write and sing about the Franco-Ontarian reality. The works of François Lemieux, Robert Paquette, André and Robert Paiement (Coopérative des Artistes du Nouvel-Ontario), Robert Dickson, Claude Belcourt not only refer to this emerging identity but also keenly describe its precariousness, as well as the anxiety and stimulation it produces.

Designations Utilized by Group Members

Another indicator of group identity can be found by examining the terms used in everyday conversation by the members of the groups when referring to their collectivity. We will now discuss the use of the terms "Franco-Ontarian" and "French Canadian" made by the subjects of our sample of French-speaking communities of Ontario.

The Bearers of the New Identity

Horowitz (1975: 118-19) has pointed out that an identity can be either contextual (dependent on the specific environment) or autonomous. When the criteria underlying a collective identity are well defined and solidly entrenched, it becomes "functionally autonomous of the stimuli that produced it and may become so internalized as to be invoked in contexts quite different from the one in which it was formed" (Horowitz, 1975: 119). This is the case with the French-Canadian identity. When the objective criteria underlying group boundaries undergo transformations, the fit between boundaries and identification becomes blurred. It is precisely during such a transition that the analyst can identify the contextual variables which give birth to different types and levels of identification. In this case, the main cultural criterion (French language) delineating group boundaries remains; the changes affect the structural level (territorial) of identification (Canadian to Ontarian). There is also a change in emphasis from the cultural to the structural factors. The relative importance of each context can be ascertained by identifying how various social actors define their community, how often they refer to this collectivity, and in what types of situation they do so. These contexts can be defined in terms of the location of group members in social networks and institutional spheres, their level of participation in the affairs in the collectivity, and their commitment to boundary-maintenance.

Between 1974 and 1976, we studied five multi-ethnic communities in Ontario, namely Sturgeon Falls, Timmins, Cornwall, Hawkesbury and Windsor[1]. It became clear through our participant observation and unstructured interviews that both identities coexisted but were not articulated by the same groups. Those involved in social change called themselves Franco-Ontarians; those who defined their ethnic group membership mainly in terms of cultural symbols preferred the term French Canadian.

Active in the political and educational spheres, Franco-Ontarians participated in the life of the community and were sensitized to boundary-change as well as to the legal-territorial framework within which their demands could be articulated and acted upon, namely the Ontario government. Those who called themselves Franco-Ontarians were aware that their battles had to be fought at the provincial level, that urbanization and modernization had altered the life of their community, and that new means had to be developed in order to achieve the old goal of boundary-maintenance. In this context, it is interesting to note that this group used the term "Franco-Ontarian" to refer to actual conditions and "French Canadian" when talking about the past or about their predecessors. It is not surprising that the younger generation generally exhibited a Franco-Ontarian identity and the older, a French-Canadian one.

In the media, those who had reached a higher educational level, and those who possessed a higher degree of political awareness, as well as students enrolled in French Language Secondary Schools, also defined themselves as Franco-Ontarians. The same can be said for the artists. As a group, they possess a very high level of sensitivity, and their awareness of changing group boundaries is expressed in their work. Finally, the new identity was also shared by those who are in contact with Québécois (apart from family ties). They were aware of recent changes in that province, and more important for our purposes, of their exclusion from the new group which had emerged.

A French-Canadian identity was dominant mainly among the group which expresses the evaluative dimension of culture, such as those involved in the religious sphere. They were more sensitive to traditional definitions, and they valued the maintenance of existing patterns. They seemed to consider themselves as descendants of the original group (which must be kept intact) from which the Québécois have unfortunately detached themselves. Those who had kept strong ties with their Quebec side of the family (which constitutes a basis of solidarity) also emphasized the cultural rather than the structural criterion of belongingness. They felt that all francophones in Canada formed a collectivity which should be united by a common bond of solidarity. On the other hand, those who called themselves Franco-Ontarians were much more ambivalent towards their Quebec counterparts.

The new definition of "we-feeling," group belongingness, and solidarity was and is crucial since it influences the means chosen for boundary-maintenance and affects the strategies utilized for achieving this goal. Franco-Ontarians emphasize structural rather than cultural pluralism; they seek to broaden the institutional completeness of their collectivity and to increase their control over its internal functioning. In terms of their analysis, survival requires the development of a strong collectivity capable of creating new cultural expressions rather than maintaining old patterns which no longer correspond to its changing social organization. The emergence of new collectivities (Québécois, Franco-Ontarian) has also modified political strategies; battles are now fought within the provincial sphere.

Franco-Ontarians and "Ontarois"

Since 1976, the Franco-Ontarian identity has become the dominant one as the French in Ontario have pursued their struggle for the recognition of their rights in this province. But their future remains uncertain, as the implementation of these rights progresses rather slowly. The referendum held in Quebec in 1980 has weakened considerably their bargaining position.

Although Premier William Davis has consistently opposed the application of Article 133 to Ontario (thus refusing to recognize French as an official language in Ontario), his government has extended French language services. Criminal courts are bilingual since 1979, and a great proportion of civil courts are expected to follow suit. Furthermore, by 1985, all children requiring special instruction, such as the physically and/or mentally handicapped, will be able to receive it in French or in English. There have also been some "victories" in the educational sphere: two French language secondary schools were opened after bitter struggles, one in Essex in 1977, and more recently, one in Penetang, in 1981. But there is still a heated controversy concerning the creation of "les conseils scolaires homogènes de langue française," a tool which would allow the French collectivity to exert greater control over its schools. This on-going debate reflects the changing status of the power struggle between francophones and anglophones in Ontario.

While the former managers of the French-Canadian community were located in the cultural sphere, the new Franco-Ontarian elite is located in the political arena where it faces a State controlled by another historical community (Juteau-Lee, 1982). This lack of control over the State apparatus contributes to reinforce its minority status. The minority status also expresses itself at the symbolic level, since the term Franco-Ontarian emphasizes "la différence"; there are Ontarians who form the dominant group and embody the norm, and Franco-Ontarians who are different. It is in this context that we can understand the new appellation "Ontarois." This term invented by Y. Grisé in 1980 in response to Paul Lapointe's film *J'ai besoin d'un nom*, has been adopted by some members of the Franco-Ontarian elite. There is a refusal to define the community in terms of the dominant group, a refusal of the symbolic dimension of its minority status; it expresses a wish to abolish its subordinate status. It is too early to make any predictions concerning its future, but once again it becomes clear that changes in the collective identity of a community reflect changes affecting its relationship to other collectivities as well as its collective goals. Many Franco-Ontarians now realize that majority-minority relations cannot be significantly modified within the existing capitalist and State framework.

Conclusion

The examination of the factors responsible for changes in group boundaries and collective indentification has shed some light on the emergence of a Franco-Ontarian identity. It has demonstrated that ethnic groups do vary over time and, consequently, that communal relations are not writ in stone. Because these changes affect the distribution of resources between the groups and their relative statuses, the importance of examining the criteria which underlie group boundaries has been stressed. Since ethnic groups are more than an epiphenomenon, it is crucial to understand the basis of their formation and transformation. Furthermore, too many analyses of assimilation (incapacity to maintain group boundaries) deal only with indicators such as language spoken in the home, language spoken at work, and media consumption. While these variables allow us to understand the linguistic patterns of individuals, they tell us very little about the viability of an ethnic community. Further studies must emphasize the collective dimension (the structural basis of a collectivity), the factors that support its boundaries, and its capacity to maintain them. They must also examine the relationship between different types of boundaries and the overall distribution of resources within them.

END NOTES

1. Further details concerning the methodology of this study may be obtained by contacting the authors.

SELECTED REFERENCES

Arès, Richard. "L'oeuvre des Etats généraux," *Relations* 337 (April 1969), pp. 99-100.

Association Canadienne-française d'Education d'Ontario (ACFEO). "Congrès d'Education des Canadiens Français d'Ontario – 1910: Rapport officiel des séances tenues à Ottawa," Ottawa, du 18 au 20 janvier 1910.

_____ . "Rapport général des fêtes du Cinquantenaire et du quinzième Congrès général de l'Association canadienne-française d'Education d'Ontario," Ottawa, Cinquante années de vie franco-ontarienne, les 20, 21 et 22 avril 1960.

Association canadienne-française de l'Ontario (ACFO). "Bottin des Organismes franco-ontariens," Ottawa, 1976.

Barth, F., ed. *Ethnic Groups and Boundaries.* Boston: Little, Brown and Company, 1969.

Bellah, R. *Beyond Belief: Essays on Religion in a Post-Traditional World.* New York: Harper and Row, 1970.

Breton, R. "Institutional Completeness of Ethnic Communities and Personal Relations of Immigrants," *American Journal of Sociology* 70 (1964), pp. 193-205.

_____ . "Types of Ethnic Diversity in Canadian Society." Paper presented at the VIII World Congress, ISA, Toronto, 1974.

Cano. *Des artistes du Nouvel-Ontario.* Sudbury: Les Editions Prises de Parole, 1973.

Census of Canada, Bulletins, 1.3-2, 1.3-4 and 1.3-5, 1971.

Clement, Wallace. *The Canadian Corporate Elite: An Analysis of Economic Power.* Toronto: McClelland and Stewart Limited, 1975.

Eisenstadt, S.N. *Modernization: Protest and Change*. Englewood Cliffs, N.J.: Prentice-Hall, Inc., 1966.

Fédération des francophones hors Québec (FFHQ). *Les Héritiers de Lord Durham*. Ottawa, 1977.

Guindon, R.G. "Essai d'analyse interne d'un discours idéologique." Unpublished Master's Thesis, Université d'Ottawa, 1971.

Horowitz, D.L. "Ethnic Identity," pp. 111-40. In N. Glazer and D.P. Moynihan, eds. *Ethnicity: Theory and Experience*. Cambridge: Harvard University Press, 1975.

Jackson, John D. *Community and Conflict: A Study of French-English Relations in Ontario*. Toronto: Holt, Rinehart and Winston of Canada Limited, 1975.

Joy, Richard. *Languages in Conflict*. Toronto: McClelland and Stewart, 1972.

Juteau-Lee, D. "The Impact of Modernization and Environmental Impingements upon Nationalism and Separatism: The Quebec Case." Unpublished Doctoral Dissertation, University of Toronto, 1974.

_____. "The Franco-Ontarian Collectivity: Material and Symbolic Dimensions of Its Minority Status." In R. Breton and P. Savard, *The Quebec and Acadian Diaspora in North America,* Toronto: The Multicultural History Society of Ontario, 1982.

Naylor, R.T. "The Rise and Fall of the Third Commercial Empire of the St. Lawrence," pp. 1-42, in Gary Teeple, ed. *Capitalism and the National Question in Canada*. Toronto: University of Toronto Press, 1972.

Rioux, M. *La Question du Québec*, Paris: Seghers, 1969.

Smelser, N.J. *Essays in Sociological Explanation*. Englewood-Cliffs, N.J.: Prentice-Hall, Inc., 1968.

Vallee, F. "Multi-Ethnic Societies: The Issues of Identity and Inequality," pp. 162-202, in D. Forcese and S. Richer, eds. *Issues in Canadian Society: An Introduction to Sociology*. Scarborough: Prentice-Hall of Canada, Ltd., 1975.

van den Berghe, P. *Race and Racism*. New York: John Wiley and Sons, Inc., 1967.

CORNELIUS J. JAENEN   University of Ottawa

French Roots in the Prairies*

Three Phases in French Canadian History Prior to the Present Era

Bilingual and Bicultural Communities (Circa 1768-1890)

> "Thirty years ago, we who speak French were called by everyone purely and simply 'Canadien.' Others were known as English, Scotch or Irish. Lately the fashion has grown up of calling others Canadians and distinguishing us as French."
>
> *Father Lewis Drummond*, 1886[1]

In the first phase of Prairie ethnic history, Manitoba and that section of the Northwest Territories which eventually became Alberta and Saskatchewan, were bilingual and bicultural communities. Their francophone and anglophone communities were balanced (with a slight French preponderance) in demographic, institutional, and constitutional terms. This is an aspect of our history which is often ignored. It may explain as much about the present as it tells us about the past.

Multiculturalism (Circa 1890-1917)

In phase 2, the Prairies received a large influx of Eastern Canadian migrants (mostly from Western Ontario) and continental European immigrants. This radically altered the demographic base, gave rise to demands for institutional changes and even constitutional changes, and resulted in a flirtation in the school system with cultural pluralism and multilingualism. From 1897 to 1916, Manitoba had a public school system which permitted instruction in English and any other language on the bilingual pattern. This system also gave rise to a number of non-English teacher training schools, to ethnic teachers' associations, school trustees' organizations, and others. In Saskat-

---

* A revised version of two papers, "The Manitoba School Question: an Ethnic Interpretation," *Proceedings of the National Conference on Ethnic Studies and Research,* Regina, October, 1976; and "Prairie Schooling and Bilingualism," *Proceedings of the 12th Annual Convention of the Canadian Association for the Social Studies,* Regina, October, 1976. Reprinted from *Ethnic Canadians: Culture and Education.* ed. Martin L. Kovacs, Published by Canadian Plains Research Center, University of Regina, 1978.

chewan this phase was marked by two distinct, but not altogether unrelated, school issues: the emotional separate school debates starting in 1905 and the bitter bilingual instruction debates which took on national proportions in 1917.

Anglo-Celtic Dominance (Circa 1917-1962)

The Anglo-Celtic dominant society asserted itself in phase 3 through such institutions as the centralized provincial school systems, civic indoctrination, and cultural reorientation so as to assimilate immigrant groups and homogenize the community according to its Anglo-Conformist ideology. This is related historically to the anti-alien feeling of World War I, the war hysteria and the postwar reactionary politics. It was a difficult time for the minorities in Canada – ethnic, cultural, religious, occupational. It was the period in Prairie educational history when the task of the rural country school, staffed by zealous, young Anglo-Saxon teachers, was to assimilate what was thought to be "the hordes of foreigners' children," while "keeping the French-Canadians in their place," with the effect that the position of the Anglo-Celtic dominant sector was consolidated.

Phase 1: French/English Dualism

Each phase is marked perhaps more by its passing than by any single event in its short duration. Principal Robert Falconer of the University of Toronto saw the first phase, a transplantation of Eastern Canadian society, as a perpetuation in the West of the dualism which had characterized Central Canada and produced Confederation. He wrote:

> Older Canada sent out her sons to possess new lands, and these first settlers belonging to the stronger races from which the older portions of Canada were colonized established the type of new life. Older political, social and religious ideals are so essentially inherent in the character, that, like hardy seeds wafted by ocean current to distant shores, they reproduce in the new environment fruit similar in quality to that which was found in their former home.[2]

Unfortunately, the old prejudices, dissensions and factionalism of the East were transferred along with the better qualities to the new seedbed of Western Canada where they took good root and flourished.

The Manitoba School Question marked the end of the first phase. It can be regarded, apart from the religious argument of the feasibility of confessional streaming within a public system, as marking the end of practical dualism (biculturalism) in the West. It had not been possible to maintain the dominant dualism through either migration or immigration. The francophone community was the first to lose its position, until by 1891 it was a small minority. There were unsuccessful efforts to attract Quebec settlers, to repatriate Franco-Americans and to induce francophone Europeans to help maintain parity with the Anglo-Celtic community and so keep alive the bilingual and bicultural community which the federal Conservatives had enshrined in the Manitoba Act of 1870 and which the federal Liberals had enshrined in the North-West Territories Act of 1875.

The Catholic schools were not taught exclusively in French because there was a recognition on the part of the clergy that immigration, and especially migration from Eastern Canada, was altering the demographic balance, which had existed in Manitoba at the time of Union, in favor of Anglo-Celtic peoples and Protestants.[3] As early as 1877, *Le Métis* sounded the alarm, calling on all francophones to unite "to resist tyranny and to defend liberty of conscience and the rights of the minority on the school question, as well as on all other questions."[4] There was no hostility to English settlement *per se*, only fear that the bicultural character of the West would be undermined. In that same year (1877), Father Lacombe, in correspondence with Bishop Taché concerning the colonization of the West by francophones, deplored the difficulty in obtaining bilingual teachers for Catholic schools. He went to Europe to recruit because Quebec was a very unfruitful source of bilingual teachers. In 1883, thanks in good measure to Lacombe's efforts, a French (Breton) order of teaching sisters which operated schools in England sent five bilingual teachers to Brandon, five to Prince Albert and four to the Métis settlement of St. Laurent. In rural homogeneously French settlements such as Ste. Anne or St. Pierre, Taché could continue to send unilingual teachers.[5]

As criticism of the dual confessional school system grew, in large measure because the system no longer comfortably fitted the sociocultural contours, there developed an ethnic tension. Superintendent T.A. Bernier of the Catholic public schools in Manitoba warned in his annual report for 1886 that immigration was threatening dualism and therefore francophones would have to mount an "eternal vigilance."[6] Electioneering politicans sometimes called for the abolition of the official use of French. One widely circulated pamphlet of 1887 called for the exclusion of French "from our legislature, from our courts, from our statutes, and from our public schools."[7] The francophone community, at least its clerical leaders, seemed to place faith in the alleged visit of Messrs. Alloway and Greenway to the Archiepiscopal palace in St. Boniface in 1888 to deliver a Liberal pledge to Rev. Father Joachim Allard, Vicar General, that the official status of French and the dual school system were not in danger.[8]

There would develop the hypothesis that the federal and provincial Liberals – Mowat, Laurier, Greenway – deliberately provoked the Manitoba School Question in 1890 in order to break the basis of Conservative power, i.e., the alliance between tolerant Ontario Toryism and the conservative Quebec Bleus. According to this conspiracy thesis, which Rev. Father Gonthier expounded in a letter to *abbé* Lindsay, and which was sent to the Vatican Secretary of State on the occasion of Prime Minister Laurier's visit to Rome in August 1897, the Manitoba Liberals undertook to restore or retain the rights of French instruction under a centralized non-sectarian school system.[9]

The arrival of the Mennonites and the Icelanders in the 1870s had given rise to the assumption that these ethnic bloc settlements would eventually have their schools incorporated into the Protestant/English school system. There was little in the austere pietistic religion of the Mennonites or the Lutheranism of the Icelanders to indicate any affinity with the Catholic brand of public schooling. Furthermore, many of the Ontario migrants to Manitoba, adherents for the most part of the Methodist or Presbyterian churches, spearheaded fundamental changes in the Manitoba constitution: the abolition of the Legislative Council; changes in the system of representation, substitution of the municipal for the parish system of local government; and abrogation of the status of French in the provincial courts, legislature and official records. These changes altered the bicultural basis of Manitoba and moved it away from the Quebec model to the Ontario model.

The Icelandic immigration which began in 1875 was marked by a strong attachment to public schooling and a steadfast determination to learn English and to become assimilated. This was all the more remarkable because they had founded their ethnic reserve, New Iceland, on the west shore of Lake Winnipeg in the territory of Keewatin just north of the Manitoba provincial boundary.[10] Swedes and Russian Jews also trickled into the province, but they did not acquire reserves of land and they, like the Icelanders, did not attempt to establish their own school system. In other words, in 1890 there were immigrant groups which did not challenge the model of Anglo-conformity or the institution of common non-sectarian public schools.

It is significant that when Manitoba passed an act creating a centralized Department of Education, to replace the dual confessional Board of Education, and an act to abolish Catholic public schools, much of the rhetoric revolved around the concept of "national" schools. It was not only the French, but also Mennonites, Icelanders, Germans, Poles, Swedes, and Jews who had to be channelled into the assimilating experiences of the public school, somewhat on the model of the American public school. Archbishops Taché and Langevin responded to the abolition of the dual confessional system by opening "free schools" (écoles libres) in opposition to "national schools" in areas of heterogeneous settlement and by encouraging taxpayers, trustees and teachers to retain the essential religious and ethnic qualities in areas of homogeneous settlement. The school legislation was still silent on the matter of language(s) of instruction so that French could be employed with equal justification in the public school system and in the private or parochial schools.

Although francophone colonizing agents, especially the colonizing clergy, redoubled their efforts to find suitable teachers as well as settlers, Langevin's resistance movement against the legislation of 1890 ran into problems. First, the Manitoba government brought down further legislation in 1894 requiring that any school not operating according to the Act would not be called a public school and therefore would not qualify for the legislative grant. Municipalities could no longer grant money to, or levy and collect taxes for the support of, schools operating as francophone *écoles libres* or Mennonite church schools. Second, the European immigrants did not always see eye to eye with their French-Canadian coreligionists on matters of public schooling; they often required what Dom Benoit of Notre-Dame de Lourdes called "re-educating".[11] Third, many teaching orders in - Quebec and continental Europe which were approached with a view to staffing schools in Manitoba and the Northwest Territories showed little interest in the Canadian West. The immediate result was that a number of schools in francophone districts – e.g., St. Claude, St. Alphonse, St. Eustache – decided to come under the public school umbrella. Finally, although most Mennonite elders had as strong objections to the school legislation as had Archbishop Langevin, they failed to form a common front with the francophone Catholics against the "godless schools."

Soon after becoming Prime Minister in 1896, Laurier expressed his pessimism about restoring the francophone dominant role in the West:

> . . . for my part I have never had . . . a great confidence that we could ever have many immigrants from France. The French people do not emigrate, but remain at home. If it were possible to have from France an immigration, not from towns and cities, but from the rural portions of the country, we would certainly have a most valuable class of settlers. I think, however, that a good deal more is to be had from the British Isles themselves.[12]

As continental Europeans began to respond to the Sifton immigration policy, some Canadians expressed the fear that the Anglo-Celtic group might share the fate of its French founding partner in the West. In 1899, W.F. McCreary, the Commissioner of Immigration at Winnipeg (to cite but one example), informed Clifford Sifton that there was a prevalent feeling in the West that the "charter groups" were being neglected in the immigration efforts. McCreary warned the minister:

> There is a cry, unfortunately, very prevalent throughout this Province and the West generally, not only among our enemies but among our friends, that the Government are doing more for the Doukhobors and the Galicians than they are for either French or English settlers – and even our papers here do not put this matter in the correct light.[13]

The defeat of the federal Conservative government in 1896 and the assumption of power by the Laurier Liberals made possible the famous Laurier-Greenway Compromise (more accurately it was a Tarte-Sifton agreement) which was announced on November 19, 1896 and which was incorporated into the new School Act of 1897. Clause 10 of the agreement read: "Where ten of the pupils in any school speak the French language (or any language other than English) as their native tongue, the teaching of such pupils shall be conducted in French (or such other language) and English upon the bi-lingual system".[14]

For the first time, Mantitoba legislation laid down specific provision for language(s) of instruction. Although each school district could have only a single bilingual character (e.g., English-German, English-Ruthenian), the province could have an unspecified number of bilingual systems according to the ethnic communities which petitioned the authorities. The legislation invited the development of inspection services, teacher training programs, curricula, centralized examinations and authorized textbooks for each of these bilingual fragments. The Icelanders openly favored the English public schools, but the "French" (Canadiens), "Germans" (mostly Mennonites) and "Ruthenians" (Ukrainians) organized their own teachers' associations and conventions and their own school trustees' associations and conventions.

The Compromise of 1897 could be interpreted as a shift in emphasis from religion to ethnicity. The *Manitoba Free Press* was later to publish the following explanation of this bilingual provision:

> In order to avoid exciting anti-French prejudices in Ontario and elsewhere, the concession as to bilingual teaching was not limited to the French, but was made general to all non-English residents in the Province of Manitoba in the expectation that it would be taken advantage of only by the French and by them in a limited degree and by a few and diminishing number of Mennonite communities.[15]

The Catholic hierarchy, at least its ultramontane bishops, had not been a party to this compromise. On the contrary, the negotiations carried on with Manitoba Liberal officials by Israel Tarte and Henri Bourassa did not satisfy Archbishop Langevin, largely because he was excluded from their confidence. Langevin attacked the language clause which placed Franco-Manitobans "on the same basis as the coming hordes of the future that Sifton saw." In a sermon delivered in his cathedral church, he protested:

> . . . we who came as the pioneers into the country, who discovered it, have not more than the last arrivals, we whose rights are guaranteed by the constitution, are placed on the same footing as those who came from Ireland or the depths of Russia, we are not better apportioned than the Chinese and the Japanese.[16]

Henceforth, bilingualism would mean English and any second language and would not be restricted to French-English dualism that historically had preceded the flow of foreign immigration.

But this did not necessarily work to the disadvantage of the francophone communities. Whereas in 1896 there had been only 25 French schools in the public system, by 1900 there were 84 schools under the jurisdiction of Robert Goulet, inspector of French-English schools. Two years later, there were 105 such schools and only six *écoles libres* in Manitoba. In the provincial election of 1899 the Conservatives called for the defeat of the Greenway government and the *règlement défectueux*, i.e., a "defective, imperfect, in-sufficient" remedy as Leo XIII's encyclical *Affari Vos* called it.[17] But the Liberals argued that a vote for them was a vote for the certainty of preserv-ing their present concessions and the hope of obtaining further ones. The provincial trend was for the Conservatives, but the three predominantly French-Canadian constituencies of St. Boniface, La Vérendrye, and Carillon all returned Liberal members.

The French-English bilingual schools continued to experience problems in finding qualified teachers as those who were eager to leave France, because they viewed the secularization of education there as persecution, knew no English, and Quebec teachers seemed increasingly unwilling to learn English or come West. Moreover, the bilingual teachers in the system were not always fully qualified and it became increasingly difficult to obtain provisional authorizations or to dissimulate their true professional status. In 1902, for example, one third of the teachers in the French-English bi-lingual schools had no diplomas. Moreover, Archbishop Langevin acknowledged in 1908 that he sometimes had to employ threats to convince parents and trustees in francophone districts to maintain French instruction.[18]

In the Northwest Territories the only concession to the immigrant ethnic communities was what remained of the language of instruction clause which the French-Canadian charter group had enjoyed. When Manitoba set up what were virtually French, German, Ukrainian and Polish teacher training institutes or normal schools, Saskatchewan followed cautiously with a Training School for Teachers for Foreign-speaking Communities in Regina, and Alberta with an English School for Foreigners at Vegreville. It appears that the farther one went West the greater was the insistence that Canada was British and English-speaking. Manitoba called her school for Ukrai-nians a Ruthenian Training School, Saskatchewan said hers was for Teachers for Foreign-speaking Communities, while Alberta insisted hers was an English School for Foreigners!

Phase 2: Multiculturalism

In this second phase – a virtual first experiment with multiculturalism – there was misunderstanding as to the goals or purposes of the school legisla-tion and practice. At the inauguration of the new provinces of Alberta and Saskatchewan in 1905, Sir Wilfrid Laurier gave the immigrants his ideal for their integration into the host society:

> Let me say to one and all of our new fellow-countrymen . . . Let them be Bri-tain's subjects . . . We do not anticipate, and we do not want, that any individuals should forget the land of their origin, the land of their ancestors . . . Let them become Canadians, British subjects, and give their heart and soul, their energy, their vows to Canada, to its institutions, to its king, who like his illustrious mother, is a model constitutional Sovereign . . .[19]

What the provincial bureaucrats expected from the bilingual system was ethnic social disintegration and assimilation, not cultural transmission of group values and ethnic perpetuation. The arrival of the first wave of Ukrainian and Polish immigrants in 1897, ostensibly to engage in farming but forced by circumstances to turn also to the railways, mines, and lumber camps, gave the bilingual system a new dimension. Those who settled in rural Manitoba, east of the Red River in marginal farm lands, in the Interlake country, and in the parkland belt west from Clan William along the south of the Riding Mountains and around Dauphin could be expected to make some demand for bilingual schools. The parents although largely of peasant origins, gave the impression of being sufficiently motivated to realize the benefits of schooling for their children. A typical inspectoral report read: "The large number of Galicians who have lately settled in the vicinity of Stuartburn has increased the school population of this district to a considerable extent. The children are bright, intelligent and most anxious to acquire a knowledge of the English language. They are well-behaved in school and easily managed." [20] As the Ukrainians became aware of the possibility of organizing bilingual schools they naturally favored these. The provincial authorities were faced with the immediate problem of finding qualified teachers to staff such schools, also with the long-range problem of ascertaining the results of an expansion of the bilingual system to encompass an undetermined number of ethnic groups.

However much Archbishop Langevin had deplored the granting of equal school rights to all ethnic minorities, he very soon rallied to the concept and sought to exploit it to Catholic advantage. He obtained from Premier R. Roblin in 1901 a promise for support of Ukrainian, Polish and German schools.[21] In public addresses he strongly defended the teaching of the mother tongues of the immigrant communities, telling Catholic audiences in particular that in preserving the Ukrainian, Polish, and German tongues the faith was being preserved.

> Schools must be established among them in which the English language will be taught according to the requirements of the law, but since the law concedes bilingual instruction, that is to say instruction of another tongue besides English for those who do not speak the latter, these strangers have the right to have their children taught in their own language, and that is their most ardent wish. But if all admit that English must be taught in Manitoba schools, not all are also of the opinion that one must teach also the mother tongue of the Galicians; a few even have proclaimed very loudly that it would be better to teach only English everywhere! An exhorbitant, unjust and dangerous pretention which endangers the peace of our country.[22]

This was an extension of the traditional French-Canadian ultramontane ideology of the inseparable relationship between language and religion.

Similarly, the Anglo-Celtic Protestants were not unaware of the advantages to be gained through support to the ethnic minorities. The

Presbyterians in particular promoted an interest that had developed in 1898 when two young "Galicians" called on the Principal of Manitoba College requesting entrance in order to obain "an English education." Dr. James Robertson, Superintendent of Home Missions in Western Canada, indicated in a public interview that the Ukranians "should be put into the great Anglo-Saxon mill and be ground up" because "in the grinding they lose their foreign prejudices and characteristics."[23]

It was only a matter of time before the Archdiocese of St. Boniface and the Home Missions Board of the Presbyterian Church found themselves in open competition for the souls of Slavic immigrants and for the control of their schools, including control of the teacher training institutions and the inspection services which were natural bureaucratic outgrowths of the legislative provisions of 1897. In 1901, Archdeacon Fortin and Dr. Reid, a medical missionary at Sifton, called a closed meeting to discuss the possibility of bringing all Ruthenian-English bilingual schools under the direction of Manitoba College; Archbishop Langevin called a mass meeting of Catholic educators on January 5, 1902 to publicize his opposition to this segment of public schools coming under sectarian Protestant control. About 10 days later, a joint meeting of Catholic and Protestant representatives was held at the Winnipeg City Hall to discuss the question of education of immigrant children. No new solutions were proposed, but at least the Fortin-Reid plan had been blocked.

In February 1905, the Roblin Conservative government opened a Ruthenian Training School in Winnipeg for the preparation of Ukrainian and Polish young men who would teach in the bilingual schools. The school was headed by a Yorkshireman who initially viewed the enterprise as "an act of self-preservation on the part of the state," but who later came to view his task as one of great national service in character building, civilizing, and Christianizing teacher-candidates. The school was soon relocated in Brandon, near an English Normal School, away from the seat of Catholic strength, and in the Minister of Education's predominantly Anglo-Celtic riding. The few Ukrainian instructors associated with the institute were of known Protestant leanings.

Archbishop Langevin protested vigorously and extracted the promise that a training school for Polish teachers would be organized in Winnipeg. But he was filled with bitterness when a Protestant was proposed as principal of this second institute. He wrote confidently to Premier Roblin:

> If things are such, and if you cannot see your way through granting us a Normal School for Galicians with a principal and, perhaps, an assistant, that we can trust, my idea is that we better leave aside the scheme; but the feeling of our Galicians, Poles and Ruthenians in Winnipeg and outside, and the feeling of other Catholics will be bitter against the Government and I will not blame them. Why did Mr. Rogers promise me so positively a Normal School for *our* Galicians if this school falls in the hands of our adversaries as it was the case with the first normal

school now in Brandon and when Catholic pupils are under a Presbyterian ruling.[24]

The assumption of the chief officials in the Department of Education was that Manitoba would be an English-speaking and British province. Bilingual schools were a stage in the achievement of this ideal and were not conceived as being a permanent feature of the multilingual and multicultural province.

Archbishop Langevin and his clergy, by seeking to unite all Catholic ethnic minorities in order to obtain a recovery of the school rights enjoyed prior to 1980, failed to counterbalance the Anglo-Celtic dominant group. More important, they failed to obtain parity between francophone and anglophone communities. Indeed, through identification of the Franco-Manitoban cause with that of the immigrant groups, they paved the way for a permanent identification of Franco-Manitobans as just another fragment of the multi-ethnic mosaic.

Phase 3: Anglo-Celtic Dominance

The phase of experimental multiculturalism came to a close during the heated legislative debates on education in the three Prairie Provinces at the time of World War I. The Mennonites were under particular pressures because of their pacifism, "separation from the world," and their use of the German tongue which was declared to be an "enemy language." In fact, the pressure on them had begun in Manitoba in 1907 with the flag-flying legislation. The Hon. Colin Campbell, in moving second reading of the patriotic legislation, quoted a London speech of Henry Ward Beecher in which he was alleged to have said:

> It takes them (emigrants to USA) a little time to get used to things, but whenever the children from foreign immigrants, of whom we have eight million born and bred in our land, whenever these children have gone through our common schools they are just as good Americans as if they had not had foreign parents. The common schools are the stomachs of the republic, and when a man goes in there he comes out after all, American.[25]

By 1918, Dr. Harold Foght, the American educator who was asked to evaluate the Saskatchewan public school system, advised that all Mennonite children should be brought forcibly into the public schools and that their private schools should be shut down by the government.

> Once the crust is broken, the Old Coloniers will probably learn as did their brothers in the United States, that it is quite impossible to retain their religion in its old-time purity, even though they accept the tongue of the land in which they and their children live.[26]

It might surprise you to know that more than one Quebec bishop opined that these persecuted Mennonites might make good settlers in the Eastern Townships of *la belle province.*

The inter-war years were marked especially by the Anglo-conformist attempt to gradually integrate the New Canadians, as they were now being called, through the education of their children in schools which were specifically designed for the purpose. The rural one-room school as conceived by educators like J. T. M. Anderson was to become a social, cultural, and educational center for the whole community. Anderson explained his concept of the schools to a national education convention in Winnipeg in 1919:

> The paramount factor in racial fusion is undoubtedly the school. It is the national melting pot. We must give it our undivided support. The great battle for better Canadian citizenship is being fought by our school teachers. They are the generals in the home field.[27]

In these schools the pupils would be instructed in good English usage, proper civic attitudes, and in such ancillary matters as personal cleanliness, proper dietary habits, good sportsmanship, and patriotic lore. To achieve these objectives it was essential to recruit for each community the "ideal young teacher" imbued with a strong sense of mission, also to exclude the poorly qualified teacher of the community's ethnic background. In numerous districts, especially in Ukrainian and Mennonite communities where the school trustees were quite adept in the democratic administration of their public schools and the hiring of teachers from their own ethnic group, the Departments of Education of the three Prairie provinces arbitrarily suspended local self-government, appointed an Official Trustee and sent in "strong young teachers of a better class." In some areas, notably in northern Alberta, the reaction was the so-called Ruthenian School Revolt.

There was some feeling that not all ethnic groups should have been permitted to come to Canada. Even Stephen Leacock disapproved of immigrants from Slavonic and Mediterranean lands because he believed they were peoples of a so-called lower industrial and moral status. One aspiring poet expressed the Anglo-conformist attitude to non-Nordic peoples;

> They are haggard, huddled, homeless, frightened at – they know not what
> With a few unique exceptions they're a disappointing lot;
> But I take 'em as I get 'em, soldier, sailor, saint and clown
> And I turn 'em out Canadians – all but the yellow and brown.[28]

Phase 4: Multiculturalism

Now we seem to have come full circle. The narrow and bigoted phase 3 has been replaced with a new attempt at multiculturalism, a partial recycling of the earlier phase 2. Without facing head on the dimensions of phase 4 and the current issues surrounding multiculturalism in the West, let us ask the question: why did phase 3 occur? In other words, where did the concept of a compulsory, unilingual British Canada upon which phase 3 was based originate? If these sentiments are still with us today, the chances of a successful phase 4 multiculturalism are nil.

The notion that Canada is a unilingual British country can be traced to a number of historical experiences. First, and this is obvious, the Anglo-Celts were among the early European colonizers of what later became Canadian territory. Everyone is aware that, after the Amerindian and Inuit immigrants, the French and the English were the earliest colonizers.

Second, the concept is rooted in what I would term the Conquest mentality. There lingers the idea – and I even hear it expressed today by otherwise well-informed people – that the Acadians were conquered in 1713, that the Canadiens were conquered in 1760, and that the Métis and Canadiens in the West were conquered in 1885. The implication seems to be that conquered peoples are second-rate citizens, that they have lost their rights and their identity, that they must forever be servants in their own house. Historically, of course, *the French-Canadians are British subjects by choice and not by conquest*. France did not have to cede Canada in the peace negotiations of 1762 – she threatened in fact to re-open the hostilities of the Seven Years' War if Britain did not accept Canada rather than Guadeloupe as the prize of war! And the French-Canadians, by the capitulation and the later peace treaty, were entitled to relocate in French territory if they wished. They chose not to. They reaffirmed their choice, as a majority, to be British subjects at the time of the American Revolution, the War of 1812, the rebellions of 1837 and at Confederation. Anglo-Celtic reaffirmations of loyalty to the British North American institutions have been no more numerous.

Third, the United Empire Loyalist experience has traumatically marked British North America and it has even influenced subsequent British immigrants. When the Loyalists came to Canada they came as a minority, as displaced persons, to a British colony which was French-speaking, which had Canadien institutions and civil law. Naturally, they wished to be themselves, to order their society along their traditional lines. They were a people still tied to "old country" apron strings. Britain was once again perceived as their homeland. In this they were different from French-Canadians whose European ties were already largely severed and who regarded Canada as their homeland. *The United Empire Loyalists became our first political separatists*. They agitated for separate and special status, and they won! Thereafter, Canada was dualistic, each section of which had its own set of institutions and dominant language. But they also had a concept of minority rights and guarantees in each section. This was carried over into the Confederation charter and later into the Canadian West. And, not surprisingly, it is a concept which many Anglo-Celts have never abandoned. When Premier W. M. Martin was hard-pressed by patriotic societies, Orange lodges, trustees associations, Grain Growers associations, and others in 1918-19 to remove all permissive legislation for the teaching of French along with other languages in Saskatchewan, he answered:

> The question of the French language, however, raises an entirely different question. The people of Canada are made up of two nationalities and each of these nationalities, to my mind must be prepared to be generous to the other. Only in this way will unity of the two races be created and a better understanding exist.[29]

On another occasion he wrote about the "historical position of the French people in Canada." He argued they were native-born Canadians and not immigrants. On another occasion he said:

> It has never been the policy . . . of the British Empire to attempt to force down the throats of any people who came under its charge their own language. The policy has been the opposite.[30]

Thus, while the United Empire Loyalist experience contributed to the development of a concept of a British and English-speaking Canada it also influenced a significant number of the elite to see Canada as a bicultural community.

Fourth, the mythology of a Canadian northern character is closely tied in with the belief in Nordic or Aryan superiority, with British imperial sentiment, with Social Darwinism combined with a concept of a civilizing mission towards lesser breeds, with Protestant libertarianism and aggressive missionary zeal, and with unabashed Anglo-Saxon racism. These sentiments were publicly proclaimed by such organizations as Canada First, the Imperial Federation League, the Orange Lodge, the patriotic societies, and the Ku Klux Klan. At times, benevolent societies, teachers and trustees organizations, farmers organizations, religious corporations, and political groups lent their support to and became the vociferous mouthpieces of such views.

Finally, there was a fear that Canada would become Balkanized and lose all national identity and national direction unless an integrated society were created. The United States often served as the model for Canadians in dealing with the integration of immigrants. Not that the melting pot thesis was necessarily adopted, but at least the necessity for common public schools, civic indoctrination and inter-group contact through occupational and professional organizations, through cultural and social associations, through political activities, was adopted.

The assumptions of the immigrants relative to what was required of them could be at variance with the assumptions of the dominant group. Many of the European immigrants assumed that in Canada they would be permitted to retain their language and customs, that there would be no pressures for rapid assimilation similar to what was experienced by immigrants in the United States. Canada did not have an organized program of republican indoctrination, citizenship courses, and the like, which characterized American reception. Some of the newcomers to the Prairies may have been aware of the heterogeneity of the British Isles, of the multilingualism and multiculturalism of the far-flung British Empire, of the historic dualism of Canada, and of the concept of unity under the Crown which was more tolerant of diversity than was consensus-based republicanism. There had never been just one way to be British, nor for that matter to be Canadian, therefore their cultural identity did not seem threatened in adopting a new political allegiance. When this kind of understanding of Canada – a Canada which was multicultural – was challenged, especially during World War I, some of the New Canadians reacted by demanding their "rights" and privileges.

It may well be asked on what grounds were such assumptions about multiculturalism and diversity, with no pressures for integration or assimilation to be exerted upon them, founded. The view that in Canada there would be no need to renounce "old country" folkways first originated in the immigration propaganda of the various agents who, in competition with American and Argentinian agents, were recruiting settlers. The Ukrainians certainly were not ignorant of the special concessions and formal guarantees that had been made to the Mennonite and Doukhobor communities as a condition of their establishment on the Prairies. Indeed, the existence of such special concessions for certain ethnic communities readily could be assumed to imply no forced assimilation for any immigrant group.

Furthermore, many immigrants discovered their homestead lots on the Prairies with little in the way of structured, organized social, political and economic life to demand their conformity. There was a sufficient lack of organization and preparedness on the part of the host society to permit the newcomers to interpret the laissez-faire situation as one which encouraged cultural pluralism.

Moreover, the settlement pattern in bloc ethnic rural communities and in city ghettoes may have reinforced the interpretation that Canadian policy was for the retention of ethnic identity. Ethnic reserves encouraged retention of the mother tongue, traditional institutions, patterns of social intercourse, and established folkways. To conclude that the Canadian authorities, in planning the settlement of the Prairies, accepted cultural pluralism as the pattern of society, and that they rejected forced assimilation or integration, was both logical and evident. At least, so it may have seemed to many immigrants.

Finally, if any further proof was required on the part of immigrants for such an assumption of multiculturalism, it seemed to have been clearly indicated in the bilingual school system introduced in Manitoba in 1897, and the special provision for instruction in languages other than Englsh in the rest of the Prairies. Given this tradition, perhaps there is sufficient ground for optimism that the new multiculturalism may be more solidly institutionalized and durable than the old.

Conclusion

The history of Prairie settlement is similar to earlier European patterns in Eastern Canada in the sense that the French preceded the British, but fate ordained that they should form a dual community. This duality distinguishes Canada from the American replubic where unity has been predicated, at least since the Revolution, on uniformity and a certain degree of homogeneity. The Canadian West's French roots made the Prairies more receptive to polyglot and multicultural development. However, the multi-ethnic *épanouissement* eventually aided in the reduction of the francophone community's status from a founding and charter member to that of a minority among numerous minorities. Only the Anglo-Celtic community profited, in the long run, from the integration of immigrant groups on the Prairies. Today, only a lack of historical perspective could obscure the fact that multiculturalism has arisen out of dualism in Canada and that bilingualism reinforces our northern and distinctively Canadian identity on a continent which tends to emphasize homogeneity rather than minority rights.

END NOTES

1. L. Drummond, "The French Element in the Canadian North-West," *Transactions of the Historical and Scientific Society of Manitoba*, No. 28 (1887), p. 14.
2. Sir Robert A. Falconer, "The Unification of Canada," *University Magazine,* Vol. VII (February 1980), p.4.
3. The decennial census of 1891 indicated that out of a population of 108 017 in Manitoba, only 7 555 had been born in Quebec, while 46 630 had been born in Ontario. The total number of Roman Catholics was 20 571 or less than one fifth of the total population.
4. *Le Métis*, January 18, 1877.
5. I am much indebted to Professor Robert Painchaud of the University of Winnipeg who generously shared information relating to schools.
6. *P.A.M.,* PR 10/7, Department of Education, Letterbook of Superintendent of Catholic Schools, Report for 1886.
7. P.H. Attwood, *A Jubilee Essay on Imperial Confederation as affecting Manitoba and the Northwest* (Winnipeg, 1887), p. 15. I differ with Lovell Clark and others who maintain that there was little or no dissatisfaction with the school system prior to 1889 and that D'Alton McCarthy's intervention provoked a sudden assault on the system. W.L. Morton puts it into its correct historical

context: ". . . the feeling was there. The grievance existed. The people's mind had only to be directed to it, and the moment attention was drawn to it, the province of Manitoba rose as one man and said 'We want no dual language – and away with separate schools as well'." W.L. Morton, *Manitoba: A History* (Toronto, 1957), p. 244.

8. Jean Des Prairies, *Une Viste dans les Écoles du Manitoba* (Montreal, 1897), pp. 10-12. I am much indebted to M. Gilbert Comeault of the Provincial Archives of Manitoba for bringing to my attention important documents on this subject.

9. "Mémoire sur la question des Écoles de Manitoba," *Revue d'histoire de l'Amérique française*, Vol. VI, No. 3 (décembre 1952), Gontheir to Lindsay, July 3, 1897, pp. 440-42.

10. F.H. Schofield, *The Story of Manitoba* (Winnipeg, 1913), Vol. 1, pp. 380-82; James A. Jackson, *The Centennial History of Manitoba* (Winnipeg, 1970), pp. 118-19, 151.

11. *A.A.S.B., Fonds Langevin,* Dom Benoit to Msgr. A. Langevin, October 1, 1896.

12. House of Commons, *Debates*, September 24, 1896, pp. 1934-35.

13. Public Archives of Canada (*P.A.C.*), MG 27, Sir Clifford Sifton Papers, II D 15, W.F. McCreary to Sifton, April 13, 1899.

14. *P.A.M.*, RG2, D1, Executive Council, "Memorandum of Settlement of School Question," Ottawa, November 16, 1896.

15. *Manitoba Free Press*, January 13, 1916.

16. *Winnipeg Tribune*, November 23, 1896.

17. *Le Manitoba,* October 25, 1899. The text of the encyclical is given in the *American Catholic Quarterly Review*, Vol. XXIII, No. 2 (April 1897), pp. 189-95.

18. *A.A.S.B.*, Fonds Langevin, Msgr. Langevin to Armand Lavergne, n.d., 1908.

19. Cited in J. Castell Hopkins, "Educational Problems and Conditions in Alberta," *Canadian Annual Review of Public Affairs, 1905* (Toronto, 1906), pp. 224-25.

20. Manitoba, *Report of the Department of Education, 1897* (Winnipeg, 1898), Inspector A.L. Young's report, p. 35.

21. *A.A.S.B.*, Fonds Langevin, Langevin to R. Roblin, January 28, 1901; also, Memorandum to Hon. Roblin, 1901, Letterbook 1900-1901, p. 646.

22. *Les Clôches de Saint-Boniface*, Vol I (January, 1902), p. 8. Langevin had already obtained the promise of Belgian Redemptorists to serve as priests in Ukrainian parishes. The clearest statement from Archbishop Langevin concerning the policy of linking the School Question, European Catholic immigration, and Franco-American repatriation is contained in a letter to a colonizing priest in 1898. CF. *A.A.S.B.*, Fonds Langevin, Letter Book, I, Msgr. Langevin to abbé Jean Gaire, April 5, 1898. Clarification of the question of francophone immigration to the West and the role of the Catholic Church will have to await the publication of the doctoral thesis of Professor Robert Painchaud, University of Winnipeg, to whom I am grateful for the above reference. In a memorandum to the Canadian hierarchy and to two East European cardinals, Langevin maintained that a common front would force a favorable settlement of the School Question. *A.A.S.B.*, Fonds Langevin, Memorandum to the Canadian episcopate and to Cardinals Rampalla and Ledowchowski, September 27, 1901.

23. *Manitoba Free Press*, November 15, 1898.

24. *A.A.S.B.*, Fonds Langevin, Msgr. Langevin to R. Roblin, February 6, 1909, pp. 331-33.

25. *Manitoba Free Press*, January 15, 1907.

26. Harold W. Foght, *A Survey of Education in the Province of Saskatchewan, Canada* (Regina, 1918), p. 150.

27. *Regina Leader*, October 25, 1919.

28. R.J.C. Stead, "The Mixer," quoted in R.C. Brown and Ramsay Cook, *Canada 1896-1921: A Nation Tranformed* (Toronto: McCelland and Stewart, 1974), p. 73.

29. *Archives of Saskatchewan (A.S.)*, M4, Hon. W.M. Martin Papers, FIle 53 (7), Martin to H.R. Walker, Kindersley, January 2, 1919, folio 18444.

30. *Ibid*, Debate of December 19, 1918, p. 18534.

NANCIELLEN DAVIS Mount Saint Vincent University

Acadian Women: Economic Development, Ethnicity, and the Status of Women*

Contrary to popular opinion, women in modern industrialized societies do not necessarily have a higher status than those in egalitarian and/or pre-industrialized societies (Tomeh, 1975: 44-48),[1] and modernization in some Third World areas has been described as creating "modern [sexual] inequality, the devaluation of female labor, and economic dependence" (Bossen, 1975: 595). If this is so, the relation between development and the status of women in Canadian regions such as northeastern New Brunswick, where federal-provincial development programs have been extensive, may be problematic.

Status may be described in at least two ways – in terms of prestige and in terms of power; although, of course, the two are not mutually exclusive. "High status may be inferred from deferential treatment, or may consist of an actual position of power over basic resources and important decisions" (Brown, 1970: 152). Assessment of socioeconomic change in Saint-Simon[2], an Acadian village in northeastern New Brunswick, indicates that the power and prestige of local women have been eroded, and that development has contributed to this erosion. It is a truism that the effects of development may be unforeseen and even unfortunate, but that women may be especially vulnerable deserves explanation. What is the basis of women's vulnerability in developing areas, particularly in Saint-Simon and northeastern New Brunswick?

Women and Development

Recent contributions to the anthropology of women relate the status of women to a variety of socioeconomic factors. Sacks, in her reexamination of Engels' account of women's status, suggests the usefulness of distinguishing between women's status as social adults and as wives, each position being affected by different criteria. Sacks suggests that "basically, women are social adults where they work collectively as part of a productive

---

* A revised version of a paper presented at the Conference on Women, Mount Saint Vincent University, Halifax, Nova Scotia, November, 1976. Sincere appreciation is expressed to Patrick L. Baker who made numerous valuable suggestions regarding this paper.

group larger than or separate from their domestic establishment," and their status as wives seems to depend on whether or not (family) estates are owned privately by males (1974: 218-19). Rosaldo similarly stresses implications for women's status arising from the restriction of females' activities to the domestic domain, as opposed to the public (economic and political) domain in which men are active (1974). These points are highly relevant in assessing contexts where sex roles related to work are undergoing modifications and are central to this discussion of the status of women in modernizing societies.

According to Bossen, modernization often brings "under-development" for women (1975: 595). This is particularly apparent in societies, like those in West Africa, where women traditionally held considerable economic power as traders. In this role, women controlled capital and displayed expertise in performing work which was recognized as valuable within the society. Today, women are progressively excluded from this occupation (Bossen, 1975: 593-94). Development strategies used in these situations have often been structured on Western models which stress specialization and hierarchical organization in which men have the most important roles.

Less striking, but perhaps more common, are the effects of modernization in societies where both men and women had traditionally contributed equally to the production of goods for the subsistence and maintenance of the household, or where women largely supported the household through their agricultural activities. In certain cases new means of production have been made available to males, although the productive activities themselves were those customarily allotted to women. Where the redefining of the activity as male rather than female has been accepted, men have gone on to gain control of a larger portion of production and thereby gradually lessened women's importance in such areas (Boserup, 1970: 53-64). Bossen is thus led to conclude that often in developing nations "modernization results in a smaller share for women in the total economy due to restrictions against their entry into many modern occupations and a devaluation of traditional subsistence activities." (1975: 595).[3]

These observations on development and the status of women in the Third World are relevant when we examine development strategies in nations like Canada where particular groups and regions are the focus of planned socioeconomic change. The importance of native groups' definitions of sex roles, and their reciprocal relationship to development strategies, is apparent. Less obvious questions involve development strategies and their relation to role systems of residents in economically depressed areas like the Maritime provinces. In the Maritimes most persons are descendents of the charter groups and probably share many of the same assumptions regarding the sexual division of labor as do development agents. Nonetheless, questions remain, for this assessment of socioeconomic change in northeastern New Brunswick suggests that the industrialization of the traditional division of labor contributes to an erosion in women's status.

Village, Region, and Development

The northeasternmost part of New Brunswick dips down and forms two islands, Lameque and Miscou. Lameque Island is about a mile from the mainland, to which it is connected by a bridge; the village of Saint-Simon is located on Lameque's eastern coast. Just north of Lameque is the smaller and less populated Miscou Island. These two islands and the narrow peninsular mainland south and west of Lameque make up Shippegan (civil) Parish.

Saint-Simon is similar to many northeastern New Brunswick villages in terms of the ethnic, demographic,[4] and economic features of its residents. Many area residents are descendents of Acadians who, on returning from the *grande dérangement* of the mid-1750s, settled along New Brunswick's northern and eastern coasts and riverways, the least accessible and agriculturally productive areas of the province, where anglophone settlers were few. Today New Brunswickers of French origin make up 37 percent of the province's population, but in Gloucester County (wherein Saint-Simon is located) francophones comprise 83 percent of the population. Like most other residents of Shippegan Parish, the 387 villagers of Saint-Simon are francophone, Roman Catholic, and descendents of Acadians.

Fishing and fish processing employ about 60 percent of the rural labor force in Shippegan Parish, and villagers of Saint-Simon rely very heavily on the fishery. Women represent about 90 percent of the workers in parish fish processing plants (or *usines*) which is practically the only source of employment available to local women.[5] In this area, fishing and fish processing are limited to the warmer months, and there is thus high unemployment from December through April, when residents must depend on unemployment insurance payments and social assistance. Area incomes are low; in 1961 the average family income in Shippegan Parish was about 37 percent of the average for Canada as a whole ($1,807:$4,906).[6]

Compounding the poverty of northeastern New Brunswick are serious problems in health and education. In order to tackle some of these issues, the federal and provincial governments, in the mid-1960s, approved the expenditure of $100 million for area development (Poetschke, 1971). School and highway construction have been relatively recent developments and longer-range goals include the rationalization of the inshore fishery and the relocation of rural dwellers into approved urban centers. In general, the strategies seem to have been aimed at economic growth, "a change in the volume of goods and services produced, [and] of purchasing power" (Belshaw, 1974: 521) of area residents.

These strategies were also implicitly aimed at increasing the complexity of social organization, that is, increasing the specialization and interdependence of roles and institutions. Thus, a rationalization of the inshore fishery entails decreasing the number of fishermen. But as an outcome of this strategy, men become dependent on other kinds of labor, especially that in local *usines*.[7] The human costs of such development are that men as wage laborers may experience alienation, either in terms of actual loss of control of economic livelihood, or in the felt loss of control and associated dissatisfaction in work.

Villagers dislike *usine* labor; it is described as boring and tiresome. Men say that they prefer fishing as they are their own bosses – free to come and go as they wish. With "development," this possibility of working for oneself and with those of one's household has diminished. In the Shippegan area, both men and women engage in wage labor at *usines*. So it is not men alone who experience the "benefits" of development.

Changing Economic Participation of Saint-Simon Women

Development programs in northeastern New Brunswick have accelerated processes of change similar to those occurring elsewhere in the world where traditional communities have been progressively modernized and industrialized. Traditionally, villagers in Saint-Simon engaged in a combination of inshore fishing and farming. Farming was largely for subsistence purposes and fishing for the production of marketable goods. Fishermen exchanged their catches for supplies and equipment at company stores. Through the early decades of this century, cash realized from fishing seems to have been negligible for most households.

Prior to 1940, fish catches were salted and dried before sale, and much of this processing labor was performed by women.[8] Women daily spread and turned the fish drying on the stages, and, on the return of the boats each day, aided in cleaning and preparing the fish for preserving. Women were also responsible for a wide range of activities in the farm and home – caring for stock and garden, processing and preserving food-stuffs, making clothes and other household items. In short, women were active partners in the production of goods for consumption and sale. At the same time, of course, they often bore and cared for eight, 10 or more children.

Around 1940 several fresh fish processing *usines* were founded in the area. Groundfish no longer had to be salted and dried prior to sale, but could be turned over directly to a *usine* representative. Coupled with the creation of the fresh fish processing industry was the increasing mechanization of the inshore fishery and the reemergence of an offshore fishing industry, both of which were stimulated by government funding. The fishing industry received a needed boost from the government at midcentury, and its effects were felt in the form of higher returns for fish sales and increased opportunity for men to purchase expensive boats and equipment, again made available via the provisions of the Fishermen's Loan Board and similar government agencies. Government monies were also provided for building and enlarging *usines*, thus further expanding the fishery and local job opportunities. These developments contributed to the decline and eventual demise of farming interests.[9]

The implications for women's role have been several. The household no longer cooperates in pluralistic economic activities; some men have several occupations, but in few households do men and women jointly engage in economic enterprises. Women at home have become increasingly specialized; their work is largely restricted to the care of house and children. Some women still maintain vegetable gardens and preserve large quantities of foodstuffs; however, this is less characteristic of younger village women. Compared to their mothers and grandmothers, these younger women are "unemployed"; they produce few goods for household consumption or sale.

Village women denied the traditional role of co-producer may become dependent on their husbands or seek wage labor, usually in *usines*. Such employment is taken during periods when responsibilities for children are lightest – before the woman marries and has children or after her children are of school age. Most women yearly earn only a few thousand dollars through wages and unemployment insurance payments; however, this makes considerable difference in households where the man's income is also low.[10]

Development and the Erosion of Women's Status

Local women's increasing participation in the labor force might suggest that change and development have benefited them. Nearly three and a half times as many women in Gloucester County reported income in 1971 as in 1961 (11 225:3 314), and this compares favorably with the increase of slightly more than two times as many men receiving income in 1971 as in 1961 (20 665:9 580). The lifestyle in Saint-Simon has improved; most households have televisions, many others have major appliances such as refrigerators, deep freezers, stoves, and even dishwashers. A few village fishermen have prospered in the offshore fishery, and one such villager has recently purchased a $250 000 fishing vessel. In what ways may women's position be described as eroded?

Ethnicity and Women's Status

The traditional status of Acadian women is closely related to elements of class, age, and a complex of cultural traits which may be equated with ethnicity. As socioeconomic change and development affect these elements, so do they affect the status of local women.

Basic components of Acadian ethnicity are the French language, Roman Catholicism, and a sense of common regional and historical origins. The significance of these components varies according to historical and sociocultural context. Religious influence within schools constituted a conflict issue between Acadians and their non-Catholic neighbors in the 19th century. In this century language has supplanted religion as a contentious issue, but differences in demography, settlement pattern, and historical inter-ethnic group relations influence actual language-based conflict in provincial regions (Sealy, 1977; 1978). All Saint-Simon residents are Acadian, and so the intravillage structuring of interaction is not based on ethnic identity. However, ethnicity does color local life and women's status. This becomes apparent by comparing household and community roles of Saint-Simon women with those of women in Cat Harbour, an Anglo-Canadian outport in Newfoundland.[11]

The roles women play in Saint-Simon and the ecclessiastical parish are those in which household or domestic specializations involving children, education, and religion are conducted at a community level. In general, if a Saint-Simon woman fills the appropriate role within household and community – as responsible wife and mother, as member interested in the running of parish and school – she is accorded a measure of respect that seems absent for women in Newfoundland outports like Cat Harbour (Faris, 1966). In Cat Harbour, life is decidedly "male dominated" with women having little authority within household and community; they are little compensated for their hard work, and instead are the first to be suspected of being "witches" or "jinkers." Female characteristics have negative connotations there, and things that are negatively perceived, such as potentially leaky boats, are symbolically identified as being female (Faris, 1966: 95-99).

Although life in Cat Harbour and Saint-Simon is similar in ways related to the residents' techno-economic adaptations, other sociocultural factors differ and contribute to a more elevated position for women in Saint-Simon, as reflected in deferential treatment of women, the symbolic and public honor accorded to women as mothers and wives, and the representation by women on parish committees. Contributing to this higher status in Saint-Simon are religious affiliation and marriage and residence patterns, factors which are based in, or related to, the ethnic origins of villagers.

The Cat Harbour residents are anglophone and Protestant, either United Church of Canada or Jehovah's Witnesses, and neither seems to supply underlying positive evaluation of women in Cat Harbour (Faris, 1966: 164-73). In comparison, in the parish Catholic church, Saint-Simon residents are regularly exposed to sermons and celebrations honoring the Mother of God, motherhood, and women's role in local domestic life.

Marriage and residence patterns also affect the status of women in the two fishing villages. In Cat Harbour, residence tends to be virilocal; about 65 percent of the wives are outsiders (Faris, 1966: 95) and fall in the category of "strangers" whom native residents of Cat Harbour generally suspect and mistrust. In Saint-Simon, on the other hand, choice of marriage partners is made largely from within the ecclessiastical parish and/or village. Although outsiders are negatively perceived in both Saint-Simon and Cat Harbour, most women in Saint-Simon are not outsiders and, hence, are not negatively perceived for that reason.

Although Saint-Simon women have a higher status than do women in Cat Harbour, they do not have the highest positions in the community and household. Nuns serve various functions in the church and local schools, but in these cases it is the priest who has the primary respect and authority. Though women are elected to serve on various administrative bodies in the parish, a man is traditionally chosen to be the president or the chairman of that body. Thus, deferential treatment is not equivalent to the possession of power, and women's roles remain subordinate to those of men.

In Saint-Simon and in Acadian communities in Nova Scotia (Hughes, et al., 1960: 126-28; 148-49) women are highly valued for their domestic or familial role, which is complementary to, and not necessarily less prestigious than, that of men. As discussed above, the evaluation of women as important household workers has a strong historical basis in fact – women traditionally made a large contribution to subsistence and market economies. However, both domestic-familial and economic bases of prestige have been undermined with socioeconomic change. Today, local women are increasingly involved in wage labor, and the effect of this on their highly esteemed traditional role is not clear. It seems that as women increasingly participate in wage labor, such work comes to be expected of them, at least at certain stages of their life cycle, and within the village the ideal role of women may be in the process of redefinition. Working women are alternatively praised or criticized, and they themselves are ambivalent about their employment.

Related to this increase in the proportion of working women is a reduction in the average size of families in the village. Fewer children are due to a variety of reasons, including the reliance today on wage labor as opposed to subsistence activities (in which children were productive and useful members) and the local church's diminished role in encouraging large families. Village women married prior to 1940 had approximately twice as many children as their daughters (an average of 10 live births per woman as compared to a projected five or six live births per woman married between 1960 and 1970). Although rearing four to six children is a considerable task, it is obviously less than that of older women who are highly praised for their work, sacrifice, and devotion to their large families. As domestic roles alter in response to societal change and development, the ideal role will either alter, or the younger women may have to choose on the one hand to elaborate their actual housewife-mother role so that they are as busy and as valued as earlier village women, or on the other hand to receive less prestige than their predecessors.

Age and Women's Status

Age is related to the control of power, and in Saint-Simon middle-aged and young adults run community affairs. Older persons maintain households as long as their health allows, but their last years are often spent in children's

TABLE 1 *Average income by sex*

	1961		1971	
	M	F	M	F
Rural non-farm				
Gloucester County	$1 584	$ 908	$3 509	$1 769
New Brunswick	2 807	1 569	5 042	2 282
Canada	3 679	1 995	6 538	2 883

Source: Census of Canada 1961, 1971.

households or in the nearby senior citizens' home. In the former case, social changes have modified their role in these households from the traditional norm. For example, reduced family size has curtailed the importance of grandparents as babysitters and thereby reduced their overall influence in the home. Thus, the elders return to the relatively powerless position of their youth and childhood.

Saint-Simon women of different generations vary in their educational and work experiences. Development includes increasing specialization of labor and demands skills and training which older women usually do not possess. Thus development creates restrictions on older women seeking work and limits their access to positions of decision-making and control over resources.

Social Class and Women's Status

"The most important feature of class is the asymmetrical distribution of power" (Harris, 1975: 396). This asymmetry is reflected in ideology, relationships, and material goods, and one indicator of the latter is income. Northeastern New Brunswick has experienced economic growth; more people are working and for higher wages, and more goods are being purchased than 10 years ago. However, area incomes still lag behind those of Canadians elsewhere, and women lag behind men, with the size of the income gap between men and women increasing. The data for the 1961-71 period is shown in Table 1.

When 1961 and 1971 incomes in rural, non-farm Gloucester Country are compared, it is evident from Table 1 that the average income of men in 1971 is 2.2. times greater than their 1961 income, and the income of women in 1971 is 1.9 times greater than their income in 1961. However, when this increase for both sexes in the county is placed in perspective with the average income in the province and county, it is found that in 1961 the average incomes of men and women in rural, non-farm Gloucester county represented 56 percent and 58 percent of those of men and women in New Brunswick, and 43 percent and 46 percent of those of men and women in Canada. In 1971 comparable incomes were 70 percent and 78 percent of those of men and women in the province, and 54 percent and 61 percent of those of men and women in Canada. (See Table 1.) In New Brunswick as a whole, women in 1961 earned slightly more than half (56 percent) of that of men, and in 1971 the gap had increased such that women earned less than half (45 percent) of that of men.

Between 1961 and 1971 the consumer price index increased by one third.[12] Villagers' "style of consumption" has altered (Runciman, 1969: 48), but the prosperity of households reflects combined incomes, which are individually low, and government transfer payments. Although some villagers enjoy material possessions like those of many Canadians elsewhere, they do so at a much greater cost.

In spite of development programs, the relative position of area residents has not altered, and the position of women has actually deteriorated; average incomes of women in rural (non-farm) Gloucester County has declined in the 10-year period from 58 percent to 50 percent of the income of men. Furthermore, in 1971 in Gloucester County, over seven times as many men as women earned $7 000 or more; in rural Gloucester County nearly eight times as many men as women earned $7 000 or more. More women are working today than in 1961, but their earnings continue to compare unfavorably with those of men.

Development programs have been aimed at stimulating growth in traditionally defined male activities, namely fishing. Today, both capital and expertise are controlled by men, but this was not always the case. Traditionally, there was minimal capital to be controlled by men and women, and men were not the exclusive holders of skills and knowledge in economic enterprises. If class differences are defined in terms of differential access to power, basic resources, and decision-making (Harris, 1975: 396-97), then development programs have undermined the class position of women.[13] Thus, a hidden cost of development in the region appears to be a widening differential in the socioeconomic position of the sexes.

Implications

The socioeconomic changes in Saint-Simon and the region represent a microcosm of the changes occurring elsewhere in North America as rural communities have been progressively incorporated into a larger, industrial, and market-oriented society. A similar pattern occurs in the Third World where Western social and economic models of progress have been continuously imposed. Contrary to what might be expected, such change has often been associated with the erosion in the status of women in both domestic and public contexts.

In northeastern New Brunswick women have an increased opportunity to obtain wage labor in *usines*. However, women's participation in the labor force does not reflect an improved status in comparison to that previously held by them or that held by today's men; it indicates the contrary.

Development programs in this region are aimed at improving and expanding regional industry, particularly the fishery in which males hold the most powerful and prestigious positions. Employment in the *usines* is little valued by men or women.

Socioeconomic change and development also affect the basis and maintenance of ethnicity in previously distinct groups, and this may partially occur through women. Acadian women have been considered the repository of traditional values and the conveyors of values to children (Hughes, et al., 1960: 128). Women were a source of stability and continuity in the ethnic group and specifically in Saint Simon. Although men left Saint-Simon to work elsewhere in the province or in the offshore fishery, women had little experience beyond the village. As one measure of that isolation, no older village women are bilingual in French and English, while several men of that generation are.

Although Saint-Simon was never isolated from the outside world, the village women experienced a degree of isolation and probably represented a conservative force locally. However, as a result of development, some women, like men, now work beyond the village and island. Women have become the conveyors of extra-village influences, some of which weaken cultural features traditionally distinguishing Acadians from others. This does not imply that Acadians will lose their ethnic identity, but only that their ethnicity may be redefined according to existing sociocultural conditions (Barth, 1969). However, if features associated with ethnicity provide the rationale for the sexual division of labor and for the allocation of power and prestige to women and men, change in these features may alter or even undermine the traditional status of women. In the absence of real opportunities for advancement in the developing society, women may be denied both traditional and modern bases for obtaining high status.

Development programs may have an extra cost for certain individuals and groups, and in northeastern New Brunswick those extra costs have been borne especially by the women. Furthermore, it appears that development strategies may help maintain, rather than eradicate, social inequalities and the exploitation of disadvantaged groups, as indicated within this one Canadian region.

END NOTES

1. For an example of a pre-industrial society in which women held positions of considerable power and influence, see Brown's (1970) discussion of women among the Iroquois.
2. Fieldwork took place for seven months in 1971 and 1972. "Saint-Simon" is a pseudonym.
3. See also, Human Resources Development Division 1975; Tinker, et al., 1976; Wellesley Editorial Committee, 1977.

4. Northeastern New Brunswick is predominantly rural and is characterized by high out-migration of working-age adults, high birth rates, and concomitantly, a population in which a great number are economically non-productive young people; 60 percent of the population in northeastern New Brunswick (defined as Gloucester County, Restigouche County, and Alnick Parish of Northumberland County) is less than 25 years of age (Even, 1970: 76-109 passim). In Saint Simon 62 percent of the population is less than 25, and 5 percent is 65 years of age or more; hence, only a third of the villagers are active adults, a proportion similar to that of active adults for the area as a whole.

5. See Community Improvement Corporation Planning Department 1968.

6. In 1971 the average family income in Shippegan Parish had risen to 51 percent of the average for Canada as a whole ($4 913; $9 600).

7. Some fishermen resist specialization; they fish 12 weeks, and then work in *usines* for another two to three months, depending on job opportunities.

8. Inshore fishermen in recent decades have fished lobster, groundfish, and herring; today lobster fishing provides their main source of income.

9. Much of northeastern New Brunswick does not constitute good farmland, and at mid-century the area as a whole began a decline in farming activity. Villagers in Saint-Simon considered that the decline and absence of local farming today was due to its being no longer financially advantageous.

10. Most households receive various types of transfer payments from the government, such as child and youth allowance, unemployment insurance payments, and pensions.

11. It is preferable to compare Saint-Simon women with women of an anglophone Protestant fishing community in New Brunswick; however, appropriate studies of such communities are not available. Newfoundland outports like Cat Harbour differ from Saint-Simon in ways other than their residents' ethnicity. As a result of historical, demographic, and geographical factors, the Newfoundland outports have remained more isolated and have maintained a more traditional, near-peasant way of life than have New Brunswick's Acadian fishing villages. Faris' study of Cat Harbour is a "classic" in the anthropologial literature on Atlantic Canada and provides a rich description against which comparisons can be drawn.

12. *Canada Yearbook 1973*, p. 842.

13. Sex stratification entails at least two dimensions. Housewives derive a status from that of their husbands, and employed women derive a status from their employment. It is this latter dimension to which my comments are related. For a discussion of women as a minority group, caste, and class, see Eichler, 1973.

SELECTED REFERENCES

Barth, Fredrik, ed. *Ethnic Groups and Boundaries.* Boston: Little, Brown and Company, 1969, pp. 9-38.

Belshaw, Cyril S. "The Contribution of Anthropology to Development." *Current Anthropology* 15:4 (1974), pp. 520-26.

Boserup, Ester. *Woman's Role in Economic Development.* London: Allen and Unwin, 1970.

Bossen, Laurel. "Women in Modernizing Societies." *American Ethnologist* 2:4 (1975), pp. 587-601.

Brown, Judith K. "Economic Organization and the Position of Women Among the Iroquois," *Ethno-history* 17 (1970), pp. 151-67.

Canada Year Book 1973. Ottawa: Statistics Canada, 1973.

Census of Canada 1961, 1971. Ottawa: Statistics Canada, 1961 and 1971.

Northeast New Brunswick, Outline Community Plans: Shippegan. Fredericton, N.B.: Community Improvement Corp. Planning Department, 1968.

Eichler, Margrit, "Women as Personal Dependents." In Marylee Stephenson, ed., *Women in Canada*. Toronto: New Press, 1973, pp. 38-55.

Even, Alain. "Le Territoire Pilote du Nouveau-Brunswick ou les blocages culturels au développement économique." Thèse pour le doctorat en économie du développement, Rennes, 1970.

Faris, James C. "Cat Harbour: a Newfoundland Fishing Settlement." *Newfoundland Social and Economic Studies No. 3*. St. John's Newfoundland: Institute of Social and Economic Research, Memorial University of Newfoundland, 1966.

Harris, Marvin. *Culture, People, Nature*. New York: Thomas Y. Crowell Inc., 1975.

Hughes, Charles C., et al. *People of Cove and Woodlot*. New York: Basic Books, Inc., 1960.

Poetschke, L.E. "Regional Planning for Depressed Rural Areas – The Canadian Experience." In John Harp and John R. Hofley, eds., *Poverty in Canada*. Scarborough, Ont.: Prentice-Hall of Canada, Ltd., 1971.

Rosaldo, Michelle Z. "Women, Culture and Society: A Theoretical Overview." In Michelle Zimbalist Rosaldo and Louise Lamphere, eds., *Women, Culture, and Society*. Palo Alto, California: Stanford University Press, 1974.

Runciman, W.G. "The Three Dimensions of Social Inequality." In Andre Beteille, ed., *Social Inequality*. England: Penguin Education, 1969, pp. 45-63.

Sacks, Karen. "Engels Revisited: Women, the Organization of Production, and Private Property." In Michelle Zimbalist Rosaldo and Louise Lamphere, eds., *Women, Culture and Society*. Palo Alto, California: Stanford University Press, 1974, pp. 207-22.

Sealy, Nanciellen Davis. "Diverses perspectives dans l'étude de la survivance du groupe ethnique acadien." *Les cahiers* 8:2 (1977), pp. 53-64.

———— . "Language Conflict and Schools in New Brunswick," in Martin L. Kovac, ed., *Ethnic Canadians: Culture and Education*. Regina, Sask.: Canadian Plains Research Centre, University of Regina, 1978.

Tinker, Irene, et al., eds. *Women and World Development*. New York: Praeger Publishers, 1976.

Tomeh, Aida K. *The Family and Sex Roles*. Toronto: Holt, Rinehart and Winston of Canada, Ltd., 1975.

Women and National Development in African Countries: Some Profound Contradictions. Human Resources Development Division of the African Training and Research Centre for Women, United Nations Economic Commission for Africa, *The African Review* XVIII:3 (1975), pp. 47-70.

Women and National Development, The Complexities of Change. Wellesley Editorial Committee, *Signs 3:1 (1977)*.

ERIC WADDELL   Laval University

CLAIRE DORAN   Association culturelle franco-canadienne de la
Saskatchewan, Régina

The Newfoundland French: An Endangered Minority?*

Introduction[1]

There are three concentrations of French-speaking people in Newfoundland – Labrador City, St. John's, and the Port-au-Port peninsula. It
is only in the third area, however, that one finds authentic Newfoundlanders of French origin (Figure 1); that is, people deeply rooted in
their villages who profess no other "homeland." Thus, although the francophones in Labrador City constitute almost one quarter of the population
and have access to French schooling, they are basically a transient group of
Québécois and Acadian workers attracted by the high salaries associated
with the extraction of iron ore and firmly intent on returning home one day.
In St. John's one finds a somewhat similar situation with, once again,
Québécois constituting the vast majority of francophones. They are
employed by the federal government and crown corporations, the schools
and university and some large businesses. It is a predominantely professional class that can afford to travel home frequently on visits and regards
the Newfoundland capital as only a temporary place of residence. There
are, of course, a number of francophones established on a permanent basis
in St. John's. Tradesman drawn in from Labrador City and St. Pierrais are
attracted by the more abundant employment opportunities and higher standard of living in the city. But in general such people consider themselves to
be strangers in an English-speaking world, and they are little concerned with
the affirmation of French rights.

Ignored by French Canada until the start of the 1970s and, above all,
overlooked by the Royal Commission on Bilingualism and Biculturalism in
the 1960s, the "true" French Newfoundlanders of the west coast are only
now beginning to make themselves known to the rest of the country, and
furnishing in the process, to the evident delight of certain politicians in Ottawa, the "proof" that a French Canada exists from coast to coast and in

---

* A slightly revised and abbreviated version of "Les Franco-Terre-Neuviens: Survie et
Renaissance Équivoques," *Cahiers de géographic du Quebec*, Vol. 23, No. 58, (1979), Les
Presses de l'Université Laval, Quebec.

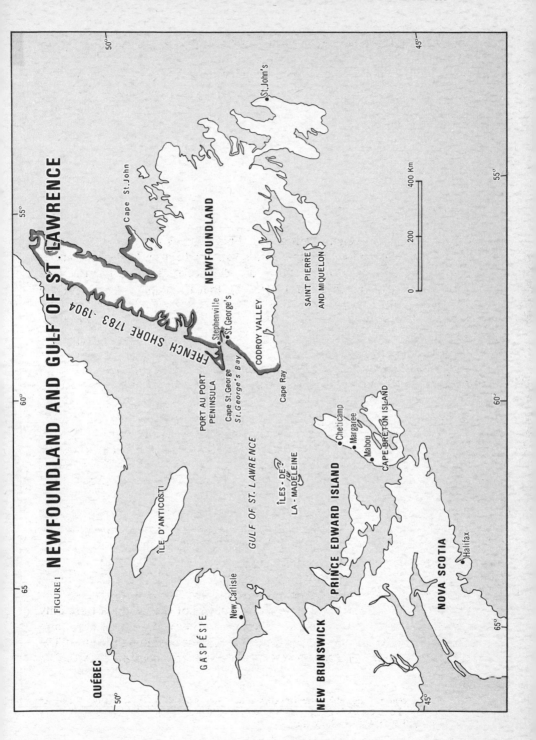

FIGURE I **NEWFOUNDLAND AND GULF OF ST. LAWRENCE**

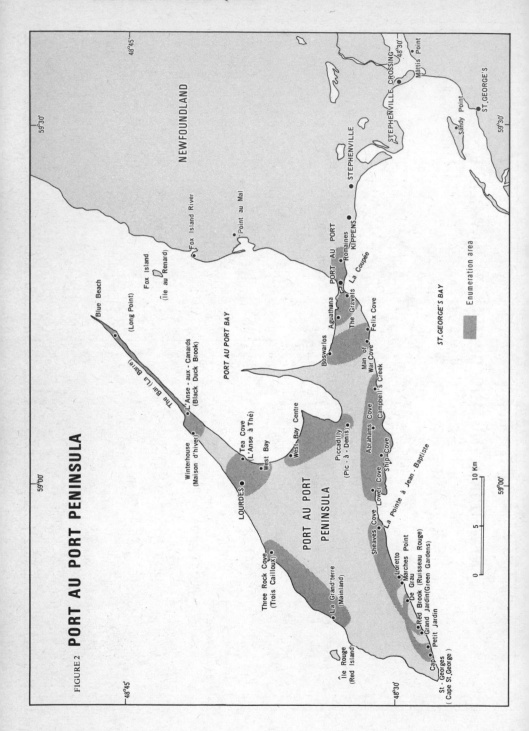

FIGURE 2   **PORT AU PORT PENINSULA**

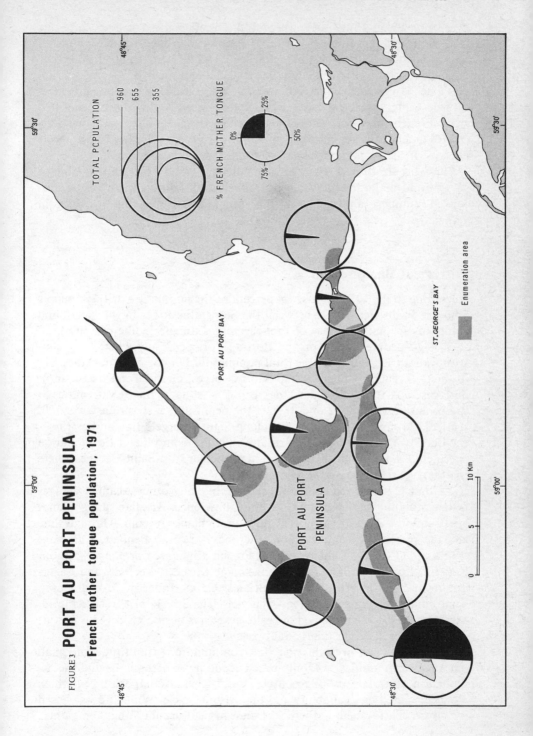

FIGURE 3 **PORT AU PORT PENINSULA**
French mother tongue population, 1971

every province. Thus, they were able to entice the Secretary of State (Pelletier) on a fact finding tour in 1973, and the Prime Minister (Trudeau) for the opening of their first bilingual school in 1975. In the meanwhile they supplied the last link in the interprovincial chain of the Fédération des Francophones Hors-Québec (FFHQ) and the Association Canadienne d'Éducation de Langue Française (ACELF). More recently they have benefitted from French television relayed by satellite from Montreal and have attracted Quebec filmmakers seeking to portray yet another tiny francophone enclave virtually submerged in a vast English-speaking continent.

But who are these French Newfoundlanders, and how are they able to survive and make themselves heard, albeit only faintly, when they are so few in number, and living in the most English-speaking province in Canada?[2]

Historical Background

According to the 1971 census, 4.4 percent of the population or 1 260 people who live in district No. 4[3] between the Serpentine River in the North and Cape Ray in the South are of French mother tongue. Some two-thirds of them (820 people) reside on the Port-au-Port peninsula where they constitute about 13 percent of the total population. For the most part they live in three "French" villages – Cap-Saint-Georges, Grand'Terre (Mainland), and Anse-aux-Canards (Black Duck Brook) – situated on the extremities of the peninsula (Figures 2 and 3). Off the peninsula, there are a few small, scattered groups of francophones along Saint-George's Bay and as far as the Codroy Valley. However, virtually all cultural and linguistic animation is centered in the three villages, and in particular Cap-Saint-Georges where there is a solid French-speaking majority.

At first glance these communities look like any other Acadian villages found along the banks of the Gulf of St. Lawrence. Acadian family names are common – Benoit, Cormier, Chiasson, Leblanc, Aucoin. Through time and the pressure of anglicisation, they have become Bennett, Chaisson, White and O'Quinn. Other names of French origin are Formanger, Simon, Retieffe, Rouzes. From Brittany have come Cornect, Kerfont, and Lagatdu; from Saint-Pierre – Morazé, Briand, Ozon. Indeed, there are even some that originated in the Channel Islands – Leprieur, Lecointre, Messervey. However, the region really never has been considered a part of *Acadie*, either in earlier times or at present.

The traditional lifestyle was one common to a multitude of small maritime communities: a family-based economy structured around the exploitation of a diversity of resources, the particular composition of which was determined by availability and the seasonal cycle. While life was based mostly on coastal fishing, there was some argiculture, hunting, and gathering as well as work in lumber camps during the winter months. Inevitably the words of Antonine Maillet come to mind in describing her Acadian people, "Fishermen, lumberjacks, blacksmiths, jacks of all trades or people without work."* And today they exploit, effectively, the resources of unemployment insurance and welfare benefits as much as those of the sea.

This population is an ethnic minority (with the exception of the three communities of Cap-Saint-Georges, Grand'Terre, and Anse-aux-Canards), small in number, it is without its own institutions or with any that might link it to Acadia; it has no tradition of a local elite, and consists of people of diverse origins that settled in a somewhat anarchic fashion along the coast. Nevertheless, it has succeeded in preserving a certain French personality for over three generations. This is all the more remarkable if one considers that the provincial government has never officially acknowledged a French presence in Newfoundland, and that, at the regional level, the ethnic boundary separating the francophone minority from the anglophone majority is very diffuse by virtue of both groups belonging to the Catholic Church. Thus, linguistic exogamy always has been permitted by religious authorities in contrast with Quebec and Acadia where up to the 1960s francophones were typically Catholic and anglophone Protestant.

To better understand the circumstances of group survival, it is necessary to consider the particular circumstances surrounding the settlement of the Port-au-Port peninsula.

(1) A Brief History and Geography of the West Coast

In the 19th century, the west coast of Newfoundland was part of two different worlds. One world was an outpost of metropolitan France as there was a French presence on the coast until 1904. The other world centered upon the Gulf of St. Lawrence which had experienced an Acadian penetration as a result of great seaborne migrations that originated in Cape Breton, Prince Edward Island, and the Magdalen Islands.

The French and Acadian groups had distinctly different interests in the area. As the coast was under their jurisdiction, the French started appearing at the end of the 18th century, first to fish for cod and later, towards the end of the 19th century, for lobster. Cod fishing was an undertaking organized by the State on a seasonal basis around a series of island and peninsula-based fishing stations. At the end of the year, in 1904, six stations remained on the French Shore between Cape St. John and Cape Bay, of which three were located on the Port-au-Port peninsula. The most important one was Red Island (Île Rouge), opposite la Grand'Terre, which attracted between 100 and 150 fishermen each summer.

---

* "Pêcheurs, bûcherons, forgerons, hommes à tout faire ou hommes à ne rien faire du tout."

In order to avoid the military draft, Frenchmen (from Saintonge and Normandy), men from St. Pierre and Breton often volunteered for service on the fishing boats. The hardship associated with this life encouraged some to desert and settle along the coast. In addition, a few St. Pierre families were established on the French Shore to look after the fishing installations. Towards the end of the 19th century they were joined by other St. Pierre families, attracted by the lobster fishing which was particularly profitable along the peninsula. As schooner owners who had come by their own means, these families often directed the fishery, served as merchants, and built their own lobster canneries. The small local population, consequently, found work in the canneries and ready buyers for their catch.

The last French arrived in 1903, on the eve of the extinction of the fishing rights accorded by the Treaty of Utrecht. The resulting population was predominantly masculine. If it were to grow, it would have to look for wives elsewhere.

The movement of the Acadians towards the west coast of Newfoundland in the mid-19th century was part of a wider migration in the direction of the Gulf of St. Lawrence's northern shore. Arriving in family groups aboard their own schooners from Cheticamp, Margaree, and Mabou (Cape Breton), occasionally via the Magdalen Islands, they were looking for good agricultural land. Hence they were drawn to the larger bays and inlets, and in particular Saint George's Bay and the Codroy Valley. Thriving communities emerged at Saint George and even Stephenville (formerly called l'Anse-aux-Sauvages). Before long, trade as well as matrimonial ties were established between the Acadians and the French. During this period the Acadian community was sufficiently vigorous to request a resident priest and, around 1850, Father Bélanger from the Magdalen Islands, assumed this role.[5]

The Acadian milieu of the bay differed in several respects from the French of the peninsula. First, there was a more favorable sex ratio in the Acadian settlements. Second, they lived off the land rather than off the sea. Third, there was a greater ethnic diversity in the Acadian communities. Of these two groups, the one of French origin was better able to resist assimilation. Their cultural tenacity is to be explained by the greater geographic isolation of the inhabitants of the peninsula, the relative linguistic homogeneity of the population, an economic organization centering on the family, and the presence in the first generation of a number of educated people. The equilibrium of the Acadian area was repeatedly upset, first by the arrival of railroad at the end of the 19th century and later by the trans-Newfoundland highway. Sawmills were established in the early part of the 20th century and an enormous military base was built during World War II at Stephenville, which literally eliminated l'Anse-aux-Sauvages from the map. All these enterprises drew in local manpower but also attracted large numbers of outsiders to the area.

(2) The Progressive Erosion of the Francophone Community, 1904-70

Two complementary developments explain the ethnic trajectory experienced by this population. At first, with respect to culture, there was a progressive isolation from the larger francophone world, an impoverishment of indigenous cultural resources, and a gradual penetration of the provincially dominant English culture. Then, in so far as the economy was concerned, the traditional way of life of the Newfoundland outports (family-based and relatively self-sufficient) was transformed in to a marginal capitalistic economy involving the progressive proletarization of labor and greater economic specialization. These twin processes can be viewed in two stages, each equivalent to a generation in the life of the population: from 1904 to the 1930s, and from the 1930s to the 1960s.

1904-1930. Even though 1904 marks the rupture of formal ties with France, not all links with the francophone world were thereby cut. Thanks to a nucleus of educated individuals, letters were exchanged with relatives in France and Saint-Pierre. The same people received newspapers from France and Quebec (notably *La Patrie* and *La Presse*) the contents of which they related to other members of the community. Having kept their French nationality, several men returned to France in order to serve in World War I. Ties with Saint-Pierre were maintained through the frequent visits of the "old smugglers" who brought liquor and other luxury products. During this same period the first links were established with French Canadians working as lumberjacks in the camps around Cornerbrook and elsewhere, and pilgrimages were made to the shrine at Saint-Anne-de-Beaupré near Quebec City. Because of the Acadian presence, the Catholic Church provided limited acknowledgement of a French presence: from 1912 to 1928 an Acadian priest from Prince Edward Island served in Lourdes and, for a while, he was assisted by a teacher, Miss Poirier, from the Codroy Valley. Thus, without entirely losing sight of their mother country across the Atlantic, the inhabitants of the Port-au-Port peninsula gradually became aware of a North American *francophonie*. However, their knowledge of it was fragmentary and they in no way identified with it.

1930-1960. With the passing away of the first generation of settlers including the few that were literate, all written communication with the francophone world ceased. Other fragile links crumbled with the Great Depression and the organization of a coast guard determined to put an end to smuggling. Subsequent economic recovery and World War II led to the progressive integration of the francophone communities into a larger regional system. No longer isolated from the rest of the province, they experienced, for the first time, a disadvantaged minority status. Wage labor assumed greatly increased significance with the founding of the American military base at Stephenville in 1941. The presence of the base completely destroyed the physical integrity of the Acadian communities in the Saint George's Bay area. With the generalised availability of wage labor, fishing and subsistence activities were abandoned by many, and the household-based economy was thereby seriously undermined. It is at this point that one can observe the beginnings of a significant language shift at the family level. Through wage labor it became evident that English was the language of work, of the majority, and of power. Although the communities remained geographically and sociologically intact, families opting for outside salaried work were increasingly exposed to the use of English. And a tendency to opt for English in preference to French found willing support among a clergy that was exclusively of Irish background. Priests urged parents to baptize their babies with English names and to speak only English to them.

In spite of these economic and cultural transformations, the geographical isolation of the francophone communities located on the tip of the Port-au-Port peninsula persisted. Even if individuals left their villages in increasing numbers and for longer periods of time to find work, the traditional culture remained strong and the institutions of the anglophone majority (school, church, and State) held little sway over them.

One development which strengthened the affective bonds with French Canada was the radio station CHNC New Carlisle on the Gaspé Peninsula in Quebec which started broadcasting on December 23, 1933, and was listened to attentively on the west coast for some 20 years. Everyone would gather in those houses that had radios in order to hear their favourite programs, the accordionist Tommy Duchesne, "Séraphin,"[6] and the daily prayers. It was natural for them to identify with the rural, Catholic Quebec culture that all this represented. The old people in the community recall with love their radio heroes and the events of a period during which CHNC came clearly over the air waves and evoked a distant world that was relevant to their daily lives.

Newfoundland's entry into the Canadian Confederation in 1949 increased the ethnic marginality of the people and their dependence on a larger economic order. Henceforth, all the "resources" (or sources of revenue) exploited by the local population, ranging from the fishery to welfare and passing by local initiative projects and adult education, were controlled directly or indirectly by the central government. And this integration within the regional structures was reinforced by the local English language media that furnished all the necessary information. French broadcasting from New Carlisle, while entertaining, was now irrelevant to the economic needs of the people.

With the end of the period of relative isolation and the imposition of cultural and linguistic marginality on the francophones, they began to encounter more and more frequently situations in which their own language was not only inadequate but also scorned. An inequality characterized by humiliation and a loss of initiative on the part of the minority and contempt and prejudice on the part of the majority became commonplace in the growing number of interactions between the two groups. Exchanges between the two groups occurred exclusively in English, a language that the francophones mastered poorly, and virtually all the adult population was now involved in the process.

Even in the heart of the francophone communities, thanks to the power of the Catholic Church, their ethnic identity was under attack. With the creation of a network of church schools, competence in the English language was now required at age five rather than at the time of one's first job. A child entering school without a working knowledge of English was immediately sent home. The 1950s and the 1960s constituted a period of rapid assimilation on such a large scale that only the most traditional families (placing little value on formal education, practising coastal fishing on a kinship level of organization, and continuing to engage in subsistence activities) were spared.

By the end of the 1960s, the francophone communities were characterized by a severe *anomie*. As in most Newfoundland out-ports, the traditional household economy had collapsed and, with it, the local autonomy of the people. Without an elite of their own, they saw a foreign leadership imposed on them that did not recognize their separate identity; the population was in the throes of a complete cultural disintegration. French became a private language used only among friends and kin and in traditional activities, and many people in the networks were now only passive bilinguals. The English language had extensively penetrated the homes of the communities as a result of the young being instructed in English in school, and of the constant presence of English television.

In the final analysis, this integration into the regional structures has served to create a Newfoundland identity to the extent that when the young leave the area to seek work in the city, they choose Halifax or Toronto rather than Montreal. And when they travel within Quebec, they use English in preference to French in their exchanges with people.

Recent Developments

Until the 1970s it was usual to deny the existence of francophones on the Port-au-Port peninsula. Regional authorities insisted it was strictly a question of folklore. Then, suddenly, the situation took an unexpected turn: francophones began to demand French schools and French television, the recognition of their linguistic and cultural rights, and they became increasingly visible within French Canada. The impetus came both from inside and outside the community. The coincidence was fortuitous and served to give the new movement more strength, but without eliminating any of its inherent contradictions.

With the establishment of schools and the training of local teachers there emerged, for the first time, a small indigenous elite of perhaps 20 persons who considered themselves both francophones and Newfoundlanders and openly asserted themselves as such. This new consciousness was strengthened through their studies at Memorial University in St. John's where the teachers invariably chose French as a "major" with a view to reappropriating and becoming literate in their language. The process was painful inasmuch as only standard (metropolitan) French was taught, Newfoundland French being judged an obscure *patois* of no relevance. But this indifference only served to sharpen their consciousness as French Newfoundlanders, while at the same time often encouraging them to hide their real identity in the university's French department.

Returning to their villages these teachers began to confront the language policies of the church and the School Board. Judged as troublemakers and unable to influence the authorities, they were obliged to resort to passive resistance, for instance confessing in French before a unilingual English priest.

About the same time (1970), the federal government, through the Department of the Secretary of State, became interested in this population. The objective of the government was to assure the survival and the *épanouissement* (flourishing) of the official language minorities from coast to coast. Delighted with the discovery of francophones in Newfoundland, the Secretary of State encouraged the creation at Cap-Saint-Georges of a group dedicated to cultural promotion, *les Terre-Neuviens francais*. Eligible for federal funding within the context of the Official Language Minorities Group Program, the group was conceived as a vehicle for social animation.

This federal initiative served to legitimize the claims of the local elite through the creation of a formal association to represent the minority and the provision of the means to intervene at regional and provincial levels. Inevitably, the whole process of animation and lobbying quickly fell into the hands of the teachers.

Federal intervention, by its very nature, also assured a certain integration within French Canada: student exchange programs, participation in the activities of ACELF and FFHQ, and so on. The support of the other francophone minorities in their demands was thereby assured. The results were not slow in coming: a French immersion program at Cap-Saint-Georges, French television relayed by satellite from Montreal, and federally-funded social animators.

However, if all these efforts have served to institutionalise a new elite that affirms itself as Newfoundland French, that travels constantly to participate in various activities across French Canada, and that is provided with the means to assure its own survival, it is in no way clear that the lot of the vast majority of the Port-au-Port French has been changed thereby. The population continues to be ravaged by assimilation and few manifest any interest in revitalising their identity – historical, cultural, or linguistic. The logic underlying their behavior is all too evident. As inhabitants of a peripheral region, their basic preoccupations are economic. For the most part, federal language policies are totally irrelevant, except as a supplementary source of income for a few privileged members of the community. So, in the eyes of the ordinary French Newfoundlander "One fishes for French in the same way as one fishes for (unemployment) stamps!" In Newfoundland, as elsewhere, power, in terms of the language of work and of social advancement, speaks English, and in order to facilitate integration into this new order the local workers, unable to share the geographical mobility of their own elite, find that it is in their best interests to aspire towards linguistic and cultural conformity.

Formerly French, Breton, St. Pierrais, or Acadian, thereafter fishermen and residents of Cap-Saint-Georges, Grand'Terre or Anse-aux-Canards, they are now in the process of becoming simply Newfoundlanders. And it is doubtful whether it will be possible for them to be at once Newfoundlanders and French Canadians. For the elite this double identity is possible, because of a high degree of mobility that is assured through federal aid. But how long can an ethnic elite survive without a popular base in its home villages?

Postscript 1982

Since we wrote the above three years ago, little has changed in terms of ethnic revival, and the future of French on the west coast of Newfoundland remains as equivocal as ever. Certainly, a second local association has been formed, *l'Ordre du Bon Temps*, that serves the St. George's Bay area from Stephenville; an annual folklore festival has been instituted at Cap-Saint-Georges; and the French immersion program in this village now runs from kindergarten to Grade 6, serving over 100 children in 1981-82, more than half of whom claim French mother tongue. That this much has been achieved, is almost entirely attributable to massive federal intervention via the Secretary of State's department. Thus the provincial federation receives the largest per capita grant of any of the nine federations serving francophone minorities across the country. Still, the Port-au-Port French are scarcely visible in its structures while, for its part, the Newfoundland government manifests little sustained interest in the French immersion program.

Mother tongue statistics, too, give little cause for hope. Cartwright notes that "within Port-au-Port the percentage of the francophone minority declined from 15.4 percent in 1971 to 9.0 percent in 1976" leading him to affirm that the subdivison lacks "the population and significant language vitality to withstand alterations in lifestyle (Cartwright, 1980:103)." Time and "modernisation" have clearly taken their toll, and a plethora of institutional arrangements and a policy of "cultural welfare" cannot hide the fact that, according to one local animator, intervention is "twenty years too late."[7]

Finally, the new Canadian Constitution, insofar as the Charter of Rights offering educational guarantees to official language minorities is concerned, is hardly likely to redress the balance. In a demographically fragile and regressive situation the critical clause "where numbers warrant" is more than likely to justify continued inaction on the part of the Newfoundland government.

Not surprisingly, certain FFHQ officials admit, in private, that the Newfoundland French have passed the point of no return on the road to total assimilation and that they should be abandoned to their lot in order to concentrate efforts on more viable minority communities in other provinces. That is a bitter pill to swallow given the rich heritage and tenacity of these out-porters.

END NOTES

1. The research on which this article is based is part of a larger project concerned with ethnic minorities in the Gulf of Saint Lawrence (funded by Canada Council: S71-1560) as well as an inquiry into the needs of the francophones of Newfoundland and Labrador (commissioned by the Secretary of State). Visits were made to the area in the summers of 1972, 1974, and 1975. An earlier version of this article was presented to the Acadian Studies Section of the 43rd Congress of ACFAS held in Moncton in 1975. Eric Waddell is responsible for the final version of the text.
2. The French Newfoundlanders have been almost totally ignored by social researchers. There are three notable exceptions: Biays (1952), Lamarre (1971), and Matthews (1976: Ch. 5).
3. This figure should be treated with some caution since numerous francophones refrained from declaring themselves as such before the authorities as the result of a certain "francophobia" that is still noticeable in Newfoundland.
4. Under the Treaty of Utrecht (1713), Newfoundland became English, but seasonal rights to catch and dry fish along the west coast were retained by France until 1904. Called the French Shore, it was established in 1783 as extending from Cape St. John to Cape Ray. During this period of French control the coast was closed to settlement.
5. It is possible that the migrations between Cheticamp and the Codroy Valley continued to the end of the 19th century. Some links were maintained between these two places until as late as 1920—people from Cape Breton crossing the strait in schooners each autumn to sell cattle and butter to their Newfoundland relatives (Father Anselme Chiasson, personal communication, May, 1975.)
6. Séraphin is the principal character in Claude-Henri Grignon's novel *Un homme et son péché* (1933), dramatised as *Les belles histoires des pays d'en haut* and so popular throughout French Canada that his name became virtually a household word.
7. Joseph Benoit, quoted in *Le Soleil* (Montreal), 20 January, 1982.

SELECTED REFERENCES

Biays, Pierre. "Un village terreneuvien: Cap-Saint-Georges," *Cahiers de Géographie*, 1. Quebec: Les Presses de l'Université Laval, 1952.

Cartwright, Donald G. *Official Language Populations in Canada: Patterns and Contacts.* Occasional Paper No. 16. Montreal, The Institute for Research on Public Policy, 1980.

Doran, Claire. *Adaptation et economie familiale dans une petite communauté rurale francophone de Terre-Neuve.* M.A. Thesis, Department of Geographie, McGill University, Montreal, 1974.

Lamarre, Nicole. "Parenté et héritage du patrimoine dans un village français terre-neuvien," *Recherches sociographiques*, 12(3): 345-359, 1971.

Matthews, Ralph. *"There's No Better Place than Here": Social Change in Three Newfoundland Communities.* Toronto: Peter Martin Associates, 1976.

Waddell, Eric. *The Francophones of Newfoundland and Labrador.* Report submitted to the Program for Official Language Minority Groups, Department of the Secretary of State, Ottawa, 1975.

PART THREE

The Other Ethnic Groups:
The Non-English in English Canada

Introduction

The Multicultural Mosaic

Canada has had a federal multicultural policy for 10 years, and "the multicultural heritage of Canadians" is noted in the Constitution.[1] What is multiculturalism? What effect, if any, has it had on Canadian life? What were the events which gave it birth? These are some of the matters Jean Burnet addresses. Similar questions are raised by Keith McLeod with the schools as a referent. Given the nature of Canadian society, what role can the school play – actually or ideally – in line with a multicultural policy?

If multiculturalism is to be more than hollow words, it must find institutional supports within the community such as the schools and the churches. David Millet assumes the church to be a key institutional structure for a multicultural Canada. Having made this theoretical assumption, he then asks: What is an ethnic or minority church? To what extent does it exist in Canadian society? Of what consequence is it for the multicultural mosaic?

It is common to confuse multiculturalism with the lifestyles found in vibrant ethnic communities formed by newly arrived immigrant groups. Broadly conceived, multiculturalism is a policy for all Canadians as we all have an ethnic heritage. What role has immigration to Canada played in the shaping of the multicultural mosaic? Canadians have tended to view immigration with a large measure of ambivalence. The one exception to this general ambivalence, perhaps, is the immigration from the country of one's own ancestors. Immigration from countries unrelated to our Old World roots has met more relative disfavor. The uncertainty of our response to immigration may be highest in regard to the "other ethnic groups"[2] – immigrants who are neither British nor French. J.L. Elliott relates the evolution of immigration policy to the more general social and economic conditions present at the time. The spin-off effects of immigration are not always apparent at the time the policy is formulated.

The final essay in this section is by Anthony H. Richmond, "Ethnic Nationalism and Post Industrialism." In this theoretical investigation, Richmond focusses upon the larger picture and poses the question which is logically prior to all those above: Are some types of societies – on the level of their basic social integration – more conducive to a tolerance of ethnic nationalism or multiculturalism than others? Richmond answers this in the affirmative and goes on to argue that the post industrial society is the most tolerant of all, although competition among local and regional elites may prevail.

European Immigration

European immigrants, the traditional source of settlers for North America through the first half of the 20th century, may be referred to as the "old" immigrants as opposed to the "new" immigrants in the current period from non-traditional source countries in the Third World. The old immigrants were selected with reference to such criteria as the ease with which it was believed that they would assimilate into Canadian life. Immigrants recruited under the "preferred nations" guidelines tended to come largely from Germany, the Netherlands, Scandinavia, and especially from the British Isles.

The smallest Scandinavian country, Iceland, has a history of emigration to Canada. The Icelandic emigration to Canada, J. Matthiasson argues, has resulted in an "assimilation paradox." While one might expect the Icelandic Canadians to be prime targets for assimilation, given their relatively small numbers and early history in Canada in which they did not oppose Canadianization, such is not the case. Icelandic Canadians have developed a "cultural dualism" that enlivens and gives a new direction to their ethnicity. In many respects the Icelandic Canadians are a study of controlled assimilation.

Large-scale immigration from the Mediterranean region stems from the beginning of the postwar era. Although the Italians have been by far the largest group represented, all Mediterranean countries have participated. Both the Portuguese and Italians share a pattern of migration characterized by an early phase of male contract labor followed by a later phase of chain migration involving the sponsorship of family members. R. Harney traces the development of the Italian community in Toronto; its origins predate the rise of Mussolini in Italy. Since the Italian community has experienced various streams of migration, its internal differentiation is greater than the Portuguese community's, for example, the latter being smaller and more recent in origin.

The Slavic peoples evidenced a high degree of internal differentiation in Europe. Upon migration, some of the Old World loyalties as well as conflicts carried over; others disappeared or were modified through encounters with the new society. Likewise, a new ethnicity arose in some instances to meet their needs and fit the reality of the new social structure. A. Matejko uses the term "double identity" to characterize the Poles. Given the recent experience of martial law in Poland, this identity for many has been galvaniz-ed. The Ukrainians have a very strong sense of their identity in Canada coupled with a significant participation in mainstream institutions. Roman March examines the participation of the Ukrainians in politics. What has been the political mobility of Ukrainians in Canada?

The Jews in Canada belong to a myriad of ethnic groups. The Jewish emigration to Canada spans the "old" and the "new" immigration in terms of the source countries involved. The Jews from North Africa and the Mid-dle East have come in recent times while the earliest Jewish settlers were from Europe. The most active migration to Canada from Europe, of course, occurred at the time of the holocaust. Although the Jews have settled in all provinces, the bulk of the population lives in Montreal and Toronto. A.J. Arnold's paper, "The Jews of Western Canada," is an interesting treatment of Canadian regionalism as it affects Jews. With the focal point the Jewish community in Winnipeg, Arnold catalogs the standard laments that westerners have regarding easterners; only in this instance the analysis is limited to the power differentials found within the various Jewish com-munities. Nevertheless, the Winnipeg Jewish community, for example, has exerted a force in Canadian life greater than its number might lead one to believe.

Third World Immigration

Asian immigration in the time of the "old immigration" was governed by a series of double standards. The Chinese immigrant, viewed as a source of cheap labor, was recruited under some economic conditions and discouraged under others. A series of "head taxes" regulated the flow of Chinese emigration into Canada until 1923 when the Chinese were completely bar-red from entry. The early discriminatory regulations, the predominantly male migration, and the prohibition of female immigration made normal family life out of the question. When the immigration policy was liberalized in the 1960s, the "new" Chinese immigration commenced. Who are the Chinese Canadians in the 1970s? Graham Johnson provides us with a hint to the answer in the title of his paper, "Chinese Canadians in the '70s: New Wine in New Bottles."

The most recent Asian immigration involved the "boatpeople" – Indo-chinese refugees who were casualties of the Vietnam War. C. Michael Lan-phier examines this period in our immigration history by showing how our refugee policy evolved and why, in spite of good intentions, it was unable to respond to a larger scale of need. Nevertheless the arrival of more than 60,000 refugees by 1981, nearly three quarters of whom were Vietnamese in origin, is the largest single yearly refugee intake in recent history.

The Chinese are one of eight ethnic groups studied by Raymond Breton and his colleagues in Toronto. The other visible minority in the sample survey was the West Indians; in addition there were six European ethnic groups for purposes of comparison. The objective of the study was twofold. How do ethnic groups perceive their problems and how are they perceived by others? In addition, to what extent is each ethnic community able to act as a resource in the alleviation of problems experienced?

From the recent West Indian immigration in Toronto, we turn to some of the oldest black settlers in Canada. S.E. Williams provides a descriptive account of the growth and development, over a 200-year period, of the Afro-Canadians in Nova Scotia. The unifying force in the community, the source of its strength, is the Baptist Church. Yet the researcher also points out that the church at times is an agent of the status quo in the community rather than an agent of progressive social change. The Afro-Canadians and the Baptist Church in Nova Scotia seem to be married for better or worse. Only the future will tell which force will gain the ascendancy.

Until recently, Arab immigration to Canada was heavily male in composition. As such it was similar to the Chinese. Migratory streams that are not composed of complete family units tend to be heavily male. B. Abu-Laban traces the evolution of Arab immigration from the period when Arab countries were on the "nonpreferred" list to the present day when they enjoy an equal status with the traditional European source countries.

Although equal to European countries in terms of formal status, immigrants from Arab countries continue to be poorly understood since information about their cultures is generally lacking in the larger Canadian society. It should be remembered, though, that the Arabs themselves are varied, containing cultural, national, linguistic, religious, and ethnic subgroups. One only has to examine events in the Middle East today in order to substantiate this observation.

END NOTES

1. Canadian Charter of Rights and Freedoms, section 27.
2. This phrase was chosen by The Royal Commission on Bilingualism and Biculturalism to designate the ethnic mix in Canada that is neither Charter group French/English nor Native People in origin. *Report on the Royal Commission on Bilingualism and Biculturalism*, Book IV, "The Contribution of the Other Ethnic Groups." (Ottawa: Queen's Printer, 1970).

SELECTED REFERENCES

Abu-Laban, Baha. *An Olive Branch on the Family Tree: The Arabs in Canada*. Toronto: McClelland and Stewart, 1980.

Anderson, Alan B. and James S. Frideres. *Ethnicity in Canada: Theoretical Perspectives*. Toronto: Butterworths, 1981.

Anderson, Grace M. and David Higgs. *A Future to Inherit: The Portuguese Communities of Canada*. Toronto: McClelland and Stewart, 1976.

Avery, Donald. *"Dangerous Foreigners": European Immigrant Workers and Labour Radicalism in Canada, 1896-1932*. Toronto: McClelland and Stewart, 1979.

Awan, Sadiq Noor. *The People of Pakistani Origin in Canada*. Ottawa: Canada-Pakistan Association of Ottawa-Hull, 1976.

Caroli, Betty B., Robert F. Harney, and Lydio Tomasi, eds. *The Italian Immigrant Woman in North America*. Toronto: The Multicultural History Society of Ontario, 1978.

Dahlie, J. and T. Fernando, eds. *Ethnicity, Power and Politics*. Toronto: Methuen, 1981.

Harney, Robert F. and Harold Troper. *Immigrants: A Portrait of the Urban Experience, 1890-1930*. Toronto: Van Nostrand Reinhold, 1975.

Hill, Daniel G. *THe Freedom Seekers: Blacks in Early Canada*. Agincourt, Ont.: The Book Society of Canada, 1981.

Isajiw, Wsevolod W. *Ukrainians in American and Canadian Society*. Cambridge, Mass.: Harvard Ukrainian Institute, 1976.

Ishwaran, K. *Family, Kinship and Community: A Study of Dutch Canadians*. Toronto: McGraw Hill-Ryerson, 1977.

Kallen, Evelyn L. *Spanning the Generations: A Study in Jewish Identity*. Don Mills, Ont.: Longman, 1977.

Kallen, Evelyn. *Ethnicity and Human Rights in Canada*. Toronto: Gage, 1982.

Kovacs, Martin L. *Ethnic Canadians: Culture and Education*. Regina, Sask.: Canadian Plains Research Center, 1977.

Kurelek, William and A. Arnold. *Jewish Life in Canada*. Edmonton: Hurtig, 1976.

Lupul, Manoly R. *Ukrainian Canadians, Multiculturalism and Separatism: an Assessment*. Edmonton: University of Alberta Press, 1978.

Ng, Roxana and Judith Ramirez. *Immigrant Housewives in Canada*. Toronto: Immigrant Women's Center, 1981.

Palmer, Howard. *Immigration and the Rise of Multiculturalism*. Toronto: Copp Clark, 1975.

Reitz, Jeffrey G. *The Survival of Ethnic Groups*. Toronto: McGraw-Hill Ryerson, 1980.

Ujimoto, K. Victor and Gordon Hirabayashi. *Visible Minorities and Multiculturalism: Asians in Canada*. Toronto: Butterworths, 1980.

Weinfeld, M., William Shaffir, and I. Cotler, *The Canadian Jewish Mosaic*. Toronto: John Wiley, 1981.

The Multicultural Mosaic

JEAN BURNET   York University

Multiculturalism 10 Years Later*

October 8, 1981, was the 10th anniversary of the Canadian federal government's policy of multiculturalism within a bilingual framework. It was an occasion for politicians and public servants to review an impressive list of accomplishments. It was also an occasion for social scientists to review the problems of conceptualization of multiculturalism and the relations between the policy and the ever-changing state of Canadian society.

Social scientists who have discussed the policy so far have attempted to analyse the circumstances out of which the policy grew, to explain its intentions, and to attack or defend it. Much of their discussion has hinged on three concepts: ethnicity, culture, and language. I should like first to sketch the background of the policy, then to deal with the three concepts, and finally to say something about the situation concerning ethnic groups in the 1970s.

Background

Canada has always been ethnically heterogeneous, although it has not always been fully conscious of the fact itself nor been recognized by others as heterogeneous. Before European contact there were in the territory about 50 distinctive Indian and Inuit societies; from the time of contact the number of peoples has increased, at first slowly but later rapidly, to include groups that have emerged in Canada such as the Acadians, the Métis, and others that have come from every part of the globe. Ethnic voluntary associations, ethnic lobbies, ethnic newspapers, schools, and churches all attest to the diversity of the population.

For most of its history, however, the diversity has received little popular or official recognition. The policy of the government has been assimilation, or Anglo-conformity (Gordon, 1964, 84-114). It is true that politicians and after-dinner speakers have delighted in contrasting the Canadian mosaic with the American melting pot, but there has been little governmental support for the mosaic; for example, broadcasting has been oriented towards integration and not cultural maintenance (Royal Commission on bilingualism and Biculturalism, 1970, 186). Lately, since it has been acknowledged that the melting was not as thorough as was once thought, it has been apparent that differences between Canada and the United States have resulted largely from different rates of development rather than from differences of policy.

Differences have also resulted from the fact that the largest minority ethnic group in Canada has been quite different from the largest ethnic minority in the United States. The French Canadians resemble the Blacks in being among the oldest inhabitants of their country, and in having a sense of oppression, expressed by one French Canadian in calling his people the "white niggers of America" (Vallières, 1968). They resemble them also in having called into question the bargains they or their forebears accepted in the past at just about the same time, as a result of urbanization and industrialization, and in having signalled their new conception of themselves by choosing a new name: French Canadians in Quebec became Québécois, Negroes became Blacks. But the French Canadians are about 30 percent of the Canadian population, not 11 percent or 12 percent; they are more heavily concentrated in a particular geographical area, where they have long controlled the provincial government, the civil service, and their communal institutions; and they have provided Canada with three of its prime ministers and two of its governors general, as well as many other luminaries. These differences are probably more important than the fact that the badges or ethnic markers distinguishing the French Canadians have been culture, language, and religion rather than color; however, it is not so long since French Canadians called themselves and were called a "race," and since a social anthropologist thought it necessary to argue that there were no physical differences between English and French Canadians (Bailey, 1947).

The tension between French Canadians and English Canadians in the 1960s played a part in leading to assertiveness among other ethnic groups in Canada. The Quiet Revolution, the birth of separatism, and the outbreak of terrorism led to the setting up of the Royal Commission on Bilingualism and Biculturalism in 1963. The Commission's mandate had to do with relations between "the two founding peoples" of Canada, the English and the French. It was charged also with "taking into account the contribution made by the other ethnic groups to the cultural enrichment of Canada and the measures that should be taken to safeguard that contribution," but intended to fulfil that charge rather casually by commissioning a few essays on the contribution of particular ethnic groups, and by paying some attention to the attitudes of certain groups to French-English relations. However, briefs submitted to the Commission and stormy discussions at its hearings revealed that there was a host of ethnic interest groups who would not be satisfied by off-hand treatment. The Commission felt constrained to devote one volume of its five-volume report entirely to "the other ethnic groups." That volume, Book 4, appeared in March 1970, and the policy of multiculturalism within a bilingual framework was announced a year and a half later as a response to Book 4.

Central Concepts

Ethnicity, culture, and language were central concepts in the work of the Royal Commission, and the way in which they were employed greatly influenced the formulation of the policy of multiculturalism. Ethnicity, or rather, ethnic group, was defined as expressing "a sense of identity rooted in a common origin . . . whether this common origin is real or "imaginary" (Royal Commission on Bilingualism and Biculturalism, 1967, xxii), and membership in an ethnic group was recognized as applicable to English and French as well as others, as indeed the terms of reference implied in speaking of "*other* ethnic groups." However, several aspects of the term worried the commissioners. One was its lack of familiarity; another was the tendency to use it as an epithet; a third was the implication that ethnicity was ascribed and immutable; a fourth was the practical difficulty of ascertaining the ethnicity of individuals whose grandparents and great grandparents may have belonged to many different groups. For these reasons they tried to avoid the term ethnic group, substituting for it cultural group. They did, however, use the term ethnic origin category; arbitrary as they recognized ethnic origin to be, they had to do so if they were to make use of the Canadian census.

Ironically, in the years since the Commission did its work the term ethnic has come up in the world. It has become commonly used; it is found in the titles of numerous books and journals in Canada and elsewhere. It is no longer an epithet, but a badge of pride, wearers of which are not confined to minorities and immigrants; on the other hand, a social science term for those who used sometimes to be considered non-ethnic, the term WASP, is now an epithet (Allen, 1975). Further, an element of choice in ethnicity has become increasingly recognized. Thus, all may participate in ethnicity, and many if not most people may select which identity they will stress when, and in what circumstances.

It may not have been because of the Royal Commission's use of the term cultural group that the framers of the response to Book 4 called the policy they devised a policy of multiculturalism; as historian Howard Palmer has pointed out, "Once Canada had been defined as bicultural, its redefinition as multicultural was inevitable, if the 'other ethnic groups' were to be given recognition" (Palmer, 1976, 117). But the choice of name was unfortunate.

Whereas the essence of ethnicity is a sense of peoplehood, culture is, in the Royal Commission's words, "a way of being, thinking, and feeling . . .

a driving force animating a significant group of individuals united by a common tongue, and sharing the same customs, habits, and experiences" (Royal Commission on Bilingualism and Biculturalism, 1967, xxxi); more succinctly, it is a style of living. It is "the sum of the characteristics particular to a group common to its individual members" (*ibid.*, xxxii). If this definition seems imprecise, it was selected from more than 300; the most recent definition I have found proposes that "culture is just another term for a mystery factor" (Beck, 1980, 10). Among other things, the Royal Commission's definition, like most others, does not indicate how distinctive or "particular" a style of life must be to constitute a culture. This is not a quibble. It has for decades now been argued that cultures are converging, and that indeed culture has become a myth (Porter, 1969). Nor does the Commission indicate how the significance and the unity of a group are to be established.

The assertion that members of a cultural group are united by a common tongue also gives rise to problems. Are all of the speakers of French or German or English or Chinese united by a common tongue and therefore sharers of a culture? The question has an interest for English-speaking Canadians and Americans, who, however permeable the border between them is, usually are insistent on their separate ethnic identities. What about people who share an ethnic identity but speak mutually incomprehensible temporal or regional dialects or even languages, such as, for example, those from different parts of Italy, or, for that matter, those who have retained and those who have lost their ancestral tongue? One may suspect that the drive to have ancestral languages taught in the schools, invariably in their standard or literary forms, may be an attempt to bring together those who have hitherto shared an ethnic identity but not a means of communication.

The Commission went further concerning the relation between language and culture. It held that "language is in the first place an essential expression of a culture . . . the most typical expression of culture. . . the natural vehicle for a host of other elements of culture" (Royal Commission on Bilingualism and Biculturalism, 1967, xxxiv). Such statements sharpen the impression that culture is viewed as inseparable from language.

It becomes difficult, then, to understand how a response to the Commission could be labelled multiculturalism within a bilingual framework, and introduced by the statement that in Canada "although there are two official languages, there is no official culture, nor does any ethnic group take precedence over any other" (House of Commons Debates, 1971). Certainly it was difficult for at least two groups of people with a vital interest in the policy to understand. The two groups, speaking for French Canada on the one hand and for "the other ethnic groups" on the other, accepted the stand of the Royal Commission on the inseparability of language and culture. The first, the French Canadians, therefore complained that multiculturalism within a bilingual framework was nonsense, and the policy an attempt to subvert the English-French dualism that they had been striving to make a more and more equal partnership (Rocher, 1973). The spokespersons for the other ethnic groups decried the small amount of assistance afforded their languages and cultures, as compared to the massive aid to the French; one extremist among them even attacked the program for implementing multiculturalism because it promised assistance to immigrants in acquiring at least one of Canada's official languages, on the ground that such assistance gave an unfair advantage to the English and French linguistic communities over others.

In fact, the primary aim of the policy was not the maintenance of cultures. The first of four ways in which the government proposed to implement the policy was, it is true, "resources permitting . . . to assist all Canadian culural groups that have demonstrated a desire and effort to develop a capacity to grow and contribute to Canada"; but it is preceded by the hypothesis that muticulturalism leads to "confidence in one's own individual identity," and "out of this can grow respect for that of others and a willingness to share ideas, attitudes and assumptions" (House of Commons Debates, 1971). However plausible this hypothesis is, it must be noted that scientific evidence does not entirely support it. The emphasis on sharing is repeated in the three other ways of implementing the policy, which speak of overcoming cultural and linguistic barriers to full participation in Canadian society, and of "creative encounters and interchange among all Canadian cultural groups."

Cultures – as distinctive styles of living – and ancestral languages can hardly be shared; on the contrary they flourish best in isolation. This was recognized by the Canadian Consultative Council in Multiculturalism, a body composed of representatives of Canada's ethnic groups, set up to advise the minister responsible for multiculturalism. In its *First Annual Report* (Canadian Consultative Council on Multiculturalism, 1975) it condemned multicultural centers, on the grounds that they promote use of a common language. From the emphasis on sharing, then, it seems evident that it was ethnic identity rather than culture that was to be fostered, as an aid to group understanding and interchange.

That is not to minimize the importance of ancestral languages. The first major research project carried out under the federal policy of multiculturalism had to do with non-official languages (O'Bryan et al., 1976), and it found that for the 10 groups included in the study ancestral languages were cherished symbols of ethnic identity, for some groups the most cherished symbol, and were also valued on the grounds that knowing more than one language is a priceless asset. The support of ancestral languages has been one of the major emphases of the policy, and I devoutly hope it will continue to be. Knowing more than one language means having more than one perspective, more than one intellectual tradition upon which to draw: a valuable asset for anyone, an indispensable asset for a scholar.

Ethnic Groups in the 1970s

The policy of multiculturalism has not won ready acceptance in Canada. In addition to the critics already mentioned, the late John Porter, one of Canada's most distinguished sociologists, persistently argued that ethnic and cultural differences are a fraud perpetrated by the British upon all other Canadians in order to maintain the social order he called a vertical mosaic, and therefore no recognition whatsoever should be given to such differences (Porter, 1965); however, by 1975 he did grudgingly agree to bilingualism (Porter, 1975). It is unnecessary to present all the evidence against Porter's conspiratorial view; it is enough, perhaps, to point out that he had to invoke cultural differences to explain the status both of the top-ranking group in the hierarchy, the Jews, and the bottom group, the Native Peoples (Porter, 1967, 397, 398-9). Other scholars and members of the general public also saw multiculturalism as a hoax, committed by the federal Liberal government in the interest either of retaining power, or, to those who saw the Liberals as WASPish, of containing the other ethnic groups (Jansen, 1978; Peter, 1979). In the 1970s, Canadians have been as inclined as Americans, whose media they share, to view politicians with cynicism. It may be noted, however, that the lack of success of the Liberals on the provincial level has not prevented the adoption of multicultural policies by the provinces: the governments which have done so have been Social Credit, Conservative, and New Democratic.

Certain changes in the ethnic situation in Canada that began before October 8, 1971 have become more pronounced since that time. Whereas the number of immigrants has declined with worsening economic conditions, and in some groups of postwar immigrants return migration has swelled, since 1967 those who have been entering, either as immigrants or as refugees, have increasingly come not from Europe but from Asia and the Caribbean. A growing proportion of them have on arrival known one or other of the official languages of Canada; many have also participated, in at least some areas of life, in British or French culture. They have joined the Native Peoples, now urbanizing, and earlier Asian and Black arrivals to constitute visible minorities far larger than Canada has been accustomed to. For them, the problem of learning English or French or maintaining ancestral languages and cultures is far outweighed by the problem of winning the right to be treated like everyone else by judges, policemen, teachers, employers, landlords, neighbors, and fellow-passengers in buses and subways. It is a serious problem: incidents involving racism have been frequent in the large cities to which most immigrants have gone, as well as in some communities where Native Peoples are conspicuous. The problem continues long after the newcomers pass, three years after their arrival, from being the concern of the Department of Employment and Immigration to being the concern of the Multiculturalism Directorate.

The sensitivity of the federal government to the new ethnic situation was evident in late 1975 when the minister who was at that time responsible for multiculturalism, the Hon. John Monro, announced that henceforth priority would be given to group understanding and the combatting of discrimination rather than cultural survival. The suggestion of Reitz (1980, 395) that either French-Canadian pressure or austerity rather than a perceived need led to the announcement seems to be gratuitous. The degree to which cultural survival was the concern of the Canadian Consultative Council on Multiculturalism was clear in the vituperation with which it greeted Munro's statement. Nonetheless, it appears that the federal government has stood firm and given intergroup tension considerable attention in recent years.

In spite of widely publicized racial incidents, a major study of the attitudes of Canadians of various ethnic groups toward one another (Berry, Kalin and Taylor, 1977) found a fairly positive climate of opinion in Canada regarding immigrants and members of most ethnic groups, and in particular a considerable acceptance of "colored immigrants." A major finding was that attitudes regarding immigrants, ethnic groups, and multiculturalism were all less favorable among French Canadians than among Anglo-Celts and members of "other ethnic" groups as a whole. However, the pace of social and political change in Quebec, where most French Canadians reside, since the research was done in early 1974 has been so rapid that attitudes may have changed considerably by now: the election of the Parti Québécois in 1976, the passage and implementation of Bill 101, the referendum campaign of 1980 and the immigration of francophone Haitians and Vietnamese are among events that may have had repercussions on ethnic attitudes.

The policy of multiculturalism within a bilingual framework is handicapped by its name and by its lack of unambiguous conceptualization in dealing with its critics and with the new ethnic composition of the population. Its basic aims are, however, to such a degree a response to the Canadian situation that it seems to be inevitable. It survived the changes of government in May 1979 and February 1980 unscathed, and it must be expected to continue for some time, although with the modifications that experience indicates to be desirable. For those who value equality, variety, and change, this is a happy prospect.

SELECTED REFERENCES

Allen, Irving Lewis. "WASP – From Sociological Concept to Epithet," *Ethnicity*, 2:2, 1975, 153-162.

Bailey, A.G. "On the Nature of the Distinction between the French and the English in Canada: An Anthropoligical Inquiry," *Report of the Annual Meeting of the Canadian Historical Association*. Toronto: University of Toronto Press, 1947, 63-72.

Beck, Brenda E.F. "Asian Immigrants and Canadian Multiculturalism: Current Issues and Future Opportunities." In K. Victor Ujimoto and Gordon Hirabayashi, eds., *Visible Minorities and Multiculturalism: Asians in Canada*. Toronto: Butterworths, 1980, 1-12.

Berry, John W., Rudolf Kalin and Donald M. Taylor, *Multiculturalism and Ethnic Attitudes in Canada*. Ottawa: Supply and Services Canada, 1977.

Canadian Consultative Council on Multiculturalism. *First Annual Report*. 1975.

Gordon, Milton M. *Assimilation in American Life*. New York: Oxford University Press, 1964.

House of Commons Debates, Statement of P.E. Trudeau, October 8, 1971.

Jansen, Clifford J. "The Italian Dilemma over Multiculturalism and Separatism." Paper presented at meetings of the Canadian Sociology and Anthropology Association, London, Ontario, 1978.

O'Bryan, K.G., J.G. Reitz, and O. Kuplowska. *Non-official Languages: a study in Canadian multiculturalism*. Ottawa: Information Canada, 1975.

Palmer, Howard. "Reluctant Hosts: Anglo-Canadian Views of Multiculturalism in the Twentieth Century." In *Multiculturalism as state policy*. Ottawa: Canada Consultative Council on Multiculturalism, 1976, 81-118.

Peter, Karl. "The myth of multiculturalism and other political fables." Paper presented at the Canadian Ethnic Studies Association Conference, Vancouver, B.C., 1979.

Porter, John. *The Vertical Mosaic*. Toronto: University of Toronto Press, 1965.

"The Human Community." In J.M.S. Careless and R. Craig Brown, eds., *The Canadians: 1867-1967*. Toronto: Macmillan, 1967, 385-410.

"Bilingualism and the Myths of Culture," *Canadian Review of Sociology and Anthropology*, 6, 1969, 111-119.

"Dilemmas and Contradictions of a Multi-Ethnic Society," Royal Society of Canada *Transactions* 4:10, 1972, 193-205.

"Ethnic Pluralism in Canadian Perspective." In N. Glazer and D.P. Moynihan, eds., *Ethnicity: Theory and Experience*. Cambridge: Harvard University Press, 1975, 267-304.

Reitz, Jeffry G. "Immigrants, Their Descendants, and the Cohesion of Canada." In Raymond Breton, Jeffry G. Reitz, and Victor Valentine, *Cultural Boundaries and the Cohesion of Canada*. Montreal: The Institute for Research on Public Policy, 1980, 329-417.

Rocher, Guy. "Les ambiguités d'un Canada bilingue et multiculturel." In *Le Québec en mutation*. Montréal: Hurtubise, 1973, 117-26.

Royal Commission on Bilingualism and Biculturalism. *Report, General Introduction*. Ottawa: Queen's Printer, 1967.

_____. *Report*, Book IV, *The Cultural Contribution of the Other Ethnic Groups*. Ottawa: Information Canada, 1970.

Vallières, Pierre. *Nègres blancs de l'Amérique*. Montréal: Parti Pris, 1968.

KEITH A. McLEOD   University of Toronto

Multicultural Education: A Decade of Development*

Introduction

Attempts to transfer the sociocultural reality of pluralism and policy into educational practice in the past 10 years are a mixture of success and failure. The following analysis shall examine the meaning of the idea of multiculturalism as it has emerged in the past 10 years, the approaches to multicultural education, and adoption by the schools of multiculturalism as an ethic.

When the federal policy was announced on October 8, 1971, Prime Minister Trudeau indicated that "although there are two official languages, there is no official culture, nor does any ethnic group take precedence over any other. . . . A policy of multiculturalism within a bilingual framework commends itself to the government as the suitable means of assuring the cultural freedom of Canadians." He also stated that, "Canadian identity will not be undermined by multiculturalism. Indeed, we believe that cultural pluralism is the very essence of Canadian identity. Every ethnic group has the right to preserve and develop its own culture and values within the Canadian context." He added that "a policy of multiculturalism must be a policy for all Canadians."[1]

The first fundamental principle of the policy, as stated, is *equality of status*. In many respects this has not been achieved although some progress has been made. There has been a tendency to regard multiculturalism as a policy for immigrants and "ethnics"; not for all Canadians. Some Anglo Canadians still persist in viewing themselves as superior, and French Canadians have been loath to regard themselves as an ethnic group. In the first instance, some Anglo Canadians do not want to recognize that Anglo-dominance is an ideal and policy of the past and that Canada has become increasingly diverse. In the second instance, French Canadians have aimed at securing equality of status with the Anglo Canadians. The increased power of French Canada, exemplified in the strength of the province of Quebec and in the nationalism of the Québécois, which other Canadians

---

* Reprinted from D. Dorotich, ed., *Education and Canadian Multiculturalism: Some Problems and Some Solutions.* Canadian Society for the Study of Education's Eighth Yearbook, 1981, (Saskatoon: February, 1981).

have had to reckon with, has meant that they have been preoccupied with bilingualism while neglecting multiculturalism.[2] In some cases they see cultural dualism as a logical consequence or corollary to linguistic dualism. Sometimes the two concepts are used interchangeably.[3]

A second basic principle that is part of the policy of multiculturalism is the emphasis on *the Canadian identity*. One of the questions most frequently posed regarding multiculturalism is, "How does it provide for being Canadian?" The answer to this question is in the 1971 announcement and in the practice of the past 10 years. Multiculturalism was to be seen within a bilingual framework and Canadian society. Thus to be Italian Canadian, English Canadian or Japanese Canadian was not to deny Canadian identity, but to recognize a component of it, pluralism – "the very essence of Canadian identity." First, the assumption, which people who ask the question often do not analyse, is that what they regard as "simply Canadian" is really part of their particular ethno-cultural heritage. Second, notwithstanding such faulty assumptions, multiculturalism does not relegate or deny commonality. On the contrary it postulates that all Canadians be recognized as part of mainstream society.

Another major aspect and principle of multiculturalism is that people would have greater *choice* of lifestyles and cultural traits. Discrimination and stereotypes have limited peoples' conceptions of themselves and of others. By living an ethnocentric life, we limit our own opportunities to experience cultural variety and enjoy it. At the group level people may not be able to fully understand, or participate in other cultures, but they can be secure enough in their own identity to transcend cultural boundaries and appreciate other groups' perspectives, traits, and behavior without feeling threatened. Even in relatively homogeneous societies there is cultural variety which must be understood; the same understanding must be extended to life in a pluralistic society. At the personal level, choice means that to be Scottish Canadian, for example, one is not "required" to eat oatmeal or haggis, play bagpipes, dance reels, read Burns, or even speak Gaelic.

The concern for the protection of *civil rights and human rights* that has developed strongly in Canada since World War II is another fundamental aspect of multiculturalism. The common law has been the traditional protection for rights but a brief examination of Canadian history will find many instances where legislatures and courts have neglected to protect basic human rights with reference to schooling, public service, private business, property, and general civil rights including the right to vote.[4] Segregated schooling, the seizure of the property of Japanese Canadians, denial of service in restaurants and hotels, the disfranchisement of Chinese Canadians, the exclusion of Jews from clubs and associations, and discrimination against Pentacostals and Hutterites in the exercise of their religious beliefs are but a few examples of prejudice and discrimination.

In the 1940s there was a trend to enact specific legislation to prevent discrimination. Manitoba and Ontario were among the initiators of anti-discriminatory legislation. The Ontario Racial Discrimination Act in 1944 prohibited signs and notices that restricted the use of public facilities on the basis of race or creed. Fair accommodation practices acts, fair employment acts, and later full human rights codes have been enacted to protect people from discrimination on grounds of race, creed, and color.[5] In the final analysis, human rights are dependent upon an educated and informed public. The paucity of literature and research on human rights, the violations by the media, the inability of human rights commissions to act, the absence of human rights education, and the increasing number of subversive organizations such as the Ku Klux Klan indicate that more attention needs to be given to human and civil rights.

Multiculturalism, as a concept and in practice, has grown in scope and depth in the past 10 years but has not been unchallenged as the resistance and as the examples of stereotyping, prejudice, and discrimination attest. In the field of education there have been some successes and failures. Before examining specific examples of what has been attempted or neglected in education, I shall analyse the three major types or forms of multiculturalism education that have most commonly been suggested or implemented in Canada.[6]

Approaches to Multicultural Education

(a) One type of multicultural education has been the *ethnic specific*, the purposes of which have been to counteract assimilative forces, extend the familiar socialization, or generally broaden the child's or adult's knowledge, involvement, or acquaintance with the ethnic heritage. Ethnic schools (full-time or after school, public or private), and ethno-cultural programs, that usually include language courses, are the most common examples. By extending the contact of the person with the ethnic culture, greater immersion is achieved. The ethno-cultural communities, by providing or securing such facilities, extend the institutional completeness of the community, and consequently promote cultural continuity and development.

In a very real sense, this type of ethno-cultural education antedates the adoption of the policy of multiculturalism. Ethnic groups established private schools based on their heritage as a defense mechanism against assimilation.[7] Part-time schools have been the most common instrument for cultural survival. Operating after public school hours and on weekends, these schools teach language and cultural courses in such languages as Chinese, Portuguese, Italian, or German. Less common institutions promoting cultural retention are the full-time schools. These have usually attempted to meet provincial curricular regulations and, at the same time, to provide partial immersion in the ethnic culture. Hebrew and Anglo schools have been the most common examples, although other ethnic groups such as the French, Scandinavians, Germans, Ukrainians and Mennonites have also supported private institutions.[8] Particular agreements have been made between Hutterite communities and provincial authorities whereby the schools on their communes are ethnically exclusive but teach the provincial curriculum as well as provide the dogma and language (low German) of the Hutterite Brethren, (a form of anabaptism).[9] Other examples of where communities have adopted linguistic and cultural programs for their children can be seen among the Native People. Native children were educated at day schools on reserves or in boarding schools which provided programs that were blatant attempts at deculturation and assimilation. For a brief period in the late 1960s and early '70s, integrated schools, invariably off reserves, became policy. Native Peoples criticized these schools because they provided a one-way integration, or as some claimed, covert assimilation. The failure of schooling among the Native Peoples has been spectacular; until recently only about 10 percent of their children secured senior matriculation. Most recently, Native control of Native education has become the policy. The Native Peoples, with governmental support, increasingly provide for education in the Native languages. In Saskatchewan, for example, 40 to 60 percent of the school day may be instructed in their languages.[10]

Ethnic specific forms of multicultural education have achieved some important purposes. They have bolstered the sense of security and continuity of the communities and they have enabled children, by increasing their sense of identity and security, to bridge gaps that have existed between their ethnic communities and the larger society. They have enabled many children to cope with both the ethnic culture of their families and community, and the cultures beyond.[11] Insofar as such programs have assisted children and communities, people recognize their importance and success. However, ethnic specific programs are not the most feasible form of multicultural education in mixed communities, although Canadian society could easily accommodate many more ethnic specific programs than exist at present.

(b) A second major type of multicultural education is *problem oriented:* specific programs are developed to answer particular perceived needs or demands associated with schooling and the assimilation or integration of people of diverse backgrounds. English as a second language or as a second dialect courses and compensatory programs for the "disadvantaged" are the most common forms.[12]

The growth of English as a second language (ESL) programs, established in response to high rates of immigration during the early post-World War II years, failed to meet the demand. Many provincial and local school systems were unprepared to meet the needs of immigrant children and their parents.

Immigrant children were abandoned in the back rows of many classrooms, left to fend for themselves, placed in lower grades, or placed in vocational courses.[13] The evidence is quite clear; school systems were simply not sensitive to the needs and demands of immigrant children. The haphazard nature of Canada's immigration policy which provided little or no assistance for settlement and adjustment compounded the problems of the school authorities. In other instances, the sheer weight of the number of immigrants overwhelmed the schools.

Nor was the situation any better for the adults. Programs for adults had not been a strong feature of education in Canada. Immigrant adult males tended to learn English on the job while females, often confined to the home, had difficulty learning one of Canada's main languages. Again it took time, too much time, for institutions to respond to obvious needs.[14] The training of teachers for children and adult programs was equally inadequate. Faculties of education, as an examination of their calendars demonstrates, did not develop programs for training ESL teachers until some 20 years after the post-war immigration began.

The most critical aspect of the school ESL programs was that they were assimilative, not integrative. They were assimilative in that the stress was on English as a substitute for the mother tongue. It has taken many systems a long time to think of English as an "additive" language rather than "substitutive" language; the same may be said for the cultural aspects of the programs. The result was that children were often alienated from the security of their families and communities. The substitutive ethic of the program was one reason many teachers demonstrated such frustration when students continued to identify with their ethno-cultural heritage.[15]

In the case of adults, additional frustrations were evident. There was only sporadic support and funding for the courses. Moreover, some institutions resisted providing programs which they did not see as part of their function. Often the only assistance came from voluntary and semi-voluntary agencies that were willing to operate programs on inadequate funding. The lack of training of the teachers in human relations also led to frustration in understanding the cultural backgrounds which the adults brought to the class. Voluntary agencies, like the school systems, tended to regard the immigrants and their cultures as a "problem." This perspective made it difficult for the immigrants to relate to the agencies and teachers in a positive manner. They did not perceive their language and culture as a problem.[16]

The increased immigration of people from English-speaking countries whose dialect was quite different from Canadian dialects necessitated the establishment of English as a second dialect course (ESD). At first the children were placed in ESL classes, but dissatisfaction with placing English-speaking children in ESL resulted in ESD. Again sufficient care was not taken to adopt an additive philosophy instead of a substitutive one.

The preschool programs were designed for "disadvantaged" children. The fundamental idea was to establish institutional care in order to supplement the disadvantaged environment of the child. Again the assumption was made that the cultural environment of the family was incorrect or at least inadequate. When the general society and teachers had this negative attitude, the perspective became a self-fulfilling prophecy; the children came to see their culture and themselves as inadequate. There were few early childhood programs that adopted a different set of assumptions, namely, to provide for the development of the children in their own linguistic and cultural milieu while gradually introducing the dominant language and culture on an additive basis.[17]

On the other hand, a genuine recognition of the economic handicaps of "disadvantaged" families could provide support and attention. Economic and social inequality are world-wide human phenomena, and are related to educational achievement. Schools are only one agency that can respond to inequality and they are incapable of solving the problem.[18] Those schools, however, that are supportive, consistent, caring, and demanding, tend to secure greater success and mobility for their students; but, in a society demarcated on the basis of social inequality, head start programs for young children are not likely to create equality of educational opportunity; they tend to be palliative.

Unfortunately, even compensatory programs that consciously attempt to bolster the chances of older children for success in society, face much the same chances of success and failure. Inasmuch as they provide assistance to children who have persisted, encouragement to children who are on the verge of leaving school, and to others who have returned to school, the programs are valuable. Often they are bandaids that allow inflexible and insensitive school systems to continue. The best assistance that the compensatory programs provide is crucial cognitive knowledge, and skills for dealing with the larger society. Other compensatory programs which stress ethnic heritage can also assist students by bolstering their sense of pride in their culture and heritage. Their self-concept improves and this increases their "ability" to learn. In the latter type of program it is often the ethnic group that provides the programs to counter the neglect of the public school.

Another form of problem oriented multicultural education is the antidiscrimination program. It is usually crisis connected. Violence, name-calling, stereotyping, and other forms of prejudice manifest in the society are countered through crash programs or units of sensitization that are made part of the school curriculum. Regrettably, such programs are often short-term and intermittent. In that they focus upon a problem they can raise peoples' consciousness; however, care must be taken that the "reasons" for the problem are not laid at the feet of the victims. Another difficulty is that "crash" programs may be superficial; they fail, because they see human relations only in simplistic ethnic or racial terms rather than in the broader context of the economic, political, and social *power* relationships. Another difficulty that has been discovered with some of the antidiscriminatory units or programs is that they may emphasize the differences to the exclusion of similarities and, consequently, highlight the improbability of improving human and group relationships.[19] Placed in a broader context and as part of a more pervasive approach, antidiscriminatory content can play an important role in improving education.

(c) The *cultural/intercultural* is the third major type of multicultural education. The focus is upon developing capabilities that will enable people to live in a pluralistic society: individuals who will be capable of transcending the boundaries of their own ethnic cultures. Skills, knowledge, attitudes, and emotions are developed so that persons acquire a sense of security of their own being and group identity, a knowledge of other cultures and sub-cultures, and the facility to behave and act capably in more than one culture. The most significant aspect of this kind of multicultural education, in its ideal form, is that multiculturalism becomes an ethic that pervades the educational or school system.[20]

In practice, school systems in several provinces appear to be attempting to implement this form of multicultural education. The bilingual and bicultural programs that are open to children of all backgrounds, the heritage language programs that are part of publicly supported school systems, and the schools that stress cultural understanding in their curricula and activities, are part of this kind of multicultural education. It is the easiest and most practical type of multicultural education for the mixed communities that are so characteristic of Canadian society.

In contrast to problem-oriented multicultural education, the cultural/ intercultural oriented approach is not crisis-based, but grounded in a realistic appraisal of the nature of Canadian society. Nor is it dependent upon the ethnic mix or the extent of heterogeneity or homogeneity that exists in a particular community or school. It recognizes that the mobility of families and of maturing adolescents often results in their moving into a new cultural milieu. It is a broad approach to multicultural education but it is not amorphous because it is based upon the fundamentals of the policy of multiculturalism. Thus the school systems stress the official languages of Canada and at the same time provide for instruction in, or the learning of, other languages. Several anglophone provinces now provide for teaching in French and the teaching of French as early as kindergarten or primary school. Similarly, several provinces allow local school systems to teach in, or teach, heritage languages as part of a child's education. The development of language programs is evidence of a greater sense of equality of status while recognizing official bilingualism. English and French are the *link* languages of Canada and the "property" of all Canadians; heritage languages give linguistic recognition to the idea that there is no official culture or dominant cultural group.

The cultural/intercultural form of multicultural education also provides recognition of other basic aspects of multiculturalism. Ethnocultural groups see themselves as sharing public institutions (schools or libraries), and see these institutions as supportive of their familial and ethnic cultures. The school, by building upon the familial-ethnic culture instead of ignoring it, or countering it, improves the possibility of assisting the children to maintain and develop positive self-concepts, which are so crucial to learning and development. Institutions and programs that reflect cultural variety also enable students to develop some sense of the variety of values and attributes that Canadians, individually or collectively, hold. From an early age children can learn positive attitudes that will enable them to transcend the boundaries of their ethnocultural heritages. By relating their school experience to social diversity, students can see that there are alternative life styles that are valued, and that individuals can make choices regarding the values and behavior that they wish to adopt or practise.

The examination of the cultures and languages of Canada gives students a better knowledge and appreciation of what Canada is, and who Canadians are. In other words, it can give students an understanding of Canadian citizenship, of our commonalities, as well as our differences. The combination of equality of status and shared development, which can be found in school programs, gives a greater meaning to citizenship in a pluralistic society. The cultural/intercultural approach to multicultural education also gives scope for the development of sound concepts of human and civil rights. The study of civil and human rights gives students a cognitive basis upon which they can examine their own society as a means of understanding other societies. Such questions, as, "Are human and civil rights culturally based?" are important. The practice of a sense of human and group equality in the school also provides students with the ethical bases of social and community practice.

The implementation of the cultural/intercultural type of multicultural education has been somewhat hesitant. One major reason for this is that it requires a broader examination or reexamination of the assumptions of education. Bureaucratized schooling involves several levels of policy makers and administration that move slowly. Some educationists resist revision of policies, program and curricula, and the adoption of new resources and materials. The complexity of educational change has frustrated many attempts at change.[21] Instead of examining these impediments, some of the ideas and practices which indicate areas of positive progress need to be looked at.

Multicultural Education in Practice

Several provincial ministries of education have supported, to varying degrees, cultural/intercultural education. Few provinces, however, have adopted a comprehensive policy on multicultural education that outlines basic principles and areas of concern. The lack of provincial policies is a serious deficiency because the responsibility for overall policy in Canadian education is vested in the provincial governments and the legislatures. Among the most advanced in establishing an overall approach are the provinces of Ontario, Saskatchewan, Nova Scotia and, in a special sense, Quebec.[22] The last mentioned has been particularly noted for its support of anglophone education in a province that is predominantly (approximately 80 percent) French-Canadian; however, there has been less of a commitment to other forms of multicultural education.

The Province of Ontario has outlined its concern for multicultural education in a document of "Special Populations in Education."[23] While this title sounds restrictive, the actual policy is not.

> It has been recognized that the responsibility for preparing all Ontario students to live in Canada's multicultural society has significant implications in terms of general approaches to education, as well as in provision for special populations. In meeting the common needs of all students, publicly provided education has the task of encouraging general system sensitivity, while ensuring that individual and group needs are met in a way that will facilitate full participation by all students in the educational opportunities of the system.[24]

With reference to implementation, the Ontario Ministry of Education has been active in the area where it exercises the greatest control-curriculum. The Ministry has sponsored the development of guidelines for publishers and authors to promote bias-free texts and curriculum materials, disseminated documents to schools outlining a cultural/intercultural basis for education in the early elementary years, adopted a special certificate for teachers who secure additional training or qualifications in multicultural education, and instigated and adopted a history course for secondary education entitled "Canada's Multicultural Heritage."[25]

The aspect of the Ontario policy and programing that engendered the greatest controversy was the implementation of the Heritage Language Program which provides for the teaching of languages other than English and French on an extended school day or after school hours basis.[26] As of 1978-79 there were some 50 languages being taught to about 75 000 students. In response to the francophone community in Ontario the Ministry has assisted in the establishment of opportunities for a complete French language education where numbers warrant. In addition the Ministry of Education has promoted instruction in French as a school subject for all elementary students from grade 4 on; the Ministry has recently encouraged school boards to extend this program from 20 to 40 minutes per day. Perhaps the greatest success has been the immersion programs for students who wish to develop a greater proficiency in French. By 1982 some 62 percent of students in Ontario elementary schools will be enrolled in the regular programs, while 11 percent will be in the French immersion.[27] Finally, in the area of language, there are the ESL programs for immigrant and Canadian-born children who do not speak English, or whose dialect is sufficiently different from the Canadian to warrant special attention. The ESL language programs are provided for adults as well as for school children.

The Ontario policy and programs also include schemes for continuous evaluation of existing curriculum resources and textbooks, in-service professional development, resource materials for classroom use, consideration for racial and religious minorities, and general citizenship education. Within the Ministry of Education, there is a section specifically responsible for francophone education with specific officers whose main responsibility is multicultural education.

Although the education of Native People is a federal responsibility, the federal agreements with the provinces have placed many Native children in provincial schools. The Province of Ontario has provided for special membership of Native People on local boards of education, developed curriculum resources regarding Native People for schools, and appointed a ministry official who has special responsibility for overseeing the province's responsibilities in Native education. While many of the essential policies, programs, and structures are in place, much remains to be done in implementation at the local level. Secondary schools have been slower than elementary schools in adopting multicultural education, because they are more discipline and subject oriented, and their teachers have been less innovative.

A somewhat different policy, in relation to language, exists in the provinces of Alberta, Saskatchewan, and Manitoba. These three provinces with legislature provisions and government policies that provide for languages other than English and French as languages of instruction, have maintained a more linguistic view of multicultural education. However, there appears to be an interest in Manitoba in broadening the definition of multicultural education. The Manitoba Teachers' Society at their annual general meeting in March, 1980, debated adopting a multicultural education policy. While the decision was deferred, indications are that a cultural/intercultural type of multicultural education will receive their support. The original resolution included the concept that "each cultural group in Canada had a right to maintain and promote its continued existence and to have the obligation to respect other cultures," and that this recommendation be fostered through the education system by means of teacher awareness, curricula, heritage languages, resources, texts, exchanges, and the cultural programs.[28] The annual meeting was also asked to recommend action by the Department of Education and its minister. There are indications that the Ministry is now considering a more general approach to multicultural education.

The Manitoba Teachers's Society has published a background paper entitled *Multiculturalism and Education in Manitoba* which indicates that the implementation of multicultural education

> is not simply a matter of introducing a new course nor is it just the teaching of another ancestral language. Although it may include these aspects, it should be viewed as an all-encompassing approach with three major components: mainstream multicultural education, immigrant orientation and New Canadian awareness, [and] ancestral languages of established ethnocultural groups.[29]

A similar thrust appears imminent in Nova Scotia. In 1979, the Nova Scotia Teachers' Union (NSTU) provincial executive established a committee on multiculturalism whose function was to examine multiculturalism in that province and to recommend a policy. The policy was duly established. Again a broad cultural/intercultural thrust was adopted, based upon ethnocultural awareness, equality of opportunity and equality of access, teacher sensitivity, curriculum reform, and the development of support services, programs, materials, and resources. In order to disseminate these ideas, the NSTU is now mounting a Multiculturalism In-Service Workshop to be carried out over the year in cooperation with the Ethnic Services Division of the Department of Education. Fifty teachers from different areas of the province will be trained to handle sensitivity workshops, to use techniques for implementing multiculturalism, and to disseminate information about multicultural education resources.[30] This project of the Nova Scotia Teachers' Union, like the action of the Manitoba Teachers' Society, is an important step in the general promotion of multicultural education in the provinces.

Let us now turn our attention to the individual school boards that operate the local schools in most provinces. To illustrate positive action, the efforts of two particular boards will be highlighted – the Winnipeg School Division No. 1, and the Toronto Board of Education. School boards are important in that they provide additional direction, establish policy priorities at the local level, and determine funding allocations. In 1978, the Winnipeg School Division No. 1 adopted a policy to encourage multicultural enrichment programs, to promote immigrant education, and to maintain liaison with the various ethnic communities.[31] In March, 1980, the Board outlined further action. A Committee on Multicultural Education (C.O.M.E.) was organized to establish goals and objectives. A draft report of the Committee set out that the schools should "create units, programs, [and] courses on many facets of multiculturalism to be used interdisciplinarily and crossgrades in Winnipeg schools for children and adults (e.g., maintenance of cultural heritage, interaction of cultural heritage, maintenance of mother tongue, bilingual programs, etc.)"[32]

The Winnipeg School Division has begun to implement the policy while it is still in the final stages of definition. For cxample, teachers' aides of various ethnic backgrounds have been employed in the schools to supplement and support the regular teachers. The Winnipeg School Division has also published brochures in various languages to inform the parents of the school system, and it has given encouragement to language instruction and to the inclusion of multicultural content.

Beginning in 1972, the Toronto Board of Education sponsored a series of studies and issued a series of reports that culminated with a final report on multicultural education in March, 1976. The process included a series of community hearings where parents could make their views known. Teachers within the system participated in the discussions and reacted to the briefs and reports. Until the review process took place there had been isolated programs but "some trustees felt that these programs would remain isolated – and perhaps serve only as tokenism – unless they existed as part of a broad Board policy on multiculturalism."[33] In essence the Toronto Board found that it was operating a system based upon a single cultural orientation (anglo-Canadian), while in reality the community was ethnoculturally pluralistic. The system was out of touch with the cultural basis of the community.

The review process itself increased awareness and sensitivity. "One of these teachers who held to her view made an about-turn. After working with some youngsters she said, 'Now I realize what you are talking about. The kids respond so much more readily when their background is taken into account.' Here is a teacher trained in England with 20 years of experience and who probably has about 10 years left. She was dead against the briefs, but she had seen how a few words in Polish helped to light up the eyes of a child."[34]

In the process of reorienting the Toronto school system to multiculturalism, the committee found varying understandings among the educators and community as to what multicultural education should be. Some saw it as the maintenance of language and culture, others as a means of dynamically developing a Canadian culture through a combination of different ethnic cultures, while another group saw it as a means of assimilation.[35] The interpretations mark the significance of having clearly stated board policies, and the importance of involving the teachers in the process so that they reorient their thinking rather than just place a new label on what they continue to do or have always done.

The Toronto Board proceeded to implement a list of recommendations and changes that identified three main areas of concern: language education, system sensitivity, and school-community relations. Greater concern and stress were placed upon ESL and ESD programs. A New-Canadian student was now defined by the Toronto Board as "any student who may be unable to achieve academic success with regular programs because his or her language dialect or culture is different from that of the school system."[36] Reception classes, transition classes, and withdrawal classes received greater support and attention. The final report advocated "a staff sensitive to the needs, hopes, and aspirations of its community, and familiar with the deep and abiding meanings of its traditions, heritage, and race."[37] There was to be in-service education to achieve these ends.

Perhaps the most dynamic changes came in the area of school-community relations. Early in the process, in the summer of 1975, the Board established a School-Community Relations Department. It was to act not only as a liaison between the school and community but also between the curricula and programs and the needs of the community. One prime change that was extremely important was the willingness of the Board to provide students and community service (social workers, psychologists) personnel with the ability to speak community languages. The Board was intent on providing the services and support which the very heterogeneous population required – more than 50 percent of the students entered the school with a mother tongue other than English.

Conclusion

School boards in Canada, in the past 10 years, have given greater attention to multicultural concerns. However, most boards have not developed comprehensive policies but have shown greater interest in educational costs. The combined effect has been that multicultural programs have been viewed as added extra costs. It can be argued that immigrant parents, minorities, and multicultural education for mainstream students have not received their just share of the educational tax dollars. Education for diversity, human rights education, programs for immigrant students, language instruction, and general support services should receive greater board priority to assist the schools under their jurisdictions.

The greatest successes in multicultural education have occurred where the school staffs have collectively examined their educational goals, objectives, and programs in the light of the diversity in Canadian society, including their particular community. Some school staffs considered administrative, program, teacher, student, and community needs as a part of a comprehensive picture. Some examples of implementing multicultural education in each of these areas will be examined.[38]

First, administrators have the leadership responsibility to be continually working with the community and staff to answer particular needs. Specifically, principals can provide the time and means for explaining the school to parents. In communities with New Canadian parents, principals have adopted practices such as: sending information to parents in appropriate languages, utilizing interpreters and community liaison workers, adjusting school events to community concerns and values, and providing outreach programs to encourage reticent parents to participate.

Second, in the area of programing some schools have become sensitive to language needs, to curriculum adjustment, and to considering extracurricular activities. Such schools try to bridge cultural gaps, and, in general, base their programs on both long-and short-term needs. Interesting and successful programs have been built around "human and group identity." Such programs acknowledge that it is insufficient to regard each child simply as an individual because children bring their group identities to the schools. These identities or cultures must be recognized if the schools are to provide the best learning environment.

Third, the teacher factor in schooling is crucial to the success or failure of multicultural education. Teachers are not generally curriculum developers; they teach curricula that are usually ready-made. Consequently, a multicultural curriculum is most successful if the teachers' attitudes and assumptions are somewhat congruent with those of the program. It is important for individual teachers to realize that they need not be hamstrung in implementing their awareness and sensitivity by a dated or biased curriculum. The teachers' attitudes and behavior towards students, their verbal and non-verbal communication, their skills and strategies, the emphasis and examples within the curriculum, their preparation and approach to topics or content, and their use of texts and resources all have potential to develop or to stultify the students' sense of worth and identity, their belief in their future, and their view of their chances of success or failure.

Fourth, students have played important roles in the implementation of multicultural education. Students have suggested establishing cultural clubs which give support to their identities and needs. Clubs developed around Black, Italian, Indian, or Chinese cultural concerns have a legitimate role in schooling. They have sometimes been the stimulus that has led to curriculum or extracurricular adjustment. Similarly, students of various backgrounds can be a positive teaching resource if they are approached and worked with in a sensitive manner. They become involved and concerned in school activities that promote human relations, personal identity, and group development.

Finally, the community has played a major role in some schools, and its involvement can reinforce and support multicultural education. Are parents utilized as resource persons or volunteers? Are the cultural values and institutions in the community recognized? Is the school demonstrating an interest in all segments of the community? Are "we" reaching out to parents and the community? Are there special needs in some groups? These are a few of the questions that school personnel ask when they implement multicultural education. Community involvement has been a major complement to the professionalism of teachers in developing multicultural education.

In conclusion, multiculturalism as a policy is only 10 years old. The policy has broadened and developed during that time. While it has been developed in cultural, social, and political spheres, it has also developed in the field of education. Whereas initial efforts in the educational area were problem oriented or ethnic specific, there has been a visible shift toward emphasizing a more comprehensive cultural-intercultural approach. One hundred years of public schooling that stressed uniformity and conformity has not been nor could be altered in 10 years. The shortcomings of education in relation to social class, ethnic diversity, race relations, the handicapped, the gifted and the slow learners are the shortcomings of society. Schools which do not provide for individual and group particularities limit social growth, human development, and group dynamics. Multicultural education is an important aspect of Canadian efforts to come to terms with our diverse self. Multicultural education should be judged by its successes not by its failures, though these must be recognized. Measured by the increased attention to human relations, group development, language teaching, teacher awareness and sensitivity, administration adjustments, student interests and concerns, and community involvement there have been successes. If multiculturalism is a Canadian concept, why should there not be more attempts to implement multicultural education? Schools need not be part of the problem.

END NOTES

1. House of Commons, *Debates*, October 8, 1971. For a brief history of multiculturalism see Harold Trooper, "An Uncertain Past: Reflections on the History of Multiculturalism," and Keith A. McLeod, "Schooling for Diversity; Ethnic Relations, Cultural Pluralism, and Education," in *Test Talk*, Vol. 10, No. 3, Summer 1979.
2. J. Rudnyckyj, "Multiculturalism – A Way Foreward," *Language and Society*, No. 3 Autumn, 1980; and G. Rocher, "Multiculturalism," as State Policy. Report of the Second Canadian Conference on Multiculturalism, Ottawa, Canadian Consultative Council on Multiculturalism, 1976. For the New Brunswick case see Donald J. Loree, "Multiculturalism in a Bicultural Province," *Multiculturalism*, Vol. 2, 1978.
3. See Government of Quebec, *Quebec-Canada: A New Deal*, (The Quebec government proposal for a new partnership between equals: sovereignty-association, 1979).
4. N. Bruce McLeod, "Human Rights and The Law," in Keith A. McLeod, ed., *Multiculturalism, Bilingualism and Canadian Institutions* (Toronto: Guidance Centre) 1979.
5. *Ibid*.
6. Margaret Gibson, in "Approaches to Multicultural Education in the United States: Some Concepts and Assumptions," *Anthropology and Education Quarterly*, Vol. 7, No. 4, 1976, outlines six approaches to multicultural education but these don't really fit the Canadian situation despite the attempts to apply her categories. For examples of the attempts and difficulties see Vandra L. Masemann, "Multicultural Programs in Toronto Schools," *Interchange*, Vol. 9, No. 1, 1978-79, and Jonathan Young, "Education in a Multicultural Society: What Sort of Education? What Sort of Society?", *Canadian Journal of Education*, Vol. 4, No. 3, 1979.

7. Ethnic groups and organizations have been the mainstay of this type of multicultural education. This also applies to the anglo-Canadians who not only wanted their own children to be inculcated with anglo-Canadian values but utilized the school system to assimilate others.

8. There are many of these anglo-Canadian private institutions particularly in Ontario – e.g. Upper Canada College, Trinity Port Hope, Havergal, Lakefield, etc. They have been utilized in boundary maintenances not only in relation to ethnicity but particularly with reference to class.

9. John W. Friesen, *People Culture and Learning* (Calgary: Detselig Enterprises) 1977.

10. See the articles by Manoly Lupul and Barbara Burnaby in Canadian Society for the Study of Education, *Yearbook*, Vol. 3, 1976.

11. John R. Young, "Multiculturalism and Its Implication for Youth," in Keith A. McLeod, ed., *Multiculturalism, Bilingualism and Canadian Institutions*.

12. This type of multicultural education either assumes there are problems in carrying out education for assimilation or when instigated by ethnic groups it has been seen as a means of countering the bias inherent in a school system which is based upon assimilation.

13. See such studies as E.N. Wright, *Student's Background and Its Relationship to Class and Program in School* (Toronto Board of Education) 1970; and Mary Ashworth, *Immigrant Children and Canadian Schools* (Toronto: McClelland and Stewart Ltd.), 1975.

14. See "Immigrant Women," Vol. II, No. 4, 1979 issue of *Multiculturalism*, published by the Guidance Centre, Toronto.

15. Loren Lind, "New Canadianism: Melting The Ethnics in Toronto Schools," in G. Martel, *The Politics of the Canadian Public School* (Toronto: James Lewis & Samuel), 1974.

16. When I became involved with an organization in metropolitan Toronto dealing with immigrants and migrants the organizations who were part of this coalition could not understand why ethnic organizations would not participate. Invariably the members of the coalition looked upon immigrants and migrants as problems.

17. See the article by T. Grande in Aaron Wolfgang, ed., *The Education of Immigrant Students* (Toronto: Ontario Institute for Studies in Education, 1975).

18. The work of Michael Katz and others indicates how schools have not come to terms with inequality.

19. Jack Kehoe, "Multiculturalism: The Difficulty of Unpredictable Strategies," *Test Talk*, Vol. 10, No. 3, Summer 1979. There are many difficulties with these studies that use pre-testing and post-testing to assess attitude change. One major factor is that attitudes are developed over a long term and one or two weeks of "ethnic content" will not change them but it may raise their consciousness of the "problem" hence more negative attitudes are found on the post test. These kinds of programs and their tests demonstrate the shortcomings of the problem-oriented approach which Kehoe has been so involved with at the University of British Columbia.

20. T.R. Morrison, "Transcending Culture: Cultural Selection and Multicultural Education," in Keith A. McLeod, ed., *Intercultural Education and Community Development* (Toronto: Guidance Centre, 1980), and Keith A. McLeod,

"Schooling for Diversity: Ethnic Relations, Cultural Pluralism, and Education," in *Test Talk*, Vol. 10, No. 3, Summer, 1979.

21. Douglas Myers, *The Failure of Educational Reform in Canada* (Toronto: McClelland & Stewart), 1973.

22. Regarding the thinking in Quebec see Camille Laurin, "Nationalism, Diversity and Quebec," in *Multiculturalism*, Vol. 1, No. 5, 1978. Saskatchewan is a bit of an anomaly. It is the only province in Canada that has enacted multiculturalism in statute but it has maintained, so far, a rather narrow linguistic approach. However, a broader approach has been implemented by the Saskatoon School Board.

23. Ontario Ministry of Education, *Review and Evaluation Bulletins*, Vol. 1, No. 3, 1979, "Special Populations in Education."

24. *Ibid.* p. 23.

25. Another recent development is Ontario Ministry of Education "A Resource Guide For Teachers," *Black Studies Across The Intermediate Curriculum*. Draft Manuscripts #3.

26. Marshall Amphlett, "The Ontario Heritage Language Program," *Multiculturalism*, Vol. 1, No. 4, 1978.

27. Max Yalden, "Language Policy in Ontario's Secondary Schools." Notes for a speech by Max Yalden, Commissioner of Official Languages, to the Ontario Secondary Education Review Project Toronto, September 16, 1980.

28. Typescript copy of the resolution.

29. Manitoba Teachers' Society, *Multiculturalism and Education in Manitoba*, March, 1980. p. 10.

30. Peter McCreath, "Focus on Multiculturalism," in *The Teacher*, Nov. 7, 1980, and "NSTU Statement of Policy and Beliefs" re multiculturalism.

31. Copy of Board resolution.

32. Winnipeg S.D. #1, Proposal of Goals and Objectives Re: Committee on Multicultural Education, Draft #2, May 1980.

33. See Toronto Board of Education, *The Bias of Culture: An Issue Paper on Multiculturalism*; and Work Group on Multicultural Program, *Draft Report*, 1975 and *Final Report*, 1976.

34. "We Are All Immigrants To This Place," Toronto, October 1976. A case study prepared mainly by the staff of the Toronto Board of Education for IMTEC. p. 130.

35. *Ibid.* p. 90 ff.

36. *Ibid.* p. 78.

37. *Ibid.* p. 84.

38. The following analysis is based upon reports and studies of a variety of school boards and schools such as those in metropolitan Toronto, Winnipeg, Saskatoon, Vancouver, etc.

DAVID MILLETT   University of Ottawa

Ethnic Survival in Canada:
The Role of the Minority Church*

Introduction

It is now 20 years since Raymond Breton introduced and began to popularize the notion of institutional completeness in Canadian sociology. In the interim, notions such as bilingualism and multiculturalism have not only developed but become official government policy. The federal government, in its continuing effort to avoid complete absorption of the country by the American empire, abandoned its ideological and economic dependence on the "British connection," because this no longer provided a sufficiently strong counterweight to the American influences, and shifted instead to the ideology of an ethnic mosaic – "vertical" or otherwise – according to the social location of the person using the term.

This initiative was a relatively adequate response to "immigrant" minorities who had opted for English as their official language. Canada was at last defined in such a way that they could feel a part of it. For Native People and French Quebecers, federalist or not, it was irrelevant. Native People had no intention of being "accepted" by Europeans, *all* of whom they regarded as immigrants; and French Quebecers no longer saw themselves as a minority.

For francophones outside Quebec, multiculturalism was a positive threat. The provincial governments (except New Brunswick) had all refused federal efforts to make French a co-official language on the provincial level, and the federal sanctioning of multiculturalism amounted to approval of the provincial attitude that they were a minority "just like the others." By the time French was restored to official status in Manitoba, the action was irrelevant as the franco-Manitoban community had virtually disappeared.

Ironically, it was the success of Quebec in establishing its own francophone immigration policy during this period which aroused new pressures for multiculturalism. Haitians, Moroccans, and a host of other French-

---

* A revised version of a paper, "Minority Churches, Institutional Completeness, and Ethnic Survival in Canada," presented at the annual meeting of the Western Association of Sociology and Anthropology, Calgary, Alberta, December, 1977.

speakers spoke up for their right to be seen as "real" Québécois; and when the language legislation known as Bill 101 began to be implemented, the old English Quebecers were amazed to find that, like francophones outside Quebec, *they* were seen as a minority, "just like the others."

They also discovered, as their members migrated *en masse* to Ontario and the West, that their institutions were closing up one by one, and that their declining institutional completeness made it more and more difficult to survive as a community. The "invasion and succession" process which Aileen Ross had described in the Eastern Townships in the 1940s, in which French migrants had gradually taken over "English" towns, had finally reached the west end of Montreal Island, the last bastion of English Quebec.

A curious byproduct of the ideology of multiculturalism is that people who study "ethnic minorities" have been encouraged to perpetuate the illusion that Canadians of British origin are always and everywhere the "dominant group." Furthermore, the focus on relatively new arrivals, by students of "institutional completeness" gives the impression that minority communities are always expanding.

Although considerable research and indeed theorizing has been carried out, no one has attempted to work out a national inventory of the ethnic communities which do exist and to ask whether in fact they are institutionally complete. As is the case with so much Canadian work, it has been confined to one ethnic group (almost always that of the author) or to an isolated geographical area. Breton's work itself, although based on a multi-ethnic study, was initially confined to the city of Montreal. His continuing work, shared with Warren Kalbach and others,[2] is confined to Metropolitan Toronto. Studies of French-English relations both inside and outside Quebec, although numerous and increasingly sophisticated, usually ignore all languages other than English and French, and all ethnic variables other than language.

The result of this is that in the sociological literature one cannot find any attempt to assess the national potential for identifiable ethnic communities to survive – with or without institutional completeness. This paper takes a first step towards providing such an assessment.

Selection of an Institution

Since the scope of this study is national, only a massive project could uncover all the institutions of every minority community in the country. The problem, then, is to select a single institution likely to be found in every minority community which is at the same time a significant factor in the development of institutional completeness. The institution I have selected is the Minority Church.

As I have indicated on a number of occasions,[3] a Minority Church, in the Canadian setting, usually consists of one or several parishes or congregations affiliated with a major church, but which are subject to some kind of discrimination. Despite this discrimination, which might be expected to lead them towards sect-like behavior, they continue to exhibit church-like behavior. That is, they tend to accommodate to and speak positively of the surrounding society, rather than see it as a threat from which they must retreat, or as an ignorant or sinful population in need of "the truth."

The explanation offered for this church-like behavior is to be found not only in the theology of the Minority Churches but in the fact that they find a sense of security in a number of reference groups holding to the same religious faith, even though the reference groups may be living in another country. The discrimination which leads to minority status may be strictly religious, as was the case of the Eglise Réformée de France, which Mehl (1965) described when he first popularized the concept of Minority Church. The discrimination could, however, be based on the language used during worship, on race,[4] on national origin – in short, on any kind of ethnic labelling.

This paper has as its goal to bring together the results of previous studies as well as a 1977 study on "Official-Language Minority Churches," so as to present a reasonably comprehensive picture of the number, type, and distribution of minority ethnic communities in Canada that have some potential for survival. It should also provide a corrective to some of our presuppositions about the size and distribution of particular ethnic communities. The following statements were held to be axiomatic, before this research was begun:

1. That the people we usually think of as minority groups are mainly immigrants from Europe or their descendants. While we are becoming aware of non-White immigrants and of Native Peoples, we do not have any clear idea of how these groups compare in size or strength to the Europeans. And this is worth finding out.

2. Although the census provides figures on origins of the people, we are becoming increasingly skeptical as to the meaningfulness of these figures. Only when people take their origins seriously enough to form communities, or dominant groups discriminate against them seriously enough to force them into communities, are figures on origins socially meaningful.

3. The hard core of an ethnic community (except certain cases where race is crucial) is the group which speaks a language different from the surrounding population. When such a group has difficulty in coping with the larger society, one of the institutions it is most likely to establish is its own church. This church may or may not be sponsored by a larger church.

4. The subjective experience of Native Peoples, of White immigrants, of non-White immigrants and of official-language minorities is so different that they should be examined separately for some purposes. Yet they are all minorities, and within each region of the country they compete for power, both with one another and with the dominant group. Their first struggle for power, however, is simply to survive. An inventory of their churches suggests their potential to survive and their relative power in each region. Groups that are strong in one region, and make major claims on the dominant group, may be quite weak in another region.

5. Accordingly, if we can establish the number of ethnic churches of each major type, in each region, we should have a good indication of the potential for survival of minority communities in Canada.

Ethnic Labelling

The operational definition of "ethnic" used here is a modified version of that used by Milton Gordon (1964) when he characterized as ethnic "any group which is defined or set off by race, regligion, or national origin, or some combination of these categories."[5] To his credit, Gordon restricted this definition to "a type of group contained within the national boundaries of America."[6] It is obvious in Canada (and indeed has subsequently become obvious in the United States) that one cannot exclude language from the list of ethnic labels. This point deserves a certain amount of elaboration.

The Primacy of Language

While it is not difficult to find cases where religious labels (Ireland), national origin labels (Slavs in North America), or racial labels (South Africa) are used as independent justifications for discrimination, it is also the case that language differences create a barrier which not only may operate independently but also reinforces the impact of any of the other labels which may be used. Where an institution and its general environment operate in different languages, and one or both are dominated by unilingual members, communication is so difficult and mutual ignorance so great that alleged differences can be magnified without limit, and labelling by language can be used to express any sort of cultural grievance. For those deploring inter-ethnic conflict, the fact that someone has another color or national origin becomes a minor issue compared to the fact that one is completely unable to speak to him or her.[7]

On the other hand, for those groups willing to pay the price of a low standard of living, this inability to communicate is one of the best guarantees of cultural survival. Fernand Dumont has in fact argued that Quebec will remain French only so long as a large proportion of the province remains *unable* to speak English. In such a state of mutual ignorance it becomes essential that a minority create as many of its own institutions as possible, not in pursuit of some abstract cultural goal, but to satisfy the everyday needs of its members.

If this line of reasoning is pursued, one arrives at the conclusion that, historically, the main reason for the existence of the Canadian mosaic, in the first instance, has been the slowness with which minority groups learned the languages of the dominant groups. This ignorance of English or French, according to region, forced them to preserve or even to develop their own institutions, not by choice but by necessity. Only when they learned the official language did the institutions of the dominant groups become open to them, and only in the presence of this option did the preservation and enlargement of their own institutions become a conscious act.

Discrimination on the basis of race, religion, or national origin could either hinder or encourage this access to institutions of the dominant groups, but has not changed the basic dynamics of this interaction, which depends primarily on language. It is for this reason that, for Canadian use, I am defining minority groups first by language and only secondarily on the basis of race, national origin, and religion.

The Basis of Classification of Minority Churches

The first distinction to be made is between official and non-official languages. The presumption is that the use of non-official languages in an institution is likely to lead to discrimination on the part of the dominant group. In many cases this discrimination is reinforced by mutual awareness of racial differences, or the language itself implies national origins different from the dominant group. The same treatment is accorded large unsponsored churches which operate in non-official languages. Hence, data on non-official languages have been divided into four sub-groups: Native Peoples (non-White understood); White immigrants; non-White immigrants; and unsponsored non-official language churches. I am using the term immigrant to refer to everyone who has arrived on this continent after the Native Peoples.

Official-language groups may also find themselves in minority situations, as when English-speakers are isolated among French-speakers or, more commonly, the reverse. They are then potentially subject to discrimination. This situation will be examined at the level of provinces, counties, and within neighborhoods of metropolitan areas.

The one major omission in this paper is the specifically religious factor – the practice of a religion which serves as a source of discrimination. This will serve as the basis of a later study; meanwhile, we will examine only Christianity, and only churches, rather than sects or cults. *We are, therefore, looking at churches which tend to attract discrimination for non-religious reasons, and which are central to the survival of various minority groups.*

Research Method

a) *Non-official language churches*

As a first step in our research we contacted a number of major churches and asked if they sponsored any non-official language parishes or congregations. As a test of whether the group in question really operated as a Minority Church, we asked whether they thought that a newcomer, unable to speak either English or French, would "feel at home" in such a congregation or parish. Their response might be a clue as to whether the Majority Church was providing a sense of strength and security to the people in it – the kind of security which prevents the group from becoming a sect, or from joining existing sects.

Initially we thought that the churches most likely to sponsor Minority Churches would be the largest and oldest ones in Canada. This assumption seemed indicated by a 1968 study.[8] Certain changes were discovered which led us to modify our selection of churches. When all was said and done, we found ourselves with usable information from the following:

Anglican Church
Baptist Church (3 kinds): United Baptist Convention of the Atlantic Provinces (1905); Baptist Convention of Ontario and Quebec (1887); Baptist Union of Western Canada (1909). Together these formed the Baptist Federation of Canada (1944).
Latter Day Saints (Mormons)
Lutheran Council in Canada (includes the 3 major synods): Lutheran Church in America, Canada Section; Evangelical Lutheran Church in Canada (1967); Missouri Synod – Canada.
Presbyterian Church
Roman Catholic Church
Seventh Day Adventists
United Church of Canada

In the 1971 census these churches[9] accounted for over 86 percent of all Canadians. The response to our survey from these churches revealed over 700 congregations and parishes operating in more than 60 languages. They also, of course, offer services in English and French; these will be dealt with later.

b) *Official-language churches*

Here we are dealing with a quite different situation. The parish or congregation in question was not a sponsored one, or one which operated in a non-official language. It was a normal parish or congregation of a dominant group which for any one of a number of reasons found itself in a neighborhood inhabited primarily by a different official-language population. Typical situations involved old downtown English-language churches in neighborhoods vacated by the English and replaced by French-speakers, or downtown French neighborhoods whose members moved to the suburbs and were replaced by new immigrants, destined eventually to speak English. Conversely, on arrival in the suburbs, downtown French people might set up new parishes in formerly homogenous English-speaking areas, or English-speaking city-dwellers might move to housing developments in French-speaking rural townships, and set up English-speaking congregations or parishes.

Despite the official federal ideology (accepted by all federal political parties), there is no concensus among the general public that English and French should both be recognized as official languages in all parts of the country. In fact, the official policy of most provinces recognizes only English, and the recently-adopted Quebec policy (Bill 101) recognizes only French.

It follows, then, that the type of population movement described above may operate as a stimulant to discrimination, especially if it involves such a visible ethnic symbol as a church. The French-language takeover of certain neighborhoods is a relatively new experience for English-speakers; its counterpart, the English takeover of French areas, is an old story both inside and outside of Quebec.

This tolerance of what are supposedly official languages gives rise to the treatment of parishes and congregations which worship in the "wrong" language of the neighborhood as Minority Churches. But there is still another complication to be considered.

In certain areas of the country bilingualism is so institutionalized that its practitioners find some difficulty in labelling either English *or* French as the dominant local language.[10] For them it is "normal" to use both languages, and "different" to operate solely in one or the other.[11]

Finally, in considering the reference groups which supposedly give support to Minority Churches, one must consider the fact that the headquarters of almost all Majority Churches have in practice recognized English as the only official language of the country.

Alone among Canadian churches the Roman Catholic Church has "always"[12] had sufficiently strong representation of both official languages that neither could be ignored at the top levels of its administration. All other churches, if they offer services in French at all, have traditionally treated it as "our French work," or "our mission to the French." Only very recently have certain churches developed semi-autonomous French administrations.

The interplay of differing regional attitudes with attitudes of church administrations reveals how arbitrary are our attempts to provide an "objective" (in this case demographic) base for determining whether in a given locality one or the other language group occupies a minority status. Only when we have some reason to believe that the language of a congregation or parish is considered illegitimate in the local neighborhood can we conclude that the potential for discrimination exists, and only then may we say that we are examining a Minority Church.[13]

In seeking this objective base, we consulted a number of census materials on "language of the home," to ascertain the linguistic composition of particular counties, municipalities and urban neighborhoods across the country,[14] and assessed the data according to the following criteria:

1. A county or census district may be labelled by whichever official language group is in the majority, e.g. if over 50 percent of the residents use French as the main language of the home, French is considered to be the dominant language of the county, and the county is labelled "French." Any English-language church in such a county accordingly is a Minority Church.

    The same applies to a census tract in an urban area. Thus, there are "French" and "English" census tracts.

2. Nevertheless, if only one or two counties of a province, or only a few tracts of a metropolitan area are dominated by one or the other language, the people in that area are likely to feel that they are a minority and churches in their neighborhood may be considered Minority Churches. For example, even in areas of Saint Boniface where most people speak French at home, they will feel a minority because they know that this is highly exceptional in Manitoba. The same would apply to English-speaking neighborhoods in Quebec City.

3. It follows, *a fortiori*, that English churches in counties or tracts where even locally the English-speakers are not dominant will be Minority Churches; the same will be true for French churches in the reverse situation.

4. Where several contiguous counties of a province, or several contiguous tracts of a large city are dominated by a different official language from their surroundings, it may be possible for residents to feel that they are a co-majority of the province or of the city in question. Thus some French counties in Northern Ontario, and some English areas of Montreal may feel relatively secure, and their churches should not be considered Minority Churches. It is especially in this situation that intellectuals and political leaders will differ with the public in their assessment of the situation; those defining the situation locally are likely to feel secure, while those defining it provincially or nationally are likely to feel threatened. For purposes of this study we will define the area by the local situation. Hence English churches in Quebec City will be Minority Churches, but those in one large area of Montreal will be assumed to feel dominant.

The application of these criteria to the metropolitan areas of Ottawa-Hull and Montreal is somewhat complex, and is described in detail in Appendix "A." Applied nationally, the criteria provide us with the following locations in which to look for Minority Churches. English-language churches will be Minority Churches in:

(a) *Entire provinces*   – none

(b) *Selected counties* – New Brunswick: Gloucester, Kent, Madawaska, Restigouche

Quebec: all counties except Brome and Pontiac

Ontario: Prescott and Russell

(c) *Metropolitan areas* – Quebec City: all tracts

Montreal: all tracts east of a line along Saint Laurent Boulevard, Park Avenue and Bloomfield, to Metropolitan Boulevard and east of Laurentian Boulevard; all tracts south of Montreal West and Westmount; 10 tracts in the Outremont area. (See Appendix B, Figures 1 and 2.)

Ottawa-Hull: Quebec side; all municipalities
Ontario side; tracts 50, 53-57
Vanier 101-104; Gloucester 122. (See Appendix B, Figure 3.)

French-language churches will be Minority Churches in:

(a) *Entire provinces*   – Newfoundland, Nova Scotia, P.E.I., Manitoba, Saskatchewan, Alberta, B.C., Yukon, N.W.T.

(b) *Selected counties* – New Brunswick: Albert, Carleton, Charlotte, Kings, North Cumberland, Queens, St. John, Sudbury, Victoria, Westmorland, York

Quebec: Brome, Pontiac

Ontario: all except Prescott and Russell

(c) *Metropolitan areas* – Lennoxville, P.Q.

Montreal: the area implied in (c) above, bounded on the west by Dorval and Lachine; on the south by the Lachine Canal and Rue St. Jacques; on the east by St. Laurent, Park, and Bloomfield; and on the north by Metropolitan Boulevard; and excluding 10 tracts in Outremont.

Ottawa: all tracts except those specified above in (c).

Observations

1. *Non-official Language Churches*

a) Native Peoples. Table 1 provides an indication of the languages and distribution of Minority Churches among Native Peoples. It may be noted that some linguistic groups are much stronger than others, ranging from the Cree, with 105 Minority Churches, to the single tiny congregations of Car-

TABLE 1 *Native language parishes and congregations sponsored by major churches, Canada and regions, 1977*

Language	Region						
	Atlantic	Québec	Ontario	Prairies	B.C.	Arctic	Canada
1. Algonquin		5					5
2. Beaver-Slavey				2			2
3. Blood				1			1
4. Blackfoot				3			3
5. Carrier					1		1
6. Chipewan				1			1
7. Cowichan					1		1
8. Cree*		2	16	68			86
9. Coastal Cree			3			1	4
10. Moose Cree		2	6				8
11. Swampy Cree			1				1
12. Plains Cree				6			6
13. Inuit	1	10				48	59
14. Gitkshan					3		3
15. Haida					1		1
16. Kwakwala					2		2
17. Loucheux						4	4
18. Micmac	1						1
19. Mohawk		2	1				3
20. Montagnais	2	7		4			13
21. Nishga					3		3
22. Ojibway			28				28
23. Oneida			3				3
24. Peigan				1			1
25. Saultax			3	4			7
26. Sioux				1			1
27. Six Nations*			3				3
28. Stony				1			1
29. Tsimpsean					5		5
30. Tuscarora			1				1
TOTAL	4	28	65	92	16	53	258

*Not specified

TABLE 2 *White immigrant parishes and congregations sponsored by major churches, Canada and regions, 1977*

Language	Atlantic	Québec	Ontario	Region Prairies	B.C.	Arctic	Canada
1. Armenian		2	1				3
2. Croatian		1	9	4	2		16
3. Czech		1	4	1			6
4. Danish			2	2	1		5
5. Dutch		1	1				2
6. Estonian		2	13		1		16
7. Finnish		1	7		1		9
8. German		3	13	45	8		69
9. Greek			1				1
10. Hungarian		3	24	8	3		38
11. Icelandic				1			1
12. Italian	1	9	57	3	7		77
13. Latin			2				2
14. Latvian		2	11	1	1		15
15. Lithuanian		2	6	1			9
16. Maltese			1				1
17. Polish	1	4	25	9	2		41
18. Portuguese		2	26	6	3		37
19. Roumanian		1	3				4
20. Russian		1	2				3
21. Slovak		1	14		1		16
22. Slovene		1	4	1			6
23. Spanish		1	7	1	1		10
24. Swedish			1				1
25. Ukrainian			4	4	1		9
26. Yugoslav*			1				1
TOTAL	2	38	239	87	32		398

*Not specified

rier, or Kwakwala. Such small groups may not find sufficient protection from the White man's world in the White man's church, and may eventually retire from "the world" into little introverted sects. The stronger tribes may evolve into large Indian Christian churches, or may use their growing sense of strength to break out of the colonialism of the White churches (however benevolent and secure) and return to their own religion, or to develop some synthesis of Native religion and Christianity, as has happened in many areas around the world.[17] Many Inuit, for example, have affiliated with the Baha'i World Faith, which permits retention of most of their original beliefs. The Baha'i do not, however, provide services in Native languages to date.

b) *White immigrants.* Table 2 shows how European Whites have formed Minority Churches over the years. The pattern of recent immigration is sug-

TABLE 3 *Non-White immigrant languages in parishes and congregations for major churches, Canada and regions, 1977**

Language	Atlantic	Québec	Ontario	Prairies	B.C.	Arctic	Canada
1. Arabic	1	2					3
2. Chinese	5	12	5	9			31
3. Creole	1						1
4. East Indian		3					3
5. Ge'ez (Coptic)	1						1
6. Japanese	3	8	3	6			20
7. Korean	2	13	4	5			24
8. Vietnamese	1	1					2
TOTAL	14	39	12	20			85

*It should be made clear that many members of these churches are Can.. 'an-born, and that often the numerical majority are Canadian citizens. The fact remains that such parishes and congregations exist ahd tend to survive because of continuous immigration. See end note 19 for an explanation of the expression "non-White."

gested by the 77 Italian parishes and the 37 Portuguese. At the other extreme are large but longer-resident groups such as the Dutch, now mainly assimilated with only two surviving Dutch-speaking parishes, both Roman Catholic. This means that virtually all Dutch members of the United, Presbyterian and Baptist churches are now anglicized.[18] Between these extreme cases, however, we find moderately-sized but persistent groups which cling to churches in their own language, such as the Croations, Estonians, and Slovaks, with 16 each, and the Latvians, with 15. Either these groups are very attached to their churches for religious or other reasons (perhaps political), or there is a heavier flow of immigration than may appear obvious.

The regional distribution of European-speaking Minority Churches approximates closely to the national distribution of population.

c) *"Non-White" immigrants.* Let us now examine the languages of "non-White" immigrants, as presented in Table 3. This group includes not only people who are visibly non-White but certain nationalities which Europeans regard as so foreign that they actually perceive them as non-White and discriminate against them on this basis.[19]

The Table shows that, at least as measured by Minority Churches, Ontario now surpasses British Columbia as an area of new non-White (primarily Asian) settlement. The total number of Minority Churches involved (shown in more detail in Table 4) reflects the change in immigration policy which has taken place since 1964. Even in the case of the Chinese there has been a sharp rise, resulting in 31 parishes and congregations. Most striking of all is the appearance of 24 Korean churches, starting from zero in 1968.[20]

TABLE 4 *Sponsors and growth of non-White immigrant minority churches*

Language	Adv.	Ang.	Bap.	L.C.C.	Mor.	Pres.	R.C.	U.C.	Tot. 1977	Tot. 1968	Net Increase
Asian											
Chinese	1	2	3	3	2	5	6	9	31	21	10
E. Ind.			3						3	0	3
Jap.	1	6					1	12	20	18	2
Kor.	1	2	3		1	6	4	7	24	0	24
Viet.							2		2	0	2
Total	3	10	9	3	3	11	13	28	80	39	41
African											
Arabic							3		3	2	1
Ge'ez (Coptic)							1		1	4	-3
Total							4		4	6	-3
Caribbean											
Creole							1		1	0	1
Over-all Total	3	10	9	3	3	11	18	28	85	45	40

*Adv. Adventist
Ang. Anglican
Bap. Baptist
L.C.C. Lutheran Council of Canada
**Adventists and Mormons not included.

Mor. Mormon
Pres. Presbyterian
R.C. Roman Catholic
U.C. United Church of Canada

Table 4 also groups these same churches by Asian, African, and Caribbean origins, showing which major church has sponsored which group, and indicates in more detail the growth of each group since 1968,[21] the date of an earlier study. To the 45 parishes and congregations of 1968 have been added 40 new ones, representing close to 100 percent growth.

The Jehovah's Witnesses and Pentecostal Assemblies also support a considerable number of Asian congregations (as well as European-language congregations), but details on their regional distribution are not yet available.

"Non-White" immigrants, then, have come to constitute a significant part of the Minority Church scene in Canada. Just how important they are is shown in Table 5, which groups all sponsored churches by region.

d) *Unsponsored non-official language churches.* The non-official language churches described to this point have been sponsored by official-

TABLE 5 *Sponsored minority churches by region, Canada, 1977*

Population				Region			
	Atlantic	Que.	Ont.	Prairies	B.C.	Arctic	Canada
Native People	4	28	65	92	16	53	258
White Immigrants	2	38	238	87	32		398
"Non-White" Immigrants		14	39	12	20		85
All Sponsored churches	6	80	343	191	68	53	741

language churches. There also are in Canada a number of churches which were formerly sponsored from outside the country and operated in languages other than English and French, and which have now evolved into major churches in their own right. In the process some have become uniformly English-speaking while others have not. The most visible, historically, have been the various Lutheran synods, sponsored from outside Canada, and operating in a number of Scandinavian languages, plus German and Finnish. These are now almost 100 percent English-speaking and Canadian-based. They therefore no longer occupy the status of Minority Churches.

The Mennonites have come to occupy a somewhat similar position, operating as an English-speaking church rather than a German-speaking sect. They do, however, continue to maintain a certain number of German-speaking congregations which could be characterized as Minority Churches. In Waterloo they also sponsor an English-language Chinese congregation.

Slightly different again are the Orthodox churches – Ukrainian, Greek, Russian, Syrian, Romanian, and others – which have all existed in Canada for several generations and which may be regarded as Canadian-based institutions, but which have *not* shifted to either the English or French language, even as their language of administration.[22] The Ukrainian Catholic church is also in this situation.

These churches have survived in their own languages despite the fact that nowhere in Canada are they located in neighborhoods where the majority of the residents speak these languages in their homes. Indeed, most of the people attending them speak English primarily, at home and elsewhere. Nevertheless, they continue to worship in the "ethnic" language, and by doing so are at least potentially subject to discrimination on the ground of being "un-Canadian."

Together, these churches represent hundreds of parishes which serve as centers of ethnic communities in various stages on the road towards institutional completeness. Table 6 shows how many parishes are involved.

TABLE 6 *Unsponsored non-official language churches, by region*

Church	Region					
	Atlantic	Quebec	Ontario	Prairies	B.C.	Canada
Orthodox						
Ukrainian	—	2	19	29	2	52
Greek	4	8	20	6	1	39
Russian	—	3	6	13	4	26
Serbian	—	1	7	3	1	12
Rumanian	—	1	4	6	—	11
Syrian-						
Lebanese	—	5	3	—	—	8
Other*	—	2	9	—	—	11
Total Orthodox	4	22	68	57	8	159
Greek Catholic:						
Ukrainian	—	3	30	54	7	94
Other**	—	1	6	—	—	7
Total Gr. Cath.	—	4	36	54	7	101
Total Unsponsored	4	26	104	111	15	260

*Includes 6 Macedonian, 2 Byelorussian, 2 Armenian, 1 Coptic
**Includes 5 Hungarian and 2 Slovak

We are now in a position to ascertain the total number of Minority Churches which operate in non-official languages in Canada. These are represented in Table 7, grouped by sponsor and region.

We now turn to official-language churches which are located in minority communities.

2. *Official-Language Minority Churches*

a) *English-language churches in French areas.* As has been indicated, there are no provinces in which all counties are French, although Quebec comes very close. We therefore turn immediately to French-dominated counties of various provinces. English-language churches in these counties will, at least potentially, be Minority Churches, and are likely to be major institutions supporting small English-language communities. In Table 8 such churches are grouped by province and counties or groups of counties.

Looking at French cities and metropolitan areas, we find that these are also a considerable source of English-language Minority Churches.[23]

b) *French-language churches in English areas.* Information on this question was considerably more centralized than that for Tables 8 and 9, for the simple reason that the vast majority of French Canadians are Roman Catholics, and that other denominations sponsoring French congregations

TABLE 7 *All non-official language churches, by sponsor and region*

Sponsor	Atlantic	Quebec	Ontario	Region Prairies	B.C.	Arctic	Canada
Adv.	—	—	7	7	3	—	17
Ang.	—	15	41	31	10	32	129
Bap.	—	—	37	—	2	—	39
L.C.C.	—	7	35	41	12	—	95
Mor.	—	1	6	—	1	—	8
Pres.	—	2	14	2	4	—	22
R.C.	6	48	167	84	22	21	348
U.C.	—	7	36	26	14	—	83
Total Sponsored	6	80	343	191	68	53	741
Total Unsponsored	4	26	104	111	15	—	260
Total N.O.L. Churches*	10	106	447	302	83	53	1001

*Non-official language

TABLE 8 *English-language churches in French counties, by province*

Location	R.C.	U.C.	Ang.	Denomination Pres.	Bap.	Luth.	Total
New Brunswick							
Gloucester	—	1	6	1	1	—	9
Kent	—	2	4	—	2	—	8
Madawaska	—	1	2	—	—	—	3
Restigouche	—	4	4	3	4	—	15
Total	—	8	16	4	7	—	35
Quebec							
West Quebec	15	10	3	1	3	—	32
Townships	6	25	47	13	8	—	99
Gaspé	—	3	25	3	—	—	31
North Shore	15	3	15	2	—	—	35
Total	36	41	90	19	11	—	197
Ontario							
Prescott-Russell	4	3	7	2	4	—	20
ALL COUNTIES	40	52	113	25	15	—	245

confine their French work almost exclusively to Quebec. Such congregations, being French-speaking in a French environment, are not minorities in the terms we are using here.[24]

The Catholic church is, however, organized into 68 separate dioceses, a number of which cross provincial boundaries, and most of which include both urban and rural parishes. While over 50 of these were contacted, the following tables must be considered tentative. Rural and urban parishes will be combined until a breakdown between the two types of location is possible.

This completes our enumeration of official-language Minority Churches. They may now be grouped by regions, as shown in Table 12.

This allows us to group Minority Churches of *all* the types we have chosen to consider (remembering that we have decided to ignore those which are a minority on a religious basis). In order that this table conforms to the original categories in terms of which minorities were classified, it is necessary to recognize that the unsponsored non-official language churches in fact fall under the heading of White immigrants (with the single exception of the Egyptian Copts). Such unsponsored churches can therefore be grouped with the sponsored churches of the same type. We thus arrive at the final table, which is also represented graphically in Appendix B Figure 4.

TABLE 9 *English-language churches in French cities and metropolitan areas, by province*

Location	Denomination						
	R.C.	U.C.	Ang.	Pres.	Bap.	Luth.	Total
Quebec							
Quebec City	3	1	5	3	1	—	13
Montreal	16	29	13	6	3	—	67
Total	19	30	18	9	4	—	80
Ontario							
Ottawa-Hull	8	3	3	3	2	2	21
ALL METRO.	27	33	21	12	6	2	101

TABLE 10 *English-language minority churches, by region*

Location	Region			
	Atlantic	Quebec	Ontario	Canada
Fr. Counties	35	197	20	252
Fr. Metro. Areas	—	80	21	101
Eng. Minority Churches	35	277	41	353

TABLE 11 *French-language churches in English areas, by region*

| Location | Region | | | | | |
	Atlantic	Quebec	Ontario	Prairies	B.C.	Canada
R.C.	19	4	148	102	5	278
U.C.	—	—	1	—	—	1
Bap.	1	—	—	—	—	1
Total	20	4	149	102	5	280

TABLE 12 *Official-language minority churches, by region*

| Language of church | Region | | | | | |
	Atlantic	Quebec	Ontario	Prairies	B.C.	Canada
French	20	4	149	102	5	280
English	35	277	41	—	—	353
Total	55	281	190	102	5	633

TABLE 13 *Minority churches by type and region, Canada, 1977*

| Type of minority | Region | | | | | | |
	Atlantic	Quebec	Ontario	Prairies	B.C.	Arctic	Canada
N.O.L.*							
Native People	4	28	65	92	16	53	258
White Immigrants	6	64	342	198	47	—	658
Non-White Immigrants	—	14	39	12	20	—	85
Total N.O.L.	10	106	447	302	83	53	1001
Official Language	55	281	190	102	5	—	633
All Minorities	65	387	637	404	88	53	1634

*N.O.L. denotes Non-Official Language.

Analysis and Reflections

Looking at these results, we might first ask, "How does the picture of the relative strength of minorities obtained by counting churches compare to our general impressions, and to census figures on origins?" The answer seems to be that while nationally the Europeans are largest, as we might expect, there are some significant differences in the order of size of the other groups. Most striking, perhaps, is the fact that Native Peoples occupy a strong third place.

In Eastern Canada, and perhaps everywhere, a good deal of publicity has been given to non-White immigrants, to the English Quebecers, and to the French outside Quebec; yet we find here that the French communities outside Quebec are almost the same in number as those of the Indians and the Inuit, and the English and French Minority Churches are equal in number. Non-White immigrants are undercounted, because non-Christian religions have not been considered, but the groups practising Native Indian religions have not been counted either.

As to our impressions of regional distribution, it may readily be remarked that the Atlantic region has a striking absence of non-official language minorities of any kind. This makes it more comprehensible that French-English relations should loom large in the preoccupations of Maritimers.

It is somewhat amusing to find that in Quebec, which people tend to consider such an anomalous province, there exists the distribution of types of minorities which most closely approximates the national distribution. Again, the number of Native communities is striking. It will probably take some time yet to grasp the fact that English Quebecers are so thoroughly confined geographically and have so completely moved into a minority position. As Richard Joy observed some time ago, the French areas of the country continue to become more French.

The Ontario scene is surely that of a boiling pot, with little indication of much melting going on. All types of minorities are strongly represented, non-White immigrant churches twice the number of their second strongest region – British Columbia. Native Peoples are strong, with churches numbering two-thirds of those on the Prairies, and more numerous than those of the entire Arctic region.

What is striking in the Prairies is the small number of non-White immigrants as compared to other minorities. The low importance attached regionally to French-language communities also becomes understandable when their strength is compared to that of Native People (highest in Canada) and White immigrants (second highest in Canada).

The Arctic might best be regarded as a separate country, in a classic colonial situation. All "immigrants" come from "the South," and all are White colonizers, speaking only one official language. Thus the only minority is the Native population, which constitutes the numerical majority of the residents. Such a situation exists nowhere else in Canada.

This, then, is the broad picture of minority communities in this country. Whether these communities can or should persist is something each of them will have to consider both individually, collectively, and in negotiations with the dominant groups, both English- and French-speaking. They will also have to determine to what extent they have interests in common.

To the extent that minorities decide to cooperate, however, they will challenge the power of the dominant groups.

But what *of* the dominant groups, which is to say most of us? One useful result of clarifying the types, distribution, and strength of the minority communities is that it obliges us to seek a clearer definition of the dominant groups, both English- and French-speaking. In 1965, John Porter destroyed the myth that access to the top decision-making positions in Canada is open equally to all. He showed that Canadians of British origin were solidly in control. Even as he wrote this, the ideology of multiculturalism was gathering strength, and soon came to public attention as a challenge to the bilingual and bicultural definition of Canada. Aided by the multicultural ideology, Canadians of non-British origin tried harder than ever to force their way into the private British preserves of decision-making, in business and in government. They made little visible headway at the elite level, as Wallace Clement was to demonstrate a few years later, but they made considerable progress at the professional level, and the multicultural wave began to weaken the will to resist of those in power. Meanwhile, inside Quebec, the British were forced out of their monopolies and a more legitimate French-speaking elite was installed. The English were reduced to a troublesome minority.

As these processes continued, the ideology of a British Canada began to appear absurd. The rapid rise to wealth of the West during the '70s forced Ontario to recognize what it had always denied – that other regions had a right to define Canadian identity, and that the major concern of most regions was economic injustice.

We have always assumed that the dominant group is somehow "national" – from sea to sea. This remains true for international issues – except that Quebec must often be subtracted out. But on domestic issues the old ethnic dominant group is gone. The old WASPS are now divided as Westerners, Central Canadians, Maritimers, and Newfoundlanders, identifying themselves by their regional economic interests, and the Quebec elites are doing the same.

Each region's ethnic relations between dominants and minorities will henceforth be worked out independently of the others. What this paper has indicated is the enormous variety of linguistically-defined communities that will be involved.

END NOTES

1. The first step has been taken in several instances, but has not been followed up with the notion of depicting a community in mind. In this connection my thanks should be recorded to Penny Geldart, of the Department of the Secretary of State, who maintains a catalogue of ethnic institutions. Use was also made of the book by V. Markotic and T. Petrunic, *Ethnic Directory of Canada*, Western Publishers, Calgary, 1967.

2. "Variations of Corporate Action Among Ethnic Collectivities," Sub-Project "C" March, 1977. Other works of Raymond Breton, Wallace Clement, and John Porter may be found in standard library collections, the *Canadian Journal of Economics and Political Science* (CJEPS) and the *Canadian Review of Sociology and Anthropology* (CRSA). Aileen Ross's work was her M.A. thesis at McGill, circa 1943, as well as an article in the *CJEPS*. Fernand Dumont, a prolific writer in French, has not been translated into English. See especially his numerous articles in *Recherches Sociographiques*, 1962-1964. Richard Joy is the author of *Languages in Conflict*, McClelland and Stewart, 1972. His major thesis is that French and English speakers are separating territorially.

3. Millett (1969, 1971, 1975, 1978). In the '60s, churches were still central to many communities. Since then, religiosity in all its forms has declined, and many aspects of cultural maintenance have been transferred to school systems, the mass media, and even restaurants. The local church remains useful, however, for locating linguistic communities, since it performs such a variety of functions.

4. As indicated in the 1978 article, certain ethnic groups are considered so "foreign" that, while biologically Caucasian, they are actually perceived as non-White. The practice of non-Western religions enhances the image of foreignness and thus the perception of them as non-White. Two examples are Arabs and Sikhs.

5. Milton Gordon, *Assimilation in American Life*, p. 27. There are, in Canada, a very small number of parishes and congregations which appear to have arisen due to identification by color and nothing else. A case in point is Union United Church (Black) in Montreal. Even here, however, a large proportion of the congregation consists of immigrants. Apart from Native Peoples, the only non-Whites whose congregations are not strongly supported by relatively recent arrivals are the Blacks of Nova Scotia, most of whom are Baptists. Research on the role of the African United Baptist Association in Nova Scotian communities is being carried out by Prof. Savannah Williams of Dalhousie University. Since language is not involved, such congregations are omitted from this study.

6. *Ibid.*, p. 27.

7. This is a generalization. In some locations racism between groups of the same language is so traditional that different languages could not make the situation worse, e.g. Blacks, Métis and Indians in many locations.

8. In 1968 the two most aggressive sponsors of Minority Churches appeared to be the United and Baptist churches. At present they appear to be the Roman Catholic Church, the Jehovah's Witnesses and the Pentecostal Assemblies of Canada.

9. This raises the empirical problems of establishing at what point a sect becomes a church, and particularly whether theology should be considered an important criterion. Traditionally, the sociological literature has found that informal struc-

tures and fundamentalist theology go hand in hand. Currently, however, we find the same theology being employed in huge sophisticated bureaucracies of the church type, especially in the Pentecostal Assemblies and in the Jehovah's Witnesses. Our research on the Assemblies and Witnesses is not complete. I have accordingly decided to include the Adventists as a church, and have left the status of the other two in suspense.

10. In most dioceses of the Catholic Church a "bilingual" parish is one which offers some masses in English and some in French. But the diocese of Alexandria (in Glengarry County, eastern Ontario), sometimes uses both languages in the same mass. For a striking view of the linguistic situation in Glengarry, see the film *Rien qu'en Passant*, National Film Board, 1976.

11. This also occurs in areas where the locally dominant group speaks a non-official language, such as Italian-dominated areas of Toronto, Chinese in Vancouver, or Ukrainian, German, Blackfoot or Cree areas on the Prairies or in the North.

12. Since the massive Irish immigration of 1820-1870. This is not to say that the French and Irish enjoyed being in the same church. Their continuing conflict has been well documented by Robert Choquette in *Language and Religion, a History of English-French Conflict in Ontario*, University of Ottawa Press, Ottawa, 1975.

13. It should be noted that the case of French Protestants in Quebec and English-speaking Catholics in extreme Protestant areas outside Quebec is being deliberately ignored here. In these cases the main source of minority status is not linguistic but religious discrimination. This will be dealt with in a later paper.

14. Census Bulletins used were: 1971 Census, Vol. 1, 3, Tables 28-32, and Census Tracts for Montreal and Ottawa. For a previous study employing such terms as "English in French districts" and "French in English districts," see Howard Roseborough and Raymond Breton, "Perceptions of the Relative Economic and Political Advantages of Ethnic Groups in Canada," *Canadian Society*, 3rd Edition, 1968, p. 604-628.

15. We will therefore ignore the fact that English is the main home language in the following smaller areas: Montreal census tracts 72, 74; Verdun 310, 313-317; Lasalle 322, 325; Lachine 396, 397; St. Laurent 419-421; Deux Montagnes 728, 729; Chateauguay 800-802 and Caughnawaga Indian Reserve; Saint Lambert and Greenfield Park 860-862 and 864; Rosemere and Otterburn Park. The only French tracts isolated in English areas are Notre Dame de Liesse 414, and Ste. Geneviève 515. All of these will be treated as if they were minority tracts.

16. For an account of the Kwakwala Anglican Parish, see the popular novel by Margaret Craven, *I Heard the Owl Call My Name*, Clarke Irwin, Toronto, 1967.

17. Both these phenomena have occurred on the Hobbema Reserve in Alberta. In this type of situation our definition of Minority Church is revealed to be somewhat defective. Whereas it assumes that affiliation with the church of the dominant group, in this case the Roman Catholic Church, provides a sense of strength and security, a certain number of Hobbema Indians (in the Ermineskin Band) have decided that this is a liability, and have returned to their own religion. The reference groups which give them a sense of strength are no longer White Canadians but other Indians and, more generally, Native Peoples around the world. The headquarters for the World Council of Indigenous Peoples is located at the University of Lethbridge, Alberta.

18. The Reformed Church in America (originally Dutch) also reports that all its Canadian congregations now operate in English.
19. This is particularly true of people from countries which have traditionally been non-Christian. Even when such people are biologically Caucasian, as in the case of Arabs, and until recently, Jews, a person obsessed by a sense of their "foreignness" may actually come to perceive them as being non-White, and subject them to specifically racial discrimination. On these grounds, I have included Arabic-speaking immigrants as non-White, but with the term in quotation marks to indicate that the category is due to a perceptual distortion. In the case of Coptic Egyptians there is a double distortion. There is first the assumption that they are Arabs, a label which they tend to hotly deny, and then the lable of non-White, on the grounds that they are Arabs.
20. This is a revised version of a table appearing in "The Religion of Immigrants," a paper delivered at a conference entitled "Two Nations at Prayer," University of Waterloo, May 1-3, 1977. Some corrections have since been made.
21. Reported in Paul Migus, ed., *Sounds Canadian* (Toronto: Peter Martin), 1974. The two major "surprise" groups were the Jehovah's Witnesses and the Pentecostal Assemblies of Canada. From material received they appear to be the two largest sponsors of Minority Churches, after the Roman Catholic Church, but their information is not yet in a form that permits a regional analysis. On the question of whether they should be treated themselves as churches, see end note 9.
22. In the case of the Ukrainians and Syrians this may be an overstatement. There appears to be a steady shift towards the use of English and French. Source: Markotic and Petrunic (see end note 1).
23. Bathurst and Edmunston, New Brunswick, are not included here, as they are covered under Gloucester and Madawaska counties respectively. In Ontario the city of Kapuskasing and two townships adjoining Timmins and Sudbury are also French, but are in a dominantly English-speaking census district. They are covered in any case under the list of French churches for the appropriate Catholic diocese. Sources used here are the 1971 Census, Vol. 1.3, Tables 31 and 32; *United Church of Canada Yearbook*, 1976, Vol. II, Toronto, 1976; *Le Canada Ecclésiastique, 1973-74*, Beauchemin, Montreal; *Year Book of the United Baptist Convention of the Atlantic Provinces*, 1970; *Anglican Year Book*, 1976; *Directory of Lutheran Churches in Canada*, 1977.
24. They are minorities in religious terms, but as already mentioned this will be left to a later paper.

SELECTED REFERENCES

General

Breton, R., W. Kalbach and others. "Variations in Corporate Action Among Ethnic Collectivities." Unpublished monograph, Toronto, March, 1977.

Choquette, Robert. *Language and Religion, a History of English-French Conflict in Ontario*. Ottawa: University of Ottawa Press, 1975.

Craven, Margaret. *I Heard the Owl Call My Name*. Toronto: Clarke Irwin, 1967.

Gordon, Milton. *Assimilation in American Life*. New York: Oxford University Press, 1964.

Markotic, V., and T. Petrunic, *Ethnic Directory of Canada*. Calgary: Western Publishers, 1976.

Millett, D. "A Typology of Religious Organizations Based on the Canadian Census," *Sociological Analysis*, Summer, 1969, p. 108-119.

_____ . "The Orthodox Church: Ukrainian, Greek and Syrian." In Jean L. Elliott, ed., *Minority Canadians*, Vol. 2 "Immigrant Groups." Toronto: Prentice-Hall, 1971.

_____ . "Religion as a Source of Perpetuation of *Ethnic Identity*." In Paul Migus, ed., Toronto: Peter Martin, 1975.

_____ . "Religious Identity: The Non-Official Languages and Minority Churches." In Jean L. Elliott, editor, *Two Nations, Many Cultures: Ethnic Groups in Canada*, Toronto: Prentice-Hall, 1978.

Roseborough, Howard, and Raymond Breton. "Perception of the Relative Economic and Political Advantages of Ethnic Groups in Canada." In *Canadian Society*, 3rd ed., Toronto: Macmillan, 1968.

Reference Sources

Anglican Church of Canada. *Anglican Year Book*, 1976. Toronto: Anglican Book Centre, 1977.

Baptist Convention of Ontario and Quebec. *Yearbook, 1975-76*. Toronto: 1976.

Government of Canada. *Census, 1971*, CT-15B (Ottawa-Hull).

Government of Canada. *Census, 1971*, CT-4B (Montreal).

Lutheran Council of Canada. *Directory of Lutheran Churches in Canada, 1977*. Winnipeg: L.C.C. Division of Information Services, 1977.

Presbyterian Church in Canada. *Yearbook, 1976-77*. Toronto, 1977.

Roman Catholic Church in Canada. *Le Canada Ecclésiastique*, Montreal: Beauchemin, 1973-74.

United Baptist Convention. *Yearbook of the Baptist Convention of the Atlantic Provinces*. Baptist Building, Saint John, N.B., 1970.

Appendix A

Ascertaining "French" and "English"
Neighborhoods in Ottawa and Montreal

Technique. Lists of French-speaking church parishes and congregations were obtained from yearbooks, telephone books and other sources, and then plotted on maps of Ottawa and Montreal, using street addresses from telephone books and city directories.

The locations were then compared to the boundaries of census tracts, as indicated on the maps of tracts CT-15B and CT-4B of the 1971 census. All tracts of each census were checked to see which had over 50 percent of families using English as the language of the home, and which had French. French parishes plotted in English tracts and English parishes plotted in French tracts were then counted, to give the total for each type of Minority Church.

Grouping the results. In Ottawa the picture was relatively clear. All the French tracts on the Ontario side of the Ottawa River are located in the north-east corner of the city of Ottawa, and adjoin Vanier city, which is almost entirely French-speaking. The only isolated French tract is in the suburban area of Carleton County east of Vanier, and it touches the adjoining county of Russell, which is itself French-speaking. On the Quebec side of the national capital area, all tracts except West Hull and Lucerne are French. Nowhere do we find a single French tract completely surrounded by English, or an English tract completely surrounded by French tracts.

This last statement is true for most of Montreal as well, but the vastness of the city means that two or three contiguous tracts of one language surrounded by dozens of tracts of the other language are nevertheless isolated. A detailed examination of the linguistic map, coupled with some knowledge of the history of French-English conflict in the city, leads to the conclusion that we are examining a battle over "turf." English-speaking Montrealers have traditionally felt that the part of the city west of a line running along Saint Laurent Boulevard and the Canadian Pacific right-of-way was "theirs" in residential terms (while the whole city was "theirs" in economic terms). The two traditional exceptions were the French elite neighborhood of Outremont and the poverty-stricken neighborhood of Saint Henri, literally "on the other side of the tracks" from Westmount.

What the 1971 census indicates, in these terms, is that "the French are taking over." They are taking over from the north, occupying all but three tracts above Metropolitan Boulevard; and they are taking over from the south, occupying everything except two tracts in Ville Lasalle, and five tiny tracts in Verdun. While the west end of Montreal Island is still English-speaking (it should be recalled that we are using 1971 figures, ignoring the massive emigration which has since taken place), the main downtown area described appears to be a vulnerable peninsula attached to the West Island by a slim corridor running through Dorval and Saint Laurent.

The 10 French tracts of the wealthy Outremont area no longer appear as a French island in "English" Montreal, but as a French wedge coming from east of Saint Laurent Boulevard, supporting the invasion from the north and the south.

For all these reasons it seems fair to say that in downtown Montreal one can only speak of one large area where English-speakers are "dominant." West of this downtown area they control the towns of Dorval, Pointe-Claire, Dollard-des-Ormeaux, and the other municipalities of the west end of Montreal Island. Other small islands of English-language dominance are therefore treated as being in a minority situation.

Appendix B

FIGURE 1 *Boundaries of downtown "English" Montreal, 1971*

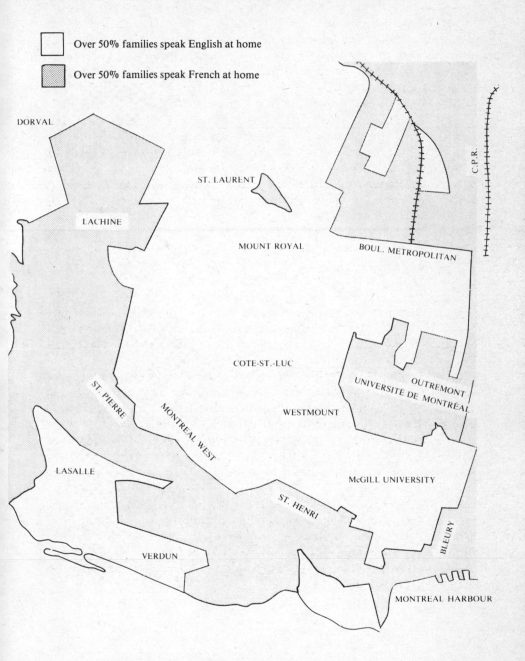

Over 50% families speak English at home

Over 50% families speak French at home

DORVAL

ST. LAURENT

LACHINE

MOUNT ROYAL

BOUL. METROPOLITAN

C.P.R.

ST. PIERRE

COTE-ST.-LUC

OUTREMONT

UNIVERSITÉ DE MONTRÉAL

MONTREAL WEST

WESTMOUNT

LASALLE

McGILL UNIVERSITY

ST. HENRI

BLEURY

VERDUN

MONTREAL HARBOUR

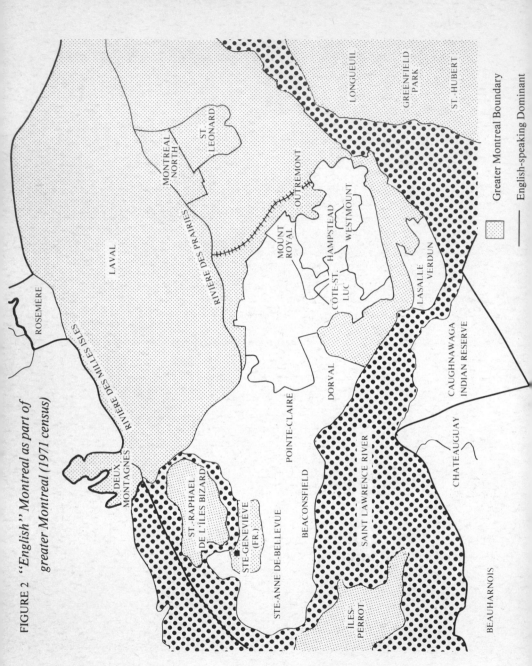

FIGURE 2 "English" Montreal as part of greater Montreal (1971 census)

FIGURE 3   *Census tracts in Ottawa-Hull metropolitan area, in which English-language churches are minority churches, 1971*

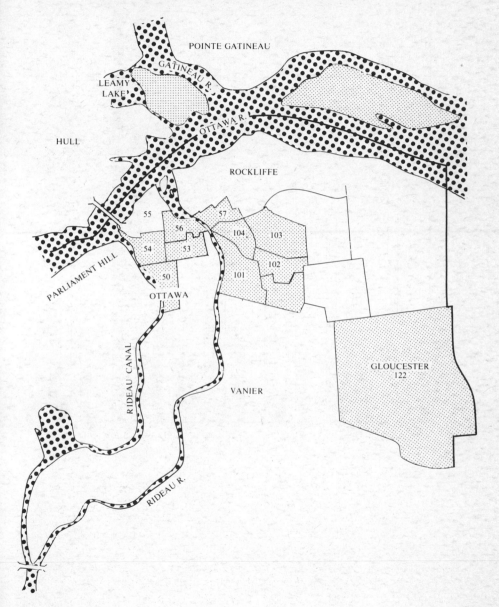

FIGURE 4 *Linguistic minorities by type and region, 1977*

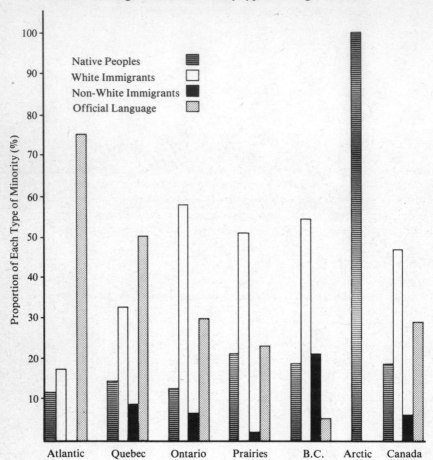

J.L. ELLIOTT   Dalhousie University

Canadian Immigration: A Historical Assessment

Introduction

While no one would question the significance of immigration for the development of Canadian society, one may not be as readily aware that immigration has served Canada in ways that extend beyond the original need to populate a vast territory, supply a labor force or add cultural diversity to the life of the whole. The greater reality surrounding immigration is not fully reflected in our nation-building myths and our image of our society as an ethnic mosaic. Over and above the usual costs and benefits that we tend to associate with immigration, the mass movements of people to Canada over the years have had an impact on what many of us might consider to be some of the more pressing issues confronting us today – national unity and minority language rights.

Canada in the 1980's is beset with conflicts. In addition to the problem of national unity, the conflicts arising from such issues as aboriginal rights and regional disparities do not stem solely from broken promises and good intentions gone astray. The conflicts that plague us today may be traced, in part, to the immigration policies of our past and the economic concerns that shaped them.

Impact of Immigration

If we were to begin an assessment of the impact of immigration with the Confederation era, we would see immediately the consequences of immigration for the Native Peoples. When the Canadian Pacific Railway was completed in 1885, the West was "opened" to immigrants. Before the land could be "opened," the Native Peoples had to be "cleared" from it. Some would see a tragic irony in the fact that in order to populate the Prairies, the existing settlements of Métis and Cree were first destroyed. The West was populated with immigrants in orderly bloc settlements; the orderliness obscures the fact that before "free land" could be offered generously to the land-hungry peasants from central Europe, it was confiscated from its prior inhabitants.[1]

The ultimate development of the West as an extension of English Canada undermined the balance of power between the French and English segments of the country. Legitimate nationalistic concerns of the French in the West were gradually eroded through legislative changes at the provincial level; French was relegated to the status of a foreign language in the schools and its use denied in the courts.

The losses sustained by the French outside Quebec were a close match to the ground lost within Quebec as a result of immigration. Immigrants to Quebec typically have assimilated to the anglophone community, succumbing to the lure and security of the anglophone-dominated economic sector. Native-born French Quebecers as well as immigrants have been swayed by economic enticements, often to the detriment of their culture. Being bilingual has been traditionally a prerequisite to economic advancement in Quebec if one's mother tongue were French. Bilingualism on the part of minority cultures is often the first step toward assimilation.

Not only has the Quebec culture been diluted by immigration, but it also has been numerically weakened by mass French-Canadian emigration to the United States. In the last decades of the 19th century, concurrent with the settlement of the Prairies, there occurred in Quebec what Richard Joy has termed "the fatal hemorrhage;"[2] the U.S. Census of 1900 indicated that one third of all French Canadians in North America resided south of the Canadian border. Many settled in New England textile communities. The Canadian Census of 1901 showed French Canadians as constituting 5 percent of the population of what are now the three Prairie provinces. One of the major "ifs" of Canadian history is: if the French Canadian migration had been encouraged to go West instead of South, would the "two-nation" aspect of the Canadian identity have proved to be a more broadly-based reality?

It was not until the Great Depression of the 1930s that Quebec emigration to the United States and European emigration to Canada ceased sufficiently for Quebec to begin to recoup demographic losses through excessive fertility. The phenomenally high birth rate in Quebec has been termed "the revenge of the cradle" because of its potentially important political implications. However, *la revanche* was short-lived. In the postwar years the birth rate fell; emigration to North America resumed, and Quebec's efforts to rebuild its numerical strength *vis-à-vis* English Canada were for naught.

Although Quebec has suffered from immigration, Ontario has benefited. After immigrants were recruited to secure the hinterland in the West, they were sought to meet the labor needs of the burgeoning industrial economy of Ontario. Aided and abetted by immigration, the industrialization of Ontario's "golden horseshoe" proceeded to the relative exclusion of the rest of the country. From the Confederation era to 1911, the largest clusters of immigrants were found on the Prairies which held 41 percent of the total foreign-born population of Canada. Sixty years later, the Prairies were the domicile of only 16 percent of the foreign-born with over 50 percent living in Ontario.[3] Ontario's growth and development would not have been possible without the majority of postwar immigrants settling there.

Industrialization in central Canada, made possible and strengthened by immigration, fostered regional disparities as well as the development of "the vertical mosaic" documented by Porter.[4] The vertical mosaic describes the outcome of certain historical processes like immigration that resulted in the hierarchical ordering of the various ethnic groups in the social structure. Individuals on the top-most rungs of the social ladder tend to be members of the British charter group. The British elites traditionally have monitored the mobility of the other ethnic groups in Canada, including the French charter group, with the exception of some francophone elites in Quebec. Thus, the process of immigration has favored some regions over others and has encouraged the growth of a vertical, social class dimension in Canadian life. Social class in Canada tends to be highly related to ethnicity.

While immigration has had a fundamental impact on ethnic stratification, Freda Hawkins reminds us that Canada is not simply "a 'nation of immigrants'. . . . this is not the central fact of Canadian history. The fact is the existence of the two founding races (sic) and the relations between them."[5] The stresses and strains associated with the immigration process have occurred within the context of uneasy French/English relations. Immigration policies have evolved in this context.

The Evolution of Immigration Policies

The impact of immigration in any historical era is related, in part, to the immigration policy in force at the time. The management of immigration in Canada spans several distinct eras (see Table 1). It is useful to think of the Confederation era through 1895 (the free-entry period), the beginning of selective immigration in 1896 up to World War I (the old immigration), the period between the wars when immigration ebbed, and the post-World War II era to the present (the new immigration).

The charter group designation for the French and British refers to the fact that the first permanent settlements in Canada were either French or British. The earliest census in New France in 1608 records 28 settlers. By 1765, the population had reached 69 810. Since French emigration virtually halted after the Treaty of Paris, the French Canadian nation tends to be descended from this early nucleus.[6]

The French and the British, however, were not the only settlers in the early period of Canadian history. During the first census following Confederation, the Blacks ranked fifth among the ethnic groups, with only the Germans and Dutch more numerous (Census of Canada, 1870-71, Vol. 1, Table 3). The Blacks came to Canada with their Loyalist masters during the American Revolution and the War of 1812 and settled largely in the Maritimes. It was not until the current era, however, that Blacks emigrated in sizable numbers from the Caribbean (see Table 2). The Maritime provinces never regained their popularity as a destination for immigrants, consistently losing population through out-migration.

TABLE 1 Canadian immigration policy and change (1861-1981)

Historical period	Decade	Population at start of decade (000's)	Immigration as a percentage of average decade population	Migration (000's)			Immigration policy	Primary destination and type of immigrant
				Immigration	Estimated Emigration	Net Migration		
Confederation to 1895	1861-1871	3 090	7.5	183	375	—192	free entry (exception: first B.C. "head tax" on Chinese. 1885.)	Eastern Canada settled by immigrants from British Isles. N.W. Europe and U.S.A.
	1871-1881	3 689	8.8	353	440	—087		
	1881-1891	4 325	19.7	903	1 109	—206		
The Sifton era to W.W. I 1896-1914	1891-1901	4 833	6.4	250	380	—130	selective immigration. objective: land settlement	Prairies settled by farmers, many from Central Europe
	1901-1911	5 371	28.0	1 550	740	810		
War and economic depression (1914-1945)	1911-1921	7 207	20.2	1 400	1 090	310	restrictive measures.	Urban settlement as well as rural.
	1921-1931	8 788	12.6	1 203	974	229	Chinese Immigration Act. 1923.	War refugees. Jewish and other displaced persons.
	1931-1941	10 377	1.4	150	242	—092	visas first issued. "sponsorship" begins.	

Postwar era (1946-1961)	1941-1951	11 507	4.4	548	379	169	liberalization. 1952 Immigration Act. objective: population increase to "absorptive capacity".	Urban areas in Central Canada. Southern European immigration begins many in manufacturing occupations.
	1951-1961	14 009[1]	9.6	1 543	462	1 081		
The Current phase	1961-1971	18 238	7.2	1 429	705	724	"points system". 1967, objective: universalistic criteria.	Urban settlement continues. Third World immigration begins. many professional and technical workers.
	1971-1979	21 568	—	1 297	—	—		

Sources: W.E. Kalbach and W.W. McVey, *The Demographic Bases of Canadian Society*, Toronto: McGraw-Hill, 1971, Tables 1.4 and 2.2.
W.E. Kalbach, *The Effects of Immigration on Population*, Department of Manpower and Immigration (Ottawa, 1974), Tables 1.1 and 1.2.
1972 *Immigration Statistics*, Dept. of Manpower and Immigration (Ottawa, 1974), Table 1.
1976 *Immigration Statistics*, Dept. of Manpower and Immigration (Ottawa, 1977), Table 2.
Immigration and Population Statistics, Dept. of Manpower and Immigration (Ottawa, 1974), Table 1.4.
1. Includes Newfoundland.
1979 *Immigration Statistics*, Employment and Immigration Canada (Ottawa, 1981), Tables.

TABLE 2 *Selected major source countries of postwar immigrants*[a]

Country (rank order 1979)	1979	1976	1973	1970	1946-69
Great Britain	11 806	19 257	23 533	23 688	836 349
China[1]	9 858	13 301	15 997	5 647	64 139
USA	7 821	14 278	21 391	20 859	229 121
West Indies[2]	6 535	15 066	19 809	13 286	62 767
India	5 486	8 562	11 672	7 089	36 406
Portugal	3 742	6 194	14 417	8 594	75 330
Italy	2 134	4 008	6 176	8 659	455 424
France	1 547	2 415	2 411	2 958	72 984
Greece	1 187	2 429	5 800	6 440	97 626
Total	50 116	85 510	121 206	97 220	1 930 146

[a]The immigrant is recorded by country of birth.
1. Includes the People's Republic of China, Hong Kong and Taiwan.
2. Includes total Caribbean area.
Source: *Immigration Statistics*, Employment and Immigration Canada, 1973, Table 12; 1976, Table 8; 1979 Table 10.

Canada's first Immigration Act was passed in 1869 but a period of free entry lasted until 1896, with the appointment of Clifford Sifton, a Manitoba businessman, as Minister of the Interior. The period of free entry ended sooner for the Chinese, however. Since the Chinese had been allowed entry into Canada primarily for work on the CPR, its completion in 1885 meant that they had become surplus laborers. British Columbia responded in 1885 with a "head tax" of $50 on every new Chinese immigrant. This tax was raised several times in the following years until the Chinese Immigration Act in 1923 barred their entry.

Sifton inherited an economic situation which demanded the immediate settlement of the West. His selective immigration policy tended to place prior agricultural experience over national origin concerns. It was a selective policy in the sense that non-agriculturalists were not wanted. Sifton's Deputy Minister in 1900 stated: "If a settler is one who has been engaged in agricultural pursuits in the old land . . . whether he is rich or poor, Galician, Austrian, Russian, Swede, Belgian or French, we believe it most desirable to encourage him to occupy our land and to break up our soil . . ."[7]

In spite of Sifton's vigorous efforts to attract and keep settlers, Canada registered a negative net migration during the period 1861-1901. As inducements to farmers, such as the Doukhobors, Sifton may have made promises which were later impossible to keep. The rural, pacifist communal sect of Doukhobors numbering about 7 000 entered Canada in 1899 on Sifton's invitation. Fleeing Tsarist persecutions in Russia, the religious group hoped it could live life in Canada without interference from the government. By 1905, however, Saskatchewan confiscated more than half their land holdings because their religious convictions prevented the Doukhobors from taking the oath of allegiance to the Crown that was necessary to acquire final title to the land.[8]

The unconfirmed expectations experienced by the Doukhobors may have been repeated by other ethnic groups that came to Canada with the thought of recreating their cultural life as they had known it in the old country. Although Sifton left office in 1905, his successor Frank Oliver continued the expansionist immigration policy up until the start of World War I. The all-time peak was reached in 1913 when over 400 000 people came to Canada. Faced with integrating this diverse mass of immigrants into a coherent social system, voices favoring cultural pluralism did not win out.[9] By World War I, German was considered as an "enemy language," and French was just another foreign tongue among many. If promises of a cultural mosaic were incentives to make the long trek to Canada, "anglo-conformity" was among the harsh realities the newcomers faced.

During the war years and the Great Depression, immigration came to a standstill with the exception of refugees and displaced persons. More Jews came to Canada in this era than in any other. Despite the influx of refugees, Canada lost more people in the decade 1931-41 than it gained. Promotional efforts had stopped in 1930, and restrictive immigration measures were introduced. Visas were issued for the first time in order to control immigration at its source.

The gradual transition in the economic structure from a rural to an urban base in the early part of the 20th century meant that the labor needs of the postwar era would be different from those known by Sifton. The rural-to-urban migration within Canada commenced to be followed by an international rural-to-urban migration that would see Europeans from rural areas seeking a new life in Canadian cities.[10]

Prime Minister MacKenzie King set the tone of the postwar immigration policy in 1947 when he advocated immigration as an avenue to population growth and economic development to be pursued up to the "absorptive capacity" of the country. Racial and ethnic selectivity continued, with France in 1949 for the first time joining Britain and the United States on the list of "preferred nations."[11] Some liberalization took place, however, regarding Asians who were allowed to sponsor family members. The immigration from southern Europe began with urban settlement as their destination.[12]

In the postwar period, the sponsorship of Italians snowballed. One study showed that every Italian meant 49 relatives.[13] Only the British were responsible for more arrivals in the postwar period that the Italians, and in the period between 1958 and 1961, the Italian immigration surpassed the British. The chain migration of family members suggested that sponsored immigrants who did not have to be self-supporting might create an intolerable economic burden for their sponsors. The need for control of the sponsorship program became obvious to those concerned with economic questions and social problems associated with the growth of ethnic neighborhoods.[14]

The sponsorship "problem" was resolved in 1967 when the immigration policy underwent a major revision. Sponsored immigrants would now be classified as dependent or non-dependent, with separate regulations applying to each. The modification in sponsorship, however, was overshadowed by the introduction of the "points system" which was also part of the new 1967 policy. Discrimination on the basis of race or national origin was eliminated for all classes of immigrants. Immigrants were to be selected on the basis of points that they earned in nine areas such as education, occupation, and language. At this juncture in immigration policy, the characteristics of the future immigrants were set.

The new immigrants from 1967 to the present have tended to come in greater numbers from the professional, technical, and managerial occupations, and from the Third World countries that previously were discouraged from applying. The changes occurring after 1967 in the rank ordering of the "source countries" is presented in Table 2. By 1974, the West Indies had climbed to number 2 position behind Great Britain in the number of immigrants coming to Canada. In fact in any two- or three-year period after the points system, the West Indies contributed approximately as many immigrants as during the entire 20-year postwar period from 1946-67.

The adoption of the universalistic points system, however, did not put an end to attacks aimed at the racist character of Canada's immigration policy. With the emphasis placed on occupational and educational achievement, Canada was accused of discriminating against developing nations who by definition did not have the manpower and potential that immigrants of the more developed societies had. Furthermore, Canada was accused of robbing the talent that did exist and was not easily replaced; for example, medical and scientific personnel. The points system which was basically a manpower recruitment strategy did seem to encourage "the brain drain."

Inasmuch as policy reflects ideologies within a society, the "anglo-conformity" mentality that reached its zenith in the pre-World War I era gradually had been replaced over the years with official notions of cultural pluralism.[15] That is, the reality of the two-nation concept for Canada was reviewed in the mid-1960s along with the case for fostering multiculturalism. The modernization of Quebec and the "quiet revolution" within her borders in the early 1960s caused a resurgence of nationalism. The Pearson government responded by creating the Royal Commission on Bilingualism and Biculturalism which eventually reported under Prime Minister Trudeau.[16] In 1968 the Official Languages Act established French on an equal footing with English on the federal level. Since the shoring up of the two-nation Confederation was not intended to slight the contributions of the "other ethnic groups,"[17] a multicultural policy for Canada was announced in 1971.[18] Thus, the backdrop of the points system was the continuing internal questioning within Canada concerning the dimensions of its own bicultural or multicultural identity.

If Third World immigrants are being welcomed to Canada in keeping with the spirit of multiculturalism, the overall numbers of immigrants may be greatly reduced in the future if the high levels of unemployment that have hit the Canadian economy in the mid-1970s continue. The 1977 Immigration Act called for more provincial input concerning labor needs.[19] All in all, it would seem that MacKenzie King's concept of "absorptive capacity" has been retained in Canadian policy as it pertains to economics and rejected as it pertains to notions of ethnic or racial assimilability.

Immigration and the Canadian Identity

A Canadian identity in a collective sense would have to reflect core aspects of life as shared and experienced by Canadians. Inasmuch as some of the core aspects of life may relate to ethnicity and Canada is not ethnically homogeneous, it may be more accurate to speak of Canadian *identities* rather than identity.

Much ambiguity shrouds the issue of identity in Canada. Even the British charter group whose members tend to occupy the elite positions in the Canadian social structure seem to have an identity that, if not riddled with self-doubt, is far from clear-cut. It has been suggested that the fuzzy Canadian identity can be attributed in large measure to Canada's colonial background and heavy immigration from the mother country, on the one hand, and the diffuse cultural boundaries and two-way traffic of considerable scope between Canada and the United States, on the other hand. The influence of American capital and mass media in Canada should not be underestimated. In addition, the United States is high on the list of "source countries" that have contributed significant numbers of immigrants to Canada consistently over the years (see Table 2).

Compared with the United States, for example, Canada has a higher proportion of foreign-born in its total population.[20] When we consider the complexities involved in internalizing a culture so that one is left with a sense of belonging or identity, we may wish to conclude that the transmission of cultural myths and values and the teaching of history and citizenship may present more of a challenge to a country actively engaged in immigration than to one with a homogeneous population or a static ethnic mix.

It is not clear whether immigrants to Canada and the United States are able to distinguish between the two countries in an accurate fashion on a cultural and political level or whether they tend to view North America as a classic, undifferentiated "land of opportunity." In such a context, distinctions between the "two nation" vision of Macdonald and Cartier and the "one nation under God" to the South may seem trivial. It is precisely such distinctions, however, that would have to be widely known if the Canadian identity were to be set apart from the American.

The warmth of the reception received by immigrants to Canada has depended on whether "anglo-conformity" or cultural pluralism was in vogue. The future of Canada as a multi-ethnic society, however, rests on more than the presence or absence of an "official" ideology of multiculturalism on the part of the government. It is in the order of an experimental question whether the concept of Canada as a multicultural society can fit comfortably into a bilingual framework. If multiculturalism were enthusiastically endorsed, might not the logic of the "two nation" premise become confused? Such fears have been behind the reluctance of the French-Canadian nation to actively support multiculturalism.[21]

Sociologists have been split on their reactions to multiculturalism. While they may recognize the inherent value of different cultures, they may have some reservation as to their equal utility in modern society. As Warren Kalbach has noted: "Perpetuation of cultural forms may . . . provide an important source for emotional gratification. Yet, successful retention of language and culture on the part of minority ethnic populations may impede social change by preventing their members from acquiring the skills they need to effectively compete in the ongoing industrial and technological revolution."[22]

Social theorists once assumed that as modernization and industrialization progressed, the ethnic dimension in life would assume less salience.[23] The urban culture, it was thought, would move toward homogeneity. In fact the concept of a world culture or "global village" was not that remote, given the pervasive influence of the mass media. As ethnic concerns became minimized, social differences would find expression along social class lines.

If the relative importance of racial and ethnic factors were superseded by a broader social class-based consciousness, the potential for social class conflict rather than racial or ethnic conflict would be present. Although predicted to occur in industrial societies, a class conflict scenario on a revolutionary scale has not been enacted in Western countries. On the contrary, a "new ethnicity"[24] has asserted itself. In the United States the failure of the melting pot is recognized.[25] On the part of Blacks, demands for integration have been somewhat tempered by the emergence of "Black pride" and the development of a parallel "Black soul culture." In Great Britain the Scotch and Welsh nationalists are active, and in Quebec, of course, nationalism is strong.

In addition to nationalistic mass movements, a concern with one's "roots" continues to interest individuals and families. The study of genealogy has achieved much popularity. Instead of ethnicity's dying with the development of modern social classes, it has staged a recovery. Perhaps for some, ethnicity literally does function as roots, providing stability and continuity amidst bewildering encounters with the forces of social change that challenge traditional identities and customs. The future of ethnicity, however it may evolve with respect to substance and modes of expression, seems assured, regardless of whether it may impede or enhance the mobility of its adherents.

END NOTES

1. When the Hudson's Bay Co. in 1869 sold Métis land to the new Dominion of Canada, the local autonomy of the Métis was placed in jeopardy. Fearing possible American intervention, Sir John A. Macdonald in 1869-70 assured Louis Riel, the elected leader of the Red River settlement, in the Manitoba Act that religion, language, land title, and local government would be honored. In time, however, the Métis stood in the way of the CPR and the grand economic design of Canada. The last so-called Métis rebellion took place in 1885, the year the CPR was completed. See Mason Wade, *The French Canadians* (Toronto: Macmillan of Canada, 1968), Vol. 1, Ch. 8.

   The Canadian business class wished to bolster staple exports by promoting wheat farming and immigration. For the staple approach to the theory of economic growth, see Harold A. Innis, *Essays in Canadian Economic Theory* (Toronto: University of Toronto Press, 1956).
2. Richard Joy, *Languages in Conflict* (Toronto: McClelland and Stewart, 1972), Ch. 11.
3. W.E. Kalbach, *The Effect of Immigration on Population* (Ottawa: Department of Manpower and Immigration, 1974), Table 2.7.
4. John Porter, *The Vertical Mosaic* (Toronto: University of Toronto Press, 1965).
5. Freda Hawkins, *Canada and Immmigration: Public Policy and Public Concern.* (Montreal: McGill-Queen's University Press, 1972), p. 34.
6. Warren E. Kalbach and Wayne McVey, *The Demographic Bases of Canadian Society* (Toronto: McGraw-Hill, 1971), Table 1.1.
7. House of Commons Journals 1900, 308 as cited in Robert C. Brown and Ramsay Cook, *Canada 1896-1921: A Nation Transformed* (Toronto: McClelland and Stewart, 1974), p. 55.
8. For a general history of the Doukhobors, see George Woodcock and Ivan Avakumovic, *The Doukhobors* (Toronto: McClelland and Stewart, 1977) esp. Ch. 6. The land in question near Prince Albert was "not far from the region of Louis Riel's last rebellion (p. 148)." Elsewhere, the confiscation has been described as a deliberate "expediency by a new federal Minister of the Interior to break up the Doukhobor communal reserve." Koozma J. Tarasoff, "Doukhobors: Their Migration Experience," in *Canadian Ethnic Studies* Vol. 4, no. 1-2 (1972), p. 2 According to Tarasoff, a similar fate had previously struck the Old Order Mennonites in Manitoba.
9. In 1918, an Order-in-Council from the Borden government prohibited "the publication of books, newspapers, magazines or any printed matter in the language of any country or people . . . at war with Great Britain." *Canadian Annual Review, 1918*, p. 580. The Order was in effect until January 1, 1920. Bil-

ingual schools were disallowed in Manitoba in 1916; 61 German/English schools and over 100 English/French schools, for example, were permanently closed. For an account of the events in Manitoba and other provinces, see Werner A. Bausenhart, "The Ontario German Language Press and Its Suppression by Order-in-Council in 1918," *Canadian Ethnic Studies* Vol. 8, no. 2 (1976).

10. A focus on European immigration to major cities has tended to overshadow an analysis of rural poverty. The rural migrant in Quebec and Atlantic Canada seeks "livelihood in the urban centers the nearest to his home community. These are urban centers the least caught up in forces of economic growth." S.D. Clark, "The Disadvantaged Rural Society: New Dimensions of Urban Poverty," *Canadian Society in Historical Perspective* (Toronto: McGraw-Hill, Ryerson, 1976), p. 77.

11. P.C. 2743, June 2, 1949. Laval Fortier was appointed as Deputy Minister of the Dept. of Citizenship and Immigration on January 18, 1950. This appointment was an attempt to involve the previously opposed or indifferent francophones in expansionist immigration. For a historical account, see Jacques Brossard, *L'Immigration: les droits et pouvoirs du Canada et du Quebec* (Montreal: Presses de l'Université de Montreal, 1962).

12. It is an oversimplification, however, to view immigrant streams as farmers followed by urban dwellers. H. Troper, *Only Farmers Need Apply* (Toronto: Giffin Press, 1972). This source focuses on the pursuit of agricultural workers. Between 1906 and 1914, however, occupational intentions of the immigrants were 37 percent farming and farm labor, 34 percent general labor, 15 percent mechanical, 6 percent clerical and trade, 2 percent mining, and the remainder unspecified. Donald Avery presents this data in "Continental European Immigrant Workers in Canada 1896-1919: from "Stalwart Peasants' to Radical Proletariat," *Canadian Review of Sociology and Anthropology* Vol. 12:1 (February 1975).

13. Hawkins, *op. cit.,* p. 51.

14. Harney and Troper call our attention to a distinct anti-urban bias which tends to equate immigrants in cities with "social problems." R.F. Harney and H. Troper, "Introduction: Immigrants in Cities," *Canadian Ethnic Studies* 7:1 (1977).

15. Historical data relating immigration history with shifting ideologies is provided by Howard Palmer, *Immigration and the Rise of Multiculturalism.* (Toronto: Copp Clark, 1975).

16. *Report of the Royal Commission on Bilingualism and Biculturalism* Vols. 1-4 (1967-1969). Ottawa: Queen's Printer.

17. *Report of the Royal Commission on Bilingualism and Biculturalism,* Book IV: "The Cultural Contribution of the Other Ethnic Groups," Ottawa, 1969.

18. In response to Book IV of the Royal Commission, Prime Minister Trudeau on October 8, 1971, announced a policy of multiculturalism within a bilingual framework whereby the government would assist various cultures and ethnic groups. A discussion of this policy and Canadian ethnicity in general is provided by Jean Burnet, "Ethnicity: Canadian Experience and Policy," *Sociological Focus* Vol. 9, no. 2 (April, 1976).

19. The new Immigration Act came into effect April 10, 1978. Applicants are awarded 5 points if they go to a location where their job skills are in short sup-

ply. Almost one half of the maximum 100 points are given for employment-related factors. The maximum education rating dropped from 20 to 12 points.

20. In the United States, the percentage of foreign-born had fallen to 4.9 percent in 1965. Ernest Rubin, "The Demography of Immigration to the U.S.," *Annals of the American Academy of Political and Social Science,* Vol. 367 (Sept. 1966), p. 15. In Canada, the percentage of foreign-born has not fallen under approximately 13 percent which it attained in 1901. In 1971, it was 15.3 percent. Kalbach, *op cit.,* 1974, Table 2.6.

21. Guy Rocher, "Les ambiguités d'un Canada bilingue et multiculturel," *Le Quebec en Mutation* (Montreal: Hurtubise, 1973).

22. Warren E. Kalbach, "Demographic Aspects of Canadian Identity," *Sounds Canadian* Paul Migus, (ed.), Toronto: Peter Martin, 1975), pp. 145-46. The same concern has been voiced by others; for example, John Porter, "Ethnic Pluralism in Canada," *Ethnicity, Theory and Experience,* Nathan Glazer and Daniel P. Moynihan, eds., (Cambridge: Harvard University Press, 1975).

23. The assimilationist perspective, as well as the conflict perspective, argued that ascriptively oriented relations would lessen in importance as modernization progressed. Universalistic rather than particularistic criteria would determine social mobility. *Cf.* Peter Blau and Otis Duncan, *The American Occupational Structure* (New York: Wiley, 1967); Parsons.

24. The "new ethnicity" is an emergent phenomenon; as opposed to the "old ethnicity," the new is not thought to be transmitted in a static state from one generation to the next. For a theoretical assessment of the new ethnicity, see William Yancey, Eugene Ericksen and Richard Juliani, "Emergent Ethnicity: A Review and Reformulation," *American Sociological Review*, Vol. 41, no. 3, (June, 1976), pp. 391-403.

25. Data disconfirming, in part, assimilationist theory is presented in Nathan Glazer and Daniel P. Moynihan, *Beyond the Melting Pot* (Cambridge: Massachusetts Institute of Technology Press, 1963). On a policy level, the response to the melting pot's "failure" has been the creation of "affirmative action" programs. In turn, their "shortcomings" are reviewed by N. Glazer, *Affirmative Discrimination: Ethnic Identity and Public Policy* (New York: Basic Books, 1976).

ANTHONY H. RICHMOND York University

Ethnic Nationalism and Postindustrialism*

The rise of ethnic nationalism in the last two decades is associated with the emergence of the supranational state of a postindustrial global economy. This is not purely coincidental. All three phenomena are closely linked with important structural and technological changes in contemporary societies. By ethnic nationalism, in this context, is meant the struggle for recognition, higher economic and social status, and political power by minorities which had previously been exposed to the assimilatory pressures of industrialization. The ethnic minorities in question may define themselves in terms of race, religion, language or former country. In some cases their aspirations for greater autonomy have a territorial basis; the movements then may assume a separatist form. However, in many cases the resurgence of ethnic consciousness has been independent of any geographical boundaries. Nevertheless, there has been a significant emphasis upon ethnicity as a force to be reckoned with both economically and politically (Glazer and Moynihan, 1975; Reitz, 1980).

This resurgence of ethnicity in advanced industrial societies has surprised sociologists and political scientists in the conservative functionalist tradition, as well as those who espoused more radical conflict theories derived from Marx. The former assumed that the developmental tendencies inherent in the industrialization process would ultimately assimilate all ethnic minorities into a single homogeneous culture defined by the boundaries of the nation-state. Marxian theorists, while rejecting the view that industrial societies would achieve harmonious integration through the functional division of labor, nevertheless expected that class conflict would eventually override ethnic divisions. Ethnic differences might be exploited by the capitalist class to weaken the solidarity of labor movements but, eventually, a socialist revolution would render ethnic differences anachronistic through the dictatorship of the proletariat (Lenin, 1970; Cox, 1948).

Neither functionalists nor conflict theorists anticipated the technological consequences of postindustrialism, the economic consequences of the emergence of a global division of labor, and the power of multinational

---

* A revised version of a paper presented at the Joint International Seminar on "After the Referenda: The Future of Ethnic Nationalism in Britain and Canada," University College of North Wales, November, 1981.

companies. In turn, these have given rise to the emergence of supranational states that threaten the sovereignty of older nation-states. The latter were the characteristic political organizations associated with an earlier stage of industrialization. As both economic and political power shift from the national to the multinational and supranational level, a vacuum is created into which the emerging ethnic elites can move. How successful they will be in mobilizing support for their ethnic power and nationalist movements will depend upon a variety of situational determinants that must be examined case by case (Dofny and Akiwowo, 1980). The last quarter of the 20th century is clearly an era of transition in which nation-states that achieved their independence and autonomy in the 18th and 19th centuries are struggling to come to terms with the new global systems of economic and political hegemony. The success or failure of ethnic minorities in maintaining their separate identities, institutions and organizations will depend upon the outcome of that power struggle.

Political and Social Integration

The central problem facing sociologists and political scientists has always been the problem of integration. Ever since the problem was first stated in Plato's Republic, two solutions have been expounded. The first represents societies as being held together by the coercive power of the dominant groups whose interests are, in the last resort, maintained through military force. This force is used to repel external sources of threat as well as for the maintenance of order within the society. The alternative view emphasizes the importance of a common value system which binds people together in a social contract or consensus concerning the necessity for order (Parsons, 1952; Cohen, 1968). In practice, of course, both principles operate simultaneously and with varying degrees of emphasis. Even the most coercive regime must endeavor to translate naked force into legitimated authority, if all its energies and resources are not to be dissipated. Once achieved, a position of power can only be maintained if there is effective control over the agencies that disseminate information and influence human consciousness. The central value system must include legitimating principles that justify the existing differential distribution of economic status and political power. At the same time, varying degrees of economic division of labor and social differentiation give rise to mutual dependency, which also contributes to the maintenance of social cohesion (Durkheim, 1947; Weber, 1946).

The precise form of this relationship between economic and political power, on the one hand, and types of legitimation and social integration on the other hand, varies with levels of technological and economic development. The abstract relationship is represented in Figure 1. Political power is exercised through control over the coercive forces, including the police and

FIGURE 1 *Power, legitimacy, and social integration*

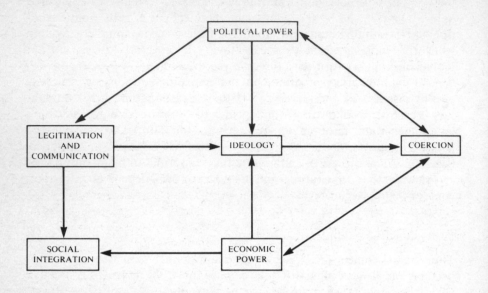

FIGURE 2 *Power and legitimacy in a gemeinschaft society*

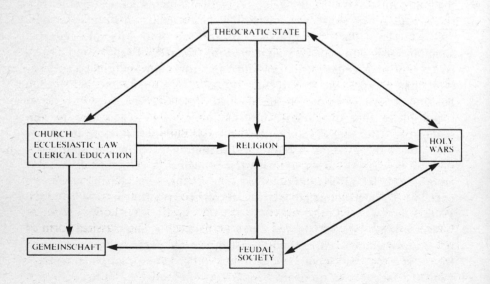

the military. The state is the supreme coercive power and those who control the armed forces ultimately exercise sovereignty. These forces are normally required to protect the territorial boundaries of the state but, in times of crisis, may also be used to quell internal threats to the ruling elites. However, in order to maintain their position, the elites must also exercise control over the agencies that legitimate their power and convert it into authority and the rule of law. The legitimating agencies include the judicial system, the education system and all those organizations concerned with the dissemination of information and the generation of belief systems containing core values. They are responsible for generating dominant ideologies which justify and sustain the existing distribution of political and economic power. These ideologies also rationalize and mobilize support for the use of coercion, for both external and internal purposes. There is a close link between the nature of the economic system, including the division of labor and the distribution of economic status, and the particular forms of social integration characteristic of the society in question. In the last resort the economic elites also rely upon coercive measures to maintain the *status quo* but, in normal conditions, legitimating agencies such as education and the law are sufficient to maintain social order.

Figure 2 illustrates the relationship between economic and political power and the typical mode of social integration characteristic of a feudal economy and a theocratic state. Under these conditions there is a close alliance between church and state in which the agencies of legitimation are dominated by the clergy, who also exercise direct political power. The king or other head of state rules by "divine right" and is generally autocratic. The church exercises effective control over both the judicial and the educational system. The dominant ideologies are those of the religion in question which sanctifies the use of military force in holy wars against the infidels. Internal rebellion will be coercively controlled by a ruler who is a "defender of the faith." Although such theocratic states have lasted to the present day they have their origins in a feudal-type economy in which economic and social roles are essentially ascriptive. The characteristic form of social integration associated with such a system is that of territorial community or *"gemeinschaft"* (Tonnies, 1957). Such communities are comparatively small, often involving an extended kinship or tribal system with a restricted division of labor and little social differentiation. The value systems binding such a community together are those of the dominant religion, generally imposed by the priesthood through oral tradition on an often illiterate population. In such a system the law courts are ecclesiastical. Orthodoxy is maintained through inquisitions and harsh punishments. The classical form of the theocratic system was to be found in medieval Europe as it conducted its holy wars against Islam. Today some Islamic countries still exhibit the characteristics of such a theocratic state although their stabilty under the conditions of rapid industrialization and social change is threatened (Warburg, 1978).

Figure 3 illustrates the relationship between political and economic power in the secular states that replaced the theocracies, following the decline of feudalism and the rise of the modern capitalist industrial system. The secular state retained many of the trappings of its predecessor but effective power shifted from autocratic monarchs to more democratic parliamentary institutions, and a generally independent judiciary. At the same time, control over the education system shifted from the church to the state. A process of functional differentiation occurred between the various agencies of legitimation. Nevertheless, there was a general consensus on the dominant value system, whose central unifying principle was nationalism. In the industrialized countries the unity of church and state was replaced by a unity of nation and state. In fact, those two concepts came to be linked in a way that is critical to our understanding of the emergence of ethnic nationalism in the later postindustrial societies. The nation-state was by its very nature an assimilating agency that was intolerant of ethnic variation within its boundaries. The internal cohesion and social integration of the nation-state depended upon an elimination of previous local, tribal or provincial attachments and the inculcation of loyalty to the larger territorial unit dominated by the secular state. Eighteenth- and 19th-century nationalism was a unifying force which brought together people of diverse backgrounds at the price of subordinating their ethnic loyalties to the larger entity. The dominant ideology was that of nationalism which idealized the state and deprecated the maintenance of any linguistic, religious, or other sentiments that might conflict with loyalty to it (Deutsch, 1953; Smith, 1971; 1976). The holy wars of an earlier era were replaced with the patriotic wars of the 19th and 20th centuries which determined and maintained boundaries of these newly forged nation-states. These countries also engaged in imperialist expansion outside Europe, in competing for access to raw materials in less developed regions. The agencies of legitimation were unified in support for patriotic wars against other nation-states. Ethnic loyalties, which sometimes transcended the boundaries of these states, were seen to be subversive and every attempt was made to suppress them.

The division of labor and the social differentiation that accompanied the rise of industrial capitalism created a new type of social integration, based upon economic and social interdependence, formal organizations, bureaucratic structures and *Gesellschaft*. As the economic system became more complex and technologically advanced, the franchise was extended to lesser property holders and eventually the adult population at large. A literate work force and electorate became essential. The public (state) school system became an important instrument of legitimation, an essential assimilating force in polyethnic societies, and the means of inculcating patriotic values. Nationalism in its most extreme forms glorified the state

FIGURE 3 *Power and legitimacy in a gesellschaft society*

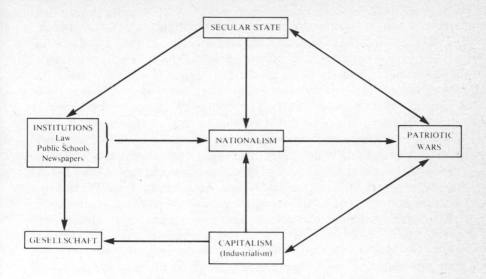

and, in its fascist manifestations, used genocidal policies to eliminate ethnic diversity.

The rise of capitalist industrialism also forged even stronger links between the economy and the military. Even under a feudal system the pursuit of holy wars had important economic and technological consequences. Taxation was never sufficient to pay for the wars in question, thus giving rise to inflationary pressures. However, these also provided an economic stimulus that reduced unemployment and created much profit for the craftsmen who made the armor and weapons used in the crusades and other religious wars. Later, the capitalist economic system became highly dependent upon the growth of an armaments industry whose enormous expenditures not only contributed to many technological advances but were a source of tremendous profit to the companies that manufactured the increasingly sophisticated weaponry. Wars, and the necessary prepartion for them, were closely associated with the trade cycles of the 19th century. The rearmament that occurred in the mid-1930s provided the necessary anti-deflationary stimulus that brought Europe and America out of the Great Depression. The capitalist system became increasingly dependent upon the exploitation of nationalism, not only in the advanced industrial countries but also in the Third World. Patriotic support for ever-growing defense budgets led to a world-wide industry in new and second-hand armaments that has now reached astronomical proportions (Myrdal, 1976; Sampson, 1977).

Postindustrial Developments

The concept of postindustrialism has been used to describe a variety of technological, economic, and social changes that are currently taking place in advanced industrial societies, whether they are of the capitalist, free-enterprise type or the socialist, state-controlled form. There is evidence that these advanced industrial states are converging in their increasing interdependence as sub-systems within a global economy (Bell, 1973; Galbraith, 1971; Touraine, 1971). The roots of this global economy go back to the beginning of the industrial revolution and the mercantalism which established trade connections between Europe and the rest of the world (Wallerstein, 1974; Kumar, 1978). The expanding nation-states of Europe established a colonial domination, involving economic exploitation backed by military force, in many parts of Africa, Asia, and the New World. What distinguishes the global economy of the postindustrial era is the emergence of multinational companies whose capital investments take advantage of cheap labor supplies outside the already industrialized countries. This has given rise to a designation of the global economy into "core" regions, "semi-peripheral," and "peripheral" areas, with varying degrees of dependency upon the metropolitan centers. in fact, the system is more complex than this trichotomy suggests as the boundaries between core and periphery are constantly changing. Furthermore, the industrialized countries themselves are undergoing rapid economic change and do not constitute a unitary system. There is a global division of labor even among industrialized countries. However, these postindustrial developments and the emergence of a global economy have threatened the viability of the traditional nation-state. North America and the countries of Western Europe are clearly in transition, but the movement toward supranational states is threatening national sovereignty (Cameron, 1981).

Figure 4 illustrates the relationship between the economic and power structures of the emerging supranational states and corresponding forms of social integration. The ultimate coercive power rests with military alliances that transcend the boundaries of nation-states. The world is now divided by the confrontation of superpowers and by a precarious balance of nuclear terror. Each side has the capacity to totally annihilate the other and to destroy much of the rest of the world. Through the genetic damage which the use of nuclear weapons would entail, the destructive capacity extends into future generations of the whole human race. Under these conditions no nation-state, not even the largest and most powerful members of these opposing military alliances, can act independently (Kaldor, 1978).

The power of the old nation-states is on the wane as they become more and more dependent upon military, economic, legal, and social structures that transcend their territorial boundaries. In the case of Britain, and a growing number of countries in Western Europe, the North Atlantic Treaty

FIGURE 4 *Power and legitimacy in a verbindungsnetzschaft society*

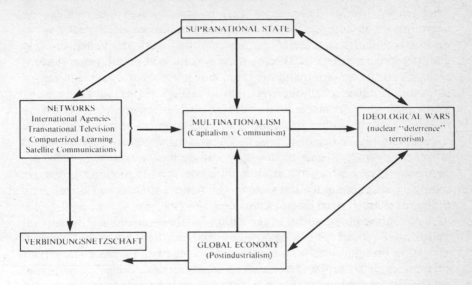

Organization (NATO), the Treaty of Rome, and the European Common Market place severe restrictions upon their autonomy. New judicial agencies are emerging that restrict the freedom of nation-states and require conformity to international laws and agreements. Agencies such as the International Monetary Fund and the World Bank use powerful economic sanctions to demand conformity to economic and social policies that are against the interests of particular countries but maintain the global economic system. New bureaucratic structures are springing up which will eventually supercede those of the old nation-states. Similar developments are occurring in the Communist-dominated countries although the struggle for independence from the Soviet Union continues, just as Western countries resent the growing domination of the United States. War, and the justification for military build-up and nuclear deterrents, is no longer legitimated in terms of patriotic sentiments of a nationalistic type. Global confrontation is now expressed in terms of the overriding ideologies of Communism and anti-Communism.[1]

Technological Changes

The postindustrial era has been brought about by technological revolution. This revolution has been most evident in the spheres of computerization and automation, on the one hand, and in communications systems on the other. The full impact of this revolution has yet to be experienced. Previously labor-intensive industries, in both the manufacturing and the service sectors, will come to depend increasingly upon these new technologies. Already, world-wide telecommunications systems link individuals and organizations in complex networks of information exchange. Banks, insurance companies, stock markets, and multinational companies, in every industrial sector, are now linked by these systems that permit instantaneous exchanges of information and the rapid movement of currency and capital from one country to another. At the domestic level our lives are being revolutionized by transnational radio and television networks aided by satellite communication systems. The education system is also being transformed by the use of television and various systems of computerized information storage and retrieval. Computerized learning systems are beginning to take over from traditional classroom instruction. Interactive computerized communication systems will remove the element of passivity which has characterized listening and viewing in the past.

A new principle of social organization has been introduced which will transform the social systems of postindustrial societies. When the industrial revolution brought with it formal organizations of the *gesellschaft* type it did not completely replace territorial communities of the *gemeinschaft* type, but the former diminished in importance as people became more involved in transactional relationships and specialized economic and social roles. By the same token, the complex social and communication networks, the *verbindungsnetschaft*,[2] that are characteristic of postindustrial societies will not entirely replace territorial communities or formal organizations. However, relationships based upon interpersonal, interorganizational, international and mass communication networks, will be the characteristic mode of social interaction in the future (Nora and Minc, 1978; Serafini and Andrieu, 1980; Toffler, 1980).

The dominant ideologies of the postindustrial period are those which endeavor to rationalize and justify the activities of multinational companies, on the one hand, and multinational socialist regimes, on the other. In economic terms, the interests of national power elites are no longer aligned with the interests of nationally-based economic organizations, whether under private enterprise or state socialism. Instead, the supranational power elites are aligned with the interests of multinational economic organizations, whether these are capitalist or socialist. The military-industrial complex is no longer an instrument of the nation-state for the pursuit of patriotic wars. It has become the instrument of the supranational state for the pursuit of ideological wars between the Capitalist and Communist superpowers. Even the civil wars within existing nation-states have become ideological rather than patriotic. They involve economic and military support from external supranational states. Insurgent movements, whether in the advanced industrial countries or the Third World, are linked through complex communication networks with each other and with the dominant suprastate agencies that encourage them. This is true whether the insurgent movements identify with the ideologies of Capitalism or Communism. Terrorism no longer operates within national boundaries but has become an international phenomenon involving bombing, hi-jacking, and hostage-taking in almost every country of the world.

The Future of Ethnic Nationalism

The emergence of postindustrialism has profound implications for the future of ethnic consciousness, ethnic organizations, and ethnic nationalist movements. In a theocratic state, variations in language, national identification, and ethnic group formation are acceptable as long as all the sources of variation are subordinated to a single religious ideology. The ultimate power structure depends upon a close relationship between the religious, military, and economic elites. There can be no religious toleration. Sectarian movements or competing religious faiths, including secular political philosophies, must be ruthlessly suppressed. Ethnic nationalism can survive under the conditions created by theocratic states as long as the ultimate power rests with the religious authorities. This was evident during the Catholic domination of Europe up to the Reformation and, to some extent, is characteristic of Islamic states today.

However, the theocratic structure of power was undermined as feudal economies gave way to industrialization. New power elites emerged that were no longer identified with the old religious order. The secular state, characteristic of industrialized countries, could afford religious toleration. The vestiges of established religion may have lingered on but religious reformist groups, new sects and widespread agnosticism or atheism were compatible with the new nationalist ideologies. However, the old link between church and state was replaced by a link between nation and state. The process of industrialization was a powerful assimilatory force that compelled people to relinquish the *gemeinschaft* attachments of the rural community in favor of the *gesellschaft* relationships of the city. No matter how heterogeneous the ethnic origins of the city-dwelling industrial workers may have been, new loyalties were generated that ensured the solidarity of the new nation-state. The 19th century, and the first half of the 20th century, in Europe and in North America, was a period during which old ethnic identities gave way to new nationalistic loyalties.[3] Wars of religion were replaced by the Napoleonic era, and two world wars in which the patriotism of the linguistic and ethnic minorities within the nation-states were severely tested. The willingness to be conscripted into the military became a critical issue. Ethnic minorities that resisted conscription, or who were suspected of less than total loyalty to the nation at war, were subjected to severe penalties. In Britain the loyalty of Scottish and Welsh minorities was rarely in question but the Irish were less inclined to fight in the British cause. In Canada, there was a similar disinclination on the part of French-speaking Quebecers. In other parts of Canada, European immigrants and their children were often unjustly suspected of unpatriotic sentiments and behavior. During the World War II, the Canadian treatment of Japanese Canadians is evidence of coercive assimilation and relinquishment of ethnic loyalties that was demanded. The McCarthy era in the United States was probably the last attempt to impose a single nationalistic ideology and to regard any nonconformity as evidence of "un-American activities." Already, the ideology of the new supranational state was emerging, that of anti-Communism.

Ethnic Power

Among first-generation immigrants in an industrialized society the maintenance of strong ethnic loyalties was seen as unpatriotic. In Europe, where changing boundaries of nation-states left many linguistic minorities politically isolated from those with whom they had cultural links, the incorporation of minorities into a single unit ready to fight in defense of the country concerned, became a major question in the 19th and 20th centuries. At the same time, in the New World, waves of immigrants were to be incorporated as citizens of their new countries. In both the United States and Canada, the question of inculcating loyalty to the state continued to be an important political issue until after the World War II. As the second and later generations, of various ethnic origins, established themselves in the countries concerned, they sought to overcome the prejudice and discrimination which previous generations had suffered.

The "Black Power" movement in the United States led the way, and other ethnic groups followed in their attempt to gain recognition. In many cases, the ethnic minorities in industrialized countries identified closely with the independence movements in formerly colonized territories in the Third World. Political imperialism was replaced by economic imperialism within the framework of the global economy. Ethnic minorities within the industrialized countries began to regard themselves as having been exploited in the interests of dominant groups within the industrialized nation-states. Their situation has been interpreted as one of internal colonialism (Blauner, 1969; Hechter, 1975). The second half of the 20th century has seen a reaction against the assimilatory pressures of industrialization and, at least among the elites within the ethnic populations concerned, a struggle for greater autonomy and even independence.

The emerging supranational states can afford to make concessions to the ethnic nationalist movements within industrialized countries as long as one overriding condition is fulfilled. That condition is an unswerving loyalty to the dominant ideology of the supranational state. In Western countries, this means unquestioning support for the economic philosophy of multinationalism, Capitalism, and anti-Communism. For countries within the

Communist bloc the reverse is the case. Varying degrees of autonomy can be permitted for the constituent national groups as long as there is unswerving loyalty to the dictates of the Communist Party. Any deviation from this is likely to be immediately suppressed, if necessary by military force.[4]

It is not only ethnic groups which are geographically concentrated, and can establish an historical claim to particular territories, who will succeed in promoting their interests within the framework of the supranational state. The very nature of postindustrialism, with its technological advances in communication networks, facilitates the maintenance of language and cultural differences, even in remotely scattered populations. The immigrant minorities in countries such as Canada and Australia are already able to take advantage of multilingual radio and television channels. New developments in Pay TV and in satellite communications will further assist and promote the maintenance of linguistic and ethnic diversity. Mass communication networks will be supplemented by interpersonal networks, with kith and kin, maintained through rapid transportation and transnational telecommunications systems. Just as the emergence of the industrialized nation-state facilitated religious toleration, so the emergence of the postindustrial supranational state will facilitate the maintenance of ethnic diversity. However, those ethnic nationalist movements that identify themselves with the opposing ideology (multinational capitalism versus multinational communism) will be regarded as subversive and subject to coercive controls.

Ethnic Power Elites

The transition from nationalism to multinationalism, and its associated multiculturalism, will not take place without a struggle between competing power elites. Already, the traditional power elites of the secular states are resisting incorporation into the new structures being created at the supranational level. The growing threat of a nuclear war on a global scale must eventually overcome the resistance of the weaker units who depend for their defense upon larger and more powerful countries. However, encroachments on national sovereignty will continue to be resisted even as independence is undermined by the technological revolution of postindustrialism.[5]

Meanwhile, within the old nation-states both ethnic and regional interests are asserting themselves. The emerging struggle for power has two major dimensions. The first is economic. Generally, it is a struggle for access to and control over natural resources, particularly those relating to energy. In this context, industrial and commercial elites will ally themselves with emerging ethnic or regional movements for autonomy and independence. In some cases, as in Scotland and Western Canada, the economic advantages of greater independence, and even separation, will be emphasized. Questions of mineral rights, export controls and taxation will be controversial.

However, the economic elites may fail to gain popular support for their separatist policies which may not be perceived as in the best interests of the population as a whole (Breton and Breton, 1980).

The second dimension of the struggle for power concerns the agencies of communication and legitimation. Specifically, the struggle focusses upon constitutional questions relating to devolution, the judicial system, the education system, and the agencies of mass communication. The constitutional issues are fought out in the political arena through the electoral system and by the use of referenda. Again, the interests of regional and ethnic elites may not coincide with those of the electorate. The latter may be suspicious of the motives of the ethnic leaders; they may retain a lingering attachment to the larger nation-state, or they may consider that their economic interests will continue to be better served by remaining part of the wider society in its federal or other more centralized form. Much will depend upon the ability of the separatist movements to gain control of the socializing agencies that influence attitudes and public opinion. Teachers and journalists play an important part in this respect and are often among the strongest supporters of ethnic nationalism.

Next in importance to the legitimating function of the constitutional debates are those relating to the control of education. Where regional and ethnic interests converge, and are focussed on the maintenance of language and culture, the education system becomes a center of controversy. In the earlier industrialized nation-states a single language of instruction was regarded as imperative and led, in some cases, to the use of coercive measures to eliminate ethnic languages in schools (Khleif, 1980; Brown, 1969). Now, newly merging ethnic elites may adopt equally coercive means to impose their own language requirements. Bilingualism may be imposed upon members of the former dominant group, rather than being a functional prerequisite for ethnic minority. In some cases the ethnic minority may succeed in imposing monolingual rules upon former majority group members, as in the case of recent Quebec legislation (Guindon, 1978). Where the ethnic minority groups do not have a territorial base they may, nevertheless, succeed in establishing the legitimacy of separate ethnic schools or bilingual instruction.

As the postindustrial revolution transforms the systems of communication in contemporary societies, a struggle for control of the networks also takes place. Access to and control over the instruments of mass communication becomes an important issue. Both child and adult socialization takes place through exposure to the information and the value systems transmitted through these networks. The school system itself becomes increasingly dependent upon televised and computerized learning systems. Many children actually spend more hours exposed to television viewing than they do in conventional classroom learning. Adults are also exposed increasingly to the flood of verbal and visual communications transmitted through the new technologies. At one time, the number of channels was strictly limited. The effect was essentially assimilatory and homogenizing. Hence the resistance to American domination of mass communication networks in Canada. However, as the new technologies evolve a much greater variety of linguistic and cultural information will flow through these channels. Ethnic minorities will seek and generally obtain control over one or more television channels. This will permit the transmission of distinctive educational, informational, cultural, and recreational programs in a variety of different languages.

Supranational states of the authoritarian or totalitarian type will have a special interest in controlling the mass communication networks and the educational systems. While some linguistic and cultural variation may be permitted, the networks will be the vehicle for transmitting a single dominant political ideology. In more democratically organized societies, there may be greater freedom of expression and more evidence of political discussion and dissent. However, ultimate control over licensing for broadcasting and reception is likely to rest with authorities who will not tolerate the use of the networks for active propaganda in favor of an opposing ideology. Nor will they permit the networks to be dominated by any one foreign source.

As the influence of *verbindungsnetschaft* replaces that of *gemeinschaft* as a characteristic mode of social organization in postindustrial societies, the maintenance of ethnic identity will become less dependent upon either a territorial base or formal organizations. It will be possible for ethnic links to be maintained with others of similar language and cultural background throughout the world. Interpersonal networks may be sustained through videophones and other telecommunication links that will function much as the "ham" radio networks have functioned in the past. Mass communication networks will also transcend the boundaries of former nation-states to link people of many different linguistic, cultural, and national origins wherever they may be located throughout the world. International migration will still occur but it will no longer be necessary to compel immigrants to assimilate culturally to the majority group in the receiving society.

Ethnic nationalism will merge with the claims of other provincial and regional interest groups seeking greater economic and political influence, wherever numbers and territorial concentration make such an alliance advantageous. Even where ethnic minorities are widely dispersed they will still be able to maintain their links with others of similar ethnicity, wherever they may be. The complex communication networks of postindustrial societies will create the possibility of a new type of society, free of both religious and ethnic intolerance, by permitting great diversity within the structure of a supranational state. Reactionary movements, endeavoring to reassert national sovereignty and seeking to impose ethnic and cultural uniformity will likely occur. The transition from nationalism to multinationalism and from industrialism to postindustrialism will not take place without conflict. Eventually, a new era of ethnic and cultural diversity may be predicted. Its achievement will depend upon one overriding condition, namely, that the supranational states do not destroy themselves, and the rest of the world with them, in a nuclear configuration precipitated by the combined forces of militarism and multinationalism.

END NOTES

1. This does not mean that there are no divisions between the adherents of these two ideologies. Clearly, there are serious conflicts between the Soviet Communist block and the Chinese Communist sphere of influence. Furthermore, there are actual and potential conflicts within the multinational capitalist countries. This is the theme of Mary Kaldor's study *The Disintegrating West*. A major thesis of her book "is the passing of the nation-state, or, rather, its struggle for survival in the face of increased interpenetration of Western societies and dissipation of national constituencies. In particular, the multinational corporations are seen to play a key role in changing the rules of the international economy and upsetting the national balance of political forces" (p. 10). She does not exclude the prospect of renewed American hegemony but argues that this is conditioned by the rivalry of the United States with Europe and Japan. She anticipates a new division of the world into super-nation states "a new global constellation of continental groupings" (Kaldor, 1979: 12).

2. I coined this term in Richmond (1969: 278). I noted that, "*verbindungsnetschaft* is an "ideal type" concept or abstract representation not necessarily corresponding exactly with the conditions in any actual society, which is likely to contain elements of *Gemeinschaft* – and *Gesellschaft*-like social systems as well. A *verbindungsnetzschaft*-like social system is one in which the characteristic forms of social interaction take place through networks of communication maintained by means of telephone, teleprinter, television, and high speed aircraft and spacecraft, etc. Such relationships are not dependent upon a territorial base or face-to-face contact, nor do they involve participation in formal organizations. Behavior is governed by a constant feedback from highly efficient information storage and retrieval processes based upon diffuse networks of inter-dependent communication systems."

3. Reitz (1980: 8) quotes Teddy Roosevelt as stating, in 1915, "the foreign-born population of this country must be Americanized population – no other kind can fight the battles of America either in war or peace. It must talk the language of its native-born or fellow citizens, it must possess American citizenship and American ideals. It must stand firm by its oath of allegiance in word and deed and must show that in very fact it has renounced allegiance to every prince potentate or foreign government".

4. The situation in Poland is a critical case in point. The greater freedom accorded to the Catholic Church and the Solidarity labor union movement was tolerated as long as there was an ultimate conformity to the dictates of the Communist Party, which in turn took its direction from the Soviet Union.

5. In a recent study of *The Information Revolution and its Implications for Canada*, Serafini and Andrieu (1980:28) note that the nation-states have relinquished some of their powers to plurinational or international bodies and that the information revolution may accelerate the erosion of national sovereignty by further increasing the dominance of multinational corporations in the world economy. "The new advances in computer communications, by significantly reducing the cost of managing large and complex organizations, may tend to increase the optimal size of firms . . . the new information technology may also help multinationals to increase control by their headquarters over corporate planning and operations by centralizing computing resources. Such a step might, indeed, become necessary to coordinate the activities of the more specialized branch plants." Later they emphasize that the information revolution is international and reflects a fundamental structural change causing increasing international interdependence. They note that "in response to the consequent erosion of national sovereignty, many countries have been experiencing a trend towards economic nationalism" (p. 94), but they argue that the effects of the new technologies cannot be stopped at the border.

SELECTED REFERENCES

Bell, D. *The Coming of Post-Industrial Society: A Venture in Social Forecasting.* London: Heinemann Educational Books Ltd., 1973.

Blauner, Robert. "Internal colonialism and the ghetto revolt." *Social Problems 16*, 4:393-408, 1969.

Breton, A. and R. Breton. *Why Disunity? An Analysis of Linguistic and Regional Cleavages in Canada.* Montreal: The Institute for Research on Public Policy, 1980.

Brown, Craig, ed. *Minorities, Schools and Politics.* Toronto: University of Toronto Press, 1969.

Cameron, David, ed. *Regionalism and Supranationalism.* Montreal: Institute for Research on Public Policy, 1981.

Cohen, P.S. *Modern Social Theory.* London: Heinemann Educational Books Ltd., 1968.

Cox, O.C. *Caste, Class and Race: A Study in Social Dynamics.* New York: Monthly Review, Press, 1948.

Deutsch, Karl Wolfgang. *Nationalism and Social Communication: An Inquiry Into the Foundations of Nationality.* Cambridge: M.I.T. Press, 1953.

Dofny, J. and A. Akiwowo, eds. National and Ethnic Movements. Beverley Hills: Sage Publications, 1980.

Durkheim, E. The Division of Labor in Society. (Translated from the French by George Simpson.) Glencoe, Illinois: The Free Press, 1947.

Galbraith, J.K. *The New Industrial State.* Boston: Houghton Mifflin Co., 1971.

Glazer, N. and D.P. Moynihan. *Ethnicity: Theory and Experience.* Cambridge: Harvard University Press, 1975.

Guindon, Hubert. "The modernization of Quebec and the legitimacy of the Canadian State," in D. Glenday, N. Guindon and A. Turowetz, eds. *Modernization and the Canadian State.* Toronto: Macmillan, 1978.

Hechter, Michael. *Imperial Colonialism: The Celtic Fringe in British National Development*. London: Routledge, 1975.

Kaldor, Mary. *The Disintegrating West*. Harmondsworth: Penguin Books Ltd., 1978.

Khleif, B.B. *Language, Ethnicity and Education in Wales*. The Hague: Mouton Publishers, 1980.

Kumar, K. *Prophecy and Progress: The Sociology of Industrial and Post-Industrial Society*. Harmondsworth: Penguin Books Ltd., 1978.

Lenin, V.I. *Questions of National Policy and Proleterian Internationalism*. Moscow: Progress Publishers, 1970.

Myrdal, A. *The Game of Disarmament. How the United States and Russia Run the Arms Race*. New York: Pantheon Books, A Division of Random House, Inc., 1976.

Nora, S. and A. Minc. *The Computerization of Society*. Cambridge, Mass: The MIT Press, 1978.

Parsons, Talcott. *The Social System*. London: Tavistock, 1952.

Reitz, J.G. *The Survival of Ethnic Groups*. Toronto: McGraw-Hill Ryerson Ltd., 1980.

Richmond A.H. "Sociology of migration in industrial and post-industrial societies," in J.A. Jackson, ed. *Migration*. London: Cambridge University Press, 1969.

Sampson, A. *The Arms Bazaar. The Companies, the Dealers, the Backers: From Vickers to Lockheed*. London: Hodder and Stoughton, Ltd., 1977.

Serafini, S. and M. Andrieu. *The Information Revolution and its Implications for Canada*. Hull, Quebec: Supply and Services Canada, 1980.

Smith, Anthony D. *Theories of Nationalism*. London: Duckworth, 1971.

_____ . *Social Change: Social Theory and Historical Process*. London: Longman, 1976.

Toffler, A. *The Third Wave*. New York: Bantam Books, Inc., 1980.

Tönnies, F. *Community and Society*. (Translated and edited by L.P. Loomis.) Michigan: Michigan State University Press, 1957.

Touraine, A. *The Post-Industrial Society*. New York: Random House, 1971.

Wallerstein, I. *The Modern World-System: Capitalist Agriculture and the Origins of the European World-Economy in the Sixteenth Century*. New York: Academic Press, 1974.

Warburg, Gabriel, *Islam, Nationalism and Communism in a Traditional Society*. London: Cass, 1978.

Weber, Max. *Max Weber: Essays in Sociology*. (Translated and edited by H.H. Gerth and C.W. Mills.) London, Oxford University Press, 1946.

European Immigration

ABRAHAM J. ARNOLD

The Jews of Western Canada*

In May 1969, two events in Winnipeg epitomized the enthusiasm and mystique that have marked Western Jewry for nearly a century. More than 900 people gathered at a kosher banquet in Winnipeg's Marlborough Hotel – then owned by the Rothstein family whose progenitor, Nathan, homesteaded at Lipton, Saskatchewan in 1904 – to celebrate the 50th anniversary of the first Canadian Jewish Congress. It was the only public celebration of that anniversary anywhere in Canada.

Winnipeg Jewry has always considered itself one of the founding communities of the CJC, but the gathering at the Marlborough was more to celebrate the Western Jewish mystique than the national achievement. For the participants, the most important part of the banquet was the honoring of some 300 pioneer Western Jews. The glittering guest list included Maitland Steinkopf, the first Jewish cabinet minister in Manitoba; Saul Cherniack, a former CJC regional chairman and then deputy leader of the provincial New Democratic Party, and Justice Samuel Freedman, soon to become the first Jew named a chief justice in Canada; all three had helped shape the Western Jewish community and had parents among the earliest settlers.[1] Guest speakers included two from Montreal: Louis Rosenberg, who had lived in the West for 30 years, beginning in 1915 as principal-teacher of Tifereth Israel, a prairie school in Lipton, Saskatchewan, and Rabbi Solomon Frank, who had served from 1926 to 1947 as spiritual leader of Winnipeg's Shaarei Zedek synagogue.

While 900 people were publicly celebrating these past Jewish achievements in the West, a private political meeting was taking place in the provincial capital building; a month later it would result in the famous election that brought the provincial NDP to power with three Jewish cabinet ministers, dramatizing thereby the mystique of Western Jewry.

---

* Reprinted from "The Mystique of Western Jewry," in M. Weinfeld, W. Shaffir, and I. Cotler, eds., *The Canadian Jewish Mosaic*, (Toronto: John Wiley and Sons, 1981).

Less than 15 percent of Canada's Jews live in the four Western provinces. In absolute terms, the Jews of Western Canada accounted for only about 36,600 of the total of 276,000 Jews-by-religion recorded in the 1971 census. On a statistical basis, it would, therefore, be all too easy to overlook the importance of this part of Canada's Jewish population. Considered from a sociological viewpoint, however, Western Jewry emerges as more important than its numbers relative to the nation's total Jews and as surprisingly influential in the overall history of the West.

It is this influence and the concurrent vibrancy of Jewish life in the West that is sometimes called the mystique of Western Jewry. That mystique is no more unfathomable than the facts of history, geography, and politics than all Westerners have had to grapple with. Jewish experience and tradition found it much easier to assert itself in conditions of pioneer freedom than it did in the contemporary East, and it was, therefore, able to contribute to moving the West forward from its status as "the colony of a colony." That subcolonial status, which held the seeds of Western alienation, applied not only to the general relationships of the Eastern government authorities to the West and its people but also to the dealings of Eastern Jewish leadership with Jewish settlers in the West. Thus, Western Jews have been part of the larger struggle against Eastern domination, while also fighting for an equal place in Canadian Jewish leadership.

A brief history plus a description of the present-day situation seems sufficient to prove the point, which is so rarely appreciated in the East.

Early Beginnings

The Jewish mystique of the West began in Winnipeg in the summer of 1882 with the arrival of Russian Jewish refugees, who first thought they had come to a new *Mitzrayim*, a new land of Egyptian bondage. They had been told that land would be granted to them, houses built, and ploughshares and other supplies provided to enable them to live and work as farmers. Instead, one of the newcomers recorded, "They have sent us to a desolate place to become servants and maids." Some also went to work on the railway, where they were soon attacked, beaten, and robbed in a vicious reminder of the persecution they had fled. But Kiva Barsky, one of the victims, succeeded in pressing charges against his assailant, who was convicted and sent to jail for a month.

By September, many of the immigrants recognized that hard work did not mean slavery, and that they could enjoy religious freedom even if it meant conducting holy day services in a tent near a railway station 40 miles from Winnipeg. Their hope for a New Jerusalem began to grow. And after the turn of the century, Winnipeg did indeed begin to acquire a reputation as the *Yerushalayim* of Canada; the development of its synagogues, Jewish schools and other institutions kept pace with and often set precedents for the much larger Jewish communities of Montreal and Toronto. Moreover, as prairie settlement expanded, Jews showed they could cope with the frontier as homesteaders and peddlers, as small-town storekeepers and pioneer entrepreneurs. In the spirit of Judaic traditions, they founded synagogues and Hebrew schools in many small settlements, while adapting to the harsh natural conditions and participating in the life of the ethnically mixed human community that surrounded them.

The Russian immigrants who developed the New Jerusalem and the vibrant Jewish life of the prairies were not, however, the first Jews in the Canadian West. Those arrived on the Pacific coast in 1858 with the opening of the British Columbia territory to general settlement at the time of the Fraser River gold rush, and on the prairies at the beginning of the land rush of the late 1870s. In both cases, the first-comers were immigrants from Eastern Europe. Many of them had first tried their luck in different parts of the United States and gradually moved westward, then north. Some were already living in California when they heard about the gold rush. On the coast, they followed the ocean-shipping route north from San Francisco to Victoria, while on the prairies they came via the inland trade route from St. Paul, Minnesota to Winnipeg. They differed from other contemporary pioneers mostly in their chosen occupations. There was hardly a gold prospector among the early Jews in the Pacific colonies, and there were no would-be farmers before 1882 in Manitoba. Just as the first permanent Jewish settlers in Lower Canada came as suppliers to the British army in the 1760s, so the first Jews in the Pacific territory served as traders and provisioners for the gold-seekers, and the first Jews in Manitoba were suppliers to the homesteaders.

The first Jews on the Pacific coast, therefore, centered in the fledgling town of Victoria, and they did very well in all sorts of business enterprises. They also soon founded the first Jewish institutions west of Toronto: a cemetery in 1859 and a synagogue in 1863 (both are still in use). When the latter opened, it reported some 65 members and claimed a Jewish population of 300 or more for Victoria,[2] though the 1881 census was to record only 104 Jews in British Columbia.

The Jews of Victoria also quickly established their political rights. In 1856, Governor James Douglas found that he had to amend a naturalization proclamation that included the words "on the true faith of a Christian" in the oath. The following year Selim Franklin, an English Jew who was BC's first government auctionneer, was elected to the legislature of Vancouver Island. Once again the oath of office became an issue, but the protracted debate had a satisfactory conclusion, unlike Ezekiel Hart's experiences of expulsion from the Lower Canada Assembly in the early 19th century.

Lumley Franklin, Selim's brother, served as mayor of Victoria in 1866; although some Jews were signing a petition for favoring the annexation of BC to the United States, he supported BC's joining Confederation. And when BC became a Canadian province, one of the first two MPs elected from Victoria was Henry Nathan, another Jew. Jews were also among the founders of the city of Vancouver in 1886. David and Isaac Oppenheimer were elected to its city council in 1887, and a year later David began a four-year term as mayor.[4]

After these early years, no Jew became prominent in BC politics until David Barrett was elected to the legislature in 1960. In 1972 he became the first Jew to serve as a provincial premier and he is now leader of the NDP Opposition.

By comparision with BC, the earliest years of Jewish settlement in Manitoba were undistinguished, although the lowly immigrants to the prairies would eventually have a far greater influence on the course of Canadian Jewish development than did the group that so quickly scaled the political heights on the Pacific coast. Between 1877 and 1881, only 33 Jews settled on the prairies, including 21 in Winnipeg. They held high holy day services, first in a private home and later in rented halls, but there is no evidence of any other communal activity before 1882. During the next decade, however, the Manitoba Jewish population greatly outstripped that of British Columbia in numbers and organization. By 1891, the Jews of Manitoba had increased to 743, including 645 in Winnipeg, while the BC had only 277, including 148 in Victoria and 85 in Vancouver.[5]

The watershed event was the arrival in Canada in 1882 of some 500 Jews fleeing czarist persecution. Most were channelled westward, and the Jews of Winnipeg, who were not yet sufficiently established to conduct weekly Sabbath services, were immediately drawn into the front line of immigrant aid. Stephen Speisman has described the provision of temporary care for 70 Jewish immigrants in Toronto in June 1882 as "a mammoth task considering that there were only about 500 Jews in the city."[6] How then should one describe the task that faced the 23 Jews of Winnipeg who had to cope with the more-than-temporary influx of 350 destitute immigrants in a city with a total population of about 8 000?

The motive for sending so many Jews out West so quickly was mixed. It was suggested that they all wanted to take up land, and it was naively expected that the government would quickly make homesteads available. Complying with the official view that Canada had opportunities only for farm settlers, Jewish leaders in Montreal and Toronto sought to restrict, as far as possible, the numbers of immigrants settling in the cities. Nonetheless, the government's failure, at this point, to assign quarter-section homesteads for the Jews led to the growth of a new urban community in Winnipeg, which quickly became the third largest Jewish center in the country.[7]

Jewish Agriculture

Of course, some Jews did get involved with the prairie land rush, especially in what is today Saskatchewan. Before the turn of the century, there were Jewish settlement efforts in the southeast, at Moosomin, Wapella, and Hirsch. After 1900, several more notable Jewish farm colonies began at Lipton-Cupar in the Qu'Appelle Valley, at Edenbridge along the Carrot River, and at Sonnenfeld-Hoffer near the U.S. border. Only the colony at Moosomin was a total failure. The others established Saskatchewan as the only Canadian province in which a number of Jews became successful farmers for half a century or longer. (Several Jewish farm settlements were also started in Manitoba and Alberta, but none of these worked as well as those in Saskatchewan.[8])

Some Jewish leaders in the East, however, were unhappy with what they saw as too low a level of achievement in Western argiculture. In the 1890s they had fostered the idea of settling as many as 2 000 Jewish families on homesteads. Some even believed that the Canadian government might grant some kind of autonomy to a major Jewish argricultural community. The government clearly denied this in the early 1900s, but the idea continued to be described as a "missed opportunity" for many years.[9]

Some of those Jews who did not go on the land in the West looked to the Jewish Colonization Association (JCA), which was founded in Paris in 1891 by Baron de Hirsch to assist in agricultural settlement efforts. However, the leaders of the JCA maintained a colonialist attitude like that of the federal authorities towards the West as a whole. Moreover, for years, the JCA gave help not in the spirit of assisting people who were struggling to meet the challenge of cultivating unbroken land, but as though it were charity, like that doled out to the Jews of Montreal or Toronto who could not find jobs.[10] The JCA and the government alike showed little recognition of the difficulty of homesteading or of the fact that Mennonites, Ukrainians, Poles, and others might be more persistent and successful at farming because of their peasant background in the old country.

Under such circumstances, it is not surprising that some Jewish homesteaders left the land to follow the familiar pursuit of peddling, though many Gentiles and even some of their fellow-Jews considered such an occupation to be base. (Indeed, in April 1895 the "Jew pedlars" of Calgary were the subject of an abusive debate in the House of Commons.) In the pioneer decades of the 1880s and 1890s, the itinerant peddler probably did little better than the homesteader waiting for his crop or the trapper counting on his catch, but at least the hope for improvement was there. And soon the peddler who achieved a degree of success moved up to become a storekeeper. In this way Jews became an important part of the rural population; by the 1920s, they were living in over 200 rural communities in Manitoba, Saskatchewan, and Alberta.[11]

Nevertheless, the Jewish population of the West continued to be largely urban, as it had been from the beginning, concentrated in the major center of Winnipeg, with outposts in the developing cities of Calgary and Edmonton, Regina and Saskatoon.

The Development of Jewish Organizations

No matter where they lived in the prairie West, Jews found that the vastness of the land and its sparse population made it difficult to develop and maintain community institutions and religious practices, especially in centers outside Winnipeg. The Jews of the West, therefore, had to be hardier, more determined, and more resourceful than their Eastern counterparts, not only to succeed economically but to maintain their rituals and to build synagogues, schools, and other communal institutions.

Organizational growth in Winnipeg, however, was very rapid, though it involved some conflicts. At first, the tension was between the strongly Orthodox, who dominated the community by the end of the 1880s, and a Reform element of the pre-1882 arrivals, who received few reinforcements. By 1893, Winnipeg had two synagogues, both officially Orthodox although one followed the Sephardish Minhag (an East European version of the Sephardic ritual).

The Orthodox population continued to grow as the 20th century began, but qualitative changes began in 1905. First came immigrants infused with the ideal of Zionism, then several varieties of socialists – Bundists, Labour Zionists, Territorialists, and even anarchists – most of whom had turned their backs on Jewish religious practice and became known collectively as secularist-Yiddish radicals. They were all "alumni" of the 1905 Russian revolution, and those who settled in Winnipeg probably had a greater influence than did their counterparts in Montreal or Toronto. It was the newest of the three major Jewish centers and the one that experienced the largest proportional growth during this decade.[12] Moreover, the radical Jews who came there found it easy to ally themselves with the growing socialist-labor-oriented element in the total population, a group that made the city the Canadian center of the social dissent that culminated in the Winnipeg General Strike of 1919.

By 1912, all parts of the Winnipeg Jewish community, including the substantial Orthodox groups, the growing number of Zionists, and the secularist-Yiddish groups were actively involved in the development of Jewish institutions. The first Talmud Torah (also known as the Hebrew Free School) had opened in 1901; the Jewish Radical School, which quickly became the Peretz School (emphasizing Yiddish) was started in 1914. *Landsmanshaften* (societies of Jews who had emigrated from particular geographic areas), a B'nai Brith lodge, various charitable and mutual aid groups, an orphanage, a home for the aged, a YMHA center, and new synagogues were all organized as the population grew.

Political Development

Jewish participation in the general political life of the prairies did not begin with the arrival of the secularist-Yiddish radicals. In fact, the sparseness of population in the vast Western territories and the Jewish presence during the earliest days of many new cities and towns made it possible for Jews to become involved in public life more quickly than was usually the case in Eastern Canada. Those who became well established economically found it relatively easy to develop business and political relationships with members of the Anglo-Celtic branch plant of the Upper Canada establishment (who had themselves only begun to settle in the West in the 1870s). Max Steinkopf, for example, whose family settled in Winnipeg before 1890, articled with Sir Hugh John MacDonald (Sir John A.'s son), became the first Jewish lawyer in Manitoba, and remained a life-long Conservative, as did other prominent Jews. After the rise of the Liberals under Wilfrid Laurier, however, more Jews began to support that party.

The first Jew on Winnipeg's city council was Moses Finkelstein, a Conservative, who was chosen in 1904. In 1910, S. Hart Green, a Liberal, was elected to the Manitoba legislature, the first Jew to sit in a provincial parliament after Confederation. By 1917, however, a Jewish Conservative, Alter Skaleter, who had been on city council for five years, lost his seat to A.A. Heaps, a labor candidate who later became one of the General Strike leaders and eventually the first Jew elected to the House of Commons from Winnipeg. And after the General Strike, Conservative Max Steinkopf, who had been involved with the anti-strike Committee of 1000, lost his seat on the Winnipeg School Board to Rose Alein, a labor candidate.[13]

The ideological influences at work in Winnipeg were significant. By the mid-1920s, large numbers of Jews had turned to socialist or labor candidates, breaking with the Eastern Jewry's tendency to support the Liberals, particularly at the federal level. This became clear with the 1926 election of Heaps, who later joined the Co-operative Commonwealth Federation (CCF). Support for labor and socialist candidates became a tradition in Winnipeg, not only among Jews, and helped to build the power base of the NDP.

Anti-Semitism in the West

During the early days of prairie settlement, some immigration agents made anti-Jewish statements, some Canadians signed protest resolutions against reserving land for Jewish homesteaders, and a good many people expressed prejudice against "Jew pedlars". But the Jews learned to fight back, as did Kiva Barsky, who won his court case in 1882 against a non-Jewish assailant.

In the 1920s, the Ku Klux Klan had a brief upsurge in Saskatchewan and Manitoba; anti-Semitism was part of its baggage. Anti-Semitic elements were also involved in the coming to power of the Social Credit party in

Alberta in the 1930s and even in British Columbia in the 1950s. Moreover, before the World War II, Winnipeg became a center for pro-Nazi anti-Semitic activity, which included a publication called *The Nationalist*. But as a result, the Manitoba legislature adopted the first group-anti-defamation legislation in Canada. Passed in 1934, it was an amendment to the provincial libel law and provided for injunctions against the publisher of racially defamatory material. (The bill was introduced by an opposition member, Marcus Hyman, a Jewish MLA who belonged to the Independent Labour Party.)[14] Attempts were made during this period to introduce group libel laws in Quebec and Ontario as well as in Manitoba, but only in the western province was the effort successful. Ten years later a debate in its legislature also led to the end of the quota system that had limited the entry of Jews and members of other minority groups to the Manitoba Medical School.[15]

In reality, of course, the West is no more immune to the virus of anti-Semitism than any other part of the country. The swastika-daubing of synagogues and cemeteries that began in Cologne, Germany in December 1960 reached all the way to Vancouver. And six years later, the synagogues of Winnipeg experienced another outbreak of defacement with swastikas, apparently unrelated to anything that was happening elsewhere at the time. On the whole it must be said, however, that the establishments of Western Canada do not seem to have been influenced by anti-Semitism in the same way as have parts of the Roman Catholic hierarchy in Quebec, the Protestant Orange Order in Ontario, or some of the ruling political groups in Ottawa, especially before the World War II.[16]

The Present – and the Future

Today the Winnipeg Jewish community is still the largest in the West by far, with more than half the total Jewish population of the four Western provinces. And it continues to be a pace-setter on the national scene, even though its population stood at only 18 300 – about the 1931 level – in the 1971 census (Montreal and Toronto then had over 100 000 Jews each).

The Jews of Winnipeg have long played a significant part in the development of Canadian Jewish life, from providing active support for all branches of the Zionist movement, to helping found the Canadian Jewish Congress in 1919, to promoting the establishment of Canada's first permanent Judaic Studies Department at the University of Manitoba in 1952. Local community organization continues apace. In 1973, Winnipeg established a unified Jewish Community Council structure by merging the Winnipeg Jewish Welfare Fund (which had operated since 1937) and the local branch of the CJC. The Winnipeg Jewish Council has led the way in unified school management by bringing the four local Jewish day schools (three primary schools, one high school) under the aegis of a central board of Jewish education.

Elsewhere in the West, the Jewish population figures for 1961 and 1971 censuses reflected the overall shifts of westward movement and urbanization. The Vancouver community was growing (from 7 300 to 8 900), though in 1971 it still stood at little better than half of Winnipeg. Calgary's was also expanding (from 2 900 to 3 300). Edmonton had held its own at 2 500. Regina and Saskatoon had dropped from 1 600 to 1 300 between them.

Despite their small size, Calgary and Edmonton have Jewish community council structures and are developing Jewish community center programs. They each have several synagogues, conduct annual campaigns for Israel and local institutions, maintain services for families, children, and the aged, and support university studies and student and other youth activities, as well as Zionist endeavors. As the 1980s begin, the Jewish communities of both cities are in the midst of building sprees, but these are probably more the result of the direct and indirect benefits of the Alberta Heritage Fund than of population growth.

Vancouver is also highly organized, with all the services and facilities of larger Jewish centers. The Jews of Regina and Saskatoon maintain themselves as communities based on a single synagogue apiece. Each of these communities retains its affiliation with the Canadian Jewish Congress.

In the religious sphere, the West has seven Conservative synagogues and at least 13 Orthodox congregations. Reform congregations are just beginning to get a foothold in Winnipeg and Vancouver. Although the physical partitions between men and women have come down in Conservative synagogues, the men still do most of the top-level community and fundraising, while the women, with some notable exceptions, are still largely involved as grass-roots workers in Hadassah, the National Council of Jewish Women, the Pioneer Women or B'nai B'rith.

The smaller towns have fared less well. On the prairies, many Jews left the small centers in the general population exodus between 1961 and 1971.[17] The result is that, outside the major cities, Jewish life on the prairies has all but disappeared, and virtually every synagogue has been closed. In British Columbia, the small-town Jewish population has grown somewhat, but only in Victoria, with its 117-year-old synagogue, has numerical increase led to renewed community endeavors.

Today, the Jews of the West continue to represent the Western Canada mystique within the national Jewish community and the Canadian community at large. Some of them are active in the struggle for Western ascendancy in Canada, though a Western Jewish separatist would be a rare bird indeed. Many others have shown the initiative and ability needed to win personal recognition in the East and elsewhere in competitive arenas such as politics, the federal bureaucracy, the arts, and big business.

For example, the Senate now includes three Jews from the West: Sidney Buckwold from Saskatoon, Jack Austin from Vancouver, and Nathan Nurgitz from Winnipeg. Sylvia and Bernard Ostry, among many other Westerners in Ottawa, have become household names. Many Western expatriates, from Winnipeg in particular, have been successful in the world of arts and letters; a partial list must include Norman Mittlemen in opera, David Steinberg and Monty Hall in American TV, John Hirsch in theatre, Paul Kligman in Canadian TV, Miriam Waddington in poetry, and Jack Ludwig and Adele Wiseman in novel writing. And to cite just one example of Western success in the corporate board rooms, Senator Buckwold sits beside Charles Bronfman on the board of the Bank of Montreal. Bronfman is, of course, the scion of the best-known Jewish family to move from the West to the Eastern pinnacle of economic power.

There is really no special secret to the success of Western Jewish expatriates; for most of this century, the able person who wanted to get to the top in a specialized field often had to go East. For several decades, people have been a major export of the Western provinces, a fact that has been much resented.

As the 1980s begin, however, the tide is turning. Alberta has joined BC in gaining rather than losing overall population, and Saskatchewan is catching up. The Canadian Jewish population has known a Western movement for several decades, and it undoubtedly accelerated during the 1970s with increasing numbers of Jews from Montreal and Toronto, as well as Winnipeg, moving to the Alberta oil capitals and to the lotus-land of Vancouver. It remains to be seen, however, whether the growth of these communities will lead to a lessening of Western Jewry's alienation from the East or to a reinforcement of isolation within new city-state structures. To assess these possibilities, one must realize that the Jewish communities farther west may now group Winnipeg with the East from which they feel alienated. This is partly because the Jewish community of Winnipeg, in spite of being much smaller than Montreal and Toronto, has achieved structural equality with the two eastern centers and plays a growing role in national leadership. Moreover, communities farther west, perceive it as part of the national Jewish establishment.

The West has always been noted as an incubator for both rugged individualism and movements for social progress; Jews have been active both as individual shapers of economic opportunity and social reformers. As economic power and opportunity draw more people to the West, more Jews will be there too. It is unlikely, however, that the Jewish population balance between East and West will be greatly affected; in the short term, in fact, the shift from Montreal to Toronto will be more significant than the shift from Eastern to Western centers. The growing economic strength of Calgary and Edmonton will enlarge their Jewish communities but probably not enough to enrich their Jewish life and culture significantly or to bring them to a position of greater influence on the national Jewish scene. They may even end up feeling more isolated. Jewish Winnipeg, on the other hand, can hold its own, even if it remains in a no-growth situation, and the city may long continue to be the only true oasis of Jewish culture between Toronto and Vancouver.

END NOTES

1. Many of the pioneers did not come just to receive accolades; they also contributed personal memoirs that became a basis of the archives and oral-history programs then being launched by the newly established Jewish Historical Society of Western Canada.

2. See "Trials and Tribulations of Victoria Synagogue Builders in 1863", *Jewish Western Bulletin*, 25 September 1957, pp. 4, 6, 80, 82.

3. See *Jewish Western Bulletins*, 30 June 1958, p. 5ff, and A.J. Arnold, "Was Amor de Cosmos the Louis Riel of British Columbia", *Transactions, Historical and Scientific Society of Manitoba, 1971-72*, series 3, no. 28, p. 50.

4. *Jewish Western Bulletin*, 30 June 1958, p. 9.

5. See Max Bookman, "Jewish Canada by Numbers", in Max Bookman, ed., *Canadian Jewish Reference Book and Directory* (Ottawa: E. Gottesman, 1963).

6. Stephen Speisman, *The Jews of Toronto* (Toronto: McClelland and Stewart, 1979), p. 58.

7. A.J. Arnold, "The Earliest Jews in Winnipeg 1874-82", *The Beaver Magazine*, autumn 1974.

8. A.J. Arnold, "The Contribution of the Jews to the Opening and Development of the West", *Historical and Scientific Society of Manitoba 1968-69*, series 3, no. 25, pictorial supplement, and "Jewish Pioneer Settlements", *The Beaver Magazine*, autumn 1975, and "Jewish Immigration to Western Canada in the 1880s", *Journal of the Canadian Jewish Historical Society* 1, no. 2 (October 1977).

   The high point for Jews in agriculture in all of Canada came in 1921, when there were 631 Jewish-owned farms accounting for a total population of 2 568; well over half of them were in Saskatchewan. Even in 1931, when the drought and locust years arrived, Saskatchewan still maintained its lead position, with a total of 196 Jewish farms out of 348 in the West and 477 in all of Canada. See Louis Rosenberg, *Canada's Jews: A Social and Economic Study of the Jews in Canada* (Montreal: Bureau of Social and Economic Research, Canadian Jewish Congress, 1939).

9. Arthur Chiel, *The Jews in Manitoba* (Toronto: University of Toronto Press, 1961), pp. 54-5, and Abraham Arnold, *Jewish Life in Canada* (Edmonton: Hurtig Publishers, 1976), p. 51. See also note 8 above.

10. Abraham J. Arnold, "The Jewish Farm Settlements of Saskatchewan", *Canadian Jewish Historical Society Journal* (spring 1980): 330-9.

11. Rosenberg, *Canada's Jews*, p. 26.

12. From 1901 to 1911, the number of Jews in Winnipeg increased more than eightfold (1 164 to 9 408), while Toronto Jews grew close to sixfold (3 103 to 18 294) and Montreal's just over fourfold (6 924 to 28 838).

13. Mrs. Alcin was not the first Jewish woman elected to public office in Canada. That distinction appears to belong to Mrs. Hannah Director, elected to the school board in Prince George, British Columbia in 1917. See Cyril Leonoff, *Pioneers, Pedlars and Prayer Shawls: The Jewish Communities in British Columbia and the Yukon* (Vancouver: Jewish Historical Society of British Columbia, 1978).

14. See Rosenberg, *Canada's Jews*, p. 303; Chiel, *Jews in Manitoba*, p. 180; Lloyd Stinson, *Political Warriors* (Winnipeg: Queenston House, 1975), p. 87-8; Arnold Ages, "Antisemitism: The Uneasy Calm", in this volume.

15. See Percy Barsky, "How Numerus Clausus Was Ended in the Manitoba Medical School", *Canadian Jewish Historical Society Journal* 1, no. 2 (October 1977).
16. See Speisman, *The Jews of Toronto*, pp. 320-35, and Irving Abella and Harold E. Troper, " 'The Line Must Be Drawn Somewhere': Canada and Jewish Refugees, 1933-39", in *The Mystique of Western Jewry, op. cit.*
17. According to the 1971 census, Manitoba then had 500 Jews living outside Winnipeg, down from 600 in 1961; Saskatchewan had 500 living outside Regina and Saskatoon, down from 1 100, and Alberta had 500 outside Calgary and Edmonton, down from 600. During the same years, British Columbia's small-town Jewish population went from 300 to 500.

JOHN S. MATTHIASSON   University of Manitoba

The Icelandic Canadians: The Paradox of an Assimilated Ethnic Group*

Introduction

The people of Iceland live within the circumpolar region of the world. Unlike the Inuit, Chukchee, or Lapp, they are not native to the region. They are displaced Norwegians who migrated there in a.d. 874 in search of political freedom. Centuries later in 1875, their descendants migrated to Canada and established a republic of New Iceland in the interlake region of Manitoba north of Winnipeg. Today, in such communities as Gimli, Riverton, and Lundar, people may be found who speak English with an Icelandic accent and some may, in fact, be bilingual. Subsequent Icelandic migration settled in Winnipeg. These people were joined by families of New Icelanders fleeing smallpox epidemics which struck the interlake region. In time, Winnipeg became the urban center of Icelandic culture in Canada.

I hope to identify some of the cultural patterns which Icelandic Canadians in Winnipeg brought with them from Iceland, but over the years adapted to their new environment. These patterns of adaptation are uniquely Icelandic, reflecting the basic structural features of Icelandic culture dating back to the Viking past and the writing of the sagas.

Historical Background

Visitors to Iceland who are used to tree-covered landscapes find this island a barren place of lava, volcanic mountains, and sparse vegetation. Others find a rugged beauty in its austerity. The country has never been an easy place to eke out a living; its inhabitants have suffered countless natural disasters and epidemics in their more than 1 000 years of history. The bubonic plague between 1402 and 1404 reduced the population by two thirds (Kristjanson, 121). By 1708, the population was 34 000, not enough to populate a city the size of Brandon, Manitoba. After the initial Norwegian settlement in a.d. 874, the Icelanders were subjected to an extended period of colonialism between 1262 and 1918 when Iceland was ruled by Denmark.

Before the colonial era, the Icelandic spirit of nationalism and independence was demonstrated by the founding in a.d. 930 of the *Althing*, the oldest functioning parliament in the Western world. In 1944, Iceland

331

formally severed political connections with Denmark when members of the *Althing* voted to restore Iceland to the status of a republic (Ruth, 10).

Halldor Laxness, an Icelandic writer, characterized Icelanders in his Nobel Prize-winning book, *The Independent People*, as aggressively independent. His sardonic portrayal of this urge for independence aptly captured the main psychological and cultural theme of his fellow islanders. With the restoration of the *Althing* to an independent status, the Icelanders had regained a position of self-determination. Nevertheless, conditions were such that in spite of their deep attachment to their small island, a vanguard of 285 Icelanders chose to break their European ties in 1875 and become participants in the social and cultural experiments taking place in Canada. After a brief time in Ontario, they settled in New Iceland.

In moving to Canada, the Icelanders hoped to find a new land which would allow them to preserve traditions which they felt were basic to their home society. At the same time, they were prepared to sacrifice tradition when it conflicted with assimilation to a new social order. This apparent contradiction or paradox has characterized their life in Winnipeg. While resisting the categorization of "ethnics," they have attempted to continue to be "Icelanders." Two related traditions they sought strongly to preserve were literary writing and publishing, and education.

Icelandic Traditions

Literary Writing

The history of both written and oral literary traditions among Icelanders goes back in time to the original settlement of Iceland, and has played a significant role in the type of adaptations which Icelandic immigrants made to Canada. Traditional history pays homage to the sagas and family eddas recounting early times in Iceland. Watson Kirkconnell, a prolific translator of Icelandic poetry, once wrote, "The sagas, taken as a whole, constitute the most important contribution to European literature in the twelve centuries between Virgil and Dante" (Kristjanson, 121). Rich in literary terms, the sagas also provide the scholar with early source material which is rare for any European population.

The New Testament was translated into Icelandic in 1540, only 15 years after William Tyndale's English translation (Kristjanson, 121). On a more mundane level, literary activities were found in the homes of farmers in isolated homesteads, where it is common to have readings each evening by some member of the family while others went about their work of weaving or repairing implements. It is said that in modern Iceland, more books and periodicals are published yearly *per capita* than in any country in the world.

When the first Icelanders settled in Manitoba, their first goal, other than to make a living, was to create a basis for the continuation of the Icelandic literary tradition in the new world. In 1877, the first issue of *Framfari*, one of the first newspapers in Manitoba and the first ethnic paper west of Ontario, appeared. Because of a factional split among supporters, which was in part responsible for the movement of Icelandic Canadians from New Iceland to Winnipeg, it ceased publication in 1880; it was soon replaced by others. *Leifur*, named after Leif Eirikson, son of Erik the Red, had a brief life, dying after three years of publication also as a result of factional division among subscribers.

In Winnipeg, two Icelandic language weeklies were born within two years of one another. *Heimskringla* was first published in 1886, and *Logberg* in 1888. The names of the two reflect the conflicting tendencies of Icelandic Canadians toward both assimilation and ethnic status. *Heimskringla* is roughly translated as "the round world," symbolizing for its first editors the communality of humanity, while *Logberg* means "the Mount of Laws," suggestive of Icelandic devotion to the *Althing*, the parliament at which each year the laws of the Icelanders were read and used to settle disputes among litigants.

The first editorial in *Heimskringla* was addressed to the question of whether or not, and to what extent, Icelandic Canadians should participate in the Canadian political scene. The conclusion reached was positive. The editorial also asked if Icelanders would be able to maintain their cultural identity in Canada with an increasing involvement in the larger fabric of Canadian society. The answer given was equally positive. Icelandic Canadians were urged to create a political front which would allow them to continue to be a unified community with a common cultural heritage, and at the same time to be Canadians to the fullest extent possible. Later editorials encouraged the formation of an Icelandic labor union and the creation of means to assist new immigrants to adjust to Canadian life (Kristjanson, 124).

Heimskringla began, then, with a strong political orientation. Its editorial policy was to support the Conservative Party in Canada and the Democratic Party in the United States. *Logberg* took the side of the Liberal Party, and the two papers continued through the years to disagree with one another, and each to claim their own supporters in an ideological rift which in time left all Winnipeg Icelandic Canadians on one side or the other.

Over the years, with the rapid assimilation of Icelandic Canadians, it became increasingly difficult to maintain two Icelandic language newspapers. In spite of their opposing ideological and political orientations, *Heimskringla* and *Logberg* were merged in 1959, under the combined name *Logberg-Heimskringla*. Both papers had attempted to retain contacts between Iceland and the new settlements in Canada by regularly publishing news from Iceland and items for their small numbers of subscribers in Iceland of life in the New World. Both the two original newspapers and their amalgamated successor created a forum for the publication of Icelandic poetry and prose, and in a sense were almost more literary journals than traditional newspapers. With the decline of the use of the Icelandic language in Winnipeg, however, the need for a new organ in English was recognized. Even substantial underwriting by wealthy patrons was not enough to maintain the vitality of *Logberg-Hemiskringla*, and it continues its life today with heavy subsidization, facing the growing reality of eventual death. The patterns of adaptation of a generation and more of Icelandic immigrants were to a large extent determined by the editorial policies of the paper which tended to urge Canadianization above ethnic retention. At the same time, they sustained and nurtured an internally directed perspective which encouraged inadvertently the very ethnic awareness which, on one level, they seemed to oppose.

Although these were the most prominent and influential publications, more than 30 were published by Icelanders in Manitoba. Regardless of their life span, all attempted to preserve the Icelandic literary traditions in the Canadian setting. The most vital one today is the *Icelandic Canadian*, a quarterly published in English which was founded in 1942 in an effort to retain the interest of younger Icelandic Canadians who had never learned Icelandic. The *Icelandic* has as an audience those Icelandic Canadians who have achieved some degree of recognition in the arts, academia or business; it has a heavy literary bent and is one of the main outlets for Icelandic Canadian poets and prose writers who want an Icelandic Canadian audience.

Many Icelandic Canadian writers have made a major impact on Canadian and international literature. Names such as Laura Goodman Salverson, William Valgardson, Stephen G. Stephansson, and Guttormur J. Guttormsson are striking examples. They have continued the saga tradition by demonstrating in a literary idiom the adjustments which Icelandic immigrants made to their new life in Canada. The poetry is rarely psychological. Instead, it typically extolls the dramatic features of the landscapes of Iceland or Canada. Short stories and novels on the other hand, vividly demonstrated in writings such as Valgardson's *Bloodflowers*, dip into the personalities of pioneers and their offsprings with analytic knives which may wound their Icelandic Canadian readers and tarnish the memories within the Icelandic Canadian psyche. They are reminiscent of the Icelandic writings of Halldor Laxness and Gunnar Gunnarsson which Icelanders found to portray their independent nature accurately, and whom they admire as national heroes, while being disturbed by the sometimes brutal accuracy of their identification of the themes of Icelandic society and personality. Both Icelanders and Icelandic Canadians seem more comfortable with images of the rigors of the landscape they selected for themselves on both sides of the Atlantic than the psychological mirror in themselves which is a reflection of those landscapes. Writing in the New World personifies contradictions inherent in the theme of cultural dualism, a theme I shall return to later.

Education

Icelanders have always cherished education as much as their literary tradition. Marriage in Iceland required literacy; a knowledge of the sagas and eddas was expected of all. Even with the recent introduction of state schools, children were generally literate before entering them, being tutored by parents or grandparents on isolated farmsteads.

NEW ICELAND   Emphasis on reading and writing skills was transplanted to New Iceland with the first Icelandic immigrants. It was a mere nine days after their arrival in the interlake area, and before homes had been constructed, that the Icelandic immigrants made a request to the Lieutenant-Governor of Manitoba to have a school provided for their children (Ruth, 1964). In 1875 the first school was opened, with 30 students enrolled (Ruth, 1964). Due to a smallpox epidemic, it was shortly closed, but reopened in 1876 with enrollment increased to 63 students. Emphasis was placed on the learning of English as a second language. Sunday schools for Christian education were founded as soon as ministers arrived to lead the new congregations, and students attending them were given instruction in reading as well as the catechism.

During this early period of settlement, New Iceland was essentially an independent political entity. A constitution drawn up in 1878 made New Iceland virtually a republic of its own, with internally controlled legal and political structures and mechanisms and the right to do everything possible to retain Icelandic traditions and the continued use of the Icelandic language (Ruth, 19). Ultimately, however, the republic was responsible, during its 12-year life, to the overriding control of the Government of Canada, but because of their geographic isolation, settlers were able to function largely independently. In 1881, the boundaries of Manitoba were extended to the north, and the republic of New Iceland became part of the larger province.

Although efforts were made to retain the use of Icelandic in New Iceland, the first schools in the area also emphasized the acquisition of reading, writing, and verbal skills in English. After a visit to the settlements in 1878, the Federal Minister of Agriculture stated in the House of Commons that he had been impressed with the quality of English spoken by both children and adults (Ruth, 21). Although Icelandic was the official language of new Iceland, from 1875 on it was not used as a language of instruction in day schools. Even in this early period, then, the Icelandic settlers, although given an almost unique opportunity to develop boundary maintenance mechanisms to protect their ethnicity, were beginning to move along the path to assimilation, and apparently consciously so.

In 1889 all schools in New Iceland were taken over by the provincial government's Department of Education. By that time there were five school districts, and in the next few years more were added.

The first immigrants had settled along the western shore of Lake Winnipeg, with fishing being the mainstay of their economy, but gradually they moved inland and farther south, replacing fishing in part or completely with farming. Eventually some settled in large towns such as Selkirk. During this period concern had developed over the possible loss of the Icelandic language among members of the younger generation. In 1901, in response to requests by the Icelandic High School committee, the provincial Department of Education approved the teaching of Icelandic in schools where parents wished it, and the University of Manitoba, where by this time several students of Icelandic background were enrolled, accepted Icelandic as a second language for incoming students and granted credit to these students for previous course work in Icelandic instruction.

WINNIPEG   The first Icelandic immigrants to Winnipeg, who arrived in 1875, found themselves in a growing urban environment in which the mechanisms for cultural preservation which existed in New Iceland were not available to them. Their children began almost immediately to attend regular city schools which differed from others in Winnipeg only because of their high ratio of Icelandic to non-Icelandic students, which was an artifact of the Icelandic immigrants' congregation in the western part of the city in what was to some extent an Icelandic enclave, although in no way a ghetto. Members of the Icelandic community were undismayed by this early exposure of their children to an alien educational system, and in fact encouraged the anglicization process by providing additional instruction in English for children and adults alike in homes, churches, and other meeting places in the evenings.

Soon after the first settlement by Icelanders in Winnipeg, several cultural and social organizations were formed which, while having social and recreational aims, also had educational overtones. One in particular, the Icelander's Society, was created to assist newly arrived immigrants to adapt to Canadian urban life. For a while, extra-school educational instruction continued to be carried out by educated individuals acting as individuals, but in 1881 the Advancement Society, which had been founded in 1877, began to coordinate the night school activities. That same year they founded a full-time day school, which at the time was the only separate ethnic day school in Winnipeg. However, the purpose of this school was not to perpetuate Icelandic culture and language in Canada, but rather to speed the process of acquisition of skills believed necessary for adaptation to a new social environment in which the Icelanders were socially, politically, legally, and in all other ways a part of a larger, non-Icelandic society. The school was closed in 1883, when it was felt that it had served its purpose, with students now able to compete successfully in the regular school system and fewer adults needing instruction in English.

Children of Icelandic immigrants in both New Iceland and Winnipeg were strongly encouraged by their parents to aspire to university. This goal was a central determining factor behind the efforts in both areas for the emphasis on the learning of English and of other parts of the standard Manitoba educational curriculum. The first Icelander in Canada to earn a university degree graduated from the University of Manitoba in 1885. Soon there were others. Typically, these university students aspired to careers in teaching, law, and medicine. Few of them took programs geared toward business. Academic and professional avenues seemed to have been ways of reemphasizing the Icelandic traditions of learning and literature, but it must also be recalled that mercantilism had not been a strong theme in Icelandic economic life. For centuries, most merchants in Iceland were Danes operating in a colonial system. There were travelling merchants in Iceland, but outside of major urban centers such as Reykjavik, the capital of the country, there was little involvement in a capitalistic way of life. To a large extent, the people of Iceland were farmers and fishermen, and it was from the rural areas that most immigrants to Canada came.

During the latter part of the 19th century, the Icelandic community in Winnipeg experienced a desire for an Icelandic college of their own. Several abortive attempts were tried, but in 1913 public dissension about the college and what it would do were settled with the opening of the Jon Bjarnason Academy. For the first two years the academy was housed in the Lutheran church which was a central meeting place for the community, and in 1915 it was moved to new quarters in a rented part of a building in the heart of the Icelandic area of Winnipeg. Classes to Grade 11 were offered. Most students were from Winnipeg, although there was a smattering of rural enrollments as well. By this time, a religious rift within the Winnipeg Icelandic community was becoming crystallized, with Unitarians on one side and Lutherans on the other. The students at the academy, because of its church connections, were for the main part Lutheran. It had a typical curriculum, but also emphasized a "Christian influence" and training in the Icelandic language and literature. In time, the academy became a center for many cultural activities carried on by voluntary associations dedicated to the retention of Icelandic culture in Canada. It closed in 1940, and the library which had been built up was donated to the University of Manitoba. More of a high school than a college as such, the academy was nevertheless a cultural and educational focus for the Icelandic community, providing a vehicle for ethnic inner-directedness which countered the increasing rates of out-marriage and general cultural and social assimilation.

One last Icelandic Canadian educational venture should be mentioned. The University of Manitoba had accepted Icelandic as a second language, and had given credit for previous instruction in Icelandic to incoming students, but the community was not yet represented at the university level through university courses in Icelandic language or history. Icelandic had been taught for several years at Wesley College, an affiliate of the University of Manitoba, and most Icelandic Canadian students pursuing degrees in the arts attended it, but some prominent members of the community thought that a permanent place for Icelandic studies should be established at the university itself. As in almost all community-wide issues, the community was divided about the feasibility of the establishment of an Icelandic chair. Gradually, however, and in the face of numerous obstacles, funds were raised and in 1952, classes were inaugurated in Icelandic language and literature at the University of Manitoba as part of the new program of the Department of Icelandic Literature and Language. The possibility of the Icelandic language being retained at least as an academic subject in Manitoba had been realized, in spite of an increasing loss of knowledge of it by the children and grandchildren of immigrants. Never heavy in enrollments, the department has swelled in recent years with the enhanced sense of ethnicity among the new generation of the 1970s, who seek an ethnic identity which their parents have lost, or possibly, never had.

Dualism: An Icelandic Cultural Theme[1]

Iceland – a land of "fire and ice" – is a land of contrasts. Volcanoes erupt periodically with their lava encrusted tops and moltenly alive interiors juxtaposed to mute but slowly moving glaciers. Frigid waters from glacial rivers spill over gigantic waterfalls such as fabled *Gullfoss*, while the cities of the nation are often heated by boiling water from underground, and people in Reykjavik bathe year-round in warm springheated outdoor pools. Iceland is a country still experiencing geological evolution and formation.

The theme of contrast in the Icelandic landscape is reflected in the personalities of the people who inhabit it, and the social and cultural forms they have evolved. It is a country of contrast and rarely of compromise. I have touched on this theme in an earlier discussion of the literary and educational traditions of Iceland and their transformations in immigrant adaptations to life in Manitoba. On the *emic* (or personal) level, many Icelanders and Icelandic Canadians dispute its existence. On an *etic* (or cross-cultural) level, it is a reality which must be examined in an anthropological or sociological analysis of either population.

I have decided to call this cultural theme of contrasts "dualism." Its expression in personality and social and cultural forms is more one of "two-sidedness" than of contrast as such. On the social and cultural level, whenever there is one form of an institution, for example, there must also exist another, often identical in form, yet standing in structural opposition to the first. A few examples are all that can be given here, but it is hoped they will illustrate some of the pervasiveness of the theme.

Kin Groups

Closed corporate kin groups, identified with larger farmstead units and their geographical location, composed the basic structural features of

Icelandic society. These units (at least in recent times) did not easily cooperate with one another, even when joined by marriages. This pattern may go back to the earliest settlement of Iceland by maverick Norwegian chiefs, and the farmsteads may be a modern continuation of these early chiefdoms. Kin groups, farmsteads and, on a broader level (although not as pronounced), regional groupings such as "the people of Northeast Iceland" stood in structural opposition to one another. This pattern is retained today and is evident in Icelandic political behavior and business practices in the larger centers such as Reykjavik which have experienced extreme population growth in recent years as a result of the increasing urbanization of Iceland. That is, the structure of rural Iceland continues in urban Iceland in the late 1970s.

These kinship-based features are one evidence of the dualism, at least on a social level, which was brought to Canada by Icelandic immigrants in the last century. Their communities were structured around them, and many of the examples of factionalism over issues of education and journalism which I identified earlier were products of this. A deeper analysis of the role played by kin (farmstead and regionally-based) in early Icelandic Canadian adaptations is needed.[2]

Church Organization

Another example of the dualism theme involves church organizations. In virtually every Icelandic Canadian community in Manitoba there were two churches: the Unitarian and the Lutheran. Every North American Icelander saw the first light of day in a Unitarian or Lutheran home, and forever remained a member of one or the other. Families were lined up against one another in political as well as religious issues. A Unitarian did not marry a Lutheran, for the one was Godless and the other a True Believer. But they were brought together through an ancient Icelandic love of debate. A debate over the Trinity supplanted in Icelandic Canadian communities other issues which created both factionalism and cohesion in communities in Iceland.

Voluntary Association

Many Icelandic Canadian voluntary associations have been formed in Manitoba communities and Winnipeg in particular. Many duplicated one another's goals and purposes. When a group of Icelandic Canadians in Winnipeg formed a temperance organization in 1887, a second association was soon formed, and the two worked in opposition to each other while striving for the same aims. Several other examples could be given. A people who have for more than a 1 000 years struggled to create a society which allowed for independence of spirit and of selfhood have, from the time of formation of the society from which Icelandic Canadians came, thus built and perpetuated a society with built-in structural features which have seemed to militate against the achievement of these goals.

Nevertheless, Icelandic Canadians have consistently worked together to preserve their cultural identity. Perhaps this is seen best in an amalgamation in 1977 of the last two surviving Icelandic Canadian social organizations in Winnipeg which have had large but dwindling memberships: the *Fron* chapter of the Icelandic National League and the Icelandic Canadian Club. The former used the Icelandic language exclusively at meetings, while the latter used English. There was a heated and drawn-out debate about the name of the new organization, but it was resolved. It would not have been a true venture of the Icelandic Canadian community in Winnipeg without it.

Ethnic Identity

Finally, dualism helps us understand why Icelandic Canadians, who for more than 100 years have sought to become non-hyphenated Canadians, still exist as an ethnic group in Winnipeg and elsewhere in Canada. The inward thrust created by structural oppositions has worked against the outward pull of assimilation. The debates have concentrated interest inward. They have militated against total assimilation, while allowing a degree of it to occur. The ultimate example of dualism in Icelandic Canadian culture has been the paradox of a simultaneous drive towards assimilation and cultural retention. The internal factionalism, found on many fronts and a product of structural features brought with them from Iceland has fostered this, and at least in the case of this one ethnic group, helps explain why Icelandic Canadians retain ethnic status within the larger Canadian society.

END NOTES

1. My use of thematic analysis varies in some respects from that of Morris Opler, who first used the concept of themes in anthropology. Whereas Opler's approach is highly psychological, mine is both psychological and structural. However, I hope that I still do justice to his concept (Opler, 1945).
2. A joint long-range interdisciplinary research project being carried out by the University of Manitoba and the University of Iceland is investigating this topic along with many others. The research was initiated in 1976.

SELECTED REFERENCES

Gjerset, Knut. *History of Iceland*. New York: Macmillan, 1924.

Kirkconnell, Watson. *North American Book of Icelandic Verse*. New York: Little and Ives, 1930.

Kristjanson, Wilhelm. *The Icelandic People in Manitoba: A Manitoba Saga*. Winnipeg: Wallingford Press, 1965.

_____ . "Icelandic Canadian Publications in Manitoba." In *The Multilingual Press in Manitoba*. Winnipeg: Canada Press Club, 1974, pp. 121-29.

Lindal, Walter J. *The Icelanders in Canada*. Ottawa and Winnipeg: National Publishers and Viking Printers, 1967.

Opler, Morris. "Themes as Dynamic Forces in Culture," *American Journal of Sociology*, Vol. 51 (1945), pp. 198-206.

Ruth, Roy H. *Educational Echoes: A History of Education of the Icelandic-Canadians in Manitoba*. Winnipeg: Columbia Printers, Ltd., 1964.

Stefansson, Vilhjalmur. *Iceland: The First American Republic*. New York: Doubleday, 1947.

ROBERT F. HARNEY   University of Toronto

The Italian Community in Toronto*

The Pre-World War I Community (1900-14)

Between 1900 and 1914, more Italians entered Canada than any immigrant group except those from the British Isles. They came from the ports of southern Italy or through Swiss border points. Others arrived at random, as members of wandering labor gangs or as petty entrepreneurs from the Little Italies of the American east coast. In Italy, the myth of the New World included all of America. For the migrants who wandered throughout the continent looking for work and a reassuring south Italian *ambiente*[1] crossing national boundaries meant less than the first tentative steps from their villages. In 1903, 2 000 of an estimated 3 000 who worked for the Canadian Pacific Railroad came from the United States.[2] The very causes of Italian emigration produced a capricious pattern of settlement. Not only *la miseria* but also the chance to make good wages drew the sojourner. Chain migration, word of mouth about work on North American railroads, and the activities of a variety of agents combined to increase the flow. In 1892, one line, the Inman Steamship Company, was reputed to have 3 500 agents in Europe.[3] Emigration and migration had become a commerce in Italy, where middle class "brokers" served or preyed on their countrymen.

The Commerce of Migration

Canada had her share of men engaged in this commerce. They came from the trickle of Italian settlers who preceded the new immigration. The most important were immigrant bankers and steamship agents who became employment brokers providing unskilled workers for the railroads and the mines.[4] During the 1904 Royal Commission investigation of Italian immigrant labor in Montreal, an agent for one company admitted that "We pay 25¢ a head for rounding them (Italian laborers) up."[5] The men who did the rounding up were known as *padroni*. It should be noted that the immigrants were often peasants from southern Italy who did not see a job as their right but as something to be wheedled from the employer. Accustomed

---

* A revised version of "The Italian Community in Toronto," in *Two Nations, Many Cultures: Ethnic Groups in Canada*, first edition. Some of the material in different form appeared in *Attenzione* (December 1979, 1:6).

342

to feigning servility in the face of *signori* and petty bureaucrats at home, they fell easily into the *padrone* system.

The railroads and other labor-intensive industries sought a docile and cheap work force while Italian migrants wanted high-paying seasonal work. Many of them had come to Canada not to settle but to amass enough capital to improve their petty holdings at home, to provide a sister's dowry, or to gather passage money for other relatives. Between North American industry and the pre-industrial labor force of rural Italy, it was natural that the *padroni* go-betweens should emerge. Men like Antonio Cordasco and Alberto Dini of Montreal had offices or agents in Toronto, New York, Boston, at clandestine migrant depots like Chiasso on the Swiss-Italian border, and in the small towns of Italy. They owned or influenced Italian-language papers in eastern North America, and they provided track gangs for the railroads and electric street railroads of Canada and the north-eastern United States. Because the railroads and other industries (often culpable because they used the Italian labor gangs as strikebreakers) hired exclusively through the *padroni*, the immigrants were at the mercy of their exploiters. A notice from the boss, Cordasco, to the labor force reflects the extent of his control.

> To the army of the pick and shovel
>
> Italian labourers, bosses and underbosses do not show a double face but only one (be true) have a soldiers courage. Apply to the elegant and solid Italian Bank of Antonio Cordasco if you do not want to weep over your misfortunes in the Spring when the shipments of men will begin. Do not believe that with your dollars or dollar you will be able to get work like your comrades who have been faithful. No, we will inspect our books and money orders and our passage ticket book, and those who will not have their names entered in them in their despair tear out their hair and will call Mr. Cordasco lordship, Don Antonio, let me go to work. No never, will be answered to them, go to those through whom you sent money and so on. A forewarned man is forearmed.[6]

Men, collected in American Little Italies or met by scouts where the Naples steamers docked, then shepherded by interpreters or foremen to remote track work sites, never left their own cultural *ambiente*. Communicating in their own dialect, living on moldy Italian-style bread and over-priced sardines in oil supplied by the *padrone*, they dreamed most often not of the rich North American earth around them but of an impoverished *paese* far away. Indeed, CPR officials admitted that it was the clannish and migrant mentality that made the Italian gangs a reliable work force.[7] Initially, cities like Toronto played a small role in the life of the migrants. They knew its main railroad stations and dock areas since they waited there before being thrust into the hinterland work force. Staying in "inns" and boarding houses owned by *padroni* or by independent older Italian settlers, hampered by ignorance of English, the migrant worker had little sense of the city as a place of opportunity. Still an Italian immigrant *ambiente* began to emerge in Toronto by the 1890s. Centered first around the train station, wharves, and market, and later in St. John's Ward, a neighborhood developed. There were church services in Italian, but in Toronto it was often a Methodist one at the Little Flower mission before it was a Catholic mass.

For many years, the migrants outnumbered the stable town dwellers in the Italian community.[8] Toronto's Union Station had a superintendent of immigration, the powerful Montreal *padrone* Alberto Dini, who maintained one of several Italian employment agencies on York Street.[9] The city had representatives of 21 railroads and after the great fire of 1903 there was much urban construction work. Still, the Italian community grew slowly. Montreal was closer to the trans-continental routes and the spurs and interurban lines of Northern Ontario. One Italo-Canadian writer, reinforcing the image of "Toronto the Good," claimed that Toronto did not appeal to the young migrants because of the absence of liquor and women. Montreal had both. "It was the center of attraction for the Italians who came from the West. Instead of facing a dull winter in Toronto, they pushed into the gay port city."[10]

The Growth of an Ethnic Neighborhood

While the Italians in Toronto did not constitute a massive foreign invasion – there were only about 1 000 permanent settlers in 1900 and less than 10 000 by the end of World War I – myth and stereotypes about the Italian and some competition with native artisans did create an atmosphere that reinforced the need for an ethnic neighborhood. Before the influx of unskilled labor, Italians practised trades and lived symbiotically within Canadian society so that their presence was little noticed. Several things were happening that threatened this symbiosis. A subtle change in the new Italian arrivals corresponded to the growth in North America of racial hostility toward southern Europeans.[11] Settlers with small artisan skills were apparently giving way to unskilled migrants. The latter thought like sojourners, did not learn English, were often bachelors and were clearly "lower class" workers. Anti-Catholic feeling and the xenophobia of a small homogeneous city existed in Toronto, but there was no dangerous competition for work in a city recovering from a terrible fire and replete with labor-intensive enterprises.[12] Yet, as early as the late 1880s even the Italian artisans had been stamped with a double stigmata: scab laborers and excitable Latins. An exchange between the counsel and a witness to the Royal Commission on the Relations of Capital and Labour will illustrate the problem.

Q. Are there any Italians doing laboring work?

A. They take the work home, and they run what are known as sweating shops. They are making quite a pile of money, and have a few slaves under them in the shape of women.[13]

Goldwin Smith who wrote at roughly the same time could not resist noting the arrival of Italians in Canada and gratuitously confimed the stereotype. "There are scatterings of other races, the last arrival being the Italian with his grinding organ and, we hope, without his knife."[14] Within this atmosphere of latent hostility, it was natural for the Italians of Toronto to overcome regional antipathies and to gather together in an "ethnic community".

World War I and its Aftermath (1915-35)

The arrival of an increasing number of women and children required more elaborate institutions. The seasonal nature of some work, combined with a pre-industrial sense of the family as a single economic unit and of the need for a number of minor sources of income, gave diversity to the community. Men who worked as common laborers in summer found work removing snow or hauling in winter; some were scavengers, street entertainers, knife-sharpeners, or fruit peddlers in their spare time. Women picked greens, gathered mushrooms, or did piece work in the nascent garment industry. They had come from a setting where work was seasonal, cyclical, marginal. While few of the new Italian Canadians dreamed of rolling wheat fields, they did buy and cultivate arable patches of ground in and immediately outside of Toronto. These properties played a role in the later development of Italian wealth and suburbs in Toronto.

St. John's Ward became the center of Toronto Italian life, a street life with a pace and purpose at variance with the dour and "indoors" north European city around it.[15] From the outset, Italians shared the Ward with the other major group of newcomers to Toronto, the east European Jews. The relationship was not unusual. Humbert Nelli showed that even in Chicago's Little Italy, the Italians rarely exceeded 50 percent of the total.[16] In New York and Chicago, Jew and Italian lived side by side. R. Glanz claims that the basis of the relationship was an essential lack of competition: Jews tending to trade and Italians to laboring and both to the garment industry.[17] The number of street corner stores that passed from Jewish to Italian hands as the latter moved into the Ward suggests, however, that competition did exist, but that there was a rapport at other levels. Neither group worried excessively about threats to endogamy; initially the strength of religion and family was too great on both sides. Both groups accepted a high level of street activity as the inevitable noise, "hustling," and crowding that preceded the "take-off" from greenhorn to successful immigrant. Jews in numbers had come north into the Ward before the Italians and had, in modern usage, "blockbusted" for the Italians to follow. Still, a typical street of the Ward had Jewish, Italian, and older stock on it. The latter were often "mechanics" (artisans) while the Jews and Italians dominated the storefront and residential pattern. Many older Italians can recount serving as "shabbes goy," the lighters of sabbath fires and runners of errands, for the Orthodox Jews of the neighborhood. Toronto's Little Italy had – along with the Italian Methodist Mission on Elm Street and eventually a parish, The Church of Our Lady of Mt. Carmel – Rumanian and Russian synagogues, some smaller congregations, several Protestant missions to the Jews, and an African Methodist Church. In that sense. St. John's Ward was not just Little Italy, it was the foreign quarter of Toronto.[18]

Occupational Diversification

The growing number of Italians produced both diversity of occupation and upward mobility within the community itself. There were ethnic bankers, postal agents, interpreters, grocers, notaries, steamship agents, and boarding housekeepers. The special food needs of the Italians, although not as likely to cause the proliferation of small shops that ritual required of the Jews, did encourage enterprise. For example, successful pasta factories were started on York Street and later on Centre Avenue in the Ward.[19] Typically, too, a certain number of fruit dealers and merchants began to import provisions (Italian-style cheese, canned fish, vegetables, and pasta), and importing led to travel agencies. Bakeries, confectionaries and a few meat markets and grocery stores sprouted to serve the community. Over the years, the Ward had few hotels (*saloni*) because of Toronto's blue laws; nevertheless, small clubs, boarding houses and a restaurant or two allowed for a glass of wine within the *ambiente*. There was an importer of wine-making equipment as well. Along Elm or Gerrard Streets, Italian was the language of the sidewalks.

Upward mobility in Little Italy was not associated initially with either assimilation or outward mobility. As the choice between laboring in the city and small commercial enterprise grew, status and income varied greatly within the Ward and often within the Italian extended family itself. Brothers living together on Elm or Centre Street might leave their flat in the morning, one to be a brewery worker or street laborer, a second to peddle fruit, and a third to run a grocery and give music lessons downstairs. Only strong parents or expanding business could keep the family destiny a shared one. It was most often the children of the merchants who became the doctors, lawyers, and professionals of the next generation, and, while there did tend to be families that were more successful than others, independent nuclear families emerged.[20]

Only an impression of the relationship of upward mobility, residential patterns, and assimilation is possible now. If we divide the occupations of Toronto Italians in the period into (1) those self-employed who served the *ambiente* for their fellow Italians (the provisioners, grocers, notaries, steamship agents), (2) those who serviced the non-Italian community (the fruit peddlers and later, the storekeepers, musicians, cobblers and shoeshine men, tailors, and barbers), and (3) laborers in the nascent industrial structure and those in varieties of street, railroads, sewer, and construction work, we can see the social history of the Ward and the outlying Italian neighborhoods more clearly.

First, one must record the courage and enterprise of men who spoke no English yet chose to live outside the Ward among their clientele.[21] Dependent on the *ambiente*, a high percentage of the barbers, tailors, and peddlers daily commuted back to the Ward, but others dared to move out. Fruit men rose before dawn to buy produce directly from the arriving freight trains and pushed carts many miles through alien streets to sell to the non-Italian community.[22] The logic of "time as money" caused them, as their business prospered, to settle and open stores outside the Ward. By 1912 half the fruit dealers in the city were Italian; by 1924, more than half. In the same period, Italians represented only 5 percent of the barbers and 3 percent of the grocers in the city, while the City Directories showed that the Greeks and the Syrians provided sharp competition in shoeshine and cobbling work as well as in producing and selling confectionaries. A very high percentage of the fruit vendors operated outside the Italian receiving areas. They opened stores first in response to the non-Italian consumer, but such shops later became the nuclei of new Italian residential areas. Men who started as fruit vendors then moved on to open grocery stores, then steamship agencies, boarding houses, and even subcontracting – always from one corner store – mediated in many ways between their less city-wise compatriots and the hazards of Toronto. New neighborhoods then were partly artifice, partly spontaneous. Following other groups such as the Jews from the worst to the better housing areas of the city, Italian housing patterns then depended on commerce and industry, from the heavier street construction and primary industries to the sale of fresh fruit.[23]

One sort of distribution that may have been as important as the fruit vendors was that set by the street railway development and by the construction of sheds and warehouses in the train yards of greater Toronto. Just as the railroads played a key role in the settlement of various ethnic groups across the continent, so the substations and junctions created little clusters of foreign laborers, and later their dependents, in various outlying parts of the city. Track maintenance in the severe winter further attenuated the settlement pattern. In the city itself electric street railroads served to distribute the once clustered and alien population. Motormen and conductors who worked the long $11^{1}/2$ and 12-hour shifts on the street railroads found it logical to reside at different turns and junctions on the line.

Not only did subcolonization go on in relation to jobs or better housing, the Ward also began to lose its Italian flavor. At the southern margins along Dundas, the Chinese began to encroach. The old Little Flower Mission became a Mission to the Chinese. The Ukrainians, exiled supporters of Hetman Skoropadsky's government, moved into the top floors of the Ward's two- and three-storey houses. Italian stores in the center and north of the neighborhood gave way not before a new ethnic group but in the face of a growing Bohemia along Gerrard-Hayter, a conscious and striking parallel to the Italian *avant garde* confrontation in New York's Greenwich Village.[24]

Although the Ward remained as Little Italy to many outsiders, it lost to the Clinton-Mansfield section as the primary receiving area for newcomers. By 1935 that area had a United, an Evangelical, and two Catholic Churches with largely Italian communicants. A hotel, the Venezia, steamship agents, and Italian grocery stores were also there. A third neighborhood – following the general northwesterly development of the city and near a major CPR junction – grew up around Davenport and Dufferin. It had fewer storefronts but St. Clements (later Saint Mary of the Angels) and a United Church Mission served the newcomers.[25]

Immigration Disrupted

The war years interrupted Italian immigration to Toronto, but heavy immigration resumed until 1924. Then the combination of Fascism in Italy, fear and hostility over the new American immigration quota, the tightening of Canadian restrictions on the unskilled, and the Depression stemmed the flow to Toronto almost completely.[26] The consequences for Italo-Toronto were twofold. The Ward and its successors in the west end could no longer be sustained by the continuing flood of greenhorns. As a result, certain stores and institutions in the ethnic neighborhood either atrophied or had to alter their nature. For example, immigrant bankers disappeared or moved into real estate and Toronto-centered activities. The amount of money transmissions to Italy and money changing declined. Ownership of boarding houses and inns passed on to other ethnic groups or disappeared as families became more affluent and immigrant *paesano* boarders dwindled in number. Steamship agencies failed or found their alternatives in importing Italian goods or preparing junkets for the affluent *Americani* of Toronto who wanted to show off their respectability to the newly respectable Fascist Italy. When the Volstead Act in the United States brought Prohibition, restaurant and liquor activities increased in the Italo-Canadian community.[27] Because of all this change, Italians in Toronto by the late 1920s had a full social pyramid. Sons of early settlers were entering the professions, many men who had started as peddlers or manual laborers had become prosperous. For many, community meant only "weekend ethnicity," a trip to one of the Little Italy areas for cheese, pasta, and veal. Others, however, continued to cling to an *ambiente* that they found comfortable, and to a preference for cultural dualism over assimilation.

As their occupation status and levels of acculturation had changed, the associational life of Toronto Italians also changed. From small *paese*-based clubs and mutual aid (burial) societies, they had moved to new institutions that were both more Italian and more Canadian than the initial organizations. Where once there had been clubs such as the Trinacria for Sicilians, there were, side by side with the "home-town clubs", clubs open to all Italians such as the Circolo Colombo and the Società Italo-Canadese, an amalgam of three mutual aid societies. Those who, 20 or 30 years earlier in Italy, had counted a man from a village miles away as a *forestiere* (stranger) now, in the new environment, developed fellow feeling for other Italians. *Campanilismo* did not disappear, hostility particularly between northerners and southerners continued. Still the small size of the Toronto community and the fact that, unlike New York or Montreal, it was not an entrepôt for all people and goods passing from a given village to its colonies in America, meant that continued localism was neither as possible nor as desirable. The struggle against such diverse enemies as Protestant temperance societies and Jansenist Irish clergy increased solidarity among the city's Italians.

The New "Nationalism"

World War I heightened the New "nationalism" among overseas Italians. The so-called *treno degli italiani* that gathered volunteers from Vancouver to the East Coast to serve Italy against the Triple Alliance stopped in Toronto where it was met both by more volunteers and Italian bands.[28] Indeed, there were many varieties of identification. One could be Italian, Italo-Canadian, or a Canadian of Italian descent. Although much of this was self-definition, a statement from the Casa Metodista (Italian Methodist Mission) showed some of the receiving society's confusion about identity. "Our aim is to make good citizens out of Italians and we know that by preaching the Gospel and endeavoring to bring the newcomers to a high spiritual life, they will become good citizens."[29] In World War I, service to the Italian ally was an acceptable form of Canadianism. Dual loyalty would be more difficult later on.

Most of the community stayed suspended between full assimilation (in the form of Protestantism and the changing of patronymics on the one hand) and the remembered Italian origins on the other. Visitors back to Italy found their fractured North American dialect and confident manner alien to their own kinsmen who had stayed behind. At the same time, in Toronto, most felt that prosperity and reasonable acculturation did not require giving up Catholicism or fully giving in to Anglo-conformity.

Men, mostly of humble and petty capitalist origins possessing a high level of Umbertine propriety and respect for property, nonetheless had undergone that part of the North American experience baffling to all immigrants. In Italy, they were used to being despised as *contadini* (peasants) by city people, and as *cafone* (rubes) or *bestie* (manual laborers) by their own upper classes. In Canada they had not expected to be looked down on simply as Italians. Even if they were humble peasants, they came of Europe's "mother culture." As success came to the individual Italian, his need for dignity was heightened. It was proper that part of that dignity should relate to ethnicity, to the place of the Italian nation and of Italians in the world.

It is in such a setting that we should understand the response of Toronto's Italians to the rise of Fascism in Italy. Many, particularly unionists, immediately saw Mussolini as a counter-revolutionary thug. Others, however, could not help but see the new Italy through their own immigrant eyes. Ignazio Silone captured the pathos of their view.

> "Descendants of eternal Rome," he began, "O thou my people. . . . Tell me . . . Who was it who brought culture and civilization to the whole Mediterranean and to all known Africa?" "We did," voices replied. "But the fruits were gathered by others." "Tell me again, I pray you, who brought culture and civilization to the whole of Europe, even to the misty shores of England, and built towns and cities where savages had grubbed for food with wild hogs and deer?" "We did," voices replied "but the fruits were enjoyed by others." "Tell me again I beg you, who discovered America?" This time everybody rose to his feet and shouted, "We did! We did! but others enjoy it. . . ." "And tell me again, if you please, who are the people who have emigrated to all the countries of the world to dig mines, build bridges, make roads, dry swamps? . . ." "We did. We did," they shouted. "And thus you have explained the origin of all your ills. But now, after centuries of humiliation and injustice, Providence has sent us the man who will give our country all its rights that others have usurped."[30]

Mussolini, the champion of the middle classes against Bolshevism, seemed to have won respect and approval for Italy in the world. His solution to the problem of the "red flaggers" and later, the Depression, found support from part of the press in Canada and from many businessmen, academics, and veterans. Respectable Italo-Canadians, full of the patriotism of World War I, could, between 1922 and 1935, support Fascism with the full approval of their fellow Canadians. At last for the Anglo-Saxons, who had never understood the importance of Dante or Verdi, there was an Italian and an Italy to obliterate the image of ragged street musicians and *cafoni* track laborers.

In Toronto, *Il Bollettino*, a paper published from Elm Street, was Fascist-controlled. Attempts to mount anti-Fascist organizations such as Matteotti Clubs met only limited success.[31] For a time a socialist newspaper, *L'Unita*, fought against the official line. With the Lateran Pact and Mussolini's increased popularity in church circles, Fascism became equated with respectability in Toronto's Little Italy. Clergy, businessmen/advertisers in the local Italian press, *Il Bollettino* itself, Italian officials in the city, and, until the invasion of Ethiopia in 1936, much of non-Italian public opinion in Toronto, made life difficult for "unpatriotic" or "leftist" elements in the Italian community. True to the city's general tendency to a colonial mentality the Italians of Toronto remained under the influence of Montreal organizations such as the Italian United Moral Front or New

York organizations like the Sons of Italy. *Il Progresso Italo-Americano*, published in New York, led all other Italian language papers in circulation in Toronto. By 1927, the Fascist government had replaced the Commissioner of Emigration with a Director General of Italians Abroad. Italo-Canadians were considered overseas Italian subjects and not emigrants lost to the mother country.[32] This wooing of the overseas Italians was one reason for Fascism's relative popularity. Centering on the *Casa d'Italia* at Dundas and Beverley Streets, Fascists controlled the life of the community with educational, social, and ideological organizations more familiar among displaced persons or political exiles than among immigrants.[33]

Fascism, then, was an acceptable political belief in the Toronto of the 1920s and 1930s. Although many Italo-Canadians paid no attention to politics, the lack of sophistication of the immigrant aided the Fascist regime's efforts to reach them. Monarchism, Catholicism, the esteem of their Canadian neighbors, and the general desire for propertied respectability colluded to make it so. For example, the triumphal passage of Italo Balbo and his squadron of hydroplanes on the way to the Chicago World's Fair was a major event for Italo-Canadians, as important as the appearance of a great musical maestro like Caruso. At one level, of course, the roar of huge Savoia-Marchetti seaplanes was a harbinger of Fascism's bombast and belligerence, for Italo-Canadians it was a source of pride in the new Italy: industrialized, a great Power, and yet evoking Columbus, Vespucci, and the Cabots. The point is that if few Italo-Torontonians were Fascists, fewer escaped some contact with the regime or its programs.

The Chaos of the World War II Era (1936-45)

As Fascist foreign policy became aggression, Canadian public opinion, following that of Great Britain, grew hostile to Italy and to the overt political activity in the Toronto and Montreal Italian communities. At a time when Toronto's Italian women were sending their wedding rings to be melted down to pay for Italy's new imperialism, the Canadian press was denouncing Mussolini's aggression in Ethiopia. Between 1936 and 1940 Italians recognized the possibility of conflict between their primary loyalty to Canada and sympathy for the mother country and her politics. When Italy declared war against Great Britain and her allies, Italo-Canadians were confused and apprehensive. One old Italian, interned as a dangerous enemy alien at Petawawa, had to ask a fellow prisoner whether Italy declared war with France or Germany.[34]

Non-Italians who had flirted with the varieties of Fascism overcame their indiscretions by loyalty and sacrifice during the war. It was not so easy for Toronto Italians. On June 13, 1940, the Minister of Justice announced to the Commons the government's policy toward known Fascists and all those of "Italian racial origins who have become naturalized British subjects since September 1, 1929." The Honourable Minister Lapointe explained that "the very minute that news was received that Italy had declared war on Great Britain and France he signed an order for the internment of many hundreds of men whose names were on the list of the RCMP as suspects. I cannot give the House the number; I have been asked by the head of the mounted police not to do this because it might hamper his work."[35]

One can imagine the terror and upset among the city's people of Italian descent. The RCMP raids were directed only against potential fifth columnists but they appeared inclusive and retrospective in their definition of Fascists. The rumor persisted in Toronto that the RCMP confiscated the guest book of the Casa d'Italia (Casa Fascista) and rounded up everyone on it. More frightening was the violence and vigilantism of the Toronto public. It was reported in the House and in the press that at least 16 Italian storefronts in the city were vandalized when the war broke out.[36] Instances of harassment and estrangement occurred with painful frequency in the first days of the war. Then too, while Members of Parliament assured the government that various German groups were loyal Canadian citizens, no Toronto voices there were raised on behalf of the Italians. Far from it. The Member from Broadview warned that "During the Spanish trouble, Italian submarines found shelter on the southeast coast of that country, and Italy has modern submarines that can cross the Atlantic Ocean and return without refueling."[37] Continued American neutrality and the ties of kinship and commerce between Toronto and New York Italians also troubled the legislators.

> "This writer goes on to say that we must watch out when Italy enters the war, because of the number of foreigners in the United States, and the German-Italian-Russian spy propaganda. He also says that there are more coloured people in that country than there are in Africa and urges that some organizations in the Dominions should cope with these questions before it is too late."[38]

The Member for York West congratulated the government on the absence of sabotage in his riding which was "an industrial constituency one in which we have a large number of foreigners.[39] Thus, the disloyalty of the Italian population was assumed.

The impact of internment on Toronto Italians is hard to assess. It cannot be compared with the removal of the Japanese. No one's property was confiscated. More political and random than racial, the cost to the community was nonetheless terrible. Men who one day held government contracts to produce war material, the next day found themselves shipped to Camp Petawawa where they languished or wasted their talent on road gangs. A Montreal Italian, Mario Duliani, wrote a moving account of life at Petawawa in La Villa Sans Femmes.[40] Fascists and Italo-Canadian leaders were interned at the camp, but the real hardship fell on their dependents.

Families were left with no livelihood during the difficult first months of the war. Although the church and other organizations cared, help came slowly from group charities lest their efforts be interpreted as support for Fascist sympathizers. During the war, numbers of Italian families from outlying areas and from isolated rural or mining communities moved into the College-Grace and the Dufferin-Brandon areas. They came because of apprehension but also, like others, because of the defense production boom. Paradoxically, some sought rapid assimilation, while others sought shelter in concentrated Italian populated areas.

Migration Resumes (Post-World War II to the Present Era)

The instinctive gathering in of Toronto's Italians during the war had important consequences for the new mass migration of the 1950s. During the war more Italian entrepreneurs had moved from subcontracting and the skilled building trades into heavier and larger construction work. This, in turn, provided some network of job opportunities for unskilled countrymen in the postwar era. The obvious loyalty of Italo-Canadians and the fact that Italy itself by 1943 appeared to be more a victim than a member of the Fascist Axis facilitated the healing of wartime wounds.

The Canadian government's search for unskilled labor in the postwar boom and the possibility of sponsorship renewed the flow of immigrants from Italy. Although the Italo-Canadian community was more Neapolitan and Sicilian in its origins than were the newcomers, it is possible to see that many family chains from the Abruzzi, Molise and Calabria, long interrupted by exclusionist legislation in North America and Fascism in Italy, became operative again. Large numbers of northern Italians, particularly Friulians and Venetians with little or no connection with the Italo-Canadian community, also arrived.

In a single year like 1956 or 1957, the arriving Italian immigrants outnumbered the 20 000 Italo-Canadians of Toronto.[41] A declining ethnic neighborhood in the west end burgeoned into new "Little Italies", and men who a few years earlier found their *italianità* a liability, now found it an avenue to commercial success. Professionals, children of the Ward's families, relearned Italian or struggled with dialect in order to reach the newcomer.

No careful analysis exists of the role of the Italo-Canadians in the postwar Italian community of Toronto. Even accepting the natural advantages of speaking English and being wise in the ways of the land, one gets the sense that their role was disproportionate. At the same time, it is incorrect to envisage an idyll in which Italo-Canadians led and the newcomers followed. The historical and cultural distance between the two groups was immense. To the newcomers, Italo-Canadians were more like Canadians than Italians or they were "umbertine", that is, fossils of the Age of King Umberto (roughly the equivalent of Victorian). Their sense of probity and even of Italy was remote from that of immigrants who had lived through Fascism and the Allied occupation. The Italo-Canadians, in turn, found the greenhorns blatantly Italian, obtuse, and ungrateful.[42]

Although there are obvious changes in the *ambiente* and ecology of migration, the idea of a commerce of migration and of a *borghesia mediatrice* similar to that which existed at the beginning of the century, can be pursued in contemporary Toronto.[43] The most important changes are probably the aeroplane, the heightened consciousness of Italian nationality and higher literacy in the post-Fascist period, and the presence in the Canadian-Italian migration of more northern Italians and more urban people.

Despite higher literacy and the benign welfare state, immigrants still use a "middle class go-between" in the same manner that migrants once used *padroni*. Signing the wrong papers can bring anything from unwanted aluminum siding to deportation. It was estimated in 1961 that 25 percent of the Italians in Toronto spoke no English at all. Many others were surely functionally illiterate in English; most are more comfortable in dialect than in Italian itself.

There is in Italo-Toronto, dependence on middle-class "brokers" ranging from ethnic driver education schools and realtors to consulting only doctors from one's *paese*. The most typical broker in the community is probably the travel agent. The Italo-Canadian Commercial Directory for 1971 lists about 50 agents in Toronto, although the number would be far greater if it included formal and informal sub-agents.[44] Toronto agencies often have business or familial ties with sub-agents in Italy, and some also tend to serve a specific *paese*: e.g., the Trinacria agency for Sicilians, the Venezia agency for people from the northeast of Italy. The following, in order of frequency, are the services that first-generation Toronto Italians expected a travel agent to render: (1) tickets, prepaid tickets for relatives in Italy and other travel arrangements, (2) arrangement of passports, (3) "going to immigration," (4) remittances, (5) helping with unemployment insurance, (6) making out income tax forms, (7) dealing with the Workmen's Compensation Board, OHIP, Old Age Pensions, and (8) dissolving partnerships and other notarial work.[45] It is estimated that before the introduction of the current points system, 80 percent of the migrants to Toronto from Italy were "sponsored." Sponsorship constitutes the most obvious form of chain migration. Yet 60 percent of the people interviewed had consulted travel agents about sponsoring relatives, and some had depended on agents to find them sponsors. All had paid for the services rendered over and above the price of prepaid tickets.

All this is not intended to suggest the existence of an especially exploitative bourgeoisie or to justify the "waspish" response of those who always dismiss immigrant problems as the exploitation of "one dirty foreigner by another." It does maintain that a coherent class analysis can cross oceans in a way that the random and episodic study of separate kinds of enterprise cannot.

Along with problems of generational change and the persistence of regionalism among Toronto Italians, the differences between the old Italo-Canadians and the recent immigrants have not disappeared. The latter naturally tend to date the Italian presence in the city from their own arrival, and fail to realize that Toronto has seen all phases of Italian migration to North America. Properly understood, the continuity of the Italo-Canadian story reaches back across the war years and the arrival of new masses of Italians to the first migrant laborers of the late 19th century.

Metropolitan Toronto ranks today with Sao Paolo, New York, Chicago, and Buenos Aires as one of the largest Italian settlement areas outside Italy. Estimates as to the number of Italian descendants among Toronto's two million residents vary from 250 000 to half a million – that is, up to 25 percent of the city's total population. The remarkable feature of Toronto's Italian community is not its size, however, but the closeness of its ties with Italy. It is unique in North America because most of its inhabitants are post-World War II immigrants and their children. The vast majority of them live in the densely populated corridor in the western part of the metropolitan area known as Toronto Italia. There, residents can read one of a half-dozen Italian-language newspapers, tune in to Italian radio and television stations, attend Italian plays and movies, and know that their children will learn Italian, as well as English, in school.

Italians live their ethnicity as their natural culture; they are perplexed by, and a bit disdainful of, comparable Little Italies in the United States, where concern with ethnic identity lacks any connection with today's Italian culture. (The director of an Italian school and cultural center in Toronto who attended an "Italian Week" in Philadelphia recalled it as "a pathetic, commercialized mix of cheap ethnic T-shirts, Caruso records, and pizza that only a non-Italian could eat.") Toronto Italia is an immigrant quarter, much like those in the United States at the turn of the century. But postwar immigrants brought a sense of values reflecting the urban, national life of contemporary Italy, rather than the localism of the small towns and regions.

Greengrocers still advertise local Italian town names on their company signs, but the array of businesses and shops along St. Clair Avenue or any other thoroughfare in Toronto Italia reveals the change that has taken place. Along with the usual restaurants, cafés, soccer-supporter bars, travel agents, Franciscans and Scalabrini, one also encounters the names of Necchi and Olivetti, and establishments catering to the demand for the latest Italian-made goods, from business machines to fashions. Fiats – slowly being replaced by Ladas, the Fiat-franchised cars assembled in the Soviet Union – compete with Mustangs as status symbols among young Italian Canadians.

The complexity of Toronto Italia is also evident in its social and political organizations, where the leadership is often an uncomfortable alliance of prewar Italian Canadians and postwar professionals and technicians. Both groups seem to interpret the issues of North American life in a dizzying variety of ways, and possibilities for misunderstanding (based on transplanted political ideologies, local Ontario politics, Italian regionalism, and on which immigrant cohort one comes from) lurk within every community organization. Thus, there is always the danger of a group's collapsing into name-calling factionalism and ineffectuality. It is common to hear members of organizations dismissing those who disagree with them as "pawns" or "paid agents" of the Italian Consulate, the Italian Communist Party, the Christian Democrat Party, or even of the Ontario Progressive Conservatives now in office. Inside and outside the community there are some who dismiss such factionalism as typically Italian; but these critics contribute mindlessly to anti-Italian sterotypes, while missing the point that a community as large and variegated as Toronto Italia cannot be reduced to a political monotone. Little Italies in the United States may place a higher value on ethnic solidarity and cohesion – as politics reduced their ethnicity to mere pressure-group tactics – but Toronto's Italian ethnoculture is too rich and healthy to succumb to such a strategy.

At a recent conference on heritage language education (a government-supported program that teaches Italian to children of Italian descent), both the factionalism and the ethnic creativity it can produce were apparent. A representative of the Italian government, introduced as an educational expert, referred throughout her speech to the pupils as "figli dei lavoratori italiani emigrati all'estero" (children of Italian workers migrated abroad). The phrase implied the Italian government's view that immigrants to Canada are merely sojourners, whose children will naturally maintain the Italian language, gravitate to Italy for their higher education, and generally act as cultural wards of the Italian state. The educator was obviously drawing a parallel between Italian Canadians and the seasonal Italian guest-workers in West Germany and other European countries. Her approach, if taken seriously, would have been insulting to Italian Canadians who are preserving their heritage through local initiative. The Ontario government, on the other hand, sees the Italians as "new Canadians" free to celebrate their *italianità* for a generation or so within Canada's multicultural society before they eventually join the mainstream.

Between the cultural imperialism of the Italian government and the honey-coated rim of the Canadian melting pot, there are those who believe that a Toronto Italia, or at least an Italian-Canadian culture, lasting over many generations, can come into being. The Italian density of the city has in fact fostered a cultural separatism which sees in Quebec's survival as a French-speaking entity a model for Toronto Italia's future. Italian-Canadian intellectuals profess to take Ottawa seriously when it accepts their

right to maintain their heritage; but few can honestly believe, after prolonged contact with Anglo-Canadian officials and other ethnic groups, that
such a future is possible.

Whether Toronto's intense Italian *ambiente* now is simply a latter-day
echo of New York's Mulberry Street or Boston's North End at the turn of
the century, or whether it in fact signals the beginning of a cultural enclave
like Quebec, there is no doubt that Toronto Italia today has an unusual
degree of institutional completeness. In Toronto Italia, it is possible for a
man or woman to work, enjoy leisure and cultural activities, gain access to
government agencies and social services, and retire to an Italian rest home
without ever using the English language.

The changes in Toronto Italia and the new respectability of *italianità* are
startling and confusing to pre-World War II Italian residents, who endured
the suspicion of the Fascist period. The older residents had been the natural
intermediaries between the newcomers and Canadian society in the 1950s,
but in succeeding decades they found themselves being eased out of positions of influence in the community by the successful postwar immigrants.
The Italian-Canadian professional or businessman who, as a teenager may
have walked a grandmother downtown once a month so that she could
report in as an enemy alien, was now brought face to face with immigrants
who had lived under Fascism for 20 years. Not only did the newcomers seem
blatantly Italian, there was also the specter of either Fascism or Marxism in
their background. To the newcomers, the Italian Canadians were either integrated to the point of eating like Englishmen, or humble oafs who had
never dared to ask the host society for anything beyond a hot meal. *Non
Dateci Lenticchie*, "Don't Feed Us Lentils," was the derisive title of the
first book published in Toronto by a postwar Italian immigrant. One marked
result of the dynamic conflict in ideas between the new and old immigrants
has been the change in power relations between the city's Italians and
authorities. For example, even though Toronto Italians had served before
the war on the Catholic school board, and even though Rome government
agencies had succeeded in creating some Italian language classes in the
schools in the 1930s, no one then could have conceived of the massive
alliance between Catholic school power and *italianità* that exists in the city
today.

In Ontario, Catholic schools receive tax dollars from the familes that use
them. Thus, they are neither parochial nor private institutions, nor are they
in any financial difficulty. In fact, they are booming. An alliance has
emerged between the clergy and the ethnic intelligentsia, the former seeming
to believe that retention of the Italian language will ensure retention of the
faith, and the latter seeing the Catholic schools as institutions for animating
Italian cultural values. The result is a situation in West End neighborhoods
where Catholic schoolyards are crowded with temporary classroom
buildings while nearby public schools atrophy.

At least 3 000 students now take college-level Italian courses in the city's major universities, and many hundreds have majored in Italian studies over the past few years. These people – grammar and secondary school teachers, librarians, the cultural bureaucrats of government and community organizations – want to encourage the maintenance of separate ethnic neighborhoods and schools, and they have the political power to impose heritage language programs.

Only a veteran observer of Toronto Italia can follow the community's institutional life. A host of organizations, represented by acronyms like FACI, ICBC, and CIBPA dominate the pages of the ethnic press, and no glossary of acronyms is provided for the casual reader. Accounts of their activities vary according to the political commitments of the newspapers: Corriere Canadese (progressive conservative), Il Giornale di Toronto (liberal), Forze Nuove (socialist), Nuovo Mondo (communist), and a half-dozen less well-defined publications. Trying to follow the struggles that have surrounded such community issues as the attempt to form a single Italian Canadian cultural center to monitor the influence of the Italian government, or to create an effective umbrella organization is a bit like attending an Italian version of the Mad Hatter's tea party in *Alice in Wonderland*. Issues and rivalries intermesh so that only the regular party-goers know who is being pleasant to whom at any given time.

In 1969, an attempt was made to create an umbrella organization for Toronto Italia called FACI (Federation of the Association of Italian Clubs). The organization was to include a considerable array of institutions, whose representatives ranged from crusty old infighters to hobbyists and social workers.

The Ontario government inadvertently noted how difficult FACI's task would be when a Cabinet minister remarked that until the organization was founded there was nowhere to "obtain a responsible, responsive, and representative viewpoint of the Italian community in Metro Toronto." But within a few years FACI had run into trouble. At a time when legislation to restrict immigration was being put forward and when ethnic community briefs would have been crucial, FACI did not respond, and instead seemed to many to be concentrating on award nights, big dinners, and Columbus week celebrations. FACI has, however, had positive results in the development of the National Congress of Italian Canadians and in establishing a school and learning center in Toronto, the *Centro scuola e cultura italiana*.

CIBPA, the Canadian Italian Businessmen and Professionals Association, has not submerged its identity in FACI and carries on its own programs, as do the Sons of Italy and other fraternal orders. The most important group still carrying on a separate social and cultural effort is ICBC, the Italian Canadian Benevolent Corporation. Led by savvy, successful businessmen and developers, with a strong Friulian contingent, ICBC sometimes seems impatient with the ideological and cultural preoccupations of FACI and has developed a power base of its own in the northwestern part of the city, with a showpiece retirement home, Villa Colombo, and the massive Columbus Center as a base for the community's social and cultural activities.

Although the community is at times hamstrung by its internal conflicts, it has so far managed to sustain debate without becoming debilitated. In the long run, however, it seems unlikely that Toronto Italia will be able to support separate cultural centers, one uptown, one downtown, one dominated by ICBC, the other by some combination of the Congress and the Centro.

Lately, a special problem has emerged for Toronto Italia, which, although itself disturbing, has brought a degree of unanimity to the community. Canada's mass media have, only in the past few years, broadcast a series of pseudo-documentaries about the role of Italians in organized crime. One, a three-part, prime-time effort, strongly implied that certain Calabrian colonies in Canada were actually secret criminal societies. Another besmirched the reputation of an Italian political figure by suggesting that a letter he had written on behalf of an imprisoned constituent linked him to criminal activities. Senator Peter Bosa of Toronto has undertaken the difficult and important task of fighting anti-Italian stereotyping in the media. The Senator acted after a Gallup poll showed a startling rise in the number of Canadians who identified Italians with crime.

Bosa and others recognize that, if the mass media and Anglo-Canadian society promote a lack of self-esteem among younger Italian Canadians, no amount of language courses or community organizing will be sufficient to slow assimilation or prevent intergenerational conflict. In fact, Toronto Italia may not be able to long afford the luxury of internal discord. Although in its diversity it may resemble Florence or any of the great Italian cities, it operates in an uncomprehending, occasionally hostile, North American environment.

In a late 1970s issue of *Toronto Life* magazine, some Torontonians of Italian descent complained that the popular image of Italians was still the old stereotype of the undereducated construction worker and fruit peddler. The new image, they felt, should be that of successful developers, lawyers, and importers of Milanese chrome furniture. Obviously, such a characterization of Italian Canadians misses the truth as much as the older stereotypes do. Toronto Italia, with a population the size of Florence, drawn from all the provinces of Italy and all the waves of immigration, has no typical people, no valid stereotypes. It differs as much from contemporary Italy as it does from the North American Little Italies of 70 years ago. The task of its present leadership will be to preserve for future generations Toronto Italia's special combination of modern *italianità* and prewar immigrant experience.

END NOTES

1. The term *ambiente* is used in this paper to designate a social and cultural atmosphere present in the ethnic neighborhood that was an evocation of the small towns of southern Italy and yet something that became a uniquely Italo-American setting.

2. *Royal Commission To Inquire into the Immigration of Italian Labourers (Montreal).* Ottawa: Ministry of Labour, 1904, p. 44. Cited henceforth as *Royal Commission (Italian).* Vol. VI. *The Cultural Contribution of the Other Ethnic Groups,* of the *Report of the Royal Commission on Bilingualism and Biculturalism* (Ottawa, 1969) has convenient tables on yearly immigration. The statistics do not account for seasonal Italo-American work gangs or tally the rates of sojourning, return, and repatriation among young Italian laborers. The best general studies are R.F. Foerster, *The Italian Emigration of Our Times* (Harvard, 1919) and the articles in S.M. Tomasi and M.H. Engel, eds., *The Italian Experience in the United States.* (New York, 1970).

3. H.P. Fairchild, *Immigration* (New York, 1913), p. 148.

4. For the workings of the *padrone* system, see. L. Iorizzo, "The Padrone and Immigrant Distribution," in S.M. Tomasi and M.H. engel, eds., *The Italian Experience in the United States*; and H. Nalli "The Italian Padrone System in the United States," in *Labor History* No. 2 Spring 1964. The chief employers were the CPR, the Grand Trunk, Dominion Coal Co. and a number of mining operations.

5. *Royal Commission (Italian)*, p. 168.

6. *Royal Commission (Italian)*, pp. 106-7.

7. Testimony of Mr. Burns, CPR hiring agent, to the *Royal Commission (Italian)*, p. 55.

8. M. Zaslow, *The Opening of the Canadian North, 1870-1914* (Toronto, 1971), p. 192. The author estimates that over 25 percent of the Ontario Italian population in the 1900s was in the North. That figure would be higher in summer. A spokesman for the Italian Immigrant Aid Society told the *Royal Commission (Italian)*, p. 12, that the Montreal Italian population went from 2 000 in summer to upwards of 10 000 in winter. The parallel seems to have held for Toronto's 1 000 permanent Italian residents.

9. First called A. Dini and Bros. and later known as the International Employment Association Ltd. Unless otherwise noted, detail about the Toronto community is drawn from the *Might's Toronto City Directory* and the Toronto Public Library Collection of Newspaper clippings on Immigration. The only scholarly narrative about Italians in Toronto can be found in the first chapters of Samuel Sidlofsky's *Post-War Immigrants in the Changing Metropolis with Special References to Toronto's Italian Population*, Ph.D. Thesis, University of Toronto, 1969. As the title indicates, the thesis is concerned with the later immigration.

10. A. Spada, *The Italians in Canada* (Ottawa, 1969), p. 265.

11. See J. Higham, *Strangers in the Land: Patterns of American Nativism, 1860-1925* (New York: Atheneum, 1963) and O. Handlin, "Old Immigrants and New," in his *Race and Nationality in American Life* (New York: Little, Brown & Co., 1957). The same views are expressed in J.S. Woodsworth, *Strangers Within Our Gates* (Toronto, 1909).

12. See the comments of the Secretary of the Charity Organization Society of Montreal in *Royal Commission (Italian)*, p. 27.

13. *Royal Commission on the Relation of Capital and Labor*, Vol. 5 *Evidence Ontario* (Ottawa, 1889), p. 628, cited henceforth as *Royal Commission (Capital and Labor)*. Italics are mine.

14. Goldwin Smith, *Canada and the Canadian Question,* ed. by C.C. Berger (Toronto, 1971), p. 34 (first published in 1891).

15. The intersections of Elm and Bay, Elm and Elizabeth, Elm and Centre had predominantly Italian storefronts. They represented the geographical center of the *ambiente*.

16. H. Nelli, *Italians in Chicago, 1880-1930. A Study in Ethnic Mobility. New York: Oxford University Press, 1973, p. 25.*

17. R. Glanz, *Jew and Italian: Historic Group Relations and the New Immigration.* New York: Ktav Publishing House, 1971, p. 9.

18. The decine of the Ward as a Little Italy, usually attributed to the expropriation of properties for hospitals, seems much more related to the arrival of new immigrants, the Chinese and then the Ukrainians pushing up from Dundas Street. Given the under-enumeration of transients and boarders in the City Directories, it is difficult to measure and record the impact of the newcomers.

19. The local enterprise was bought up by Catelli, the Montreal-based Italian food producer. Control of Toronto Italian foodstuffs showed the dualism between Montreal and New York influence. For example, the Tuscan-style cigars that the immigrants enjoyed were either De Nobile, made in New York, or Marca Gollo, produced in Montreal.

20. Some of these tendencies can be found in C. Ware, *Greenwich Village, 1920-1930: A Comment on American Civilization in the Post-War Years* (New York: Octagon Books, 1965), p. 153. See also L. Tomasi, *The Italian American Family.* Staten Island, N.Y.: Center for Migration Studies, 1972. For this study, a number of Italian extended families in Toronto were followed over time, occupation, and residential change through city directories and interviews.

21. M. Puzo, "Chasing a Dream: Italians in Hell's Kitchen," in T.W. Wheeler, ed. *Immigrant Experience: The Anguish of Becoming American*. Baltimore: Penguin Books, 1972, pp. 47-48.

22. Attempts to see fruit vending as natural to former peasants or as indicative of entrepreneurial spirit lacking among the track laborers fail (1) to realize how many such peddlers were seasonal laborers looking for an extra hustle and (2) that pushing a fruit cart could be as heavy as track work.

23. Many of the families in the Ward had family members doing business in the Clinton-Mansfield Street area, just as other people of the Ward held jobs in the first settlement areas around Union Station and the Market. In turn, people from Clinton-Mansfield Street area commuted back to work in the City Dairy and the garment area. The correlation between work and residence is only loosely possible.

24. C. Ware, *op. cit.*

25. In the late 1920s and early 1930s, Brandon and Beaver both had higher Italian residential density than streets in the Ward, but there were few storefronts and little *ambiente*.

26. Regular emigration from Italy stopped, few political exiles arrived, but they moved on to more active centers of anti-Fascism.

27. Money made during Prohibition may have had connections with American organized crime; often it related to legitimate "chains" of extended family that provided a natural avenue for such commerce.

28. G.G. Napolitano, "Il Treno degli Italiani" (Milan, 1933), quoted in G. Mingarelli, *Gli italiani di Montreal. Note e Profilo,* Montreal, 1957, pp. 64-66. The volunteer's cry, "Brittani accoci qua" demonstrates that there was no conflict between loyalty to Italy and to Canada.

29. *The Toronto Star,* 12 Dec. 1920.

30. I. Silono, *Bread and Wine,* (N.Y., 1962), p. 169.

31. A. Spada, *The Italians in Canada,* pp. 118-19.

32. The change came in May, 1927. For a statement about emigrants as overseas Italians, see. B. Mussolini, *Onera Omnia,* Vol. XXIII, p. 187.

33. Now the home of C.O.S.T.I., the building was confiscated during the War years. Some of the Fascist organizations later outlawed by the Minister of Justice were the *Fasci italiani all 'estero, Depolavoro, Associazioni Combattenti Italiani, Organizzazioni Giovanili degli italiani all' estero,* and the Italian United Moral Front.

34. M. Duliani, *La Ville sans Femmes* (Montreal, 1945), p. 54.

35. Speeches of the Minister of Justice, 11 June and 13 June, 1940, *House of Commons Debates,* Vol. 1 (1940), p. 657 and pp. 744-45, respectively.

36. *Toronto Telegram,* 11 June 1940.

37. Speech of Mr. Church, Member for Broadview (12 June, 1948) *House of Commons Debates,* Vol. 1 (1940), p. 718.

38. *Manchester Guardian* article quoted by Mr. Church in *House of Commons Debates,* Vol. 1 (1940), p. 717.

39. Speech of A.R. Adamson, Member for York West (13 June 1940) *House of Commons Debates,* Vol 1 (1940), p. 757.

40. M. Duliani, *op cit.*

41. Canadian Dept. of Citizenship and Immigration, *Annual Reports,* Ottawa, 1951-1959. See *Annuario Statistico Italiano* for the early 1950s. On the Friulians, see B.M. Pagani, *L'Emigrazione friulana dalla meta del secolo XIX al 1940,* Udine, 1968.

42. G. Mingarelli, *Gli Italiani de Montreal,* pp. 59-61, and O. Bressan, *Non Dateci Lenticchie. Esperienze, Commenti, Proseettive de Vita Italo-Canadese* (Toronto, 1958), pp. 106-10.

43. The impressions of Toronto's Italian community in this part of the paper are drawn mainly from two sources. For eight years, students in my Italian history course at the University of Toronto have written term papers on "anonymous immigrant history" subjects. Palmacchio Di Iulio, pre-Law student and Immigration Receiving Counselor at the Malton Airport, and Joseph Cornacchia, Law student, helped interview over a hundred first-generation Toronto Italians.

44. *Italo-Canadian Commerical Directory,* pp. 50-51.

45. Of a hundred people interviewed, 90 percent expected services 2 and 3 from a travel agent; about 70 percent expected service 4, and 40 to 60 percent expected the other services. To the migrant, the phrase "going to immigration" meant that the agent solved a problem or "arranged a difficult case." The agents seemed to protect their role as mediators by affecting an air of mystery about the nature of such transactions.

ALEXANDER J. MATEJKO University of Alberta

The Double Identity of Polish Canadians*

Introduction

The Polish-Canadian ethnic group is comprised of various local groups in limited communication with one another. A substantial number of the more than 300 000 people of Polish origin have no contact with the Polish-Canadian ethnic institutions. Four-fifths of them do not speak Polish at home (Radecki, 1976: 131)[1] Ethnic organizations are divided along ideological, educational, and social class lines (Matejko and Matejko, 1974). Nevertheless, Polish-Canadians as a whole show a high degree of interest in their heritage. The dramatic political events in Poland since 1980 have revived a Polish identity among many. The huge public interest in North America shown for the labor movement, Solidarity, and the struggle of the Polish people for freedom in their home country have had an obvious impact on the social and political conciousness of Canadians of Polish origin in Canada.

Politics in Poland

People of Polish descent in Canada have to face several questions which are widely asked in the mass media: Is it really so important what happens in Poland? Was it worth it, in December 1981, to bother so much about the Polish government's introducing martial law which it justified by saying it has to pacify the country and stop the strikes initiated, or at least tolerated, by Solidarity? Was there any real reason for the Soviet Union to intervene by proxy using the Polish army it had largely trained and equipped? (Matejko, 1981).

The events in Poland should be understood within the context of the growing tensions within the Soviet empire orginating from the ambition of several nations to liberate themselves from Soviet dominance, the deterioration of the Soviet model of society totally run from the top, the food shortage and the rulers' inability to improve the situation, the economic mismanagement cultivated under the guise of central planning, and the

---

* A revised version of "Multiculturalism: The Polish Canadian Case," reprinted from the *Polish Review*, 1976, Vol. 21, No. 3, pp. 177-194 in *Two Nations, Many Cultures*, first edition.

alienation of the young generation from the communist system (Matejko, 1980a). Furthermore, the Soviet Union as a global power feels endangered by the growing demand for civil rights among Poles. Poles want to have free trade unions, be exposed to variety of views in the daily press, have the opportunity to establish associations of various kinds free from direct state control, travel abroad when they wish, and have free elections (within some acknowledged conditions). The Soviet intervention by proxy in Poland shows that the attempted democratic arrangement in Poland is treated by the Soviet leaders as totally unacceptable.

However, the Soviet leaders have been hesitant so far to run Poland themselves. Poles have to be fed, allocated to various jobs according to their skills, rewarded for what they do, and trusted at least to some extent. The Polish military leadership trained in the USSR and loyal primarily to headquarters in Moscow can order mass imprisonments or even killings but in the long run they are not qualified to run the economy.

The fact that the country is in a state of economic collapse results from the bureaucratic centralization of decision making and the suppression of market relations. Even the top leaders of the ruling communist party in Poland have admitted, much before the introduction of martial law at the end of 1981, the necessity to have in Poland a much more liberal economic system. It would be difficult to discount these official promises, as well as the very pessimistic official evaluation of the state of the Polish economy. It is in the vested interest of the ruling communist establishment in Poland, including the military high ranks, to improve economic performance.

The rulers of Poland do not seem to have a ready program for dealing with all these issues and the Soviet authorities are not able to give any good suggestions in this respect, not having answers themselves to their own domestic problems. The political establishment in Moscow fails to acknowledge the changing reality and tries anxiously to reverse historical trends. Their own Marxist creed has become so ossified that it does not help them anymore to understand what really happens in the countries belonging to the Soviet empire (Kolakowski, 1978).

The developments in Poland since 1980 have several important consequences for Polish Canadians. First of all, the large number of Poles who left Poland, mostly illegally, have been shown good will by Canadians generally, and Polish-Canadians have sponsored Polish refugees to Canada. Second, because of the deteriorating food situation in Poland, many Polish Canadian families have become very active in shipping food parcels to Poland, inviting temporary guests from Poland, collecting money, and pressing the Canadian authorities to offer help to hungry Poles. Third, since 1980 Polish Canadians have been constantly inspired by the heroic events in Poland to take a public position in defense of democratic freedoms for their compatriots in the motherland. They are proud that Poland has become the first communist country with a free trade union movement and that Poles have shown great courage in pushing for their civil rights.

Of course, all these factors have much strengthened the *double identity* of Polish-Canadians. However, its significance differs with the various generations of Poles who have settled in Canada.

Generations of Polish Canadians

The new arrivals of the 1970s and the early 1980s still have mostly a Polish identity even if they show the best will for becoming Canadian landed immigrants and citizens. They speak Polish at home and are busy arranging the basic conditions for successful adaptation: learning the English language, finding a job suitable to their professional background, saving enough money for permanent accommodation and upgrading occupational qualifications. Most Polish new arrivals have a professional or semiprofessional standing and are anxious to find an appropriate occupation as soon as possible. They are hard working, industrious, flexible and ambitious. At the same time they do not have much time and interest in becoming active in the local ethnic life.

The new arrivals are very sensitive to events in Poland; they listen to news and react to Polish happenings by participating in demonstrations, writing letters to the media, and sending food parcels to Poland. The fact that they do not join existing ethnic associations in large numbers does not mean they are ethnically unconscious or insensitive. Rather the problem is that the ethnic organizations are unable or unwilling to respond to their specific problems.

A considerable gap remains between new arrivals and previous generations of Polish-Canadians who have created the organizational structure of their ethnic life (Radecki, 1979; Heydenkorn and Rusinek, 1979). This structure has a whole variety of important functions, and sometimes also dysfunctions, not only for the associated members whose material, social and emotional interests are satisfied within the ethnic voluntary organizations, but also for the Polish ethnic group as such (as well as for the host society). The Polish case is in this respect particularly interesting because Polish-Canadians have a long-established tradition of organizational life, as well as because there have been some very significant transformations inside this group. The share of the Polish primary mother tongue group in the total Canadian population has diminished in the period from 1941 to 1976 from 1.1 percent to 0.4 percent, and the percentage rate of Polish as the mother tongue has diminished in the Polish ethnic group in the period from 1941 to 1971 from 77 percent to 38 percent. In the early 1970s only one fifth of the Polish ethnic group spoke Polish most often at home, and probably since then this number has further diminished.

The Poles who settled in Canada before World War II were predominantly peasants, and their whole ethnic lifestyle was very much influenced by the values of the traditional peasantry (Matejko and Matejko, 1975). In the old country, the scarce material resources and the "limited good factor" (Forster, 1965) favored the acceptance of the authoritarian rule imposed on peasants. The traditional peasant community[2] transplanted to North America reappeared in a multitude of self-help associations and ethnic parishes. Priests served as external brokers in dealing with the Anglo-Canadian environment (Matejko, J., 1974a).

The poverty of peasants in northern and western Poland was in marked contrast with the "better-off" people. In Russia this differentiation was even more evident (Shanin, 1972) and justified the statement that there were two different societies: one poor and helpless, the other rich and powerful. The tensions which grew in Canada between the older peasant immigration and the postwar intelligentsia immigration may be related to a large extent to the unhappy recollection of class distinctions. But although the social dualism which originated in the distant past may exist today, it is less evident (Radecki and Heydenkorn, 1976; Heydenkorn and Rusinek, 1979).

The traditional Polish intelligentsia exists in Canada only as a remnant of the past because the young Polish professionals acquire early the characteristics of the local middle class (Matejko, 1977, 1982). The "governance of souls" as the main moral responsibility of the traditional intelligentsia has lost its sense in Canadian conditions where the leadership of Polish ethnic life is elected at the grass-roots level. In order to succeed in their local organizational life, Poles had to simulate the pattern established by Anglo-Canadian organizations. The aspirations typical of the traditional intelligentsia in the home country did not have much application to the new socio-cultural and political conditions.

In Canada, where Anglo-Canadian urbanites predominate, there was no long-range possibility for Polish peasant immigrants to continue traditional patterns of behavior. They became urbanized, especially after the Second World War when the new tide of refugees from Poland consisted mostly of urbanites who had temporarily settled in Great Britain or in Germany. Closer integration into the Canadian urban-centered society has become simply unavoidable for the Poles. However, the general style of ethnic life originally established by peasant immigrants has remained, at least for a period of time. The segmentation into local units which do not have very much in common with one another may be interpreted as the continuation of traditional villages.

Social relations among Poles are still particularistic and diffuse; the organizational commitment is relatively weak; most common activities are of local importance; ethnic politics is highly personalized. The proliferation of local organizations may be partly explained by a demand for honorific social positions among people who are traditionally status-oriented and who are not able to find this status in the Anglo-Canadian world.[3]

Early Polish immigrants have gained much materially and politically[4] but at the same time they have paid for it heavily by conformism to the Anglo-Canadian environment and the abandonment of most of their Polish identity. It is true in general that conformity for European immigrants, including the Poles, was a way of guaranteeing respectability (Richmond, 1967b). "Ironically, then, in light of nativist fears that these immigrants would undermine middle-class patterns of life and threaten democratic political institutions, these (immigrant) ethnic and religious groups are among the principal defenders of the status quo" (Palmer, 1972:247). This is evident in many respects: strong anticommunism, very little political support of the NDP, uncritical acceptance of many Anglo-Canadian customs, strong consumerism, little understanding and tolerance of any deviance and praise of hard work at the expense of leisure.

Social Distinctions among Poles

It is necessary to make a clear distinction between Polish Canadians who have improved their status and security by resettling in Canada, and those who have good reason to feel less fortunate. For the peasants who entered Canada before World War II and went through the long crisis of the 1930s, what they have now is seen as a great achievement. "An experience of immigrants of downward occupational status mobility, followed by recovery or improvement of status, leads to higher levels of their satisfaction and adaptation of Canada" (Richmond, 1967b:175). In general, the lower-rank immigrants to Canada in the period 1945-65 were more satisfied with life in Canada than those who had high rank in their native country. This observation is valid, among others, for Poles.

After the Second World War, the middle-class Polish people who refused to return to communist Poland and settled for good in Canada suffered the loss of their traditional status. In the late 1960s and in the 1970s many of them managed to improve their positions in the Canadian society. Already by the 1950s and early 1960s, the Polish working class people also became well-established in their occupations. The generation of the arrivals to Canada during the late 1940s and the early 1950s still remains the backbone of Polish ethnic life. They have established most of the ethnic organizations, parishes, halls, Saturday schools, women's associations, veterans' groups dating from World War II, scouts, etc.

Still most of the ethnic leadership consists of these people who did not want to return to communist Poland and opted for the West. This group is becoming older and their children mostly show little interest in Polish affairs; many among them have lost fluency in the Polish language; also many marry outside the Polish group. There is a serious problem of ethnic continuity when you take into account the fact that the new arrivals from Poland become active in Polish ethnic life relatively rarely. Who will take over the organizations constructed by previous ethnic generations?

With the progress of Polish-Canadians in education and income, and the entrance of young generations into the scene, the traditional ethnic neighborhood integration ceases to exist or at least becomes much weaker. This is generally valid not only for Poles, but for all immigrants in North America (See Neumann et al., 1973:97). The young and educated Polish-Canadians, who are ambitious enough to prove their worth, typically move into the English-Canadian environment. "To young people fired by curiosity and equipped with a cosmopolitan education, the ethnic community can be intensely stultifying. It is likely to be suspicious, narrow-minded, riddled with prejudices" (Higham, 1974:69).

For Polish-Canadians, an additional difficulty derives from the ideological conflict between state socialism in Poland and the anti-communist orientation of the Poles in exile. This political orientation is particularly strong among veterans from World War II who have their own association ties, still maintain political aspirations, and support the Polish government in exile located in London (U.K.). The decision of these people at the end of the war not to return to a Poland controlled by communists, changed the social structure of the Polish community in Canada, which before had been dominated by the lower classes. Now also some among the new arrivals from Poland appear in the first line of anticommunist activities. Their resentments are still fresh and also they feel more obliged than other Polish Canadians to show solidarity with suffering compatriots in Poland.

Before the 1950s the Polish middle class in Canada was very small because most of the Polish immigrants were blue collar workers or peasants. Among the war veterans of middle class background many had to accept in Canada much lower-status jobs than before and become members of the lower-middle class. By being active in ethnic life they defended to some extent their previous status and maintained it at least in the perception of their compatriots.

The educational boom of the late 1950s and the 1960s was much utilized by the young generation Poles. The Polish middle class already started to expand and play an important role in the 1950s by establishing new associations, being more devoted to common ideals and values, and strengthening patriotic fervor. Many more Poles than before started to view themselves as an ethnic group that matters in Canada. The whole Polish ethnic group became more self-conscious and mature as a social entity.[5]

One of the obvious reasons for Poles to be proud was their participation in the growth of a "Third Power" in Canada. The ratio of the non-British and non-French population in Canada had grown from one in ten in the last quarter of the 19th century to one in four in the 1960s. Catholics, which includes most Poles, had grown from 39 percent to 46 percent of the total population in the period 1921-71 (only one fifth with an English background). These numerical gains made it possible to achieve some "bargaining power", especially when the Liberal Canadian government found in the policy of multiculturalism a vital support for its own political survival.

The Costs of Ethnic Identity

The stress experienced perhaps by some Polish Canadians as members of a non-statutory ethnic group in Canada may lead to several possible outcomes. Poles have been for a long time "marginal people." However, "marginality may provide a perspective which enables one to gain keener insight into society and human behavior and can contribute to urbanity and sophistication. The challenge of marginality for the individual is to exploit the opportunity rather than to become a victim of it" (Martin and Franklin, 1973:48).

With the progressing educational and socio-economic upgrading of Polish Canadians there is less reason for them to feel marginal. Visits to Poland have shown them that even with economic deprivation a lot was done by the Polish nation to promote its culture. Poles feel proud of their scientists, artists, writers, poets, intellectuals, actors, musicians, film directors, and other creative people.

This national pride encourages young Polish-Canadians to think that ethnicity should not be treated merely as a remnant of the past. "Even though modern development brings with it tradition-rending change, such as the rational division of labor and secularization, ethnicity per se may be equipped to adapt to the new conditions . . . The mobilization of ethnic groups may reflect the traumas of casting off tradition, but it may also portend innovative political forms for the future, beyond modernity" (Enloe, 1973:274).

The ethnic group must have the will, ability and courage to become progressive, open-minded, up-to-date. The influx of new immigrants from Poland, much better educated, more intellectually flexible and open-minded, has contributed very considerably to the innovative processes within the Polish-Canadian ethnic group. They are more outspoken and also more willing to go beyond their own ethnic ghetto than were the previous generations. They are also more critical of the dominant Canadian values and traditions which they confront with their own values brought from Poland. For example,the new arrivals complain about the lack of genuine interest and appreciation in Canada of people who are located in inferior positions (see the testimony of household servants in Ciesielska, 1981 and Spirala, 1981). People belonging to the older generations of Polish Canadians do not like this criticism and there have been heated exchanges of views in the Polish-Canadian press or even in the mainstream press.[6]

From the perspective of new arrivals, the existing set up of Polish-

Canadian ethnic life looks somewhat parochial, ghetto-like, status-oriented, benefiting primarily a limited number of permanent leaders, anti-intellectual and devoid of any self-criticism. On the opposite side, the new arrivals are criticized by the older generations of Polish-Canadians for not appreciating enough what has been done, as well as for being hesitant to make their own contribution.

The parochialism that is often attributed to ethnic groups appears primarily to be the result of stereotyped thinking; this manifests itself in little concern for facts, prejudice, and impatience. Stereotypes "take less effort and give an appearance of order without the difficult work that understanding the true order of things demands. They are a way of classifying, which in itself is a necessary process for any kind of thinking . . . The traits assigned to a stereotype are selected for their ability to produce some desired effects or on the basis of an emotional predisposition" (Simpson and Yinger, 1972: 153-54). For example, some intellectually oriented new arrivals from Poland have been labelled "communists" because they do not conform to the cliché views common among the older generations of Polish-Canadians.

Parochialism among majority and minority groups takes the form of keeping oneself at a distance from anything new. Since the first wave of Polish immigrants were mostly peasants who shared with other rural immigrant groups a lack of education and skills, maladaptation to urban life, lack of mobility and an inadequate consumption pattern, these factors contributed to the prejudice of Anglo-Canadians against such rural arrivals as Poles or Ukrainians (Krawchuk, 1966:28-42). This prejudice was strengthened by the fear on the part of some Anglo-Canadians[7] that the unfamiliar Slavic culture would undermine the status quo (Matejko, A., 1974b). The intensity of personal attacks usually tended to be greater when the minority was seen as a political threat.

The lower class Poles who settled in North America came to consider their own status as a very touchy issue (Znaniecki-Lopata, 1976), especially when they started to enter the ranks of the middle class. (The Jews tend to use their jokes as part of their survival kit, while Polish jokes in North America are very often made about but not by Poles). With improvement in their economic status, more contact with other ethnic groups, and better acculturation, lower class Poles are now increasingly losing their feeling of isolation or parochialism and the sociopsychological vulnerability related to it.

Better contact between the Poles and other ethnic groups is partly related to the changing cultural content of ethnic life. The Polish immigrants who came after World War II brought some new elements and stimuli. Once in Canada, they tended to stay; in the period 1946-1961, Canada succeeded in retaining 70 percent of immigrants from Britain, 60 percent of those from the United States, but 80 percent of those from other countries including Poland. In that period, the Poles and other immigrant groups contributed heavily to the growth of the country. The postwar immigration to Canada up to 1961 constituted a third of the population increase and half of the labor increase. While the postwar immigration substantially strengthened Polish ethnic identity, it also contributed to some confusion as to the exact place of Poles in Canada. It is not the belonging to many groups that causes the difficulty, but an uncertainty of real belonging.

Polish-Canadians share with Polish-Americans[8] mixed feelings about their ethnic identity. Michael Novak has spent considerable effort in the U.S. to convince people that ethnic consciousness is not regressive; that it is not only for the old; that it must not be necessarily illiberal and divisive, and breed hostility; that it will not disappear; that intermarriage does not hopelessly confuse ethnicity; that intelligent sensitive ethnics, proud of their heritage, should not go around thumping their chests in ethnic chauvinisim; that emphasis on the ethnic must not conflict with American patriotism; and that ethnicity is all right not only for minorities, but also for the mainstream of society (Novak, 1971; 1972). In Canada, Poles may have had much less reason to feel inferior and therefore, may have had less ground for hiding an ethnic background. The arrival of many well educated Poles in the 1970s and the educational advancement of local Poles have improved very considerably the Polish share in the local middle class.

Ethnicity as the desire to uncover one's roots has become fashionable in North America, and the views held by Novak (1972) are quite popular. In the 1950s religion was popular not only because of a deep interest in its doctrines, but also because religion was a more respectable way of maintaining ethnic primary ties than ethnicity itself (Herberg, 1965). However, during the 1960s the status of being ethnic became upgraded. The wave of ethnic feeling was evoked by domestic development such as the Black Power movement in the U.S. Religion declined as a focus of ethnic identification (Glazer and Moynihan, 1970). In Canada the government policy of multiculturalism has contributed considerably to the improvement of ethnic status. Polish-Canadians now feel free to use their language, cultivate their national traditions and help their compatriots at home. More and more often they are using the collective power of their ethnic group in order to articulate demands of a general nature, especially regarding the situation in Poland.

Is it realistic to expect that Polish-Canadians will gain a political leverage similar to that already enjoyed by Ukrainian-Canadians? (Petryshyn, 1980:213-240). There are some affirmative trends in this respect. Ethnic voting increases when the ethnic group has produced a middle class and this has already happened with Polish-Canadians. However, Poles entering the middle class ranks become more dispersed territorially. One thing that may bring them together are moral, political and cultural issues of a very strong appeal. For example, with world public opinion paying great attention to political developments in Poland, Canadians of Polish origin gained a common cause which may further stimulate them to act jointly.

Assimilation

Until the 1950s, the assimilation process of Poles in Canada was relatively slow. The percentage of those of Polish origin who spoke Polish had decreased only slightly in the period 1921-51 from 83 percent to 78 percent (Weinfeld, 1974:21). However, among the Canadian-born of Polish descent, the retention of the Polish mother tongue went down in that period from 82 percent to 39 percent and later in 1971 to 17 percent. The mother-tongue Poles have decreased in the period 1951-71 from 7.8 percent to 4.8 percent of the total non-English and non-French population (Ukrainians from 21.2 percent to 11. 1 percent). Only about half of mother-tongue Poles spoke Polish at home in the early 1970s. By contrast, the retention of the Ukrainian mother tongue among the Canadian-born of Ukrainian descent declined in the period 1921-71 from 98 percent to 43 percent, and the retention of the Italian mother tongue among the Canadian-born people of Italian descent declined in the same period from 54 percent to 44 percent. The percentages for Canadian-born people of German descent were 78 percent in 1921 and 27 percent in 1971. It seems that Canadian-born Polish-Canadians are less inclined to retain the use of their native language than other ethnic groups, with the exception of the Germans and Scandinavians who lose their native languages particularly fast (Weinfeld, 1974:21, 23). The upgrading of Polish-Canadians to the middle class position together with more commitment in the cultural field could reverse this trend. Data on Polish-Canadians show that among young people who are proud of their background, language retention is quite strong (Matejko, 1977).

Intermarriage with other ethnic groups represented almost two thirds of all the marriages in 1961 contracted by Polish males; for Ukrainians, slightly more than half their marriages (57 percent) were formed with outsiders. It is significant that the percentage of Polish males marrying Anglo-Canadian females has risen from 3 percent in 1921 to 25 percent in 1961 (among Ukrainians, from 0.5 to 25 percent and among Jews, from 1.5 to 5 percent). Among Canadian-born Poles in 1961, only a quarter had Polish wives in comparison with 88 percent of Canadian-born Jews with Jewish wives and a half of Canadian-born Ukrainians with Ukrainian wives (Weinfeld, 1974:51, 52). Even among the Jews the ratio of intermarriages is growing (from 2.5 percent in the late 1920s to 14 percent in 1970),[9] but the intermarriage rate among the Polish people is particularly high. This trend toward intermarriage ultimately may undermine the existence of the Polish ethnic group.

Language ceases to be an important basis of social differentiation in the second and subsequent generations, at least in large urban centers like Toronto (Richmond, 1972:61), and Poles in this respect are not different from other ethnic groups. It is religion rather than ethnic allegiance which may remain (Richmond, 1972:17; Herberg, 1955). With the progressing acculturation there is less reason for Poles to stay in "Slavic" areas or to limit their social contacts to their own compatriots. In a sample of householders in Toronto in 1970, only 16 percent of Slavs expressed a preference for living in an area where most people were of the same ethnic group – in comparison with 27 percent among British and 29 percent among Jews and Italians (Richmond, 1972:52). It is also significant that the most important reasons for such preference were language difficulties (33 percent of responses) and, to a much lesser extent, the presence of friends, relatives and closer acquaintances (12 percent of responses) (Richmond, 1972:53a). Most Slavs found living outside of their own ethnic group more interesting, although ironically, they rejected the idea of "total" Anglo-conformity. With the general educational and cultural advancement of Polish-Canadians, and Slavs in general, there will be probably less reason to avoid each other as neighbors.

Poles and other Slavs become more cosmopolitan in their general outlook following their socioeconomic advancement, fluency in English, higher security, and the broader societal contacts outside their own ethnic group. However, this does not necessarily mean that they rigidly conform to a Canadian lifestyle. The concept of "ethnic community" is no longer equal to an ethnic ghetto but is an extended social network "not necessarily confined to the immediate neighborhood" (Neumann, et al., 1973:84). Such an ethnic community is highly differentiated internally, and fluency in English, educational level, income and class membership count a lot (Richmond, 1967a:97). With the territorial dispersion of middle class Poles, the role of an ethnic parish is diminishing, except in the case of an emergency such as the collection of money for hungry compatriots in Poland or community action to sponsor refugees from Poland.

The relative position of Poles in the class structure of Canada improves with the progress of their adaptation, but it still is less favorable than the position of some other ethnic groups. Among people of Polish origin in 1971, managerial, administrative and related occupations represented 2.8 percent in comparison with 3.6 percent among Germans, 5.2 percent among British, and 10.7 percent among Jews. The generally poorly paid services represented 13.1 percent among Poles in comparison with 10.6% among British and 4.9% among Jews (Perspective Canada, 1974: 279-80). New arrivals of the 1970s also quite often started their careers in low-level job positions but due to their good educational background they advance relatively fast. They are also fully aware of the necessity to learn English as soon as possible and look actively for contacts with the Anglo-Canadian environment instead of sticking together only with Poles. It is also true in this respect that Polish-Canadian organizations in general are of little help for them in occupational matters. Now in the 1980s the situation has started to change with the sponsorship of refugees by several Polish ethnic organizations.

Upward social mobility is more open to the young generation of Poles than to the old and it is accompanied by their rapid assimilation to English Canada. Thus, there is not much hope for the preservation of ethnic language on the North American continent. (The recent arrivals from Poland, however, are fully aware of their Polish identity and far from ready to change it for an Anglo-Canadian identity – (see several testimonies in this respect in Heydenkorn, 1980; Spirala, 1981; Kolodziejczyk, 1981a, 1981b.) With increased general mobility, there are no longer strong communal supports in retaining distinctive ethnic cultures. Children of immigrants begin to lose their ethnic languages when they enter school. Everything which is relevant in life and work is conducted in English (or in French in Quebec). The immigrant cultures and languages are abandoned (Glazer, 1966). "These fragments of ethnicity that are retained in a disjointed and altered fashion are usually insufficient for the maintenance of functional bilingualism beyond the first generation" (Fishman, 1966:395). Ethnic language retention is strongest among immigrants who have maintained the greatest psychological, social, and cultural distance from the institutions, processes and values of the Anglo-Saxon core society (Fishman, 1966:396).

Poles and Anglo-Canadians

If "the fundamental variable in majority-minority relations is a condition of unequal power between two more or less self-conscious groups" (Yetman and Steele, 1971:XIII) then in the relationships between Poles and Anglo-Canadians such a condition does not have substantial explanatory value. Anglo-Canadians do not impose their will on Poles. Poles do not threaten the Anglo-Canadians, and vice versa. Nevertheless, differences exist that alienate the two. For example, traditional Poles put heavy emphasis on status-orientation (Matejko, A., 1970, 1973, 1974b), Roman Catholic background, nationalism, the gentry tradition, and collectivistic values. These factors also create a ground for tension between the traditional older generations of Polish-Canadians, and the new arrivals who are much more goal oriented, tolerant of opinion diversity, open to innovation, and still able to bring up their children in a Polish spirit.

Inequality of placement in the social hierarchy tends to entrench ethnic differences. Canada's elite of non-Anglo and non-French origin, including Poles, constituted in the early 1970s only 5 percent of the economic elite, 8 percent of the political elite and 4.5 percent of the bureaucratic elite. They constituted 27 percent of the total population while Anglo-Canadians constituted 45 percent; the latter represented 87 percent of the economic elite, 68 percent of the political elite and 72 percent of the bureaucratic elite (Clement and Olsen, 1974:23). During the 1970s, Polish representation has been considerably strengthened among academics, medical staff, politicians, lawyers and businessmen. The traditional relatively low-class standing of

Polish-Canadians has improved as it has in the case of Ukrainian-Canadians (Petryshyn, 1980:53-106).

Of course, certain specific traits of Poles distinguishing them from the Anglo-Canadian environment do not disappear easily. For example, the concept of public interest differs among various ethnic groups, including the Poles. Their experience in the last 200 years, based on the partitions of the Polish state and long foreign rule, taught the members of the enlightened Polish strata to make a very clear distinction between "national" interest and "state" interest. Such a distinction is blurred in the Anglo democracies. Although Poles are in general law-obedient citizens, they place the common welfare higher than blind acceptance of formal rules. They have a long tradition of bending the latter in order to achieve what they regard as proper and satisfying ends.

The social distance between the people is also experienced differently among Poles than with Anglo-Canadians. The social distance people are inclined to see and accept between themselves and their superiors, as well as the value they place on informal group relationships, depends on the nature of the socio-cultural setting.[10] Historically, Poles had more exposure (in comparison with the British in North America) to social structures founded on nepotism and favoritism in which there was not much room for formalized participation. Informal pressures effectively encouraged Polish people to act in a way which was socially prescribed for them. Social distance has been very much entrenched among Poles so that there is a distinction between "our people" ("our" family, "our" close friends, members of "our" stratum) and "strangers". (Podgorecki, 1976; Nowak, 1981).

Poles in Europe today are exposed, on the one hand, to the influence of the gentry tradition on which the whole Polish culture is built, and, on the other hand, to the current bureaucratic patterns of state socialism brought from Russia. In this respect the problems of young-generation Poles differ substantially from those of young Canadians (Matejko, 1982). For the second or third generation of Polish-Canadians, it is relatively easy to conform to the patterns sponsored by the dominant Anglo-Canadian group. However, vivid interest in Poland is still cultivated at least in some Polish-Canadian circles, primarily the Polish scouts and groups of university students. Young Polish-Canadians visit Poland; some of them even study there, and the cultural influence of Poland is quite substantial. It is the ambition of at least some Polish-Canadian intellectuals to play the role of middlemen between nonofficial Poland and Canada.

The Multicultural Commitment

The issue of multiculturalism in the case of Poles in Canada is mainly limited to the preservation of at least a bicultural identity. The fact that the Anglo-Canadian majority sets the cultural patterns and sustains them does not necessarily eliminate for Poles their own chance to survive as a socio-cultural entity. The critical issue in this repect is how Poles can cultivate their dual identity in a creative manner, and offer their own contribution to Canadian culture. For Canadians, it is a matter of recognizing the creative potential in Slavic "strangers". Poles must make a realistic evaluation of their own abilities as well as deficiencies. As long as they are not forced to accede to the demand of ultra-conformists for full cultural assimilation, there is no reason to worry. However, it is not an easy matter to preserve the ethnic self in a highly conformistic society manipulated by the mass media and not very tolerant towards deviance or diversity (Matejko, 1980b). Squeezed between two cultures, English and French, other ethnic groups may not find much place for themselves. Great courage and determination is needed under such circumstances to promote ethnic specificity beyond folklore.

Bringing the Polish ethnic group from a relic of the past to the "movement of self-knowledge" (Novak, 1974:18) is probably the most critical problem of this group. For the young generation of Polish Canadians it is a choice between becoming "like everyone else," namely an average Anglo-Canadian, or becoming truly bicultural and conscious of one's own ethnic identity. The climate today in Canada for ethnic "deviation" has, for several historical reasons, become more suitable than it used to be. There is now a place on the North American continent for a new type of ethnic movement not of a purely defensive nature, but oriented to the highest self-awareness.

Individuals should find enough opportunities in ethnic culture to achieve personal growth, and any "ethnicity" that is reduced to mediocrity does not make much sense. There is a necessity to stimulate among Canadians a healthy curiosity about each other and to sensitize them to the variety of ethnic cultures available in the country. "A sense of belonging to a racial or ethnic group possessing its own distinct culture is a necessary factor in personality formation process" (Bouraoui, ed., 1980: 100).

The multicultural policy of the Federal government in Canada, as well as of the provincial governments, still needs some clarification. According to H. Bouraoui (1980), transculturalism should be applied as a positive alternative to either the melting pot or mosaic, and multiculturalism is the suitable way to avoid homogeneity and conformity dictated by the manipulated mass culture. It is necessary to enrich the understanding of ethnic cultures beyond dance, folklore, and food, as well as to transcend factionalism.

Multiculturalism in order to become a permanent asset of the Canadian society needs some spiritual basis. Unity in diversity is impossible without exchanging parochialisms for an universalistic set of values, norms and attitudes. However, all of us remain under the pressure of commercialism and cheap mass culture; both of them contribute to mediocrity and narrowmindness when taken to extremes. Multiculturalism understood seriously, and not used for the political manipulation of people, is based on the spiritual enrichment of individuals through their exposure to a variety of cultural values.

The spiritual potential of various ethnic groups expresses itself in the ability to utilize a given ethnic background as a vehicle to effect self-development. It does not have anything in common with "the upper-class intellectual romanticism" which must serve, according to Myrdal, conservative and reactionary interests (Myrdal, 1974:30). It is rather, as in the case of Italian-Americans, the result of the emergence of an ethnic intelligentsia which is bicultural, but at the same time rejects the melting pot concept (Vecoli, 1974:39).

A new intellectual elite has emerged from the ranks of Ukrainian-Canadians which is committed to the resurgence of ethnic consciousness. For Polish-Canadians it is still an open question whether, and to what extent, they will be able to go in the same direction. The old generation still occupies all important positions in the Polish ethnic movement and the problems specific to this generation dominate everything else. There are political divisions brought from Poland to Canada just recently or many years ago. The question is if, when, and how the young generation will take over the control of the Polish-Canadian ethnic group. The Canadian Polish Congress which represents most Polish-Canadians, already has in its ranks some leaders of the new generation. However, there are still some intergenerational cleavages. Some Poles in Canada accept the Polish emigré government in exile, and some of them do not. Some maintain contacts with the authorities of the Polish People's Republic, and others do not. Some want to cooperate with the Ukrainians, while others are still preoccupied with whether the western Ukrainian territory now in Soviet hands should be returned to Poland in the event of a future major political upheaval in Eastern Europe. The dividing lines are numerous (Matejko and Matejko, 1974); it is not easy for various generations of Poles to find common ground. However, the difficult political situation in Poland may serve to inspire unified action among Polish-Canadians for the sake of the national interest.

END NOTES

1. In the early 1970s, mostly English was spoken at home in Canada by almost all Scandinavians, 9/10 of the Dutch, Germans and Jews, three quarters of Ukrainians and Poles, a half of Asians, but only 2/5 of Italians, and 1/7 of French. Among Canadians who spoke Slavic languages at home only 1/10 was under 15. Among all Canadian Slavs only one fifth spoke their native language most often at home (Statistics Canada).

2. "Community of descent and relatively low territorial mobility, primary personal contact and lack of anonymity, low division of labor and simple cooperation seem to underlie the high cultural cohesion of rural communities." (Shanin, 1972:33).

3. For similar trends in other parts of the world, see Kuper, 1972:140; Hunt and Walker, 1974. On Poles in the United States, see Znaniecki-Lopata, 1976; Sanders and Morawska, 1976.

4. Three quarters of immigrants to Canada in the period 1946-61 felt that they improved their standard of living. The British immigrants to Canada, compared with non-British immigrants, are less likely to be strongly positive in their attitudes to the Canadian way of life. English-speaking immigrants in Canada in the period 1945-65 tended to be recruited from skilled manual and white-collar occupations. They tended to enter the middle and higher levels of the Canadian social structure (Richmond, 1967b).

5. I use the term "ethnic group" after Greeley (1972). The characteristics of an ethnic group are: (1) a consciousness of kind rooted in a sense of common origin; (2) interaction with each other most of the time; (3) sharing of ideals and values; (4) moralistic fervor and a sense of being persecuted; (5) distrust of those outside and a massive ignorance of them; and (6) tendency to view themselves as the whole of reality that matters. The arrival of Polish combatants to Canada has particularly contributed to points 3 and 6, while the previous ethnic experience of the lower class Polish people was focused in points 1, 2, and 5.

6. For example, in December 1981 a group of young Polish hunger strikers in Edmonton felt, rightly or wrongly, that they did not receive enough moral support from the local Canadian Polish Congress. Rick Peterson, "Local Hunger Strike Starts Polish Rift," *The Edmonton Journal* (December 23rd, 1981), p. B2.

7. According to the Harris Survey conducted for the Urban League in the U.S. in 1970, prejudice exists more among Anglo-Americans than among European ethnic groups (Krickus, 1971).

8. In 1971, 2.5 percent of Americans were of Polish origin (*Statistical Abstract of the U.S.*, 1972:33).

9. In the U.S. intermarriage is greater for every Jewish generation born in the U.S. and rises even more sharply among the college-educated. The intermarriage rate among college-educated U.S. Jews is 2/5. Jewish men have a much higher intermarriage rate than Jewish women.

10. For example, in the field of industrial relations, "a man who does not expect to be consulted by his superior and is not inclined to trust either his superior or his peers will see little value in participating in decisions on a man-to-group basis" (Williams et al., 1970; see also A. Matejko, 1976).

SELECTED REFERENCES

Allardt, Erik & W. Wesolowski, eds. *Social Structure and Change. Finland and Poland. Comparative Perspective.* Warsaw: Polish Scientific Publishers, 1978.

Anderson, A.B. & J. Frideres, *Ethnicity in Canada.* Toronto: Butterworths, 1980.

Bouraoui, Hedi, ed. *The Canadian Alternative: Cultural Pluralism and Canadian Unity.* Downsview: ECW Press, 1980.

Brodzki, Maria and Stanislaw Brodzki, eds. *Polonia 1978. Polonia Jutra,* (Polonia 78. Polonia of Tomorrow), Toronto: The Canadian Polish Congress (no year of publication).

Ciesielska, Anna, Dziennik Anny Sluzacej "The Diary of a Home Servant", *Alliancer,* 98/99: 31-32, 1981.

Clement, Wallace and Dennis Olsen, "Official Ideology and Ethnic Power: Canadian Elites 1953-1973." Paper presented at the Annual Meeting of the American Sociological Association, Montreal, 1974.

Crysdale, Stewart and Les Wheatcroft, eds., *Religion in Canadian Society.* Toronto: Macmillan of Canada, 1976.

Enloe, Cynthia H. *Ethnic Conflict and Political Development.* Boston: Little, Brown, 1973.

Fishman, Joshua A. "Language Maintenance in a Supra-Ethnic Age: Summary and Conclusions" in J.A. Fishman et al. *Language Maintenance in the United States.* The Hague: Mouton, 1966.

Forster, G.M. "Peasant Society and the Image of a Limited Good." *American Anthropologist,* 67, 1965.

Glazer, Nathan, "The Process and Problems of Language-Maintenance: An Integrative Review." in J.A. Fishman, et al. *Language Maintenance in the United States.* The Hague: Mouton, 1966.

Glazer, Nathan and D.P. Moynihan. *Beyond the Melting Pot.* Cambridge: The MIT Press, 1970.

Goldfarb, J.C. *The Persistence of Freedom: The Sociological Implications of Polish Student Theater.* Boulder: Westview Press, 1980.

Goldstein, J.E. and R.M. Bienvenue, eds. *Ethnicity and Ethnic Relations in Canada.* Toronto: Butterworths, 1980.

Gross, Feliks, *The Polish Worker. a Study of A Social Stratum.* New York: Roy Publ., 1945.

Heine, Marc E. *The Poles. How They Live and Work.* Toronto: Griffin House, 1976.

Herberg, William, *Protestant-Catholic-Jew.* New York: Doubleday, 1955.

Heydenkorn, Benedykt. *Przywodztwo w Polonii Kanadyjskiej* (Leadership in the Canadian Polonia). Toronto: Futura Graphics, 1980.

_____. *Memoirs of Polish Immigrants in Canada,* Toronto: Canadian-Polish Congress. Canadian-Polish Research Institute, vol. 16, 1979.

_____. *Organizational Structure of the Polish-Canadian Community. The Federation of Polish Societies in Canada,* (introduction by Robert F. Harney), Toronto: Canadian Polish Research Institute, 1979.

_____. *Topics on Poles in Canada.* Toronto: Canadian-Polish Research Institute, 1976.

_____. *From Prairies to Cities.* Toronto: Canadian-Polish Research Institute, 1975.

_____. *Past and Present.* Toronto: Canadian-Polish Research Institute, 1974.

Heydenkorn, Benedykt and Zygmunt Rusinek, "The Executive Board of the Polish Canadian Congress." in *Organizational Structure of the Polish-Canadian Community,* ed. B. Heydenkorn. Toronto: Canadian Polish Research Institute, 1979.

Higham, John, "Integration versus Pluralism: Another American Dilemma." *The Center Magazine,* VII: 4, 1974.

Hunt, Chester L. and Lewis Walker, *Ethnic Dynamics: Patterns of Intergroup Relations in Various Societies.* Homewood, Illinois: The Dorsey Press, 1974.

Jablonska, Marie A. "My Cultural Shocks in Canada," in *Polish Settlers in Alberta. Reminiscences and Biographies,* ed. J. Matejko. Toronto: Polish Alliance Press, pp. 336-345, 1979.

Kogler, Rudolf K., "The Canadian Polish Community in the Light of the 1976 Census Results" in the *Canadian Alternative,* ed. H. Bouraoui, Downsview: ECW Press, 1980.

Kolakowski, Leszek. *The Main Currents of Marxism.* Oxford: Clarendon Press, 1978.

Kolodziejczyk, Zygmunt, Batorym do nowego etapu zycia (On 'Batory' to the new life stage), *Alliancer,* 97.6, 1981a.

_____ . "Pierwsze kroki (First steps)". *Alliancer,* 98/99:54, 1981b.

Krawchuk, P., "The Ukrainian Image in Canadian Literature." *A Tribute to Our Ukrainian Pioneers in Canada's First Century.* Proceedings. Special convention of the Association of United Ukrainian Canadians and the Worker's Benevolent Association of Canada. Winnipeg (May, 1966), pp. 28-42.

Krickus, J. "The White Ethnics." *City* (May-June 1971).

Kuper, Leo. "Relition and Urbanization in Africa", in Anthony H. Richmond, ed., *Readings in Race and Ethnic Relations.* London: Pergamon Press, 1972, pp. 129-148.

Manczak, K. "Spoleczny rachunek sumienia" (Examination of Social Consciousness). *Glos Polski-Gazeta Polska,* 40, 1974.

Martin, James G. and Clyde W. Franklin *Minority Group Relations,* Columbus: Charles E. Merrill, 1973.

Matejko, Alexander. "Task versus Status." *International Review of Sociology,* VI, 1-3 (1970), pp. 329-354.

_____ . "Gestures or Deeds?" *International Review of History and Political Science,* X;4 (1973), pp. 18-33.

_____ . *Social Change and Stratification in Eastern Europe: An Interpretive Analysis of Poland and Her Neighbours.* New York: Praeger, 1974b.

_____ . "Adaptation of Polish Engineers to Canada." *Bulletin of the Association of Polish Engineers in Canada,* XXX1, 1:18-21, 1976.

_____ . "The Polish-Canadian Intelligentsia." *Migrant Echo,* VI, 3 (1977), pp. 142-157.

_____ . "Multiculturalism: The Polish Canadian Case." in *Two Nations, Many Cultures,* ed. J.L. Elliott. Scarborough: Prentice-Hall of Canada, pp. 237-249, 1979c.

_____ . "Canada and Poland, Two Countries, Two Big Brothers," *The Jerusalem Journal of International Relations,* 4, 4(1980a), pp. 31-55.

_____ . "The Manipulated Freedom in Mass Societies (West and East)," *International Review of Sociology,* XVI, 2-3 (1980b), pp. 238-276.

_____ . Economic Deterioration Gave Impetus to Solidarity, *Edmonton Journal,* December 22nd, (1981), p. A5.

_____ . "Between the Myth of East European Intelligentsia and the Reality of the North American Middle Class" in *Proceedings of the Conference on Poles in North America,* Toronto: The Multicultural History Society of Ontario, 1982.

Matejko, Joanna. "Rola Misjonarza wsrod polskich pionierow w Albercie (Role of missionaries among the Polish pioneers in Alberta)," *Migrant Echo*, III:1 (1974), pp. 41-51.

———. "Polscy pionierzy w oczach Auglosasow (Polish pioneers in Canada as seen by the Anglo-Saxons)." *Zwiazkowiec* (Alliancer), 1974b, issues no. 70-74 (in Polish).

Matejko, Joanna and Alexander Matejko, "Polish Canadians." in B. Heydenkorn, ed., *Past and Present*. Toronto: Canadian-Polish Research Institute, 1974, pp. 37-60.

———. "Polish Peasants in the Canadian Prairies." in B. Heydenkorn, ed., *From Prairies to Cities*, Toronto: Canadian-Polish Research Institute, 1975, pp. 9-34.

Myrdal, Gunnar. "The Case Against Romantic Ethnicity." *The Center Magazine*, VII:4, pp. 26-30, 1974.

Neumann, Brigitte, et al. *Immigrant Integration and Urban Renewal in Toronto*, The Hague: Nijhoff, 1973.

Novak, Michael. "White Ethnic." *Harper's* (September 1971).

———. *The Rise of Unmeltable Ethnics*. New York: Macmillan, 1972.

———. "The New Ethnicity." *The Center Magazine*, VII:4, pp. 18-25, 1974.

Nowak, Stefan, "Values and Attitudes of the Polish People," *Scientific American*, 245:1, 1981, pp. 45-53.

O'Brian, K.G., J.G. Reitz, and O.M. Kuplowska, *Non-Official Languages. A Study in Canadian Multiculturalism*. Ottawa: Supply and Services Canada, 1976.

Origins of the Canadian Population. Census of Canada 1966, Bulletin 7. 1-6, Ottawa: Dominion Bureau of Statistics, 1961.

Palmer, Howard. *Land of the Second Choice. A History of Ethnic Groups in Southern Alberta*. Lethbridge: The Lethbridge Herald, 1972.

Perspective Canada. Ottawa: Information Canada, 1974.

Petryshyn, Roman, ed. *Changing Realities: Social Trends Among Ukrainian Canadians*. University of Toronto Press, 1980.

Podgorecki, Adam. "The Global Analysis of Polish Society." *The Polish Sociological Bulletin*, 4(1976), pp. 17-30.

Potichnyj, Peter, ed. *Poland and Ukraine. Past and Present*. University of Toronto Press, 1980.

Radecki, Henry. "Cultural Mosaic: A Micro View." in B. Heydenkorn, ed., *Topics on Poles in Canada*. Toronto: Canadian-Polish Research Institute, 1976.

———. *Ethnic Organizational Dynamics. The Polish Group in Canada*, Waterloo: Wilfrid Laurier University Press, 1979.

B. Heydenkorn. *A Member of a Distinguished Family: The Polish Group in Canada*. Toronto: McClelland and Stewart, 1976.

Richmond, Anthony H. "Immigrants and Ethnic Groups in Metropolitan Toronto." York University (Institute for Behavioural Research mimeo), 1967a.

———. *Post-War Immigrants to Canada*, Toronto: University of Toronto Press, 1967b.

———. "Ethnic Residential Segregation in Metropolitan Toronto." York University (Institute of Behavioural Research mimeo), 1972.

Samulski, Jozef. *Pamietnik emigranta polskiego w Kanadzie* (Memoirs of a Polish emigrant in Canada). Wroclaw: Ossolineum, 1978.

Sanders, Irwin T. and Ewa T. Morawska. *Polish-American Community Life: A Survey of Research*. New York: The Polish Institute of Arts and Sciences in America, 1976.

Shanin, Theodor. *The Awkward Class: Political Sociology of Peasantry in a Developing Country: Russia 1910-1925*, Oxford: Clarendon Press, 1972.

Simpson, E.S. and J.M. Yinger. *Racial and Cultural Minorities*. New York: Harper and Row, 1972.

Spirala, Malgorzata A., Kariera Canadian Kuchta (Career of a Canadian House servant) *Alliancer*, 98/99, (1981), p. 47.

Statistical Abstract of the U.S. Washington, D.C.: The U.S. Government Printing Office, 1972.

Thomas, W.I. and F. Znaniecki. *The Polish Peasant in Europe and America*. Boston: R.C. Badger, 1918-1920.

Vecoli, Rudolph. "The Italian Americans," *The Center Magazine* VII:4 (1974) pp. 31-45.

Weinfeld, Mort. "Multiculturalism and Canadian Ethnic Groups." Manuscript. Ottawa: Department of Sociology, Carleton University, 1974.

Williams, Lawrence K., et al. "Do Cultural Difference Affect Workers' Attitudes?" in Henry A. Landsberger, ed., *Comparative Perspectives on Formal Organizations*. Boston: Little, Brown, 1970.

Yetman, Norman R. and C. Hay Steele, eds. *Majority and Minority*. Boston: Allyn and Bacon, 1971.

Znaniecki-Lopata, Helana, *Polish Americans*. Englewood Cliffs, N.J.: Prentice-Hall, 1976.

ROMAN R. MARCH McMaster University

Political Mobility of Ukrainians in Canada*

The rise of a variety of "ethnic consciousnesses" that no longer accept the old assimilation model are a recent and fascinating North American phenomenon. While "Black Power" and "Quebecois nationalism" have been extensively examined, various forms of "Slavic consciousness" have received only minimal scholarly treatment. This essay is a contribution to this relatively new, but increasingly important, area of study and activity.

Commenting on the phenomenon of developing Ukrainian communities in the United States and Canada, Myron B. Kuropas of the Ukrainian National Associaiton said:

> Both of our communities were founded by pioneers who arrived in North America with little appreciation for their Ukrainian ethnonational heritage. Occupied and divided by foreign powers for centuries, Ukrainians had little opportunity to raise the level of their national consciousness and to develop a national will which reflected the sentiment of all segments of the population. . . . The ethnic climate in the United States began to change dramatically a few years ago as the result of the rise of Black Power. Other ethnic groups benefited from this development because it heralded the beginning of a new era of understanding for the ethnic phenomenon. In a very real sense it meant the demise of the melting pot and the rise of cultural pluralism as the model for American unity. "We are preserving our cultural heritage in an environment which appears to be significantly more amenable to ethno-national diversity. And we are gaining – slowly in America, more rapidly in Canada – a modest degree of political influence."[1]

It is the intent of this paper to look at the political success of the Ukrainian community in Canada by examining the Ukrainian participants in the 11 legislative bodies.

It has been relatively simple to collect data on participation rates of ethnic groups in political institutions at the federal, provincial, or municipal levels.[2] This information is used in time-series analyses conducted to measure and compare the extent to which various ethnic groups are represented in such institution as legislatures, courts, cabinets, and the civil service.

---

* Reprinted with permission from *Changing Realities: Social Trends among Ukrainian Canadians*, ed., W.R. Petryshyn, Edmonton: The Canadian Institute of Ukrainian Studies, 1980.

TABLE 1 Summary of election results for Ukrainian candidates in federal and provincial elections, 1904 to 1975

Area	Period covered	Ukrainian candidates		Number of constituencies	Elected Ukrainian candidates	
		Total	Female		Total	Different[a] candidate
Federal						
Manitoba	1911-74	77	1	60	15	6
Saskatchewan	1904-74	46	1	41	9	3
Alberta	1926-74	78	5	49	25	10
Ontario	1942-74	52	2	45	12	4
British Columbia	1940-74	9	—	9	—	—
Quebec	1953-65	4	—	4	—	—
Canada	1904-74	266	9	208	61	23
Provincial						
Manitoba	1914-73	233	6	147	69	28
Saskatchewan	1912-75	113	2	91	37	17
Alberta	1913-75	207	4	136	67	32
Ontario	1945-75	51	—	48	14	4
British Columbia	1941-75	16	2	15	1	1
Total Provincial	1912-75	620	14	437	188	82
Federal and Provincial	1904-75	886	23	645	249	105

Source: Darcovich and Yuzyk, *Statistical Compendium*, Table 33.2, 321.
Note: [a]Some candidates are elected more than once and this column shows the number of different candidates elected. For example, four different candidates were elected (or re-elected) 14 different times to the Ontario Legislature.

The "Statistical Compendium on the Ukrainians in Canada, 1891-1976" provides this kind of data from over 600 federal and provincial constituencies in which Ukrainian candidates ran for office between the years 1904 to 1975.[3] In Appendix A the numbers of those Ukrainians appointed, rather than elected, to higher political office are presented through 1981.[4] The Compendium defines political participation as "running for or seeking election to political office." It claims that

> this definition implies more political participation than may be apparent at first sight. It implies an awareness of local or "grass root" problems and of larger provincial and national issues, the existence of a political philosophy on the part of the candidates and a motivation to stand for election. It also implies that considerable preparatory efforts have been undertaken: running for office in local governments, being active in business or community affairs, joining or being active in political parties, going through the nomination procedures and conducting the campaign itself.[5]

The Compendium found that "886 Ukrainian candidates, 23 being women, contested 645 federal and provincial elections in the period 1904-1975. . . ."[6] This data is summarized in Table 1 opposite.

Federal Elections

The time-series data of all federal elections from 1904, when the first Ukrainian candidate ran, to 1974, when 42 Ukrainian candidates ran and eight were elected, show that the number of Ukrainian candidates for federal office increased incrementally. At first the overall success rate was quite modest. The first Ukrainian member of Parliament, Michael Buchkovich, was elected from Vegreville, Alberta, in 1926. He was a United Farmers Party (UFA) candidate and the only Ukrainian candidate. Eight Ukrainian MPs were elected in 1968, in 1972, and in 1974. This was the maximum. The number of Ukrainian candidates increased from one candidate in each of the elections from 1904 to 1926 to six in the elections from 1930 to 1940, and rose rapidly from 10 in 1945 to 42 in 1974 (Table 2).

In view of what is known about the prejudice of the Anglo-Celtic and French groups against the other ethnic groups, it is not surprising that the first Ukrainian candidates ran for such non-establishment parties as the UFA and the Co-operative Commonwealth Federation (CCF). Commenting on this phenomenon with respect to the rise of the CCF in Saskatchewan during the 1930s, S.M. Lipset wrote:

> Urban middle-class leaders of the CCF differ signficantly from farming and working-class leaders in one essential respect – ethnic origins. They belonged, predominantly, to minority ethnic groups; these groups were not part of the urban "upper class," which in Saskatchewan is largely Anglo-Saxon. This is true

TABLE 2 *Ukrainian candidates and Member of Parliament in federal elections and by-elections*

Year of election	Number of Ukrainian candidates	Number of Members of Parliament elected
1904	1	0
1911	1	0
1921	1	0
1926	1	1
1930	6	1
1935	6	0
1940	6	1
1945	10	2
1949	15	1
1953	18	4
1957	19	6
1958	20	7
1962	20	5
1963	21	5
1965	26	4
1968	22	8
1972	34	8
1974	42	8
Total	266	61

even in areas where the population of the surrounding countryside is composed overwhelmingly of members of minority ethnic groups. The non-Anglo-Saxon businessmen are often newcomers to the business life of the towns, being former farmers or children of farmers. They tend to retain their ties with the minority ethnic group of the surrounding countryside, and remain socially marginal to the business community. This was clearly brought out in a study of a small, predominantly Anglo-Saxon town in a Ukrainian farming district. According to one young Ukrainian merchant, "The Anglo-Saxons made it plain that they were better than the Ukrainians and didn't want us, so the Ukrainians said 'To hell with you, we can get along by ourselves.' " The two CCF Ukrainian members of the Saskatchewan legislature in 1944 were small town merchants who came from farm families. Both reported close ties with the Ukrainian rural community.[7]

The first Ukrainian Liberal candidate was not elected until 1949, while the first Ukrainian elected as a Progressive Conservative (PC) did not win until the 1953 federal election. In 1957 one CCF, two Social Credit and three PC Ukrainians were elected MPs. From 1958 to 1965 every Ukrainian elected federally was a PC. This underlined John Diefenbaker's ability to attract strong support among Ukrainian Canadians, because he supported the civil rights of non-establishment groups and championed the causes of the "little man" long before he became leader of the PC party. It also reflects increasing conservatism of western Canadian voters.

Pierre E. Trudeau was able to break the PC stronghold in Ukrainian communities when four Ukrainian MPs were elected as Liberals in 1968. However, the pattern established under Diefenbaker was strongly reasserted in 1972 and 1974, when Ukrainians won 13 seats for the PCs, one for the NDP and two for the Liberals. It would appear that Ukrainian Canadians are now indistinguishable from others in Manitoba, Saskatchewan, and Alberta in their united support for the Progressive Conservative Party.

Provincial Elections

The Political experience of Ukrainians in the provincial area has been extensive. Political participation has been heaviest in Manitoba where there have been 245 Ukrainian candidates and 66 seats won. The second greatest activity has been in Alberta where 206 candidates won 66 seats, followed by 111 candidates in Saskatchewan and 35 seats won; 51 candidates in Ontario and 14 seats won; and 16 in British Columbia with one seat.

For all five provinces the CCF/NDP attracted 146 Ukrainian candidates and won 53 seats; the Liberals had 132 candidates of whom 27 won; the Conservatives had 109 candidates and won 31 seats; Social Credit had 79 candidates and won 35 seats (33 in Alberta); and 75 independent candidates won only four seats. The farmers' parties were the most successful, running 10 candidates and scoring seven victories.

Theoretical Considerations

John Porter, a pioneer in the analysis of political participation and mobility in Canada, defines the admission of ethnic groups to the power structure as "entrance status."[8] He found that the English and French "charter groups" relegated most other ethnic groups to low status occupational roles and subjected them to assimilation. In addition to the concepts of "entrance status" and "charter groups," Porter explored the question of whether a Canadian-style ethnic mosaic is less conducive to social mobility than the American melting pot. "The melting pot," he wrote, "with its radical breakdown of national ties and old forms of stratification, would have endangered the conservative tradition of Canadian life, a tradition which gives ideological support to the continued high status of the British charter group."[9] Porter's assumption is that an ethnic group either assimilates or remains locked into a position of limited social status.

His initial findings were rather pessimistic and implied that non-charter groups would not move rapidly out of a low entrance status into higher income and occupation status. This pessimism was based on his assumption that only a drastic alteration in the North American Anglo-Protestant capitalist system toward a more social-democratic form would open up North American society to increased upward mobility among non-charter

TABLE 3 *Ukrainian candidacies and seats won in provincial elections by political party*

Candidates and elected Members	LIB	PC	CCF/ NDP	SC	IND	F	LP[a]	Other	Total
Manitoba 1914-73 candidates	44	31	53	5	56	3	31	23[b]	246
Elected as MLAs	9	3	21	1	4	3	20		61
Alberta 1913-75 candidates	39	43	39	55	8	7		16[c]	207
Elected as MLAs	5	21	3	33	0	4			66
Saskatchewan 1912-75 candidates	30	20	40	10	7	0	0	4[d]	111
Elected as MLAs	8	0	27	0	0	0	0		35
Ontario 1945-75 candidates	14	14	11	4	3	0	0	5[e]	51
Elected as MPPs	5	7	2	0	0	0	0		14
British Columbia 1941-75 candidates	5	1	3	5	1	0	0	1[f]	16
Elected as MPPS	0	0	0	1	0	0	0		1
Total candidates	132	109	146	79	75	10	31	49	631
Total elected	27	31	53	35	4	7	20		177

Notes: [a]The party affiliation of candidates is given according to the following abbreviations:

Communist Party	(CP)	Labour	(L)
Conservative	(PC)	Labour Progressive Party	(LPP)
Co-operative Commonwealth		Liberal	(LIB)
Federation	(CCF)	Liberal Progressive	(LP)
Farmer	(F)	New Democratic Party	(NDP)
Farmer Labour	(FL)	Other	(O)
Government Coalition	(GC)	Progressives	(P)
Independent	(IND)	Social Credit	(SC)
Independent Liberal			
Progressive	(ILP)		

[b]Other candidates include: ILP — 4; LPP — 5; CP — 4; O — 1; L — 1; DK — 3; CP — 3; GC — 2.
[c]Other candidates include: CP — 12; O — 4.
[d]Other candidates include: P — 2; FL — 1; LP — 1.
[e]Other candidates include: LPP — 5.
[f]Other candidatebinclude: O — 1.

groups, such as Ukrainian, Poles, and Italians. Nowhere in his extensive research does Porter acknowledge that very rapid upward mobility is possible for non-charter groups within the existent liberal-democratic social and political structures.[10]

Recent studies of occupational mobility among non-charter ethnic groups suggests that the process is more rapid than Porter anticipated.[11] The model of assimilation which lies behind these findings is based on the assumption that "all [ethnic] groups enter a linear and cumulative unitary process of cultural assimilation . . . ." with upward mobility being a slow, multi-generational process.[12] This model envisages that minority ethnic groups begin at the lowest educational, occupational, and income levels and slowly filter upwards, all the while shedding their linguistic and cultural baggage as they assimilate into the dominant culture. Thus Ukrainians and other ethnic groups will initially enter dominant group institutions at the local, then provincial, and finally federal political levels.

In sharp contrast to these linear and cumulative assumptions, William Newman writes that "the most dramatic cases of minority social mobility in the U.S. appear to have been facilitated through the creation of minority-group-controlled parallel structures, not through structural assimilation."[13] As an example of this process, let us examine briefly the basic unit of American political structures, the precinct, which is a neighborhood encompassing 100 to 700 voters. Dan Nimmo and Thomas Unger write:

> Party organization begins with the precinct. The principal functionary is the precinct committee person, captain, or leader, who is elected either in the party primary or by the precinct party members assembled in convention; in some areas, he or she may be appointed by party leaders of countrywide organizations. The precinct leader workers to increase voter registration and achieve a respectable turnout of party identifiers on election day. Moreover, he or she preaches party doctrine, passes along information, and performs social and economic services.
>
> The constituency is next above the precinct; it is the lowest level from which a public official is elected. In larger cities, this level is the ward; in rural areas, it is the township; in some sections of the country, it is a state legislative district; and in some states, it is the congressional district. The basic organization is the country committee, usually composed of the precinct leaders. The head of this committee is the country chairperson who is chosen either by the committee or in the party primary. He or she is charged with seeing that precinct leaders mobilize majorities in their precincts and that the party as a whole carries the constituency for local, legislative, congressional, senatorial, gubernatorial, and presidential candidates.
>
> The coordinating level is above the precinct and constituency; it is usually composed of the state central or executive committee and includes representatives from constituency committees.[14]

Since neighborhoods are usually highly homogeneous, ethnic groups could and did come to control precincts, then wards, counties, and even states. Precinct power was the means for ethnic communities to amass political power. However, no such permanent grass-roots political organization exists in Canada. Very few Canadian polling divisions have been as strongly organized or decentralized as are their precinct counterparts in the United States. In Canada, political power rests in the hands of the small, usually self-selecting constituency executive, which in turn is jealously guarded by the incumbent member of the Legislature or Parliament. Only during elections are ephemeral polling organizations established. Once the election is over, the Canadian poll organization disappears, whereas in the United States the precinct remains intact. One consequence of these fundamentally different approaches to the structuring of political parties in Canada and the United States is that Canadian ethnic groups have not created permanent bases of political power in areas where they are numerically dominant. Nathan Glazer and Daniel Moynihan see the development of political organization along ethnic lines as the primary mechanism of assimilation and social mobility in the United States and a prelude to political and economic assimilation.[15] Other studies suggest that total assimilation is not inevitable, and that group diversity is a permanent fixture of many modern societies.[16]

The study of ethnic groups in America requires careful reconsideration of the theories that have arisen to account for sociological and historical developments. The experience of the Ukrainian community in Canada suggests that it is possible for an ethnic group to overcome severe restrictions and prejudices against it in a relatively short period. But the political success of Ukrainians in Canada suggests that the success rate of different ethnic communities is quite varied. Ukrainian Canadians have made remarkable progress in achieving political office at the federal and provincial levels in Canada. In doing so, they have avoided the incremental model. Why the Ukrainian community, however, has been able to achieve this high level of political success remains to be explained.

APPENDIX A *Ukrainian appointees to political office in federal and provincial governments, 1950-1981[1]*

Time period[2]	Provincial governments				Prov. Total	Federal Gov.	Total[3]
	Ont.	Sask.	Man.	Alta.			
1950-1970	1	1	5	2	9	5	14
1971-1981	0	3	1	6	10	5	15
Total	1	4	6	8	19	10	29

1. While I have examined the period from 1904 to the present, the first entry occurs in 1950 in Manitoba. N.V. Bachinsky, Liberal Party. was appointed Deputy Speaker by Premier Campbell. He served a six year term. Darcovich and Yuzyk, "Statistical Compendium," Table 33.3, 323.
2. The terms of some appointees overlap the two time periods represented. Such individuals have been counted twice.
3. The names of all appointees, their position in the government, their term of service, and party are available from me upon request.

Appendix B

Identification of Ukrainian Canadians

The procedure used in identifying Ukrainian ethnicity consisted of examining the list of candidates for each constituency and selecting those with Ukrainian surnames. The easiest candidates to identify were those generally known to be Ukrainian by the Ukrainian community at large and these formed a significant portion of the total. Other candidates were identified by reference to biographical summaries in the Parliamentary Guide. These provided the ethnic origin or birthplace of the candidate or of the parents or gave the Ukrainian surname of the parents if the candidate's name had been Anglicized. *Who's Who* publications provided ethnic background for additional candidates and the *Dictionary of Ukrainian Surnames* provided a check on doubtful surnames. Individuals in provinces familiar with local political affairs were provided with lists of possible Ukrainian candidates and their knowledge was helpful in resolving doubtful cases.

An identification procedure based on surnames is only approximate. The classification may include some non-Ukrainian candidates who are Poles, Russians or Jews as persons of different Slavic origin sometimes have common surnames. On the other hand, Ukrainian candidates may be excluded due to poor transliteration or Anglicization of their surnames. In mixed marriages the practice is to include a candidate if either of the parents is Ukrainian; some omission of candidates can be expected on this account, especially where the one Ukrainian parent is the mother.

Since the classification is based on the ethnicity of either parent, it is broader than that in the census, which is based on male ancestry. In common with the census, however, it is mainly an objective classification. It may therefore classify candidates as Ukrainian who do not feel or identify themselves as such and who may not be sympathetic to such a designation.

END NOTES

1. Remarks to the Twenty-Sixth Convention of the Ukrainian National Federation, Toronto, 7 October, 1978. The Ukrainian National Association is the largest Ukrainian fraternal insurance company in North America.
2. R.R. March, "Political Mobility of Slavs in the Federal and Provincial Legislatures in Canada," in *Slavs in Canada*, 3 vols. Toronto: Ukrainian Echo Publishing Co., 1968, 2:16.
3. William Darcovich and Paul Yuzyk, eds., "Statistical Compendium on the Ukrainians in Canada, 1891-1976" (Unpublished typescript, Ottawa, 1977), 316-60. For a later revision of this work, see William Darcovich, "The Statistical Compendium": An Overview of Trends," in *Changing Realities: Social Trends among Ukrainian Canadians*, ed. W. Roman Petryshyn (Edmonton: The Canadian Institute of Ukrainian Studies, 1980), pp. 3 - 17.
4. Ibid., p. 323. The figures for the period 1976-1981 are from my own research.
5. Ibid., 317.
6. Ibid.
7. S.m. Lipset, *Agrarian Socialism: The Cooperative Commonwealth Federation in Saskatchewan: A Study in Political Sociology* (Garden City, N.Y.: Anchor Books, 1968). 233-4.
8. John Porter, *The Vertical Mosaic: An Analysis of Social Class and Power in Canada* (Toronto: University of Toronto Press, 1965).
9. Ibid., 71.
10. Elia Zuriek and Robert M. Pike, *Socialization and Values in Canadian Society* (Toronto: McClelland and Stewart, 1975), 51.
11. Merrijoy Kelner, "Ethnic Penetration Into Toronto's Elite Sructure," in *Social Stratification in Canada*, eds. J. Curtis and W. Scott (Scarborough, Ontario: Prentice-Hall, 1973), 140; Wsevolod W. Isajiw and Norbert J. Hartman, "Changes in the Occupational Structure of Ukrainians in Canada," in *Canada: A Sociological Profile*, 2 vols., ed. W.E. Mann (Toronto: Copp Clark, 1969), 1:96-112.
12. William Newman, "Theoretical Perspectives for the Analysis of Social Pluralism," in *The Canadian Ethnic Mosaic: A Quest for Identity*, ed. Leo Driedger (Toronto: McClelland and Stewart, 1978), 43.
13. Ibid.
14. Dan Nimmo and Thomas Unger, *Political Patterns in America* (San Francisco: W. H. Freeman, 1979), 236, 258.
15. Nathan Glazer and Daniel P. Moynihan, *Beyond the Melting Pot: The Negroes, Puerto Ricans, Jews, Italians and Irish of New York City,* (Cambridge, Mass.: MIT Press, 1963.
16. Driedger, 44.

Third World Immigration

GRAHAM E. JOHNSON University of British Columbia

Chinese-Canadians in the 1970s: New Wine in New Bottles?*

Introduction

Chinese have been resident in Canada since the mid-19th century. they worked first in the goldfields of British Columbia and then labored, under appalling conditions and at great human cost, on the westernmost segment of the CPR, contributing handsomely to the realization of a Canada *abs mare usque ad mare*. From the beginning, Chinese immigrants were the objects of prejudice and discrimination. Once their difficult task of building the railroad was complete they were subject to a variety of discriminatory laws and regulations at all levels of government. For the greater part of their history in Canada, the Chinese were unable to participate fully in Canadian social life. They were excluded from the franchise and from the practice of certain professions and were obliged to pay a head tax for the privilage of entering Canada. They were finally subject to a law which excluded Chinese from entry into Canada. Only in 1967 were the final marks of discriminatory immigration legislation removed.

One consequence was that Chinese communities in Canada developed in curious, imbalanced ways. Chinese-Canadian history is marked by a constant effort to remove the disabilities that characterized Chinese-Canadians and their communities. That those communities met the threats to their continued viability, and ultimately prevailed against substantial odds, is largely because of a strong sense of organization, not merely in Canada but in other overseas Chinese settings, where Chinese residents were typically subject to prejudicial legislation.[1] The 1960s mark a watershed in the history of Chinese in Canada. Above all, immigration legislation reflected a different

---

* Written expressly for *Two Nations, Many Cultures: Ethnic Groups in Canada,* second edition.

view of Chinese Canadians and other groups that had formerly been subject to prejudicial treatment. Its outcome was to create within a decade a Chinese ethnic group in Canada which differed markedly from that of a previous generation.

Immigration Policies: the Background

Immigration legislation has always been a key element in determining the character of the Chinese population of Canada. The infamous 1923 Act, which had excluded Chinese from entering Canada as permanent residents was repealed in 1947. But disabilities for Chinese remained for 20 years after repeal. The Diefenbaker government had introduced new regulations in 1962 which shifted the direction of immigration policy away from that laid down by MacKenzie King in 1947. The regulations removed the emphasis on country of origin as a major criterion for admission to Canada and stressed the economic contribution that a potential immigrant could make. For immigrants from Asia and Africa, however, disabilities remained in regard to sponsorship.[2]

In 1967, regulations free from the discriminatory elements that characterized the 1962 initiatives were introduced. They gave less discretion to individual immigration officers and via the "points system", spelled out precisely the criteria to be used in assessing potential immigrants. The possibilities for a new kind of Chinese immigrant were opened in 1962; the 1967 changes allowed their full realization. Not only did larger numbers of Chinese start coming to Canada but fewer came as sponsored immigrants and more because of the skills they possessed. The prototypical Chinese migrant before 1923 was rural-born, poorly educated, and without a knowledge of English. In the 20 years following the repeal of the Chinese Exclusion Act the characteristics of Chinese migrants did not alter substantially. The change came after 1947. Urban, well-educated, English-speaking migrants arrived in increasing numbers from such centers as Hong Kong, Manila, Johannesburg, and the Caribbean. Very different from their compatriots of an earlier generation, the new migration stimulated and renewed Canada's major Chinese communities.

Immigration and Settlement Patterns: 1967-79

The new immigration regulations in 1967 coincided with some important changes. The old relationships between Canada and China had ceased to exist in 1949 following the proclamation of the People's Republic of China. Direct migration from China to Canada stopped then, and was not restored until 1974, three years after official Canadian recognition. Meanwhile, the most important source of Chinese migration had become Hong Kong, with some Chinese arriving from a variety of Chinese communities in Southeast Asia, southern Africa, Latin America (especially Peru), and the Caribbean.

Hong Kong was significant to Chinese migrants to Canada for several reasons. By the mid-1960s, the Chinese émigrés in Hong Kong with either family or the promise of a job in Canada were altogether different from the migrants of a previous generation. Many had lived in Hong Kong for a decade or more, and many had acquired English-language education there. They were used to an urban environment, in contrast to their kinsmen and fellow-countrymen of an earlier generation, who were country folk with peasant skills. Their general sophistication allowed for relatively easy entrance into Canada and pointed to a potential for adaptation that their predecessors could rarely hope to possess.

The year 1967 is important not merely because of the changes in Canada's immigration regulations. That summer the Great Proletarian Cultural Revolution spilled across the border from Guangdong province into Hong Kong. From May until the autumn, Hong Kong experienced bombs, strikes, demonstrations, and martial law. For a brief period it seemed that the colony might revert to China long before the New Territories lease was due to expire. Thus, as immigration legislation had considerably eased access to Canada, internal pressures in Hong Kong generated additional motivation. Canada became a highly desirable destination for substantial numbers of Hong Kong residents.

The abolition of restrictions coincided as well with changed conditions facing Chinese communities in other parts of the world. In Southeast Asia, the Chinese had traditionally held a dominant economic position. That dominance came under increasing pressure in the 1960s and 1970s. Political conditions in the Malay Peninsula were such that Singapore – a largely Chinese settlement – felt obliged to withdraw from a nation dominated by Malays to form a new city-state in 1963. Elsewhere in Malaysia, life for the Chinese population grew increasingly complex with the "Bumiputra-policy," which favored the Malay at the expense of the Chinese citizen. In 1969 there was ugly communal rioting in Kuala Lumpur and other parts of West Malaysia which left several hundred Chinese dead.

In the Philippines, pressure against the Chinese intensified with the declaration of martial law in 1972. Internal difficulties, notably in South Africa, Peru, and the Caribbean, were important in causing Chinese to look to migration as a long-term solution to their problems. Canada became increasingly attractive throughout the 1960s and into the 1970s.

The Chinese population of Canada doubled between 1961 and 1971, when it was 118 815. Immigration to Canada as a whole fluctuated in the 1960s and into the 1970s, but Chinese migration continued to increase. The provenance of chinese migrants changed dramatically over the three decades after repeal of the Exclusion Act (Table 1).

From the early 1970s, Chinese made up between 7 percent and 10 percent of all immigrants to Canada. Hong Kong ranked third or fourth behind the traditionally large sources of immigration, the United Kingdom and the United States. With the post-1967 influx, the major centers of British Col-

TABLE 1 *Immigration to Canada by China, Taiwan, and Hong Kong Various Years, 1946-79*

	1946-57	1958-62	1963-67	1968-75	1976-79	1946-79
China	16 817	1 958	701	1 941	4 333	25 750
Hong Kong	3 222	6 052	17 130	69 213	27 802	123 419
Taiwan	—	—	885	8 485	3 421	12 721
Total	20 039	8 010	18 716	79 639	35 556	161 960

Source: Department of Manpower and Immigration.

umbia, Alberta, Ontario, and Quebec continued to attract new Chinese migrants, with Ontario and Quebec leading. (Table 2). The largest Chinese communities continued to be in Vancouver, Toronto, and Montreal, with Toronto gaining an increasing share of the new migrants.

Some of the smaller urban Chinese settlements grew only modestly during the period. Victoria, the dynamic center of Chinese immigration in the 19th century, certainly reflected the over-all changes in immigration patterns, but the impact seemed slight. Its 19th century past was manifested in a "bachelor society" in the old center of Chinese settlement. Its 20th century present was marked by the immigrants and second and third-generation Chinese Canadians living in the suburbs, taking on distinct (and bourgeois) occupational characteristics, and using the "Chinatown" as a marketing center.

In Ontario secondary Chinese communities such as Kingston, Hamilton, and London went through a process not unlike that of Victoria. The smaller communities of the 1920s that had experienced a sense of liveliness and had borne with stoicism the difficulties of the 1930s and 1940s, did not participate in the revival of the larger ones like Toronto and Vancouver. The smaller communities did not die as did those in B.C.'s interior, but what change did occur was not dramatic.

Despite their increased concentration in Canada's major cities, Chinese also remained scattered throughout most of the land. The stereotype Chinese resident in Canada was a laundryman, restaurateur or pedlar, occupations that can be described as "solitary."[4] Such occupational niches have been preserved into the modern period and account for Chinese living in the more remote parts of Canada's provinces. In Northern Ontario, for example, there are clusterings (*i.e.*, up to 50 persons) of Chinese to be found in Kenora, Sioux Lookout, Cochrane, Elliot Lake, and Espanola. Timmins, Sudbury, Thunder Bay, and Sault St. Marie have Chinese populations in excess of 250.[5]

One of the most important economic bases for these settlements of Chinese is the restaurant business. Chinese hand-laundries ceased in Sudbury in the 1960s, a trend seen throughout the region as the early migrants

TABLE 2 *Distribution of Canada's Chinese population by provinces, 1961-71*

	1961	1971	% Change
Newfoundland	445	610	39
P.E.I.	43	25	-41
Nova Scotia	637	935	46
New Brunswick	274	575	110
Quebec	4 794	11 905	148
Ontario	15 155	39 325	160
Manitoba	1 936	3 430	77
Saskatchewan	3 660	4 605	26
Alberta	6 937	12 905	86
British Columbia	24 227	44 315	83
Yukon	100	85	-15
N.W.T.	34	115	540
	58 197	118 815	104

Source: *Census*, 1961. *Census*, 1971.

grew old, retired and moved to large urban centers. The Chinese population of Northern Ontario's smaller towns is very different from a generation ago: sex ratios are almost equal, in contrast to the "bachelor" communities of 50 years ago; there are families rather than single men. The population is heavily concentrated in restaurants, grocery stores and, increasingly, in hotels and other tourist-related enterprises. There is still a quality of "isolation" but in the larger settlements, such as Sudbury, there are the beginnings of community organization.

The dramatic changes in Chinese settlement patterns in the late 1960s and 1970s occurred in the two major centers – Vancouver and Toronto. On the eve of the 1967 changes in immigration regulations, the center of Toronto's Chinese community was threatened with physical extinction by the forces of urban renewal. As a consequence, the Toronto Chinese population was unusually dispersed in its settlement pattern as the decade of the 1970s began.[6] The post-1967 influx of Chinese into the Toronto area began a transformation of the community which substantially affected the settlement pattern. It led, by mid-decade, to a reestablishment of a community center ("Chinatown") several blocks away from the traditional center. In a classic example of residential succession, a Chinese population, consisting largely of immigrants from Hong Kong, displaced another ethnic group, the Jews.[7]

In Vancouver, a different picture emerges. The influx of Chinese immigrants into the city saw two tendencies. On the one hand, traditional Chinatown and its adjacent "inner city neighborhood," Strathcona, were substantially renovated. On the other hand, a process of residential dispersal occurred whereby the Chinese population, previously clustered in one or two pockets, particularly in the eastern part of the city, moved to neighborhoods throughout the city, just as in Toronto in the 1960s and in Montreal even earlier. Parallel with residential dispersal, Chinese immigrants came to dominate the corner grocery store business. By the middle '70s, Chinese were running other types of small retail business – hair salons, hardware stores, dress shops – which served the non-Chinese population and were therefore located outside Chinatown or largely Chinese parts of the city.

Chinese settlement patterns by the 1970s differed substantially from those of the late 1940s. The changes were due, in large measure, to alterations in immigration regulations, which allowed the declining or stagnating Chinese communities across Canada – at least those that had survived the destructive effects of the Exclusion Act and the Great Depression – to take new leases on life. Chinese communities in the 1970s were larger, more vibrant, and they no longer exhibited the isolation and imbalance that characterized settlements of Chinese at an earlier generation in Canada.

A New Kind of Chinese?

By the mid-1960s, the sojourner Chinese was becoming a social type of the past. An atmosphere no longer marked by prejudice and discriminatory regulations allowed Chinese-Canadians to participate in Canadian social and economic life to a degree denied to an earlier generation. As one consequence, Chinese residents in the period after the mid-1960s were able to cope effectively with the complexities of Canadian society, expressed few reservations about their decision to move to Canada, and suggested that the difficulties of adaptation to Canadian society were not widespread. By 1971, although the bulk of Canadians of Chinese ethnic origin had been born in China, a substantial number (37.8 percent) were "local born." The Chinese population of Canada was still predominantly a migrant population but its commitments to Canada seemed strong. In 1971, 70 percent were citizens.

Changes in immigration regulations had allowed the migration to Canada of Chinese on the basis of universalistic criteria, such as level of education, rather than on the more particularistic ties of kinship. Chinese in Canada after 1967 came from Chinese communities scattered throughout the world. A variety of skills, sophistication, and *savoir faire* was therefore brought to Canada's Chinese communities, which reflected the diverse cultural traditions that Chinese migrants from the mid-1960s had been influenced by, prior to their move to Canada. That variety was most marked in the larger urban centers, especially Toronto, where a process of accommodation and adaptation was necessary not merely to Canadian society in general but also to existing Canadian-Chinese communities. In the post-1967 period, Chinese communities in Canada changed substantially under the impact of new migrants, one of whose contributions was to help rejuvenate the major Chinese communities across the country. The Chinese communities in Canada became much more heterogeneous in their composition during the 1970s – birthplace was but one index of this – and that markedly affected aspects of traditional social organization.

By the mid-1970s the impact of new migration began to make itself felt in a number of spheres of Chinese community life, not the least of which was in local "Chinatown" policies. This is not to suggest that certain traditional principles of affiliation did not continue to exert a substantial influence. The impact of new migration has to be seen as increasing the richness and the complexity of Chinese community organization. Little was rejected, although sometimes the old was transformed. By the mid-1970s new forces exercized a decisive effect within Chinese communities, but the assumptions of their behavior were rooted in the history of Chinese communities in Canada.

The points of origin of Chinese residents in Canada by the 1970s were diverse. More of them than at any other time were Canadian-born, but the largest group was still China-born. The China experience was filtered through Hong Kong or some overseas Chinese community, but the links with the homeland were, nonetheless, still emotionally tinged and part of the self-definition of the Chinese Canadian. The links were different from those which an earlier generation of Chinese residents had enjoyed with the Chinese homeland. They were, nonetheless, still present. The great difference was that now Chinese-Canadians could enjoy a more intense and committed relationship to Canada than was ever possible for Chinese of an earlier generation. The isolation that characterized the survivors of the pre-1923 period was not an option which the new migrants were willing to accept, nor was the ambivalence towards things Chinese *and* Canadian, which was often a part of the personality of the small second generation that grew up in the period of exclusion and came to maturity in the immediate post-war period. Chinese in Canada in the post-1967 period were no longer homogenous. Social class, point of migration, date of migration all served to distinguish groups within the ethnic population. But the fundamental distinction inevitably related to immigration history and the division between pre- and post-1960s migrants became the critical one.

The centrality of Chinese politics (specifically the conflict between Communists and Nationalist) was muted by the political events of the 1950s and 1960s. Sympathy for the achievements and goals of the People's Republic of China was publicly expressed over a broad area only after Canadian recognition in 1970 and China's entry into the United Nations in 1971. The physical presence of an embassy from the People's Republic of China in Ottawa, and, in the mid-1970s, a consulate in Vancouver, gave legitimacy to positive sentiments about China's achievements since 1949. As the 1970s progressed it became common for Canadians to visit China and many

TABLE 3 *Vancouver Chinese: Birthplace of fathers and where informants were raised, 1974*

	Fathers' birthplace	Where informant raised
	%	%
Yin-ping	5.3	3.4
Hoi-ping	6.7	5.8
Toi-san	33.2	20.7
Sun-wui	6.7	3.8
Chung-san	15.9	14.4
Nam-hoi		
Poon-yue	6.7	4.8
Sun-dak	1.4	6.7
Tung-koon	1.4	1.0
Other Guangdong	12.0	2.9
Hong Kong	1.4	14.4
Other China	7.2	3.4
Asia	0.5	2.5
Elsewhere	0.5	1.0
Vancouver	12.5	
Other Canada	9.1	15.2
		N = 339

Source: *Vancouver Chinese Community Study, 1974.*

Chinese Canadians were able to make physical contact with their ancestral areas, many for the first time since childhood. Changing attitudes towards China did have some consequences for the structure of the community and gave rise to alternatives to traditional sources of authority within the inventory of community associations. This feature of change in Chinese communities was significant.

At a more general level, however, an older, a political, version of the *Chinese* roots of Canada's Chinese population was a salient element in the character and sentiments of the new population. The population after 1967 was a migrant population, coming from a broader spread of cultures than had been the case in a previous generation. And yet, the bulk of migrants traced their origins, not merely to China, but to that small fragment of China that had provided migrants to Canada and North America since the 1850s.

A sample survey of Vancouver's Chinese population was made in 1974. In terms of where the fathers of the sample population had been born, and where the informants had been raised, the links with the traditional points of migration were clear (Table 3). The dominant emphasis in the history of Chinese in Canada from the late 1960s and into the 1970s is one of rejuvenation of, and change in, the Chinese communities. But those communities are rooted in a particular history and their members, even after 1967, have shared common culture. To be sure, the experience of Hong Kong, Manila,

TABLE 4 *Chinese population of Canada: Male/Female by age groups, 1971*

	0-10	11-20	21-30	31-40	41-50	51-60	61-70	70-85	80 plus
Male	41.2	55.6	49.8	57.1	50.5	42.5	31.7	69.8	73.7	51.8
Female	50.8	44.4	50.2	42.9	49.5	58.0	61.3	30.2	26.3	48.2
	24.6	15.4	18.2	16.7	8.4	6.6	5.1	3.5	1.5	N = 1226

Source: *Census*, 1971.

or Lima has its effects. But the ties with a particular part of South China are extant and meaningful. The basic distinction between pre- and post-1960s' migrants (and their offspring) is real. The shared-culture experience is the basis for cooperation when other attributes are distinct, and goes some way to explain why certain traditional community organizations can persist – even flourish – in a historical period which is marked by such sharp contrasts with other periods of Chinese-Canadian history.[8]

If continuity is an underlying theme, the dominant characteristic of development after 1967 is the extent of change, and the nature of the contrast with earlier periods. The greater part of Chinese-Canadian history had seen a preponderance of males in the population and strangely lopsided communities as a consequence. Increasingly, liberal immigration regulations allowed the Chinese population of Canada to correct the grosser imbalances in sex ratios. By 1971, there was only a slight preponderance of males, although history gave to certain age categories a certain peculiarity (Tables 4 and 5). The preponderance of males at older ages is a reflection of discriminatory legislation and the last aging remnants of "traditional" sexually imbalanced Chinese communities that were formerly preponderant. The large numbers of younger men possibly reflect the attractiveness of Canada for higher education, for those who are not migrants. The relatively larger number of women between 50 and 70 reflects the reality of late marriage for pre-1923 immigrants and perhaps also the role of grandmothers in the process of migrant adaptation.

TABLE 5 *Chinese population of Montreal and Toronto: Male/Female by age groups, 1971*

	0-10	11-20	21-30	31-40	41-50	51-60	61-70	70-85	80 plus
Male	56.6	68.1	48.6	52.1	64.3	46.7	45.8	85.7	66.7	55.2
Female	44.4	31.9	51.4	47.9	35.7	53.3	54.2	14.3	33.3	44.8
	23.1	13.1	20.1	26.2	3.9	4.2	6.7	1.9	0.8	N = 359

Source: *Census*, 1971.

TABLE 6 *Chinese population of Canada: Educational achievement, household heads, 1971*

	(%)
None	8.1
Less than grade eight	23.1
Grades 8 - 10	25.2
Grade 11	4.3
Grades 12 and 13	17.9
Some university	7.0
B.A. degree	9.2
M.A./Ph.D. degree	5.3
	N = 775

Source: *Census*, 1971.

Chinese migrants to Canada in the pre-1923 period were typically from rural China with little or no facility in English and with skills that gave them limited opportunities outside Chinese ethnic niches. Chinese with skills acquired in a Canadian context were restricted by discriminatory rules. Change gradually lessened the disabilities as the basic thrust of Canadian immigration policy after 1945 was to encourage skilled migrants who could contribute to the economy, which was still growing substantially by the mid-1960s. As one consequence, the educational level of Canada's Chinese population by the early 1970s appeared quite high. In the country as a whole, over 20 percent of household heads had some university education, although, it must be added, a somewhat larger proportion (32 percent) had had less than a grade 8 education. This reflects, in part, the dual character of the Chinese population by the early '70s. There was a part of the population that had entered as kinsmen of those already resident in Canada. Such "sponsored" immigrants were likely less competent in English, and had

TABLE 7 *Chinese population of Montreal and Toronto: educational achievement of household heads, 1971*

Educational achievement	(%) Montreal	Toronto	
None	35.7	64.3	6.5
Less than Grade 8	45.1	54.9	23.8
Grades 8 - 10	25.9	74.1	25.2
Grade 11	21.4	78.6	6.5
Grades 12 and 13	17.4	82.6	15.4
Some university	19.0	81.0	9.8
B.A. degree	21.1	78.9	8.9
M.A./Ph.D. degree	37.5	62.5	3.7
	28.0	72.0	N = 214

Source: *Census*, 1971.

TABLE 8 *Chinese population of Vancouver: educational achievement of household heads, 1974*

	(%)
None/Illiterate	5.3
Traditional — Literate	6.8
Elementary	19.8
Some high school	27.2
High school graduate	16.9
University	24.0
	N = 338

Source: *Vancouver Chinese Community Study, 1974.*

fewer educational qualifications when compared to migrants who had entered Canada independent of kin ties and on their own, possessing needed skills, which were indexed by educational achievements. The general picture in the country as a whole (Table 6) is magnified in the context of the major centers of Chinese population. Montreal, which had grown substantially in the 1950s, likely through kinship-related migration, stood in contrast to Toronto in terms of the educational levels of the Chinese population (Table 7). Toronto, as the center of southern Ontario economic power, was an attractive location for Chinese migrants whose skills could be readily utilized. A comparable group from Vancouver in 1974 suggests a similar pattern of educational achievement (Table 8). If the general social environment no longer disallowed Chinese participation in all but a handful of sectors, the Chinese population had the capacity to take advantage of the economic opportunities that were presented.

Chinese in Canada by the early 1970s were engaged in a broad range of occupations in a variety of contexts (Table 9 and 10). The great majority of gainfully employed Chinese were wage earners; less than 10 percent were employed on their own account. Certain occupational characteristics traditionally associated with a Chinese population, whether in Canada or in other parts of the world, were apparent. Almost two-fifths were to be found in the sales and personal service categories. In terms of an industrial classification, almost 60 percent of the Chinese labor forces were involved in either trade or service industries. But not a significant number – almost one-fifth – were engaged in occupations that are clearly "white collar." It is the case, however, that only a relatively small proportion were engaged in either manufacturing or primary industry, such as farming, fishing, mining, or the timber industry. Chinese market gardeners have continued to play a significant role in the Vancouver and Victoria regions – the great bulk of Chinese involved in agricultural pursuits in Canada are located in British Columbia – but their overall role in this sector has been in decline for some decades.

TABLE 9 *Chinese population of Canada, Montreal and Toronto: Occupational profile, 1971*

	% Canada	% Montreal	% Toronto
Manager	1.1	9.3	2.2
Science/Engineering	7.1	9.3	9.7
Medicine	5.3	—	4.4
Religion	0.4	—	0.7
Teaching	2.6	2.3	5.2
Social Science	0.7	—	0.7
Artistic, Recreational	0.5	—	1.5
Clerical	12.1	11.6	21.6
Sales	9.7	2.3	7.5
Services	27.9	32.5	22.4
Farming	2.2	—	0.7
Primary production	0.2	—	—
Processing	3.1	2.3	0.7
Fabricating	7.3	9.3	9.7
Construction	0.7	2.3	0.7
Transport	0.7	—	1.5
Other	4.8	2.3	3.0
Not stated	13.1	16.3	7.5

Source: *Census*, 1971.

TABLE 10 *Chinese population of Canada, Montreal, Toronto and British Columbia: Industrial sector of economically active, 1971*

Industrial Sector	Canada	Montreal	Toronto	B.C.
Agriculture	2.2	—	0.7	5.6
Forestry	0.4	—	—	0.9
Mining	1.2	—	—	1.9
Manufacturing	12.1	20.9	20.9	14.8
Construction	1.2	—	0.7	0.9
Transport	5.0	—	7.5	8.8
Trade	14.1	9.3	11.9	20.4
Finance	4.1	7.0	3.0	4.2
Service	43.5	46.5	37.8	32.9
Public administration	2.2	—	6.7	—
Other	13.6	16.3	8.2	9.7

Source: *Census*, 1971.

TABLE 11 *Chinese population of Vancouver: occupational profile, 1974*

Occupation	%
Professional	10.7
Businessman	16.3
Manager	0.3
Clerical	6.2
Sales	2.7
Service	18.0
Craftsman	2.7
Operative	4.7
Laborer	8.0
Unemployed	2.7
Farmer	1.8
Student[1]	3.0
Homemaker[1]	3.8
Retired[1]	19.2

Source: *Vancouver Chinese Community Study, 1974*
1. This was a survey of household heads. Inevitably, it included some who were not economically active. The data are thus not strictly comparable to census data. It was felt useful to include those not in the labor force. In 1971 approximately 25 percent of those between 16-64 were not in the labor force.

The Chinese of Canada are overwhelmingly an urban population with urban skills. An earlier generation had roots in China's countryside and brought to Canada peasant skills. The Chinese population in Canada from the late 1960s suggests a close association with an urban milieu. The points of migration are major urban concentrations and even for the local-born second generation, their provinces of birth contain Canada's major urban centers.

Chinese involvement in the lesser centers of population also suggests an involvement in service-oriented occupations. This is reflective of the status of the Chinese population as an immigrant population. Immigrants whose mother tongue is neither English nor French, coming from distinctive cultural backgrounds, may move into particular economic niches. Such niches allow the immigrants to adapt to the new culture by either doing unpleasant work requiring little skill (such as working on the railroad) or working very long hours. Chinese in Vancouver and Victoria, and, to a lesser degree, in other Canadian cities, have a substantial domination of corner grocery stores. Hard work, long hours, diligence, and the use of long-established Chinese wholesaling networks, allow the establishment of a secure economic foothold for the Chinese immigrant who can bring suffi-cient capital together for such an operation.

At both national and metropolitan levels, although certain occupational characteristics traditionally associated with the Chinese population are

TABLE 12 *Chinese population, Canada, Montreal and Toronto: Income,*
       1971

Income ($)	Canada %	Montreal/Toronto %
Less than 2 000	4.5	4.8
2 000 - 3 499	7.8	6.9
3 500 - 4 999	9.8	11.4
5 000 - 7 999	20.4	19.1
8 000 - 10 999	16.3	16.2
11 000 - 13 999	10.3	10.0
14 000 - 19 999	7.0	6.7
20 000 - 24 000	2.7	1.4
*Over 25 000	2.1	2.0
Loss/None/Not Applicable	18.8	20.3
	N = 1241	N = 369

Source: *Census*, 1971.

prominent, Chinese are involved in a broad range of occupations (Tables 9, 10, and 11).

Because of the recency of migration and the consequent problems of adaptation, the population is not a wealthy one. In 1971 modal income was in the $5 000-$7 999 range with only about 20 percent earning in excess of $11 000 (Table 12).

Canada's Chinese population is characterized by dualities the roots of which lie in changing immigration regulations. Thus the population is structured around those who came to Canada before 1923 and those who came after the great regulation changes in the 1960s. The overwhelming impression of Chinese in Canada in the 1970s is that of an immigrant population. But to see the population only as a set of immigrants is to ignore the reality of the older, if numerically smaller, group of descendants of the pre-1923 migrants. The Chinese migrants of the earlier period developed communities and community organizations that newer migrants have had to take into account. The newer Chinese residents have tended to add onto existing structures and sometimes to revive extant ones.

Immigration was, nonetheless, one of the dominant themes in the organization of Chinese-Canadian communities in the 1970s. It is not easy to pinpoint precisely why Canada became such an important area for Chinese migration in the 1960s. Certainly the places that provided migrants were becoming increasingly unattractive in that decade. It is also important to indicate those factors that make a given destination appear attractive to potential migrants. The two factors that predominate are the presence of kinsmen and the possibility of social or economic conditions that migrants can adapt to. In Vancouver in the middle 1970s, Chinese informants gave

TABLE 13 *Vancouver Chinese population: Reasons for migration to Canada, by age, 1974*

	Reason for migration to Canada						
Age	Family links	Economic prospects	Social stability	Generally better	Education system	Other	
20 - 29	35.7	10.7	3.6	10.7	26.0	17.8	10.6
30 - 39	42.4	22.0	8.5	13.6	5.1	8.5	21.3
40 - 49	39.0	19.5	11.0	15.9	9.7	4.9	29.6
50 - 59	43.6	2.6	5.1	23.1	12.8	12.8	14.1
60 - 69	50.0	7.1	10.7	17.9	7.1	7.1	10.1
70 - 79	48.3	31.0	6.9	6.9	—	6.9	10.5
80 & over	27.3	54.5	—	18.2	—	—	4.0
	41.5	18.1	7.9	15.2	9.0	8.3	N = 277

Source: *Vancouver Chinese Community Study, 1974.*

family ties as the single most important factor that impelled migration. But also economic conditions were seen as attractive, as was the general aura of peace and tranquility that migrants believed characterized Canada. Also of significance was the nature of the educational system and the opportunities for their children within it. The educational system of Hong Kong and, to a lesser degree, also of Singapore and Malaysia, was extremely competitive. The strain on pupils and parents alike was substantial. The less pressured, more open, system of Canada was a not insignificant element in the decision to migrate. Reasons to migrate vary with education and age. The young tend to come with less attention to kinship considerations. For those with higher educational levels, educational opportunities (for children) or the economic and social climate tend to figure more prominently than kinship in the decision to migrate (Tables 13 and 14).

For most migrants, however, it appears that kinship links were very important – at least in the Vancouver sample. Indeed, three-quarters of this sample were sponsored migrants. Further, a typical pattern in Vancouver seems to have been one in which an individual came alone, to be followed by someone he sponsored, typically, spouse and children. There was, of course, some variation with age. Elderly informants were victims of immigration regulations and were recruited with spouses, or married only after migration. Younger migrants were typically single, marrying only after accommodating to the new environment.

In general, the process of adaptation did not seem unduly traumatic. Difficulties could be expected to arise in the contexts of employment, education, housing, food, and language. In Vancouver 54.3 percent reported language problems; 23.7 percent reported no problem. In 1971, in Canada as a whole, 77.2 percent of the population was able to speak English, 0.4 French and 3.2 percent both official languages; 19.2 percent were able to speak neither. In terms of the language of the household, the great majority

TABLE 14 *Vancouver Chinese population: Reasons for migration to Canada, by educational level, 1974*

Educational level	Family links	Reason for migration to Canada					
		Economic prospects	Social stability	Generally better	Education system	Other	
University	24.2	17.2	9.7	16.1	19.1	12.9	22.3
High school graduate	29.7	16.2	8.1	27.0	10.8	8.1	13.3
Some high school	50.6	14.8	6.2	11.1	7.8	9.9	29.1
Elementary	46.6	22.4	8.6	12.1	3.4	5.1	20.9
Traditional — literate	36.3	31.8	4.5	27.7	4.5	—	7.9
Traditional — illerate/ None	72.2	5.6	11.1	5.6	—	5.6	6.5
	41.5	18.1	7.9	15.2	9.0	8.3	N = 277

Source: *Vancouver Chinese Community Study, 1974.*

spoke a language other than French, English, or a European language commonly spoken in Canada (presumably Chinese). In the Vancouver sample, 14.2 percent spoke no English, 24.8 percent spoke it "poorly," 37.4 percent comfortably, and 23.6 percent fluently. The language of the home in Vancouver reflected the subcultural diversity of the population. Of those born in Vancouver, less than one-third spoke Chinese exclusively, one-third spoke a mixture of Chinese and English, and the rest (37 percent) spoke English only.

In the larger urban centers of Canada, which were the primary points of settlement for new Chinese migrants, housing was, in general, at a premium. Population growth rates in both Vancouver and Toronto, and, to a lesser extent, Calgary, Edmonton, and Montreal, were substantial. This was especially so in the early 1970s when Chinese migration to Canada was increasing. In Vancouver, however, 67.1 percent of the sample population reported no problems with finding a house. In 1974, only 18.4 percent were renting accommodation. Although it does seem to be the case the migrants lived with relatives or in rented accommodation initially, the purchase of a house was a priority. Almost 30 percent of the Vancouver sample bought a house outright with cash. Difficulties associated with borrowing money were thus alleviated in a substantial number of cases. By the 1970s, restrictive covenants limiting the areas where Chinese could live in Vancouver were a thing of the past. Chinese were scattered throughout the city and adjacent municipalities. There were certain districts, however, that became popular. This was in part due to cost – other immigrant groups lived in these areas as well – but was also related to public transportation networks. The early 1970s saw the Chinese population of Toronto scattered throughout the metropolitan area. After the development of a new "Chinatown" to replace the old which was effectively demolished by urban "renewal" in the middle 1960s a new residential area, adjacent to the reestablished "Chinatown," grew. The development of this residential concentration and the quality of life there became an important issue in Chinese ethnic politics in the middle 1970s. These disputes in Toronto were reflected in other major centers of Chinese population from the late 1960s on.

Given the generally substantial levels of educational achievement of Chinese migrants to Canada after 1967, and the significance of Canada's educational system in the decision to migrate, it is not surprising that difficulties with education did not rank high. Younger children coped easily with the system and parental encouragement saw the entry of large numbers of "visa students" from Hong Kong, Singapore, and Malaysia, the vast majority of whom were Chinese. Cantonese became a second language in many student cafeterias. Chinese students were numerically dominant in certain disciplines, especially in applied science, medicine, and dentistry, but as the 1970s progressed, commerce, law, and the arts became attractive alternatives. As Chinese communities grew in complexity, the demand for Chinese professionals grew. Only in the late 1940s had the maturing second generation successfully argued for the Chinese right to be represented by ethnic Chinese in such professions as law, pharmacy, and accountancy. A quarter-century later the universities produced an array of Chinese professionals, whose ranks were swelled by highly qualified immigrants. Unlike their kinsmen of a generation earlier, they were not hemmed in by restrictive professional rules. While the ethnic community became an important point of reference in their professional commitments, they were not limited by it.

The generally high levels of educational achievement are one set of reasons which account for the relative ease with which Chinese in Canada coped with a steadily worsening labor market in the 1970s. In the Vancouver sample almost one-half reported no problems in finding employment; 22.5 percent suggested they had substantial difficulties. Vancouver, with its relatively lower manufacturing capacity when compared to Montreal and Toronto, presumably presented special difficulties. One reason for the attractiveness of Toronto for Chinese migrants in the 1970s was the economic opportunities throughout southern Ontario.

One of the problems for migrants was that skills and training acquired outside Canada were not always readily transferred to the Canadian environment. Civil engineers with a training at a Chinese university and job experience in Hong Kong or some other part of Asia, found it difficult to practise their profession in Canada without some effort to upgrade skill levels. Initial jobs were thus often in contexts that were not wholly appropriate to their training or expertise. And those jobs were often located within an ethnic context – for example, restaurant manager. Indeed, the immediate consequence of migration was to suffer a loss in occupational prestige. Certain Chinese cultural norms seemed to prevail in seeking jobs. A significant portion of the Vancouver sample (45.9 percent) relied upon introductions by friends or relatives to find jobs. Relatives were particularly significant in introducing informants to jobs within the ethnic community. Ties within the ethnic community, or kinship networks, were thus important in assisting Chinese migrants in the 1970s to adapt to the difficulties posed by the Canadian occupational system.

Conclusion

All ethnic groups change their character over time. The typical process of change is one in which the first generation of a migrant population establishes its base and allows the second generation to take on the major characteristics of the dominant culture, albeit while retaining certain aspects of homeland culture. Canadians of German, Dutch, or English origin have only few elements of distinctiveness among them in the second and third generation. Chinese Canadians did not follow this typical development pattern. It was not a question of their cultural distinctiveness. Rather, for so much of their history they were denied participation in the larger society and the Chinese ethnic group developed in a highly unbalanced way as a consequence of immigration legislation. Only after 1967 was the possibility of a more typical development sequence realized. Free of the petty restrictions of a previous generation, Chinese were free to come to Canada insofar as they satisfied certain universalistic criteria contained within the new immigration regulations. A portion of the increasingly large numbers of Chinese immigrants that came to Canada in the 1970s were the kinsmen of those already present. But a significant number arrived independently of kin ties – scoring high in terms of education, English-language competence, and having the wherewithal to support themselves in the Canadian context. The new Chinese migrants were of urban origins and highly sophisticated. They were able to fully contribute to Canadian society in general and to become involved in the renewal of Chinese communities in the major centers.

The restrictions of a previous generation had resulted in a ghetto-like existence for Chinese Canadians who, deprived of the possibility of family formation in Canada, sought resolution to their major problems within their male-dominated communities. After 1967, new migrants were no longer restricted by "Chinatown" although they contributed to the renewal of Chinatowns as the locus for cultural items that were distinctively Chinese and the major course of a distinctive Canadian-Chinese identity. The new migrants transformed the Chinese ethnic group into a vital title in Canada's ethnic mosaic.

END NOTES

I would like to acknowledge the research support provided by the Secretary of State and Canada Council and the wise guidance of Prof. E.B. Wickberg of the Department of History, University of British Columbia, and the counsel of Prof. W.E. Willmott and the Department of Sociology, University of Canterbury, New Zealand.

1. The most comprehensive summary of the issues is L. Crissman, "The Segmentary Structure of Urban Chinese Communities," *Man* 2, 2 (June 1967), pp. 185-204.

2. For an excellent discussion of immigration policy see Freda Hawkins, *Canada and Immigration: Public Policy and Public Concern* (Montreal and London, 1972), esp. pp. 71-173.

3. For a brief assessment see my "Chinese Family and Community in Canada: Tradition and Change," in J.L. Elliott, ed., *Two Nations: Many Cultures* (Scarborough, Ont.: Prentice-Hall of Canada, 1979), pp. 385-371.

4. Paul C.P. Siu, "The Isolation of the Chinese Laundryman," in E. Burgess and D.J. Bogue, eds. *Contributions to Urban Sociology.* (Chicago, 1964), pp. 429-442.

5. Chang, Lee, "Chinese in Northern Ontario," unpublished paper given at the Annual Meeting of the Canadian Society for Asian Studies, Guelph, Ont., May 1978.

6. Vivien, Lai, "The Chinese Immigrants in Toronto," in J.L. Elliot, ed. *Minority Canadians: Vol 2. Immigrant Groups.* Scarborough, Ont.: Prentice-Hall of Canada, 1971, pp. 120-140.

7. See P.S. Levine *Historical Documentation Pertaining to Overseas Chinese Organizations*, unpublished Thesis, University of Toronto, 1975, pp. 118-119.

8. One of the intriguing features about a visit to Toisan *xian*, the major point of migration for Chinese to Canada, is how the county town is reminiscent of a Canadian "Chinatown." The architectural links between Canada and China are clear. In one household in a village that I visited in Dun-fen commune, I noted a photograph of one of the grandchildren of the household head – in the graduation robes of Simon Fraser University!

C. Michael Lanphier[1] York University

Indochinese Resettlement and the Development of Canadian Refugee Policy*

Historical Background

Throughout Canadian history immigrants have arrived in Canada for political reasons. With curious irony, however, a policy of refugee intake, *per se*, has existed formally only since the Immigration Act of 1976. Prior to that time, Canada's continuing involvement with persons who immigrate as refugees required special action of the federal government and the Cabinet. Such political urgencies were considered as non-recurring issues. That a government should establish a policy within which refugee intake would be accommodated was a proposition which dawned only after the waves of post-World War II displacements. Political action slowly but inexorably occurred thereafter (*cf.* Dirks, 1977).

The term "refugee" itself remained a flexible category until the implicit adoption of the U.N. High Commission for Refugees (UNHCR) Convention relating to the status of Refugees of 1951. Despite easily recognizable distinctions in social status, the official status of "refugee" was absent in Canadian legislation (cf. Dirks, 1977, Ch. III).

Even large blocs of refugees immediately after the close of World War II required *ad hoc* measures of order in council for admission to Canada. Yet, this cumbersome procedure resulted in Canada's first massive immigration (some 40 000 displaced persons by the end of 1948) in recent history (Dirks, 1977, 154-5). Efforts in the creation of any coordinated policy on refugees, *per se*, were halting, despite the creation of a Department of Citizenship and Immigration in 1946. That department was unable to accede to the provisions of the UNHCR Convention on the Status of Refugees in 1951; rather, it remained an implicit set of working definitions for the Canadian government until final ratification of the Convention in 1969 (Dirks, 1977, 181-2, 232). This movement from a nation-centered to an internationally-centered commitment developed gradually since World War II, but little change would have been noted had political upheavals not

* A revised version of "Canada's Response to Refugees," C. Michael Lanphier, *International Migration Review* (Center for Migration Studies of New York, Inc.) Vol. 15, No. 1 Spring-Summer, 1981.

aroused the attention of Western nations in unrelieved succession in the past two decades.

The experience of the early 1970s provided initial affirmative answers to two disparate but cardinal questions: (1) Do selected refugees adapt well to Canadian society within a relatively short period of resettlement? (2) Is there a need for a policy initiative especially for refugee assistance? As for the first, it was apparent that not only persons from European origins, but also those from Asiatic and African origins showed initial signs of adaptation similar to those of other immigrants to Canada. In other words, ethnic origin has little or no direct effect on speed or degree of refugee adaptation in Canada.

The affirmative answer to the second question relating to refugee policy remained rather complicated in light of existing practices. Breadwinners were selected on the basis of their youth and education or occupational training, including language facility in English or French. This consistent practice served as a functional equivalent to policy, as these guidelines, or operating procedures, yielded a type of selectivity of refugees in each cohort. The need for a more clearly articulated policy was manifest. Operating procedures, however standardized over time, remained to be applied in an *ad hoc* manner on each occasion in which comprehensive aid to political refugees was required.

Evolution of Refugee Policy

The evolution of refugee policy in Canada has developed in increasingly broad and detailed ways in recent years. This evolution may be highlighted by the following four points:

1) Adoption of the UN definition of Convention refugee;
2) Differentiation in legislation of refugees into Convention and other "Designated Classes";
3) Development of methods of sponsorship for refugees in both Convention and Designated Classes; and
4) Formulation of annual refugee plans.

Adoption of Convention Refugee Status

Canada did not sign the UN Refugee Convention upon its formulation in 1951. Rather, it opted to use the definition as an operating guideline for identifying refugees. Decisions regarding the admission of refugees fell squarely, according to the government of the day, within the terms of national sovereignty (Dirks, 1977, Ch. VIII). The formal adoption of the Convention refugee definition in 1969 implicated Canada in an international commitment, however tenuous, to assist such refugees as a continuing, rather than *ad hoc*, undertaking. Correspondingly, the government has responded, since 1969, to 10 refugee movements of differing sizes, in comparison with three (very large) movements in the two decades prior.[2] These responses stand largely outside the legal frame of the UNHCR Convention, as they relate to activities undertaken abroad, whereas the Convention specifications relate to rights and privileges of refugees within the bounds of the country.

Differentiation of "Designated Classes" from Convention Refugees

The specific requirements which conform to the Convention Refugee status cannot be met in every situation in which large numbers of persons experience or perceive political retribution in their home country. As a result, the Immigration Act of 1976 enabled the government to establish "Designated Classes" for persons whose collective situation placed them in a *de facto* refugee situation, even if the Convention criteria might not all be met. The use of "Designated Classes" overcomes the brittleness of a single definition, so that definitions used by Canadian visa officers can more closely fit the characteristics of the particular group of displaced or persecuted persons.

Currently there are three different "Designated Classes" in vigor for a two-year period.
1) Indochinese (citizens and residents of Kampuchea, Laos, Vietnam, leaving after April 30, 1975);
2) Latin American (citizens of Argentina, Chile, Uruguay still residing there); and
3) Self-exiled (citizens and residents of Albania, Bulgaria, Czechoslovakia, GDR, Hungary, Poland, Romania, USSR, applying outside Eastern Europe; and Haiti).

Development of Sponsorship Arrangements

Over and above the intake of Convention and Designated Class refugees planned by the federal government, the legislation has included provisions enabling groups of individuals and organizations to sponsor refugee individuals or families. Groups of five or more persons or a corporation may undertake support of the refugee and dependents for a period of one year. In addition national organizations may sign "master agreements" with the federal government enabling their constituent groups (in the case of a church, its local parishes or congregations) to sign sponsorship undertakings with minimal formalities. Policy development has therefore encouraged participation of the private and organizational sectors in sponsorship while maintaining the centralized procedure of admissions. Numbers of refugees admitted to Canada may thereby vary not only with international political conditions but also the level of participation of the private sector within Canada, as private sponsorships are supplementary.

Formulation of Annual Refugee Plans

With the development of attention to refugees as a separate category of immigrants, has come the annual planning exercise specifically addressed to the Canadian commitment to refugee intake in the following year. In the first instance, the planning endeavor is conducted independently of other immigration concerns. Prior commitments are assessed with a view to their possible extension, and new sources of refugees are evaluated. Quotas are attached for each category of refugee. Over the past four years, the annual plans, announced in November of the year preceding, have appeared as follows:

	1979	1980	1981	1982
Indochina	5 000	10 000	8 000	4 000
East Europeans	2 300	3 000	4 000	6 000
Latin America and Caribbean	500	500	1 000	1 000
Other areas	200	500	500	1 000
Contingency reserve	2 000	1 000	2 500	2 000
Total	10 000	15 000	16 000	14 000

Source: (Employment and Immigration, Annual Reports, 1981 and 1982).

During the year, plans are revised upwards, with the contingencies applied to particular categories. In the case of Indochinese refugee intake, the quotas were successively revised during 1979 and 1980 to numbers which quadrupled the originally planned target figures.

Refugees Admitted to Canada

The period 1970-71 (Table 1), witnessed relatively low refugee movement to Canada. With the expulsion of ethnic Asians from Uganda early in 1972, however, the intake resumed its increasingly undulating yearly pattern, followed in 1973 by the beginning of reception of Chilean refugees – a flow which has continued until the present. The ascending totals of refugees from 1975 onwards is attributable to multiple movements from Chile, Indochina (especially Vietnam), Lebanon, and Mozambique. Not until early 1979, however, did the movement from Indochina assume its presently

TABLE 1 *Refugees admitted to Canada, by year and birthplace*

Birthplace	1970	1971	1972	1973	1974	1975	1976	1977	1978	1979	1980
Vietnam										18 390	24 274
Kampuchea										1 605	3 092
Laos										3 459	6 390
Other										1 374	1 465
Subtotal Indochina						3 576	2 602	777	1 315	24 828	35 221
East Europe										2 225	4 116
Tibet		187									
Uganda			41	2 075	119						
Latin America			4 875	20	1 054	1 857	1 351	1 214	729	432	437
Lebanon							6 116	3 661	1 078		
Mozambique							691	750	271		
Others	1 361	614	324	288	483	1 023	1 023	951	868	394	587
Subtotal refugees	1 361	801	5 204	2 383	1 656	6 331	11 783	7 353	4 261	27 879	40 361
Other immmigrants	146 352	121 099	116 766	181 817	216 809	181 550	137 646	107 561	82 052	84 217	102 756
Total	147 713	121 900	122 006	184 200	218 465	187 881	149 429	114 914	86 313	112 096	143 117

Source: Employment and Immigration Canada, Refugee Policy Division.

predominating place as a source of refugees. The figure in 1979 of 18 390 refugees from Vietnam represents the largest intake of people from any single country to Canada since 1976, when immigrants from Great Britain totaled over 21 000 persons.

Since World War II Canada has received more than 365 000 immigrants as refugees, displaced persons, or "Designated Classes." The largest proportion, 71 percent, were from Central and Eastern Europe, especially immediately after World War II. Refugees from Asia accounted for 19 percent of the total; with the exception of Tibetans, they have all been very recent arrivals. Africa and South America accounted for 3 and 2 percent respectively, with the remaining 5 percent from various other parts of the world.

Indochinese Refugees

As a result of priority selection of families with children, Indochinese refugees arriving in Canada in 1979 clustered in the younger age ranges, with about 14 percent being under school age and another quarter of school age (6-17 years inclusive). On the other end of the age continuum, only 2 percent was age 60 or over. A Dependency Ratio the number of young and old as a fraction of those eligible for the work force of .50 represents a relatively high proportion of dependents.

As one-half of the males and about three-fifths of the females age 18 and over are married (although the partners may not have both arrived in Canada in some cases), it can be estimated that couples average more than two dependents each. Thus dependents are by no means evenly distributed over the population of adults; rather, almost half the adults arrive with responsibility mainly for themselves, even though they may be part of an extended family group.

While educational background of Indochinese refugees appears low in the overall, a certain amount of those having no formal education experience may be attributable to the unusually young age profile. Thus the data on educational background in Table 2 are classified separately for "principal" arrivals (heads of households and unaccompanied adults) to adjust for the age disparity. Nearly all "principals" have elementary education, with a median of nine years. Roughly about one in five of the "principals" has some trade or (para-) professional education. About one in eight have some university education.

By birthplace, the profile for persons born in Vietnam is similar to that discussed above, as refugees from that origin constitute the largest number of refugees to date. Among those from Kampuchea, their numbers are concentrated in the secondary-or-less category, with trade or university training being rare. The profile for persons born in Laos differs in that a greater proportion have taken trade or (para-) professional training.

TABLE 2 *Education, intended occupation and official language capability Indochinese refugee arrivals, 1979-1980[a]*

| | Education (%) | | | | | |
	None	Secondary or less	Trade school	University	Total	Number cases
Principal[b]	3	79	9	9	100	25 309
Total	24	66	5	5	100	60 049

| | Intended occupation (%) | | | | | | |
	White collar[b]	Mid range[d]	Blue collar	New[f]	Other[g]	Total	Number cases
Principal	6	7	49	27	11	100	25 309
Total	3	4	26	16	51	100	60 049

| | Official Language Capability (%) | | | | | |
	English	French	English and French	Neither English or French	Total	Number Cases
Principal	8	4	3	85	100	25 309
Total	5	2	1	92	100	60 049

Source: Employment and Immigration Canada, Special Tabulations.
Notes: [a]Arrivals January 1, 1979 — January 5, 1980
[b]Heads of families or single, unaccompanied adult
[c]Managerial, professional
[d]Clerical, sales
[e]Service, manual, repair
[f]No previous job; no stated intention
[g]Students, homemakers, nonworkers

Information about occupation is derived from responses on visa applications. Correspondence between these intentions and occupations which refugees will have obtained either in launching or later on in their careers in Canada is unknown. Yet the data in Table 2 indicate availability and a first approximation as to status levels to which refugees may orient themselves in the Canadian labor market.

Overall, only 27 percent of the 1979 arrivals indicated an occupational intention which was codable according to the codes normally used in occupational classification in Canada. Among "principals" this codability reaches a level of only 54 percent. Thus a substantial majority of persons destined for labor force participation and a majority of other refugees have no *prima facie* orientation in terms of the Canadian occupational structure.

Among the refugees who indicated an occupational intention, blue-collar occupations, especially relating to repairing and manufacturing, predominate. By contrast, only small minorities indicated either white-collar or middle level occupational intentions. By far the largest uncodable category among "principals" was that of "new worker," a category indicating intention to join the labor force but with insufficient training or work experience to provide an occupational orientation.

Variation in intended occupational orientation by birthplace is only slight. The Vietnamese profile corresponds to that noted above. By comparison, Kampucheans are "new workers" in greater proportion. Similarly, among Laotians, the largest single category is that of "new worker," with proportionally more cases than average falling into blue-collar manufacturing.

Refugees who indicated a substantive occupational intention were reflecting a moderate-to-considerable number of years of work force experience. If "new workers" are excluded, only 11 percent of the prospective labor force entrants had no prior formal work experience. Rather, some 42 percent of them had more than five years work experience, with only slight variation in that proportion by birthplace.

Thus there is only a loose and very much *ad hoc* "fit" between the profile of occupational intentions expressed by refugees and the present structure of occupations in Canada. The implications of this disjuncture are somewhat mitigated by the significant proportions of "new workers" many of whom are young entrants to the labor force. In practical terms, however, the urgency both of occupational training and counseling is paramount. The orientations of the recently-arrived Indochinese refugees appear vague and labile. The resolution into a clearer profile of occupational intentions remains one of the greatest challenges in the resettlement process in Canada. Most refugees face the work world as yet another new experience to encounter.

In terms of language abilities, only about 10 percent of all immigrants could communicate with even minimal proficiency in either of Canada's official languages, English and French. Data in Table 2 indicate that the low levels of knowledge of English or French characterized not only dependents, but also to a lesser extent, the "principals." As only 15 percent of the "principals" could express themselves with any degree of fluency in either of those languages, mainly English, the need for training in either English or French has surfaced as one of the immediate requirements. In practical terms, all arrivals of school age and beyond were candidates for language classes.[3]

Sponsorship: Government and Private

As previously indicated, Canada's refugee assistance for Indochinese refugees especially represents a mix of governmental and private sponsorship. Although such a combination has occurred in response to earlier refugee movements, notably the Hungarian movement in 1956-57, the present arrangements appear more broadly based both geographically and organizationally. Not only have local groups, religions and voluntary organizations undertaken individual initiatives of sponsorship of refugee families, but they have provided a network of services to sponsors and families over and above that offered from governmental sources. Collaboration with federal, provincial, and local governments has been close enough to coordinate delivery of services with minimal or no overlap; it has been distant enough to permit criticism of policy (Adelman, *et al.,* 1980).[4]

The processing of refugees in camps and until arrival at the final destination is identical for all refugees unless the sponsor has nominated a particular individual or family. Most private sponsors, however, have requested a family group of a certain size with the option of accepting or rejecting any particular refugee family group so matched.

The response of the private sector to sponsorship of Indochinese refugees commenced in quantity midway through 1979, after active encouragement by the federal government, including the agreement which committed the government to sponsor one refugee for each one privately sponsored, as discussed above. Through March, 1980, some 36 000 requests for sponsorship were made by private groups. By the end of December, 1979, some 13 400 privately sponsored refugees had arrived in addition to another 11 200 under governmental sponsorship auspices. As the time lapse between initiation of sponsorship request and arrival has varied from three weeks to five months or more, it is not possible to reconcile numbers of requests with numbers of arrivals even in an approximate fashion.

While the private sponsorship system was widely diffused throughout all provinces of Canada, the proportions of requests follow population size. A month-by-month analysis of applications indicates, however, a definite wave moving from West to East in a period of six months. Requests in 1979 from sponsors in the Prairies and the West were proportionally heavier through June. The wave of sponsorship requests moved easterly within two months, so that Ontario sponsors predominated in the third quarter of 1979.   By September the rate of applications had grown considerably in Quebec. Applications from private sponsors in the Atlantic regions increased in turn during the fourth quarter. In the first quarter of 1980, the sheer number of sponsorship applications dropped noticably but evenly across provinces. Presently, the provinces with the higher rates of private sponsorship are those with large metropolitan areas. In overall numbers of private sponsorship applications it appears that they have superceded even the upwardly revised expectations of the federal government. By December, 1980, the private sector had sponsored more than one half of an expected total of 60 000 Indochinese refugees.

Summary and Conclusions

Canada's response to refugee problems has oscillated both in level of intake and in degree of organization of activity since World War II. Positive responses to refugee movements from Central and Eastern Europe following the cessation of hostilities and subsequent political upheavals represented a series of *ad hoc* responses yet with substantial numbers received.

The notion of refugee as defined by the UNHCR Convention was adopted only in 1969 by Canada, although it had been used implicitly since 1951. Two implications followed from this ambivalence. First, Canada as a government appeared reticent to assume responsibility for refugees as an international commitment, above and beyond national goals, until late in the 1960s. Second, and more important, the definition was somewhat maladaptive if used exclusively.

Canada adopted a broader if more complex position. Recent legislation has accommodated both Convention refugees and Designated Class provisions as general categories. The existence of the definition of four different "Designated Classes" – Indochinese, Latin American, Haitian, and Self Exile (East European) – each with different specifications, indicates a distinctly innovative and flexible governmental approach in determining eligibility for selection under relaxed admissibility criteria.

Analysis of a series of refugee movements during the past decade indicates that success in adaptation, if measured in terms of socioeconomic adjustment, varies somewhat independently of particular cultural background. Rather, "success" of adaptation depends on a substantial provision of services to refugee arrivals, including language instruction and prolonged, if informal, supervision *by sponsors*.

More recently, both public and governmental attention has concentrated on Indochinese refugee aid. The arrival of more than 60 000 refugees by 1981, nearly three-quarters of whom were Vietnamese in origin, is the largest yearly refugee intake in recent history. Compared with immigration of persons from all other countries to Canada in the same year, it is the largest identifiable group.

This responsiveness had diminished during 1981 and even more in 1982, with governmental intake tapering off as public enthusiasm for private sponsorship has waned. Despite this diminution by the end of 1982, the numbers and diversity of refugees especially in the developing world have augmented even more dramatically. Which refugee groups will be better served by resettlement in Western nations than in neighboring areas of first asylum remains a much-debated question. Even an innovative and broadened policy, as that demonstrated in Canada's recent experience, appears woefully ethnocentric and restricted in an international perspective of growing demand for assistance to refugees.

Epilogue

The Minister of Employment and Immigration struck a Task Force on Immigration Practices and Procedures in September, 1980 to investigate a variety of problems in the process of determination of refugee status. The wide-ranging report in 1981 criticized not only the general rigidity of the process, but more significantly, focussed upon the importance of careful examination of claims to refugee status, including the elimination of the practice of rejecting large portions of refugee claims as being "manifestly unfounded" without individual review by committee. Secondly, the report advocated the extension of the range of credibility to the prospective refugee in two important ways: burden of proof and the issuance of a variety of temporary status measures. As for burden of proof, it was asserted that all claims should be regarded as true and valid in the first instance. Thus it was the burden of proof on the part of the Government of Canada to disqualify any and all such claims. During what might be a very lengthy process of such determination, refugee applicants, if already resident in Canada, would be permitted to remain with family and hold jobs. The Task Force also recommended a far wider interpretation of notions of "persecution" and recommended that assistance in making such claims should be provided as a service by the very government from which the refugee status is being sought.

In February, 1982, the Minister of Employment and Immigration, Lloyd Axworthy, announced the implementation of several of the Task Force's recommendations ("New refugee status advisory guidelines on refugee definition and assessment of credibility" – Press Release, February 20, 1982). The guidelines were implemented to act retroactively on a large backlog of cases before the Refugee Status Committee. Likewise, appeals from that committee were to be governed by the same guidelines. The content of the guidelines relates to claims for refugee status, burden of proof, and interpretation of circumstances of "persecution."

It is argued that claims for refugee status may vary both in their timing and location. Persons may claim refugee status well after having left the country under circumstances which might not have been related directly and tangibly to persecution prior to the time of departure. The burden of proof for the claimant's argument would be assumed as recommended by the Task Force; the claim would be considered valid unless serious evidence to the contrary was brought forward; and temporary asylum would be granted until such time as the final determination of each case would be made. The circumstances of persecution may be interpreted broadly so as to include events that could potentially place the person in jeopardy at the time the claim is made, even though such circumstances did not exist at the time of departure. Persecution may likewise be defined to include periodic harassment, impersonal deprivation, and group-related discrimination.

Thus the Government of Canada has broadened the criteria for eligibility for refugee status that will allow significantly more claims on an *individual* basis. Whether or not a country may have been categorized in one of the "designated classes," individuals may make claims relating to similar circumstances of impersonal or indirect persecution or terrorism, previously recognized as valid only among persons within the "designated class" category. Thus not only is it likely that the number of refugees admitted under the newly revised criteria governing eligibility of Convention refugees will increase, but also that the origins of refugees will be more diverse, both by nations and by circumstances of persecution or fear thereof.

As the levels of refugees to be selected on a yearly basis, including Convention refugees, is a resultant of a deliberative process by the Minister involving consultations in and out of the government, the selection of the number of refugees to be admitted in any given year is an issue that still extends beyond the scope of that report. Changes will be reflected far more in terms of the criteria for eligibility for refugee status than in an overall growth in the number of persons admitted as refugees to Canada in any given year in the near future.

END NOTES

1. The writer is indebted to members of the Refugee Task Force and Refugee Policy Division of the Department of Employment and Immigration, especially Michael Molloy, C. Thorlakson and T. Falsetto for invaluable information and data. Joan Brown, of the Ontario Ministry of Culture and Recreation, also provided many of the data sets. None of these persons or departments bears any responsibility for errors or interpretations herein. Support for this work was given by the Faculty of Arts, York University.
2. The recent movements are the Tibetan (1970), Ugandan Asian (1972-73). Special South American 1973-79, Cypriots (1975), Special Vietnamese-Cambodian (1975-78), Iraq Kurdish (1976), Angola Mozambique (1976-77, Lebanese (1976-79), Argentine political prisoners (1978) and Indochinese (1979-present).
3. Although services in Cantonese are widely available in Canada, services in Vietnamese were initially available only in larger metropolitan areas. They were quickly diffused as the year progressed. Services in Khmer, Mandarin and Lao were diffused in the larger metropolitan areas only late in the year. Gaps in coverage remain.

   The Government of Canada was prepared for provision of English or French classes to refugees upon arrival through a combination of subsidized language classes, special classes in regular schools and some supplementation through volunteers. The Government of Quebec established its own network of French language classes for all immigrants. Private sponsors were assisted in finding these classes both through voluntary organizations and the branches of the Department of Employment and Immigration. They were advised categorically to insist that all adults and school-age children be enrolled in such programs. Refugees who were sponsored by the Government of Canada risked losing their subsidy if they failed to attend language classes regularly.

4. Organizations were vociferous, for example, when the federal government announced in November, 1979, a veritable curtailment of its own sponsorship of refugees on a matching basis with the private sector. This curtailment was rescinded and the governmental sponsorship program augmented in April, 1980, after a federal election brought a change in political party in power. In any case the voluntary organizational sector spearheaded the resistance at the risk of losing a certain margin of popular support (Adelman, 1980).

5. Technically, it has not been possible to obtain a "flow" table which traces the cases from initiation through interview, visa and arrival in Canada to date.

SELECTED REFERENCES

Dirks, G. E. *Canada's Refugee Policy: Indifference or Opportunism?* Montreal: McGill-Queen's University Press, 1977.

Facts for Canadian Groups and Organizations. Ottawa: Employment and Immigration Canada, 1979.

Smith, W. *Tibetan Refugees: A Second Life in a New Land.* Ottawa: Employment and Immigration, 1976.

RAYMOND BRETON   University of Toronto

West Indian, Chinese and European Ethnic Groups in Toronto:
Perceptions of Problems and Resources*

Introduction

In the course of their experience in the larger society, ethnic groups pursue certain values and encounter problems to overcome, costs to meet, and opportunities to exploit. It is the combination of aspirations, costs, problems, and opportunities that constitute the basis of the group's system of interests in relation to the rest of the society.[1] These can be collective phenomena because they are part or would be part of the individual experience of a significant number of members of the group as, for example, are aspirations and problems related to the search of a satisfactory job. If they are sufficiently frequent, if they have a symbolic value for the group, or if individuals experience problems or face opportunities because of their group membership, individual problems and opportunities can become group problems. However, groups can also face circumstances that affect them as a group, such as immigration laws, antidiscrimination programs, cultural policies, job specifications, and police protection.

In order to assist their members in connection with individual goals, problems, and opportunities or in order to pursue collective goals, ethnic groups may develop a more or less elaborate sociopolitical organization. At least three basic processes are involved: the identification of matters as being of collective interest and the articulation of related issues; the mobilization of commitment and participation, including the investment of resources; and the organization of the action itself to deal with problems identified or objectives formulated.

The components of social organization required include leadership; structures for decision-making, communication and social control; and mechanisms for conflict resolution and coordination. The organization of action also requires the availability of money, social cohesion, ideology,

---

* A revised version of "The Ethnic Community as a Resource in Relation to Group Problems: Perceptions and Attitudes," Research Paper No. 122, Centre for Urban and Community Studies, University of Toronto, May, 1981. The larger research project is entitled, "Ethnic Pluralism in an Urban Setting: A Study of Some Toronto Ethnic Groups."

425

and social norms. Once established, the organizational system constitutes a resource that members can use to cope with the problems they encounter.

The results presented in this essay deal with a limited number of the above dimensions, namely with some of the perceptions and attitudes of individuals with regard to problems faced by their group and its members in becoming fully incorporated in Canadian society. Two aspects of incorporation are considered: social acceptance and discrimination.[2] The essay also considers the perceptions as to the types of action that would be effective to deal with some of these problems, in particular the use of community organizational resources.[3]

Sources of Data

The results presented in this paper come from a survey of 2,338 respondents in Toronto.[4] An important feature of the study is that it is comparative in nature. The study includes a total of nine groups: eight minority groups and the "Majority Canadian group." The minority groups are the following: Chinese, German, Italian, Jewish, Portuguese, Ukrainian, West Indian, and "other English." This last group comprises first and second generation persons of English origin. The Majority Canadian group includes third-or-more-generation persons of English, Irish, and Scottish origin.

Since generation is an important source of variation in ethnic identity and behavior, it is incorporated in the study design. Some of the groups include only one generation either because significant immigration to Toronto occurred only recently (West Indians, Portuguese, and Chinese) or because of the way the group was defined (Majority Canadian group.) For the other groups, the study was designed so as to allow comparisons across generations. The sample is restricted to persons aged 18 to 65 years who were in the labor force or students.

The persons included in the sample were interviewed with the use of a schedule. On the average, interviews lasted one hour and a half. The interviews were carried out in 1978 and 1979.[5]

I – Perception of Problems of Social Incorporation

The incorporation of individuals and groups in a community and the social equality that full incorporation implies have an instrumental and an expressive dimension. They involve both matters pertaining to the position one occupies in the social structure with its associated benefits and matters related to the acceptance, respect, and status one receives from others. Thus, in attempting to improve their condition, ethnic groups and their members will seek social acceptance and will attempt to avoid discrimination.

(a) *Social Acceptance*

Two sets of indicators are used to explore possible problems of social acceptance: one pertains to personal acceptance in social relations and the other to acceptance expressed by the community-at-large through its immigration legislation.

Respondents were asked "how easily the Majority Canadian group" accepts them as neighbors and as "close relatives by marriage." In addition, members of the Majority Canadian group in the sample were asked if they would have someone from each of a number of groups as a next-door neighbor or as a close relative. The results for both sets of questions are presented in Table 1 for each of the groups.

The upper panel of the table on acceptance as neighbors reveals considerable variations but primarily in the *degree* of easiness with which people perceive the Majority Canadian group as accepting them. That is to say, the percentages who feel they are accepted very easily vary between 21 and 68, with the West Indians, Jews, and Chinese showing the lowest percentages and the Germans and Ukrainians the highest. If however, we combine the very easily and somewhat easily categories, variations are considerably reduced. The second part of Panel A shows that acceptance as neighbors as expressed by Majority Canadians themselves is not very different from what the group themselves perceive.

There are, however, a few discrepancies worth noting. Jewish respondents are *less* likely to feel accepted than what the Majority Canadians declare (a 12-percent difference). On the other hand, West Indian respondents seem to over-estimate their acceptance by Majority Canadians by 10 percent.

Generally and as expected, the level of acceptance as relatives tends to be lower than as neighbors (Table 1, Panel B). The differences in these two areas of social acceptance, however, are not the same for all groups.

Some members of the various groups also declare that they have personally experienced difficulties of social acceptance. Table 3, Section C shows the percentages, for each group, of those who have experienced problems of social acceptance. The "other areas" include the following items: (1) "socially, by people of other ethnic groups who did not want to associate with me"; (2) "when I was trying to rent an apartment, or buy or rent a house"; (3) "by not being accepted by a school I wanted to go to"; and (4) "other." The variations among groups in the experience of such difficulties correspond roughly with the variations in social acceptance just presented.

The degree to which various groups are accepted in a society is also reflected in its immigration legislation. Such legislation reflects the official attitude of a country vis-à-vis immigration generally and the immigration of various groups in particular. Because of this, it will usually be a matter of

TABLE 1 Perception of social acceptance by majority Canadian group and attitudes of majority Canadians and of others vis-à-vis each group (%)

	Chinese %	German %	Italian %	Jewish %	Portuguese %	Ukrainian %	West Indian %
A. 1 Perception of acceptance as neighbors							
Very easily	33 } 85	68 } 94	45 } 89	22 } 77	52 } 85	58 } 92	21 } 57
Somewhat easily	52	26	44	55	33	34	36
Not easily	5	3	8	17	9	4	35
Don't know	10	3	2	6	6	4	8
Number of interviews	(152)	(321)	(351)	(348)	(161)	(353)	(150)
A. 2 Acceptance as neighbors by							
Majority group*	83	92	85	89	84	91	67
Others**	84	82	83	84	83	85	66
Number of interviews	(1861)	(1706)	(1696)	(1698)	(1844)	(1643)	(1862)
B. 1 Perception of acceptance as relatives							
Very easily	11 } 56	62 } 89	41 } 89	8 } 41	42 } 77	49 } 84	10 } 33
Somewhat easily	45	27	48	33	35	35	23
Not easily	23	3	7	45	8	7	45
Don't know	21	8	5	14	15	9	21
Number of interviews	(152)	(320)	(350)	(347)	(162)	(353)	(150)
B. 2 Acceptance as relatives by							
Majority group*	65	87	84	77	68	87	49
Others**	50	64	65	66	62	69	38
Number of interviews	(1887)	(1727)	(1699)	(1699)	(1863)	(1664)	(1883)

*The number of interviews for the "Majority Group" ranges between 224 and 229.
**"Others" include all non-Majority Canadians except the respondents for the group concerned. Since this combined category changes with each group, the base of the percentage varies from column to column.

TABLE 2 *Views about immigration policies and changes in the relative size of groups by ethnic groups (%)*

	Chinese	German	Italian	Jewish	Portuguese	Ukrainian	Majority Canadian	West Indian	Other English
	%	%	%	%	%	%	%	%	%
A. Present laws make it too difficult for group to come to Canada									
Agree	46	8	32	14	69	25	64	8	24
Neutral	11	1	2	4	1	2	3	1	1
Disagree	37	78	55	69	21	56	25	74	64
Don't know	6	13	11	13	9	17	8	17	11
Number of interviews	(152)	(321)	(351)	(344)	(163)	(345)	(150)	(230)	(267)
B. Concern that group is becoming too small compared to others									
Very much and somewhat	18	11	10	24	13	25	28	45*	51*
A little	10	7	10	12	10	13	14	21	16
Number of interviews	(147)	(306)	(344)	(339)	(156)	(347)	(143)	(230)	(262)

*The question asked of the respondents of British origin referred to "the non-English groups becoming too large" in relation to the English-Canadian group.

some concern to many members of ethnic minorities and to the Majority Canadian group. This is so because it affects their relative sizes and thus their relative importance in society and because it may have an impact on the allocation of scarce resources and social status among them. There are, of course, other reasons why people may be concerned with immigration, such as the possibility of having relatives, friends, or simply people of one's own cultural background come to Canada.

An attempt was therefore made to ascertain if respondents see the legislation as presenting a problem from their perspective. Specifically, they were asked if present immigration laws make it too difficult for their own group. The results appear in Table 2. Given the previous results, it is to be expected that West Indians and Chinese respondents will be among those who are the most likely to feel that present laws make it too difficult for people from their home country to come to Canada. This is indeed what we observe, although the percentage is still higher among the Portuguese. For these three groups the percentage who think that the laws are too restrictive (for their group) vary between 46 and 69. Other groups show significantly lower percentages.

On the other hand, there is also the feeling that the immigration of certain groups is facilitated by present laws. The groups for whom that feeling exists in three categories of respondents (Majority Canadians, "other English", and all minority groups combined) are listed in Table 3. Pakistani and West Indians are the two groups for whom the percentage are the highest: 50 and 40 respectively. A third of minority group members feel that the law makes it too easy for people from the British Isles. About one-fourth (24 percent) of Majority Canadians feel this way for all groups. The percentages are relatively low for the Chinese (14 percent) and Jews (3 percent), a result that is somewhat surprising given the previous results on social acceptance.

Related to immigration and to the view that immigration laws may be too lenient or restrictive is the matter of size of one's group compared to the size of other groups. In other words, immigration laws may be a concern not only because of the kinds of people they directly or indirectly select, but also because of the number of people admitted. Thus members of certain groups may come to feel that their group is becoming too small relative to others (or that others are becoming too large).

The views of the sample on this question are presented in Table 2, Panel B. Among the minority groups, the view that they are "becoming too small a group in Toronto compared to other groups" is not a prevalent one. It is most frequently held among West Indians, Ukrainians, and Jews: about a third in each of these groups are at least a little concerned about this possibility. In the other four groups the percentage is somewhat lower, varying between 18 percent and 28 percent. What may seem surprising is that two of those four groups (Chinese and Portuguese) show fairly high

TABLE 3 *Percentage who feel that present immigration laws make it too easy for certain groups to come to Canada*

	Majority Canadian %	Other English %	Minority Groups %	Total %
Too easy for:				
"All groups"	24	20	14	16
Pakistani	58	53	49	50
West Indians	40	49	39	40
British	13	3	33	27
Chinese	15	16	13	14
Italians	13	16	14	14
Portuguese	8	7	5	5
French	5	1	7	6
Greek	4	2	3	3
German	2	1	4	3
Jewish	1	1	3	3
Ukrainians	1	1	*	*
Other groups	11	22	14	15
Number of interviews	(136)	(146)	(911)	(1193)

*Less than 1%
Note: The table excludes those who do not think that immigration laws are too easy and those who did not answer.

percentages who feel that present immigration laws make it too difficult for their group to come to Canada, yet reveal low percentages as far as concern for the possibility of their group becoming too small. It would seem that for them, immigration is not seen in terms of building numerical strength but rather in terms of reunion with friends and relatives.

What is less surprising is that it is among the Majority Canadians and the "other English" that the concern with the relative size of groups is significant: two-thirds of each category are at least a little concerned "that the non-English ethnic groups are becoming too large in Toronto compared to the English-Canadian group." Indeed, the Census shows that, for the last few decades, it is the population of British origin that has declined. The percentage of the Toronto Census Metropolitan Areas population whose origin is classified as "British Isles" declined from 81.1 percent to 56.9 percent between 1941 and 1971.

(b) Discrimination

At a general level, respondents were asked if "discrimination against members of their group as far as jobs, pay, or other working conditions are concerned" is a problem in Toronto. The percentages of those who feel that job discrimination is a problem for their group appear in Table 4, Section

TABLE 4 Perception and experience of discrimination by members of minority ethnic groups and by Majority Canadians (%)

	German	Italian	Jewish	Portuguese	Ukrainian	Chinese	West Indian	Majority Canadian	Other English
	%	%	%	%	%	%	%	%	%
A. Discrimination as far as jobs, pay, or working conditions are concerned									
As very and somewhat serious problem	31	3	19	16	31	9	60	5	8
Not too serious problem	46	17	41	45	26	32	22	18	15
Not a problem	20	77	39	36	36	55	13	76	76
Don't know	3	4	1	4	7	3	5	1	1
Number of interviews	(153)	(320)	(350)	(348)	(163)	(354)	(150)	(230)	(267)
B. Employers perceived as discriminating a lot or somewhat									
By the group itself*	57	19	32	43	36	27	75	—	—
	(140)	(301)	(338)	(312)	(128)	(334)	(132)	—	—
By the majority group	51	19	40	43	56	20	79	—	—
	(212)	(209)	(223)	(212)	(201)	(184)	(218)	—	—
By others	45	23	37	34	48	23	70	—	—
	(1569)	(1353)	(1536)	(1440)	(1543)	(1086)	(1682)	—	—
C. Have experienced discrimination									
When trying to get a job	15	5	6	12	5	11	21	1	5
In other areas	15	20	20	31	6	14	17	5	12
Number of interviews	(153)	(321)	(351)	(348)	(164)	(354)	(150)	(230)	(267)

*In this case, the data pertains to those who are English (Majority Canadian or other).

A. The West Indian group is the only one with a large percentage who think that it is either a very serious or a somewhat serious problem: 60 percent. The next highest percentage who think it is a very or somewhat serious problem for their group is found among the other non-European group, the Chinese, and among the Portuguese (31 percent).

Respondents were also asked if various groups are treated fairly by employers or if they experience discrimination. Table 4, Section B shows that the rank order of groups along the percentage perceiving some or a lot of discrimination by employers is about the same as the one obtained with the previous question.

Another observation to be made from the table is that with one exception, the Majority Canadian group appears to agree with each group's perception of its treatment by employers. Thus, the minority groups who perceive discrimination by employers and, as seen earlier, who perceive problems of social acceptance do not appear to be under the influence of a persecution complex: generally, Majority Canadians and members of other minority groups tend to agree with them. Moreover, it would seem quite doubtful that those in the majority and minority groups who declare that there are problems of discrimination and of social acceptance are all under some sort of delusion. There clearly are problems to be dealt with, especially in the case of certain of the minority groups.

Other groups not included in our sample are also perceived as being discriminated against by employers in varying degrees. The question asked included seven other groups. A sizeable majority believe that Pakistani and Canadian Indians are the object of discrimination as it was the case for West Indians. A much lower but still significant proportion think that employers discriminate against French and Greeks.[6]

The above questions deal with perceptions of the experience of entire groups. Information was also obtained on the respondents' own experience; they were asked if they had "ever been discriminated against in Canada because of (their) ethnic or cultural background." The type of situation in which discrimination occurred was also ascertained. Concerning job discrimination, it can be seen from Table 4, Panel C, that the rank ordering of the group tends to be similar to the ones obtained earlier; job discrimination is more frequently reported by Chinese and West Indians, followed by Jews and Ukrainians, and then by Germans and Italians. Although the rank order is about the same, the percentages of the groups which experienced discrimination are significantly lower than those groups which perceived discrimination by employers. This is not surprising; it only indicates that in the latter case, people are referring to cases they have witnessed or have heard about in addition to their own experiences. It could also reflect the influence of the media which, to a degree, shape popular perceptions.

Summary

The rank order of the groups included in the study is similar with regard to the various instrumental and expressive aspects of social incorporation in Canadian society. Generally, the non-European origin groups (Chinese and West Indians) are those who are the most likely to experience problems of social acceptance and job discrimination and to perceive their groups as unequally treated by immigration laws. Jews tend to be next highest in the experience of such problems (except with regard to immigration laws, about which they are not likely to perceive problems). Italians and Portuguese follow. Finally, Ukrainians and Germans are close to the Majority Canadians and the Other English who are the least likely to experience problems.

It is noteworthy that the perceptions of the Majority Canadian respondents tend to be the same as those of the respondents from the groups themselves. That is to say, West Indians and Chinese are the most likely to report problems of social acceptance and job discrimination; it is also these groups that are the most likely to be perceived as experiencing problems by Majority Canadians and other English respondents.

II – The Ethnic Community as a Resource: Types of Action Favored

There are a number of ways in which a community can be a resource[7] for its members. It can be a source of relationships for the satisfaction of one's socioemotional needs; of assistance in dealing with matters related to jobs and housing; of services performed in the context of a familiar cultural context. It can be a milieu in which one finds social acceptance and is given respect and recognition, especially if such advantages are not forthcoming from the larger society; a milieu in which individuals can find support in correcting situations which harm them. As an organized social unit, it can also provide leadership and promote action to combat discrimination and pursue objectives with regard to culture maintenance and immigration policies. In short, it can be a resource in relation to individual and community needs or problems such as those discussed above.

This section examines some of the ways in which the ethnic (and the larger) community is seen as a potential resource in relation to some of the problems faced by ethnic groups. This is done by focusing on the channels respondents think would be effective in dealing with certain matters. Two problem areas have been selected: job discrimination and immigration laws and procedures. The question is what actions and, by implication, what types of resources the respondent favors in terms of getting results with regard to cases of discrimination or to changes in immigration laws and procedures.

1. *In Relation to Instances of Discrimination*

There are various ways of dealing with problems encountered or of seeking certain objectives. In order to explore the views of the respondents in this area, they were asked about various courses of action in relation to a case of discrimination at work and to a desired change in immigration laws or procedures. The question dealt with the perceived effectiveness of these actions, that is, the likelihood that they would get results.

In the instance of job discrimination, the possible actions presented to the respondent can be grouped under three headings:

a) Individual action:
   - Complain directly to the boss or personnel manager;
   - Say nothing, but work harder than the others so as to impress the boss.

b) Activation of social networks:
   - Get together with co-workers to complain to the boss;
   - Deal with the situation by contacting a friend one happens to have in the company.

c) Use of organizational resources:
   - Take case to the union or employee association, if there is one in the company;
   - Take case to an organization of the ethnic community;
   - Take case to a community agency like the Ontario Human Rights Commission whose purpose is to handle cases of discrimination.

The distribution of responses appear in Table 5 for each of the ethnic groups. Taking one's case to a "community agency like the Ontario Human Rights Commission whose purpose is to handle cases of discrimination" is the action that appears to be the most frequently seen as most likely to give results. Taking one's case to the union comes as a close second most-favored action. Generally, then, the use of organizational resources appears to be the most favored.

An important observation, however, is that the organizational resources favored appear to be those of the community-at-large, not of the ethnic community. The latter are not the least favored of all types of action, but they are thought, on the average, as significantly less efficacious than society organizations. They are among the least-favored actions in two of the groups whose members are the most likely to be victims of discrimination, as we have seen earlier: only 26 percent of the Chinese and 23 percent of the West Indians think taking the case to an ethnic organization would help very much or somewhat to change the situation. However, the percentage for this type of action is more favored relative to other non-organizational actions among the Jewish respondents (42 percent) who are also among the most likely to experience problems of social rejection and discrimination.

TABLE 5 *Percent feeling that various actions with regard to a case of discrimination would help to change the situation very much or somewhat by ethnic group*

	Chinese	German	Italian	Jewish	Portuguese	Ukrainian	West Indian	Majority Canadian	Other English
	%	%	%	%	%	%	%	%	%
Complain directly to the boss	39	52	52	36	40	47	31	46	48
Get together with co-workers to complain to the boss	43	49	52	38	40	46	26	45	35
Deal with situation through a friend in the company	27	35	35	28	23	34	21	32	25
Work harder to impress the boss	36	46	42	35	28	38	29	45	47
Take case to union or employee association	52	70	73	64	52	71	59	76	70
Take case to an organization of the ethnic community	26	34	46	42	24	27	23	44	38
Take case to an agency that handles cases of discrimination	53	71	71	70	70	69	72	80	73
Number of interviews*	(153)	(321)	(351)	(348)	(164)	(354)	(150)	(230)	(267)

*These numbers apply to each row of percentages.

TABLE 6 *Type of action considered effective* by ethnic groups*

	Chinese	German	Italian	Jewish	Portuguese	Ukrainian	West Indian	Majority Canadian	Other English
	%	%	%	%	%	%	%	%	%
A. In relation to case of discrimination									
Individual	45	59	55	41	38	49	37	54	56
Social Networks	41	50	55	37	41	48	29	48	37
Organizational	52	70	76	70	62	71	64	80	70
B. In relation to a change in immigration laws and procedures									
Individual	58	43	43	37	29	42	35	38	46
Social Networks	44	58	58	53	44	61	50	67	61
Organizational	49	56	56	51	32	56	39	60	58
Number of interviews**	(146)	(320)	(348)	(343)	(160)	(349)	(150)	(230)	(267)

*Percentage with a relatively high score of an index combining each set of items.
**These numbers represent the total for *each* of the three categories under A and under B.

TABLE 7 *Percent feeling that various actions would help change immigration laws or procedures*

	Chinese	German	Italian	Jewish	Portuguese	Ukrainian	West Indian	Majority Canadian	Other English
	%	%	%	%	%	%	%	%	%
Write to Member of Parliament or government official	50	38	35	32	34	38	30	30	38
Work through a political party	43	43	46	42	24	44	31	45	49
Write letters to the editors of newspapers	29	34	32	27	12	29	25	32	34
Work through an organization in the community	29	42	47	41	26	45	33	46	45
Get as many of one's friends and neighbors as possible to write to MPs or government officials	38	53	55	47	42	52	37	61	54
Organize support for or opposition to certain candidates at election	34	50	47	43	29	46	37	56	46
Number of interviews	(153)	(321)	(351)	(348)	(164)	(354)	(150)	(230)	(267)

Much of the literature on collective action suggests the importance of organization in translating discontent, grievances, or aspirations into collective action. In social psychological terms this means that individuals will favor the type of action that they perceive as having the best organizational apparatus and support system for its execution. This may be the reason why societal institutions like the Human Rights Commission are the most favored. This may also be why Jewish respondents are more likely to favor action through their own organizations than members of most other minorities: indeed, Jewish communities tend to be among the better organized for a variety of purposes, including combatting anti-Semitism.

Dealing with the discrimination through a friend in the company is generally the least frequently selected course of action, although in several groups (Chinese, Germans, Portuguese and West Indians) it is at par or close to other actions. Among Portuguese and Ukrainians, it is almost at par with working harder to impress the boss.

A view of the overall pattern of preferences emerges if the responses for the items corresponding to each type of action are combined (Table 6). When this is done, it can be seen that the use of organizational resources to deal with discrimination is significantly more favored by all groups except that among the Chinese the difference is not as pronounced.

2. *In Relation to a Change in Immigration Laws or Procedures*

A similar classification can be made of actions oriented to a change in immigration laws or procedures:
   a) Individual action:
       – Write to a member of parliament or to government officials;
       – Write letters-to-the-editor of newspapers.
   b) Mobilization of social networks:
       – Get as many of one's friends and neighbors as possible to write or talk to the Member of Parliament or to government officials;
       – Organize support for or opposition to certain candidates at election.
   c) Use of organizational resources:
       – Work through one of the political parties to get something done;
       – Work through an organization in the community to get something done.

As can be seen from Table 7, the tabulation of responses by ethnic groups does not reveal as clear a pattern as in the case of discrimination: the range of percentages favoring each type of action is not as wide and, frequently, different types of action are equally favored. A reason for this may be simply that the different types of actions presented to the respondents can fairly easily overlap. That is to say, writing to a Member of Parliament or to government officials can be seen as part of an organized campaign. Similarly, the organization of support for or opposition to a political candidate can involve one's personal networks but it can also extend to action through organizations. However, even though patterns are less pronounced, they are not absent.

First, it appears that the mobilization of social networks is a little more likely to be perceived as the most effective in bringing about a change in immigration laws or procedures. The Chinese are the only exception in this case. The individual action items, on the other hand, seem to reap the lowest percentages, with few exceptions. The use of organizational resources falls in between or close to the use of social networks.

Thus, some respondents may have taken it to refer to the larger community and others to the ethnic community. This ambiguity may explain the higher percentages. It is also plausible that people feel that their ethnic community organizations would get more results in this area than in the area of discrimination. In any case, it should be noted that for *both* areas, the Chinese and West Indians are the least likely of all groups to think that this type of action would help.

What is the relationship between the propensity to favor working through community organizations and the perception and experience of problems? In the sample as a whole, those who perceive job discrimination as a problem for their group in Toronto are more likely to favor taking a case of discrimination to an ethnic organization than those who do not perceive a problem for the group. This is true for all groups taken separately except the Chinese (table not presented). It should be noted, however, that generally, those who have themselves experienced discrimination are less likely to favor the use of organizational resources than those who have not. There appears to be a distinction between the perception of discrimination as a community problem and its experience by individuals. A reason may be that those who perceive discrimination as a group problem are also those who are the most likely to be involved in their community and thus would be more oriented toward the use of group resources. Another reason for the difference noted may be that those who have experienced discrimination have also had the experience of attempting to use organizational channels to deal with their problem without much success. A personal failure in attempts to obtain redress may lead to disaffection with regard to particular courses of action.

As far as a change in immigration laws is concerned, there is not much of a relationship between the perception of the present laws as too restrictive for one's group and favoring action through community organizations.

Conclusion

This essay has attempted to describe some of the problems encountered by ethnic minorities as perceived by members of the minority groups themselves and by Majority Canadians. The propensity to favor the use of the organizational resources of the ethnic community was also described and related to the perception and experience of problems. By way of conclusion, the situation of each of the groups included in the study will be reviewed briefly, with regard to the dimensions considered.

Chinese

The problems that the Chinese are the most likely to face in Toronto are problems of discrimination: a significant proportion declare having experienced discrimination in the past. They are also likely to perceive employers as discriminating against members of their group; a perception with which an equal proportion Majority Canadians agree. Close to a majority of them perceive present immigration laws as making it too difficult for their group to come to Canada. Also, a significant proportion perceive problems of social acceptance as relatives.

Relatively few of the Chinese favor the use of ethnic community organizational resources to deal with the problems faced: about one-fourth favor the use of such channels to deal with discrimination and a slightly larger proportion favor them with regard to immigration laws and procedures.

Germans

Relatively few Germans perceive problems for their group in Toronto with regard to social acceptance and discrimination although about one-fourth declare having experienced discrimination themselves in Canada at one time or another, mostly in areas other than work. German respondents are moderately likely to favor the use of ethnic organizational resources to deal with problems of discrimination or immigration legislation and procedures.

Italian

Present immigration laws and discrimination appear to be perceived as group problems of moderate magnitude by Italians. About one-fourth mention having personally experienced problems of discrimination. Acceptance as neighbors or as relatives by Majority Canadians seems to be a negligible problem for them. Almost half of Italians favor the use of community organizational resources to deal with discrimination or to obtain changes in immigration legislation.

Jews

Jewish respondents are quite likely to perceive problems of discrimination and problems of acceptance as relatives. The next frequently mentioned problem is the possibility that their group is getting too small in relation to other groups in Toronto (one-third). Jews are among the most likely to favor the use of the organizational resources of their community.

Portuguese

The problem that Portuguese respondents perceived with the greatest frequency is that present immigration laws and procedures make it too difficult for members of their group to come to Canada (almost 70 percent). Other areas seem to pose moderate problems for the members of this group. In fact, Majority Canadians are more likely than the Portuguese themselves to perceive problems of discrimination for Portuguese or to report difficulties in accepting them socially. In spite of this perception of problems, only about one-fourth of the Portuguese respondents favor the use of community organizational action to obtain changes in immigration laws and procedures. The same proportion favor such channels in relation to problems of job discrimination.

Ukrainians

Few Ukrainian respondents perceive problems for their community: problems of discrimination are mentioned by one-fourth or less of the respondents as is the concern that the group is getting too small in relation to other groups in Toronto. Problems of social acceptance are mentioned by even a smaller proportion of respondents. Almost half of Ukrainian respondents favor the use of community organizational resources to obtain changes in immigration laws and procedures, but only one-fourth favor such channels to deal with discrimination problems.

West Indians

In contrast with Ukrainians, West Indians perceive and experience problems in almost all areas except with regard to cultural maintenance: discrimination is mentioned by about three-fourths the respondents; immigration laws and procedures by about two-thirds; the actual experience of discrimination by over one-third. Problems of social acceptance either as neighbors or as relatives are also frequently mentioned. About the same percentage of Majority Canadians share this perception of the situation of West Indians. On the other hand, the propensity to favor ethnic organizational action to deal with problems appears to be low among West Indian respondents relative to perceived magnitude of the problems.

END NOTES

1. For a discussion of ethnic interests in relation to ethnic group structure and behavior, see for example Zielyk (1975), Breton (1978), Siegal (1970), and Cohen (1974) (especially the papers by Cohen himself, Deshen, Hannerz, and Charsley).

2. Another broad category of problems pertains to dimensions of cultural loss or maintenance. These are dealt with in the larger study, but are not included in the present essay.

3. The propensity to favor the use of ethnic organizational resources to deal with problems is related to the respondents' involvement in community affairs and relationship with community leaders. It is also related to various features of the sociopolitical organization of their ethnic group: the decision-making structure, the efficacy of the community leadership and their relationship with societal institutions; and the factors that divide the group. For instance, some groups show an awareness of problems facing the community, but a community organization that seems to fail to mobilize its members may be perceived as unable to get results. Other groups perceive few problems to be dealt with, but reveal a fairly well organized community that presumably could launch action in the event that the group became confronted with problems of one sort or another. Finally, there are communities with both sets of characteristics: they face a number of problems and show a willingness to use its organizational resources to deal with them – a phenomenon reflected in the high degree of involvement of their members and in the favorably perceived decision-making structure and leadership. A systematic analysis of these relationships is beyond the scope of this essay. However, some are considered in the paper on which this essay is based.

4. Grants from the Social Sciences and Humanities Research Council of Canada made the study possible. Its support is gratefully acknowledged.

5. The technical aspects of the sample design and selection and the field work were carried out by the York University Survey Research center. Their collaboration is greatly appreciated. For more details on the study and on the sample design, see Breton et al. (1981).

6. The seven groups are as follows (the numbers in parenthesis are the percentages who perceive some or a lot of discrimination on the part of employers vis-à-vis those groups among Majority Canadians and minority groups respectively): French (41,33); English (5,7); Irish (6,10); Scottish (5,8); Greek (39,38); Pakistani (82,76); and Canadian Indian (74,70).

7. The notion of resource is used here in its very general sense and therefore may refer to a variety of different types of resources.

SELECTED REFERENCES

Breton, R., Reitz, J., Isajiw, W., and W. Kalbach. "Ethnic Pluralism in an Urban Setting: Conceptual and Technical Overview of a Research Project." Toronto: Centre for Urban and Community Studies, University of Toronto, 1981.

Breton, Raymond. "Stratification and Conflict between Ethnolinguistic Communities with Different Social Structures," *Canadian Review of Sociology and Anthropology* 15: 148-157, 1978.

Cohen, Abner, ed. *Urban ethnicity*. London: Tavistock Publications, 1974.

Siegel, B.J. "Defensive Structuring and Environmental Strength," *American Journal of Sociology* 76: 11-32, 1970.

Zielyk, I. "Two types of ethnic communities", pp. 147-157 in Paul M. Migus, ed.: *Sounds Canadian. Languages and Cultures in Multi-Ethnic Society*. Toronto: Peter Martin Associates, 1975.

SAVANAH E. WILLIAMS Dalhousie University

Two Hundred Years in the Development of the Afro-Canadians in Nova Scotia, 1782-1982*

Introduction

The African Baptist experience in North America was first introduced to me as a child growing up in Virginia. I came to know the important role of the church in the religious and secular life of my community and other Afro-American communities in the United States. As a resident of Nova Scotia and an anthropologist, I have realized that the African Baptist Church here serves the same roles in the lives of many of the people of the community. Historically, Canada and the United States have had a different development; however, there are many parallels in the roles of the African Baptist Church in these two countries. Even though this account is not comparative in nature, it is written with extensive exposure to the African Baptists in both countries and without membership or vested interest in the Baptist Church.

People of African origin have been present in Nova Scotia for three centuries; many are descendants of those who came as United Empire Loyalists or as refugees from the War of 1812. Numerically they have always constituted a small percentage of the population. And, since the Canadian Census has classified its population by country of origin[1] and Afro-Canadians were denied that identity once they arrived in North America, a large percentage of the Nova Scotian Afro-Canadian population is listed under the category of "other."[2] Nevertheless, the current population is estimated to be between 20 000 and 25 000. Although a portion of this population has come to Canada since the 1950s, largely from the Caribbean, the Afro-Canadian presence in Nova Scotia has been felt continuously since 1749 when British settlers arrived with their slaves.[3]

Despite the historical and anthropological importance of the African Baptist in Canadian society, the literature has been sparse and scattered.[4] Because the church is the oldest and the major institution in the communities of descendants of Black Loyalists and Refugees, this paper will be an overview of the role of the African Baptist Church.

---

* A revised version of "The Role of the African United Baptist Association in the Development of Indigenous Afro-Canadians in Nova Scotia, 1782-1978," in Barry Moody, ed., *Repent and Believe: The Baptist Experience in Maritime Canada* (Wolfville, Nova Scotia: Lancelot Press, 1980).

My presentation will be divided into historical periods, introducing the leaders, the issues of concern, and the role of the church. Because the majority of the African Baptist Churches are members of the African United Baptist Association, the Association will be used as a point of reference. The Association was established in 1854, 26 years before the Negro Baptists attempted to organize in the United States.[5]

The Early Black Settlers

The first written record of a person of African descent in Nova Scotia is in 1605 when Matthew Da Costa arrived with the Champlain Expedition. In 1749, when the English settled in Halifax,[6] they evidently brought slaves with them, since two years later Africans were advertised for sale in Boston:

> Just arrived from Halifax and to be sold, ten strong hearty [N]egro men, mostly tradesmen, such as caulkers, carpenters, sailmakers, and ropemakers.[7]

By 1762, the colony had recognized slavery as an acceptable institution. Even though slave laws were not written as such, they were surely implicit,[8] and citizens held African people in bondage. As in many other colonies, public officials and members of the clergy owned slaves. One clergyman wrote an extensive letter to another urging him to set his slave free.[9] In some White Baptist Churches pews were reserved for Black slaves. As cases in Prince Edward Island prove, conversion to Christianity and baptism did not gain freedom for the slave.[10]

Free Black Loyalists and servants had arrived to add to this population by 1783. In this group were artisans and individuals with various farming skills. The hardship suffered by these people was a result of broken promises of land and provisions. Patterns of discrimination and public policies to benefit the White population evolved. Ongoing research indicates diverse skills in this population, thereby placing them in competition with White laborers for various jobs. This competition factor may be one of the variables in analyzing why their residences are outside of the centers of White settlement.

The negative activities and attitudes toward the Black Loyalists denied them a place in Nova Scotia history until recently. The title of "United Empire Loyalists" has been reserved for Whites and, even today, many people in the province and country think that all "Loyalists" who came to Nova Scotia were White.

The Refugee Blacks of the War of 1812 came in search of a new life, bringing with them numerous skills. Many were able to maintain themselves and the members of their families. In spite of the harsh climatic conditions to which they were not accustomed, they built homes, petitioned for schools and churches, used their skills to farm and find other jobs – in essence they founded Afro-Canadian communities in less than two years. They were hardworking people who were no more dependent on the government than

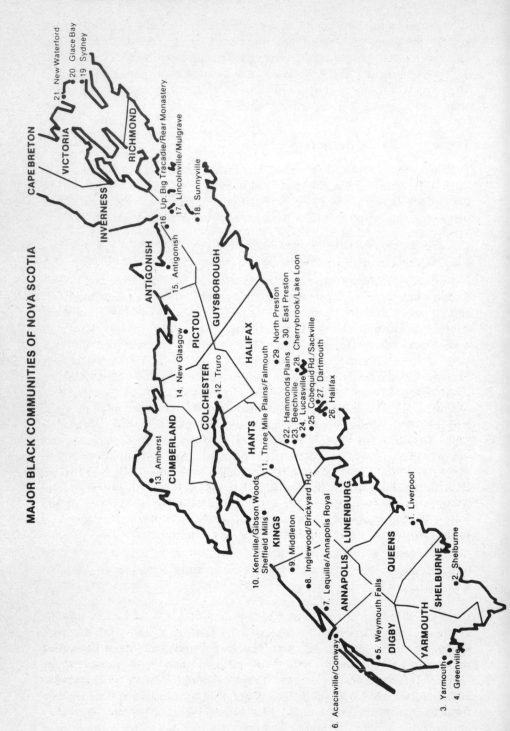

MAJOR BLACK COMMUNITIES OF NOVA SCOTIA

CAPE BRETON

VICTORIA

RICHMOND

INVERNESS

ANTIGONISH

PICTOU

GUYSBOROUGH

COLCHESTER

HALIFAX

HANTS

CUMBERLAND

KINGS

ANNAPOLIS

LUNENBURG

DIGBY

QUEENS

YARMOUTH

SHELBURNE

21. New Waterford
20. Glace Bay
19. Sydney
16. Up. Big Tracadie/Rear Monastery
17. Lincolnville/Mulgrave
18. Sunnyville
15. Antigonish
14. New Glasgow
12. Truro
29. North Preston
30. East Preston
28. Cherrybrook/Lake Loon
22. Hammonds Plains
23. Beechville
24. Lucasville
25. Cobequid Rd./Sackville
27. Dartmouth
26. Halifax
Three Mile Plains/Falmouth
13. Amherst
11. Kentville/Gibson Woods
10. Kentville/Gibson Woods
Sheffield Mills
9. Middleton
8. Inglewood/Brickyard Rd.
7. Lequille/Annapolis Royal
6. Acaciaville/Conway
5. Weymouth Falls
1. Liverpool
2. Shelburne
3. Yarmouth
4. Greenville

other immigrants. Many of today's population in Preston, Hammond's Plains, Beechville, and Halifax and descendants of the Refugee Blacks.

The Ministry of David George: From Nova Scotia to Sierra Leone

In 1782, David George, a Black Baptist minister from Silver Bluff, South Carolina, arrived with his family and others.[11] With the blessings and permission of the governor of the province, he traveled to Shelburne where many of the Loyalists had settled. There was a large Black population in this area. He established a cóngregation that was comprised of both Blacks and Whites. George's ministry in Nova Scotia lasted 10 years. During this time, he was confronted by a White group when he attempted to baptize a White woman.[12] Because of religious and racial antagonisms, it is difficult to know the basic nature of the attack. However, George left the area and went to New Brunswick where he again found opposition to his presence.[13] He was given permission to preach to "his" people.[14] From this reference, it appears that the preaching was to be to Black people only. Shortly thereafter, he returned to Nova Scotia where he found his church being used for secular purposes.[15]

Because of the overall conditions that Black people faced in Nova Scotia, Thomas Peters made an inquiry about the possibility of their leaving. Peters was a former slave from North Carolina and a member of the Black Pioneer Corps during the American Revolution.[16] The opportune moment to move came in 1792. The British needed settlers for the West Coast of Africa and Nova Scotia's Black settlers were not satisfied with the conditions under which they lived. On January 16, 1792, 1 190 people of African descent sailed for the colony of Sierra Leone, West Africa.[17] David George was one of those who went on that long voyage. With him he carried a new religion that flourishes today, and in Nova Scotia a Baptist legacy was left with those who remained. In 1794, Maroons from Jamaica arrived in Nova Scotia following their deportation. While residing in Nova Scotia, they worked on the building of the Citadel and, in 1800, many went to live in Sierra Leone.

The Establishment of the First Baptist Church: The Burton Era, 1792-1832

On May 20, 1792, four months and five days after David George and the group of 1 190 departed for Africa, John Burton, a native of England, arrived in Nova Scotia. He was "licensed in England as a dissenting minister,"[18] but had been "initiated into the Episcopal Church in infancy."[19] After spending a year in Nova Scotia, he went to the United States, which was his original destination.[20] There he was baptized and ordained as a Baptist minister. He returned to Halifax where he established the First Baptist Church. His congregation used Marchington's meeting house.[21] The meeting house had been built for Methodists, but was unoccupied when Burton arrived.[22] After Burton became a Baptist, he lost Marchington as a patron.[23] In 1795, an edifice was built with contributions from the membership and sums he had collected in different parts of the United States.[24] The congregation was integrated racially. The influx of Blacks to Nova Scotia after the War of 1812 added adherents to Burton's church.

In 1824, a leadership struggle took place in St. Paul's Anglican Church in Halifax. The dissenters joined Burton's Church.[25] Prior to the group's joining, the congregation was comprised mostly of people from the working class. The St. Paul's dissenters were of a higher class. Later, Rev. Robert Davis joined the church. These new adherents and the old members did not get along very well for reasons of class, color, and religious principles. In 1828, the first division took place in Burton's Church with Rev. Davis taking a group out. This group fought for the status of the First Baptist Church of Halifax but the title was awarded to Burton's Church.[26] By 1832, there were no less than eight churches that had originated out of Burton's Church.

A new member to Burton's Church around 1816 was Richard Preston, a former slave from Virginia. Preston had been converted in Virginia in 1815[27] and arrived in Nova Scotia in 1816.[28] According to MacKerrow, he had come in search of his mother who had "gone to Canada, but to what place he could not tell."[29] He found her "residing at a district by his own name."[30]

Preston became active in the church and worked with the Reverends John Burton and Edward Manning. "The colored brethren . . . and Father Burton gave him much information and assistance, that produced a great success to the cause of Christianity. . . . When a request was made for Preston's ordination, it was considered by some that he had not acquired sufficient knowledge of theology to be ordained. . . ."[31] As a result, Preston was sent to England in 1831 "to avoid any religious friction that might arise and to clothe him with authority to solicit aid to build a church for his brethren from the chains of sin and slavery."[32]

The Establishment of the African Baptist Association: The Preston Era, 1832-1861

One year before slavery was abolished in the British Empire, Richard Preston returned to Nova Scotia from England as an ordained Baptist minister. His credentials had come from the West London Baptist Association.[33] Unlike any other Baptist minister in Halifax, he had credentials from England. The theological question appeared to have been resolved, at least for those who had questioned his knowledge of theology before he left.

However, as one examines the legacy which Preston left, in the Minutes of the Association and activities of today's African Baptist Churches, the question can be raised again. The theological question has been raised in the Black Baptist Churches in the United States.[34]

Shortly after Preston returned, he organized the first African Baptist Church, Cornwallis Street Baptist Church. The church was established on April 14, 1832, with branches in Dartmouth, Preston, Beech Hill, and Hammond's Plains.[35] Cornwallis Street was resolved to be the "Mother Church."[36] Even though this group of churches appeared to be an organization, the official church organization was not established until September 1, 1854.[37] The birth of the African Baptist Association came 22 years after Preston's ordination and 41 years before the establishment of the National Baptist Convention, USA.[38] The Association was comprised of 12 churches, three ordained ministers, and 308 members.[39] However, there were African Baptist Churches that did not and have not joined the Preston Association. The only split in the Association was from 1867 to 1880. There are now three National Baptist Conventions in the United States.

As was traditional among African Baptist ministers, Preston was strongly involved in social issues. No less can be said of the African Baptist Churches. In 1842, Preston organized an Anglo-African Mutual Improvement and Aid Association.[40] The placement of Anglo before African must have had some significance since the word "African" has a very proud usage among African Baptists in Nova Scotia. One of the committees of this organization was concerned with political action. In 1846, Preston participated in a Negro Abolition Society.[41]

At Preston's death on July 16, 1861, there were 15 churches, 443 members, four ordained ministers, and nine licentiates in the Association.[42] The churches were located in the Halifax area and along the South Shore of Nova Scotia.

Leadership in Question: A Period of Transition, 1861-1880

The Rev. James Thomas, a Welshman, succeeded Preston as the pastor of the "Mother Church" (Cornwallis Street Baptist) and several other churches. Thomas lived in Preston and was the owner of a fur company in Halifax. He was married to Hannah Saunders, a Black woman.

Thomas had traveled extensively with Preston between 1840 and 1860.[43] He was ordained in 1857 and worked as an evangelist until Preston's death in 1861.[44] From the Minutes of the African Baptist Association, Thomas appeared to be a very important minister in the Association and was well received by the majority. However, after Preston's death, Thomas became the center of much controversy in the Association.

The first problem concerned the case of the Rev. Benson Smithers of First Preston, now known as East Preston. Smithers was a prominent minister of the Association, according to the Association's Minutes. In 1867, Smithers' credentials were revoked on the grounds of "immoral conduct."[45] Smithers not only continued to preach, but succeeded in establishing his own group which published minutes under the same name as the African Baptist Association. The 11 persons who supported Smithers against charges of immorality, which were not explicitly defined, were expelled.[46] These men eventually joined Smithers' Association. Several churches also joined Smithers. The Rev. George Neal, who moved the exclusion of Smithers, eventually was expelled himself. He joined Smithers also. This Association existed separately from the Preston Association for 13 years, 1867 to 1880.

Two years after Smithers was expelled, Thomas resigned from First Preston after "disciplined members exercised unprincipled means to impeach [him] but the plans resorted to proved a failure."[47] In the same year, 1869, Joseph Cox of Cornwallis Street Baptist Church, brought a suit against Thomas in the Supreme Court of Nova Scotia.[48] This suit was to have "Thomas removed as Trustee of the 'Mother Church.' But it was unsuccessful and Cox was excluded from the church on the grounds that he published false and defamatory statements regarding Thomas."[49] The conflict continued until May 27, 1872, when "a meeting took place in which . . . old foundations and a code of laws were sustained with their present pastor, Rev. Thomas."[50] In spite of this conflict being resolved, the African Baptists remained divided until after Thomas' death. Inasmuch as Smithers and Thomas appear to have been the two strongest leaders after Preston's death, leadership was probably the major focus of the conflict. At various meetings, presentations were alternated between Smithers and Thomas. Since Thomas and his son, the Rev. John Thomas, were the only White ministers in the Association and the majority of the Association membership was Black, color was more than likely one of the variables that contributed to the split, but just one of the variables.

In spite of the difficulties of this transition, several activities should be noted. The church doctrine was presented in written form: the Article of Faith and Practice, Concerning A Visible Church of Christ and the Discipline, and the Covenant.[51] These church documents appear in the Association which supported Thomas. In 1883, a resolution was passed to unite with the Baptist Convention meeting at Moncton.[52] The following year, representatives of the Association were in attendance at the Convention.

In the midst of the conflict and declarations, Peter E. MacKerrow, Clerk of the Association, reminded the membership that "he hoped [that] the day would soon dawn when the cloud of prejudice that . . . [hangs] over the descendants of 'Africa' in [this] province particularly would soon be dispersed when we will be able to breathe a clearer atmosphere than we now do. The condition of the people of color in the province," he said, "was deplorable, none worse throughout the Dominion, for although [their] votes are sought both in parliamental and civic elections, yet no recompense [did] they receive, but [had] to put up with the meanest of school houses that the province can afford, which deserves the greatest censure from the educated world."[53]

Growth During A Period of World Turbulence - 1880 to 1936

The Association united after Thomas's death in 1879. An influx of new ministers from the United States added to the Association's ministry from 1880 to 1936. The Reverends Wilton R. Boone and Henry H. Johnson, graduates of Newton Theological Seminary in Newton, Massachusetts, were among the first of these new ministers. By 1936, the Rev. W. A. White of Virginia had become a prominent leader in the Association. Nova Scotians such as the Reverends A. W. Jordan, Edward Dixon, A. Clements, and W. N. States left their legacies.

The Rev. A. W. Jordan, a graduate of Acadia University and McMaster Hall, with graduate studies at Morgan Park in Chicago, had at his death earned the title of Doctor of Divinity.[54] James R. Johnston, Clerk of the Associaton from 1906 to 1915, was graduated from Dalhousie Law School in 1898.[55]

The membership grew steadily from "five hundred and twenty in 1880 to six hundred and forty-eight in 1914. . . . By the end of World War I in 1920, the membership had reached seven hundred and sixty-seven and nine hundred and forty-two in 1925. . . . Even though there was a drop in membership before the Depression, there was an increase during the Depression" (1930-739; 1935-858).[56] In 1898, J. R. Johnstone, who had introduced the Baptist Young People's Union at Cornwallis Street Baptist Church, made a presentation to the Association on the establishment of Youth Unions in other churches.

By the early 1900s, the contact with African Baptists outside of the province had extended only to the United States. So when a member of the Association visited Ontario during this period, he returned to propose a relationship with the Upper Canada Association, presumably the Amherstburg Association. He felt that "the association would be productive."[57] However, no action was taken.

A strong relationship between the church and the community continued. In preparation for the Jubilee Year Celebration of the Association in 1904 at Cornwallis Street Baptist Church, there was a desire not only to recall the glorious history of the church, but to show the community at large "what religion and education [was] doing for the race. . . ."[58] Ever aware of the "corrupt and prejudice-laden atmosphere of the so-called Christian Aristocracy, who despise the poor, many of whom are made poor by their [the Christian Aristocracy's] vicious legislation . . . ,"[59] the display of this progress was of great importance to the church.

Community awareness was demonstrated in the establishment of an Aid Society for the sick,[60] as well as the Normal and Industrial Institute.[61] In 1917, "Rev. M. B. Puryear of Pennsylvania, who was Moderator of the Association, introduced to the provincial government the Association's idea of the Nova Scotia Home for Coloured Children."[62] In the same year, "a cottage was found to house the Home near the Institute with Miss Julia Jackson, a teacher recruited from Philadelphia."[63] The cottage lasted only for about a month because of the great Halifax Explosion of December 6, 1917.[64] Miss Jackson returned to her home in Philadelphia.[65]

A replacement for the cottage was established four years later, after J. A. R. Kinney was hired to raise funds for a new facility. The Rev. A. A. Wyse of Cherrybrook located the McKenzie farm just outside of Cherrybrook and in 1921 the Home's gala opening took place. The complex contained a farm and living quarters for the children and adults. A school was included as a part of the Home. The Association pledged $1 000 annually, but has never fulfilled this promise. Kinney devoted most of his life to this organization which still exists today.

In spite of the fact that the Association was involved from the initial stage of the idea, it was not until 1974 that the first Black person, the Rev. Donald Fairfax, became President of the Board of the Home. Even more recently, Blacks have come to constitute the majority of the Board. In 1978, the Home moved into new facilities.

The female society which MacKerrow spoke of in 1883 was finally established in 1917.[66] The objective of the Ladies' Auxiliary was the "stimulation of the spiritual, moral, social, educational, charitable and financial work of all the local churches of the African Baptist Association. . . ."[67] Numerically and financially, the Ladies' Auxiliary is the strength and backbone of the Association. During various years, the Auxiliary has raised more money than the total receipts of the Association. As to the other objectives, further research needs to be done. Nevertheless, it appears that the women's organization has been more productive than the Laymen's Council, which is composed of men. This seems to prove MacKerrow's conviction in 1883 that "their [women's] labors are generally more successful than the males'."[68] In addition to the church-oriented Ladies' Auxiliary, an auxiliary, composed of many of the same women, was organized to support the programs of the Nova Scotia Home for Coloured Children. The First Congress of Coloured Women in Canada was held in Halifax in 1920.[69]

In 1919, the Association was incorporated as the African United Baptist Association with the objective to "maintain the educational, moral and spiritual welfare of the African race."[70] With various programs, the Association has continued to attempt to fulfill these objectives, sometimes under duress.

During World War I, the No. 2 Construction Battalion was formed entirely of Black soldiers. The Rev. W. A. White was a captain. The Rev. M.

Puryear said in a speech to the Association: ". . . the African race was making history, and when it reached the century mark, providing it holds fast to the faith, the record would be one of which it would be justly proud . . . the time for the Coloured Canadians to enter the struggle is now. We should fill up quickly the ranks of the No. 2 Construction Battalion, for a failure on our part to comply with the request of the Government would be an insult to the Flag under whose protection we have enjoyed the fullness of freedom for over 100 years and we would also prove ourselves unfaithful as Baptists."[71] The Association placed itself on record as being "in hearty sympathy with the Empire's struggle," and pledged itself "to do all in its power to encourage colored men to uphold the traditions of their country, and of the empire to which they belonged."[72] The No. 2 Battalion is remembered as a major contribution of Black Nova Scotia in World War I.

The Association grew from one pastor and no divinity students in 1905 to five pastors and three students by 1910. By 1936, growth in membership and churches was evident. Even the number of young Nova Scotians entering the ministry increased. At the beginning of the Depression, a five-year program was recommended to support the activities of the church and the community.[73]

Three ministers who appeared to be very active during this period were the Reverends W. A. White, W. N. States, and A. A. Wyse. An international awareness was reflected in the Association by the reporting of various topics, such as the Boer War, the death of Queen Victoria, and the role of Black people in the world. The Association's Minutes have not indicated such an extensive view of international affairs since this period.

Shortly before his death in 1936 the Rev. White received an honorary Doctorate of Divinity from Acadia University, his alma mater.[74] Since then, two other Black Nova Scotians have received honorary doctorate degrees. Dr. W. P. Oliver, of Lucasville, has received degrees from the University of King's College and his alma mater, Acadia. And Dr. Carrie Best, an Anglican of New Glasgow, has received an honorary Doctorate of Law from St. Francis Xavier University. She was the first Black woman in the Atlantic region to publish a newspaper, the *Clarion*.

Challenge and Change in the Present Era

Afro-Canadian people in Nova Scotia have survived under extremely difficult conditions. They have endured slavery, two large exoduses of many of their people to Sierra Leone, West Africa, and the United States, discrimination, the Depression, and two world wars. In spite of all of these pressures, the Association and the communities have grown spiritually, educationally, and economically.

By 1945, a trickle of graduates from Normal School (Teacher's College) had begun. Today, a number of the Association members are teachers, including one of the pastors. One minister is a vice principal of a high school.

In the early part of this period the Baptist Youth Fellowship Union organized a new Youth Convention. In addition, youth oratorical contests were held in the Association. These contests gave young people opportunities to express their views on various issues. Several times, the winners went on to compete at the Maritime Baptist Convention. Today the youth participate mostly in activities that are associated with their Union.

Two changes within the Maritime Baptist Convention had an impact on the Association and on the leadership in the communities which it serves. The first change prevented the licensing of ministers lacking university training in spite of the fact that laypersons in the African Association must replace the ministers at various services in order for the churches to survive spiritually.

The second change made an exception to the university requirement provided one "had served exceptionally for five years."[75] As of today, the records indicate that only one African Baptist minister has met this requirement.

Other roles have changed during the last 25 to 30 years. The one and only woman to acquire the status of pastor in the Association was Mrs. Agnes Waring, a White missionary who served at the Second Baptist Church, New Glasgow. Four laypersons have become moderators of the Association, a position formerly held only by ministers. Deacon R. S. Symonds and Ross Kinney, of Halifax, Deacon Howard Lawrence of New Glasgow and, in 1976, Pearleen Oliver became the first woman to hold the position.

One of the most beloved women of the Association, Muriel States, of Dartmouth, served the church and community for 30 years as the organizer of the Ladies' Auxiliary. During these years, she traveled the province raising funds for the Association, while sharing the daily life and activities of the people she met. Born in 1888, Muriel States, the widow of the Rev. W. N. States, is affectionately known as the "Mother of the Association." She and Edith Samuels Sparks are two of the women who were present at the establishment of the Ladies Auxiliary in 1917. These women and many more represent the strength of the African Baptist Churches even though their roles continue to be along traditional lines.

Several community and church organizations and committees that developed between 1936 and 1956 were the Nova Scotia Association for the Advancement of Coloured People, the Committee on Social Service and Child Welfare, and the Committee on Rural and Urban Life. The NSAACP was organized to undertake concerns of civil injustices. Leaders and members of the Association were active in this organization. The two committees were established to serve community needs; however, it appears that they serve to keep community issues before the Association rather than act as instruments of social change. In 1964, "the Urban and Rural Life [Committee Report] jolted our slumbering memory on the goals we [the Association] failed to reach in [the] drive for first class citizenship."[76]

By 1964, in spite of the illustrious history of the Association, and community organizations, first class citizenship had not been obtained. The small numbers and low economic status of the majority of the Black population had prevented the people from assuming full support for their churches and community programs. It is only through the help of the Home Mission Board of the United Baptist Convention that many of the churches survive.

Since there are 22 churches and 10 ministers, several ministers serve more than one congregation and some churches are pastorless. In one case, one minister serves three churches. The years of service for the majority of the ministers range from one to 40 years, mostly between 20 and 40. These ministers represent the only generation of Black ministers present in Nova Scotia.

In 1957, the Baptist Youth built on the Education Committee's previous effort by establishing a scholarship fund. In the 1930s and '40s, funds were provided for educating ministers for the Association. Now a fund provides general university scholarships. By 1968, five scholarships had been given and as of 1974, 124 scholarships had been awarded amounting to over $14 000.[77] These scholarships continue to be given without any obligation to the Association. In fact, many recipients are young people who are not active participants in the church and quite often express the view that the church is not relevant.

The Association, not unlike other institutions of its kind, has not grown to the extent that it has been able to accommodate the old and the new, the young and the matured. Two problems appear to have had a negative impact. First, the Association has never had a full-time paid person responsible for directing its short- and long-term programs. The Moderator, who traditionally has been a minister with other responsibilities, coordinates the programs with the assistance of chairpersons of committees. Second, the problem of obtaining new leaders appears to have grown even more serious because, during the past 30 years, the Association has isolated itself by looking only within the province for leaders. Attendance at national and international conferences by clergy and laypersons is very small.

When new Black immigrants came to Nova Scotia in the early 1950s, they sought out the African Baptist Church because they were Black, not because they were Baptist. Today, the population has grown to the point that places of employment and residence determine the degree of contact newcomers have with the African Baptist Churches and the communities they serve.

With the growth of concern for civil rights in the 1960s and '70s in the United States, there was a spillover into Nova Scotia with visits from the Black Panther Party and the Rev. Ralph Abernathy of the Southern Christian Leadership Conference. Because of historical differences, the struggle for civil rights in Nova Scotia never reached the level of social or political challenge that it did in the U.S. The division over ideology and methodology dispersed the potential power which could have influenced change. Blacks became divided into two groups: "Canadian" (Nova Scotian-born, second to fourth generations) and "foreigners" (residents and citizens from the Caribbean, the U.S., and Africa). The Black United Front was established during these years as an umbrella organization for Black groups, and the Human Rights Commission of the Nova Scotia government was formed to deal with social injustices. These two organizations still exist today.

The issues of housing, education, unemployment, social injustices, and land were the major problems during this period. The Association and community groups dealt with these concerns separately and in some cases simultaneously. In several cases conflict between the young and the matured, as well as the "Canadians" and "foreigners," caused serious breakdowns in progress. The inconsistencies of the Association are best exemplified in its response to issues of controversy. Even though most people think of the African church and its community as one and the same, the Association seems to be able to separate community and church when it is not sure about the ramifications of its involvement in controversial issues.

Another separation of church and community takes place when it comes to politics. The church appears to be used for political purposes only to obtain community resources, not to challenge political and public policies, nor to further the political careers of Blacks, at least not in an overt manner. The most obvious leaders in the communities have been ministers and church officers, but none have ever run for political office beyond the local level. In a province that contains the oldest and largest indigenous Black communities of Canada, several Blacks have run for provincial and federal political offices, but none have been elected. There are several elected Black town and city council persons. However, if we consider Canada has only had one Black in Parliament in its history, Lincoln Alexander of Ontario, the Minister of Labor in the Clark Government, the phenomenon is not unique to Nova Scotia. It appears that population size and interest group pressure influence the political arena and the failure to participate fully is connected to the lack of a strong economic base and political program within the community and the Association itself.

The Association has had influence in many areas, but it appears to have less in the political and economic aspects of life. As a result, there are few businesses owned by its people that would provide the basis for political development.

"The Blacks in Nova Scotia are poorer than the average White Nova Scotian and Nova Scotians are poorer than the average Canadian."[78] However, the economic status of Blacks is diversified just as it is in the White Nova Scotian population, in spite of the image that is presented in newspapers and scholarly publications. There has always been stratification within the community and the levels of stratification depend on the proximity of the community to the urban areas where jobs may be available.

The Association's intellectual growth has not been stimulated to a point where ideas and philosophies are either reevaluated or new ones established. The lack of the continuation of family businesses or professionals has left another gap. Several conditions appear to contribute to the business problem. The most obvious is the role that covert institutional racism has played in the development of the socioeconomic conditions of many people. Covert institutional racism means discrimination in various institutions such as education, business, housing, health, and family life through socialization into expected behavior, roles, and positions. This knowledge is passed from generation to generation of both Blacks and Whites. Although discrimination is not identifiable by signs as has been the case in the United States and South Africa, the mental stigmas are difficult to remove. As a result, people pretend that discrimination does not exist while responding to all of its conditions.

Two other factors appear to contribute to the problem. One is the habit of Canadians to find elsewhere situations that are perceived to be worse than those in which they participate; two is the inability of Black people to form strong business organizations which would provide capital and mentors. This comparative outlook discourages economic efforts which could have an impact in the political arena and works to the benefit of the oppressor. Television plays a role in furthering knowledge of comparable conditions. Unfortunately, television too often presents the negative side of life with little or no emphasis on the positive aspects, showing people involved in organizations, businesses, or institutions.

The inability to provide capital and mentors is a traditional problem caused by a divide and conquer strategy because there is no organization to which individuals can turn when the system rejects them or provides for some to the disadvantage of others. The most recent example of this strategy was a program announced in 1980 to assist Black businesses. The first announcement provided no details just stated that any help that was needed would be provided. When an inquiry was made as to the specific method of assistance, a list of programs already being implemented but not applicable in the businesses of the Black community was provided. Black businesspersons throughout Nova Scotia applied for the assistance and attempted to organize as a group. When the final distribution of funds was made, only one area of the province received assistance. The selection process was never made public. As a result, the opportunity to develop a cooperative organization on a province-wide basis was once again thwarted.

In spite of the fact that many Black people know about the type of behavior that is going on in the continuous oppression of their people, few, if any, confront the problem. There appears to be a code of silence when Black people are helping White people to oppress Black people, especially in the business world. Even at the peak of Black awareness in the early 1970s, there was not a strong thrust in the community or church for economic self-sufficiency. There has not been a marked change in the economic status of the Black population in many communities over the past 20 years in terms of the development of businesses or extensive support for the Association.

In considering the economic status of Black Nova Scotians, we cannot overlook the continuous emigration since the turn of the century of many church and community persons to other parts of Canada and the U.S. The exodus of 1 190 Black persons to Sierra Leone in 1792 weakened the early economic foundation of Black communities as many of the emigrants were artisans and skilled persons. The Black community's biggest economic and cultural challenge of this century will be to administer and support in a cooperative spirit the new Black Culture Centre. William P. Oliver, the oldest minister in the Association, helped to develop the concept of the center and the programs.

In the Association's "Rural and Urban Life Report" in 1971, Oliver acknowledged the extent of change that had taken place outside of the African Baptist Church. He stated:

> It used to be said that eighty-five per cent of the Black people in Nova Scotia were Baptist. Our population was 13,000 then; today Nova Scotia has a population of close to twenty-five thousand and we list a church membership of approximately fifteen hundred. We can no longer claim 85% of the Black population. There are hundreds of West Indians, Africans, and Americans who are not Baptist, who have never been inside one of our churches. These people are Black, they are living in Nova Scotia. Many are highly educated and hold prominent positions in our province. They are unwilling to accept some of the things that we Nova Scotians have taken for granted, they want change. What consideration have we given to these newcomers, have we talked to them, do we understand their point of view? This new dimension will be of serious significance to the future of the African United Baptist Association. These newcomers represent a new voice coming from the Black community, they are knowledgeable and articulate. The program of the church should be broad and flexible enough to be able to utilize these new talents.[79]

The Association has not yet begun to deal with the concern voiced by Oliver. It must also take into account the Black community's youth who may also be "unwilling to accept some of the things" that older "Nova Scotians have taken for granted." This population is also "knowledgeable and articulate."

Blacks in Nova Scotia have not all been Baptists. They have been for example, African Methodist Episcopalians (AME), Presbyterians, Pentecostals, and Anglicans. Today there is still one AME church which is located in Amherst even though the Black Presbyterian church has ceased to exist. The visit of Black Muslims to Halifax in the mid-1970s has encouraged some young Blacks to investigate further the philosophy and practices of Islam. Although it is still too early to know the impact of this development, there is concern among the African Baptists as to the influence of Islam on secular organizations, some of which were organized by members of the Association. Many young university graduates are not attending any churches; young parents, however, are participating more as their families grow.

Conclusion

The Association faces the same problems of churches everywhere, regardless of color or creed: leadership; membership; challenges to religious practices; and economics. There is no doubt that the African United Baptist Association has played a significant role in the development of the religious and secular life of Blacks in Nova Scotia. And, although it is unique in being the oldest institution controlled by Blacks, control is only one aspect in its continuation as a useful organization to the communities it serves. It must find solutions to some of the problems listed above. The resolution of the problem of leadership is crucial to its survival. Membership and economics appear to be secondary to leadership. The Association remains the major organization for Blacks in the province of Nova Scotia. Unlike other communities in Canada and the U.S., where there are other secular and religious organizations, the African United Baptist Association of Nova Scotia still serves the dual role of fulfilling religious and secular needs. If the Association is to continue in this dual role, it needs to find solutions to some of its existing problems.

END NOTES

1. *Canadian Census* (Ottawa: Statistics Canada, 1971-1976).
2. *Ibid.*, 1971, 1976.
3. T.B. Akins, "History of Halifax City," *Collections of the Nova Scotia Historical Society*, vol. VIII, 1899, p. 235.
4. Peter E. MacKerrow, *A Brief History of the Coloured Baptists of Nova Scotia, and Their First Organization as Churches, A.D. 1832* (Halifax, 1895); Pearleen Oliver, *A Brief History of the Coloured Baptists of Nova Scotia, 1782-1953* (Halifax, 1953).
5. Joseph R. Washington, Jr., *Black Religion: The Negro and Christianity in the United States* (Boston, 1964), p. 52.
6. Thomas Raddall, *Halifax, Warden of the North* (Toronto, 1948), pp. 20-30.
7. Quoted in T. Watson Smith, "The Slave in Canada," *Collections of the Nova Scotia Historical Society*, Vol. XX, p. 9.
8. Public Archives of Nova Scotia, Halifax, N.S., Owen Scrap Book, No. 2, *Slavery Days in Nova Scotia*, p. 111; "Coloured Slave Bought in Truro," *Truro Daily News*, June 8, 1926, p. 1.
9. George Patterson ed., *A Few Remains of the Rev. James MacGregor, D.D.* (Philadelphia, 1859), pp. 169-188.

10. William Renwick Riddell, "The Baptism of Slaves in Prince Edward Island," *Journal of Negro History*, Volume 6, July 7, 1921, pp. 307-309.

11. I.E. Bill, *Fifty Years with the Baptist Ministers and Churches of the Maritime Province of Canada* (St. John: Barnes and Company, 1880), p. 20.

12. *Ibid.*, p. 22.

13. *Ibid.*, p. 23.

14. *Ibid.*, p. 23.

15. *Ibid.*, p. 22.

16. C.B. Fergusson (ed.), *Clarkson's Mission to America, 1791-1792.* (Halifax: Public Archives of Nova Scotia, 1971), pp. 13-14.

17. *Ibid.*, pp. 149,161.

18. Bill, *op. cit.*, p. 32.

19. *Ibid.*, p. 32.

20. *Ibid.*, p. 32.

21. *Ibid.*, p. 32.

22. *Ibid.*, p. 32.

23. *Ibid.*, p. 32.

24. *Ibid.*, pp. 32-33.

25. "The Baptists of Nova Scotia, From A.D. 1828 to A.D. 1838," in *Christian Messenger* (Halifax; Wednesday, January 29, 1862), p. 33.

26. *Ibid.*, p. 33.

27. *Minutes of the Eighth Session of the African Baptist Association of Nova Scotia* (Halifax, 1861), p. 6.

28. *Ibid.*, p. 6.

29. MacKerrow, *op. cit.*, p. 18.

30. *Ibid.*, p. 18.

31. *Ibid.*, p. 19.

32. *Ibid.*, p. 19.

33. *Ibid.*, p. 20.

34. Washington, *op. cit.*, Chapters 1, 3, and 4; James H. Cone, *A Black Theology of Liberation* (New York: J.B. Lippincott Company, 1970).

35. MacKerrow, *op. cit.*, p. 15.

36. *Minutes of the Session of the African Baptist Association* (Halifax, 1854), p. 2.

37. *Ibid.*

38. Washington, *op. cit.*, p. 52.

39. *Minutes of the Session of the African Baptist Association*, 1854, p. 3.

40. *The Novascotian*, 1846, p. 6.

41. *Ibid.*, p. 6.

42. *Minutes of the Session of the African Baptist Association*, 1861, p. 2.

43. MacKerrow, *op. cit.*, p. 31.

44. *Ibid.*, p. 32.

45. *Minutes of the Fourteenth Session of the African Baptist Association* (Halifax, 1867), p. 5.

46. *Ibid.*, p. 5.

47. MacKerrow, *op. cit.*, p. 33.

48. *Minutes of the Sixteenth Session of the African Baptist Association* (Halifax, 1869), p. 10.

49. *Ibid.*, p. 10.

50. *Minutes of the Nineteenth Session of the African Baptist Association* (Halifax, 1872), p. 13.

51. *Minutes of the Sixteenth Session*, pp. 1-7.
52. *Minutes of the Thirtieth Annual Session of the African Baptist Association* (Halifax, 1884), p. 8.
53. *Minutes of the Twenty-fourth Session of the African Baptist Association* (Halifax, 1877), p. 8.
54. *Minutes of the Fifty-First Annual Session of the African Baptist Association* (Halifax, 1904), p. 9.
55. Office of the Dean of Law, Dalhousie University, Halifax, N.S., list of the members of the graduating class of 1898.
56. *Minutes of the African Baptist Association* (Halifax, 1930 and 1935).
57. *Minutes of the Forty-Seventh Annual Session of the African Baptist Association of Nova Scotia* (Halifax, 1900), p. 5.
58. *Minutes of the Fiftieth Annual Session of the African Baptist Association* (Halifax, 1903), p. 17.
59. *Minutes of the Twenty-Seventh Annual Session of the African Baptist Association* (Halifax, 1880), p. 10.
60. *Minutes of the 68th Meeting of the African United Baptist Association of Nova Scotia* (Halifax, 1921), p. 39.
61. *Ibid.*, p. 39.
62. *Ibid.*, p. 36.
63. *Ibid.*, p. 36.
64. *Ibid.*, p. 39.
65. *Ibid.*, p. 39.
66. *Minutes of the 64th Meeting of the African United Baptist Association of Nova Scotia* (Halifax, 1917), pp. 29-30.
67. Acadia University Archives, Wolfville, N.S., Constitution, Ladies Auxiliary of the African Baptist Association, "Objects".
68. *Minutes of the Thirtieth Session*, p. 16.
69. *Minutes of the 67th Meeting of the African United Baptist Association of Nova Scotia* (Halifax, 1920), p. 21.
70. *Minutes of the 66th Meeting of the African United Baptist Association of Nova Scotia* (Halifax, 1919), p. 23.
71. *Minutes of the Sixty-Third Annual Session of the African Baptist Association of Nova Scotia* (Halifax 1916), pp. 4-5.
72. *Ibid.*, p. 4.
73. *Minutes of the 77th Annual Session of the African Baptist Association of Nova Scotia* (Halifax, 1930), p. 5.
74. *83rd Meeting of the African United Baptist Association of Nova Scotia* (Halifax, 1936), p. 46.
75. *Minutes of the 98th Annual Meeting of the African United Baptist Association of Nova Scotia* (Halifax, 1951), p. 33.
76. *Minutes of the African United Baptist Association of Nova Scotia, 111th Session* (Halifax, 1964), p. 16.
77. *Minutes of the 121st Session of the African United Baptist Association of Nova Scotia* (Halifax, 1974), p. 59.
78. Poverty in Nova Scotia, Brief for Special Committee on Poverty, Staff Members and Associates, Institute of Public Affairs, Dalhousie University (Halifax, N.S. 1969), p. 56.
79. 118th Session of the African United Baptist Association of Nova Scotia (Halifax, 1971) p. 52.

BAHA ABU-LABAN   University of Alberta

Arab Immigration to Canada*

Introduction

In the summer of 1883, a Syrian youth, Joseph Jebawy, was strolling along the main streets of Montreal. Nothing looked familiar. The layout of the city, the buildings, the people, the languages spoken, the culture, all these and more were radically different from Syria, the country from which he had emigrated with his father. In the vicinity of the Notre Dame Cathedral, across from the famous Place d'Armes Square, he glimpsed a face which did not look so strange. The young man with the familiar appearance was selling artifacts on the street. Peter Tady, the peddler, was a Syrian, like myself, who had emigrated to the New World. The news of Jebawy's discovery soon reached his father, and Abraham Bounadere, yet another youthful Syrian, who had arrived in Montreal a year earlier. The four Syrian men had a joyous social gathering in Bounadere's residence, a simple room located at the corner of Laguachetiere and St Andre Streets. These men were the first four Arabic-speaking immigrants to set foot on Canadian soil.[1]

The Syrian Arabs

The early immigrants from the Arab world were not in any way representative of the Arab population. They were largely males, young, and mostly unmarried. More importantly, they were overwhelmingly Christians from Syria. Although they were classified officially in Canada as Syrians, and later as Syrian-Lebanese, they were Arabs. They carried with them to Canada the Arab cultural heritage and they spoke the Arabic language. Some of these early immigrants and their descendants prefer(red) to be called *Arabic-speaking* Syrian or Lebanese rather than Arabs. There are several reasons underlying this preference, chief among which is the desire not to be mistaken for Moslems. But the fact remains that they are Arabs, both in language and culture.

---

* Excerpted from Baha Abu-Laban, *An Olive Branch on the Family Tree: A Study of Arabs in Canada*, with permission of author and publisher, the Multicultural Programme, Department of the Secretary of State, Ottawa (forthcoming).

The beginning of Syrian immigration coincided with a period during which increasing numbers of immigrants from other parts of the world were gravitating toward this country. For example, in 1882, Canada admitted a total of 112 458 immigrants, compared to only 47 991 admitted in the year preceding. Also, between 1881 and 1890, Canada admitted a total of 886 177 immigrants, compared to only 342 675 admissions during the ten-year period immediately preceding. More importantly, in the final two decades of the 19th century, an increasing number of immigrants to Canada came from countries other than the United States and those of western Europe. During this period, the proportions of immigrants from eastern, central and southern Europe were increasing.[2] Thus, Canada's ethnic mosaic began to take on a more variegated form. The admission of Syrian immigrants to this country added a new dimension to the Canadian ethnic mosaic.

The Growth of the Early Arab-Canadian Community

According to the best available evidence, the number of Syrian residents in Canada increased from four in 1883, to 10 in 1885, and to 50 in 1890.[3] The formative period for the Arab-Canadian community was toward the end of the 19th century when increasing numbers of Syrians joined their kindred in Montreal and elsewhere in Canada. On the average, about 80 Syrian immigrants arrived in Canada annually during that decade. By the end of the 19th century, the Syrian-born immigrants in Canada totaled 826.[4]

Immigration statistics show that a substantial number of Syrians crossed the Atlantic in the first decade of the 20th century. Syrian immigration to Canada in the first 12 years of this century has been recorded as follows:[5]

1900 – 1901	464
1901 – 1902	1 066
1902 – 1903	847
1903 – 1904	369
1904 – 1905	630
1905 – 1906	336
9 months ended March 31, 1907	277
1907 – 1908	738
1908 – 1909	189
1909 – 1910	195
1910 – 1911	184
1911 – 1912	144

Thus, between 1900 and 1912, a total of 5 373 Syrian immigrants arrived in this country.

TABLE 1 *Syrian-born Arabs in Canada by sex, 1911-41.*

Year	Total	Male	Female
1911	2 907	1 885	1 022
1921	3 879	2 395	1 484
1931	3 953	2 305	1 648
1941	3 577	2 057	1 520

Sources: *Census of Canada*, 1931, Vol. I, Table 24; and *1941*, Vol. IV, Table 18.

From 1911 to 1951, the rate of growth of the Arab-Canadian community was very slow and was based largely on natural increase. Arab immigration to Canada during this period was reduced to a trickle. Table 1 shows the number of Syrian-born Arabs in Canada for the period 1911-41. Part of the decline in the number of Syrian-born immigrants may be due to return migration, but we do not have information on this process.

The decline in the immigration of Syrian- or Arab-origin people to Canada in the 40-year period following 1911 is due to two sets of conditions. The first may be summarized in terms of the limitations on the free movement of people resulting from World War I, the depression of the 1930s, and World War II. During these disastrous events, Canada followed a very restrictive immigration policy. The policy was applied more or less uniformly to all national-ethnic groups except those from Britain and the United States.

The second, and perhaps more critical, set of conditions curbing the entry of Syrian- or Arab-origin people to Canada during that period were the following: the 1908 Order-in-Council, P.C. 926, which placed severe restrictions on the admission of all Asiatic immigrants[6]; the negative public attitudes toward Syrian immigrants; and the mistaking of these immigrants for Turks – Canada's enemy during World War I.

The above discussion has been confined to first-generation (i.e., Syrian-born) Arab-Canadians, which is a portion of the ethnic community. Table 2 shows the growth of this community by sex, for the period 1921-71. The effects of restrictive immigration on the size of the Arab-Canadian population are clearly reflected in this table. The figures in Table 2 show that between 1921 and 1951 the growth rate of the Arab ethnocultural group was relatively small. Specifically, it increased from a total of 8 282 in 1921 to 12 301 in 1951. In relative terms, the size of this ethnic community increased by 22 percent between 1921 and 1931; 18 percent between 1931 and 1941; and only 4 percent between 1941 and 1951. The main contributor to growth was natural increase (i.e., surplus of births over deaths).

The Postwar Arab-Canadian Community

Since 1951, the change in the size of the Arab-Canadian community has been influenced more by immigration than natural increase. Again, Table 2 shows the effects of a more open immigration policy on the size of this ethnic community. Between 1951 and 1961, the Arab population of Canada increased by about 57 percent, from a total of 12 301 in the former year to a total of 19 374 in the latter. For reasons which are discussed below, the 1971 figure of 28 550 (Table 2) is a substantial underestimate of the actual size of the Arab ethnic group. Nevertheless, between 1961 and 1971, the resident Arab population in Canada increased by over 47 percent. A more realistic growth rate for this period, involving an upward adjustment of the 1971 census figure, would be 300 percent.

The 28 550 figure for 1971 is based on the number of Arab-Canadians claiming Arabic as their mother tongue. This figure does not include those Arab-Canadians whose mother tongue is not Arabic (and there are many of those) or is not reported as Arabic. Technically, the 1971 figure is not comparable to the figures given for the preceding decennial years. Since the 1971 Canadian census does not record a total for the Arab-Canadian community, as distinct from mother-tongue affiliation, we are forced to rely on estimates. Judging from the inflow of Arab immigrants to Canada, and allowing for natural increase, there were an estimated 50 000 to 60 000 people of Arab origin in Canada in 1971; and 70 000 to 80 000 at the end of 1975.

The two significant periods of growth in the history of the Arab-Canadian community are the formative period 1891-1911, and the postwar

TABLE 2 *The Arab population of Canada, by sex, 1921-71*

Year	Total	Male	Female
1921	8 282	4 595	3 687
1931*	10 753	5 796	4 957
1941	11 857	6 288	5 569
1951	12 301	6 469	5 832
1961	19 374	10 112	9 262
1971**	28 550	16 135	12 415

Sources: *Census of Canada, 1921*, Vol. 1, Tables 22 and 25; *1941*, Vol. IV, Table 1: *1951*, Vol. I, Table 32; *1961*, Vol. 1.2, Table 35; *1971*, Bulletin 1.3-4, Table 18; and W. Burton Hurd, *Ethnic Origin and Nativity of the Canadian People*, Ottawa: Dominion Bureau of Statistics, 1941, p. 193, Table 2.
*The total for 1931 is obtained from Hurd. The corresponding sex distribution is determined on the basis of 116.9 males per 100 females, which is four points higher than the comparable 1941 sex ratio. See Hurd, p. 75, Table XXXIV.
**The 1971 figures are based on "mother tongue" rather than "ethnic origin." As such, they are an underestimate of the Arab origin population of Canada.

TABLE 3 *Arab immigrants to Canada, 1946-75*

Year of Arrival	Number	Year of Arrival	Number
1946 – 1955*	1 491	1966	3 114
1956**	571	1967	3 608
1957**	563	1968	5 437
1958**	353	1969	3 256
1959**	404	1970	2 641
1960**	337	1971	1 967
1961**	301	1972	2 123
1962	1 912	1973	3 595
1963	2 281	1974	4 533
1964	3 379	1975	3 839
1965	2 914		
TOTAL (1946 – 1975)			48 619

Sources: Department of Manpower and Immigration, *Immigration Statistics, 1956; 1957; 1958; 1959; 1960; 1961; 1962; 1963; 1964; 1965; 1966,* Table 2; *1967; 1968; 1969; 1970; 1971; 1972; 1973; 1974,* Table 3; and *1975, Fourth Quarterly Report,* Table 1.
*The figure for the period 1946-55 is taken from *Immigration Statistics,* 1970, Table 13.
**For the period 1956-61, the figures are based on "ethnic origin." For the preceding and following years, the figures are based on "country of former or last permanent residence."

period, starting in 1951. Both migration and natural increase have played a significant role in the demographic evolution of the Arab ethnocultural group, but net migration has been the more important of the two.

Postwar Arab Immigration to Canada

Between 1946 and 1975, Canada received nearly 4,000,000 immigrants. About one out of every 100 of these immigrants was of Arab origin. Table 3 shows the numbers of Arab-origin immigrants admitted annually during this period. The total number of immigrants from the Arab world is 48,619, giving an average of over 1 600 admissions annually for 30 years. The table also shows that the heaviest influx of immigrants from Arab countries came in the second half of this period (during which the average number of persons admitted annually reached about 3 000).

The statistics reported are based on "ethnic origin" for the period 1956-61, and on "country of last permanent (or former) residence" for the preceding and following years. This means that for all years, except 1956-61, some non-Arabs, whose country of last permanent residence is recorded as Arab, are included in the statistics. By the same token, some Arab immigrants, whose country of last permanent residence is recorded as non-Arab, are excluded.

The period following World War II, particularly the decade of the 1960s, has witnessed not only a substantial growth in Arab immigration to Canada, but also significant changes in the characteristics and national origins of Arab immigrants. For example, prior to 1945, virtually all of the Arab immigrants in Canada came from Syria and Lebanon. Between 1946 and 1975, the largest number of immigrants from the Arab world came from Egypt (18 115), followed by immigrants from Lebanon (16 333), Morocco (7 234), Syria (3 713), Jordan (737), and Tunisia (583). In addition, a total of 1 904 immigrants originated from other Arab countries. Of these, 441 immigrants were officially classified as "Arabian," but their countries of origin were not specified. The balance, or 1 463, originated from Algeria (391), Saudia Arabia (301), Kuwait (285), Iraq (187), Libya (87), Sudan (55), Bahrain (45), Qatar (45), United Arab Emirates (U.A.E.) (23), Somalia (13), Mauretania (12), Yemen (12), and Oman (7).

Patterns of Change in Sex Composition

In the first few years of Syrian immigration to Canada, women were almost totally absent. However, in the late 1880s, couples, some with children, as well as unattached women began to arrive in Canada.[7] Also, as men became more established socially and economically, wives reunited with their husbands, and, as well, there were marriages between Arab-Canadian men and women from the old country.

The unattached women immigrants in general did not come to Canada as fully independent persons, but rather as relatives, e.g., as a sister or daughter, or as persons sponsored by a Syrian resident or a family already in this country. This is consistent with the Arab cultural tradition of female dependency and emphasis on the nurturant role. The presence of Syrian women provided not only a secure and stable home environment in a strange land, but also a complementary economic role to that of the husband or guardian.

The sex composition of a given group of people is often depicted in the form of a "sex ratio," expressed as the number of males per 100 females. Two sets of sex ratios are available. The first set of sex ratios is for foreign-born Arab-Canadians, i.e., immigrants, and the second set of sex ratios is for Canadians of Arab origin regardless of whether they were born overseas or in Canada (Table 4).

Several important facts may be derived from Table 4. First, for any given years, the sex ratio is higher among immigrants than Arab-origin Canadians. Second, between 1911 and 1961 there was a steady decline in the percentage of men to women for both immigrants and the Arab-Canadian ethnic group. The trend toward a steady decline in the percentage of males to females may be explained in large measure by marital status. Marriage and parenthood have a decisive balancing effect on the sex distribution of a given group of people, immigrant or otherwise. The evidence points to the presence of an increasing number of married couples with children among Arab immigrants in recent years, and to the eventual marriage of those who landed in Canada as unattached immigrants.

TABLE 4 *Percentage of males to females for Arab immigrants and Arab-origin Canadians, 1911-71*

| | Males as % of Females | |
Year	Arab Immigrants	Arab-origin Canadians
1911	184	—
1921	161	125
1931	140	117
1941	135	113
1951	—	111
1961	127*	109
1971	115	112**

Sources: See Tables 1 and 2 which give the numbers of males and females for the 1911-1941 immigrant groups and for the Arab-Canadian community (1921-1961); and Department of Manpower and Immigration, *Immigration Statistics, 1956; 1957*, Table 7; *1958; 1959; 1960; 1961; 1962; 1963; 1964; 1965*, Table 8; *1966; 1967; 1968; 1969; 1970; 1971*, Table 9.
*The percentage is based on the sex distribution of the 1956-61 immigrant groups.
**This percentage is an estimate, representing the mid-point of the figures given for the Arab-Canadian community for 1961 (109) and Arab immigrants for 1971 (115).

Factors in Migration

The Early Syrian Immigrants

As discussed earlier, the Arabs who migrated to Canada in the latter part of the 19th and the first few decades of the 20th centuries had two striking characteristics: they were mostly Syrians and Christians. Estimates of the proportion of Christians among early Syrian immigrants to North America have ranged, but they have been variously set, at between 90 percent and 97 percent. The 1931 Census of Canada records only 645 Moslems in the country, out of a total of 10 070 Arab-origin Canadians. Why did emigration occur mostly from Syria? Why were Christians more inclined than other religious groups to migrate?

The larger portion of the Arab world was under Turkish control until the end of World War I. As a colonized people, Moslem and Christian Syrians were highly oppressed under the Turkish rule – more so, for example, than the geographically more distant inhabitants of Arabia. The oppression of the Syrian Moslems was mitigated by their religious affinity with the colonial administration. No such mitigating circumstance existed for Syrian Christians. Compared to their Moslem compatriots, the Syrian Christians in general felt greater pressure from the Turkish rulers.

The aversion of Canada's early Syrian immigrants toward the Turkish rule was well expressed by the Very Reverend Michael Zarbatany, parish priest of St. Nicholas Cathedral of the Syrian Eastern Orthodox Church, Montreal, who migrated to Canada in 1902.

Syrian Christians were, therefore, living under the shadow of oppression, with the massacre of the 60's [1860] still fresh in their memories, never knowing what fatal surprises the morrow held for them, and constantly discriminated against in their contacts with constituted authority. In view of all this and of their natural bent towards trade, and fondness for travel, is it to be wondered at that they should finally have found in emigration to America "the Land of Freedom", relief from all their fears and worries?[8]

In a similar vein, a Syrian-Canadian writer attributed the migration of Christian Syrians "to the pressure of the Turkish rule and the well known discrimination of that vindictive power against the Christian elements of its empire . . ."[9]

One important aspect of the Turkish government's misrule concerns the *millet* system of administration whereby non-Moslem sects were given a high degree of autonomy in matters affecting the personal status of their members. Although religious separateness was not new to the region and the goals of the *millet* system were worthwhile, the way it was applied intensified the social separation of sects and religious groups. One of the fiercest conflicts, for example, occurred in 1860, mainly between the Druse and the Maronites. The dislocations resulting from that conflict were felt for many decades and were an important factor in the migration of Syrian nationals.[10]

Another important element in the structure of Syrian society, relevant to the migration of Syrian Christians to the New World, was the presence of a large number of European (and, later, American) nationals in the region. Largely because of their presence, Westernization progressed more rapidly in that region than anywhere else in the Arab world. Lebanon, in particular, is frequently identified as the most modern and most Westernized among the Arab states. The role of missionaries was particularly important, for in addition to their religious function they opened Western-type schools and established strong social relations with the local residents. French missionaries worked closely with the Maronite communities while the British missionaries established strong relations with the Druse and the Greek Orthodox sects. Typically, it was the Syrian Christians, not the Moslems, who acquired a Western orientation.

During this period, the economy of The Lebanon (the mountainous region of modern Lebanon) was hard hit by the decline of the silk industry, low agricultural productivity and increasing population pressure. The mountain peasants, many of whom were Christians, were searching for the slightest hint of possible relief. Canada-bound Syrian immigrants came with little education and hardly any capital, but with a strong commitment to hard work and success. The goal frequently expressed by these immigrants was to live in Canada for a short period and then return to Syria with enough money to guarantee their economic security there.

Canada was seen as a land of freedom and economic opportunities. This "pull" factor was revitalized constantly in Syrian villages when remittances were received from relatives abroad or success stories were told of Syrians in the New World. Immigrants who returned to Syria, either permanently or for a short visit, provided concrete evidence of the promise which Canada held for immigrants.

The Recent Arab Immigrants

Canada's postwar immigrants from the Arab world were more heterogeneous than their earlier counterparts. For example, more recent migrants included a larger proportion of non-Christians; they came from more diverse Arab countries; they represented a wider range of educational and occupational backgrounds; and they carried varying political ideologies and orientations.

The results of our survey of Arab-origin Canadians provide insights into the reasons underlying their immigration. The following question was asked of all foreign-born respondents: "For what reason(s) did you come to Canada?" Forty-five percent of the responses centered around inducements in Canadian society. Included in these inducements are job and economic opportunities (23 percent), educational opportunities (12 percent), better future (6 percent), and better standard of living (4 percent).[11]

Postwar Arab immigrants included a large number of professionals and highly skilled individuals for whom emigration was not an economic necessity, but rather an avenue for the fulfillment of higher career and professional aspirations. Moreover, many of the occupationally well-placed among recent immigrants referred to the goal of higher education as a primary reason for coming to Canada. Some of these respondents entered the country as students and later decided to seek permanent residence. The goal of higher education was almost totally absent among the pioneer Arab immigrants.

Kin-related considerations constitute the second most important factor in postwar Arab immigration to Canada. Twenty-one percent of the responses given referred to family reunions, maintaining an intact family unit, and aspirations for children. In a few cases, friendship considerations played a role in the motivational structure of immigrants. It is interesting to note that female respondents, as well as respondents with lower educational qualifications, tended to refer to family reasons more frequently than their opposite counterparts.

The third most important contribution to postwar emigration from the Arab world is the factor of political estrangement, which accounts for about 12 percent of the responses. Such terms as political instability, insecurity, loss (or fear of loss) of freedom, political repression, discriminatory treatment, and government policy (e.g., socialism) illustrate the nature of "push" factors involved. Respondents from Palestine added expulsion from and inability to return to the homeland.

Since 1961, increasing numbers of alienated Egyptian nationals have been emigrating to different parts of the world, and a significant number of them have been non-Moslems. Immigrants from Egypt tended to verbalize political disaffection and hopes for a higher standard of living and better future more frequently, and family reasons less frequently, than immigrants from other Arab states. In some cases, respondents attributed their migration, and that of their compatriots, partly to what they considered to be discriminatory treatment of non-Moslems in Egypt, and partly to lack of opportunities for advancement. The infrequent reference to family as an underlying reason for immigration is due to the short history of this stream of immigration to Canada, and to the Egyptian immigrants' tendency to move in family units.

And lastly, 22 percent of the responses to the question on reasons for immigration to Canada refer to such miscellaneous factors as search for adventure, change, and tourist travel followed by a decision to stay permanently. This composite factor is certainly not unique to Arab immigrants, but its presence as a motivating element in this group should be acknowledged.

Summary

The history of the Arab-Canadian community is relatively short. Arab immigrants began to come to Canada in the 1880s as a part of a larger stream of Syrian immigration to the New World. By 1901, Canada had an estimated total of 2 000 people of Arab origin. By 1911, the size of this ethnocultural group rose to 6 000 – 7 000 people. For the 40-year period ending in 1951, relatively few Arab immigrants were admitted to this country because of severe restrictions on the admission of immigrants from Asia.

The second phase of Arab immigration to Canada began in the 1950s and reached its peak in the decade following. Between 1946 and 1975, 48 619 of Canada's immigrants originated from the Near East and Arab North Africa. The majority of these immigrants, or 44 599, arrived after 1961. Unlike the earlier wave which consisted almost entirely of Syrians, the recent wave consisted of immigrants from many different Arab states, notably Egypt. Today, it is estimated that there are in Canada 70 000 to 80 000 people of Arab origin. The vast majority of these people, or more than nine out of 10, live in Ontario, Quebec and, to a lesser degree, Alberta and Nova Scotia.

While the sex ratio among the Arab immigrants was about 184 males per 100 females in 1911, by 1971 it had dropped to about 115 males per 100 females. In the postwar period, there were significant differences in the age-sex composition of immigrants from different Arab states. Considering the whole of the Arab-Canadian ethnic group, the percentage of males to females declined from 125 in 1921 to about 112 in 1971. The steady decline in sex ratio is due not only to the increasingly more balanced sex ratios among Arab immigrants, but also to family formation among the resident Arab population and the possible return of some immigrants, usually male, to their ancestral homeland. The important point is that the decline in sex ratio is symptomatic of the increasing stability and permanence of the Arab ethnic group in Canada.

Since the 1880s the reasons for Arab immigration to Canada have been associated with the unfavorable social, political, and economic conditions in the ancestral homeland. The details of these conditions varied from one immigrant to another and from one country to another, but they have always been an important component of the motivational structure of Arab immigrants. For the disaffected as well as the achievement-oriented Arab migrants, Canada has offered freedom and ample economic opportunities. The nucleus of Canada's Arab community was established as early as 1901. Over the years, this community attracted increasing numbers of newcomers from the Near East, partly because of its capacity to accommodate new immigrants and partly because of the strength of filial ties among its members.

END NOTES

1. Elias Karam, "Syrian Immigration to Canada," in Elias Karam, ed., *The Syrian Canadian National Review* (Ottawa, 1935), p. 19.
2. For a relevant discussion of immigration during this period, see Norman MacDonald, *Canada: Immigration and Colonization, 1841-1903* (Toronto: Macmillan, 1966).
3. Karam, "Syrian Immigration to Canada," pp. 19, 21 and 23.
4. Baha Abu-Laban, "The Arab-Canadian Community," in *The Arab Americans: Studies in Assimilation*, Elain C. Hagopian and Ann Paden, eds. (Wilmette, Ill., 1969), p. 21.
5. Recorded by the Superintendant of Immigration, Ottawa, in a January 16, 1913, letter to Hon. Dr. Roche. See Records of the Immigration Branch, RG76, Vol. 431, File No. 622436: "Immigration from Syria and Lebanon, 1905-1910, 1913."
6. P. C. 926 required immigrants of Asian origin to have in their possession $200 upon arrival. In view of the destitution which characterized the overwhelming majority of these immigrants, the $200 requirement was severe. In practical terms, it meant debarment from entry to Canada.
7. Cf. Karam, *op. cit.*, p. 21.
8. Michael Zarbatany, "A Short History of Syria," in *The Syrian Canadian National Review*, Elias Karam, ed. (Ottawa, 1935), p. 17.
9. Karam, *ibid.*, p. 25.

10. Some non-Christians adversely affected by the civil war also were prompted to migrate. In his biography, an early Druse immigrant to Canada, for example, relates his father's experience. See Sheikh Muhammad Said Massoud, *I Fought As I Believed* (Montreal, 1976), p. 5ff.

11. The survey carried out in 1974 was based on structured interviews with 349 Arab-Canadians living in the Toronto and Montreal areas. The interview schedule was designed to yield information on background characteristics, reasons for emigration to Canada, social and economic adjustment, survival of ethnic patterns, and attitudes toward Canada and the ancestral homeland. On the average, each interview lasted for about one hour.

Appendix A

A STATISTICAL ALMANAC OF CANADIAN ETHNICITY*

TABLE 1 *Population counts of Native People*

	Registered Indian population*		Census of Canada** Indians	Inuit
1929	108 012	1881	108 547	—
1939	118 378	1901	127 941	
1949	136 407	1921	110 814	2 910
1961	191 709	1941	118 316	7 205
1966	224 164	1951	155 874	9 733
1971	257 619	1961	208 286	11 835
1974	276 436	1971	295 215	17 550

Source: *Perspective Canada* II, Statistics Canada, Ottawa, 1977.
*The Department of Indian and Northern Affairs annually counts the number of Registered Indians under its jurisdictions. Prior to 1960 this count was made every five years.
**The Census of Canada counts as Indian anyone who calls himself Indian, whether registered or not, and who can trace Indian ancestry through the father's line. Prior to 1951 people of mixed Indian and non-Indian parentage were included in the native population. In the 1951, 1961 and 1971 censuses, people of mixed parentage were counted in the same way as other ethnic groups, i.e., through the line of the father.

TABLE 2 *Provincial distribution of registered Indians and Inuit*

	Registered Indians 1974	Inuit 1971
	%	%
Newfoundland	—	6.0
Prince Edward Island	0.2	—
Nova Scotia	1.9	0.1
New Brunswick	1.8	—
Quebec	10.9	21.4
Ontario	21.8	4.3
Manitoba	14.6	0.7
Saskatchewan	14.8	0.4
Alberta	11.8	0.8
British Columbia	18.7	1.2
Yukon	1.0	0.1
Northwest Territories	2.5	65.0
Canada	100.0	100.0
Total population	276 436	17 550

Source: *Perspective Canada* II, Statistics Canada, Ottawa, 1977.
*All tables and charts are reproduced by permission of the Minister of Supply and Services, Canada.

TABLE 3 *Registered Indians by location of residence*

	On reserves %	On Crown lands %	Other* %	Total %	number
1959	73.2	9.9	16.9	100.0	179 126
1966	70.3	10.2	19.5	100.0	224 164
1968	68.1	9.1	22.8	100.0	237 490
1970	65.2	9.3	25.5	100.0	250 781
1972	63.7	8.6	27.7	100.0	264 680
1974	63.8	9.2	27.0	100.0	276 436

Source: Statistics Canada, *Perspective Canada* II, Ottawa, 1977.
*Includes Registered Indians whose type of residence was not known.

TABLE 4 *Indian and Inuit population by place of residence*

	Urban and Rural Distribution	
	1961 %	1971* %
Rural	87.1	69.3
Farm	6.8	3.9
Non-farm	80.3	65.4
Urban	12.9	30.7
Cities of:		
100 000 +	6.6	15.9
30 000 - 99 999	1.3	2.9
10 000 - 29 999	1.1	4.5
5 000 - 9 999	0.8	2.0
2 500 - 4 999	9.0	1.6
1 000 - 2 499	2.2	3.8
Totals	100.0	100.0
Number	220 121	295 215

Source: Statistics Canada, *Perspective Canada*, Ottawa, 1974.
*Does not include Inuit.
Note: The cities chosen were those which in 1971 had the largest number of Indian residents. The numbers are probably underestimated since many new arrivals in a city are itinerant and are, therefore, very difficult to count in a census.

TABLE 5 *Infant mortality in the registered Indian, Inuit and Canadian populations*
Rate per 1 000 live births

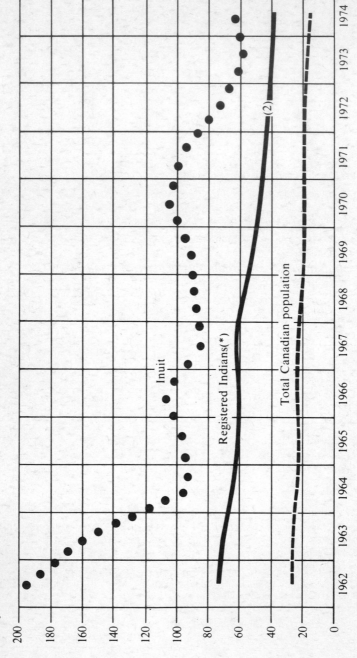

(*) See the introductory text for a short note re the source of the data for Registered Indians.
(**) No national figure was available for Registered Indians in 1972.
Source: *Perspective Canada* II. Statistics Canada, Ottawa, 1977.

TABLE 6 *Indians and Inuit in urban centers*

	1951	1961	1971*
Calgary	62	335	2 265
Edmonton	616	995	4 260
Hamilton	493	841	1 470
London	133	340	1 015
Montreal	296	507	3 215
Prince Albert	211	225	1 045
Prince Rupert	—	800	1 780
Regina	160	539	2 860
Saskatoon	48	207	1 070
Toronto	805	1 196	2 990
Vancouver	239	530	3 000
Winnipeg	210	1 082	4 940

Source: Statistics Canada, *Perspective Canada*, Ottawa, 1974.
*Does not include Inuit.
Note: The cities chosen were those which in 1971 had the largest number of Indian residents. The numbers are probably underestimated since many new arrivals in a city are itinerant and are, therefore, very difficult to count in a census.

TABLE 7 *Enfranchisements* of registered Indians*

	Enfranchisements upon application		Enfranchisements following marriage to a non-Indian		Total enfran- chisements
	Adults	Children**	Women	Children**	
1955-56 to 1959-60	912	724	2 078	484	4 198
1960-61 to 1964-65	401	239	2 198	694	3 532
1965-66 to 1969-70	207	107	2 440	655	3 409
1970-71 to 1974-75	54	20	1 823	117	2 014

Source: Statistics Canada, *Perspective Canada* II, Ottawa, 1977.
*On enfranchisement an Indian permanently gives up his rights under the Indian Act. Enfranchisement in this sense has nothing to do with the possession of voting rights which were guaranteed to all Indians in 1960.
**Prior to 1972-1973 minor, unmarried children were automatically enfranchised with their parents(s). Since 1972-1973 minor, unmarried children have been enfranchised only when it is requested by the parent(s) and when the application is approved by Indian and Northern Affairs.

TABLE 8 *Age distribution of the registered Indian population*

| | Age group | | | | | | Dependency ratios* | |
	0-14 years	15-64 years	65 years and over	No age given	Total	Population	Young	Aged
					percent			
1924	32.2	51.2	5.9	10.7	100.0	104 894	62.9	11.5
1934	34.7	55.4	6.2	3.7	100.0	112 510	62.7	11.1
1944	37.5	55.9	6.6	—	100.0	125 686	67.0	11.8
1954	41.7	53.2	5.1	—	100.0	151 558	78.5	9.6
1964	46.7	49.1	4.2	—	100.0	211 389	95.0	8.6
1974	43.2	52.4	4.2	0.2	100.0	276 436	82.4	8.1

*The dependency ratios reflect the relationship between the groups least likely to be involved in the work force, (i.e. the young and the elderly,) and the working age population. The ratios are calculated as follows:

Young- Persons aged 0-14 ÷ Persons aged 15-64 x 100

Aged- Persons aged 65 and over ÷ Persons aged 15-64 x 100

A high dependency ratio suggests that the working age population must support a larger non-productive population than a similar working age population with a low dependency ratio.
Source: Statistics Canada, *Perspective Canada* II, Ottawa, 1977.

TABLE 9 *Causes of death by international classification, 1974*

	Indians and Inuit	All Canada
	%	%
Diseases of the circulatory system	20.0	49.3
Diseases of the respiratory system	10.5	1.2
Diseases of the digestive system	5.1	3.7
Diseases of the nervous system	2.3	1.1
Neoplasms	7.6	20.4
Infective and parasitic diseases	3.1	0.7
Congenital anomalies	1.6	1.0
Perinatal morbidity	4.6	1.5
Accidents, poisoning and violence	34.8(1)	10.1
Other causes	10.4	11.0
Total	100.0	100.0
Total deaths	1 973	166 794

(*) "Accidents, poisoning and violence" includes motor vehicle accidents (8.8%), drowning (5.6%), exposure (1.7%), burns (3.8%), falls (1.2%), firearm mishaps (2.7%), drug overdoses (1.1%), and others (9.9%).
Source: Statistics Canada, *Perspective Canada* II, Ottawa, 1977.

TABLE 10 *Population by ethnic group*

	1871	1911	1921	1931	1951	1961	1971
				percent			
Austrian	—	3.8	7.3	2.4	1.1	2.3	0.7
Belgian	—	0.8	1.4	1.3	1.2	1.3	0.9
Czech and Slovak	—	—	0.6	1.5	2.1	1.6	1.4
Dutch	10.1	4.9	8.0	7.2	8.9	9.1	7.4
Finnish	—	1.4	1.5	2.1	1.5	1.3	1.0
German	69.4	35.2	20.1	22.9	20.8	22.3	22.9
Greek	—	0.3	0.4	0.5	0.6	1.2	2.2
Hungarian	—	1.0	0.9	2.0	2.0	2.7	2.3
Italian	0.4	4.0	4.6	4.7	5.1	9.6	12.7
Jewish	—	6.7	8.6	7.6	6.1	3.7	5.2
Lithuanian	—	—	0.1	0.3	0.5	0.6	0.4
Polish	—	2.9	3.6	7.0	7.4	6.9	5.5
Roumanian	—	0.5	0.9	1.4	0.8	0.9	0.5
Russian	0.2	3.9	6.8	4.3	3.1	2.5	1.1
Scandinavian*	0.6	9.8	11.4	11.0	9.5	8.2	6.7
Portuguese**	—	—	—	—	—	—	1.7
Ukrainian	—	6.6	7.3	10.9	13.2	10.1	10.1
Yugoslav	—	—	0.3	0.8	0.7	1.4	1.8
Other European	1.3	0.6	1.2	0.4	1.2	1.9	1.7
Chinese	—	2.4	2.7	2.3	1.1	1.2	2.1
Japanese	—	0.8	1.1	1.1	0.7	0.6	0.6
Other Asiatic	—	0.6	0.7	0.7	0.6	0.7	2.2
Native Indian and Inuit	7.9	9.2	7.8	6.2	5.6	4.7	5.4
Other and not stated	10.1	4.6	2.7	1.4	6.3	5.2	3.5
Totals (other than French and British)	100.0	100.0	100.0	100.0	100.0	100.0	100.0
Number in thousands	293	1 147	1 465	2 068	2 980	4 699	5 764
French	31.1	28.6	27.9	28.2	30.8	30.4	28.7
British	60.5	55.5	55.4	51.9	47.9	43.8	44.6
Other	8.4	15.9	16.7	19.9	21.3	25.8	26.7
Totals	100.0	100.0	100.0	100.0	100.0	100.0	100.0
Number in thousands	3 689	7 207	8 788	10 377	14 009	18 238	21 568

Source: Statistics Canada, *Perspective Canada*, Ottawa, 1974.
*Includes Danish, Icelandic, Norwegian and Swedish.
**Included with "Other European" prior to 1971.

TABLE 11 *Age by ethnic group, 1971*

	0-4	5-9	10-14	15-24	25-44	45+	Total	Total persons
			percent					*no.*
British	8	10	10	19	23	30	100	9 624 120
French	8	11	12	20	26	23	100	6 180 120
German	8	10	10	17	29	26	100	1 317 200
Italian	11	12	10	16	31	20	100	730 820
Ukrainian	7	9	9	17	25	33	100	580 655
Netherlands	9	12	13	18	26	22	100	425 945
Indians and Inuit	16	16	13	20	21	14	100	312 765
Scandinavian	7	9	10	18	26	30	100	384 795
All other	9	9	9	17	29	27	100	2 011 890
Canadian average	8	10	11	19	25	27	100	21 568 310

Source: Statistics Canada, *Perspective Canada*, Ottawa, 1974.

TABLE 12 *Ethnic group by occupational group, 1971*

	British Isles	French	German	Hungarian	Italian	Jewish	Netherlands
				percent			
Managerial, administrative and related	5.2	3.7	3.6	2.8	1.8	10.7	3.5
Natural sciences, engineering and mathematics	3.1	1.8	2.7	4.7	1.3	2.6	3.3
Social sciences and related	1.0	0.9	0.6	0.6	0.3	3.3	0.7
Religion	0.3	0.4	0.3	0.2	0.1	0.2	0.4
Teaching and related	4.3	4.5	3.6	3.1	1.6	5.2	3.2
Medicine and related	4.1	3.6	3.5	3.4	1.1	4.9	3.6
Art, literature, performing arts and related	1.0	0.9	0.7	1.3	0.6	2.1	0.8
Clerical and related	18.5	14.7	13.4	11.5	9.7	18.8	11.9
Sales	10.4	8.7	8.7	6.7	6.7	24.2	8.8
Service	10.6	11.2	10.6	11.9	13.0	4.9	10.6
Farming, horticulture and animal husbandry	5.4	4.4	12.5	9.4	1.8	0.4	14.2
Fishing, hunting, trapping and related	0.4	0.2	0.1	—	—	—	0.2
Forestry and logging	0.6	1.3	0.5	0.4	0.2	—	0.4
Mining, quarrying including oil and gas field	0.6	0.9	0.7	0.7	0.4	—	0.4
Processing	3.1	4.9	3.7	4.2	6.2	1.4	3.8
Machining	2.4	2.8	3.4	5.8	5.2	0.6	3.1
Production, fabrication, assembly and repair	5.9	8.2	7.6	9.7	15.6	6.4	6.9
Construction trades	5.6	6.9	7.9	7.2	15.3	1.7	8.1
Transport equipment operation	4.2	4.5	3.5	2.5	2.6	1.7	3.5
Material handling and related	2.4	2.2	2.3	2.4	3.4	0.8	2.3
Other crafts and equipment operation	1.4	1.3	1.1	1.0	0.7	0.6	1.1
Not stated and not elsewhere classified	9.5	12.0	9.0	10.5	12.4	9.5	9.2
Totals	100.0	100.0	100.0	100.0	100.0	100.0	100.0

Source: Statistics Canada, *Perspective Canada*, Ottawa. 1974.

TABLE 13 *Mother tongue and language spoken in the home, 1971*

	Mother tongue *(1)*	Language of the home *(2)*	Percentage change from *(1) to (2)*
English	12 973 810	14 446 235	+ 11.3
French	5 793 650	5 546 025	– 4.3
German	561 085	213 350	–62.0
Italian	538 360	425 235	–21.0
Ukrainian	309 855	144 760	–53.3
Native Indian	164 525	122 205	–25.7
Netherlands	144 925	36 170	–75.0
Polish	134 780	70 960	–47.4
Greek	104 455	86 830	–16.9
Chinese	94 855	77 890	–17.9
Portuguese	86 925	74 765	–14.0
Magyar (Hungarian)	86 835	50 670	–41.6
Serbo-Croatian	74 190	29 310	–60.5
Yiddish	49 890	26 330	–47.2
Other	41 835	31 900	–23.8
Finnish	36 725	18 280	–50.2
Indo-Pakistani	32 555	23 110	–29.0
Russian	31 745	12 590	–60.3
Arabic	28 550	15 260	–46.5
Czech	27 780	15 090	–45.7
Norwegian	27 405	2 160	–92.1
Danish	27 395	4 690	–82.9
Spanish	23 815	17 710	–25.6
Swedish	21 680	2 210	–89.8
Gaelic	21 200	1 175	–94.5
Slovak	17 370	9 465	–45.5
Japanese	16 890	10 500	–37.8
Inuit	15 295	15 080	– 1.4
Lithuanian	14 725	9 985	–32.2
Estonian	14 520	10 110	–30.4
Flemish	14 240	3 190	–77.6
Lettish	14 140	9 250	–34.6
Romanian	11 300	4 455	–60.6
Icelandic	7 860	995	–87.3
Welsh	3 160	370	–88.3
Totals	21 568 310	21 568 310	

Source: Statistics Canada, *Perspective Canada*, Ottawa, 1974.

TABLE 14 *Language most often spoken at home, 1971*

	English	French	Other	Total
	per cent			
CANADA	67.1	25.7	7.2	100.0
Newfoundland	99.1	0.4	0.5	100.0
Prince Edward Island	95.7	3.9	0.4	100.0
Nova Scotia	95.5	3.5	1.0	100.0
New Brunswick	67.9	31.4	0.7	100.0
Quebec	14.7	80.8	4.5	100.0
Ontario	85.1	4.6	10.3	100.0
Manitoba	82.6	4.0	13.4	100.0
Saskatchewan	89.9	1.7	8.4	100.0
Alberta	90.8	1.4	7.8	100.0
British Columbia	92.8	0.5	6.7	100.0
Yukon	95.0	0.7	4.3	100.0
Northwest Territories	58.1	1.7	40.2	100.0

Source: Statistics Canada, *Perspective Canada*, Ottawa, 1974.

TABLE 15 *Population by mother tongue, 1971*

	Linguistic Group		Provincial Population			
	English	French	English	French	Other	Total
	percent					
CANADA	100.0	100.0	60.2	26.9	12.9	100.0
Newfoundland	4.0	0.1	98.5	0.7	0.8	100.0
Prince Edward Island	0.8	0.1	92.4	6.6	1.0	100.0
Nova Scotia	5.7	0.7	93.0	5.0	2.0	100.0
New Brunswick	3.2	3.7	64.7	34.0	1.3	100.0
Quebec	6.1	84.1	13.1	80.7	6.2	100.0
Ontario	46.0	8.3	77.5	6.3	16.2	100.0
Manitoba	5.1	1.0	67.1	6.1	26.8	100.0
Saskatchewan	5.3	0.5	74.1	3.4	22.5	100.0
Alberta	9.7	0.8	77.6	2.9	19.5	100.0
British Columbia	13.9	0.7	82.7	1.7	15.6	100.0
Yukon	0.1	—	83.4	2.4	14.2	100.0
Northwest Territories	0.1	—	46.9	3.3	49.8	100.0

Source: Statistics Canada, *Perspective Canada*, Ottawa, 1974.

TABLE 16 *Official language of specified ethnic groups*

	Converse in neither English nor French		Converse in English Only		Converse in French Only		Converse in both English and French		Total
	1961	1971	1961	1971	1961	1971	1961	1971	
					percent				
British	0.1	—	95.5	94.1	0.4	0.6	4.0	5.3	100.0
French	0.2	—	8.6	8.2	61.2	60.1	30.1	31.7	100.0
German	1.3	11.2	95.7	94.0	0.5	0.8	2.6	4.0	100.0
Italian	17.4	16.6	65.2	63.3	6.8	6.0	10.6	14.1	100.0
Jewish	1.3	0.9	79.9	74.3	0.5	1.4	18.4	23.4	100.0
Netherlands	1.6	0.7	95.3	94.6	0.2	0.3	2.9	4.4	100.0
Polish	2.5	2.6	91.3	89.6	0.7	0.7	5.5	7.1	100.0
Russian	2.7	3.8	90.3	89.3	0.5	0.6	6.5	6.3	100.0
Scandinavian	0.2	0.2	97.4	96.6	0.3	0.3	2.1	2.9	100.0
Ukrainian	2.5	2.0	94.6	93.6	0.2	0.2	2.6	4.2	100.0
Other European	4.9	9.2	85.4	79.8	2.0	2.2	7.7	8.8	100.0
Asiatic	11.2	12.0	80.9	78.3	1.3	1.6	6.6	8.1	100.0
TOTALS	1.3	1.5	67.4	67.1	19.1	18.0	12.2	13.4	100.0

Source: Statistics Canada, *Perspective Canada*, Ottawa, 1974.

TABLE 17 *Educational attainment by mother tongue, 1971**

	Elementary	Secondary	Post-secondary	University
		percent		
English	26.2	42.5	17.5	13.8
French	49.5	29.0	12.8	8.7
German	47.0	25.7	18.7	8.6
Indians and Inuit	79.5	15.0	3.8	1.7
Italian	74.0	16.0	5.7	4.3
Dutch	37.6	30.7	21.6	10.1
Scandinavian	45.7	29.8	16.2	8.3
Ukrainian	54.8	27.3	9.9	8.0
All other	48.0	25.7	11.4	14.9
TOTALS	36.8	36.0	15.4	11.8

*Persons 20 years of age and over.
Source: Statistics Canada, *Perspective Canada*, Ottawa, 1974.

TABLE 18 *Population by religion*

	1871	*1901*	*1911*	*1921*	*1931*	*1951*	*1961*	*1971*
					percent			
Anglican	14.1	12.8	14.5	16.1	15.8	14.5	13.2	11.8
Baptist	6.8	6.0	5.3	4.8	4.3	3.7	3.3	3.1
Greek Orthodox[1]	—	0.3	1.2	1.9	1.0	1.2	1.3	1.5
Jehovah's Witnesses	—	—	—	0.1	0.1	0.2	0.4	0.8
Jewish	—	0.3	1.0	1.4	1.5	1.4	1.4	1.3
Lutheran	1.1	1.8	3.2	3.3	3.8	3.1	3.6	3.3
Mennonite[2]	—	0.6	0.6	0.7	0.9	0.9	0.8	0.8
Pentecostal	—	—	—	0.1	0.3	0.7	0.8	1.0
Presbyterian	16.2	15.8	15.6	16.0	8.4	5.5	4.5	4.0
Roman Catholic	42.9	41.7	39.5	38.6	39.5	42.7	45.8	46.3
Salvation Army	—	0.2	0.3	0.3	0.5	0.5	0.6	
Ukrainian Catholic	—	—	—	—	1.8	2.8	1.0	1.1
United Church	3 689	5 371	7 207	8 788	10 377	14 009	18 238	21 568

1) Includes those churches which observe the Greek Orthodox Rite such as Russian Orthodox, Ukrainian and Syrian Orthodox.
2) Includes Hutterite.
3) Includes Evangelican United Brethren.
4) Included with "Other".
Source: Statistics Canada, *Perspective Canada*, Ottawa, 1974.

TABLE 19 *Birth rates, Canada and Provinces, 1956-79*

	1956	*1961*	*1966*	*1971*	*1976*	*1977*	*1978*	*1979*
			Rate per 1 000 population					
Canada	28.0	26.1	19.4	16.8	15.7	15.5	15.3	15.5
Newfld.	35.0	34.1	28.5	24.5	20.0	19.8	18.4	17.7
P.E.I.	26.8	27.1	20.3	18.8	16.4	16.4	16.3	15.7
N.S.	27.5	26.3	20.1	18.1	15.5	14.8	14.9	14.6
N.B.	29.9	27.7	20.6	19.2	17.4	16.8	15.5	15.5
Quebec	29.4	26.1	19.0	14.8	15.5	15.2	15.1	15.7
Ont.	26.6	25.3	19.0	16.9	14.8	14.7	14.3	14.3
Man.	25.8	25.3	18.7	18.2	16.4	16.2	15.9	15.7
Sask.	27.3	25.9	19.9	17.3	17.3	17.7	17.5	17.7
Alta.	31.1	29.2	20.9	18.8	18.0	18.1	18.1	18.4
B.C.	25.9	23.7	17.3	16.0	14.5	14.7	14.7	15.0
Yukon	40.1	38.1	25.7	27.5	20.6	20.1	20.6	23.2
N.W.T.	41.3	48.6	40.3	37.0	27.8	27.5	27.6	29.6

Source: Statistics Canada, *Vital Statistics*, Vol. 1, Ottawa 1974, 1977 and 1979.

Appendix B

THE CANADIAN CHARTER OF RIGHTS AND FREEDOMS

Whereas Canada is founded upon principles that recognize the supremacy of God and the rule of law:

Guarantee of Rights and Freedoms

Rights and freedoms in Canada

1. The *Canadian Charter of Rights and Freedoms* guarantees the rights and freedoms set out in it subject only to such reasonable limits prescribed by law as can be demonstrably justified in a free and democratic society.

Fundamental Freedoms

Fundamental freedoms

2. Everyone has the following fundamental freedoms:
  (*a*) freedom of conscience and religion;
  (*b*) freedom of thought, belief, opinion and expression, including freedom of the press and other media of communication;
  (*c*) freedom of peaceful assembly; and
  (*d*) freedom of association.

Democratic Rights

Democratic rights of citizens

3. Every citizen of Canada has the right to vote in an election of members of the House of Commons or of a legislative assembly and to be qualified for membership therein.

Maximum duration of legislative bodies

4. (1) No House of Commons and no legislative assembly shall continue for longer than five years from the date fixed for the return of the writs at a general election of its members.

Continuation in special circumstances

(2) In time of real or apprehended war, invasion or insurrection, a House of Commons may be continued by Parliament and a legislative assembly may be continued by the legislature beyond five years if such continuation is not opposed by the votes of more than one-third of the members of the House of Commons or the legislative assembly, as the case may be.

Annual sitting of legislative bodies

5. There shall be a sitting of Parliament and of each legislature at least once every twelve months.

Mobility Rights

Mobility of citizens

6. (1) Every citizen of Canada has the right to enter, remain in and leave Canada.

Rights to move and gain livelihood

(2) Every citizen of Canada and every person who has the status of a permanent resident of Canada has the right
  (*a*) to move to and take up residence in any province; and
  (*b*) to pursue the gaining of a livelihood in any province.

Limitation
(3) The rights specified in subsection (2) are subject to
(a) any laws or practices of general application in force in a province other than those that discriminate among persons primarily on the basis of province of present or previous residence; and
(b) any laws providing for reasonable residency requirements as a qualification for the receipt of publicly provided social services.

Affirmative action programs
(4) Subsections (2) and (3) do not preclude any law, program or activity that has as its object the amelioration in a province of conditions of individuals in that province who are socially or economically disadvantaged if the rate of employment in that province is below the rate of employment in Canada.

Legal Rights

Life, liberty and security of person
7. Everyone has the right to life, liberty and security of the person and the right not to be deprived thereof except in accordance with the principles of fundamental justice.

Search or seizure
8. Everyone has the right to be secure against unreasonable search or seizure.

Detention or imprisonment
9. Everyone has the right not to be arbitrarily detained or imprisoned.

Arrest or detention
10. Everyone has the right on arrest or detention
(a) to be informed promptly of the reasons therefor;
(b) to retain and instruct counsel without delay and to be informed of that right; and
(c) to have the validity of the detention determined by way of habeas corpus and to be released if the detention is not lawful.

Proceedings in criminal and penal matters
11. Any person charged with an offence has the right
(a) to be informed without unreasonable delay of the specific offence;
(b) to be tried within a reasonable time;
(c) not to be compelled to be a witness in proceedings against that person in respect of the offence;
(d) to be presumed innocent until proven guilty according to law in a fair and public hearing by an independent and impartial tribunal;
(e) not to be denied reasonable bail without just cause;
(f) except in the case of an offence under military law tried before a military tribunal, to the benefit of trial by jury where the maximum punishment for the offence is imprisonment for five years or a more severe punishment;
(g) not to be found guilty on account of any act or omission unless, at the time of the act or omission, it constituted an offence under Canadian or international law or was criminal according the general principles of law recognized by the community of nations;

(*h*) if finally acquitted of the offence, not to be tried for it again and, if finally found guilty and punished for the offence, not to be tried or punished for it again; and

(*i*) if found guilty of the offence and if the punishment for the offence has been varied between the time of commission and the time of sentencing, to the benefit of the lesser punishment.

Treatment or punishment	*12.* Everyone has the right not to be subjected to any cruel and unusual treatment or punishment.
Self-crimination	*13.* A witness who testifies in any proceedings has the right not to have any incriminating evidence so given used to incriminate that witness in any other proceedings, except in a prosecution for perjury or for the giving of contradictory evidence.
Interpreter	*14.* A party or witness in any proceedings who does not understand or speak the language in which the proceedings are conducted or who is deaf has the right to the assistance of an interpreter.

Equality Rights

Equality before and under law and equal protection and benefit of law	*15.* (1) Every individual is equal before and under the law and has the right to the equal protection and equal benefit of the law without discrimination and, in particular, without discrimination based on race, national or ethnic origin, colour, religion, sex, age or mental or physical disability.
Affirmative action programs	(2) Subsection (1) does not preclude any law, program or activity that has as its object the amelioration of conditions of disadvantaged individuals or groups including those that are disadvantaged because of race, national or ethnic origin, colour, religion, sex, age or mental or physical disability.

Official Languages of Canada

Official languages of Canada	*16.* (1) English and French are the official languages of Canada and have equality of status and equal rights and privileges as to their use in all institutions of the Parliament and government of Canada.
Official languages of New Brunswick	(2) English and French are the official languages of New Brunswick and have equality of status and equal rights and privileges as to their use in all institutions of the legislature and government of New Brunswick.
Advancement of status and use	(3) Nothing in the Charter limits the authority of Parliament or a legislature to advance the equality of status or use of English and French.
Proceedings of Parliament	*17.* (1) Everyone has the right to use English or French in any debates and other proceedings of Parliament.

Proceedings of New Brunswick legislature

(2) Everyone has the right to use English or French in any debates and other proceedings of the legislature of New Brunswick.

Parliamentary statutes and records

18. (1) The statutes, records and journals of Parliament shall be printed and published in English and French and both language versions are equally authoritative.

New Brunswick statutes and records

(2) The statutes, records and journals of the legislature of New Brunswick shall be printed and published in English and French and both language versions are equally authoritative.

Proceedings in courts established by Parliament

19. (1) Either English or French may be used by any person in, or in any pleading in or process issuing from, any court established by Parliament.

Proceedings in New Brunswick courts

(2) Either English or French may be used by any person in, or in any pleading in or process issuing from, any court of New Brunswick.

Communications by public with federal institutions

20. (1) Any member of the public in Canada has the right to communicate with, and to receive available services from, any head or central office of an institution of the Parliament or government of Canada in English or French, and has the same right with respect to any other office of any such institution where
(*a*) there is a significant demand for communications with and services from that office in such language; or
(*b*) due to the nature of the office, it is reasonable that communications with and services from that office be available in both English and French.

Communications by public with New Brunswick institutions

(2) Any member of the public in New Brunswick has the right to communicate with, and to receive available services from, any office of an institution of the legislature or government of New Brunswick in English or French.

Continuation existing constitutional provisions

21. Nothing in sections 16 to 20 abrogates or derogates from any right, privilege or obligation with respect to the English and French languages, or either of them, that exists or is continued by virtue of any other provision of the Constitution of Canada.

Rights and privileges preserved

22. Nothing in sections 16 to 20 abrogates or derogates from any legal or customary right or privilege acquired or enjoyed either before or after the coming into force of this Charter with respect to any language that is not English or French.

Minority Language Educational Rights

Language of instruction

23. (1) Citizens of Canada
(*a*) whose first language learned and still understood is that of the English or French linguistic minority population of the prov-

ince in which they reside, or

(*b*) who have received their primary school instruction in Canada in English or French and reside in a province where the language in which they received that instruction is the language of the English or French linguistic minority population of the province,

have the right to have their children receive primary and secondary school instruction in that language in that province.

Continuity of
language
instruction

(2) Citizens of Canada of whom any child has received or is receiving primary or secondary school instruction in English or French in Canada, have the right to have all their children receive primary and secondary school instruction in the same language.

Application
where numbers
warrant

(3) The right of citizens of Canada under subsections (1) and (2) to have their children receive primary and secondary school instruction in the language of the English or French linguistic minority population of a province

(*a*) applies wherever in the province the number of children of citizens who have such a right is sufficient to warrant the provision to them out of public funds of minority language instruction; and

(*b*) includes, where the number of those children so warrants, the right to have them receive that instruction in minority language educational facilities provided out of public funds.

Enforcement

Enforcement of
guaranteed
rights and
freedoms

24. (1) Anyone whose rights or freedoms, as guaranteed by this Charter, have been infringed or denied may apply to a court of competent jurisdiction to obtain such remedy as the court considers appropriate and just in the circumstances.

Exclusion of
evidence
bringing
administration
of justice into
disrepute

(2) Where, in proceedings under subsection (1), a court concludes that evidence was obtained in a manner that infringed or denied any rights or freedoms guaranteed by this Charter, the evidence shall be excluded if it is established that, having regard to all the circumstances, the admission of it in the proceedings would bring the administration of justice into disrepute.

General

Aboriginal
rights and
freedoms not
affected by
Charter

25. The guarantee in this Charter of certain rights and freedoms shall not be construed so as to abrogate or derogate from any aboriginal, treaty or other rights or freedoms that pertain to the aboriginal peoples of Canada including

(*a*) any rights or freedoms that have been recognized by the Royal Proclamation of October 7, 1763; and

(*b*) any rights or freedoms that may be acquired by the aboriginal peoples of Canada by way of land claims settlement.

Other rights and freedoms not affected by Charter

26. The guarantee in this Charter of certain rights and freedoms shall not be construed as denying the existence of any other rights or freedoms that exist in Canada.

Multicultural heritage

27. This Charter shall be interpreted in a manner consistent with the preservation and enhancement of the multicultural heritage of Canadians.

Rights guaranteed equally to both sexes

28. Notwithstanding anything in this Charter, the rights and freedoms referred to in it are guaranteed equally to male and female persons.

Rights respecting certain schools preserved

29. Nothing in this Charter abrogates or derogates from any rights or privileges guaranteed by or under the Constitution of Canada in respect of denominational, separate of dissentient schools.

Application to territories and territorial authorities

30. A reference in this Charter to a province or to the legislative assembly or legislature of a province shall be deemed to include a reference to the Yukon Territory and the Northwest Territories, or to the appropriate legislative authority thereof, as the case may be.

Legislative powers not extended

31. Nothing in this Charter extends the legislative powers of any body or authority.

Application of Charter

Application of Charter

32. (1) This Charter applies
(*a*) to the Parliament and government of Canada in respect of all matters within the authority of Parliament including all matters relating to the Yukon Territory and Northwest Territories; and
(*b*) to the legislature and government of each province in respect of all matters within the authority of the legislature of each province.

Exception

(2) Notwithstanding subsection (1), section 15 shall not have effect until three years after this section comes into force.

Exception where express declaration

33. (1) Parliament or the legislature of a province may expressly declare in an Act of Parliament or of the legislature, as the case may be, that the Act or a provision thereof shall operate notwithstanding a provision included in section 2 or sections 7 to 15 of this Charter.

Operation of exception

(2) An Act or a provision of an Act in respect of which a declaration made under this section is in effect shall have such operation as it would have but for the provision of this Charter referred to in the declaration.

Five year limitation

(3) A declaration made under subsection (1) shall cease to have effect five years after it comes into force or on such earlier date as may be specified in the declaration.

Re-enactment (4) Parliament or a legislature of a province may re-enact a declaration made under subsection (1).

Five year limitation (5) Subsection (3) applies in respect of a re-enactment made under subsection (4).

Citation

Citation **34.** This Part may be cited as the *Canadian Charter of Rights and Freedoms.*

PART II

RIGHTS OF THE ABORIGINAL PEOPLES OF CANADA

Recognition of existing aboriginal and treaty rights **35.** (1) The existing aboriginal and treaty rights of the aboriginal peoples of Canada are hereby recognized and affirmed.

Definition of "aboriginal peoples of Canada" (2) In this Act, "aboriginal peoples of Canada" includes the Indian, Inuit and Métis peoples of Canada.

PART III

EQUALIZATION AND REGIONAL DISPARITIES

Commitments to promote equal opportunities **36.** (1) Without altering the legislative authority of Parliament or of the provincial legislatures, or the rights of any of them with respect to the exercise of their legislative authority, Parliament and the legislatures together with the government of Canada and the provincial governments, are committed to

(*a*) promoting equal opportunities for the well-being of Canadians;

(*b*) furthering economic development to reduce disparity in opportunities; and

(*c*) providing essential public services of reasonable quality to all Canadians.

Commitment respecting public services (2) Parliament and the government of Canada are committed to the principle of making equalization payments to ensure that provincial governments have sufficient revenues to provide reasonably comparable levels of public services at reasonably comparable levels of taxation.

PART IV

CONSTITUTIONAL CONFERENCE

Constitutional
conference

37. (1) A constitutional conference composed of the Prime Minister of Canada and the first ministers of the provinces shall be convened by the Prime Minister of Canada within one year after this Part comes into force.

Participation of
aboriginal
peoples

(2) The conference convened under subsection (1) shall have included in its agenda an item respecting constitutional matters that directly affect the aboriginal peoples of Canada, including the identification and definition of the rights of those peoples to be included in the Constitution of Canada, and the Prime Minister of Canada shall invite representatives of those peoples to participate in the discussions on that item.

Participation of
territories

(3) The Prime Minister of Canada shall invite elected representatives of the governments of the Yukon Territory and the Northwest Territories to participate in the discussions on any item on the agenda of the conference convened under subsection (1) that, in the opinion of the Prime Minister, directly affects the Yukon Territory and the Northwest Territories.